George Firestone

Holy Angel, my Conductor,
PRAY FOR US.

THE HISTORY

OF

THE HOLY BIBLE,

COMPRISING THE MOST REMARKABLE EVENTS IN THE

Old and New Testaments,

INTERSPERSED WITH

MORAL AND INSTRUCTIVE REFLFCTIONS,

CHIEFLY TAKEN FROM

THE HOLY FATHERS.

BY THE REV. JOSEPH REEVE.

ILLUSTRATED WITH
TWO HUNDRED AND THIRTY ENGRAVINGS.

NEW-YORK:
PUBLISHED BY D. & J. SADLIER, & CO.
164 WILLIAM STREET,
BOSTON:—128 FEDERAL STREET.
MONTREAL, C. E:
COR. OF NOTRE-DAME AND ST. FRANCIS XAVIER STS.
1862.

PREFACE.

An abridgment of the historical books of the Old and New Testament, was compiled in French by a noted writer of the last century, and published under the borrowed name of Royamount. It is written in a plain and easy style, suitable to the subject, and formed upon a plan judiciously chosen, as it seems, to initiate youth in the early knowledge of holy Scripture, and well calculated to point out a method of reading the sacred history with advantage: the narrative is distributed into paragraphs, and the paragraphs are concluded with such moral and instructive reflections, as are suggested chiefly by the holy fathers, to render the subject more intelligible and useful. A work of this kind in the English language had been frequently called for, and in obedience to that call, a translation of the French historical abridgment was begun, under the encouragement of a liberal and gracious patronage. The translator had not far advanced in his undertaking, before he perceived, that the author's intended brevity had made his performance in many parts defective and obscure; and that to convey any tolerably clear and connected account of the sacred history, the rules of translation were to be set aside, and the text itself more closely attended to. It likewise appeared, upon a nearer examination, that the compiler, in some of his reflections, had not less studiously flattered his friends at Port-Royal, than he had been partially severe in others, upon the dignitaries of the church, and in many of his passages had given such a turn to the thought and expression of the fathers, as was more calculated to support an enthusiastic system of theology, than to promote the interest of true piety. This seemed totally foreign to the purpose of an English reader, and an alteration was therefore judged expedient, that the instruction might be rendered more universal, and the expression less liable to exception.

In the historical account which is here given of the inspired writings, the thread of the narration is carefully connected, and carried on with as few interruptions as the nature of the work will allow. Facts are related as they occur, according to the order of time in which they happened, and not according to the arrangement of books, as they stand in the common bible. From the creation of the world to the coming of our blessed Saviour, the best chronologists reckon four thousand years, which they divide into six unequal periods, called ages. This computation of years is carefully marked at the head of each paragraph, and this division of time into ages is regularly observed, as a relief to the reader's memory, in helping him to fix and retain the date of memorable events.

The reader will undoubtedly observe, that many facts are related from those books, which in the English bible are not styled canonical, though accounted holy. How, or by what authority, some books of the sacred writings have been received into the Protestant canon, and others left out, is not the present subject of enquiry. The Roman Catholic canon takes in all those books of Scripture, which are cited and held to be canonical by the third council of Carthage, A.D. 397.

The canonical writings, being penned under the immediate influence of the Holy Ghost, contain nothing but what is most certainly true, and are to us an inexhaustible source of Christian knowledge and instruction. A history thus dictated by the unerring Spirit of God himself, is, to a lover of truth, infinitely more pleasing than any human composition can be. For there, he is not only sure that all the facts are true, he moreover finds that many of those facts are expressly foretold, long before any human marks appeared of their coming to pass: he is there informed, how second causes are directed by the hand of God, to concur in bringing all things by degrees to their appointed ends: he there sees with what wonderful wisdom the Creator presides over all his works; how sweetly and how powerfully he regulates the springs of action; and with what certainty he effects his omnipotent decrees, without infringing the privilege of man's free-will; the rewards of virtue, and the punishments of vice; the danger of prosperity, and the advantages of affliction; the social and religious duties of public and private life, are there emphatically described, and illustrated by example. These are interesting points to a Christian reader, and these points are set forth by the inspired writers, in that sublime simplicity of style, and sacred energy of expression, which no modern language can equal, and no studied composition can pretend to.

Difficult then is the task, and more precarious still must be the success of an undertaking of this kind, where the object is both to instruct and please, as far as human capacity will permit, without deviating from the spirit or from the letter of the divine original; where the sense of the sacred text may be equally injured by a word too much as by a word too little; where, in fine, a respectful deference to the Scripture phrase foregoes the ornaments of speech, and yet a certain flow, with some degree of harmony in the composition, is requisite to humour the reader's taste, and invite his attention. However short this epitome may fall of the judicious reader's expectations, his benevolence, it is presumed, will be the more readily inclined to forgive the inaccuracies and defects he meets with, when he is candidly assured, that no other than his improvement in Christian knowledge, to the greater glory of God, is the true motive and design of this publication.

The Edition now offered will have an additional claim on the attention of the Public, by the introduction of TWO HUNDRED AND THIRTY appropriate CUTS. It being universally admitted that nothing can be better calculated to impress strongly on the minds of youth indelible recollections of the sacred truths of our holy religion, than representations given in a series of Prints of such interesting circumstances as are recorded by the inspired writers.

This work, so universally and justly celebrated, as well calculated to convey to youth and the general class of Catholic readers, a clear and uninterrupted knowledge of sacred history, may also be considered a most valuable addition to the holy Scriptures, forming an approved key for the right understanding thereof.

CONTENTS.

OLD TESTAMENT.

FOURTH AGE OF THE WORLD. *Page*

SIXTH AGE OF THE WORLD.

NEW TESTAMENT

SEVENTH AGE OF THE WORLD.

THE HISTORY

OF

THE HOLY BIBLE.

FIRST AGE OF THE WORLD.

FROM THE CREATION TO THE DELUGE, CONTAINING THE SPACE OF 1656 YEARS.

A.M. 1.] *The world is created.*—GEN. i. [A.C. 4000.

GOD, having decreed to make the world, as he has, out of nothing, created in the beginning a vast and indigested mass, as it were, of matter without form, dark in itself, and void of all that order and beautiful variety of parts which appeared soon after. The holy Scripture expressly says, that Almighty God perfected this great work in six days. On the first, after having created the heaven and the earth, he made the light: on the second day he made the firmament, to which he gave the name of heaven: on the third, he separated the dry land from the waters, that were mingled with it; the waters he collected together, and called them the sea. He then commanded the earth to produce the different sorts of plants and fruit-trees. with their respective seed in them, for the reproduction and increase of each in its own kind. On the fourth day he made those great luminaries that shine in the firmament of heaven, the sun, moon, and stars; ordaining at the same time, that the sun should preside over the day, and the moon over the night; that by their stated revolutions they should also regulate the days, the months, and the seasons of the year. On the fifth day God extended his creative power from the inanimate to the animated part of the universe. From the waters he produced an innumerable variety of creatures, containing within themselves the principle of life and motion; fishes of various sizes, and birds of every kind, which he blessed, and bade to increase and multiply, commanding these to people the air, and those the watery deep. On the sixth day he commanded the earth to produce, not plants and trees, as it had already done, but animals and living creatures of every species. He chose likewise on the same day to create Man, the last and most perfect of all his works: for, of so many excellent beings which he had formed, Man was the only one capable of knowing and of loving his Creator; and therefore, for Man were they all created. The creation being thus perfected, God on the seventh day ceased from doing any thing more; for which reason that day was then consecrated to the divine service, and appointed to be kept holy in future times.

Such is the account Moses has given us of the creation; in which we find no mention made of the angels: but as those pure spirits do most certainly exist, the holy fathers are of opinion, that they were created by Almighty God when he spoke those words, *Let light be made;* and in consequence, St. Austin understands that separation which God made, of the light from darkness, to express also a division which he at the same time made, of the good angels from the bad. Thus from the first existence of the world, and in the most excellent of his creatures, it pleased the divine wisdom to let us see, that none can be happy who separate themselves from God; that to whatever degree of greatness or of glory they may be raised, they must still remain subject to their Creator, since, if they transgress, nothing can screen them from the justice of an offended Deity: therefore, as by the example of the good angels, we are encouraged in that indispensable duty of fidelity, which we owe to our Creator, so at the remembrance of those fiery torments, into which the rebel angels have been thrown, we must undoubtedly conclude that God resists the proud, and gives grace to the humble.

A.M. 1.] *Adam placed in the earthly Paradise: formation of Eve.*—GEN. ii. [A.C. 4000

THE heavens and the earth being made complete, with all their ornaments, and the man, who had been formed out of the earth, being moreover dignified with a spiritual and immortal soul, according to the image and likeness of his Maker, God constituted him the master of the universe, and placed him in the terrestrial paradise. Paradise was the seat of all earthly happiness, a garden teeming with delight, planted by the hand of God himself, and adorned with every produce of nature, that was pleasing to the taste and charming to the eye. In the middle of this garden was a tree, called the tree of life, and near it grew the tree of the knowledge of good and evil. Here it was that God placed the first man, not to be an idle inhabitant, or a mere spectator of the place, but to keep and work it, as the Scripture particularly specifies. But lest in the midst of such delights he might unwarily forget his divine benefactor, on whom he solely depended for the enjoyment of them, Almighty God restrained him in one particular point, and thereby gave him an opportunity of showing at once his obedience and his gratitude. The precept was but one; it was an easy and a just precept. You may eat, says God, of every tree that grows in paradise, excepting that of the knowledge of good and evil: that tree alone you must not touch; or, if you do, you will most assuredly die in punishment thereof. He then made all the living creatures pass in review before Adam; and Adam, for so the first man was called, gave to each a name, expressive of the nature and qualities of which each species of bird and animal was possessed. Amidst such a variety of living creatures, he saw none equal to himself, nor was there one endowed with reason to whom he could speak his thoughts. He fell asleep, and during his repose God took out one of his ribs, which he formed into a woman, filling up the vacant space in his side with flesh instead of bone. Adam no sooner saw her, but struck at her charming figure, with ecstacy cried out, "This is the bone of my bone, and the flesh of my flesh!" For this reason the husband in future times, shall leave his father and mother to cleave to his wife, and they shall be two in one.

In the first sleep of Adam, Almighty God has given us a most palpable mark of what was long after to happen in the second; and the holy fathers tell us, that the mysterious sleep of Adam was a figure of the death of Jesus Christ upon the cross. For then it was that the church was formed by our divine Saviour; and the water and blood which issued from his gaping side, mark the source from whence the sacraments of the new law derive their power to heal and cleanse our souls. This heavenly bridegroom having in some sort left his Father in heaven, came in human shape amongst us, to unite himself eternally to his church, the spouse he had taken upon earth; and having made us worthy of contracting so ineffable an alliance with him, he most truly says of his church, what Adam said of Eve, "Behold the flesh of my flesh, and the bone of my bone!"

A.M. 1.] *The fall of Adam.*—Gen. iii. [A.C. 4000

Scarce had Adam and Eve begun to enjoy the delights of paradise, when the devil, who had been already ruined by his pride, resolved to try his utmost malice against them: he resolved to deprive them at once, if he could, both of their happiness and innocence. He was galled with envy to see two creatures, whose low beginning was from the slime of the earth, thus blessed and happy in their fidelity to God, while he, an original inhabitant of heaven, was thrown down into the lowest disgrace and misery. He therefore began to execute the ruinous design which he had formed against them, and undertook to destroy the succeeding race of mankind in the very root. For this purpose he made use of the serpent, which of all animals was the most subtle; and not doubting but the easiest and most certain way to succeed, would be to seduce the woman first, he thus expressed himself to her: Why has not God permitted you to eat indiscriminately of all the fruits of this garden? He has, replied

Eve: we eat of every fruit of the garden except one, and that one God has forbidden us to touch, lest we die. It is not the fear of your dying, answered the serpent; it is the apprehension of your knowing too much, which has induced God to lay such a restraint upon you; for he knows that by eating of this fruit you will not die, but that your eyes will be opened, and you yourselves will become as Gods, like him, having the knowledge of good and of evil. Eve, instead of turning away her ear, as she ought, from such deceitful language, not only listened, but was even pleased with her seducer. She was flattered with his promise; she sucked the poison of his words into her very soul; she looked earnestly at the fruit, and concluding it to be as delicious to the taste as it was delightful to the eye, she put forth her hand—she took it—she eat it. Thus was Eve gradually led to transgress the command of her Creator, and thus did sin enter into the world. For no sooner had she herself eaten of the forbidden fruit, but she offered it to her husband, and he also eat thereof. Rather than be the cause of any uneasiness to the spouse he loved, he chose, by a sinful compliance, to renounce the fidelity which he owed to his Creator, and thereby betrayed a want of that manly virtue, even in paradise, which Job in after times so greatly displayed upon his dunghill, as the fathers remark.

This is the transgression, of which death and all the train of human miseries, are the fatal consequence. This is the sin too enormous in its guilt for words to express, since in the father it ruined his whole posterity. Sprung from rebellious parents, we are born the slaves of Satan; nor should we have ever had the possibility of recovering our forfeited inheritance, had not God himself become our deliverer. The greatness of so unmerited a mercy ought never to be forgotten by us: as on one hand it challenges our most grateful acknowledgments to God, so on the other, it admonishes us to be always upon our guard against every temptation of the old serpent. That malicious enemy of mankind still remembers, and still practises the same wiles, that succeeded once so well with him in paradise. By a thousand ways he daily tries to persuade us, that we may innocently follow our own inclinations, even against the express commands of God our Creator. But as Eve, by experience, found the threats of God to be as certain as the promises of the serpent were deceitful so we always should remember, that God is still as unchangeable as he was then, in the commands he gives; and that the specious interpretations we may be tempted to make, in order to elude their force, are no more than the artifices of a subtle enemy, endeavouring to impose upon the children, as he once did upon their parents.

M. 1.] *Punishment of Adam.*—Gen. iii. [A.C. 4000

By the fall of our first parents, vanished the pleaing prospect of their happiness. Being stripped of their original innocence, they, for the first time, perceived that they were naked: for while their minds were unstained with sin, and the appetite of their senses remained subject to reason, they had known no cause of shame; but shame now followed the inward consciousness of guilt, and made them blush at what they had not observed before: for which reason they girded themselves round with fig leaves, finding a total change was wrought within them. What had hitherto been their joy, began to alarm and terrify: they heard the voice of God walking in the garden; it was no longer the voice of gladness; it was a sound of terror in their ears: they ran off and hid themselves, trembling with fear, among the thickest of the trees. God called upon Adam by name, and asked him where he was. I heard your voice, said Adam, but was afraid of being seen by you on account of my being naked. Adam mentioned not the real reason of his fear, but soon found it was in vain to dissemble with an all-knowing God: being severely reprimanded for his disobedience, which was the real cause of blushing and confusion, he began to exculpate himself upon the weak, but cruel pretence, that the woman had first offered the fruit to him. The woman hearing her self thus accused, sought also in the same manner to shift the blame from herself, and fix it upon the serpent that had deceived her. But in a formal violation of his precepts, God admits of no such excuses: he cursed the serpent upon the spot, as the prime promoter of the sin, condemning him to creep upon his belly along the earth, and to eat of the dust thereof all the days of his life; and concluded by pronouncing his disgrace and final overthrow by the woman, who in her seed should hereafter crush his head. He then addressed himself to the other two offenders that stood before him, and sentenced them both to the most afflicting penalties which their posterity severely feel to the present day. He told the woman, in particular, that he would multiply her sufferings; that in bringing forth her children she should groan in pain, and be for ever subject to her husband's power. To Adam he said, that since he had preferred the woman's voice to the voice of God, the earth should be cursed on that account; that notwithstanding his hard labour, to render it fertile, it should produce him briars and thorns; and that by the sweat of his brow he should earn his bread, until he returned to dust, from whence he had been taken. After this he clothed them with the skins of beasts, and to make them still more sensible of their sinful folly, he ironically exclaimed: Behold! Adam is become like one of us; by experience he has now the knowledge of good and evil. He never shall come near the tree of life, lest he should be for

eating also of that fruit, and live for ever. God therefore drove them out of paradise, and at the entrance placed a cherub with a fiery sword to prevent their return.

Thus were our unhappy parents compelled to quit that garden of delights; thus were they sent out to bewail their misery in a desert land, where they met with nothing but the melancholy marks of their own disobedience. Their ideas of the happiness which they had just lost, were fresh in their minds; and having now the experience of evil, which, in the state of innocence, they had never known, they could not help making a comparison between the two extremes. The first sight of natural knowledge was not yet extinguished in them;

their notions of good and evil were more clear than any man can now form; the more sensible therefore was their affliction, to see themselves so miserably fallen from what they were. Their hearts were ready to burst with grief at the prospect of so many of their helpless children, who were eternally to perish on their account. For having once consented to the sin, they could not possibly prevent the fatal consequences of it. However exemplary their penance may have been, it could not of itself save either them or their children. The work of their salvation, moreover, required the grace and mediation of a God made man, whose merits should be equally infinite with his mercy. This Jesus Christ has done for them and us; and he has done it in so wonderful and so plentiful a manner, that, with the church, we may call the sin of Adam, in some sort, a necessary sin and a fortunate transgression. This is the redemption which our first parents hoped for: this was the thought that comforted them in all their miseries.

A.M. 128.] *Abel slain by his brother Cain.* [A.C. 3872.
GEN. iv.

ADAM, soon after his fall, began to increase his family; the first of his sons was called Cain, and the second was called Abel. Cain soon showed himself to be of a very jealous temper, naturally rough and violent; he employed his time in working and tilling the ground. Abel was more meek; his natural turn of mind led him to the more gentle exercises of piety in the employment of a shepherd. Both being instructed in the duties of religion, they both worshipped the Supreme Being by religious sacrifice; the one offered to God the best and the fattest of his flocks, the other presented him with the first fruits and gifts of the earth. But as their offerings were made with very different dispositions of the heart, so, very different likewise, was the acceptance they found in the divine sight. It stung Cain to the very quick, to see the preference given to his brother: his countenance fell, and a discontented gloom expressed the rancour of his heart. The piety of Abel was the great cause of his uneasiness; and a brother's good qualities, which he himself was wholly void of, stirred up his envy into a most violent hatred: it was the beginning of what has happened in every subsequent age of the church, where the good and virtuous are obliged to bear the unjust censures and aversions of the wicked, with whom they converse. God himself was pleased to speak, in order to gain the heart of that wretched man. He asked him why he let himself be carried away by passion? why he was cast down? and why he fretted at what did not concern him? Thou are accountable only for thy own actions, said God to him, whether good or evil: if they are good, thou shalt have thy reward; but if evil, thou alone must bear the guilt of thy sin. The divine admonition was without its effect; for, St. Gregory observes, the word of God, which is so sovereign a remedy against every other distemper of the soul, cures not the secret

wounds of envy, when applied to them; it does but exasperate instead of heal. Cain had worked his passion up to its full height: being bent upon acts of violence, he invited his harmless and unsnspecting brother to walk out with him into the fields, where he violently attacked and killed him upon the spot. Horrid as the action was, the murderer was too hardened in his guilt to be shocked at it. God soon after asked him what was become of Abel. He insolently answered, that he did not know, neither was he his brother's guardian. But to convince him that nothing can escape the eye of all-discerning Providence, God told him in reply, that the blood of his brother Abel cried to heaven for vengeance against him; that he should, therefore, be accursed upon the earth; that he should shun the society of men, and live a vagabond all the days of his life; giving an example to future ages, of the vengeance due to all who unjustly shed their innocent neighbour's blood, or by enmity murder him in their hearts.

The holy fathers consider the death of Abel as a figure of the death of Jesus Christ; and his sufferings as a beginning of those persecutions which the faithful in all ages were to bear from their jealous brethren. Therefore the true followers of their divine Master are not afraid of being exposed to the injustice of a persecuting world, knowing that if their sufferings are great, great also will be their reward; and that to repine at the first, would be to make themselves unworthy of the second.

A.M. 1556.] *Noah's Ark.*—Gen. vi. [A.C. 2444.

The descendants of Cain inherited their father's spirit, and became a very wicked race of men; the sins of the earth increased in proportion with the number of its inhabitants. About the time of Abel's death, God had given to Adam another son, whom he named Seth, and whose descendants, for their piety, are in the holy Scripture called the sons of God; till falling in love with women of the race of Cain, they also were corrupted like the rest. In process of time their wickedness became so great and universal, that scarce any remains of virtue could be discovered in them. The marks of original righteousness were either worn away by neglect, or disfigured by vice. Man, the visible master-piece of the creation, was so far degenerated from his first state, that he seemed a disgrace even to the creatures that had been made for his use and benefit. The Lord repented, as the Scripture expresses it, and was sorry for having made him; he resolved to sweep him off the face of the earth, and with him all the living creatures that had been made for his service. Amongst so many thousands of men that were then living, only one was distinguished for his innoceuce and spotless life. Noah was this man; who, being in favour with his Creator, had the happiness to be chosen by him for the restorer of a future race, when the first should be destroyed. To Noah, therefore, did God communicate the resolution he had taken, of destroying the world by an universal deluge; and, as he intended to show mercy to him and his family, commanded him to build an ark, according to the dimensions he then gave him. Noah set immediately to work, and was an hundred years in completing it. During that time men saw the preparations he was making, and could not be ignorant of his design; they undoubtedly heard the divine threat, but did not apprehend it would fall so heavily: they considered it as a distant evil, and being wedded to their passions, either would not believe, or did not regard it.

Strange as the insensibility of these antediluvians may appear, it is no more than what will again happen in the latter days, as our blessed Saviour tells us in his gospel. As suddenly and as unexpectedly as the deluge, the last judgment will likewise come upon the world. In compassion to mankind, Almighty God threatens long before-hand, that the fear of punishment may make them studious to prevent it; for he never punishes but with regret, and when the impenitence of sinners provokes his severest anger. He cannot with indifference see his threats disregarded, his admonitions slighted, and his mercy abused. Men must not fancy that their numbers, or their wealth, or worldly power will be able to screen them from the vengeance that their crimes deserve. When summoned to appear before the tribunal of an omnipotent judge, they will find, that the whole world will be as little able to stand against the fires of the last day, as against the waters of the deluge.

A.M. 1656.] *The Deluge.*—GEN. vi. [A.C. 2344.

THE fatal period fixed for purifying the earth by water being at hand, God commanded Noah to take of every kind of bird and animal, male and female, seven couple of those that were clean, and one couple only of such as were unclean, and to convey them into the ark, with provisions of all sorts sufficient for a twelvemonth. These orders being executed, Noah and his wife, with his three sons, Sem, Cham, and Japhet, and their three wives, entered into the ark, and according to the Scripture phrase, God fastened close the door on the outside. At that moment the cataracts of heaven were opened, and an incessant deluge of rain was poured out with great violence for forty days and nights together. The earth soon disappeared and the sea was no longer distinguished by any bounds; the inundation spread itself impetuously above every thing; till the surface of the waters were fifteen cubits higher than the highest mountains. Birds, animals, and men were swept away by the torrent, and lay buried beneath the deep;

and, excepting what were in the ark, all perished without distinction. The ark, in the mean time, rose with the rising flood, and rode triumphant over the raging waters. Then did those unhappy mortals who had laughed at Noah's prudent forecast, most bitterly bewail their folly; with deep despair did they then see themselves swallowed up by the resistless waves, and the more sensibly did they feel the stroke of their destruction, as they had received the power and timely notice to prevent it.

The holy fathers have considered the ark of Noah as a figure of the church of Christ, and in that view have learnedly commented, not only upon the stateliness of its hulk, but also upon the assemblage of living creatures that were contained within it. The church, like the ark, has triumphantly risen above the storms that have been raised to depress her; by the activity and vigour of her founders, she has carried salvation even to the extremities of the earth, whilst by the vocation of the Gentiles, she assembles within her pale a collective body of believers from every tribe and nation beneath the sun. This is the refuge which all must flock to, who desire to be saved; this is the sanctuary, out of which no salvation can be found; for whosoever does not believe, says our blessed Lord, will eternally perish. Singular then has been the mercy of our Redeemer, who, in preference to thousands, has not only taken us into the bosom of his church, but has moreover given us the grace to know our happiness therein. Without such a grace we had, like the rest, been borne down the torrent, which has deluged the world with vice and infidelity. By a merciful stroke of his special providence, we have been cleansed from sin in the waters of baptism; by his cross we have been rescued from perdition; and through his merits we hope to enter the haven of eternal repose

END OF THE FIRST AGE.

Names and ages of the ten Patriarchs of the first age.

1	Adam,	*born*, A.M.	1	*died*,	930	*aged*,	930
2	Seth,	——	130	——	1042	——	912
3	Enos,	——	235	——	1140	——	905
4	Cainan,	——	325	——	1235	——	910
5	Malaleel,	——	395	——	1290	——	895
6	Jared,	——	460	——	1422	——	962
7	Enoch,	——	622	——	987	——	365
8	Methusalem,	——	687	——	1656	——	969
9	Lamech,	——	874	——	1651	——	777
10	Noah,	——	1057	——	2006	——	950

SECOND AGE OF THE WORLD.

FROM THE DELUGE, 1657, TO THE VOCATION OF ABRAHAM, 2083, COMPREHENDING THE SPACE OF 426 YEARS.

A.M. 1657.] *Noah quits the ark: the Rainbow.*—GEN. viii. [A.C. 2343.

THE flood had continued in its full fury for a hundred and fifty days, when God was pleased to remember Noah and his companions in the ark. He put the wind into motion, which, blowing steadily from one point, began to dispel the clouds, and to drive the waters back to their source. The inundation visibly decreased, and in the seventh month left the ark upon the top of Mount Arrarat, in Armenia. The ark there rested for four months, when Noah, being eager to know whether the waters had subsided, opened the window, and sent out a crow; the crow, an unclean bird, and the emblem of an abandoned sinner, returned no more into the ark; but the dove, which was sent out seven days after, not finding any place to rest upon, soon flew back, and was taken in again. At the end of seven days more, she was sent out a second time, and in the evening came back with a green olive branch in her beak, which Noah joyfully received, not only as a proof that the flood was abated, but likewise as a sign that God was now reconciled with the world. He opened the top of the ark, looked around, and saw that the waters had retired,

and left the surface of the earth quite dry. By the command of God he then went out of the ark, he and his wife and sons, and every other living creature with them, after they had been shut up for a whole year. He no sooner set his foot upon the dry land, than he erected an altar, and offered to God a sacrifice, in acknowledgment of his special goodness towards him. God was pleased with Noah's gratitude, and accepted his sacrifice. He blessed him and his children, telling him to re-people the earth, which he promised never to curse again on account of the sins of men. To convince them of the care he took of their future preservation, he impressed an awe and fear of man upon the brute creation, and gave to Noah and his sons a discretionary power over all living creatures, with permission to use them as they used the vegetables of the earth, for food and nourishment. He moreover entered into a solemn covenant with the holy patriarch

and his posterity, and assigned the rainbow as a token of the peace between them. When you shall see my bow in the clouds, said he, be then assured that I am mindful of the contract, and of the promise I have made, never to destroy the world again by another flood. And in effect no such general calamity since that period has befallen mankind: though their hideous crimes have often cried, and still cry aloud for vengeance. God nevertheless continues faithful to his word, nor will his promise ever fail. The rainbow is a standing sign of his mercy towards us, and as often as that sign appears, it ought to remind us of the gratitude we owe him: for his power is still the same, nor is his arm abridged, though no longer exerted with the same visible marks of terror.

It is not simply to the painted bow, which appears in a cloudy sky, that we are to confine our view; it is the church, says St. Ambrose, on which we are to fix our attention. Brilliant as the rainbow in all its glory, the church shoots her rays of brightness on every side, through the clouds that surround her. Those brilliant rays are the various graces with which God adorns his spouse, and makes her shine so charming to the eyes of men. Faithful in her duty, she receives them all as the gifts of his divine goodness to her; she bows to God, the author of her greatness; him she adores as the sun of justice, that enlightens and sets her up, not only as a sign, but as a mediatrix of peace between God and his people.

GEN. ix.

SCARCE had the effects of God's anger ceased upon the earth, when there happened an event, which shows what little good is to be expected from man, when his heart is once corrupted, or governed only by servile fear. Of the three sons of Noah, who had been so miraculously preserved from the general wreck, there was one, who having first drawn upon himself the malediction of his father, merited also that of God; instead of being the head of a virtuous race, for which he had been preserved, he became the author of a very unfortunate posterity. Noah seeing himself in the midst of a ruined and dispeopled country, applied himself to the works of husbandry, and amongst other rural employments planted the vine. When the time of vintage came, he gathered and pressed the grapes, drank freely of the juice, and intoxication was the consequence, before he was aware of it. He fell asleep in a posture, as it happened, not decent to be seen, and lay uncovered in the middle of his tent. Cham, his second son, and the father of Chanaan, was the first to discover him in that situation. Filial piety, one would think, ought to have prompted him to conceal, or at least compassionate an aged father's disgrace, but instead of that, he impudently laughed and diverted himself at what he saw. Nor was that all; he ran open-mouthed with it to Sem and Japhet, and invited them also to come and join in the diversion. But they, more mindful of the reverence due to a parent, threw a mantle over their shoulders, and respectfully turning their faces a different way, covered in their father, what they could not innocently look at. Noah, as soon as he awoke, being informed of all that had passed, condemned the action of Cham, and pronounced the curse which his son Chanaan was to inherit on that account. Chanaan, said he, shall be a slave to the slaves of his brethren unto future generations; while, for their piety, Sem and Japhet shall be blessed with a long and prosperous posterity.

This story, in the literal meaning of the words, conveys a most important instruction for children to pay that honour and respect to their parents which God commands them, and to be always careful not to laugh at, nor expose the private failings they may discover in them; but, in its figurative sense, according to St. Austin, it inculcates to all Christians a respect for Jesus Christ, their true father, in his state of humiliations and sufferings. The bitter cup of affliction, which his heavenly Father gave him to drink; the fruit of that ungrateful vine, which he himself had planted; the nakedness and disgrace which accompanied him upon the cross; are all strongly marked in the circumstances of Noah's story; and though few, perhaps, may be impious enough to laugh openly at the cross and ignominies of Jesus Christ, yet the number of those, who by their worldly conduct throw that slight upon their suffering Redeemer, is not very small, We in effect laugh at Christ, says the same holy doctor, when by our actions we contradict the principles of our Christian profession; we despise the humiliations of Christ by indulging the pride of life; we ridicule, in fine, the sufferings and the cross of Christ, by showing our contempt of those, who are more professedly the followers of his footsteps, and the imitators of his patience.

A.M. 1757.] *The Tower of Babel.*—GEN. xi. [A.C. 2243.

THE descendants of Noah, soon became very numerous; in the space of about a single century they were so surprisingly increased, that the country they were in was too scanty for their numbers. Being obliged to extend their territories, they began to look out for a new settlement in different parts of the globe. Before their separation they proposed leaving

some monument behind them, that might make their memory famous in after ages. With that view they undertook to build a city, and in it to erect a tower, the top whereof might reach to heaven. Their intention was not merely to signalize their name, but to provide themselves moreover with a place of security against any future deluge that might happen. Extravagant as the project was, they seemed, nevertheless, determined to effect it. They set immediately to work: upon the conceited notion of human pride they foolishly laid the foundations of their own disgrace, and wickedly attempted to raise themselves above the reach of being stopped or awed from sin by the fear of punishment. God fixed his eye upon those busy sons of Adam, looked down upon the tower they were labouring at, and saw how bent they were upon finishing it. At that time they all spoke the same language, and thereby encouraged one another in their impious undertaking. Full of that thought, they did not consider from whom they had received that gift of speech, or that it was as easy for the Almighty to take away as it was to give. By a stroke of the divine power they, in a moment, lost their uniformity of accent, and were surprised to hear nothing but a confused and discordant sound of words which no one understood. The disorderly noise and tumult that ensued upon it, forced them to desist, and the tower they had begun, was, on that account, called the tower of Babel, or confusion.

That tower of confusion, says St. Bernard, is the figure of all such worldly projects, as presumptuous mortals were to form through every age, in opposition to the commands of God. More pleased with the appearance than with the reality of being truly great, men often set aside the substance of real good, and toil after the shadow of they know not what. God in this instance showed his displeasure at the presumption of men, by punishing them in that slippery part, the tongue, which was and still continues, to be the active instrument of sin. That diversity of languages which then began, and still subsists between nations, is, as it were, a continual voice that makes itself be heard over the whole earth, and intimates to all, says St. Austin, that the shortest and the surest way to heaven is not in building lofty edifices to their vanity, nor in forming vast projects in the mind, but in humbly submitting to the decrees of God; not in pretending to elude his justice by an obstinate resistance, but in endeavouring to preserve his mercy by a timely repentance.

END OF THE SECOND AGE

Names and ages of the ten Patriarchs of the second age.

1	Sem,	*born*, A.M.	1558	*died*,	2158	*aged*,	600
2	Arphaxad,	——	1658	——	1996	——	338
3	Sale,	——	1693	——	2126	——	433
4	Heber,	——	1723	——	2187	——	464
5	Phaleg,	——	1757	——	1996	——	239
6	Rehu,	——	1787	——	2026	——	239
7	Sarug,	——	1819	——	2049	——	230
8	Nacher,	——	1849	——	1997	——	148
9	Thare,	——	1878	——	2083	——	205
10	Abraham,	——	2008	——	2183	——	175

THIRD AGE OF THE WORLD.

FROM THE VOCATION OF ABRAHAM, 2083, TO THE DELIVERY OF THE HEBREW PEOPLE OUT OF EGYPT, 2513, COMPREHENDING THE SPACE OF 430 YEARS.

A.M. 2083.] *Vocation of Abraham.* [A.C. 1917

GEN. xii.

FROM the dispersion of mankind into different parts of the universe, is dated the origin of the different states and kingdoms that were formed by their enterprising leaders. Being no longer awed by the presence of their patriarchs they soon forgot the principles, and laid aside the practice of the religion they had been instructed in. Instead of God, man began to worship creatures, in which they fancied a divinity to reside. A corruption of morals became almost universal, and the true religion remained but with a few of the descendants of Sem, and they were chiefly of the branch of Heber. Idolatry had began to spread itself even amongst them, when God was pleased to select to himself a man more deserving than the rest, whom he destined to be the founder of a more faithful race. This extraordinary man was called Abraham, the tenth in a lineal descent from Noah, and lived with his father Thare, in Ur, a city of the Chaldeans. Here it was that God appeared and imparted his orders to him. Go forth from thy native country, says the Almighty; quit thy kindred and thy father's house, and pass into the land that I will show thee. Thee I will make the father of the head of a great people, and thy name shall be famous amongst them. Those that shall bless thee I will bless, and those that shall curse thee will I likewise curse; and in thee shall all the nations of the earth be blessed. Abraham gave implicit credit to the words he heard, and immediately prepared to execute the divine order. He communicated it to his wife and father, who agreed to go along with him. He therefore bade an eternal adieu to the place that gave him birth, and began his journey towards the country that God had pointed out to him. Lot, his brother's son, was one of the company. Abraham advanced as far as Haran, a city of Mesopotamia, where he seems to have made some stay. There it was he buried his father; after which he proceeded in his journey towards the land of Chanaan. Upon his arrival thither, God renewed to him his former promise of putting him in possession of all that country. Abraham erected an altar upon the spot, and adored that sovereign power, which bids the empire of nations rise or fall, as it pleases to direct. He had not long been in the country, before a raging famine obliged him to leave it, and to retreat into Egypt. But whilst he retreated from one danger, he became apprehensive of perishing by another. The comeliness of Sarah's person, he thought, would tempt the men of Egypt to make away with the husband, that they might take the wife. For that reason he desired her to say, she was his sister, as in effect she might, without any injury to truth. The event quickly showed that Abraham was not wrong in his conjectures; for the Egyptians no sooner saw Sarah, but were taken with her beauty, and described her to Pharaoh their king. Pharaoh sent for her to his palace, with an intention of making her his wife; ordering, at the same time, that every mark of civility should be paid to Abraham her brother. Sarah was in a very critical situation, which must have ended in her shame, if God himself had not been the guardian of her purity. By the most convincing proofs of his anger, he made Pharaoh sensible of the wrong he had done, and that the woman he had forced into his palace, was the wife of Abraham. Pharaoh upon this ordered Abraham to be brought before him, and without making him any other complaint, than that of his not having at first told him that Sarah was his wife, bade him take her and go his ways. So totally averse to the crime of adultery was this prince, although an idolater, says Saint Ambrose, and so tender was he of a stranger's honour, with whom he had no other connection than that of his having taken refuge within his dominions.

Thus it was, that God called to himself the man, whom he had chosen to be the father of all true believers, and such were the first proofs he made of the steadiness of his faith. He commanded him to quit every advantage which he had been born to in his native country, and go into a foreign land, where, at his very first entrance, he had all the hardships of a severe famine to struggle against. Being again forced to abandon the place he had been directed to, he retired into an idolatrous kingdom, where amidst a thousand frights, he ran a thousand risks, without any other comfort than that of having been obedient to him who was pleased to make that trial of his faith. But by experience he was in the end convinced, that he had nothing to fear under the immediate protection of a God, who knows how to turn to our advantage all those passing inconveniencies which we patiently submit to, rather than give up our allegiance to him.

A.M. 2084.] *Lot leaves Abraham* [A.C. 1916.
GEN. xiii.

ABRAHAM staid no longer in Egypt than necessity obliged him: he came back into the country which he had left the year before, and fixed his residence near Bethel. He had not been long there, when he began to experience a misfortune, which is but too often the attendant of wealth. Both he and his nephew were possessed of great riches, which consisted chiefly in their numerous herds and flocks. Many servants were, of course, employed in taking care of them, and where different interests prevail, disputes and disagreements will necessarily arise. Abraham, who was naturally of a very pacific turn of mind, being apprehensive of the evil consequences that were likely to ensue from such domestic wrangles, judged it the more prudent part to propose to his nephew a timely separation, before the quarrel should spread from the servants to their masters. He went to find out Lot, and begged, that as they were brethren, there might be no misunderstanding between them, and that every subjec of complaint between their servants might be instantly re moved. Behold, said he, the country is open to your choice; take the part you like best; if you choose to go to the left, I will take the right; or if you prefer the right, I will then retire to the left. Discreet and friendly was the proposal, as made by Abraham; but on the part of Lot there appeared neither the same friendship nor discretion. Inattentive to his uncle's goodness, and insensible of the loss that he was likely to suffer by such a separation, he eagerly catched at the offer that was made him, and so blindly threw himself, as Saint Ambrose observes, into numberless perils and misfortunes; for the desire of a present advantage seems to have excluded every other consideration. Lot fixed his eyes upon the country that lay round the borders of the river Jordan; the freshness of its verdure and the richness of its soil, watered with the most pleasing streams, gave it all the appearance of a delightful garden. The prospect was inviting; it excited his desires; it induced him to separate from the most holy personage then living, and to settle in the midst of a people, the most abandoned and infamous for their lusts; he settled in the town of Sodom.

From this story, short as it is, says the same Saint Ambrose, we may gather two very important instructions. In the conduct of Abraham, we see how very cautious we ought to be, not to enter into an dispute that may lessen fraternal charity, and how suspected ought to be the whispers of servants, whose selfish views often raise complaints and jealousies of one another. In the example of Lot, we discover of what dangerous consequences it is, for young persons especially, to break off with a sincere and judicious friend: his advice is oftentimes more essential to their happiness, than they imagine. A virtuous friendship is the source of blessings, which are not always attended to: one hasty step inconsiderately taken, is frequently productive of evils that are felt for life. Though Lot was a just man, as Saint Peter testifies, yet we cannot but tremble for him, when on the one hand we see him struggling with difficulties, which his imprudence had engaged him in, and on the other, bereft of the only man who, by his presence, either might have prevented the evils he fell into, or taught him how to surmount them.

GEN. xiv.

SOON after Lot had separated from Abraham, there happened an event, which, at once, evinced the charity of the one, and the imprudence of the other. Four kings, it seems, had united their forces together, and made an incursion into the neighbourhood of Sodom, laying waste, and plundering all before them. In order to make head against them, the king of Sodom solicited the assistance of four other petty princes, who readily accepted of the proposal, and in one body marched out against the common enemy: they came to an engagement, were defeated, and put to flight. The four confederate kings being greatly elated with their victory, and having nothing more to oppose them, directed their march to Sodom, which they took and plundered. Lot shared in the common calamity: his effects were pillaged, and he himself carried off amongst the prisoners. Fortunately for him, a messenger had escaped from the field of battle, and carried the news of his captivity to Abraham. The virtuous patriarch was grievously afflicted at what had happened, and concluding it to be no time for tears and inactive complaints, immediately collected all the force he could, and armed three hundred and eighteen of the most resolute of his dependents. With that little troop, he went in pursuit of the victorious enemy; and as it was upon the divine power that he chiefly relied for success, God was pleased to give a blessing to his arms, and to crown his courage with victory. He came up with the enemy, attacked and defeated their army, which the united force of five princes had not been able to cope with

Having broken their lines, he pursued them in their flight, and rescued Lot, with all the other prisoners that had been carried off from Sodom.

It was on this occasion that he was met by Melchisedech, the king of Salem, and priest of the most high God, as the scripture calls him. This extraordinary man sacrificed in bread and wine, which the holy fathers unanimously exhibit, as a figure of that wonderful sacrifice which Jesus Christ, the true priest according to the order, not of Aaron, but of Melchisedech, was to institute and ordain to be performed in his church as long as the world should last. He gave his blessing to Abraham, and rendered thanks to God for having given him victory over his enemies. The king of Sodom was exceedingly rejoiced at this unexpected turn of his affairs, and with a due sense of gratitude insisted upon Abraham's taking home with him the rich booty that he had recovered from the enemy. But Abraham, being as disinterested in his views as he had been successful in his enterprise, generously refused the offer, and in the most solemn manner declared, that of the spoils he would not take so much as a single thread, nor put it in any man's power to say, that he had enriched Abraham.

Thus did Abraham, as Saint Ambrose remarks, become more glorious by the use he made of his victory, than by the victory itself. His example is an instruction to all christians, that the motive of exerting their courage should be always founded in charity; that a tender compassion for the sufferings of others should make them active in their relief, that the best recompense of a good action is the merit of having performed it; and that the greatest glory of a christian is, to have co-operated with the designs of God for the benefit of mankind

A.M. 2094.] *The Flight of Agar.* [A.C. 1906.
GEN. xvi.

ABRAHAM seemed to be at the height of his temporal felicity; an heir to his great riches was the only thing wanting to make him completely happy. The great desire he had of so happy an event, could be equalled only by his humble resignation to the divine will; and that resignation made him worthy of the blessing he so earnestly wished for. In a vision God expressly told him he should have a son, though at that time there was not the least probable appearance of it; for Sarah was not only barren, she was moreover far advanced in years. Abraham was too well principled in faith, not to submit his judgment to the divine word; he knew the power and veracity of Him who spoke, to be equally great, so could not form the least doubt of the promised blessing. But to Sarah the time seemed long; she saw no sign of her having a son, and her husband was growing old; she therefore begged him to take Agar, the Egyptian, her handmaid to wife, and thereby console them for her past sterility. However singular the proposal may seem, Abraham knew, as the holy fathers observe, that it had its sanction from heaven, and therefore gave his consent. The event did not answer Sarah's expectation; for what she intended to be her comfort, became a new subject of uneasiness. Agar seeing herself honoured by her master, began to despise her mistress, and to set herself above her. Sarah complained of it to Abraham; and he, to convince her that he was far from encouraging any such insolence of behaviour, advised her to exert her authority, and to insist upon the respect which is due from a servant to her mistress. Sarah wanted nothing more; she stretched her authority to the utmost; she carried her correction to a degree of harshness and severity not to be borne with. Agar would no longer submit, left the house, and fled off into the wide country. There, in the depth o. her affliction, she sat herself down near a fountain, where an angel of the Lord appeared to her, and asked from whence she came, and whither she was going. She answered, with great sincerity, that she was flying from the anger of her mistress. The angel commanded her to go back, to make her submission to Sarah, and to respect the just authority that her mistress had over her.

In this manner did God employ an angel to brings things back into their natural order, out of which the hurry of passion had first thrown them. He saw, as the holy fathers take notice, that the cause of Agar's flight arose not so much from Sarah's severity, as from her own perverse temper; wherefore, without casting any blame upon Sarah, the angel directed his advice solely to Agar, telling her to humble herself at her mistress's feet, and to regain her good graces by a submissive and cheerful obedience. For God, who never breaks through the order established by his justice, always requires that the inferior class of mankind pay a due deference to those on whom they depend. No natural abilities or talents, however great, can authorize an insult against any lawful superior; the greater the gifts are that we have received from God, the greater should be our humility and our gratitude; for in the divine sight no man is great, but in proportion as he is little in his own.

A.M. 2107.] *Abraham entertains the three Angels.*—Gen. xviii. [A.C. 1893.

Agar, soon after her return into Abraham's house, in the vale of Mambre, was brought to bed of a son, who was called Ismael. At the end of thirteen years, God appeared again to Abraham, renewed all his former promises, and entered into a more express covenant with him. He changed his name of Abram into Abraham, and told him that his wife, who had hitherto been called Sarai, should henceforward be called Sarah. He then enjoined him the law of circumcision, which he commanded him and his posterity to observe, as a sign of that sacred covenant which he had just ratified between them. For he plainly told him, that Sarah should have a son, whom he would bless, and from whom a numerous race of kings and people should descend. At hearing this, Abraham fell prostrate on the ground, and laughing with joy, asked himself, if it were possible for a man an hundred years old to have a son, or for Sarah to conceive in the ninetieth year of her age? God repeatedly assured him it should be so, and then left him. In a promise so explicit on the part of God, Abraham could no longer doubt the event, especially as he soon after received a further confirmation of it in the following manner:—during the heat of the day he happened to be sitting at the door of his tent, and by chance looking round, he beheld three angels, in the appearance of men, coming towards him. He immediately rose up, and advanced to meet them. It was an indispensable duty with him, it seems, never to let a stranger pass without offering him hospitality He saluted his three visitors with all that courtesy and candid simplicity which bespeaks a good heart, offered them his service, begged they would let him wash their feet, and presented them with a refreshment. Upon their accepting his offer, he stepped back into his tent, and desired Sarah to prepare three hearth-cakes; then, hastening to the herd, he chose out a fat and tender calf, which he ordered his servants to kill and dress with all expedition His orders were speedily performed, and the entertainment served up under a tree, Abraham standing the whole time, and helping his guests to whatever they wanted. When they had done, they inquired after his wife Sarah, and he answering that she was within her tent, they assured him, that by the time they came that way again, she should have a son. Sarah was near enough to hear what they said, and laughed

secretly behind the door of the tent. Upon that, one of the angels, addressing himself to Abraham, asked what Sarah meant by laughing as she did; whether she disbelieved the promise, or fancied anything was difficult to God? Sarah began to be afraid, and denied her having laughed. The angels told her she had, gave her a gentle reprimand for her insincerity, rose up, and departed towards Sodom. Abraham accompanied them part of the way.

The holy fathers seem particularly delighted with the virtues that shine forth in the detail of this history. On the one hand, they seem at a loss for words to express their commendation of Abraham's benevolent hospitality; and on the other, they display all their eloquence in extolling the unaffected modesty of Sarah. Very unlike to many of her sex, who, under the pretext of charity, says Saint Ambrose, seek but an occasion of shining in public, she remained private in her apartment, without so much as appearing before the strangers that her husband was entertaining. From her example, every Christian woman ought to know, adds the same saint, that domestic retirement, and the constant care of her family, constitute the chief duty of a virtuous wife.

A.M. 2107.] *The Crimes of Sodom.* [A.C. 1893.
GEN. xviii. 19.

THE three angels discoursed in a most familiar manner with Abraham, as they went along: they first spoke of the great blessings which from him should flow upon all the nations of the earth, and then told him they were going to destroy the town of Sodom, in punishment of its crimes, that cried to heaven for vengeance. Abraham began to expostulate with them, and hoped they would not involve the innocent at least with the guilty. His charitable entreaties so far prevailed, as to engage their promise not to destroy the town, provided ten just persons could be found therein; but Sodom had them not. Abraham and the angels took leave of one another; he returned home, and they went on towards Sodom. Two of them reached the town about evening, and found Lot sitting at the gate. Lot still retained the principles of his virtuous education, and, in the midst of a corrupt people, preserved that purity of manners which he had learned from Abraham. He no sooner perceived the two strangers but he rose up to salute them; he invited them to his house, and pressed them to stay all night, that they might be fresh for their journey next day. The angels at first seemed to make some difficulty in accepting his invitation, and said they would remain in the open street. Lot would admit of no excuse; compelled them to enter under his roof, and gave them a very hospitable reception. When they had supped, and were retiring to rest, a lawless crowd of townsmen, being inflamed with an unnatural lust of sin, surrounded the house, and clamorously demanded to have the two young men that were within given up to them. Lot was grieved to the heart to find his guests thus exposed to an insult, from which he was in hopes they had been secure under the shelter of his roof. He went out to the Sodomites, and by meek entreaties tried to dissuade them from their brutal design They answered his representations with great insolence of language, bade him remember that he was but a stranger himself, and by no means qualified to advise or direct them. They grew excessively outrageous, were near forcing their way into Lot's house, and threatened the rudest violence to his person, when the angels put forth their hand to his assistance, and drew him within the door, which they instantly fastened against the mob, casting at the same time such a mist upon their eyes, that they could neither see nor find their way in after him.

Like unto this is the usage, and such is the violence, which has been frequently experienced by the faithful servants of God, who live in the midst of a corrupt and unbelieving world. To the shameless Sodomites, blinded as they were, and persisting in their attempt of breaking into Lot's house, Saint Gregory compares those wicked slanderers, who never cease to insult the fairest characters. Hurried away by the spirit of malevolence, they are blind to their neighbour's good qualities, and fancy to themselves defects which have no existence but in the wildness of their own imagination. As for those whose misfortune it is to be thus traduced by the tongue of slander, God is their protector, and his holy angels are their guardians. For by the choice they make, of preferring virtue to vice, and duty to false friendship, they secure to themselves a friend in God, who is both able and willing to support them in their utmost need.

A.M. 2107.] *Sodom consumed by fire.* [A.C. 1893.

GEN. xix.

THE angels having thus delivered Lot from the violence of a licentious mob, declared to him the commission they had to destroy Sodom and its inhabitants; they desired him to inform his sons and daughters, or any other persons who were dependent on, or connected with him, to leave the town immediately, for fear of being involved with the rest of the citizens, whose abominations were no longer to be tolerated. Lot gave notice to the two young men whom he had designed for his sons-in-law, and advised them to quit the sinful city: they laughed at his advice and treated it as a mere dream Morning being come, the angels pressed Lot to depart with his wife and two daughters; for Lot was dilatory, and seemingly unwilling to move. They, therefore, took him by the hand, and led him out of the town, expressly cautioning both him and his wife and daughters not to look back, but to retire with all speed into the mountain. Lot was afraid of going to the mountain, and begged leave to retreat into the neighbouring town of Segor: the angels consented to his request, upon condition that he would make haste thither, because they could not execute their orders till he should be in a place of safety. Lot was no sooner arrived at Segor, but God let fall a shower of fire and brimstone upon Sodom and Gomorrah, and two other towns, which, with all their inhabitants, and the country round, were entirely consumed. Lot's wife being terrified by the noise, unfortunately forgot the caution that the angel had given her, and looked back at the town. Her curiosity was punished on the spot; she was changed into a pillar of salt, to serve as a warning to those who, from fear or fickleness of mind, shall at any time cast a wishful look at the sinful objects they have once quitted. Struck at so terrible an instance of the divine justice, Lot began to tremble for the fate of Segor, and con-

cluded he should be more safe in the mountain that the angel had first pointed out to him: thither he then hastened, with his two daughters, and concealed himself for some time in a cave.

Thus, through the efficacy of Abraham's prayer, Lot was miraculously delivered from the sulphureous flames of Sodom. The punishment of that infamous people was adapted to the nature of their crimes: the stench and fury of the flames kindled for no other purpose than to punish, give us a striking figure, according to Saint 'Gregory, of those eternal fires which are reserved for impenitent sinners in the world to come: yet, dreadful as those burnings are, they frequently are no more considered, than if they were an empty dream. Senseless as the sons-in-law of Lot, men often laugh at the threats they hear, and disregard the danger that is hanging over their heads. If that example of the divine vengeance appeared to Lot so grievous and dreadful, can sinners stand unmoved, and unconcernedly hear Jesus Christ assuring them, that the inhabitants of Sodom, abominable as they were, will in the last day be treated with less severity than they who shall have heard, and not profited by his holy word.

A.M. 2107.] *Punishment of king Abimelech.* [A.C. 1893.
GEN. XX.

SOON after the destruction of Sodom, and in the same year, Abraham quitted his former place of residence in the vale of Mambre, and removed to the town of Gerara, in the southern part of the country. Here the beauty of his wife exposed him to the same danger from Abimelech, that he had once experienced from Pharaoh. Abimelech was the king of Gerara, and had an inclination to make Sarah his wife, upon the presumption that she was only Abraham's sister. But God, who had undertaken to be the protector of the virtuous pair, even against the attempt of kings, admonished Abimelech in the night, that she was Abraham's wife, and threatened him with instant death, if he presumed to touch her. Terrified at the unexpected threat, Abimelech began to plead the uprightness of his intention, aad hoped his ignorance would recommend him to the divino mercy. Almighty God received his excuse, and assured him that on account of his simplicity he had preserved his hands from sin, nor permitted him to do an action which his heart abhorred. It was the dead of the night: Abimelech was struck beyond expression at the thought of his having been so near the fatal precipice: he started suddenly out of bed, called his officers round him, and related to them the whole adventure. He sent immediately for Abraham, to whom he made his complaint for having deceived him. For what reason, said he, did you not impart to me the whole truth? and why was I to be left in ignorance? What injury, what provocation had you received, thus to expose me and my people to the hazard of being cursed for an adultery, which, as we abhor, we never intended to commit? Abraham replied, that in this he had not acted contrary to his usual custom; that in desiring Sarah to pass for his sister, he had not offended against the truth; that being unacquainted with their manners when he came amongst them, he did not know whether they had any fear of God, and was, therefore, afraid of being murdered by them, had he moreover declared her to be his wife. Abimelech seemed satisfied with his reasons, gave him back his wife, and made him rich presents, both in cattle and in money. In taking his leave of Sarah, he told her with a smile, that he had given a thousand pieces of silver to her brother, as she called him, to buy her a veil, which he advised her to wear for the future as a distinctive mark, says Saint Ambrose, of her being a married woman: he desired her to remember how her deceit had been discovered, and bade her be careful how she attempted the like again upon any other man. Abraham spoke in his turn, and finished with a prayer to God, who in consequence thereof exempted Abimelech and his family from the punishment which they had otherwise undergone on the account of Sarah.

In this manner, as Saint Ambrose observes, did God testify his abhorrence of adultery. Being the protector as well as the author of matrimony, he severely punishes whatever tends to violate its sanctity, or to defile its purity. And though the effects of his vengeance may not now-a-days be so sudden or so visible as they formerly were, yet it is not to be imagined, that his hatred of the crime can be less now than it was of old, or that his punishment of it is to be less dreaded, because less visible. The licentiousness of men may make the sin more common or more glaring at one time than at another; but the judgments of God are at all times equally just, and equally to be feared.

A.M. 2108.] *Ismael turned out of doors.* [A.C. 1892.
GEN. XXI.

CONFORMABLY to the angel's promise, Sarah brought forth a son, whom his father circumcised on the eighth day, as God had commanded, and called him Isaac. Notwithstanding the distinguished rank she held in the world, on account of her husband's wealth and eminent virtues, she suckled her own child; and in tha says St. Ambrose, has given an admirable example to all such mothers, who, upon some frivolous pretence or other, often seek to exempt themselves from a duty, which nature herself has imposed upon them: to nourish with her milk the tender offspring of her body, should be the glory and the joy of every mother; and they who decline it, can be considered in no better light, than that of being but half parents to their children, since at the breast is imbibed and strengthened that mutual love, which should subsist for life between a mother and her children. Sarah weaned her son, when he was of a proper age, and Abraham expressed great joy on the occasion. It was a day of mirth and entertainment for the whole family, and stands recorded as an emblem of that spiritual joy which the pastors of the church experience, when they see their tender flock advance in virtue, and grow susceptible of more solid food. Sarah was become one of the happiest of her sex; the reproach of her long sterility was wiped away, and all the blessings of a mother united in her. The smiling Isaac increased her joy as he increased in age, till Ismael's behaviour towards him began to give her great uneasiness. Ismael, who had been long flattered as an only child, and had been taught to look upon himself as the presumptive heir of Abraham's great riches, saw his hopes cut off at once by the birth of Isaac. A disappointment of that nature must consequently affect both Ismael and his mother Agar; the joy, moreover, and partiality that was shown to Isaac, naturally provoked Ismael's jealousy, and prompted him to vent his spleen and ill humour against his little brother. Sarah's fondness for an only son, made her too sharp-sighted not to observe what passed between them, and, being apprehensive of the consequences, desired Abraham to stop the evil at once, by turning the handmaid and her son out of doors, assuring him that the handmaid's son should never share in the inheritance with her son Isaac. The good patriarch was much hurt at the proposal, for he loved his son Ismael. But, being warned by Almighty God to act in this matter as Sarah should direct, he took a loaf of bread and a bottle of water, which he laid upon Agar's shoulder, delivered to her her son, and dismissed her. Agar, in that forlorn condition, being turned out of doors, wandered about the wilderness of Bersabee for some time, till her little provision was consumed. Her distress became extreme: she had no resource left for the preservation either of herself or son, and abandoned herself to despair. She placed her son under a tree, there to wait for death; then retiring as far as a bow can carry, not to see him die, she sat herself down upon the ground, raised a mournful cry, and wept most

bitterly. In that melancholy situation, she suddenly heard a voice, that called her by her name. It was the voice of an angel commanding her to take care of Ismael, for that he should be the father of a numerous people. The angel pointed out to her a fountain that was near; she was much comforted; she educated her son in the wilderness, who in process of time became an expert archer, and married a woman of Egypt.

St. Paul expressly tells us, that in the picture of these two sons of Abraham is clearly represented, what was in after-times to happen to Christ's church, in which the children of promise were to suffer persecution from their own brethren. Whoever would inherit the blessings of Isaac, must with him bear the envy and the insults of Ismael; far from returning evil for evil, he ought rather to deplore the misfortunes of a brother, who for his own demerits, is for ever banished from his father's house. It is God alone who in his wisdom has decreed the one to be born of her who is free, and another to be born of her who is a slave. It is a duty incumbent upon us who are free, to thank our heavenly

Father for the decree he has passed in our favour, and we must be ready to submit, with Isaac, to any persecution whatever, rather than become, like Ismael, the persecutors of our brethren: the wrath of Ismael was but short, the inheritance of Isaac is everlasting.

A.M. 2145.] *Abraham's Sacrifice.* [A.C. 1855.
GEN. xxii.

ISMAEL'S banishment restored peace to Abraham's family, and left Isaac the indisputable heir of his father's fortune. Isaac had reached the thirty-seventh year of his age, according to the Jewish tradition, when God was pleased to make trial of Abraham's faith, in a point the most decisive: he ordered him to take that very Isaac, his beloved son, and to offer him in sacrifice upon the mountain he should show him. Abraham had always looked upon his son as a special gift from God, and therefore did not hesitate a single moment to give him back in the manner that God required. He had been assured that his posterity should one day become as numerous as the sands upon the shore, or as the stars in heaven. Steadfast, therefore, in that belief, and unshaken in his hope, Abraham stifled every doubt he might otherwise have formed of the repeated promises God had made him; he rose early in the morning, and keeping his secret to himself, went silently out with Isaac and two servants. He carried with him the wood necessary to consume the holocaust, and directed his way towards the mountain. Fixed in his resolution, he went on for two days, and on the third came in sight of the destined place of sacrifice. He told his servants to remain at the bottom of the hill, while he with his son should go up to adore their God. Inflexible to the sensations of flesh and blood, he took in his hand the fire and the sword, and gave to his son the wood that was intended for the sacred fire. Charged with his load Isaac proceeded up the hill, a lively representation of Him who was afterwards to ascend the mount of Calvary loaded with a cross, on which he was to consummate the great work of our redemption. As they were going on, Isaac asked his father where the victim was? The question was too interesting not to waken all the tenderness of a father's love in such circumstances: Abraham dissembled the secret feelings of his heart, and with a manly firmness answered, that God would provide the victim. Being come to the appointed spot, he erected an altar, and laid the wood in order upon it; then having bound and placed his son Isaac thereon, he took up the sword, and stretched

out his hand to strike. The firm obedience of the father, and the humble submission of the son, were all that God required of them. An angel at that moment was despatched to stop the father's arm, and to assure him that God was satisfied with the readiness of his obedience. The angel called aloud on Abraham; Abraham answered the voice, and looking round saw a ram with his horns entangled with the brambles, which he took and offered an holocaust for his son.

This history, which is so mysterious, and in almost every circumstance so resembling the passages of our Saviour's passion, is, according to the holy fathers, an instruction for all parents to consult the will and implore the aid of God, before they presume to dispose of their children. Nothing less than the eternal welfare of their souls, and the service of Almighty God, ought to guide their intention, and regulate their conduct in this respect. Saint Chrysostom more at large deplores the misfortune of those parents who, notwithstanding their Christian profession, sacrifice their children, not to God as Abraham did, but to Satan, either by engaging them in the pursuits of a vain world, or by drawing them from the practice of a virtuous life. Abraham is the only one, says he, who consecrates his son to God, while thousands of others turn their children over to the devil; and the joy we feel in seeing some few take a Christian care of their little ones, is presently, suppressed with grief at the sight of those greater numbers, who totally neglect that duty, and by the example they give, deserve to be considered rather as parricides, than the parents of their children.

A.M. 2145.] *Sarah's Death.*—GEN. xxiii. [A.C. 1855.

ISAAC being restored to his parents by the express order of Almighty God, who had given him to them in their old age, continued to be the comfort of his mother as long as she survived: for she died soon after, in the hundred and twenty-seventh year of her age, and the thirty-seventh year of her motherhood. Abraham felt and bemoaned her death: he affectionately paid her the tribute of his tears, and gave her an honourable interment. Being a stranger in the country, without so much as a foot of land that he could call his own, he addressed himself to the people of Geth for leave to purchase a little spot of ground, wherein he might bury the remains of his deceased wife. The citizens of Geth had conceived a very high opinion of Abraham's merit, whom they styled the prince of God; they begged he would fix upon the spot which seemed the most suitable for his purpose, and take it as a mark of the respect they bore him. Abraham thanked them in the most civil terms for their offer, but from a principle of generosity refused to accept of it, unless they would permit him to pay the full value: the only favour he requested was their interest with Ephron, a principal man of the city, to sell him his field, in which their was a double cave, that would serve as a burying place both for him and Sarah. Ephron, who was present, immediately made him an offer, and even insisted upon his acceptance of the field he wanted. Abraham had taken his resolution to accept of nothing but what he paid for: he desired to know what the field was worth; it was valued at four hundred sicles of silver. The generous Ephron still refused to sell, and urged the point of making a present of his ground to Abraham: Abraham upon that counted out his purchase money in presence of the people, and positively insisted upon the contract being immediately made and signed by proper witnesses;

which being accordingly done, he took possession of the field, and there interred his wife.

It seems not a little extraordinary, that Abraham, to whom the possession of the whole country had been so repeatedly promised, never should have thought of making any other purchase, than that of a burying place for himself and children. The holy patriarch had his thoughts almost constantly fixed on heaven; the prospect of an everlasting inheritance above, gave him a contempt for all perishable things below, and made him look upon the earth only as his place of banishment and death; and therefore was not desirous to possess any more of it, than what was sufficient to serve him for a grave. So perfectly does this conduct of the patriarch agree with what St. Paul has witnessed of him, and so disinterested was his attachment to the delighful land of Chanaan! How desirable soever that country might seem to worldly men, to Abraham it served for nothing more than as a mirror, wherein he contemplated that invisible land, in comparison of which, as the same apostle speaketh, all the rest is but dung and ordure.

A.M. 2148.] *Isaac's Marriage.*—Gen. xxiv. [A.C. 1852.

Abraham was now grown old, and the happy settlement of his son Isaac became the serious object of his thoughts. He knew how much the happiness of man depends upon the woman whom he takes for his partner in life. In the consort whom he proposed for Isaac, he expected more essential qualifications than could be discovered amongst the daughters of Chanaan: he sought a woman whose piety might draw down the blessings of heaven upon his son, at the same time that she should become his wife; and such a woman he thought was not to be met with, but amongst his own kindred in Mesopotamia. Thither therefore he sent Eliezer his household steward, with instructions how to act. Eliezer being come near to the town of Nachor, he humbly prayed for success in his commission, and that by some visible sign he might know the maiden whom God had chosen for Isaac's future consort. The sign he prayed for was, that of all the young women who were then coming out of the town, according to custom, to fetch water from an adjacent fountain, whosoever upon his speaking to her, should offer to let him and his cattle drink, her he should look upon as the person chosen for his master. He had scarce ended his prayer, and taken his stand near the fountain, when behold, Rebecca, the

fair daughter of Bathuel, came in sight. Bathuel was the eighth son of Nachor, Abraham's second brother. Rebecca filled her pitcher at the fountain, and was going off with it upon her shoulder, when Eliezer asked her to let him drink. She readily consented, and moreover offered her service to help his camels to drink. The circumstance exactly answered to his wish; by this he was thoroughly persuaded, that Rebecca was the maiden whom God had chosen for the wife of Isaac, and immediately presented her with a pair of bracelets and ear-rings, in token of his acknowledgment for the kind service she had done him. He asked her whose daughter she was, and whether in her father's house there was lodging for a stranger. She answered that her father's name was Bathuel, that they had plenty of room for him to lodge in, and good store of hay and straw for his camels. Having said that, she ran back to her mother's house, showed her the bracelets and ear-rings, and related her whole adventure. Laban, her brother, went out in haste to see the generous stranger, found him near the fountain, and invited him in. Eliezer readily accepted of the invitation, but refused to take any refreshment, till he had declared his message, and settled the business he was upon. Being bid to speak what it was, he informed them, that he was the servant of Abraham, whom God had taken under his special protection in the land of Chanaan, and blessed with great wealth; that having a son grown up to man's estate, he had commissioned him to look out for a suitable match for him amongst his relations; that in obedience to his master's orders he was therefore come into Mesopotamia; that he had earnestly commended the matter to God, and by a sign, which he mentioned, had undoubtedly learned, that Rebecca was the woman designed by Providence to be Isaac's consort, and as such demanded her in marriage for him. Bathuel and Laban were convinced that the hand of God had conducted the whole affair, and forthwith consented to the proposal. Eliezer produced the rich presents he had brought, of gold and silver plate, a banquet was prepared, and the day was spent in good and cheerful entertainment. Eliezer, like a trusty servant, rose betimes next morning, impatient to return, and proposed setting off immediately. Laban and his mother insisted upon his staying at least ten days longer, which he not being willing to consent to, Rebecca was called upon to decide the point, and fix the time for their departure. Her answer was, that she was ready to go as soon as it should be determined; upon which Eliezer stood to his first resolution, and immediately set off with her towards the land of Chanaan As they drew near their journey's end, Rebecca happened to descry Isaac walking in the field; and Eliezer telling her that it was his lord, and her intended husband, she alighted from her camel, quickly took her cloak, and covered herself with great modesty. Isaac advanced to meet her, conducted her into Sarah's tent, took her for his wife, and in her love consoled himself for the grief which he still felt for his mother's death.

In the conduct of this affair we see no art employed, and no measure pursued, but what tends to constitute a virtuous and happy marriage: no mention is made of riches or of worldly interest; innocence of life and probity of manners is the sole object of inquiry. For this end not only the advice of discreet and saintly persons is asked, but God himself is consulted by frequent prayer. How charming is the circumstance of Rebecca's drawing the cloak over her face, at the sight of Isaac! In that she is an example of modesty to all young women, says Saint Ambrose, and she teaches them, with what discretion they are to behave themselves, even towards those whom they think of making their partners for life. It is not the art of finery, nor the show of dress; it is modesty alone, and simplicity of manners, that must gain the heart, and insure a lasting love.

A.M. 2168.] *Jacob and Esau.*—GEN. XXV. [A.C. 1832

ISAAC and Rebecca passed the first twenty years of their marriage without any issue: he prayed earnestly to God for a son, and as he prayed with a due disposition of heart, his prayers were heard. Rebecca became pregnant of twins, who seemed to rival each other, even before they were born: for she felt them struggling, as it were for superiority, within her. Full of apprehensions, she began to repine at her having conceived, and in holy prayer consulted the Lord to know, what the alarming prodigy foreboded. God signified to her, that she had two infants in her womb, who should be the chiefs of two different people, and that the elder of the two should become subservient to the younger. Rebecca went her full time, and was brought to bed of two sons, the first-born of whom was red and hairy, and named Esau. His brother followed close after, holding him by the heel, which gave occasion to his being called Jacob, that is, the supplanter.

Abraham shared an equal joy with Isaac at this happy increase of his family, which enlivened his hope with the prospect of a numerous and lasting progeny. He saw his two grand-children as far as the fifteenth year of their age, when having nothing more to desire in life, he died in a good old age, and was gathered to his forefathers. To his latest breath he happily preserved the same fidelity to his Creator, for which he had been so remarkable through life. Steady in his faith, and fixed in the principle of paying an unlimited obedience to the commands of God, he was not to be diverted from his duty by any human considerations. He always considered himself as a stranger in the land of Chanaan; and yet, since Providence had once called him thither, he never thought of revisiting his native country of Chaldea. His own good sense twice extricated him from the difficulties into which the beauty of his wife had thrown him, and his personal courage rescued him from the dangers to which he exposed his life for the sake of preserving Lot. Having spent a hundred and seventy-five years in one continued exercise of virtue, he died full of days, and is called the father, as he had been the model, of all true believers.

Jacob and Esau being grown up, the one was plain and simple in his manner, the other a husbandman and a lover of the chase. Esau one day returned from the field hungry and much fatigued; and observing a mess of lentil pottage, which his brother had been boiling for his own repast, earnestly begged to have it. Jacob would not part with it, but upon condition of Esau selling him his birth-right. Esau was pressed with hunger; his present want hindered him from considering the future advantages that might accrue to him from the title of primogeniture; he foolishly gave up his privilege to Jacob, ate the mess, and careless went his way.

The holy fathers observe, that in these two brothers are characterised two different sorts of men, whose principles and manners are as opposite to one another, as good is to evil. These are the virtuous man, and the sensual man; the first takes reason for his guide, the latter is swayed by pleasure. Wealth, birth, and worldly honours may seem to place the one in a higher rank, and make him as it were, the elder of the two; but neither birth, nor wealth, nor worldly honours, can entitle a man without virtue to a place in heaven, or make him great in the sight of God. The virtuous man, however mean he may appear in the eyes of an ambitious world, is preferred by God in the book of life, and whom God prefers must be truly great. Esau, in selling his birth-right for a mess of pottage, furnishes an ample subject of reflection to those, who inconsiderately grasp at the perishable goods of the earth, and for the sake of enjoying what they deem their present happiness, give up their pretensions to the future joys of heaven. Blinded by a similar stroke of folly, they seem to care as little as Esau did, about the title they forfeit; and being only intent, like him, upon gratifying their passions for the present moment, they remain equally insensible of the loss which they entail upon themselves by the bargain they make.

A.M. 2245.] *Isaac blesses Jacob.* [A.C. 1755.
GEN. xxvii.

JACOB, through the folly of Esau, having acquired the right of primogeniture, was soon after, through the contrivance of his mother, fortunate enough to have that right confirmed to him by the blessing of his father. Isaac was far advanced in years, and had lost his eye-sight; therefore thinking the time of his dissolution to be much nearer than it really was, he resolved not to defer giving his last blessing to his children. With that design he sent for Esau, his favourite son, and told him to take his bow and quiver, and to kill him some game to his liking, that at his return he might receive his father's blessing. Rebecca was in the way to hear what Isaac said, and resolved to procure that blessing for her favourite Jacob. She therefore told him to go, as soon as Esau was set out, and fetch her two of the fattest kids of the whole flock. He did so; she lost no time, she prepared and served them up in the manner she knew her husband liked. She had already dressed Jacob in Esau's best clothes, which she had in her custody, and covered his hands and neck with the kid's skin, that if, from the difference of voice in the two brothers, Isaac should suspect any fraud, he might by feeling be induced to take him for Esau. Jacob, therefore, in that disguise carried the meat unto his blind father. and asked his blessing. Isaac no sooner heard him speak. but he knew it to be Jacob's voice, and asked him who he was. Jacob answered, that he was his eldest son Esau. Isaac was not convinced; the voice instead of removing, did but increase his doubts; he bade his son approach, took him by the hand, and felt to find whom he could not see. The voice, indeed, says he, is the voice of Jacob; but the hands are the hands of Esau. Being thus satisfied, he received the meat and the wine from Jacob, and having finished his meal, desired his son to kiss him. A sweet fragrance diffused itself from the young man's clothes, which as soon as Isaac perceived, he compared him to a field full of the sweetest odours, and with his blessing wished him an abundance of all good things; that he might be replenished with the dew of heaven, and with the fat of the land. He declared him to be the lord of all his brethren, and concluded with these words: Whoever shall curse you, let him also be accursed, and whoever shall bless you, let him be replenished with benedictions. Scarce had Isaac finished the sentence, when Jacob went out of the room, and in came Esau, with the game he had killed, big with expectation of his father's blessing. Isaac, in surprise, asked him who he was; and, being answered it was Esau, it is incredible with what amazement he was struck, and how awfully he admired the mysterious ways of Providence. Thy brother, said he, has craftily obtained the blessing which I had for thee; I have blessed him, and he shall be blessed. Whereupon Esau roared out with vexation; and, in the bitterest terms, arraigned his brother Jacob's perfidy. Bathed in tears, he sorrowfully asked his father if he had not one blessing, at least, in reserve for a helpless son, who had been twice supplanted by a brother's treachery.

Esau in this point of view exhibits to us a striking figure of those Christians, as the holy fathers remark, who being desirous of uniting the service of God and the service of the world together, would be glad to enjoy the sweets of the earth without giving up those of heaven. The good old patriarch, being softened into pity at the tears of his wretched son, blessed him indeed at last, but with this express reserve, of his being ever subject to his brother; and this it was which provoked Esau's resentment to such a height, that he waited but his father's death to take away his brother's life.

This history, so curious and at once so mysterious through all its parts, marks out to us Jesus Christ clothed with the appearance of a sinner, as Jacob was with the likeness of his hairy brother; and it is, according to the holy fathers, a wonderful figure not only of the reprobation of the Jews, whose desires were wholly fixed upon the things below, but also of the pre-ordination of the faithful, who, with holy David, demand of God but one sovereign good, and confine their desires to one only blessing, which is that of inhabiting the house of our Lord for ever. We must be careful, says St. Paul, not to incur the misfortune of Esau, who, in the request he made for his father's blessing, having no other title to produce than what he had made over to his brother, deserved not to be heard; not could he, by entreaty or by his tears, prevail upon the virtuous patriarch to retract what he had once pronounced. For, as he had despised God, God in his turn despised him, and disregarded his cries, as the marks of a fictitious sorrow, that sprung only from vexation, and not from any goodness of the heart.

A.M. 2245. *Jacob's Ladder.*—Gen. xxviii. [A.C. 1755.

The violence of Esau's anger made it no longer safe for Jacob to remain with him under the same roof. Rebecca foresaw the storm, and trembled at the thought of what might be the consequence; her apprehensions for the safety of a darling son, awakened all the tenderness of a mother's affection, and put her upon the study of some contrivance to preserve him. She wisely judged that Esau's resentment might cool by length of time, if the object of it were but removed out of sight. She proposed her thoughts upon the matter to her husband, and she did it in such a manner, that it was impossible for him not to approve. She said it was time for Jacob to settle himself in life; that she could not bear the thought of his marrying a woman of Chanaan, as Esau had done; she therefore entreated him to let Jacob go to her father Bathuel, in Mesopotamia, where he was likely to find a proper match for himself amongst the daughters of her brother Laban. Isaac gave his consent; and, in taking leave of his son, repeated to him the blessings he had already given him. Jacob, therefore, quitted his native home, more like a distressed man, that was flying from the persecution of an enraged brother, than in the style of a rich heir, who was going to make choice of a companion for life. In his dress and equipage, he wore the badge of a christian and truly religious humility. Being come to a certain place in the open country, after sunset, he threw himself upon the ground, laid a stone under his head, and composed himself to sleep. During his repose, he was favoured with a vision, which

convinced him that the poor and persecuted are under the immediate protection of heaven. In his sleep he saw a ladder, the foot of which stood upon the ground, and the top seemed to reach to heaven; numbers of angels were ascending and descending by it; God himself was leaning thereon, and said to him: I am the God of Abraham thy father, and the God of Isaac; to thee I will give the land in which thou sleepest; thy children shall be as numerous as the grains of dust upon the earth, *and in thy seed all nations shall be blessed.* He promised to be with him wherever he should go, and to bring him back to the country which he was quitting. Jacob awoke out of his sleep, and being hurried with the idea of what had been represented to him, trembling cried out, How awful is this place! the Lord is most certainly here: it is no other than the dwelling place of God, and the gate of heaven!

"And Jacob arising in the morning, took the stone which he had laid under his head, and set it up for a title, pouring oil upon the top of it. And he called the name of the city Bethel, (the House of God,) which before was called Luza. And he made a vow, saying, If God shall be with me, and shall keep me in the way by which I walk, and shall give me bread to eat, and raiment to put on, and I shall return prosperously to my father's house: the Lord shall be my God. And this stone, which I have set up for a title, shall be called the House of God: and of all things that thou shalt give to me, I will offer tithes to thee."—GEN. xxviii. 18-22

This mysterious vision, of which the holy fathers have said so much, leaves no room to doubt of the special care that God always takes of his faithful servants. In all occurrences of life, he is ever present with them; in their most pressing wants his holy angels are waiting by their side, as witnesses of their conduct, ready to present their petitions to the Almighty God, for their support and comfort. Animated by such a faith and encouraged by such a hope, the faithful Christian is neither terrified by persecution, nor disheartened by affliction. The words that Jacob spoke upon his waking, are in a special manner applied to the sanctity of our churches, in which we adore the same supreme being, whose visible presence filled the patriarch with so much awe; and the holy fathers wish that every Christian, as often as he enters the house of God, would carry with him the like religious respec towards the same Divine Majesty, of whose invisible presence he is fully convinced by the faith he professes.

A M. 2252.] *Rachel and Lia.*—GEN. xxix. [A.C. 1748.

JACOB being in this manner assured of the divine protection that was watching over him, rose up with fresh confidence, and continued on his journey till he came to Haran. There meeting with some shepherds of the country, he asked them if they were acquainted with Laban, the grandson of Nachor. The shepherds answered that they were, and pointed out

Rachel his fair daughter, who happened to be then coming to water her father's flock at a well just by. Jacob advanced to salute her; told her, with tears in his eyes, who he was, and quickly removed the stone from the mouth of the well, that her flocks might drink. Rachel ran to tell her father, that Jacob, his sister's son, was come. Laban hastened out to meet his nephew, whom he heartily embraced and brought into his house. Jacob, with a simplicity peculiar to the patriarchs in those days, related to his uncle the motive of his coming, the cause of his brother's anger, and the necessity he was under of absenting himself from home for a time. Laban told him he was welcome to stay in his house as long as he pleased, and asked him what reward he should give him for his service while he. staid. You have a daughter called Rachel, replied Jacob, and if you will but suffer me to become your son-in-law, I want no other recompense: I will serve you for seven years. His proposal was accepted of: and happy did he think himself in being to receive so amiable a consort for so trifling a service. But at the end of the seven years, he found himself most grievously disappointed; for Laban being unwilling to see his second daughter married before the first, deceived him the very night of his marriage, and in place of Rachel substituted Lia, her eldest sister Jacob did not discover his mistake before morning, when he began to complain most heavily of the injustice that was done him. To silence his complaints, Laban promised to give him Rachel, and that as soon as the seven days appointed for the solemnity of his marriage with Lia were expired, he should espouse her fair sister, if he pleased, upon condition that he would agree to serve him seven years longer. Jacob acquiesced, rather than not gain the charming object of his affections. During those seven years, he had six sons by Lia, and not one by Rachel, for she was barren. Rachel grieved to see herself thus subject to a reproach, which all the fondness of her husband could not compensate. The numerous offspring of her happy sister, moreover, fixed the sting of envy in her breast, and increased the pain of her affliction. Her only resource of comfort was from God. She sent up her fervent prayers to heaven; nor did she cease from praying, till she obtained what she asked. Almighty God blessed her with a son, to whom she gave the name of Joseph. Soon after the birth of Joseph, Jacob desired Laban to let him return into his own country. He represented to him, that the fourteen years he had bargained for were elapsed; that he had demeaned himself with the strictest honesty in his service, and that it was time for him to think of settling and providing for his own family. Laban was sensible of the treasure he possessed in Jacob, and would not willingly agree to let him go. He knew what blessings he had received from God, since Jacob had had the management of his flock; he entreated him to continue in his service, and bade him name the recompense he expected in return. They came to an agreement, and Jacob, upon the condition of having a certain share in the flocks, consented to remain six years longer.

The holy fathers, in taking a view of Jacob's life, admired the wonderful conduct of Divine Providence in his regard. Almighty God had promised him the sovereignty of the whole country of Chanaan, and yet left him no less than twenty years in foreign servitude. His children were to be the chiefs of a great people, and he, their father, was compelled to pass his life in labour and painful service. By this example, say the saints, God has been pleased to teach us, that every head of a family, and every pastor of the church, ought in duty to labour for the salvation of those whom they have under their charge, with as much solicitude as for their own: to advance the good and happiness of their flock, or family, ought to be their joy and chiefest glory: with a fatherly care they ought to watch over and provide for them in their wants, that they may with truth be able to say, what Jacob said to Laban: Behold, I have not lost one of thy flock, neither has the thief nor the wolf diminished thy fold; whatever accident has happened, I have laboured to make it good; thy numbers are increased and multiplied, for this I have spared no pains, and refused no labour: day and night I have borne the heat and cold, and of their sleep have mine eyes been robbed; yet for this, and for all the service that I have endeavoured to render to men, ingratitude and evil treatment have hitherto been my only recompense.

A.M. 2265.] *Jacob's Return.*—GEN. xxxi. [A.C. 1735.

LABAN was grown extremely jealous of Jacob, on account of his great increase of wealth, which he looked upon as so much taken from himself. The prudent patriarch began to be apprehensive of the consequences that this jealousy might produce, and thought that to save his life it was as necessary to fly from Laban, as it had once been to fly from Esau. He was soon after confirmed in that opinion by a special revelation from Almighty God, who commanded him to return to his native home, and promised to be his protector against the resentment of Esau. He communicated his thoughts to Rachel and Lia; they approved of his design, and agreed to accompany him in the journey. Jacob had nothing more to do than to prepare for his departure, which he did with the utmost secrecy. Laban was gone into the country to shear his sheep; Jacob took that opportunity of collecting his substance together, and privately set off, without taking leave of any one. Rachel had secreted the idols of her father's gods, and carried them away with her. It was three days before Laban was informed of this unexpected flight of his son-in-law. He then hastily assembled his dependants, and led them out as in the pursuit of an enemy, whom he intended to reduce by open force. He followed the route that the holy patriarch had taken, and on the seventh day came up with him in the mountain of Galaad. The preceding night Almighty God had admonished him in a vision, to beware of violence and all harsh expressions against his servant Jacob They both pitched their tents upon the mountain, where they came to a parley. Why, said Laban, why do you thus run off with my two daughters, as if they were your slaves taken from an enemy? Why did you conceal your departure? Why was I not made acquainted with your design? I then might have accompanied you with honour part of the way home, and have taken leave of my children. To long after your native country, and to wish to be amongst your friends, was but natural for you, and what I cannot disapprove of; but to steal away my gods.——Here Jacob interrupted him, and, after making a short apology for the secrecy of his proceedings, boldly denied the theft, promising to agree, that if any one of his whole retinue had been guilty of such an action, he should satisfy for it by his death: so little did he think that his favourite Rachel was the person. Laban took him at his word, and entering into Jacob's own tent in the first place, he there made a diligent search after his gods. But not finding them, he proceeded in the same manner to the tents of Lia and the two maid-servants, and, in the last place, came to Rachel. Rachel had secreted the little gods under the camel's litter, and had sat down upon them. As soon as her father entered the tent, she began to make her excuses for not rising to salute him, under the pretence of her not being well, nor in a condition to stand. Laban, therefore, being unable to prove the charge he had brought against Jacob, Jacob in his turn began, with some warmth, to complain of the many and heavy grievances which he had been forced to undergo for twenty years in his service. When they had thus opened their mutual complaints, and expostulated with one another, they suddenly forgot the subject of their disagreement, entered into a solemn league, and parted good friends.

St. Ambrose considers Jacob in the house of Laban as a perfect model of that prudence and honesty which ought to direct our transactions with the world. In taking care to possess nothing but what he could easily carry with him, he remained independent to every other man; he possessed nothing which he had not honestly acquired, and which he could not strictly call his own. The manner by which he had acquired his wealth, was not only equitable in itself, but even advantageous to the person whom he served. Laban had done all he could to keep him in a state of indigence and servitude, yet could not prevent his growing rich: he had always treated him with insincerity and injustice; but was forced, in the end, to own the superior virtues of a man, who was in all things guided and supported by the spirit of God. Happy is the Christian who, in the words of Jacob, can say to the devil and the world, says the same father, Behold, there is nothing about me that belongs to you; search me round, and take it if you find it. Happy Rachel, who by flying from her father's house, trampled his idols under foot. It is the example which all Christians have to follow, in separating themselves from those who, under the mistaken name of love or friendship, would persuade them to sacrifice their souls to the idols of vanity and the world, by a violation of those sacred engagements which they made to God at baptism.

A.M. 2265.] *Esau reconciled with Jacob.* [A.C. 1735.

GEN. xxxiii.

JACOB having got free of Laban, began to consider what method he should take with his brother Esau; for he could not suppose that Esau had entirely forgot what had formerly passed between them. Therefore, to try how he might be disposed, he sent some of his attendants before, to let him know that his brother Jacob was coming home, upon the presumption that he would be glad to see him after so long an absence. Esau, at receiving this information, put himself at the head of four hundred men, and set forward to meet him. Jacob was alarmed at the report, and not doubting but his brother intended to offer violence, sought for shelter under the divine protection, and by fervent prayer implored the power of the Most High against all events whatever. This done, he resolved to try such human means as in his prudence he judged the most likely to soothe his brother's anger. He prepared him rich presents; he chose out of his herd and flocks a certain number of each sort, which he divided into two troops, and sent before him, at some distance one from another, ordering the leaders of each troop to present them successively to Esau, as they met him, with the greatest tokens of submission and friendship. The night before these orders were to have been executed, Jacob had a vision, in which he seemed to be wrestling with a man till morning. It

was an angel in human shape, who, not being able to throw him, touched the sinew of his thigh, which immediately became dry and contracted. The hardy patriarch still would not yield, and refused to let his antagonist go, unless he would first give him his blessing. The angel asked him his name; he answered, Jacob. Thou shalt no longer be called Jacob, but Israel, replied the angel; for since thou hast exerted thyself with such vigour against the angel of God, how much more easily wilt thou prevail over the efforts of men! It was now morning; Jacob cast his eyes round the country, and at a distance descried his brother coming on at the head of a formidable troop. Not knowing what might happen, he ranged his wives and children in a line behind him, and advanced towards his brother. He bowed respectfully to him as he approached, and at seven different times made his obeisance to the very ground. Esau was disarmed and mollified: unable to stand out against such marks of goodness and submission, he ran up and embraced him; with becoming kindness he saluted his brother's wives and children, and could scarce be prevailed upon to accept his presents. He expressed the greatest satisfaction in his friendship, and begged they might finish the remaining part of the journey in each other's company. You see, said Jacob, that my flocks are weak, and my children young; they travel on in very slow marches, which will be tedious to you. Let me be no burden; if I am happy enough to have your good graces, I want no more: return to Seir, where I will join you as soon as circumstances will permit.

In this manner did Jacob disarm the violence of a brother who had conspired his ruin. He considered not which of the two was most to blame; he mentioned not any thing that could renew their former subject of disagreement; his language was discreet and humble; he forgot the past; he banished from his heart every emotion of passion and resentment; or, if he retained a feeling of the injuries he had received, it did not arise from any ill-will, but from a charitable and tender concern for the mischiefs that his brother had thereby drawn upon himself, as St. Ambrose remarks. Great and trying were Jacob's misfortunes, and he bore them with fortitude:—his confidence in God raised him above the reach of human fears: amidst the terrors of an armed host, in the presence of an enraged enemy, he acted with all the coolness and deliberation of a mind at ease; amidst the threats of an approaching death, he remained unshaken and unruffled; by a timely condescension, he triumphed over his brother's obstinacy; by knowing when to yield, he broke his savage hatred. In this example we see that every thing at last must yield to true piety, though for a time oppressed by open force; and that God, who with an admirable wisdom regulates the manner and the measure of sufferings with which he tries his faithful friends, turns all to their advantage, and in their favour changes the hearts of men when and as he pleases.

A.M. 2274.] *Dina.*—GEN. xxxiv. [A.C. 1726.

JACOB, after his return from Mesopotamia, settled with his family near Salem, a town of the Sichimites, where he purchased a piece of land, and lived extremely happy, till an unlucky accident interrupted the peace of his family. He had a daughter called Dina, a fair virgin, in the bloom of youth. Being led by a curiosity which is as natural as it is often dangerous to that age, she went out to see the women of that country. Sichem, who was king of the place, saw her, and being taken with her beauty, seized and carried her off to his house. He tried every persuasive art to make her consent to his wicked desires; but not being able to prevail, he proceeded to the most criminal violence, and then told his father Hemor, that he would marry her with her father's consent. They both went to treat with Jacob upon the subject. The good patriarch, who was in great concern for what had befallen his daughter, said he could give them no answer without the approbation of his sons. The sons came in soon after and were informed of the whole affair, with all its circumstances. They were greatly exasperated at the injury done to their sister by her lover, and resolved to revenge it as soon as an opportunity should offer. They however dissembled their resentment for the present, and only said that no marriage could be lawfully contracted between their sister and the prince of Sichem, unless he and his people would first submit to the law of circumcision. Hemor and Sichem proposed it to their people, who readily came into it, and the ceremony was accordingly performed unto all the men of Sichem. The third day after, when the wound is commonly the most painful, Simeon and Levi, full brothers to Dina, without saying a word to their father, entered sword in hand into the town, and killed every man they met, without exception. This first scene of blood was scarce ended, when the other sons of Jacob rushed in, pillaged the town, and carried off the spoils. Jacob was grievously provoked at his sons, especially for their having abused a religious ceremony to obtain their revenge, and loudly complained of Simeon and Levi in particular, who by an action equally cruel and perfidious, had rendered his name odious to the neighbouring cities, and exposed their little family to the danger of being cut off by the like violence. Being under this apprehension he was inspired to go to Bethel, where God had formerly appeared to him when he fled from Esau. He marched away with his whole family, unhurt and unmolested. For the terror of his name, as the Scripture remarks, had made such an impression upon the people, that no one durst presume to give him the least disturbance. Soon after his arrival at Bethel he lost his dear Rachel, who died in child-bed. [A.M. 2288.] About the same time died also his father Isaac, aged a hundred and eighty years. Full of days, says the sacred text, the venerable patriarch slept with his [illegible] fathers, and was buried by his two sons Jacob and Esau. Esau soon after separated from his brother, for they were too rich to live together.

The history of Dina is mentioned by the holy fathers, as an instance of the danger that attends an idle curiosity. It merits the particular attention of those, says St. Ambrose, whose age and sex are most exposed to danger. The loose modes and maxims of the present age ought to make a Christian virgin extremely cautious, how she trusts herself unaccompanied abroad, what company she sees, and what places she frequents. Curiosity may be as strong in her as it was in Dina, and if indulged with the same liberty, may possibly be followed by the same fatal consequences. Curiosity led her to the spot where she lost her virginity; her curiosity was the first step towards all those horrors which her brothers committed in butchering the inhabitants, and in plundering the effects of Sichem; her curiosity, in fine, was the first cause that obliged Jacob to retire from the spot, where he could no longer stay with safety to himself or family, and where they must all have perished, had not God miraculously interposed in their favour.

A.M. 2276.] *Joseph sold by his brethren.* [A.C. 1724.
GEN. XXXVII.

JACOB, who had happily escaped the attacks of foreign enemies, began to be perplexed with domestic broils, which were the more painful to him, as they were fomented by his own children. Joseph, his son by Rachel, and the last of those that were born in Mesopotamia, had accused some of his brothers of a most shameful crime, which the sacred text does not name. This accusation procured him much ill-will amongst them all; he was his father's favourite, and that alone had been enough to make them hate him. He was an innocent, artless, open-hearted youth, in the sixteenth year of his age, and thinking his brothers to be as well meaning as himself, freely spoke his thoughts to them. Amongst other things he related two of his dreams, which added fresh fuel to their glowing envy. I dreamed, said he, that I was binding up corn in a field with you, and that my sheaf seemed to rise, as it were, and to stand upright, while yours stood round and paid homage to it. And in another dream, I saw the sun and moon and eleven stars, paying the like homage to me. The relation of these two dreams kindled up a flame in his brothers' breasts, which seemed to threaten him with present ruin, but which the Almighty rendered instrumental to that future greatness which his dreams presaged. Not long after this his father sent him to visit his brothers, who were tending their flocks in the plains of Sichem. As soon as they

saw the dreamer coming, as they called him, they formed a design against his life. Reuben the eldest of all Jacob's children would not agree to the barbarous proposal. Instead of imbruing their hands in the blood of the innocent, he advised them to let him down into a dry well that was hard by His intention was to save his brother's life, if he could, for the present, and in a seasonable hour, restore him to his father. His advice took place, and Joseph was let down into the well. Some Ismaelite merchants happening to pass by soon after, on their way to Egypt, the unnatural brothers thought it a fair opportunity to get rid of Joseph without taking away his life: they drew him out of the well, and sold him to the merchants for twenty pieces of silver, intending at the same time, to make their father believe that his darling son had been devoured by a wild beast. To make that story the more credible, they took Joseph's variegated coat, and having stained it with the blood of a kid, sent it home, as if

they had found it in that condition. Jacob knew it at first sight, and from thence concluding his son to be really dead, rent his garments through grief, and would admit of no consolation. Joseph in the mean time was carried away into Egypt, where the merchants sold him to Putiphar, the prime officer of king Pharaoh's guards.

Thus was the helpless youth plunged into a state of the deepest distress, which he had neither merited nor foreseen. God had given him an obscure glimpse of the glory that was waiting for him at a distance, but concealed from him the misfortunes that were then hanging over his head. Joseph sold by his own brothers, is a lively figure of Jesus Christ in that particular circumstance of his life, in which, by the treachery of a false apostle, he was likewise sold to his enemies. The grief that Jacob so justly expressed on this occasion is, according to St. Ambrose, a singular instruction to all parents. He wept for the loss of a son whom he tenderly loved, and whom, if he had not loved so much, he would perhaps have had no cause to weep for. For the father's excessive love was the primary cause of the son's misfortune, in as much as it first excited his brothers' envy, and whetted their spleen against him. It is a father's duty to love his children, says the holy doctor, and it is but just to love them the most, who are the most deserving: but to show that love in the presence of the rest is always dangerous; for such a show of preference to the one must naturally make the others jealous, who look upon themselves as injured by it. Hence the father's partiality often becomes a real injury to his own favourite child, as far as it deprives him of the affection of his brothers. A perfect union of heart and will, is one of the most precious advantages that a father can produce in his family. No wonder if an estate, or some less valuable present made to a favourite child, should excite the envy of the rest, continues the same saint, since a coat somewhat finer than ordinary, given by Jacob to Joseph, stirred up such a ferment amongst the brothers, that even the most moderate were eager to sell him for a slave, while others insisted upon his blood.

A.M. 2286.] *Joseph's Chastity.*—Gen. xxxix. [A.C. 1714.

Oppressed innocence never is abandoned by Almighty God. Joseph in an idolatrous country, in the midst of strangers, met with kinder treatment and with better friends than he had found at home amongst his brothers. His prudence, his fidelity, and modest conduct, gained him the affection of Putiphar his master. His genius and liberality of sentiment, was not that of a common slave. His person was comely, and an engaging sweetness of countenance and behaviour made him every body's favourite. Being appointed by Putiphar to superintend his household, he acquitted himself faithfully of the trust that was reposed in him: he was happy and enjoying the sunshine of his good fortune, when a sudden storm arose from a quarter he had the least suspected. Amongst his many admirers, was his mistress, Putiphar's wife. She beheld him with a fond eye, she grew amorous, and conceived a criminal affection for him: she discovered to him her passion, she solicited his consent, without being able to obtain it. Far from being checked by the first refusal, she returned again to the charge; she pressed and solicited with more eager warmth.—How is it possible, replied the virtuous youth, that I should think of being so unfaithful to a master, who has been so good, and placed such confidence in me? How is it possible I should consent to commit such a sin in the presence of my God?—This steady resistance increased her desires. Finding him one day alone in his apartment, she attacked him with fresh eagerness; she laid hold of him, and began to offer violence. In this situation, having no witness near, Joseph had but to fly. He rushed out of doors, but left unluckily his cloak in the woman's hands. Her slighted love then turned to fury; she became outrageous, she determined to ruin the man whom she could not gain. She screamed aloud, as if Joseph had made some violent assault upon her honour; she ran out with his cloak in her hand; she held it up and showed it to all, as a proof of her assertion. She carried it to her husband as a trophy of her fidelity to him, and impudently produced it against the man, whose innocence was his guilt, and whose conduct had been the very reverse of her own. Putiphar gave her credit for what she said, and upon her single evidence judged the innocent to be guilty. Without any further examination he ordered Joseph to be immediately secured and cast into one of the state prisons. By a sentence the most unjust and cruel, Joseph was condemned to suffer for a supposed crime, of which his accuser was really guilty. For the slander was believed, and silence imposed upon the truth.

So it is, says St. Ambrose, speaking of the orthodox Christians, who were at that time grievously persecuted by the Arians, that the prisons are now become the dwelling of the innocent; the adulterers of our faith prevail; they accuse and cast into chains all those who refuse to concur with them in their impious tenets. But let not the courage of those champions of Christianity be dejected, continues the holy doctor, God will descend with them into the dungeon, as is recorded of the patriarch Joseph, nor will he abandon them in their chains. Sufferings and persecutions are the portion of God's elect; through various tribulations and painful trials lies the way to heaven; that is the way in which our blessed Redeemer trod; that way the apostles and all the holy martyrs followed. Animated by their example, and encouraged by the hope of that happy kingdom which they have in view, the confessors of Jesus Christ receive their sufferings with joy, and think themselves honoured by the contumelies they undergo in so glorious a cause. Though innocent of the crimes of which they stand accused before men, they know that in the sight of God they are still deserving of punishment, and therefore bless the hand that strikes to heal them. Void of resentment against their persecutors, they think they are under a strict obligation of loving them the more, because they so happily contribute to make them companions of the cross, and partakers of the glory of Jesus Christ. They count the days of their affliction, amongst the most happy of their lives: under their severest trials, in the midst of their sharpest sufferings, they say with holy Job, there is One in heaven, who sees and will judge according to the uprightness of our hearts; in Him we hope for the justification of our innocence; on Him alone we rely for the reward of our labours.

A.M. 2287.] *Joseph's greatness.*—Gen. xl. [A.C. 1713.

Joseph in his prison made himself beloved and esteemed by all that came near him. Honour attended him even in the place of his disgrace. The keeper of the prison had such an opinion of him, that he put all the other prisoners under his care, and directed himself by his advice. Two of the king's officers, his cup-bearer and chief baker, had fallen into disgrace, and were lodged in the same prison with Joseph. On the same night they had each a dream, which seemed to indicate their future fortune. The cup-bearer dreamed he saw a vine, in which there were three shoots, producing first the bud, then the blossom, and at last ripe grapes; he gathered the grapes, squeezed them into Pharaoh's cup, and presented it, as usual, to the king. The baker dreamed he had three baskets of meal upon his head, and, in the uppermost, different sorts of pastry work, which the birds came to peck at. Being much troubled in mind, and anxious to know what these dreams could signify, they both applied to Joseph for an explanation Joseph, as a figure of Jesus Christ in the judgment he passed between the two companions of his sufferings upon the cross, gave two very opposite interpretations to the two dreams, declaring to the baker, that within three days he should be hanged upon a gibbet; and to the cup-bearer, that he should be restored to his former honour. When you shall stand before the king, said he to the cup-bearer, speak a good word for me; for I have been traitorously sold in my own country, and am here unjustly thrown into prison. The event answered the prediction; Joseph, nevertheless, remained two years longer in confinement; for the cup-bearer in the hurry of his prosperity had entirely forgot him, till he was put in mind by the relation of two dreams that Pharaoh had. Pharaoh, in his sleep, seemed to be standing upon the banks of the Nile, from whence came out seven fat kine, that went and grazed in the fertile marshes. Soon after there came forth seven other kine most hideously lean, which began to feed upon the rich banks of the river, and devoured the seven that were fat and beautiful. Pharaoh awaked, and composing himself to sleep again, saw in a second dream seven full ears of corn upon one stalk, that were succeeded and spoiled of their beauty by seven blighted ones. These two dreams in one night, seemed to portend something uncommon; and every man that pretended to any skill in Egypt, was sent for to interpret their meaning; and no one being able to say any thing that was satisfactory upon the subject, the cup-bearer

mentioned what had happened to him, when in prison with a Hebrew servant called Joseph. Joseph, therefore, by the king's command was brought out of prison and presented before him; the king related his dreams, which Joseph thus interpreted: From what has been shown to Pharaoh in his sleep, it appears that for seven years to come there will be great plenty in the land of Egypt; and that a seven years' famine will then succeed. Having thus declared the meaning of the dreams, he advised the king to provide himself with large granaries, and to lay up sufficient stores against the time of scarcity. Pharaoh stood amazed at the wisdom of this young Hebrew, and received his advice as an oracle from God. Amongst all his subjects he judged none so capable and so fit as Joseph, to execute a plan of that mighty consequence, and therefore created him his vicegerent over the whole kingdom of Egypt, with an absolute power to direct and command, as he should think expedient for the common weal. To insure him moreover a due respect from the people, he gave him his own ring, put a chain of gold about his neck, invested him with a silk robe, and placed

him in his second chariot, commanding the herald to proclaim aloud, that all should bend their knee to Joseph, whom in the Egyptian language he styled the saviour of the world.

In this manner was that illustrious patriarch set up to public view; thus was he drawn from the obscurity of a dungeon, and advanced to the highest pitch of worldly grandeur. So sudden and so great a change of fortune had been enough to turn the head of a man less moderate in his desires, or less steady in the principles of virtue; in Joseph it made no alteration of sentiment, no change of principle; the same natural goodness still held the direction of his heart and actions. As he never had been dejected at the frowns of fortune, so neither was he now elated at her smiles. Being invested with a dignity second to the king, over all Egypt, he received his power as from the hand of God, for the general good of mankind. Far from revenging himself upon those who by their slanders had thrown him into a dungeon, he left them to the secret remorse of their own conscience, the worst of punishments than can attend an evil action in this life. In the ordinary course of visible events, a change of fortune like that of Joseph seldom occurs; but in the invisible order of things there daily happens a change incomparatively greater, when poor suffering mortals are called from this vale of tears to the joys of heaven. Joseph's translation from his prison to a palace, bears but a faint resemblance of the glory that God confers upon his faithful servants after death. The light and momentary sufferings which they here endure, are there crowned with a happiness which is equally incomprehensible and eternal.

A.M. 2296.] *Joseph's brothers.*—GEN. xlii. [A.C. 1704.

JOSEPH being invested with an authority, as we have seen, that extended itself over the whole Egyptian empire, soon showed, by the use he made of his power, how much the happiness of a people depends upon the wisdom of their governors. His chief study was the good of his fellow-subjects, for that he knew to be the real interest of his royal master: without restraining the people in the enjoyment of their property, he prudently contrived the means that were no burden, to lay up a sufficient provision of corn during the time of plenty, for their support against the famine. At the end of seven years a raging famine began to distress the land, and it was Pharaoh's order, that all in their distress should go to Joseph. With the tenderness of a father, Joseph heard their complaints and relieved their wants. By him none were despised, none rejected; his granaries were open to all that came. The general dearth had reached as far as Chanaan, and Jacob's family with the rest was reduced to great distress. The good patriarch being told that corn was to be bought in Egypt, sent thither ten of his sons. Joseph knew them at first sight; they had not the least suspicion of his being their brother, and knew no more of him than if they had never seen him. He received them with a seeming harshness, asked them, as though they had been strangers to him, from whence they came, and whether they were not spies. They answered with profound respect, that distress alone had forced them from home, and nothing but an honest intention of buying corn had brought them into Egypt; that they were twelve sons of the same father, that one of them no longer existed, and that the youngest of all, called Benjamin, was left behind with their father Jacob in Chanaan. The name of Benjamin touched the inmost feelings of affection in Joseph's breast, and reminded him of the cruel treatment that he had once experienced from his unnatural brothers; he was apprehensive lest Benjamin also might some day or other experience the like ill usage, and therefore resolved to secure him out of their hands. He seemed to give no credit to their words, and said that to assure himself of the truth of their story he must see Benjamin; that one of them should go home and fetch him, while the rest remained his prisoners and sureties for their brother's coming. He therefore put them in prison three days, when he ordered them again to be brought out before him. They stood whispering their thoughts to one another in their own language, little suspecting they were understood by any one there; for Joseph had spoken to them by an interpreter: they discoursed of their present affliction, and considered it as a just judgment fallen upon them for their former cruelty towards their brother Joseph. Joseph listened to and understood every word they said; his heart began to beat, his bosom heaved with fraternal affection, and the tears stole down his cheeks. He was obliged to leave the room for fear of discovering himself too soon. When he had suppressed that flow of tenderness and wiped away his tears, he came back and told them, that he should content himself with detaining only Simeon as a hostage, and that the rest might depart. He had given secret orders that their sacks should be filled with corn, and that the money they had given for it should be tied up in the mouth of each sack. Upon their return home they gave Jacob an account of all that had passed, and particularly of the engagement they were under of carrying Benjamin into Egypt, where Simeon was detained, as a pledge of their promise. Such a tale wounded their aged father to the quick: he bemoaned his misfortunes, he talked over his children, he was inconsolable at the thought of parting with the last and dearest of his sons. Joseph, said he, is no more; Simeon is in chains; and must Benjamin be taken from me too? No, I will not part with him; to part with him would wring my very soul with grief, and carry my grey hairs in anguish to the grave.

The holy fathers seem charmed with the relation of this history, in which they discover such singular strokes of the divine Providence, which sweetly disposes and brings all things to their appointed ends. The sons of Jacob were jealous of the greatness that had been foreshown to one of their brothers; they used the most efficacious means, as they thought, to prevent it, and Providence directed those very means to promote it. Joseph was forewarned from heaven of his future greatness; his brothers sought to put him out of the way of it, and that was the very way which led him to it: they sold him for a slave, and the state of servitude opened him a passage to the highest honours; they caused him to be transported into a foreign country, and there he became the preserver of his own. Such incidents of human life may, by a profane writer, be passed over unnoticed, or be ascribed to chance; but by the inspired historian they are recorded to serve as a conviction to the incredulous and free-thinker, that there is a God who rules and presides over all things here below, and that no efforts or artifices of men can circumscribe his power, or defeat his designs. There is no wisdom, there is no prudence, no counsel, says the wise man, powerful enough to prevail against God. By his almighty will the very opposition that is made by men, becomes oftentimes instrumental in his hand for the accomplishment of his designs.

A.M. 2297.] *Joseph makes himself known to his brothers.*—GEN. xlv. [A.C. 1703.

THE general dearth continuing still to rage with greater violence, Jacob was obliged to consent at last to let Benjamin go into Egypt, lest he should see him die with famine in the land of Chanaan. But it was not without great persuasion that he had been prevailed upon to give his consent, Judas had in a manner extorted it from him, by pledging himself and children for Benjamin's return. By Jacob's consent, they all set out again for Egypt, with considerable presents for the governor. Joseph was no sooner told that the brothers were arrived, but he ordered his steward to receive and entertain them. They were surprised at this civil treatment, which was so very different from what they had experienced before, and knew not how to account for it. They began to suspect some artful design against them on account of the money they had found tied up in their sacks of corn, and to prevent every accusation upon that score, they informed the steward, that they had brought back the money which ought to have been left with him the last time. The steward was very courteous, bade them be under no apprehension, and as a pledge of their safety introduced their brother Simeon. They began to feel themselves at ease, they washed their feet, and set their presents in order, before the governor came in. Joseph entered at the appointed hour, to whom they paid the most respectful homage, and offered their presents. He kindly returned the salutation, and eagerly asked them whether their aged father was still alive and in good health. His brother Benjamin immediately drew his eye: is this, said he, your little brother you mentioned to me? His heart at the moment melted with affection, he could just speak to wish him the blessing of heaven, the rising tears started from his eyes, and forced him to retire into an adjoining apartment, that they might flow without restraint. When the first flutter of his spirits was abated, he washed his face, and went back to his brothers in the room where they were to dine. He sat himself down at a different table from them, for the Egyptians were not allowed to eat with Hebrews; they sat before him in order according to their age, and received the meat he sent them in great plenty: Benjamin engaged his particular attention, to whom he took care constantly to send the greatest share. The day was thus spent to the full satisfaction of the eleven brothers, and the next day appointed for their return into the land of Chanaan. Joseph in the mean time gave orders that their sacks should be filled with corn, and beside the money which was tied up in each one's sack, as before, that his own silver cup should be secretly conveyed into the sack of Benjamin. They set out in the morning, but had not gone far when Joseph's steward overtook them with a complaint of their having stolen the governor's silver cup, in return for the civilities he had shown them. They were surprised to hear so odious a crime laid to their charge, for which they did not conceive there could be the least foundation. Conscious of their innocence, they begged to be searched upon the spot, and if any one of them should be found to have the cup, they freely consented that he should die, and the rest be made slaves. The steward answered, that the innocent should not suffer for the guilty, and that none but he who had the cup should become his slave. They hastily opened their sacks, and behold, Joseph's silver cup was found in the sack of Benjamin. The unsuspected discovery threw them into the utmost consternation; they knew not what to say, or what to do; they turned back into town, hastened to the governor, and flung themselves at his feet. Having no other proof than their bare word to produce in defence of their innocence, they patiently bore his dissembled anger, and each one offered to remain his slave, if Benjamin might only be at liberty to go back to his father. You are free to go, replied Joseph, but Benjamin shall remain with me: upon which Judas, who had pledged his own children to Jacob for Benjamin's safe return, began in terms the most respectful and pathetic, to represent to Joseph the promise he had made of seeing his brother safe home again; urged the respect due to a father's grey hairs; mentioned the loss of another favourite son, whom he still mourned for, and concluded by saying, that the detention of this his last and darling child, would certainly sink his declining age to the grave. Joseph could refrain no longer; he bade the Egyptians leave the room: there, being alone with his brothers, he raised his voice, and said, I am Joseph your brother: is my father still living? Be not afraid to approach me; I am your brother, whom you sold to be carried into Egypt. It happened by the design of an all-ruling Providence, who has thus provided for your safety. Go, hasten to my father, and let him know that his son Joseph not only lives, but has all the land of Egypt at his disposal. Go, bring him and your families hither; you shall be settled in the fertile lands of Gessen; be quick, make no delay. Struck dumb with amazement, it was some time before they could make any answer. Joseph wept and tenderly embraced them all: with greater feeling he threw himself upon the neck of Benjamin, folding him in his arms, and clasping him close to his breast.

The bare narration of Joseph's history, say the holy fathers, sufficiently informs us of the goodness of his heart, and of the mildness of his disposition. He is a pattern for every Christian to follow in the pardon of injuries. He said not a word of the malice of his offenders, he excused the action, he put the best construction he could upon their conduct, and so far was he from making them any reproach, that he even tried to dissipate the fears which the consciousness of their guilt must naturally have caused within them. Invested with full power to punish offenders as he pleased, he employed it all for the good of those who had intended him the greatest evils, and their frowns of envy he repaid with the sweetest smiles of brotherly benevolence. The admirable charity of this saint is a figure of that unparalleled goodness which we adore in Jesus Christ, who being sold by his own brethren, not only pardoned them for the cruel death they put him to, but also made the blood he spilt upon his cross, the price of their salvation and the ransom of their souls.

A.M. 2298.] *Jacob goes into Egypt.* [A.C. 1702
GEN. xlvi.

THE sons of Israel, loaded with stores and rich presents from their brother Joseph, hastened home as fast as they could, to impart the happy tidings to their father. The joy and surprise of the good patriarch to hear that his son Joseph was not only alive, but also had the command of all Egypt, were so great, that he seemed in a manner stupified at first, and out of his senses. When he recovered himself, and was informed at leisure of the particulars that had happened, he said, It is sufficient, if my son Joseph be only living; I will go and embrace him before I die. Joseph had already sent wains and beasts of burden for the convenience of transporting his father and brethren, with their goods and families, into Egypt. In an expedition of such lasting consequence to his whole family, the religious patriarch would not proceed, without first informing himself of the will, and imploring the blessing of the Most High. He slew victims to the God of his father Isaac; and God in an audible manner told him not to doubt of going into Egypt, where, under the divine protection, he should grow into a numerous nation, and in process of time be brought back from thence, after his eyes should be there closed in death by his son Joseph. Being extremely comforted by this vision, Jacob loaded his whole substance upon Pharaoh's waggons, and with his eleven sons, their wives and little ones, to the number of seventy in all, began his journey towards the land of Egypt. Judas was sent before to apprise Joseph of his father's coming. Joseph set off with a becoming retinue to meet him, and proceeded as far as Gessen. The moment his father's carriage came in sight, he got out of his chariot, and respectfully advanced on foot to receive him. As soon as they met, they rushed into each other's arms, they cordially embraced, they clung for some time together, without being able to utter a single word. The excess of their joy was too high for either of them to speak what they felt. They wept, and their tears best witnessed the glowing sentiments of their hearts in this unexpected interview. Joseph conducted both his father and his brothers into the royal city, and presented them to the king. Pharaoh gave them a gracious reception, and, according to their desire, allotted them the fertile spot of Gessen for their place of residence. There they settled, unmolested and separated from the Egyptians; there, under the protection of God, and by the particular care of Joseph, they lived strangers to the famine which was severely felt by their neighbours round.

Truly admirable, says St. Chrysostom, is the conduct of Almighty God with regard to his elect. Through various trials, by continual succession of good and adverse fortune,

he trains them up to virtue. He tempers their success with affliction, lest they should swell too high; and then visits them again with comfort, lest they should sink beneath the weight of continued sufferings. It was no loss either to Jacob or to Joseph to have been deprived of each other for a time; the joy they felt at meeting again made ample amends for their past afflictions. The fortune that afterwards attended the descendants of Jacob in Egypt was the very reverse of his. They at first experienced every advantage they could wish for, and were in the end oppressed with all the evils that an infidel and barbarous people could inflict. For Egypt, that is to say the world, is always to be dreaded by every true Israelite; notwithstanding its caresses, it is not to be relied upon. It varies in its favours and its friendship, as best suits its interest. Both its promises and its flatteries are always to be suspected by the wary Christian. It often smiles whilst it fixes its sting, and pampers the body while it kills the soul.

A.M. 2315.] *Midwives of Egypt.*—Exod. i. [A.C. 1685.

Jacob enjoyed a comfortable old age, during the seventeen years he resided in Egypt. Upon the report of his being sick, Joseph, the bright pattern of filial piety, hastened with his two sons, Ephraim and Manasses, to pay the last duty to his dying father. The venerable patriarch raised himself up in the bed at his son's approach, and spoke to him of the inheritance which God had promised to his seed in the land of Chanaan, whither he desired his remains might be carried after death, and deposited with his father's. Joseph promised him they should, and presented him his two sons Manasses and Ephraim. Jacob adopted them for his own, promised them each a share

in the lands of Chanaan, and laying his hands upon their heads, blessed them both. He called his other sons around his bed, and gave to each a special blessing; the most memorable is that which he spoke to Judah. It expresses that from his race the Messias, THE EXPECTATION OF ALL NATIONS, should be born; and that this great event should happen at or near the time, when the sovereign power should be entirely taken away from the Jewish nation. Jacob died in the hundred and forty-seventh year of his age. As soon as he had breathed his last, Joseph threw himself upon the face of his deceased father, and poured out a torrent of tears. He gave orders for his physicians to embalm the body, and when the seventy days that Egypt mourned for him, were expired, he asked Pharaoh leave to see it buried, as his father had desired, in Chanaan. The king's whole court, and all the ancients of Egypt, accompanied the funeral, and Jacob was with great pomp deposited in the double cave near Mambre by the side of Abraham and Isaac. Joseph having paid these last honours to his father with a truly filial piety, hastened back into Egypt, where he remained sole depository of the royal power and authority, as long as he lived. His brethren expressing some apprehension, lest he might take an opportunity from their father's death, to repay them for the injuries they had formerly done him, he assured them, with tears in his eyes, that they had nothing to fear, that they should always find him their friend and protector, that he would feed both them and their little ones. With the spirit of prophecy he declared, that after his death God would visit and lead them forth from thence, into the land which he had promised to Abraham, Isaac and Jacob, bidding them remember, when that time should come, to carry away his bones with them out of Egypt, that they might be interred with his father's in the land of Chanaan. Joseph lived to see his sons' children unto the third generation, and then died, being a hundred and ten years old, during eighty of which he had governed Egypt with great renown of justice and wisdom. His body was embalmed and deposited in one of the Egyptian tombs, where it rested till the departure of the Israelites out of that country.

A.M. 2427.] Within a few years after Joseph's death a total change of affairs took place in the kingdom of Egypt. A new king, known also by the name of Pharaoh, a name adopted, as it seems, by most of the Egyptian kings, forgetting the glory of Joseph's administration, showed himself no friend to the Hebrew people. Far from protecting them, as his predecessors had done, he thought to afflict and destroy them. Growing jealous of their power, and seeing their progeny increase, he artfully attempted to diminish their numbers, under pretence of rendering them serviceable to the state. For that purpose he employed them in the public works which he set on foot, and imposed such heavy burdens on them as he concluded must break their strength and ruin their constitutions. But as the church was afterwards to gather strength from its worldly afflictions, so did the Israelites at that time increase the faster for being oppressed. Pharaoh took the barbarous resolution of having all their male children strangled, as soon as they were born, and charged the midwives of Egypt with its execution. The compassionate women, having the fear of God before their eyes, refused to imbrue their hands in innocent blood. Pharaoh called them to an account for not having executed his orders; they were terrified at his threats, and made use of an officious lie in their excuse, saying that the Hebrew women were not like unto those of the country, and were delivered before any midwife could come to them. The king was exasperated to find himself thus disappointed in his schemes of secret murder, threw off the mask, and gave a general order, that all the Hebrew boys, without exception, should be thrown into the river Nile.

It seems as if every tender feeling and sentiment of

humanity had been banished from the breasts of the Egyptians, excepting a few women, who out of compassion to an injured people, exposed themselves to the resentment of a cruel prince. They made indeed an excuse for their disobedience by a lie, which was a weakness; yet God rewarded them for their piety towards the helpless children. Superlatively happy would they have been, says St. Austin, if to their feelings of humanity they had united the love of truth, and had generously chosen to expose their own lives rather than save them by a lie. After having been resolute enough to preserve the lives of the innocent at the hazard of their own, glorious had it been for them to have gone one step farther, and met the final stroke, rather than have fled from it by a breach of truth. Their earthly house of clay, says the same holy father, might probably have been demolished by it, but in recompense thereof they had dwelt eternally in heaven.

A.M. 2433.] *Moses saved from the Nile.* [A.C. 1567.
Exod. ii.

Whilst the Israelites were groaning under the load of oppression, and an ungrateful king was exerting his utmost malice to extinguish a people to whom his predecessors had been indebted for their crown and prosperity, Amram, the grandson of Levi, had a son by his wife, whose name was Jochabed. Love prompted the mother to use every ingenious artifice to conceal her child, whose comely countenance made him still more dear. But as Pharaoh's order was executed with the most unrelenting barbarity, she was compelled, at the end of three months, either to give him up, or to perish with him. She therefore contrived, as it were, a cradle of bulrushes, which she twisted together, and lined the inside with pitch. In this kind of basket she laid her little infant, and exposed him on the sedgy bank of the Nile, telling her daughter to stay near the place, and cautiously wait the event. Providence so ordained, that Pharaoh's daughter, attended by her maids, should then come to that very spot with an intent to bathe in the river. She immediately espied the basket, and being curious to know what was in it, sent one of her attendants to fetch it. She opened it, and found a beautiful infant crying, and stretching out his little hands, as it were, for help. She was softened into pity, and resolved to save it. The sister of the infant, who was all

this while upon the watch, narrowly observed, and heard what was said. She drew nearer by degrees to the princess, and at last ventured to ask her if she wanted a nurse for the child, and offered her service to call one of the Hebrew women. Being told she might, she ran to call her mother. The mother came, and full of secret joy received her child from the princess, who promised to reward her well for her trouble in taking care of him. When the boy was grown up she presented him to the princess, who adopted him for her son, and called him Moses, because he had been saved from the waters; for Moses or Moyses in the Egyptian language signifies water.

The holy fathers seem lost in admiration, when they consider this saintly man, who was the minister of the old law, as Jesus Christ is of the new, preserved in the same wonderful manner as our Saviour was, amidst so many thousands of infants, whom a tyrant's fury cut off in the bud of life. It is in such instances of his fatherly providence, that God shows himself to be the sovereign ruler of all things, and that nothing is so easy to him, as to defeat the deepest schemes that human policy can form in contradiction to his eternal designs. He seems pleased to exert a more visible power against those who presume to attack him by open force. In vain did Pharaoh strive to extirpate the Hebrew people; he nourished within his palace, as his grandson, the very man who was to deliver them out of his hands. The mother, whose fears had drove her to expose her son to the merciless waves, not only received him back again into her arms, but was even paid for nursing and taking care of him, a care more precious to her than all the treasures of Egypt. The step that was intended to rob the infant of his life, was the first advance towards his future greatness. By a special providence Moses was delivered from the waters of the Nile, that at his command the son of that prince who had thrown him there, might be swallowed up in the waters of the sea. Overwhelmed in the same abyss, perished likewise those Egyptian chiefs, who had been the ministers of their master's tyranny. To all who have not given up their pretensions to reason and common sense, these instances of a superior providence must be a convincing proof that there is a God, who presides over and directs the ways of men; that the most vigorous efforts of men are but mere weakness against the divine arm, and that to dispute the power of the Most High, is a folly not less extravagant than impious.

A.M. 2473.] *The Burning Bush.* [A.C. 1527.

EXOD. iii.

MOSES spent the years of his youth in the royal palace of Egypt, where he was treated as Pharaoh's grandson. Having attained the fortieth year of his age, he began to think that a life so miraculously preserved by God, ought not to be idly spent amidst the pleasures of a court. Under the title of adoption he enjoyed every worldly comfort, though by birth a Hebrew, whilst his brethren were groaning under the most oppressive slavery. Being of the same race and religion with them, he saw no privilege that he could have to exempt him from sharing in the same fortune. As he was one day taking his walk, and musing upon that subject, he found an Egyptian man beating a Hebrew in a most cruel manner. Moses was too partial to his countryman to remain an idle spectator: in the warmth of his zeal he struck the Egyptian, and killed him upon the spot. He looked round, and seeing no one near, thought he had not been seen, buried the body in the sand, and walked off. In his round next day he met with two Israelites that were quarrelling with one another; he interfered and endeavoured to reconcile them; upon which one of them rudely asked him, what he meant, and whether he intended to kill either of them, as he had killed the Egyptian the day before? Moses by that found he was discovered, and thought it necessary for his security to leave the country. He therefore retired across the Red Sea, in to the land of Madian, which is a part of Arabia Petrosa: in Madian there lived a priest, whose name was Raguel, otherwise Jethro, who had seven daughters. These young women daily attended their father's flocks, and one day leading them to drink as usual, at a certain spring, they found Moses there. By his dress and language they took him for an Egyptian, but by the services he did them in helping their flocks to drink, they found him to be a good man. They spoke advantageously of him to their father, who desired to see him. Moses was therefore sent for, who being pleased with a certain air of goodness he saw in Jethro, consented to live with him. He took a liking also to Sephora, his eldest daughter, married her by mutual consent, and for forty years together took care of her father's flocks that fed in the desert.

A.M. 2513.] Moses had one day led his flocks into the inner parts of the desert, towards the mountain of Horeb, where he saw a bush on fire without its being consumed. Struck at the wonderful appearance, he advanced to examine it more closely, when a voice from amidst the flames bid him

stop and take off his shoes, for that sacred was the ground on which he stood. God told him that the cries of the afflicted Israelites had penetrated the heavens, that an end should be put to their labours, and that he was the man chosen to lead them out of the Egyptian slavery into the land of promise. Moses humbly begged to be excused from an undertaking, for which he deemed himself wholly unfit; but God insisted upon his obedience, and by two miracles convinced him of the divine power that should be always at hand to support him. He first of all changed his rod into a serpent, and from a serpent into a rod. After that he bade him put his hand into his bosom, which in an instant was covered with a leprosy, and as soon made clean again. Moses notwithstanding, was still unwilling to consent, till being terrified at the threat of God's displeasure, he at last accepted of the charge, which he could no longer refuse without a sin. Upon that he took leave of Jethro, and hastened back into Egypt for the consolation of his countrymen.

The holy fathers look upon the burning bush, as an emblem of what happens to the elect of God. Persecuted by a jealous world, they remain unhurt and unimpaired by the flames of affliction that surround them: For God himself is in the midst of them to support them by his grace, and to render them more illustrious by their sufferings. St. Gregory dwells upon the example of humility that Moses gave, in refusing to take upon him the charge of conducting the people of God, though so qualified with talents both of grace and nature. Little in his own eyes, he deemed himself unworthy of the honour, and unequal to the arduous task; nor was he to be prevailed upon to consent to his own preferment, but by the evidence of miracles, and express order of God himself. Instructive as such an example is to all Christians, it is particularly so to those, says the same holy doctor, who are rash enough to covet the direction and command of others. For such is the presumption of human weakness, that the less virtuous and less qualified a person is, the more desirous often is he of a charge which the greatest saints have always been afraid of, as above their abilities. Men who know not how to guide themselves, wish to have the guidance of others; unable to answer for their own conduct, they thrust themselves forward to be answerable for the conduct of others.

END OF THE THIRD AGE.

Names and ages of the Patriarchs of the third age.

1 Abraham,	*born,* A.M.	2008	*died,*	2183	*aged,*	175
2 Isaac,	——	2108	——	2288	——	180
3 Jacob,	——	2168	——	2315	——	147
4 Levi,	——	2255	——	2392	——	137
5 Moses,	——	2433,	of Amram and Jochabed,			

the grand-children of Levi, who had lived thirty-three years with Isaac, and Isaac had lived fifty years with Sem. From this and the two foregoing tables it appears, that Moses has written nothing in his sacred history, but what was then still fresh in the memory of men.

FOURTH AGE OF THE WORLD.

FROM THE DELIVERY OF THE ISRAELITES OUT OF EGYPT, 2513, TO THE FOUNDATION OF SOLOMON'S TEMPLE, 2992; COMPREHENDING THE SPACE OF 479 YEARS.

A.M. 2513.] *Moses before Pharaoh.* [A.C. 1487.
EXOD. V.

PHARAOH, the tyrant who had declared so unnatural a war against the Hebrew children, was now dead, and succeeded by his son of the same name, a prince equally cruel and tyrannical in his disposition. This is the Pharaoh, before whom Moses and Aaron his brother presented themselves, for leave to go with the people for three days into the wilderness, where God had commanded them to offer him a sacrifice. Pharaoh received them with great harshness, treated them as rebels, and said he knew nothing of the God they talked of. He ascribed their petition to a spirit of revolt, and rejected it with scorn, telling them he should give them something else to think of. He accordingly gave strict orders to his officers to impose new burdens upon the mutinous Hebrews, as he called them, and to exact their daily task with the utmost rigour. The people finding themselves thus loaded with new grievances, instead of being relieved by the remon-

strances that had been made in their favour, began to complain most bitterly, and through a strange but common weakness of mind, turned their complaints against the two brothers. They loudly murmured against Moses and Aaron, as if they had been the cause of those very evils which they had been labouring to remove. It is the treatment which the zealous pastors of the church have often met with through every age, in return for the pains they have taken for the service of their flocks.

The ears of God being always open to the cries of the poor and needy, he commanded Moses to present himself a second time before Pharaoh for the deliverance of his people. Full of confidence, Moses therefore went to the king, and on the part of God repeated the subject of his commission. He backed his petition by a miracle, as a proof of his mission from God, and in the king's presence changed Aaron's rod into a serpent. Pharaoh had his magicians ready to mimic the divine power. By the help of their black art they undertook to perform the like prodigy, and in effect changed their rods also into serpents. This prevented the good effect which Moses's miracle was likely to have had upon the king's mind, and nothing more was done at that time. God soon afterwards commanded his servant Moses to go for the third time, and in his name to make a more urgent demand on Pharaoh for his consent. The place of conference was upon the banks of the Nile. Undaunted at the appearance of savage majesty, Moses spoke with a manly firmness, but yet softened his discourse with a gentle meekness and modesty of action that was natural to him. The king answered him with boisterous threats, and sternly refused to let the people go. Upon which Moses quietly addressed himself to Aaron, bidding him stretch his rod over the surface of the Nile, and the waters not only of that river, but of all the rivers in Egypt, were in an instant changed into blood, and the fishes died therein.

This change of the rivers into blood is called the first plague of Egypt, and hardened was the heart of Pharaoh not to bend by such a stroke. His magicians indeed, by doing the like wonders as Moses did, misled his judgment, and gave a specious pretext of obstinacy to a prince, who only sought to find out reasons not to yield. Those reasons were insufficient to excuse him from guilt: he plainly saw that the magicians were not only outdone, but likewise restrained in their power by Moses, so as not to be able to remove the plague they had occasioned. They had changed water into blood as well as Moses, but they could not, like him, change that blood into water again. To see the laws of nature altered and brought back into their first state, at the word of him who spoke and acted in the name of the living God, was more than sufficient to have opened the eyes of a common infidel; but to a man who is wilfully blind, no evidence is clear; and on a heart that grows harder, like iron, by the strokes it receives, no impression can easily be made. By a terrible, though just judgment of God, such is the man who, in punishment of his obstinacy, is once abandoned to the malicious desires of his own heart.

A.M. 2513.] *Plagues of Egypt.*—EXOD. viii. [A.C. 1487

THE first plague by which God had sought to make Pharaoh sensible of his duty, having proved ineffectual, was followed

by nine others. An incredible number of frogs, that swarmed through every place, and in every house of Egypt, was the second plague, and, according to St. Austin, exhibits a striking likeness of those Christians who spend themselves in empty words, and know no piety but in the unmeaning motion of their lips. The sciniphes, a small flying insect, according to Philo, produced from the dust, were the third plague, and resembled those wrangling sectaries, who only exist and thrive by their restless spirit of altercation and dispute. The fourth plague was an infinity of flies, which terribly incommoded Pharaoh and his people, and denote those peevish sallies of a fretful temper, that tease away the peace and happiness of human society. The fifth was a grievous murrain amongst the cattle, which strongly indicates that they who, like the irrational animal, guide themselves only by their senses, shall be struck with a spiritual pestilence, that kills the soul. The sixth inflicted biles and swelling blains upon men and beasts. The purulent and angry red that appears in an ulcerated body, bears a visible resemblance to the inward swellings of a soul transported with the passion either of pride or anger. The seventh plague was a storm of driving hail, accompanied with dreadful lightnings and thunders, that broke down and destroyed every thing on which it fell. Such is the boisterous fury of the wicked in pushing on their malicious designs, till they break or melt away like hail-stones, and perish amidst the ruins they have made. The eighth plague were the locusts, that devoured

every green thing which the hail had spared. To these locusts all false witnesses are properly compared, as with their mouths, like them they equally hurt and destroy. The ninth was a palpable darkness, which sat upon the land for three days throughout Egypt, excepting where the Israelites inhabited, and represents that sad obscurity which overclouds the soul of the impious, while a bright and cheerful serenity shines upon the face of the virtuous.

Such were the first temporal chastisements by which a merciful God sought to reclaim an obdurate sinner, and to make him sensible of his duty. In this visible exertion of the divine power we are to observe that these plagues were not inflicted upon Pharaoh and his people all at once, but at certain intervals of time. A second scourge was not employed, till Pharaoh's hardened malice had rendered the foregoing void of its intended effect. Pharaoh's submission to the divine will, on any one day, would have prevented his chastisement on the next. From the very first plague the magicians saw, and on the third acknowledged, the agency of a divine power, far superior to their own. To an omnipotent God, says the wise man, it had been as easy to let loose the lions upon his enemies at first, and without any previous notice to destroy them with one blow. But in compassion to the misery of human weakness, he tempered his justice with tender mercy: he contented himself with lesser punishments in the beginning; he sought to rouse the Egyptians to a sense of their duty by degrees, and by milder strokes informed them what they had to fear, should his anger be once raised to its height. We cannot be too thoroughly convinced of the truth, that God is always to be feared, that no mortal power can pretend to resist his might, and that in asserting his own divine rights, if softer methods will not do, he will then apply the most severe. For the divine justice is not to be outdone by human malice, nor are the mercies of God to be defeated by the obstinacy of his enemies.

A.M. 2513.] *The Paschal Lamb.* [A.C. 1487
EXOD. xii.

THE nine foregoing plagues having had no effect upon the heart of Pharaoh, God resolved upon a tenth, more striking and fatal than anything that had yet happened. Before he let fall this last stroke of his vengeance upon the Egyptians, he commanded the Israelites to prepare and eat the lamb, which he had told them to have in readiness ever since the tenth day of the month; prescribing at the same time the manner and the ceremony which he would have them observe in eating it. Each family, says the sacred text, shall take a lamb, and on the fourteenth day of the month shall sacrifice him in the evening, and sprinkle the doors of their houses

with the blood thereof; that night they shall eat the flesh, roasted at the fire, with unleavened bread and wild lettuces. While they eat it, they shall stand with their clothes girt up, with shoes upon their feet, and staves in their hands, like travellers ready for their journey. The obedient Israelites punctually fulfilled every circumstance of the order. On the same night God sent his exterminating angel into every house in Egypt, that was not sprinkled with the blood of the lamb, and slew every first born of man and beast. Struck at the sudden death of his eldest son, Pharaoh rose in the dead of the night, and by the mournful cries that were heard around, he was convinced that the same melancholy disaster had befallen every family in Egypt at the same hour The consternation was universal: from the royal palace to the meanest cot, there was not a house without a dead body. Pharaoh's obduracy was at last overcome; he sent for Moses and Aaron, and in compliance with their request, bade them go with their people, with their flocks and herds, into the desert, and there sacrifice to their God for three days. The Egyptians also pressed them to be gone, and lent them the most valuable furniture they had, on that solemn occasion. The very next morning Moses led forth the whole host of

Israel into the desert, which lay in their way towards the land of promise, nor was there a single person left, or sick amongst them. To the number of almost six hundred thousand fighting men, besides women and children, the Israelites began to march out of Egypt, four hundred and thirty years since Abraham had first taken refuge there against the famine, and two hundred and fifteen, since Jacob had gone thither with his whole family. It was by the special direction of Almighty God, that they carried away the richest spoils of Egypt, the fine clothes, the gold and silver plate of its inhabitants, not only as a recompense for the painful services they had done them, but also as a figurative mark, that the Christian church should be also furnished with temporal supplies for the external support and ornament of the divine service.

This deliverance of the Israelites from the slavery of Egypt is the figure of that most singular mercy, by which the world has been since rescued from the tyranny of Satan, through the blood of Jesus Christ, the immaculate Lamb of God. If that divine victim had not been immolated on the cross for man's redemption, the unhappy sons of Adam would be only able to weep; they could not have freed themselves from the slavery of sin. Jesus Christ by his death has set them free, and by his cross has opened to them a passage to their promised country. To nourish in our hearts a due sense of gratitude for a favour so unparalleled, and yet so unmerited on our part, we cannot too often or too seriously reflect, by whom we were once oppressed, and by whom we have been so bountifully redeemed. The reflection will teach us to value our present happiness, and to guard in future against the wretched state from which we have been delivered. To be zealous in the service of Jesus Christ, who can alone preserve us in the freedom he has purchased us, and carefully to shun whatever tends to throw us back into the servitude of sin, is a duty both of gratitude to God, and of charity to ourselves.

A.M. 2513.] *The Red Sea.*—Exod. xiv. [A.C. 1487.

Pharaoh had consented, as we have seen, to let Moses go with the Israelites into the wilderness for three days, to perform their religious duties to Almighty God. The three days were elapsed, and no Israelites returned. Pharaoh began to suspect that they had imposed upon him, and intended to escape out of his hands. Full of those surmises, and regardless of the scourges which lay still heavy upon his kingdom, he resolved to pursue them; his subjects likewise being afraid of losing the costly clothes and plate which they had lent to the Israelites, were eager to second his design. Pharaoh therefore assembled his troops in haste, put himself at their head, and directed his march through the desert to the Red Sea, where he found his enemies encamped upon the shore. The approach and terror of his arms, threw the defenceless Israelites into a deadly consternation. Closely pressed on one side by an enraged tyrant, who was ready to fall upon them, and hemmed in on the other by the sea, they began to abandon themselves to despair. For they forgot the wonders which God had so lately wrought in their favour, and grew diffident of the powerful providence, which from the moment of their departure had watched over them, in the form of a cloud by day, and of a pillar of fire by night. They crowded round Moses, and insultingly asked him, if

Egypt could not as well have provided them with a grave, and what need there was of bringing them to be butchered in the wilderness? Moses in the mildest terms endeavoured to soothe them into temper, and to rouse their drooping spirits by assuring them of the divine protection.

Pharaoh had put his troops in motion, and was advancing to attack them. Moses retreated till he came to the very edge of the sea, when stretching forth his arm over the profound abyss, as God had commanded him, the waters were suddenly divided by a mighty wind, and opened him a passage to the opposite shore. The Israelites rushed into the dry

hollow of the deep, wondering at the watery bounds, that stood suspended like a wall upon their right and left, as they marched through the middle. The angel, who had hitherto gone before them at night in the form of a fiery cloud, shifted his station to the rere, and hindered the Egyptians from coming too close upon them. Pharaoh seemed insensible of the miracle; blinded by passion, he only thought of satiating his revenge; and fancying the passage to be as free and as safe for him as for the Israelites, he rushed on headlong after them with all his host. He had advanced into the middle of the abyss, before he became sensible of the distinction that God makes between his friends and enemies. For from amidst the fiery cloud there appeared such glaring strokes of the divine wrath against him and his Egyptians, that in the utmost terror and confusion they began to turn back. Moses, who with all his followers had by that time reached the other shore, stretched forth his hand again upon the sea, and called back the waters to their natural state. Shut up within the bosom of the deep, the whole Egyptian army perished, with their chariots and horses; for of them all not so much as a single man escaped.

Miracles of this nature never fail in their effect of making an impression on the human mind, as they carry with them such convincing evidence of the divine power. Prodigies that affect our outward senses seldom pass unnoticed, as the holy fathers remark: there are likewise other prodigies of a much superior, because of a more spiritual nature; prodigies in which we are more immediately concerned, and which nevertheless we scarce attend to. We stand astonished, says St. Bernard, to see the Hebrew people so miraculously rescued from the slavery of Egypt, while we take no notice of a soul, that by sincere repentance and conversion is delivered from the slavery of her passions. Pharaoh is the tyrant who was overthrown in the first instance, and the devil is vanquished in the second: in the first were overthrown the chariots and the horsemen of an earthly prince, and in the second is defeated the united force of concupiscence and sin. The victory gained by the Israelites, was over men made of flesh and blood like themselves; the triumph of a penitent soul, is over the aerial powers and the tremendous prince of darkness. To men, who judge of things as they strike their senses, the first may seem more wonderful; but to God, by whose power all things are done, the second is more glorious.

A.M. 2513.] *The Manna.*—Exod. xvi. [A.C. 1487.

The passage which had been so miraculously opened through the Red Sea, struck the most insensible of the Jews with astonishment. Penetrated with a due sense of gratitude, they joined with Moses in singing the most sublime hymns of thanksgiving to God, for his mercy towards them. The women, likewise, with Mary, the sister of Moses, at their head, turned their canticles of joy to the sound of the harp, and other musical instruments. But these good dispositions of the people lasted not long. They no sooner began to feel some inconveniences for want of provisions, than their songs were changed into murmurs and complaints against Moses, whom they made answerable for every accidental hardship they met with. Moses, like a faithful minister of the Most High, strongly reprimanded them for their behaviour, as grievously injurious to God himself. For the complaints you have made, said he, are not against us, they are against the Lord, in whose name we act. Be but convinced, that the Lord himself watches over you for your preservation, and he will give you your fill. They waited not long, before the promise was accomplished. For in the evening there came into the camp a prodigious flight of quails, of which the people killed as many as they chose; and the next morning there appeared upon the ground something like the crispy substance of a hoar-frost, small and white, which they called Manna, and which, from that time, never failed them for their support during the forty years they wandered in the wilderness. Upon showing their surprise at the first appearance of a thing so new and unexpected, Moses informed the people, that this was the bread which God had sent them from heaven for the nourishment of life, that every morning before sun-rise they were to gather as much of it as should

be necessary for the present day, but that for the more religious observance of the Sabbath, they should, on the day before, gather a double quantity. By these injunctions to his people, God has been pleased to signify to us, that we ought to anticipate the sun in our acts of prayer and thanksgiving to him, and that we are not to be over solicitous about the necessaries of life, nor anxious to hoard up a quantity of things that we shall never want. In consequence of these injunctions we must observe, that the Manna corrupted if kept longer or in greater quantity, than was requisite for any one day besides the Sabbath, and if not gathered early in the morning, it melted away soon after the sun was up.

The Manna is manifestly a figure of the holy Eucharist, as Jesus Christ witnesses in his gospel. Miraculous was its production, and most wonderful were its effects. It had both the effect and taste of delicious food, during the time that the Israelites were upon their journey to the land of promise It is by the Scripture called the bread of heaven, and the bread of angels. But as the reality is always more perfect than its figure, so still more miraculous in itself, and more wonderful in its effects, is the eucharistical food which Jesus Christ has given to his church. This is truly the living bread descending from heaven, with which he nourishes, comforts, and strengthens our souls during their pilgrimage on earth. Hence the warmest sentiments of gratitude are due to our blessed Lord for so salutary an institution. A lively faith and an ardent desire of true happiness ought to keep us so habitually disposed, that we may be worthy each day to receive and profit by it. As long as such sentiments animated the Hebrew people in the desert, they joyfully received and relished their heavenly food ; but as their piety grew cold, they also grew disgusted, and wished again for the flesh-pots and leeks of Egypt. A similar conduct is but too often visible in those Christians who, being cold in their devotion, and weary in the divine service, come to the holy table without being worthily disposed, and so eat to their own condemnation, not discerning the body of our Lord

A.M. 2513.] *Water issued from the rock.* [A.C. 1487.
EXOD. xvii.

A POWER so miraculously and so constantly displayed by Almighty God, in favour of his chosen people, ought to have removed every fear, and prevented every ground of diffidence for the future. But new trials created new fears, and rising difficulties renewed the clamours of a people naturally mutinous and inclined to rebel. The country through which they marched, was a dry and sandy desert : they came to a place called Raphidim, where no water was to be found : impatient of thirst, they grew seditious. A spirit of revolt spread itself through the camp : they vented their spleen against Moses, whom they threatened to stone to death for having brought them out of Egypt. Of all men living Moses was one of the most meek and gentle ; the critical situation he was then in, afforded him no refuge but in God. To God he had recourse by humble prayer: he earnestly begged the divine power to support him in the discharge of a duty which he never had undertaken but in obedience to his holy will. God was pleased with his humility, heard his prayer, and told him to take the rod with which he had changed the waters of th Nile into blood, and to go with the ancients of Israel to the rock of Horeb, where his name should be glorified, and the people be relieved. Moses went accordingly to the place appointed, being accompanied by the ancients, and followed by a vast crowd of the common people: he stood with the rod in his hand, he struck the rock in their presence, and an instan-

taneous stream issued out. They quenched their thirst, and were satisfied. This stream is a figure of those flowing graces that are drawn from the wounds of Christ crucified; for Christ is the rock from whence the streams of salvation flow. By these streams our hearts are softened into tears of compunction, and our souls refreshed with new vigour in their way to heaven.

On a similar occasion of discontent amongst the people, (*Numbers*, xx.) Moses repeated the same miracle in a place called Cades, where Mary his sister died. The mutineers at that time carried their insolence so far, as to forget all respect for their leaders. The two brothers seeing it was not only useless, but also dangerous, to contend with the lawless multitude, retired into the tabernacle, where, bathed in tears, and prostrate before God in prayer, they implored the divine mercy upon a hardened people, from whose violence they were obliged to fly. With the earnest tenderness of a father they prayed for the most ungrateful of men; they interceded for the preservation of a people who were persecuting them for the very good they had done them. God was pleased to comfort his faithful servants by manifesting his glory to them, and he told Moses to lead out the people before the rock, where he would give them water to drink. Moses accordingly rose up, assembled his people, and bade them follow him. He stood full before them, he addressed himself to the rock, as though it were less hard and less deaf than they; he struck it twice with his rod, and behold a plenteous stream gushed out. The people drank, and their fury was allayed with their thirst.

In this interesting miracle, the sacred writer takes notice of a circumstance which ought not to be forgotten. Moses struck the rock twice; by which he expressed a doubt of the subsequent event. Little as the fault may seem, it was most severely punished. Almighty God was offended by it, and therefore warned his servant out of life before he should enter the land of promise. Moses, who on every other occasion had been so faithful to his God, who had wrought so many and so glorious achievments in his service; Moses, who had so often obtained pardon for the most atrocious sins of his people and in whose hands the plenitude of God's miraculous power seemed to be deposited, was taken out of life for a fault apparently only venial. In punishment of some little diffidence he had shown in the execution of God's order, Moses was deprived of the only happiness that he wished to enjoy before he died. How adorable are thy counsels, and how terrible are thy judgments, O God of Israel!

A.M. 2513.] *Defeat of Amalec.*—Exod. xvii. xviii. [A.C. 1487.

Encouraged by this fresh instance of the divine goodness, which had given them water from the hard rock, the Israelites kept up their spirits for a time, till they saw themselves attacked by a formidable enemy. The Amalecites were the first who had the boldness to make war upon a nation, which God had visibly taken under his protection. They imagined that an undisciplined multitude of men, fatigued with continual marches, spent with scarcity of provisions, and almost wholly destitute of every implement of war, would make no great resisance. Upon that cowardly presumption they drew their forces together, and marched out to destroy a people from whom they had received no provocation, and could fear no harm: Moses, with his usual confidence in God, was resolved to defend himself. Neither the numbers nor the warlike show of his enemies gave him the least alarm. He called upon Josue, and ordered him to choose out some of the most valiant amongst the people, and to make head against the common enemy, assuring him at the same time that he would be answerable for the success. The next morning Josue led out his troops to battle, while Moses with Hur and Aaron, went to the top of a neighbouring mountain, that commanded the plain, to pray for the combatants. He prayed with his arms extended in the form of a cross, which was in future times to be so salutary to us, and so formidable to our enemies. By that he taught the children of Israel in their very first engagement, that victory depends solely upon God, and that he is ready to grant it to those who, with an humble confidence, ask it of him. The Israelites accordingly prevailed against the most vigorous efforts of Amalec, as long as Moses lifted up his hands to heaven in prayer for them. But when, through fatigue, he was obliged to let them fall, his people then gave way, and the Amalecites prevailed in their turn; which when Hur and Aaron observed, they obliged the man of God to sit down, and standing on each side of him, held

up his arms stretched out in prayer till sun-set, when the Israelites put the enemy to flight, and gained a complete victory. The memory of that glorious event was, by God's order, recorded to future generations, and an eternal enmity declared against the nation of Amalec, till it should be utterly destroyed.

In this example, as we see on one hand how ineffectual every human effort is of itself to insure success, so on the other we cannot but admire the force of holy prayer, which so efficaciously engages the hand of the Almighty to assist and support us. Prayer is one of the first duties of a Christian; it is an important, it is a public, it is an universal duty; a duty from which no man of whatever rank or station in life can be exempt. And though it be a duty incumbent upon all in general, yet it in a more special manner regards those who are charged with the conduct of others. Unable of themselves to fulfil their obligation, they must by fervent prayer obtain the divine help, which alone can strengthen their weakness, and make them equal to the task. To pray for those under their care, is perhaps the most important service they can do them: prayer is a source of endless blessings, which are not communicated through any other channel. If Moses had not prayed, Josue had not been victorious. The forces of Amalec, though more than sufficient to defeat the arms of the whole nation, could not stand against the prayer of Moses: the single prayer of one man contributed more to the victory than the united efforts of a great army.

A.M 2513] *The Commandments given on Mount Sinai.*—Exod. xix. [A.C. 1487.

Three months were elapsed since the Israelites had left the land of Egypt, and every day since that time had furnished some miraculous instance of the divine goodness towards them. God commanded Moses to remind them of those great wonders which he had wrought in their favour, and to declare the merciful designs that he still had upon them; for of all the nations of the earth, he promised to make them his chosen people, and special inheritance for ever, upon condition that they, on their part, would promise to be faithful in his service, and keep his commandments. Moses, in consequence, assembled the people, and related to them the words he had received from the Lord for their consent: they all, with one accord, immediately cried out, that they would do whatever the Lord should command them. Upon that public profession of their willingness to obey the divine precepts, he gave them notice to prepare for the third day, when they should hear God himself speaking to them from the summit of Mount Sinai. And that they might be worthy to appear before him, he ordered them not to approach their wives in the mean time, but to sanctify themselves, and to wash their garments. Around the foot of the holy mountain he drew a boundary, which, in the name of God, he charged them not to pass, under pain of death.

The third day now began to dawn; a clear light diffused itself over the earth; the sky was open and serene; when behold, a dark and gloomy change came on, and a solemn scene unfolded itself to the spectators. Dreadful thunders began to roll on every side of Mount Sinai, and quick lightnings flashed from the sullen cloud that hung over its top. The Lord descended in fire upon the steep summit, and called Moses to him. The whole circumference of the mountain was forthwith involved in thick smoke, and an incessant

stream of flames arose, as from a glowing furnace. The shrill and swelling clangors of a trumpet were also heard at the same time: the people trembled, and lay close within their tents. Moses went down to them, and with difficulty having prevailed upon them to move out, ranged them in order beyond the boundary that he had set round the foot of the mountain. The Lord then spoke his commands, saying: I am the Lord, thy God: thou shalt not have strange gods before me, nor make to thyself any graven things: thou shalt not take the name of the Lord thy God in vain: remember thou keep holy the Sabbath day: honour thy father and thy mother: thou shalt not kill: thou shalt not commit adultery;

thou shalt not steal: thou shalt not bear false witness against thy neighbour: thou shalt not covet thy neighbour's wife: thou shalt not covet thy neighbour's goods. The loud voice and presence of the Lord, arrayed with all that pomp of awful majesty, filled the Israelites with such terror, that, unable to stand any longer, they desired Moses to speak, and not thus expose them to the danger of being terrified out of life by the tremendous language of a God.

Thus did Almighty God for the first time publish his commandments in a solemn manner to the world. They are ten in number, and contain the sum of all our obligations both to God and man: they will, to the latest posterity, retain their full force, and no man can ever presume to transgress them without incurring the guilt of sin. It is the wish of the holy fathers, that every Christian shared a part at least of that holy fear with which the Israelites were at that time so deeply penetrated. Such a fear is the beginning of true wisdom; it checks the passions, and restrains the heart from vice. Length of time and a corruption of morals, first amongst the Jews and since amongst Christians, have almost worn out the salutary impressions, and left the world imperfectly sensible of its sacred obligations. Self-love has studied every art, and by every subtlety has tried to explain away the force of God's precepts, and to remove every bar that is a check to our corrupt inclinations. But Jesus Christ, who has assured us that not so much as the least tittle of his law can be altered, continues to be still the same God he always was, and still exacts the same respectful obedience to his precepts. No length of time can prescribe against their force, and no fashions of the age can make any change in the nature of their obligations. It is not fear, it is the nobler sentiments of love and charity, that ought to influence our obedience to the law of God. Servile fear may for a while restrain a slave from vice; it never can perfect the free-born sons of God in Christian virtue. Very different from the stiff-necked Israelites, who desired God to speak no longer, lest their fears might kill them, a Christian wishes to hear the voice of God himself; for he knows that the words of God are the words of life, and therefore begs him to accompany them with the unction of his Holy Spirit, that his yoke might be made sweet and his burden light.

A. M. 2513.] *The golden Calf*.—Exod. xxxii. [A. C. 1487.

In compliance with the request of a stiff-necked people, it pleased Almighty God to speak no more in person to them, but to employ the ministry of Moses in the future orders he had to give them. For that purpose he called him up to the mountain, where, in a private conference, he imparted many fresh instructions to him. These instructions are a collection of holy laws, full of consummate wisdom, by which he regulated the religious and civil duties of his people at that time. They are comprehended under the common title of the Jewish or Levitical law, and recorded at full length in the books of Moses. Almighty God having fully explained himself to his inspired law-giver, upon every particular, delivered to him two tables of stone, on both sides of which he had with his own finger, as the Scripture expresses it, engraved the ten commandments, as the ground-work and abridgment of all his other precepts. Forty days and as many nights were spent in this secret interview between God and Moses. During that time the people had, by an unaccountable hardness of heart, forgot not only Moses, but the very God who a few weeks before had appeared so terrible to them on the mountain, under which they still lay encamped. Not knowing, as they said, what was become of Moses, they assembled round Aaron, and in a tumultuous manner insisted upon his letting them have an idol, like other nations, to go before them. Aaron weakly yielded to their impious demand, and ordered them to bring him a collection of gold, and golden ear-rings of their wives and daughters. He melted it down together, and formed the image of a golden calf. Strange as it appears, this was the idol which the Jews, amidst the applauses of a shouting multitude, set up in the camp, and adored as the God of Israel. Moses at that very hour, by the express command of God, came down from the mountain with the two tables of the law in his hand. Struck at the unusual sound he heard, he hastened on to see what the matter was, and behold, as he approached the camp, he found the people dancing and singing round the golden calf. Grief and indignation at the sight, kindled such a flame within his breast, that he seemed in a manner to be transported out of himself. he threw down the tables from his hands, and

shivered them to pieces, for they were needless to a people who had blotted the law itself out of their hearts. In the ardour of his zeal he laid hold of the idol they had made, immediately broke it down, and cast it into the fire. As soon as he had reduced it to powder, he mixed it with water, and gave it to the Israelites to drink, that they might see how despicable a thing it was, which they had foolishly adopted for their God. He called Aaron to a severe account for having suffered such a scandal to be set up, and last of all addressed himself to the people in general. Having placed himself in the entrance of the camp, he proclaimed aloud, that all those who still retained any sense of their duty to God, should come forth and join him. The whole tribe of Levi ranged themselves immediately by his side. He turned about and told them to unsheath their swords, and to march in a straight line quite through the camp and back again, putting every one to death that should come in their way, without any distinction or respect of persons. The faithful Levites executed the order in its full extent, and by their hands about three and twenty thousand men were sacrificed, to expiate the guilt of those that survived.

To a censorious world, whose thoughts are confined to the resentment of injuries done to men only, this execution may perchance seem severe. To Christians, who consider the infinite distance that there is between the Creator and his creature, it occurs, how great a satisfaction is due to an insulted Deity. The Levites were armed with the sword of justice, and they were armed by the meek, inspired minister of a God who holds the sovereign power of life and death over all men. The whole body of the Israelites had sinned, and their sin was grievous beyond expression; a few were punished as they deserved, that the rest might repent and live. The conduct of Moses on this occasion is an instructive lesson, says St. Gregory, to those pliant parents, who are afraid of giving the least reprimand or correction to their children; who, though they see them straying from their duty, plunging into vice, and falling headlong towards the precipice of hell, yet suffer no uneasiness, no disturbance to be given them. The zealous Levites, says this holy father, had no doubt a true love for their children, though they spared them not. True paternal love has its moments of severity; it is forced to chastise sometimes even with rigour, that it may correct the faulty and save the delinquent. No father ever had a more tender love for his son, than Moses had for the Israelites; their interest, their life and happiness were blended with his own. His love had duty for its foundation, and God for its motive; it was subservient to the fidelity that he owed to his Creator: his zeal for justice was equal to his charity. He knew how heinously his people had offended: he dreaded the anger of a just God, and was therefore zealous to prevent the consequence by a timely severity.

A. M. 2513.] *The second Tables of the Law.* [A. C. 1487. EXOD. xxxiv.

MOSES was inconsolable for the prevarication of his people. The crime of idolatry seemed to him too abominable to admit of an excuse, or to leave any room for pardon. He called however the tribes together on the following day, and after having set forth the enormity of their guilt in the most expressive language, he told them, that notwithstanding their ingratitude, he would present himself before God in their behalf, and endeavour to obtain their pardon for a sin which called aloud for punishment. With a heart ready to burst with grief, he retired from their presence, prostrated himself before God, as though he had been the only guilty one, and in the sentiments of an humble penitent, begged that he might be blotted out of the book of life, rather than that his people should not obtain forgiveness. A prayer so fervent so humble, and so charitable, did not fail of its effect. God bade him rise, and tell his people, that in consideration of their fathers, Abraham, Isaac, and Jacob, he would put them in possession of the land he had promised them; but that henceforward he should be less liberal of his favours to a race of men, whose stubbornness of heart was likely to deserve his severest vengeance, before they reached their journey's end. When Moses repeated these last words to the people, they wept, seemed sensible of their crime, and, as a mark of their repentance, laid aside their usual ornaments of dress, and recovered the divine favour. Almighty God being thus reconciled with his people, commanded Moses to hew out two other tables of stone, like those he had broken, and to go with them to the top of Mount Sinai, where he should receive the same words engraven on them, as had been engraven on the first. In obedience to this order, Moses provided himself with two new tablets, and for the second time ascended the holy mountain to converse with God. As soon as he reached the top, he prostrated himself in prayer, and begged the divine blessing upon his Israelites, for the rest of their journey. The Lord descended from the cloud that hung over the summit of the mountain, heard his prayer, and promised him protection. He conversed familiarly with his servant, and gave him every instruction necessary for his own and the people's future conduct. The holy conference lasted for forty days and forty nights, during all which time Moses neither ate nor drank. The term being expired, he took up the two tables of stone, on which God had written the words of the ten commandments, and came down from the mountain, ignorant of the change that this long conversation had made in his countenance; for, as he approached the camp, Aaron and the rest of the Israelites perceived a bright blaze of glory shining from his face, which made them afraid of coming near him. Being told the cause of their not approaching, he covered his face with a veil, which he wore ever after, except when he entered the tabernacle to converse with God. Moses's conduct in this particular is a tacit admonition for us likewise to condescend to the weaknesses of others, as far as duty will permit, and carefully to avoid the show of any extraordinary gifts or talents we may be possessed of.

Thus it was that God received his people again into favour,

and delivered to them his commandments, written for the second time on two new tables of stone with his own hand. The singular favour he then granted to the Israelites, is a mark of that which he grants to all true penitents, when by the operation of his Holy Spirit he re-imprints in their souls the character of his love, which had been effaced by sin. And it is that gratuitous grace, which no one can merit, and few obtain, without great pains, and the most laborious endeavours. It is what is signified to us by the labour which Moses was ordered to employ in hewing out the second stones, with his own hands; a labour which he had not employed about the first, as the holy fathers observe. The difficulty that attends the purchase of a favour, usually makes us more sensible of its value: and this very difficulty God has annexed to the recovery of his holy grace, that it may make us more careful not to lose it a second time. For such is the weakness of our nature, that we easily resign what we can easily recover; and the greatness of a loss is not made sensible to us, but by the difficulty we find in repairing it. As the restoration of the law on stone was not to be effected but by great labour, joined with fasting and devout prayer, so neither can the loss of grace in the soul be repaired but by tears and penitential deeds.

A.M. 2513.] *The Tabernacle.*—Exod. xxvi. [A.C. 1487.

Moses having brought the tables of the law to the people, and the people having promised a faithful obedience to it, he turned his thoughts upon the execution of those special orders which God had given on the mountain. Before he set to work, he convened the tribes, and informed them of the instructions he had received; he described to them the different works and ornaments which he was commanded to prepare for the divine service; he proposed to them the expense that would be requisite for so great an undertaking, and hoped that each one would be ready, according to his abilities, to contribute towards it. They no sooner heard the proposal made but they produced their most precious effects, their costly stuffs, their rich plate and perfumes: the women likewise, unwilling to be outdone by the men, stripped themselves of their finest ornaments, their bracelets, their rings, and ear-rings; in a word, the zeal of all the people on that occasion, striving to outdo one another, was so great, that Moses was presently furnished with every material he wanted. He saw such heaps of riches lying around him, that by a public crier he gave them notice to bring no more. His next concern was to look out for proper workmen and skilful artists for the execution. The first thing he set about was the tabernacle, an oblong quadrangular tent, thirty cubits in length and nine in breadth. The back part and two sides were made of setim boards, ten cubits long, which formed the height of the edifice from the ground to the edge of the roof. These boards were placed upright, mortised at the sides, and at the bottom let into a base by two silver tenons at the corner of each board: they were fastened together on the outside with cross pieces of setim wood, and plated with gold. The roof was covered with a double row of dyed skins, laid one upon another, and fastened close together with loops and buckles of brass. This covering was made long enough to hang down a whole cubit on each side, as a fence against the weather. The inside was hung with rich embroidered tapestry, and was divided into two parts by four pillars of setim, richly gilt upon silver pediments, with capitals of gold. Before these pillars was a veil of most exquisite needle-work, variegated with the brightest colours of purple, hyacinth, and scarlet. The apartment inclosed behind this veil, was called the Holy of Holies, and the space between that veil and the entrance was called the sanctuary. The entrance itself was shut up by another veil of the same costly needle-work, which, like the other, hung by rings against the finely ornamented pillars that formed the front of the tabernacle, and looked to the east.

Such was the mysterious structure of Moses's portable tabernacle; which, according to St. Austin, was a figure of the church militant in its state of pilgrimage upon earth, as the temple of Solomon was an emblem of its immutable state of glory in heaven. The solid planks that composed the sides of the tabernacle, represent those solid virtues which have rendered the church of Christ eminent for sanctity in all ages; and the silver tenons on which they stood, denote the truth and purity of her doctrine. The various colours and works of embroidery which ornamented the inside of the tabernacle, give us an idea of the various gifts and graces that adorn the elect, and are at once the glory of God and ornament of his church. But it is not one part only, nor any separate perfection of its parts; it is the beauty of the whole, and the union of all its parts together, that is to be considered when we speak of the tabernacle of God, as the holy fathers remark. For however excellent the virtues of particular persons in the church may appear, they are nothing if not linked together by faith and charity with the rest of the faithful, whose peace and concord form the most perfect temple that God has upon earth.

A.M. 2514.] *The Ark of the Covenant.* [A.C. 1486
EXOD. XXV. XXVI.

THE tabernacle being finished according to the model which God himself had given upon the mountain, Moses in the second place, began the ark of the covenant. This ark, when finished, was considered by the Israelites as the most precious symbol of their religion, the glory of Israel, according to the scripture phrase, and the strength of the Hebrew people. It was to prepare a place suitable for its reception, that the tabernacle had been first made. The ark measured two cubits and a half in length, one and a half in breadth, which was equal to its height. It was made of incorruptible wood, plated with the purest gold, both within and without. The cover or lid of the ark was not of wood, like the rest, but of solid gold, and was called the propitiatory, or mercy-seat; because there it was that God heard the petitions of his people, and returned them his answers, whenever he was pleased to be propitious, and to show mercy to them. Upon the propitiatory stood two cherubs, face to face, with their wings extended and spread, so as to cover the ark, and formed, as it were, a throne for the God of all sanctity and majesty. Hence comes the expression which we often meet with in the holy scriptures, of God sitting upon the cherubims. At the four corners of the ark were four golden rings, in which four levers of setim, covered with gold, were always left, for the convenience of carrying it, whenever the camp moved forward. The ark was in a special manner consecrated to God, in which nothing was deposited besides the two tables of the law: it is therefore called the ark of testimony, and the ark of the covenant, by which two names the law itself is often called in holy writ.

Thus it pleased Almighty God, in ancient times, to treat his people, and to give them a visible object of religious veneration, proportioned to their capacity, and placed within the reach of their corporal senses; for some external sign is necessary to rouse our faith, to aid our weakness, and to fix our attention, in the exercise of divine worship. The propitiatory, which covered the ark, was a type or figure of Jesus Christ, who, according to St. Paul, is our propitiation, and the mediator of peace between his heavenly Father and us. Through him alone we obtain the remission of our sins, and from him we receive the oracle of salvation, when we hear him speaking by the mouth of those whom he has commissioned to teach, and commanded us to hear: for to his church he says, He that hears you, hears me. The propitiatory had its cherubims, and so has Jesus Christ in his followers. Christians themselves, as St. Austin often repeats, are those cherubims, who, by their ardent charity, are transformed, as it were, into the living seats and thrones of God. The honour to which we are raised by the sacrament of baptism, being so eminently great, we cannot stoop to the pomps of sin, without degrading our Christian character: being once formed into the living temples of the Holy Ghost, we cannot, without sacrilege, admit any other object of adoration within our hearts. The Philistines, indeed, set up the ark and Dagon in the same temple; and it is what every Christian does, says St. Austin, who endeavours to unite God and the world together, who divides his service between Jesus Christ and Satan.

A.M. 2514.] *The Table of Show-bread.* [A.C. 1486.
EXOD. XXV.

THE ark of the covenant being finished, Moses gave directions for making a table, according to the model God had shown him. It was made of the incorruptible wood setim, plated on the top and edged round with the purest gold, being a cubit and a half high, two cubits long, and one broad. Above the edge was a rich border of fret-work, four fingers high, with a small gilt rim round the top. To each foot, just under the four corners, were four golden rings to receive the bars that were made of setim, and covered with gold, for the decent convenience of carrying the table, whenever it was to be moved. It always stood in the sanctuary, on the north side, over against the golden candlestick, and on it were set the twelve loaves of show-bread, so called, because they were placed in open view before the ark of the Lord. They were set six and six, one upon another, in two heaps, one at each end of the table: they remained there for a whole week, when they were replaced by twelve fresh ones, made like them, of the finest flour tempered with oil. Upon the uppermost loaf of each heap stood a vessel smoking with the sweetest incense. The stale bread at the week's end was, according to God's order, eaten by the priests within the sanctuary; nor was it lawful for any other person to eat thereof.

This offering of the show-bread, according to the remark made by the holy fathers, was a continual sacrifice, by which the children of Israel expressed their gratitude, and acknowledged their dependence on God for the blessings they enjoyed. The number of loaves was equal to the number of tribes, that each tribe might share in that public act of thanksgiving, which was so justly due to the common Father of them all. The like acts of gratitude are not less pleasing to God now than they were then; and with far greater reason does he now expect a more grateful return, as the blessings which he has since showered down on us Christians are infinitely more precious. Amongst the many spiritual blessings which are peculiar to us, and were not granted to the carnal Jews, we have received a more excellent kind of show-bread, Jesus Christ himself, in the holy Eucharist. This is the heavenly and living bread, which is daily offered in the Christian Church to Almighty God, in thanksgiving for all his benefits, both spiritual and temporal; and for this reason it is specified by the name of the holy Eucharist. It not only is the tribute of thanksgiving which we pay to God, it also is the pledge of God's special love to us, and a standing memorial of all his other wonders. The participation of this heavenly bread is not now-a-days restrained to priests only; it is extended to all and each of the faithful, that, being animated with the same spirit, and nourished with the same divine food, we may all live, and form one body in Christ Jesus.

A.M. 2514.] *The Golden Candlestick.* [A.C. 1486.
EXOD. XXV.

OF all the magnificent ornaments and sacred utensils which God commanded Moses to make for the divine service, the golden candlestick, for its workmanship, seems to have been the chief. It was made according to the pattern which God himself had drawn and shown to Moses upon the mountain. Six branches, three and three on each side, spread themselves out in a curve from the pedestal, which was carried up in a straight line, and formed a seventh branch in the middle. The stem of each branch was ornamented with knobs, in the form of a nut, at equal distances, and those distances were filled up with leaves and cups of flowers, richly wrought and most exquisitely finished. Upon these seven branches were hung seven lamps of massive gold, which were fed with the sweetest oil of olives, and lighted up every day, by the high-priest himself, to burn during the night. The candlestick with all its ornaments, weighed a whole talent of the purest gold, which, by computation, is considerably more than three thousand pounds sterling. The seven mysterious lamps seem to have some reference to a passage we meet with in the Revelations, where Jesus Christ, after his ascension, is represented with seven stars in his hand, in the midst of seven candlesticks, which, he expressly says, are seven churches with their respective prelates. Of his ministers in the new law, our blessed Saviour says, that he has kindled them up as lamps to shine in the house of God. These living lamps must not only burn, they must also shine, as he testifies of his baptism; the bright example of good works, which shine forth in the conduct of every zealous pastor, and of every good Christian, receives its intrinsic lustre from the fire of charity which burns within his heart. The flame of divine love, which has been once kindled in a devout soul, must be diligently attended to, lest it chance to be damped by worldly communications, and at last be extinguished by growing passions. St. Gregory takes notice of the solid massiveness that composed the golden candlestick, and thinks it expressive of that steady firmness which ought to distinguish every true Christian in the discharge of his duty to God and man. He moreover observes, at the same time, that this fortitude of mind must come from Christ, who is the stock that supports the branches, and imparts life and vigour to them all. The several members of the church have nothing to fear as long as they remain united to Jesus Christ, says the same holy doctor. Men may work up storms, and strive by boisterous efforts to shake their constancy; God, who is in the midst of them, will continue to help them by his grace, and save them by his power. Under his protection they stand secure in the midst of trials; they may be oppressed, but cannot be overcome; if in his cause and for his sake they fall a sacrifice to persecuting violence, they fall to rise again; they gloriously exchange a mortal life for an eternal one.

A.M. 2514.] *The Altar of Perfumes.* [A.C. 1486.

EXOD. XXX.

To complete the furniture that God had ordered for his tabernacle, Moses made an altar, which was called the altar of perfumes, because upon it was daily offered the morning and evening sacrifice of sweet-scented gums and spices, mixed together according to God's own direction. This altar was of a quadrangular form, made of the wood setim, and covered on every part with plates of gold: it was two cubits high, one broad and one long: it stood between the golden candlestick and the table of showbread, full against the veil that divided the Holy of Holies from the sanctuary. Round the tabernacle lay a large court, inclosed with pillars five cubits asunder, finely carved, and ornamented with brass pedestals and silver capitals: costly hangings covered the four sides of the inclosure, which was extended a hundred cubits in length, and fifty in breadth: in that breadth of the court which looked towards the east, there was an entrance twenty cubits wide, hung with rich embroidered work of fine twisted linen, of violet, and purple, and scarlet twice dyed. Within the court, in the open air, and opposite to the door that opened into the sanctuary, Moses placed a great altar for the burnt-offerings, which he called the altar of holocausts. It was a square figure made of setim, three cubits high, five long, and as many broad. Thick plates of brass covered it on every side; a grate of net-work lay along the top, under the middle of which was the hearth, a cubit and a half in dimension. The altar was hollow within, that it might be carried the more easily, whenever the camp moved from one station to another.

This was the structure of the two altars, which, according to St. Gregory, represent the two different classes of men that the church embraces within her pale, the innocent and the penitent. The altar of holocausts stood in the open court, and represented the state of a sinner, who is not worthy to be re-admitted within the sanctuary, till, by a hearty sorrow, joined to external works of penance, he has mortified his flesh, and rendered himself a sacrifice acceptable to God. The altar of perfumes was placed within the sanctuary, and indicated the privilege of those happy souls, who, for their innocence, are always united to their Creator. Their charity shines like the gold which covered that altar, while their morning and evening prayers ascend like incense to the clouds. In the fervour of devotion they pour forth their souls to God, and offer him the purest homage of their love, whilst the penitents make him an humble offering of their tears, and sigh at the sad remembrance of their past offences. Thus one of these altars is for those whose consciences are still bleeding with the wounds of sin; the other is for those who have their affections fixed on heaven, and breathe after the enjoyment of their God. The priest prepares the first, when he strongly represents to sinners the faults they have committed, and exhorts them to repent: he prepares the second, when, after the sacrifice of compunction is fulfilled, he leads those humble penitents into the temple of our Lord, where their tears, that lately sprung from sorrow and regret, now more sweetly flow from a principle of gratitude and holy love. But though these altars so much differ one from the other, yet in this they agree, that by them both religious honour is paid to God, and that on them both the fire of the Holy Ghost is requisite to render the sacrifices acceptable.

A.M. 2514.] *Vestments of the Priests.* [A.C. 1486
Exod. xxviii.

Besides the principal ornaments already mentioned, there was a vast variety of other rich furniture prepared for the use of the tabernacle, such as saucers, phials, censers, and goblets of the purest gold. To inspire respect and add dignity to the sacerdotal functions, the priests had their sacred vestments made by divine appointment. Part of their vestments were common to the whole order of priests, and part peculiar to the high-priests only. That part of the dress which was common to them all, consisted of a mitre, of a close linen tunic, and a variegated girdle, that went twice round the body, and hung down to the ground at both ends. The vestments peculiar to the high-priest were a large blue robe, the ephod with its girdle, the pectoral and rich mitre. The blue robe was put over the white linen tunic, and reached down to the ancles; the bottom of it was skirted round with pomegranates and little bells of gold, that hung alternately intermixed one with another, to the number of seventy-two. Next came the ephod, which was of very rich-coloured stuff, embroidered with gold; it reached but half way down, was close on both sides, with an opening on the top for the head and neck; it was held together over the shoulders by two clasps, ornamented with two precious stones of onyx, one upon each shoulder: upon these stones were engraven the names of the twelve tribes, six upon one, and six upon the other. In the forepart of the ephod corresponding to the breast, was an open space of about a foot square, which was filled up by a rich piece of embroidery, called the pectoral; it was set with twelve precious stones, on each of which was written the name of one of the twelve tribes of Israel: the two words *Urim* and *Thummim,* that is, doctrine and truth, were there also written upon a thin plate of gold. To fasten the pectoral, there were four golden chains, one at each corner, that hooked it to the ephod. The ephod, though rightly fitted to the body, was tied round with an embroidered girdle. Upon the mitre, which was made of twisted silk, was fixed a thin plate of gold across the forehead, on which were seen these words: Sacred to the Lord, *Sanctum Domino.*

The holy fathers confine not their view to the outward richness that shone in the sacerdotal vestments, they search into, and strive to discover the mystical meaning that lay concealed within. The brilliancy of the gold, says St. Gregory, was an emblem of those bright virtues which God requires in them who approach his holy altar; virtues that may render them as pleasing in the divine sight, as their rich robes exhibit them to the eyes of men. The bells round the bottom of the blue robe, were as a perpetual admonition to the priest, that in his conduct of life, he ought to make no step, but what tended to the glory of God, and the sanctification of his people. The bells returned no sound, unless he moved: a minister of God no longer edifies his flock, when he once ceases to move on in the way of virtue. The legend on the pectoral pointed out to him who wore it, the subject on which his thoughts and words were to be employed. The twelve names of the patriarchs engraven on the twelve stones, reminded him of the illustrious chiefs of his nation, and naturally excited him to emulate those greater virtues, which had distinguished them in the divine service. For nothing has a more powerful influence upon a generous mind, than the example of those personages, who by their actions have traced out the way to true greatness, and merited a place amongst the most eminent of God's servants.

A.M. 2514.] *Nadab and Abiu.*—Lev. x. [A.C. 1486.

All things belonging to the tabernacle being finished, Moses ordered the different parts to be put together. The tabernacle was therefore set up and solemnly dedicated, in the beginning of the second year after the deliverance of Israel from the land of Egypt. By the most unquestionable signs, Almighty God expressed his approbation of the manner in which his orders had been executed: an awful cloud hung over and covered the tabernacle, as a token of the Divine Majesty that resided within. This cloud continued in the same position as long as the tabernacle rested in the same place, and only shifted when the camp was in motion. Thus it was that a regular form of worship was first set on foot; thus the God of heaven and earth began to be honoured by the sacrifices which he himself ordained. Aaron and his sons were consecrated priests, and appointed to officiate in the sacred ministry to which God had called them. Every thing relating to the exercise of their holy functions was minutely penned down by Moses, and God exacted from them the nicest observance of each religious ceremony. Amongst other things it was ordained, that the priests should, morning and evening, add fresh fuel to the fire which was to be kept constantly alive upon the altar. From that fire, which was accounted holy, the censers were to be filled with glowing coals for the sacrifice of incense. Nadab and Abiu, the two eldest sons of Aaron, had neglected that duty: on a certain occasion they filled their censers with unhallowed fire, and their neglect was followed by an exemplary punishment; during the time of incense, they both dropped down dead before the altar. A sudden flash, like lightning, darted from the hand of God, pierced into their very vitals, and without leaving any external mark, either upon their clothes or bodies,

consumed their entrails. Moses ordered the dead bodies, dressed as they were, to be carried immediately away from the sanctuary, and thrown outside the camp, forbidding Aaron or any of his sons to mourn for the deceased. He addressed himself on that occasion to the other priests, whom he desired to take warning from what they saw: he bade them remember the holy unction they had received at their consecration, and how attentive they ought to be in the performance of the sacerdotal functions.

By an example so visible and so terrible, God has been

pleased to signify that the most religious honours we can pay him, are not acceptable, unless accompanied with the conditions he requires. So adorable is he in his nature, that we cannot worthily honour him, but in the very manner that he has prescribed. Though a neglect of his holy ordinances may not now-a-days be so visibly chastised, yet it is still no less a subject of his displeasure. With the same discerning eye he views the hearts and hands of those who approach his altar, and sees with what fire their affections are enkindled. There is a fire, says St. Gregory, very different from that which Jesus Christ came to kindle upon earth; a fire, which is raised in the hearts of many by the love of creatures, and nourished by the desire of earthly enjoyments. From the example of Nadab and Abiu, he takes occasion to exhort the faithful in general, to banish from their hearts whatever is incompatible with the love of God. In the narrow heart of man, God never can admit a rival of his love: no man can serve two masters; he cannot divide his heart between God and the world.

A.M. 2514.] *The Blasphemer stoned.* [A.C. 1846.
LEV. xxiv.

THE instance that God exhibited of his justice in the punishment of Nadab and Abiu, was soon after followed by another of equal severity in the death of a blasphemer. Two of the common people had a quarrel with each other, and one of them in the transport of his anger blasphemed the sacred name of God. The by-standers were shocked to hear such language, and led the offender straight to Moses. Moses judged the matter to be of too important a nature for him to decide upon the spot. He consulted God in his holy prayer to know how to act in this matter. Lead the blasphemer out of the camp, said Almighty God; let all those who heard him, lay their hands upon his head, and the rest of the people then stone him to death. The order was immediately executed with a severity which ought to make those Christians tremble, who either speak or suffer the same impious language. A general law was then made, which condemned every blasphemer to the like punishment. Examples of such severity seemed necessary to keep that stiff-necked people within due

bounds, and to make them sensible of their duty to God. The like sentence was soon after passed against a man who had gathered a few sticks upon the Sabbath-day.—*Numb.* xv. The action, no doubt, was servile, and, as such, forbidden by the commandment; but neither Moses nor Aaron would determine whether it was a capital fault or not, or what punishment it might deserve, until by prayer they had learned from God what was to be done. God told them to have the man led out of the camp, and there stoned to death.

If the like severity of civil and religious discipline were still kept up, men would be more cautious how they offended. The fear of present punishment, though it did not inspire them with a love of God's law, might at least hold them back from daring to offend in public. To those who join the practice to the knowledge of their duty, it is a subject of the deepest concern, to see the sacred laws of God notoriously transgressed without shame or fear by the impious offender. With the eyes of faith they penetrate into the fathomless depth of eternity, and there behold those endless pains, which are more to be dreaded than any thing we can suffer in this life. With aching hearts they lament the blindness of thousands, who run laughing on towards the fiery pit that is always open to receive the falling sinner. However slow God may seem to punish during life, he still is just and immutable in his decrees. Death shall no sooner close the impenitent sinner's eyes, but he must carry with him all his sins before the tribunal of a judge, who in the end will do himself justice for his long-injured mercy. To his cost the sinner shall then find that no worldly system, no laws of men, can prevail against the law of God, nor human considerations justify a breach of the divine precepts. What God has once written, should stand recorded to the end of time. The heavens may pass away like smoke, the earth may crumble into its first nothing; but the law of God shall never vary, its obligations shall never cease to bind the consciences of men.

A.M.2514.] *The Twelve Spies*—NUM. xii. xiii. [A.C. 1486.

NOTWITHSTANDING the severity of these examples, it was with the utmost difficulty that the people were restrained within any bounds of duty. They still murmured and complained of hardships which they had to struggle with; even Aaron and his sister were not exempt from guilt; for being jealous of their brother's authority, they were bold enough to say, that Moses was not the only one whom God had spoken to; that the Lord had likewise communicated himself to them; and to palliate their conduct against the holy man, they objected as a crime the marriage he had contracted with a Madianite, the daughter of Jethro. Moses on that trying occasion behaved with his usual meekness, and said nothing. Almighty God undertook the defence of his servant, and by a visible miracle, made the two murmurers sensible of their sin. Aaron acknowledged his fault, and escaped punishment. Mary was struck with a sudden leprosy, which covered her from head to foot. This is the Mary who had formerly concurred in saving her little brother from the Nile. Moses interceded to God for her pardon, and received for answer that she should be separated from the people, and perform a seven days' penance in a state of excommunication from the camp.

The minds of the people were still very far from being quieted; the spirit of sedition spread amongst them, and became almost general. The camp was removed from the desert of Sinai to Pharon. From thence, by the command of God, Moses sent twelve spies, one out of every tribe, to reconnoitre the land of Chanaan, which was at no great distance. The messengers at their return gave a most flattering account of the beauty and fertility of the land they had seen, and as a proof, produced a huge bunch of grapes and other rich fruits thereof; but at the same time, they gave so frightful an account of its inhabitants and fortified towns, that the hearts of

the hearers were struck with a sudden panic, which filled the camp with tumult and confusion. The people mutinied against their leaders; they declared they would sooner die in the desert, than follow Moses any farther, and began to deliberate upon the choice they should make of some other chief, to conduct them back to Egypt. Their hopes of the promised land, which had hitherto encouraged them, seemed to be no more, and the power of God, which had so miraculously preserved them, was entirely forgot. Moses and Aaron had no resource but in the Lord; they were under the greatest apprehensions for their people; they dreaded the consequence of God's wrath, which they expected every hour to see fall upon a rebellious race, and therefore prayed most earnestly to avert the stroke. In the mean time, Joshue and Celeb, two of the twelve spies, exerted their utmost endeavours to quiet the people, and to convince them of the unreasonableness of their fears. They went from tribe to tribe, and assured them, that under the protection of a God who had shown himself always ready to support them, they had nothing to apprehend; and that no enemy, however formidable in appearance, would be able to stand against them. The people answered them with loud clamours of indignation, being seemingly determined to stone them to death, when God himself suddenly interposed; and over the roof of the tabernacle his glory appeared visible to all the children of Israel. Go, tell the incredulous people, said the Lord to his faithful servant Moses, that I have heard their clamours; that I will treat them as they desire; that they shall die in the desert; that of them all who have attained the twentieth year of their age, not one, except Joshue and Celeb, shall ever reach the land which so displeases them; that for full forty years they shall wander up and down the wilderness, and there die, before their children shall be permitted to enter into the promised land. The people were moved at this declaration; they wept and promised obedience, the ten seditious spies, who had been the first instigators of that popular tumult, were struck suddenly dead before the Lord; and Moses the next day marched the people back towards the Red Sea.

From this conduct of the Hebrew people, we see how shameful and how dangerous a thing it is, to let ourselves be dejected at difficulties, which are either imagined or magnified by fear. Difficulties will unavoidably occur in the way of virtue; let them not startle us; let us only strive, and by the divine aid we shall happily surmount them. There is no entering into the land of promise, but by conquering the enemies that stand in our way. So far from being disheartened at the sight of hardships, we ought rather to rely more confidently upon God, who promises never to abandon those that put their trust in him. In the law of grace, Jesus Christ promises his kingdom to those only who with pious violence shall strive to gain it. Not to strive, is to give up the crown; the crown is not to be won, but by vigorous contest, and the contest is not above our strength. Aided by the grace of God, we not only can surmount every difficulty we meet with, but we also add a new lustre to our crown, by every effort we make to gain it.

A.M. 2514.] *Core, Dathan, and Abiron.* [A.C. 1486.

NUM. xvi.

THE disturbance caused by the ten spies, was soon after followed by another of a much more pernicious tendency, as it was formed by some of the leading men in the council, and aimed at nothing less than anarchy and schism. Core, the great-grandson of Levi, Dathan, and Abiron, of the tribe of Ruben, with two hundred and fifty more chiefs of the Israelites, rose in rebellion against Moses and Aaron. Being misled by the passion of jealousy and ambition, they claimed a share of the supreme power, which they were determined to wrest out of the hands of the two brothers. They made no secret of their design, they publicly avowed it; and before an assembly of the people, began to call Moses and Aaron to an account, as if they had usurped to themselves an authority which was injurious to the rights of the holy people of God. Astonished at their boldness, Moses fell prostrate upon the ground, and implored the divine protection; then rising up, he addressed himself to the multitude in general, and told them, that on the morrow it should visibly appear whom the Lord had chosen. To Core and his Levitical adherents he spoke more particularly, and reproached them with their audacious ambition: Hear, ye sons of Levi, said he, does it seem to you but a trivial honour that the God of Israel has done you, in selecting your tribe from the rest to serve him in the ministry of his holy tabernacle? Must you therefore assume to yourselves the priesthood too? If Aaron has been preferred, was it not by the Lord's command that he had been anointed; and why do you murmur against him? Let each one take his censer in his hand, and come thou Core, and all thy associates with thee, before the tabernacle to-morrow morning, and the Lord himself shall show whom he has chosen. They accordingly appeared, Aaron on one side, and Core, with his adherents on the other. At that moment also appeared the God of Majesty in full glory, and commanded his faithful servants to separate the schismatics from the rest of the people. It was done: Core, Dathan, and Abiron, with their wives and children stood at the entrance of their own pavilions apart. Moses then called the Israelites to witness, that he had in all things acted under the special direction of Almighty God, and that his very enemies, by being swallowed up alive into the earth, should be his vouchers for the truth. Scarce had he finished speaking, when the earth opened and swallowed up

the three factious leaders, with their tents and all their substance. They descended alive into hell, says the sacred text: their bodies were inwrapped within the bowels of the earth, and they miserably perished from amongst the people. Their doleful cries terrified those that were standing round, and made them fly, for fear of being swallowed up in like manner. Fire at the same time came forth from the Lord, and destroyed the two hundred and fifty men that had presumed to offer incense; upon which Almighty God thus spoke to Moses: Tell Eleazer, the son of Aaron the priest, to take the censers out of the fire, because they are sanctified by the incense which hath been offered by them to the Lord; let him beat them into plates, and fasten them to the altar, that they may there remain as a lasting monument to the children of Israel, lest some other stranger, who is not of the seed of Aaron, may hereafter presume, like Core, to exercise the functions of the priesthood. This exemplary punishment, one would think, ought to have awed the people into a sense of their duty; but so hardened were they grown, that on the very next day they accused Moses and Aaron, as guilty of the death of their fellow-citizens. God was grievously offended at their perverseness, and threatened to destroy them all by fire. Kindled by the breath of his divine anger, the fire began

to rage amongst them; Moses hastened to the tabernacle, and in fervent prayer strove to obtain their pardon. Fourteen thousand seven hundred of the common people had already fallen victims to the spreading flames, when he bid Aaron fill his censer with burning coals from the altar, and offer incense to the Lord. Aaron immediately went, and placing himself before the flames, between the living and the dead offered up his prayers with the smoking frankincense. The flames that instant ceased, and God was pacified.

To prove the divine appointment of Aaron and his sons to the priesthood still more decisively, God commanded Moses to take twelve rods, besides that of Aaron, and to write upon each rod the name of the leader of each tribe, and to lay them in the tabernacle before the ark, where the rod of that chief should blossom, whom he had chosen for the priesthood. Moses communicated these orders to the people, and received a rod from the chief of each tribe, twelve in number, besides Aaron's for the tribe of Levi, which he marked and carried into the tabernacle, where he left them all night. Upon his entering the tabernacle next morning, he found the rod of Aaron not only teeming with buds and blossoms, but also shining with leaves and fruit. The other twelve rods were as dry as when they were first put in. Moses brought them forth to public view; the fact was evident: Aaron's priesthood and prerogative was established beyond the possibility of a doubt. The rod was carried back and deposited in the tabernacle, as a mark for the rebellious Israelites, to put a stop to their complaints.

So miraculous an interposition of the divine power, in support of the priesthood, most undoubtedly shows its origin, and stamps a sanctity upon its character. The honour of being, by divine appointment, selected from among men, to be employed in those things which immediately concern the worship of God, and to officiate at his altar, more especially in the law of grace, is so sacred, that none should dare to meddle, none thrust themselves in, who are not appointed. The dreadful punishment inflicted upon Core, Dathan and Abiron, for having taken the censer into their hands, and attempted the exercise of a function that did not belong to them, is a warning for all to be upon their guard, how they trespass upon the rights, or disrespect the sanctity of God's altar.

A.M. 2552.] *The Brazen Serpent.* [A.C. 1448

NUM. xxi.

NOTWITHSTANDING the stupendous miracles which God had wrought, for the encouragement of his people in their duty, and notwithstanding the severe instances he had given of his anger to deter them from sin, the Israelites remained still as stubborn, still as perverse as ever. Neither promises nor threats, neither favours nor punishments, seem to have any effect upon their hardened hearts. Tired with their long and tedious journeys in the desert, they grew impatient of subordination; they conspired against their leaders, they publicly arraigned their conduct, and threw out complaints against God himself: they complained as they had often done before, for having been forced out of Egypt. Why were we not permitted to remain there, said they? why have we been dragged out to die in this barren wilderness? We have not bread to eat; we are often perishing for want of water to drink; our stomachs turn at the very sight of this insipid manna. Such complaints deservedly drew upon them the severest punishments. God sent amongst them a number of venomous serpents, whose bite caused a burning pain like that of fire. Numbers of the people died; the survivors were terrified by the sufferings and groans of their dying brethren, and became sensible of their offence. Their murmurs were changed into sighs, and their clamours into acts of supplication. They went like humble supplicants, to Moses, confessed their crime, and with all the show of repentance, besought him to give them relief. Moved by the tears of a suffering people in distress, Moses undertook to intercede for them, and by his prayers obtained their pardon. As a token of their faith, God commanded him to set up the brazen figure of a serpent, so that the people might see it,

and by looking at it be healed of the bites they received. The mortality ceased, and the people were mercifully freed from an evil, which, by their sinful murmurs, they had drawn upon themselves.

The holy fathers point out the spirit of murmuring and discontentedness, as one of the most dangerous temptations that can happen even to the most perfect. If not roused by faith and strengthened by hope, weak nature is frequently inclined to complain in time of trial. Such complaints arise from a dejection of mind, and secret diffidence in God, with which the infernal serpent stings and poisons our souls. Jesus Christ upon the cross, prefigured by the brazen serpent in the desert, is the object we, then, must turn to; on Him, who is the true restorer of our health, we must fix our eyes. Jesus Christ, in the agonies of death, stretched out in pain, and nailed to a cross, uttered no complaint! his sufferings were extreme: he suffered not for himself, but for us. Shall we, then, refuse to suffer for him? or shall we dare to murmur at the sufferings we meet with in his service? Suffer what we will, our sufferings are but light in comparison of his; they are not equal to what our sins deserve. Sufferings borne with patience satisfy for sin, and add new gems to the crown of glory, which God has prepared for those who persevere to the end in his service.

A.M. 2553.] *Balaam the Soothsayer* [A.C. 1447.

NUM. xxii

THE Israelites were drawing towards the borders of the promised land; they had passed the wilderness, and entered into the inhabited country that lies stretched along the eastern bank of the river Jordan. They had sent deputies to Sehon, king of the Amorrhites, for leave to march peaceably through his territories; Sehon put himself at the head of his army to oppose their passage, and the king of Basan followed his example. Encouraged by a promise of victory from God, the Israelites attacked, defeated, and slew the two kings with their people, and possessed themselves of the whole country; then marched on with the hopes of new conquests, and encamped in the plains of Moab, opposite to Jericho. Balac, king of the Moabites, seeing what had happened to Og and Sehon, sent for Balaam, a false and famous prophet of the country, to come and lay his curse upon an enemy, whom no human power seemed strong enough to resist. Balaam told the king's messengers, that he could give them no answer before morning: in the night he was forewarned from heaven not to curse a people whom God had blessed, and, therefore, bade the messengers to return to Balac as they came. Balac would not be refused; he sent a more solemn deputation of his nobles with larger presents to Balaam. The old wizard began to stagger in his resolution; the honour of being thus courted by the king, flattered his vanity; the presents were tempting; he viewed them with a covetous eye; and, as if God, like him, had been capable of being bribed into other sentiments by force of gold, he consulted him again. God, in punishment of his impiety and avarice, abandoned him to the secret desires of his own corrupt heart, and bade him go with the messengers to Balac. Balaam rose betimes next morning, saddled his ass, and accompanied the king's servants. As he was going on, the ass suddenly turned aside, to avoid an angel that stood in

the way with a drawn sword, and ran out into the field. Balaam, not knowing what the beast had started at, for he did not see the angel, gave her hard blows to bring her back into the road. The angel then placed himself in a narrow pass between two dead walls, where, to avoid him, the ass thrust herself close on one side, and hurt the rider's foot against the wall, for which she was cruelly beaten a second time. She after that saw the same angel standing in a place where it was impossible to pass him; she fell with fright under the feet of the rider, who in a transport of anger beat her sides more vehemently with his staff. Then, by a singular miracle, did God open the mouth of the dumb animal, to complain of the cruel treatment. Balaam's eyes were opened, and seeing the angel with a drawn sword ready to kill him, threw himself on the ground, confessed his fault, and offered to return home, if such was the angel's will. The angel told him he might go on, but to take care how he uttered anything contrary to his orders. Balac being informed of Balaam's approach, went forth to meet and conduct him to the high places of Baal. Seven altars were erected and the victims slain. Balaam told the king that he could speak no otherwise than as God commanded him, and in spite of all the king could say or promise him, he persisted in declaring he could pronounce nothing but blessings and happy tidings for Israel. The fear however of losing the king's bounty, induced him to advise a measure, which he thought would defeat the blessings he had pronounced. His advice was, to make the Israelites acquainted with the women of Madian, not doubting but by forming a connection with them they would adore their idols, and so forfeit the favour and protection of the God of Abraham. This advice was followed and attended with the worst of consequences; for the idolatrous women of Madian, having gained the affections of the carnal Jews, seduced them from their duty into the most criminal engagements. Moses wept to see the Israelites abandon themselves to the superstitious rites of Beelphegos, used his strenuous endeavours to reclaim them, and by the command of God, punished many of the offenders with death. Phinees, the zealous grandson of Aaron, distinguished himself on that occasion, and by one vigorous stroke put a stop to an evil, which seemed to threaten ruin to God's chosen people.

Thus, by the zealous efforts of one true Levite, says St. Ambrose, the children of Israel were saved from the precipice, which the avarice of a false prophet had prepared for them: the artifice of the one was defeated by the piety of the other. Happy are the people, when under such guides as have the prudence to direct, and the zeal to defend them, against the criminal attempts of those who are sold to seek or advise their ruin.

A.M. 2553.] *Death of Moses.*—DEUT. xxxiv. [A.C. 1447.

THE Moabites having debauched the children of Israel from their duty, God commanded Moses to revenge himself upon them. In obediênce to the order, Moses chose out twelve thousand of the most valiant of his people, and put them under the command of the Phinees, hoping that the zeal which he had lately shown in the cause of God would draw down a blessing upon his arms. Nor did his hope deceive him. The twelve thousand Israelites fell upon the united forces of Moab, and cut them to pieces: all the chief men of the country, and the wicked Balaam amongst them, were without mercy put to the sword, their country plundered, and their cities burnt to the ground. The conquerors returned with a very rich booty, driving the women and vast herds of cattle before them into the camp. Moses went out to meet them, and expressed great dissatisfaction with the officers for having spared the women, who had been the chief agents in perverting the Israelites. He therefore gave strict orders to have them executed, as guilty of death, excepting the virgins, who had not shared in the guilt: these amounted to the number of thirty-two thousand, and with the rest of the spoils, after a certain part had been set aside for the Lord, were distributed amongst the people. This being done, Moses allotted the conquered lands to the tribes Reuben and Gad, and one half of the tribe of Manasse, upon condition that they helped their brethren to subdue the country that lay on the other side of the Jordan.

As mention of the twelve tribes is often made, and as the land of promise was to be parcelled out amongst them under that title, we may observe once for all, that the tribes take their names from the twelve sons of Jacob, viz, Reuben, Simeon, Levi, Juda, Dan, Nepthali, Gad, Aser, Issachar, Zebulon, Joseph, Benjamin, Reuben by the crime of incest, having forfeited his right of primogeniture, the privileges annexed to it were divided amongst his brethren: those privileges were the priesthood and sceptre, and a double portion of his family estate. The first was given to Levi, the second to Juda, and the third to Joseph, whose two sons, Ephram and Manasse, where by Jacob reputed as his own: hence, each of them has his share amongst the twelve divisions of the promised land, and the tribe of Levi, which was to live dispersed amongst the other twelve, and to receive the tithes of all their lands, shared no particular part of the soil.

Moses having brought the Israelites as far as the river Jordan, which he knew he was not to pass, sent to Josue, and in the presence of the people, invested him with the civil power of governing the people in his stead, from that day; for the sacerdotal power, by God's command, had been already given to Eleazer, the son and successor of Aaron, a little before his death, on the mount of Hor. The holy law-giver, knowing his end to be near at hand, repeatedly exhorted Josue to execute the trust reposed in him, with all the zeal and magnanimity he was capable of: he told him that the task he had upon his hands was nothing less than the conquest of the promised land, and an equitable distribution of the same amongst the people: he recapitulated all that had passed from the time they had left Egypt to the present day, the unwearied pains he had taken to conduct them thus far, the prodigies God had wrought for forty years together in their favour, the precepts he had given them, and the promises he had made them, upon condition that they remained faithful in his love and service. After this God commanded him to go up to the top of Mount Nebo, from whence there

was an extensive view of the land of promise. He blessed God at the sight, and humbly submitted to the divine will, which did not permit him to set his foot thereon: he there gave his last blessing to the tribes of Israel, and slept with his forefathers, having completed the hundred and twentieth year of his age. They mourned for him in the plains of Moab thirty days: he was buried in the valley over against Phogor, but the spot of his sepulchre no one knows to the present day.

Thus, in the sight, and on the very borders of the promised land, for which he had undergone so many dangers, had borne so many labours, and had been privileged with the gift of working so many miracles, died the holy prophet, the great law-giver and deliverer of the Hebrew people. Equally admirable for his meekness as for his fortitude of mind, he united a fatherly tenderness for his people, with an inflexible fidelity to God. By divine inspiration, he wrote the first five books of the Holy Bible, which he gave to the Levites, to be carefully deposited in the tabernacle, by the side of the ark. The circumstances of his death, as to time and place, seem to have been intended by the Almighty God, not for the trial only, but for the perfection of his servant's virtue. However desirous he might naturally be of entering into the land of Chanaan, a land so often promised to Abraham, to Isaac, and to Jacob; a land so fertile and so teeming with delights; yet he knew it to be no more than the figure of a more delightful and more permanent inheritance. It is by weaning our affections from the earth, as Moses did; it is by dying like him to our earthly desires; it is, in fine, by a perfect resignation to the will of God, through the various trials and afflictions of life, that we must open to ourselves a passage into that heavenly kingdom, which God has promised to those who love him and keep his commandments.

A.M. 2553.] *Passage of the Jordan.* [A.C. 1447.

JOSUE, iii.

UPON Moses's demise, Josue was acknowledged his successor in the supreme temporal command, and in that capacity received the promise of fidelity from the body of the people. He was a man of consummate wisdom, and qualified with every other virtue for the high station he was called to. The Israelites under his command lay encamped upon the bank of the river Jordan, which God commanded them to pass. Three days were employed in making the necessary dispositions: every thing being ready, Josue ordered the heralds to give public notice through the camp, that as soon as they should see the priests begin to move forward with the ark of the covenant, they should all arise and follow at the distance of two thousand cubits. The priests, who carried the ark on their shoulders, set forward at the signal given, and advanced to the edge of the Jordan. Their feet no sooner touched the stream, than the river stopped its course; the waters below ran off as usual into the Dead Sea, while those above were collected in a heap as they flowed down from their sources, and stood like a high swelling mountain in one place. A dry and open passage was hereby let across the bed of the river: the priests advanced with the ark as far as the middle of the channel, and there halted till the whole host of Israel had reached the opposite bank, near the town of Jericho. When they were over, Josue, by the express command of God, ordered twelve chosen men, one out of every tribe, to fetch twelve large stones from the spot where the priests

were standing with the ark, and to erect in the place where they were to encamp that night, a standing monument of their gratitude to God for so miraculous an event. He also ordered them to carry twelve other stones from the bank, and to pile them up after the same manner in the middle of the dry channel; which being done, he commanded the priests to come forward with the ark. The priests were no sooner come up, and began to tread upon the dry ground, than the waters of Jordan returned into their channel, and flowed as they were wont before. Thus, under the divine influence, did Josue begin to display his talents, and to signalize his name at the head of the Israelites.

In this miraculous passage of the Jordan, God has been pleased to signify to us the more spiritual wonders he has to work in after ages, when through the waters of baptism leads his children of adoption into the true land of promise which is his church. For the passage of the Jordan is a figure of baptism, by the grace of which the new-born Christian passes from the slavery of sin into a state of freedom, peculiar to the chosen sons of God. Happy is the man who, being faithful to the grace which he then received, has the will to check the torrent of his corrupt inclinations, and turns the flow of his affections towards God, the source of virtue and real happiness.

A. M. 2553.] *Taking of Jericho.*—JOSUE, vi. [A. C. 1447.

THE Hebrew people were now entered into the country which Almighty God had so often and so solemnly promised to their forefathers. The first town that stood in their way was Jericho, whither Josue had already sent two spies to reconnoitre the place. The prince of Jericho had been informed not only of their arrival, but of the very house in which they lodged, and sent to have them seized. Rahab, their hostess, concealed them upon the roof of her house till the king's messengers were gone, and then let them down the wall by a cord. The spies, very different from those who had been sent by Moses forty years before, far from being disheartened at the sight of a fortification, encouraged their countrymen to march boldly on, assuring them, that from the observations they had made, the town would quickly fall an easy conquest to them. For at the approach of a people of whom such prodigies had been related, the townsmen were thrown into so great a consternation, that they had no hope of safety left, but in the strength of their walls and ramparts. And what is the strength of walls and ramparts against the arm of the Almighty? Josue in the name of God, gave orders for his people to make a general procession round the walls of Jericho for seven days together, and on the seventh day to go seven times round: the troops under arms to march in the first place; the ark to go next, supported by priests, and immediately preceded by seven other priests, sounding their trumpets of jubilee as they went along; and lastly, the rest of the people to close the rear with sound of trumpet. These orders were punctually executed. On the seventh day, as they were making the seventh round, the trumpets sounded, according to God's order, and the people shouted. The mingled shouts and clangors were still thundering in the ears of the multitude, when the walls instantly fell down, and opened the Israelites an entrance into the city. Each one

rushed forward over the crumbled ruins that lay before him: they took possession of the town, and, as Josue had commanded, put all the inhabitants to the sword, excepting Rahab, who, for the service she had done the spies, was saved from the general massacre. Josue had moreover cautioned them not to appropriate to themselves any part of the spoils, which he had solemnly consecrated to the Lord.

In this manner fell the strong town of Jericho; at the trumpets' sound her walls tumbled down, and the strong bastions, which she fancied to be impregnable, sunk at once into dust. The holy fathers have taken particular notice of this miraculous transaction, and they tell us that the flourishing sound of the trumpets represented the glorious preaching of the gospel. The same sound which inspired the Israelites with courage, filled their enemies with terror and alarm. Nothing, says St. Ambrose, renders the people of God so formidable to their enemies, as his holy word carefully explained and deeply impressed upon their minds By that, as by the trumpet's sound, they are animated with a lively sense of their duty; by that they are encouraged to resist the enemies of their salvation with vigour, and joyfully to rely on God for victory. The followers of Jesus Christ, says the same St. Ambrose, become victorious against the powers of hell, when they devoutly listen to the truths, and faithfully follow the doctrines of the gospel that is preached to them by the pastors of their souls. Then it is that they are inspired with heavenly desires, that they are confirmed in their good purposes, and warmed with the joyful hopes of salvation; then it is that they learn to esteem their Christian profession, and to trample the world, as another Jericho, with its sinful vanities, under foot.

A.M. 2553.] *Destruction of Hai.* [A.C. 1447.
JOSUE, vii.

THE destruction of Jericho was followed by that of Hai, a neighbouring town of no great strength, and incapable, as it was imagined, of making any resistance. Josue let himself be persuaded, that it was but to harass his troops, to lead the main army against it, and, therefore, contented himself with a detachment of three thousand men, which he thought would be sufficient to reduce so insignificant a place. The troops of Israel no sooner came within sight of the enemy, than they shamefully turned their backs and fled, and in their flight lost six and thirty men. Alarmed at this unexpected check in the very beginning of his conquests, Josue threw himself upon the ground, and, in humble prayer, began to expostulate with God, why he had permitted this disgrace to befall his people. Israel has sinned, replied the Lord; they have stolen—they have taken of the consecrated spoils, and concealed them; they cannot now stand before their enemies; I will be no longer with them, till the man be punished who is guilty of the wicked deed. Josue upon that assembled the people, and having informed them of the cause of their defeat, publicly declared that the offence must be expiated by fire. Without losing any time, he applied the lots to discover who the offender was, and found it to be Achan, of the family of Zare, of the tribe of Juda. Achan seeing himself thus miraculously discovered, thought it superfluous to dissemble any longer; he quickly owned himself guilty, and confessed, that in the sacking of Jericho, he had been tempted by a scarlet cloak, a golden ruler, and two hundred sicles of silver, which he had taken home, and secreted in his tent. His tent was searched, and the things were found in the very place he had mentioned. Josue, therefore, ordered the man to be taken into custody, to be led forth into the vale of Achor, and there stoned till he was dead. The sentence was immediately executed, and all things belonging to him were committed to the flames. By this public act of justice, God was again reconciled with his people, and promised them the conquest of Hai. Josue sent five thousand men to lie in ambuscade beyond the town, while the body of the army marched in the open valley that lay before it. The townsmen being flushed with their late success, rushed eagerly out to attack them. The Israelites, with well dissembled fear, immediately turned their backs. The enemy concluding their flight to be the effect of real fear, as it had been before, pursued them to a great distance. The Israelites having thus drawn them off from the town, Josue, as had been agreed upon, lifted up his shield against the city, and they who were in ambuscade, rising at the signal, set fire to the defenceless town and then pushed on to attack the enemy's rear. Josue discovering the success, by the smoke that rose from the town, faced about with his army, and attacked also in his turn. The Chananeans seeing themselves thus enclosed between two armies, no longer thought of making any resistance. They were all cut off to a man, and their city reduced to ashes.

St. Chrysostom, in the reflection he makes upon the misfortune that befell the Israelites, on account of Achan's sin, expresses his concern for the church militant, of which that people were the figure. When he considers a whole army so severely chastised for the crime of one soldier, he is surprised at the unconcern of those who sport away their time in the midst of sinners. He therefore earnestly exhorts every Christian to shun the company of notorious sinners, and to guard against the contagion of vice. We never ought to be without fear; we are never safe against the infection of others' faults. In the midst of a corrupt world, it is no small task to preserve ourselves from being tainted by it: to be innocent, our hearts must be equally unsullied as our hands. Achan was not less guilty in the sight of God before his crime was known, than when discovered to the eyes of men. It is not the appearance, it is the reality of virtue, that constitutes the merit of a Christian: the appearance, indeed, may impose on men, who see only the outside; the reality alone is acceptable to God, who beholds the heart.

A M. 2553.] *The Sun stands still.* [A.C. 1447.
JOSUE, x.

THE name of the Hebrew people was now known as far as Mount Libanus, in the most northern part of the country. The petty kings of Chanaan grew alarmed at their rapid progress, and resolved to unite their forces together for the common safety. The inhabitants of Gabaon were the only state that refused to join in the confederacy. These people wisely foresaw the consequences of a war, that should be undertaken against a nation so cherished by heaven. Open force they perceived must inevitably end in their own ruin; they had recourse to stratagem. They sent deputies to Josue, as from a people living at a great distance, who had heard of his achievements, and solicited his friendship. To make their story more plausible, they produced a few stale loaves of hard and dry bread, which they pretended had been baked the very day they left home, and appeared in old tattered clothes, that might look as if they had been worn out by the length of the journey. Josue, at first suspected some fraud, but trusting too much to appearances and his own judgment, let himself be imposed upon. He did not consult God upon the matter, as the sacred writer observes, but unadvisedly concluded a treaty of alliance with the Gabaonites, and bound himself by oath not to destroy them. In less than three days he found himself upon the territories of those very people, which he had fancied at an inconceivable distance: his troops began to exclaim against the cheat that had been put upon them; they thought it unreasonable that such impostors should be suffered to live, and would actually have put them all to the sword, if Josue had not interposed, and alleged the sanctity of his oath. To allay the warmth of their resentment, and to silence their complaints, he told them that the Gabaonites should be the slaves of Israel, and be for ever employed in cutting wood and carrying water for their service. Gabaon being thus preserved from the arms of Israel, was, in consequence, exposed to the danger of being ruined by those of Chanaan. Adonibesec, the king of Jerusalem, had been long jealous of that city, on account of its stately grandeur, and the valour of its inhabitants; and the late alliance she had made with the Israelites, made him now look upon her not only as a rival, but as a dangerous enemy of his power. He, therefore, resolved to exert the whole force of his kingdom against her: he prevailed upon four other princes of the country to join him in the enterprise, and march at the head of a great army, as to a certain victory. The Gabaonites, seeing themselves attacked by so superior a force, applied to Josue, their new ally, for assistance. Their application gave Josue a fair opportunity of striking some decisive stroke against the common enemy, and extending the conquest over the country. He led an army against the five confederate kings, whom he attacked and defeated with great slaughter. The remains of their army endeavoured to save themselves by flight. Josue perceived the day was fast upon the decline; he saw the night coming on before he could complete his victory, and thereupon commanded the sun not to move

against Gabaon, nor the moon against the valley of Aialon. The sun and moon, therefore, stood still while he finished the overthrow of his enemies; for God obeyed the voice of man, says the holy Scripture, and neither before nor after was there seen so long a day.

So singular an effect of the divine power, exerted at the voice of man, must naturally rouse the faith, at the same time that it excites the admiration of all who read it. The same omnipotent hand of God, which gave existence to the universe, which fixed the earth, the sun, moon, and stars, and bade them move in their respective spheres according to the laws he gave them, can at pleasure alter or suspend those laws, as he shall judge expedient either for his own glory, or for the special benefit of his favourite servants. But when we see the Almighty thus condescend to the wants of weak mortals, and for their service work such stupendous changes in the order of nature, we are then called upon to renew our belief in his divinity, to adore his power, to revere his wisdom, and obey his commands, lest we seem less rational and less sensible of our duty, than the very inanimate parts of the creation.

A.M. 2570.] *Punishment of Adonibesec.* [A.C. 1430.

JUDGES, i.

JOSUE, by the might of God's arm, bore down all before him: victory attended him wherever he turned his arms, and every day was signalised by some new conquest. By the rapid progress of his arms, the Hebrew people took possession of the land of Chanaan, as of their own inheritance. At the end of six years, scarce an enemy was left to face him in the field. The Scripture mentions no less than one and thirty kings who had yielded to his arms. Most of the old inhabitants of the country fell victims to his sword: for God permitted no more of them to remain alive, than might be sufficient to exercise the courage, or to punish the infidelity of his own people. Josue having made himself master of the country by his valour, displayed an equal wisdom in the distribution he made of it amongst the conquerors. He observed so nice and impartial an equity towards every tribe, that no room was left either for censure or complaint. He had now completed the glorious work to which God had called him; he had subdued the promised land, and established the Israelites in the quiet possession of it. Finding himself to be near his end, he called the Israelites together, as Moses had done before him, and reminded them of the wonders that God had wrought in their favour; he exhorted, besought, and conjured them, till he obtained their promise not to serve any other God than the Lord of the universe. Having thus happily discharged his duty both to God and his people, Josue slept with his forefathers in the hundred and tenth year of his age, and was mourned for by all the people. To him is attributed the book which bears his name amongst the sacred writings During the whole time that he governed the Hebrew people, he was happy never to see them fall into any acts of idolatry, nor to hear them utter any complaints against the Lord. The battles he fought, and the conquests he made, have given occasion to the following remark of the holy fathers: that no one can pretend to inherit the promised blessings of Almighty God. till he has happily subdued those domestic enemies, the sinful appetites and vicious inclinations that bear dominion in his heart. By sin we are born tributary to the Chananean and the Amorrhean, that is to say, Satan; and we must first extirpate sin, and bring into subjection whatever else there is in us belonging to Satan, before we can be possessed of the kingdom of Jesus Christ.

Upon the death of Josue, Celeb put himself at the head of the tribe of Juda, and distinguished himself by many victories that he gained against the remaining enemies of his nation. Adonibesec, the cruel tyrant of Jerusalem, was the first that felt the vengeance of his arm. By a just judgment of God, this wicked prince experienced the same barbarous treatment from the sons of Juda that he had before inflicted upon others. At different times, no less than seventy kings had the misfortune to be his prisoners; he cut off the extremities of their hands and feet, and forced them to lick up the leavings of his table. The children of Juda had no sooner laid their hands upon him, than they treated him in the same manner, and sent him to Jerusalem to drag out life by a lingering death.

In the reverse of this tyrant's fortune is verified the truth of that sentence, where our blessed Saviour has since declared, that he will pass judgment upon men as they shall have passed judgment upon others. The sentence is universal; it makes no distinction between the king and the subject; if it is not executed during life, its severity is more to be dreaded after death. An impartial and all-knowing judge will then pronounce according to the merits of each particular; and by the mouth of the wisest of kings he has already declared, that the mighty if they abuse their power, shall suffer mighty torments.

A.M. 2719.] *Debora's Triumph.* [A.C. 1281.

JUDGES, iv.

AFTER the death of Josue, and of those virtuous sages who had seen the wonders that God had wrought during their forty years' pilgrimage through the desert, the Israelites fell into very great disorders. Being no longer united under one head, each tribe began to pursue a separate interest; they made war or peace, entered into treaties and alliances, as party interest and passion led them; they intermarried with the idolatrous inhabitants of the land, so by degrees grew familiar with their vices, imbibed their principles, and fell from the worship of God to the worship of idols. To punish them for their apostacy, God made use of those very people who had seduced them from their duty. By them they were at different times reduced to a state of servitude, and tyrannically oppressed, till the smart of temporal misfortunes roused them up to a sense of their duty, and made them return to God by repentance. Ever mindful of his mercies to them, God was pleased to listen to their cries: for their relief he called forth some extraordinary personages, who, from the authority they had over the people, are called Judges. The king of Mesopotamia was the first scourge that God employed to make his people sensible of their crimes. From this king the Israelites suffered bitter hardships; they at length acknowledged the hand of God in their sufferings, and repented. By the abilities of Othoniel, the nephew of Caleb, they shook off the Mesopotamian yoke, and regained the divine favour, till a run, of forty years prosperity made them forget their duty again; they relapsed into idolatry, and the Moabites were employed to chastise them for it. They suffered all the calamities of war for eighteen years, when, upon their having recourse to God, Aod rose up in their defence and restored peace to Israel. But the repentance of that unsteady people never lasted many years. They fell into fresh sins, and in punishment thereof were delivered into the hands of Jabin, king of Chanaan. Sisara, the Chananean general, poured out the evils of war upon them for twenty years together, and sc great was the number of troops and armed chariots which he led to battle, that the Israelites were afraid to face him in the open field. The Hebrew commonwealth was at that time governed by Debora, a woman full of the spirit of God, and as much renowned for her prudence in peace, as for her fortitude in war. In this dangerous situation of affairs she sent for Barac, of whose abilities she had a good opinion, made him her general, and ordered him to march with ten thousand men against Sisara. Barac refused to accept of the command, unless she would accompany him into the field. She consented, and God was pleased to strike such a panic into the Chananeans, that the army fled at her approach, and left the Israelites nothing to do but to kill and take prisoners. Sisara was borne away by the torrent, and endeavoured to save himself in the pavilion of Jahel, the wife of Heber the Cinite. Spent with fatigue, he there laid himself down upon the ground to sleep, and as he lay, Jahel took a nail, and with a hammer driving it through his temples, nailed him to the ground. By his death an end was put to Jabin's

tyranny, and the Israelites enjoyed the tranquillity of a forty years' peace.

In thanksgiving for the victory, Debora sung to God a solemn hymn, in which the highest praises are bestowed upon Jahel for her heroic fortitude. Fortitude and wisdom are the gifts of God, who at his pleasure distributes them as he pleases: by them he makes women equally capable as men of the greatest undertakings. Debora by her wisdom kept that rebellious people in obedience, which Moses with all his authority had been scarce able to effect; she was the first woman that governed the Hebrew nation, and from her government was derived every advantage that could have been expected from the wisest and most valiant of men. She took every prudent step to promote the public good; she raised the drooping spirits of her subjects, mustered her troops, chose her officers, directed their operations, and marched to battle at their head. The spirit and the hand of God carried her victoriously through the most perilous undertakings. Hence the holy fathers observe, that nothing can be truly great which is not begun and guided by the spirit of God. Under that divine influence the weaker sex become capable of the most difficult enterprizes, and without it men degenerate into the weakest of the weak. What appears the least capable in the eyes of a conceited world, God sometimes chooses, that he may confound the wise, and he chooses the weak to confound the strong.

A.M. 2759.] *Gedeon's Sacrifice.* [A.C. 1241.

JUDGES, vi.

UPON the death of Debora, the Israelites being no longer restrained by authority, fell back into such a state of licentiousness, that God abandoned them for seven years to the power of the Madianites. The Madianites were a cruel enemy, who ravaged and destroyed the whole country. The distress to which the Israelites were then reduced, became extreme, and extorted from them the cries of repentance. God heard their cries, and fixed upon Gedeon for their deliverer. Gedeon was a valiant young man, of an obscure family, of the tribe of Manasse. God sent an angel to inform him that the Lord was with him, and that upon the strength of his arm depended the safety of Israel. The angel, in the form and habit of a stranger presented himself in view under an oak tree, near the place where Gedeon was winnowing his father's corn. The heavenly messenger delivered his commission to the chosen youth, and assured him, that notwithstanding the low opinion he entertained of himself, he should drive the Madianites before him, and destroy them as easily as if they were but one man. Gedeon desired to know upon what grounds he had made him that extraordinary promise, and begged he would not go till he had taken some refreshment. The angel having accepted his offer, he quickly ran to prepare a kid and unleavened bread. He boiled the kid, and as soon as it was ready put the flesh of it into a basket, and the broth into a pot, to carry to his guest under the tree. The angel bade him lay the bread and meat upon the rock, and pour the broth thereon; which being done, he touched them with a rod he held in his hand, and behold a sudden flame blazed out of the rock, and consumed both the flesh and the loaves. The heavenly messenger vanished immediately out of sight, leaving Gedeon half dead with fright for having conversed so long with an angel, whom he had all the while taken for a common man. Almighty God inspired Gedeon with a holy confidence, and commissioned him to go and overturn the altar of Baal, to cut down the grove that surrounded it, and to erect upon the summit of the same rock an altar to the living God, where he should offer one of his father's bullocks in sacrifice. Gedeon was afraid of being murdered by the inhabitants, should he attempt any such thing by day; he therefore deferred it till night, when, with the help of his servants, he executed every part of the command. The inhabitants next morning were strangely surprised to see their grove cut down, and the altar overturned. Being much exasperated, they made diligent search after the author of the fact, and upon enquiry having found it to be Gedeon, went to Joas his father, and insisted that he should bring forth his son, and deliver him over to be punished as he deserved. Joas asked them in reply, if they were the avengers of Baal, or appointed to fight his battles? If Baal be a god, said he, let him revenge himself on the man who hath cast down his altar: it belongs not to you. The men upon that desisted from their pursuit: Gedeon escaped with impunity, and from that day obtained the surname of Jerobaal.

Gedeon, by his example, teaches those who are appointed to the care and government of others, with what exact fidelity and watchful prudence they ought to execute the commands, and promote the services of Almighty God, whatever may be the labour or the danger that attends them in the performance of their duty.

A.M. 2759.] *Miracles of the Fleece.* [A.C. 1241.

JUDGES, vi.

GEDEON being miraculously assured that God had chosen him for the relief of a distressed nation, was suddenly invested with the spirit of the Lord, at the very time that the Madianites and Amalecites were in common council plotting the destruction of Israel. He snatched up a trumpet, and sounded the alarm; he gave orders for the tribes to assemble, and follow him to battle. They immediately obeyed his summons, as from God, and unanimously acknowledged him for their chief. Thus from a private station, without interest or birth, Gedeon was raised to the supreme command of the Hebrew nation. Far from being elated by the honour of preferment, he still entertained the same humble sentiments of his own abilities; diffident of himself, he rested his trust in God, from whom he had received his authority. Not satisfied with these first assurances of the divine appointment in his favour, he suspended his military operations till, by some new miracle, God should more explicitly make known his will and intentions to him. This caution and humble diffidence which Gedeon expressed in accepting his employment, is a good instruction, says St. Ambrose, to those who fancy themselves qualified for, and eagerly grasp at every trust and honorary employment that presents itself to them. Gedeon therefore begged of Almighty God to confirm the choice he had made of him, by a miracle that he himself should specify. If the fleece of wool, said he to Almighty God, which I will expose all night to the open air, should be soaked with dew, while the grass around it continues dry, then shall I conclude that thou intendest to save Israel by my hand. The event answered his expectations; and yet so diffident was he of himself, that he wished for some further sign from heaven, and humbly besought the

Lord to exhibit a second miracle, that should be the reverse of the first: he begged that the fleece only might be dry, and the ground wet with dew. The Lord was pleased to condescend to his request, and there was dryness in the fleece that had lain exposed the whole night, and dew on all the ground.

These two miracles, according to the holy fathers, mark the difference of conduct which God had followed with regard to the Jews and the Gentiles. The Jews were once visited by that more plentiful effusion of his holy graces, by which he selected them from the midst of other nations, and made them his chosen people; till by their incredulity they rejected the divine gifts, and ungratefully abused the sacred blood which the Messias shed for their salvation. More sensible of the mercy, and more obedient to the voice that called them into the admirable light of divine faith, the Gentiles then became the special people of Jesus Christ. The mercies of our Great Redeemer extended over the face of the whole earth; his graces are poured out from sea to sea, to the uttermost limits of the globe, for the salvation of all mankind. His grace is as a celestial dew, with which our souls are refreshed against the heat of passions, and enabled to produce the fruits of eternal life.

A.M. 2759.] *Gedeon's Soldiers.* [A.C. 1241.

JUDGES, vii.

GEDEON, by the two miracles of his own choosing, was fully assured of the divine will in his regard: he was convinced that God had appointed him, not only to command the troops, but also to reap the victory, and therefore prepared to execute the important charge with as much eagerness, as he had at first shown unwillingness to accept it. Vast numbers of voluntary recruits flocked daily to his standard; his army soon made a very formidable appearance; he took the field, and encamped within sight of the enemy. Almighty God foresaw that the presumption and ingratitude of a stiff-necked people, would make them attribute to themselves the victory, if it were gained by such numbers, and resolved that they should not only owe, but moreover own their success solely to him. He therefore commanded Gedeon to disband part of his troops, and to proclaim through the camp, that every one who was not disposed to undergo the fatigue, or afraid to stand the shock of war, might peaceably return to his own dwelling. Two and twenty thousand of them readily accepted the offer, and only ten thousand remained to support the service of their country. But to answer the designs of God, that number was still too great: God commanded Gedeon to lead his army to the waters, where he would let him know the precise number that he had chosen for the service. He bade him observe the posture in which his soldiers should drink, when he came to the waters; whether they knelt down to slake their thirst at leisure, or only caught a sparing draught in the hollow of their hand, as they hastily passed along; that they, and only they, who should drink in this manner, were the men to whom he had resolved to grant the victory. When Gedeon came to the waters, he attentively observed his men; and of his whole army there were no more than three hundred who did not kneel down to

drink. He immediately disbanded the rest, and full of confidence in the divine promise, marched on with his little troop against the Madianites.

In this instance we may observe the distinction the Almighty God makes of those who engage in his service, and how small the number is of his chosen champions; since of the two and thirty thousand that followed Gedeon to war, twenty-two thousand took themselves off at once, and of the ten thousand that remained, three hundred only were reserved for victory. The mark of their election was their not bending the knee to drink: mindful of their character, even in little things, they sought no contrivance for their ease; they scooped up a passing refreshment in the palm of their hand, and were contented with a scanty draught to allay their thirst upon the march: in like manner, whoever engages in the divine service—and we are all engaged by the promises we made at baptism—ought not to stoop down towards the earth, beyond what is required to supply the wants of nature: ever mindful of our baptismal engagements, and steady in the divine service, we ought to stand always upon our ground, and to keep our affections still fixed to heaven. If compelled by necessity we make use of this world, it ought to be in the sense of St. Paul, as if we used it not. If for the comfort or support of life, which is constantly flowing off like a swift stream, we partake of the benefit of God's creatures, it ought to be without any strong attachment to them, without stop or hindrance in our way to heaven. The number of such Christians is indeed but small; but such there are; they are the chosen few, and it is in such that the Church of Christ chiefly glories; with these she stands invulnerable against her enemies, and with these she conquers

---

A.M. 2759.] *Gedeon's Victory.*—Judges, vii. [A.C. 1241.

Though nothing could be more explicit than were the promises which God had so often made to Gedeon of success, and though Gedeon did no longer entertain the smallest doubt of the event, yet it pleased the divine goodness to make him hear the same assurance of victory confirmed by the Madianites themselves. Gedeon, by advice of God, rose in the dead of the night, and being accompanied by a single servant, went into the enemy's camp to collect what intelligence he could. He listened to every sound, and caught up every word, as he stole cautiously along. He heard one of the Madianite soldiers telling his comrade a dream which he had, relative to the event of the war. I seemed to see, said the soldier, a barley loaf rolling through the camp, till it struck against one of the tents, and threw it down. It is the sword of Gedeon, immediately replied the other, that is here signified; to him the Lord has delivered our armies, and by him the tents of Madian shall be struck and overthrown. Upon hearing this, Gedeon made the best of his way back, and encouraged his troops to action by the relation of this story. He lost no time; he divided his three hundred men into three separate companies, and accoutred them with arms equally new and mysterious. He gave to each a trumpet and an empty pitcher, with a burning lamp concealed in the middle of it. He charged them to observe the most profound silence, till he should make them a signal to sound their trumpets, break their pitchers, and produce their lamps, shouting at the same time as with one voice, To the Lord and Gedeon! It was now midnight; they marched in deep silence; the three divisions took possession of the posts that had been assigned them! Gedeon gave the signal by sound of trumpet, and was answered by his men from their different stations. The Madianites between asleep and awake, were surprised at the unexpected alarm. The glittering of the lamps, the clash of the pitchers, and the clangors of trumpets, mixed with shouts of war from every quarter, made them fancy that they were surrounded by a vast army. Their fears magnified their danger, and in that confusion they turned their swords against one another, giving to Gedeon a decisive victory, without his striking so much as a single stroke.

The more singular this manner of fighting was, says St. Gregory, the more mysterious it appears; for who ever thought of going to war without arms, or who ever fancied that an earthen pitcher was a likely weapon against a coat of mail? To human wisdom, uninstructed in the sacred ways of divine Providence, such a scheme might seem ridiculous: but what appears mere folly in the eyes of men, God often chooses in his wisdom, as the most conducive to his designs. By this he teaches us in whom we are to place our greatest trust, and to whom we are to look up for success in our undertakings. It is not by any bodily or human strength, but by the virtue of Jesus Christ, that the enemies of our salvation can be put to flight. The earthen pots that were borne by Gedeon's men represent these brittle frames of our mortal bodies; and they only are to be accounted the worthy soldiers of Jesus Christ, who, like him, shall be ready to sacrifice their lives for God's service, and to conquer by their death. Death to such Christians is no more than the breaking of an earthen vessel: upon the dissolution of their mortal frame, the lustre of their virtues, which lay concealed before, is publicly disclosed, and like a burning lamp shines to all around. It is what we see in the blessed martyrs of Christ's church. However weak and even contemptible they may have appeared in their sufferings, by their virtues they are the strength, and ornament of the church. By their glorious conflicts they made themselves be admired even by their enemies and persecutors; their patience triumphed over the rage of tyrants, and their miracles confirm the truth for which they magnanimously fought and conquered.

A.M. 2768.] *Death of Abimelec.*—JUD. ix. [A.C. 1232.

GEDEON, by his prudence and military valour, having rescued his country from the hands of the Madianites, retired to his own private home, and there died in a good old age. Amongst the seventy sons that he left behind him, there was one called Abimelec, whose mother was a native of Sichem. This man being of a turbulent and ambitious temper, formed a strong party among the Sichimites, by whom he procured himself to be made king. Having thus raised himself above the reach of human laws, he committed strange disorders in the country, and amongst other cruelties, sent a band of ruffians to his late father's house in Ephra, to murder his brothers. The unhappy youths were all taken excepting Joatham the youngest, and slain upon one stone. Notwithstanding such acts of violence, the Sichimites were much pleased with the part they had taken, and assembled in a plain to make rejoicings in honour of the king they had chosen. This plain lay at the foot of a hill called Garizim. The young Joatham placed himself upon the top of it, and in an audible voice reproached the Sichimites for their ingratitude to a man who had saved their country from ruin. In a figurative style of language he compared them to the trees in a forest, who being ambitious of a kingly government, addressed themselves to the olive, to the fig-tree, and the vine, to be their king; and being refused by each in its turn, they at last chose the thorn, who promised to take them under his protection. He then turned off his discourse to Almighty God, and begged that if Gedeon and his family had been injuriously requited for their services, a flame might burst out from that thorn, for the speedy destruction both of king and people. His petition was granted him. For at the end of three years, the Sichimites growing tired of Abimelec, entered into a conspiracy to deprive him of his throne. But being too weak to execute their design, they themselves became a sacrifice to Abimelec's superior power, and their town was levelled with the ground. The citizens of Sichem being thus punished for their ingratitude, by the very man whom they had raised from nothing, the tyrant himself soon experienced the like vengeance. Flushed with the success that had hitherto attended him, he began to flatter himself that God had either forgot his crimes, or would suffer them to go unpunished. But God stretches not his patience beyond the limits that he himself has fixed: he often permits the greatest criminals to prosper for a while, that his glory may be the more manifest either in their repentance or in their punishment: he often strikes when they least expect it, and in a moment throws them down from their towering height, in which they thought themselves secure: and so it happened to the tyrant Abimelec; he was cut off at the very time that he flattered himself with the hopes of new victories. He had laid siege to the town of Thebes, and forced the inhabitants to retreat to their last hold, a tower in the middle of the city. He was eager to set fire to it, and approaching too near, was knocked down by a stone, which a woman cast upon his head.

Not less chagrined at the stroke, than confounded at the thought of dying by a woman's hand, he ordered his armour-bearer to run him through. His order was obeyed; and thus by a violent death the wretched man repaid the punishment that was due to him for the murder of his brothers.

The example of Abimelec, say the holy fathers, is a proof that no passion so disposes the mind to deeds of cruelty, as an inordinate thirst for power. Ambition, when it has once taken possession of the heart, destroys all respect for kindred, and blunts the very feelings of humanity. The sacred tie of friendship are regarded no longer; the laws of honour and common probity are violently broken through; and nothing is left untried, that can be thought to open the way to the enchanting object.

A.M. 2817.] *Jephte's Daughter.* [A.C. 1183.
JUDGES, xi.

AFTER the death of Abimelec, the reins of government passed successively through the hands of Thola and Jair; the latter was succeeded by Jephte. Jephte was the son of Galaad, a man naturally valiant, and a great warrior, but being base-born was compelled by his brothers to quit his father's house, as having no right to any part of their family inheritance. He retired into the land of Tob, where a lawless troop of banditti chose him for their leader. In the mean time the Israelites, who had left the worship of Almighty God for that of Baal and Astaroth, were grievously harassed by the Ammonites; for they were the scourge that God had chosen to chastise his faithless people for their apostacy. Sufferings made the delinquents sensible of their error. Their first concern was to appease the wrath of God by repentance, and then to look out for some able general to command their armies. They fixed their eyes on Jephte, with whose courage they were well acquainted; they sent deputies to offer him the command, and to beg his aid in the nation's distress. Jephte at first reproached the deputies for having suffered a man, for whom they professed so good an opinion, to be reduced to the necessity of seeking bread in a foreign land; but upon their promise of submitting entirely to his authority, he grew calm, and consented to be their leader. Before he entered upon action, he did all he could by treaty, to dissuade the Ammonites from acts of hostility against the Israelites; but finding his reasons had no effect upon them, who thought themselves injured, he collected an army, and prepared for battle. In order to draw down a blessing upon his arms, he made a vow to God, of sacrificing, in his honour, whomsoever he should first meet coming from his own house after the victory. He fought and conquered. Fame soon spread the joyful news through the country. His only daughter, attended by other maidens of her acquaintance, went out dancing to the sound of the tabour and other musical instruments, to meet her victorious father. But what a damp to the victor's joy, and what grief to a fond father, was the sight of an only daughter in such circumstances! With tears in his eyes, he told her the vow he had made: she consented, she even exhorted him to fulfil his promise to Almighty God, and declared herself happy to yield even her life as a holocaust to the Lord

who was the giver and disposer of it. The only thing she asked, was a respite of two months, that she might retire into the mountains with her female friends, and there bemoan her hapless virginity. The two months being expired, she came to her father, and he fulfilled his vow.

The interpreters of holy Scripture differ in the judgments they form upon the nature and performance of Jephte's vow. Some think, that Jephte's meaning was to consecrate to God whatsoever should first meet him, according to the condition of the thing; and, therefore, conclude, as human sacrifices were forbidden by the law, that he did not spill his daughter's blood, but consecrated her to God by a vow of perpetual virginity; for she lived and died a virgin. But the most common opinion is, that Jephte, in consequence of the vow he had made, slew his daughter as an holocaust to the Lord, being led thereunto either by a false and erroneous conscience, or by a particular dispensation from the law on the part of Almighty God, who is the sovereign master of life and death. However that may have been with respect to the father, we cannot sufficiently admire the dutiful behaviour and amiable simplicity of the daughter, who voluntarily submitted to her parent's will, and exhorted him to do as he had vowed. To die to sin, to resign the pomps of a licentious world, to renounce those pleasures and incentives to vice, which are inconsistent with a clean heart, is a sacrifice truly meritorious and acceptable to God; it is a sacrifice which was solemnly begun at the font of baptism, which ought to be daily renewed, and must be freely continued on till the end of life, that it may be crowned with the promised recompense of Him to whom it is religiously offered, and is justly due.

A.M. 2848.] *Birth of Sampson.* [A.C. 1152.

JUDGES, xiii.

JEPHTE judged Israel six years; after which succeeded several other judges, of whom the sacred history mentions little more than the number of their children. The next remarkable personage that occurs is Sampson, of whom many wonderful things are recorded. He was of the tribe of Dan, indued with vast bodily strength, which he exerted chiefly against the Philistines, whom God at that time let loose upon the Israelites in punishment of their sins. The birth of this extraordinary man had been foretold to his mother by an angel, who acquainted her not only that she should have a son, who should be consecrated to God from his birth, and be the first to promote the delivery of Israel out of the hands of the Philistines, but that from the hour of his conception, she should moreover contribute towards his sanctification, by abstaining from wine and strong drink, and unclean meats. She informed her husband Manue of the angel's apparition and message. Manue earnestly prayed that he might be favoured with a like vision. His petition was granted, and in a second visit, the angel not only made himself visible to him, but, moreover, told him that his son must also abstain from the same things that he had mentioned to his wife. Manue begged his guest to let him dress a kid for his repast. The angel refused to eat of his bread, saying, that if he chose to make a holocaust of his kid, he might offer it to the Lord. Manue laid the kid upon the rock, and set fire to it; as the

flame arose the angel ascended with it, and appeared to them no more. The child of promise was born soon after, and named Sampson. Every direction that God had given to his parents concerning his education, was religiously observed; his hair was not cut; neither wine nor any other liquor did he drink! the child was blessed by God, and became the strongest of men. Being of a mature age, he fell in love with a Philistine woman, and begged his father's consent to marry her. His father had an abhorrence of the very name of a Philistine, and, at first, refused his consent, not knowing that his son, in that point, acted under the immediate influence of God's Holy Spirit. For Sampson was a figure of Jesus Christ, the *strong*, the *wonderful*, who was one day to espouse the church of the Gentiles, after having been rejected by the Jews. Sampson by this alliance sought every occasion to chastise the Philistines for the many and grievous calamities they had brought upon the

people of Israel. Being one day on his way to the town where his intended spouse resided, he was met by a young lion, that came foaming with rage to devour him. Sampson, without weapon or defence, rushed forward by the impulse of the Holy Spirit, and laying hold of the lion, tore him with as much ease as he would have torn a kid to pieces. He threw the carcass aside, and there left it. Some days after, as he returned the same way, he steppeu aside to look at it, and behold a swarm of bees had settled and formed a honeycomb in the mouth of the dead lion. This singular circumstance gave occasion to a noted riddle, which Sampson proposed to thirty young Philistines, who were appointed to accompany him during the seven days' solemnization of his marriage with their countrywoman. He proposed it in the following words: Out of the eater came forth meat, and out of the strong came forth sweetness; and he promised to give each of them a suit of clothes if they solved it within seven days, upon condition that they promised also on their part to pay him the like forfeit if they failed. The condition was accepted of. They puzzled for three days about the riddle, but could not expound it: they then applied to the bride, telling her, she must obtain a discovery of the secrets from her husband, or they would burn her and her father's house if she did not. She immediately employed all the female arts she was capable of, to induce him to let her know what the riddle signified; she wept and complained, she caressed and solicited, till on the seventh day she prevailed upon him to expound the problem, which she immediately communicated to her countrymen. They hastened to Sampson before the sun went down, and said, What is sweeter than honey, and what is stronger than a lion? Sampson, by the direction of Almighty God, set off to Ascalon, where he slew thirty Philistines, whom he stripped, and gave their garments as a forfeit to the young men who had declared the riddle.

The holy fathers, in their remarks upon the honey-comb which Sampson found in the lion's mouth, take occasion to speak of that wonderful change which Jesus Christ wrought by his holy spirit among the Gentiles. Furious as a lion, the pagan people once raged and threatened destruction to the Christian Church, till being disarmed by the power of Jesus Christ, they ceased from acts of violence, and yielded to the force of truth. Softened into mildness by the doctrine and spirit of the gospel, they forgot their savage temper, and being regenerated in the waters of baptism, became the children of adoption, and were formed into one body of true believers, under one and the same head.

A.M. 2867.] *Sampson's wonderful exploits.* [A.C. 1133.
JUDGES, XV.

SAMPSON being provoked at the perfidious behaviour of the Philistine youths, and grieved at the shameful treachery o. his wife, abruptly left the house, and returned home. Her parents concluded from the manner of his going off, that he did not intend to return, and therefore married their daughter to another man. But contrary to their expectations, Sampson returned some time after and demanded his wife. Her father made him excuses for what he had done, and offered his youngest daughter in her stead. Neither his offer nor his excuses were accepted of. Sensible of the injury he had received, Sampson publicly declared, from that day he should think himself warranted to do them all the mischief he could, in punishment of their crimes. His first attempt against them was of a very singular nature. He caught three hundred foxes, and tying them by the tail two and two together, with a lighted torch in the middle, he let them out into the vineyards and corn-fields, by which means the whole produce of the adjacent country was entirely destroyed. So extraordinary a contrivance of doing mischief, made the Philistines extremely curious to know the author and the motive of it. They discovered the author to be Sampson, and his motive the evil treatment which he had received from his wife and father-in-law. These then they looked upon as the real authors of their misfortunes; against these they directed their revenge, and burned them alive. Sampson, who by the angel's express declaration to his parents, had been appointed to chastise the enemies of his country, was not yet satisfied. He performed such singular feats of valour against the Philistines, and spread such a terror amongst them, that they raised an army to oppose him. The tribe of Juda was alarmed at their warlike preparations, and sent to know of the Philistines what they meant. They received for answer, that nothing more was intended than the death of Sampson. The answer did not remove their fears. They thought a part of the storm, when it was once raised, might possibly fall upon them, and concluded the best step they could take, would be to prevent it, by delivering Sampson into their hands. Sampson had retreated into a cave in the rock of Etam. Thither they sent three thousand of their choicest men to secure him; yet such was the awful fear they had of his mighty strength, that they scarce dared to approach, much less lay their hands upon him. They told him the purport of their coming; they stood and remonstrated to him the dreadful calamities their whole nation might be exposed to, from the provoked rage of a lawless people who ruled over them: and as they solemnly promised upon oath not to take away his life, if he would only let them bind him, he peaceably yielded himself up into their hands, and willingly consented to be their prisoner. They bound him with two new cords, and led him off towards the Philistines. The Philistines shouted with joy at the sight, and began to think themselves out of all danger from their formidable adversary. Sampson was at that moment strongly moved by the spirit of the Lord, and by a sudden exertion of strength, burst his bands asunder, with as much ease as flax is consumed by fire: then snatching up the jaw bone of an ass, that lay accidentally in his way, he rushed upon his enemies, and with that single weapon slew a thousand of them. The heat and vigour of his efforts brought on an excessive thirst, he called upon God for relief in that extremity. God heard his prayer, and out of the dry bone drew a copious spring of water, with which he recruited his drooping vigour. Sampson returned his immediate thanks to God; and, as a monument of his gratitude, gave to the place a name, which would perpetuate the miracle to future ages.

To men full of that wisdom which is taught in a vain world, these facts may be a subject of profane wit and ridicule; but to the saints, who guide their thoughts and actions by the spirit of God's word, they furnish matter for devout meditation. Spiritual matters come not within the reach of the sensual man's knowledge; he judges and talks of the things of God, only as they strike his senses, and accord with his worldly notions; while the humble Christian measures them by the rule of faith, and considers them in the spirit of true piety. The great St. Gregory speaks of Sampson's victory over the Philistines, as a figurative representation of that which Jesus Christ has since gained over the pagan world. In his hand the patience and simplicity of a few fishermen, has been more efficacious, than the bone of a dead animal was in the hand of Sampson; by that he defeated the wisdom of philosophers; by that he triumphed over the rage of insulting tyrants, and put the power of superstition and infidelity to flight. The humble servants of Jesus Christ, being like him patient and prepared to die with pleasure in his service, are since their death become a source of living waters, and the instruments of many flowing graces, which God, by their intercession, plenteously diffuses through the whole church.

A.M. 2880.] *The Gates of Gaza.*—JUD. xvi. [A.C. 1120.

THE Philistines grew more active from disappointment, and the late stroke they had received did but whet their desire of revenge. They scarcely allowed Sampson any time to breathe; they narrowly observed all his motions, and diligently sought every opportunity either to surprise or oppress him. They had watched him into the town of Gaza; secure as they thought of their prey, they in a very few hours collected a considerable number of men to surround him, and posted a strong guard at the town gates, watching there the whole night in silence, that in the morning they might kill him as he went out. Sampson in the mean time had laid himself down to rest, thoughtless of the danger that surrounded him. He slept till midnight, when being apprised of his situation he arose, hastened to the town gates, and with one effort of his strength tore them up with their posts and bolts, threw them upon his shoulders, as trophies of triumph, and thus accoutred, he marched intrepidly through the midst of his enemies up the steep summit of the hill that faces Hebron, with as much ease as if he had walked upon a smooth plain, disencumbered from every weight. Struck with astonishment at such a prodigy of strength, the guards stood motionless, and all Philisthim, on the report, were seized with such panic, that they never after dared to oppose him with open force.

The lines of this surprising personage, says St. Gregory

are too strongly drawn, not to discover at first sight whom they are designed to represent. It is the figure of Jesus Christ himself whom the Jews never ceased to persecute, till they saw him dead, and consigned to the tomb. There as he slept, the guards were placed around his sepulchre, to prevent his being taken away by surprise; when behold, during the silence of night, he victoriously rose again to life, and by an unexpected, but most wonderful appearance, put the soldiers to flight, that had been placed to guard him. Triumphant over the malice of his enemies, he broke down the bolts and bars of death, which he carried with him to the holy mountain of Olivet, and from thence ascended into heaven, setting open to his followers the gates of eternal life, which till that happy time had been shut, by the sin of our first parents, against their unfortunate posterity.

A.M. 2885.] *Death of Sampson.* [A.C. 1115.

JUDGES, xvi.

HAPPY had it been for Sampson, if he had only shown as much resolution against a false woman's charms, as he had strength against lions and the armies of the Philistines. Dalila, by her allurements and treacherous caresses, proved the ruin of a man whom the united force of men had not been able to hurt. She dwelt in the vale of Sorec, and is thought by many to have been his wife. The Philistines observing how fond Sampson seemed to be of her, promised her a considerable recompense, if she could only learn and discover to them the secret of his strength. Dalila, like many of her sex, being influenced by love of gain, began to try her art to deceive and betray the man who loved her. She proposed her malicious questions, which Sampson prudently defeated by his delusive answers: he told her, that to make him as weak as other men, she had but to tie him with seven wet or with nine new cords, or to fasten him by seven hairs of his head. She tried them one after another, and found herself as often disappointed. She thereupon became more and more pressing, and continually hung upon him for many days; she reproached and flattered, she threatened and caressed by turns, till his soul fainted away, and was wearied even unto death: then opening the truth, he said to her, that being a Nazarite that is, a person consecrated to God from his infancy, the scissars had never come near his head, and that his strength depended upon his hair. The treacherous woman gave immediate notice to the princes of the Philistines, and invited them to come, as Sampson had at last opened his heart to her. She composed him to sleep, called a barber, and shaved

him both of his hair and strength at once. Sampson awoke from his sleep, little caring, as he seemed, about the presence of his enemies, but thought he would go out as he did before, and shake himself, not knowing as the Scripture says, that the Lord had departed from him. The Philistines seized him, and forthwith putting out his eyes, led him bound in chains to Gaza, and shut him up to grind in a mill. To that disgraceful drudgery Sampson was confined, bereft of his sight and the solaces of life. During his confinement his hair began to grow, and as his hair increased, his strength also gradually returned. The lords of the Philistines had at that time assembled to celebrate the feast of their god Dagon; their place of entertainment was a large hall, whither they ordered Sampson to be brought that he might play before them. Sampson was therefore brought out of prison, and made to play for the diversion of his insulting enemies. He desired the boy who guided his steps, to let him rest upon the pillars, that supported the house. There calling upon the Lord to restore him his former strength, and desiring to die with the Philistines, he took hold of one pillar with his right hand, and the other with his left, and shook them violently together, till the whole edifice fell down, and crushed him and three thousand of the Philistines under its ruins.

Sampson's death, which was severely felt by the enemies of his God and country, is, according to the holy fathers, an emblem of that great overthrow which Jesus Christ, by his death, gave to the infernal powers. For then it was, says St. Paulinus, that the temple of Satan was pulled down, and the pride of his bold associates humbled to the dust. But it is not the figurative sense only, that the fathers confine their remarks to in this history. They deplore the misfortune of an invincible hero, who, notwithstanding his invincible strength, was at last conquered by a woman. By a woman's power he became not only weak, but likewise blind, and was condemned like a beast, to grind in a mill. His misfortune gives us the striking likeness of a sinner, who being stripped of his inherent virtues, and deprived of the light of the Holy Ghost, becomes abandoned to his pleasures, and enslaved to the pomps of a wicked world; groaning under the tyranny of his passions, he toils and frets in the pursuit of what only tends to feed his desires, and increase his troubles. A sinner, in this state, has no other remedy, than to raise his voice with Sampson, and to pray that his former strength may be restored to him. It is by repentance only, says the same St. Paulinus, that the soul can recover her lost virtues, and triumph over the enemies of her salvation: by that she regains her first strength, by that she destroys the work of Satan, by that she dies to sin and self-love, that she may henceforth live to God alone.

A.M. 2570] *Death of the Levite's Wife.* [A.C. 1430.
JUDGES, xix.

In the two last chapters of the book of Judges, is related a fact, which is commonly thought to have happened soon after the death of Josue. A certain Levite, who dwelt in Mount Ephraim, had married a woman of the town of Bethlehem: upon some disagreement between them they separated, and the woman returned home to her parents. The Levite still retained an affection for his wife, and at the end of four months went over to Bethlehem, with an intention of proposing a reconciliation, and of taking her back. His father-in-law received him with great cordiality, and his wife, forgetting all that had passed between them, expressed the tenderest affection for her husband. The friendly civilities he there met with, made him prolong his stay a day or two more than he had intended. He at last took leave, and set off upon his return in the company of his wife and man servant. About sun-set they arrived at Gabaa, a town belonging to the tribe of Benjamin, where they proposed to pass the night. They remained for some time in the street, before any one would offer them a lodging. At last, an hospitable old man, who was also from Mount Ephraim, coming home after his day's work, perceived the Levite and his wife in the street, and in a friendly manner invited them to his house. After a frugal supper, they retired to rest, when some of the riotous townsmen beset the house, and demanded the stranger, with a lewd intent to abuse him. The hospitable old man used every argument to reduce them to reason, but arguments were lost on men, who were burning with lawless passion: both he and his guest grew terrified at their threats, and to stop their cries, abandoned the Levite's wife to their discretion. The wicked wretches committed such brutish violence upon her the whole night, that she was but just able next morning to crawl back to her husband's lodgings. She had scarce reached the door, when she dropped down dead, with her arms extended upon the ground, demanding vengeance, as it were, for the outrage she had suffered. The Levite rose when it was light, opened the door, and finding his wife in that posture, thought she was only taking her rest, and said to her, Arise, and let us be going; but, as she made no answer, perceiving she was dead, he took her up, laid her upon his ass, and returned to his house, meditating revenge upon the whole tribe of Benjamin, as accessary to her death. As soon as he was come home, he took a sword, and divided the dead body of his wife, with her bones, into twelve parts, which he distributed through the different tribes of Israel. All were shocked at the crime of Benjamin, and unanimously agreed to concur in washing out a stain that had disgraced the whole Hebrew nation.

St. Ambrose admires the unanimity, and extols the zeal that animated the Israelites on this occasion: they resolved to see justice done to an injured man, and reparation made to the sanctity of the law, which had been so enormously violated. An outrage done to the marriage bed, says that holy father, put them all into a flame; a single tribe had committed the crime, and they all agreed in their resolves to punish it. To remain inactive was, in their opinion, to approve the fact, and to become partners of the guilt. They were afraid, lest the tacit dissimulation of so notorious an offence might make the other tribes liable to the bolts of God's wrath, which one of them had so justly merited. The holy doctor expresses great concern at the corruption of morals that reigned in his time; he deplores the many infidelities that were committed against the sanctity of marriage, in contempt of God's law; he arraigns the shameful licentiousness of those, who not only plunge into vice themselves, but also encourage it in others; who never exert their influence or authority to condemn or correct, but as interest or passion guides. To such degenerate Christians he proposes the example of the Israelites, who being actuated by a laudable zeal for public justice, resolved upon the most vigorous efforts to chastise the delinquents, and put a stop to vice. They were influenced by no respect of persons, nor misled by any false compensation, either to palliate or excuse a notorious guilt at the expense of injured innocence.

A.M. 2570.] *Punishment of the Benjamites.* [A.C. 1430.
JUDGES, XX.

THE Israelites having appointed Maspha for the place of general rendezvous, the injured Levite there appeared, and renewed his complaint against the Benjamites. His story roused an honest indignation in the breast of all; they resolved to see justice done, in a point which concerned the community: they drew together a numerous army to support their resolves against any resistance that the Benjamites might make, and God himself named the general to command the troops. Before they proceeded to acts of violence, they tried, by deputies, to make their unhappy brethren sensible of their crime, and to prevail upon them to deliver up the perpetrators of it, that they might be punished as the Lord directed. The Benjamites not only refused to make any satisfaction for the injury they had done, but declared themselves the protectors of their friends and fellow-citizens. They raised an army of five and twenty thousand men, and a civil war was unhappily commenced. The Israelites advanced with great confidence to give them battle, in which they had the misfortune to lose two and twenty thousand of their best troops. They were surprised, but not dejected, at this unexpected overthrow; they prepared for a second battle; with tears in their eyes they begged the Lord of Hosts to give a blessing to their arms; but victory still declared against them; they were routed a second time, with the slaughter of eighteen thousand men. The Israelites began to be alarmed; to meet with two such bloody defeats in a war so just on their side, and where the numbers were so greatly in their favour, seemed unaccountable. In this unhappy state of affairs, they had recourse to God; they went in procession to the tabernacle, which had been set up in Silo, a city of the tribe of Ephraim; there they sat and wept before the Lord; they fasted, they prayed, and begged to know whether it was his will that they should still proceed against the Benjamites. Phinees, the grandson of Aaron, was high-priest at the time, and by his mouth God declared to the Israelites, that they should go for the third time against Benjamin, and gain a complete victory. Upon this assurance, the confederate tribes marched against the town of Gabaa. The Benjamites rushed out intrepidly to meet them, not doubting but they should beat them back with the same slaughter as they had done twice before. To confirm them in their rash opinion, the Israelites, designedly, gave way, and drew them off to some distance. They then faced about, and at the same time a body of their troops which had been placed in ambush near the town, rushed out upon the enemies' rear. The Benjamites were now hemmed in between two armies; whichever way they turned they met with an implacable enemy; they received no quarter and were all cut off to a man. The conquerors set fire to their towns and villages, laid every thing waste before them, and the massacre was so universal, that of the whole tribe of Benjamin, only six hundred men escaped by flying into the desert. The Israelites seemed fully bent upon the total ruin of that unhappy tribe; for in the wrath of their resentment, they bound themselves by oath not to marry their daughters to any of the miserable survivors. When the heat of passion was over, they began, upon more cool reflection, to be sorry for what they had done, and instead of rejoicing, were extremely grieved at a victory which had nearly extinguished one of their tribes. They wished to see the loss repaired: the town of Jubas Galaad furnished them with the means. The inhabitants of that town had been deficient in their duty during the late war: by general agreement it was resolved to punish them on that account. An army of ten thousand men was accordingly sent to put them all to the sword, excepting the young virgins, who were reserved and given in marriage to the surviving Benjamites.

Wonderful is the conduct of divine Providence through this whole affair. No war in appearance was ever more warrantably undertaken; it had the approbation of God himself, and yet was very unsuccessful in the two first engagements. By that, says St. Gregory, Almighty God would signify to us, how exempt from sin they ought to be, who undertake to punish it in others. Preposterous is the attempt to call our brethren to an account for faults, which we encourage by example. However great may be the provocation, and however just the cause to punish, the weapons of severity are not to be taken up but with the greatest caution, and always with regret. The severe punishment inflicted on the guilty Benjamites, as we have seen, became a subject of real sorrow to those by whom it had been inflicted. The generous Israelites were grieved to see a kindred people reduced so low; they wept to think that they had been the unhappy instruments of such severity; they had no sooner struck the fatal blow, than they repented, and turned their thoughts upon the means of repairing what they had endeavoured to destroy. It would be shameful, as the holy fathers observe for Christians in point of charity to be outdone by Jews, to be less tender of their neighbour's interest, to show less feeling, or to be less compassionate for a brother's sufferings.

A.M. 2708.] *Ruth follows Noemi.*—RUTH, i. [A.C. 1292.

THE short but interesting story of Ruth happened under the Judges, and makes a book of itself. The sacred writer tells us, that at the time when the land of Israel was sorely vexed by famine, a certain man, by name Elimelech, of the town of Bethlehem, retired with Noemi his wife and two sons into the country of the Moabites, not to starve in his own. After his death, Noemi married her two sons to two young women of that country, whose names were Arpha and Ruth. They lived ten years together, but no issue came from either of the two marriages: the two brothers died and left their disconsolate mother in a childless widowhood. Having no consolation to expect in the land of Moab, Noemi resolved to return into her own country, where the famine was no longer felt. She communicated her design to Arpha and Ruth; they both desired to accompany her to Bethlehem. She begged they would not think of accompanying a friendless widow, from whom they had neither fortune nor comfort to expect, but return to their relations, from whom they might meet with both: she represented to them, that by going along with her, they would but throw themselves into fresh miseries; that her present distress was sufficient without any other addition; that to see them suffer on her account would increase her pain; and that their sufferings would be more afflicting to her than her own. Arpha yielded to Noemi's reasons, tenderly embraced her, and returned to Moab. Ruth was too much attached to her mother-in-law to think of leaving her; with the greatest eagerness she begged that they might be never separated from each other: I will accompany you, said she, wherever you shall go, and with you I will for ever dwell; your people shall be my people, and your God shall be mine; in the same land with you I will live and die, and nothing but death shall ever part us. Noemi could not refuse so affectionate and so resolute a request; she consented to Ruth's going with her, and they both came to Bethlehem. It was then harvest time, and Ruth desired leave of her mother to go into the neighbouring fields, where she might glean some relief in their scanty circumstances. Kind Providence

conducted her into a field belonging to Booz, a near relation of Elimelech, Noemi's former husband. Her remarkable diligence drew the eyes of the reapers, and Booz, from the favourable account he had received from his overseer, of Ruth's dutiful behaviour to her mother, and of her diligence at work, ordered every kindness and civility to be shown her. He bade his reapers scatter the corn on purpose, and leave Ruth a sufficient quantity to requite her amply for the pains she took; if she should be willing to reap, he told them not to hinder her, and insisted upon her eating and drinking with his servants.

This goodness of Booz to Ruth has been considered by the holy fathers, as an emblem of that which Jesus Christ has since shown to his church. Booz did not disdain to take notice of a poor stranger; neither the present meanness of her appearance nor the past errors of her religious sentiments, excluded her from the acts of his humanity. Ruth's steady attachment to Noemi, is an example of that unshaken fidelity which every Christian owes to Jesus Christ and his church. He that loves his father, mother, or his kindred, more than me, says our blessed Saviour, is not worthy of me. Whoever will come after me, let him deny himself, take up his cross, and so follow me. If in following Jesus Christ, worldly advantages must be sometimes given up, and hardships undergone, an upright mind and a peaceful conscience will confer an inward satisfaction, which, without virtue, no riches can purchase, and no power bestow. Noemi's poverty was to Ruth of more advantage than the wealth of Moab; and they who, by a firm and generous attachment, stand steady to the principles of duty, will also receive their reward in the end. They may suffer, they may be oppressed for a time; the hour of their delivery hastens on, an eternity of joys is already prepared to console their pains, and to crown their patience.

A.M. 2708.] *Booz espouses Ruth.* [A.C. 1292.

RUTH, iii.

NOEMI being encouraged by these first favours that Booz had shown to her daughter-in-law, began to think of procuring her something more, and of providing her with a settlement for life. She told her that Booz was her near kinsman, and, according to the Mosaic law, ought to be her husband. Wash thyself, therefore, said she, and anoint thee, and put on thy best garments, and go down to the place where he is winnowing his barley; but let the man not see thee, till he shall have done eating and drinking. Mark the place where he retires to sleep; go in, lay thyself down at his feet, and he will tell thee what thou hast to do. In obedience to Noemi's commands, Ruth punctually performed what she otherwise never durst have thought of. Booz awoke in the night, and being surprised to find a woman lying at his feet, asked who she was, and what she meant. Ruth gave him a direct answer, expressing her name and her pretensions to him. Booz immediately acknowledged the affinity there was between them, and commended her conduct in the step she had taken: he praised her for her prudence in not following the young men, either rich or poor, and promised to marry her, if the man who was nearer akin than he, should refuse her. Sleep till the morning, said he; then rise, and go cautiously away, before it is light enough for any man to see or know that thou camest hither. Towards the dawn of day, Booz arose, and gave her six measures of barley to carry to her mother-in-law, then went and seated himself near the town gate, where public justice was administered according to the custom of those days. There seeing his kinsman pass by, he called him by his name, and explained to him Ruth's affair in the presence of ten respectable witnesses. He told him, that Noemi, the widow of their deceased brother Elimelech, had a share in a certain field, which she was willing to sell, and that it was his right in the first place either to take or refuse the purchase. The man said he would take it; then, replied Booz, you must take also the widow, and raise up the name of thy kinsman in his inheritance. The man made answer, that he would rather choose to forego his right, and yield up his privilege to Booz. Booz accepted the offer, and the deed of cession being immediately made according to the established form, he publicly espoused Ruth, and received the good wishes of all present upon the occasion. They wished him every blessing that can attend a happy marriage; they prayed that this young woman might prove as great a happiness to his family, as Rachel and Lia had been to that of Jacob; that she might be an example of virtue in Ephrata, and have a famous name in Bethlehem.

The issue of this marriage was a son called Obed, the father of Isai, and grandfather of David. Noemi, was looked upon as one of the most fortunate of her sex, and as completely blessed in her daughter-in-law, as she could have been in a numerous offspring of her own. Fond to excess of the little Obed, she united the diligence of a nurse with the tender affections of a mother.

In the extraordinary history of Ruth, says St. Ambrose, we see the qualifications that God chiefly regards in the choice he makes of his friends; he is not determined by the nobility of their birth, nor even by the sanctity of their ancestors, he considers their personal virtues, and views the disposition of their own hearts. A daughter of the Moabites, born of idolatrous parents, was, in reward of her piety, raised to the greatest honour which was then upon earth, the honour of being ranked in the genealogy of the Messias, and becoming one of the progenitors of Jesus Christ, according to the flesh. Her example, says the same saint, is a lesson for us not to rely upon the show and nominal profession of a Christian, as if nothing more were expected of us. Such once was the infatuation of the Jews, who solely trusted to their carnal sacrifices, and vainly glorified in the name of Abraham, as if that alone had been sufficient for their justification. Without faith, working by charity in the performance of our Christian duties, we can never please God, nor become worthy of the chaste nuptials of Jesus Christ in his glory.

A.M. 2848] *Samuel under the care of Heli.* [A.C. 1152.
1 KINGS, i.

SAMUEL, a renowned and holy prophet, was from his infancy trained up to virtue. Anna, his mother, had for many years been married to Elcana, without having any children. Overwhelmed with the excess of sorrow, she wept and prayed to God for comfort in her affliction; she joined fasting to her prayers, and bound herself by vow, if she should obtain a son, to consecrate him all the days of his life to the divine service. Samuel was the fruit of his mother's piety, and the recompense of her faith. In a son like him, says St. Chrysostom, Anna became more happy than if she had been mother of the greatest prince upon earth. She received him as a present from the hand of God, and in compliance with her vow, hastened to give him back by a solemn act of religion. As soon as she had weaned him, she carried him to the tabernacle, put him into the hands of Heli the high-priest, and consecrated him irrevocably, as she had promised, to the service of her Creator. Gratitude and piety alone guided the tender feelings of her love; she parted with her child at a time when the charms and smiles of innocence made him the more dear. She knew what was good for her son, and what was acceptable to God. Her sacrifice in some sort seems to resemble that of Abraham. She offered to God her darling, her only son; she offered him for life, and stripped herself of all future claim over him. The mother's piety was repaid by the virtues of her son. The little Samuel ministered to the Lord under Heli's direction by day, and at night slept within the tabernacle, near the ark of God, and there it was that God favoured him with a special revelation, the preparatory walk of his future greatness. During the silence of the night, he heard a voice calling him by his name; unskilled as yet in the language of the Lord, the holy youth thought it had been Heli's voice, hastily rose, and asked him what he wanted. Heli told him he had not called, bade him go and compose himself to sleep. Samuel had scarce laid himself down, when the same voice called him up again; he ran to the high-priest, who ordered him to return and sleep. Samuel was called the third time; he again rose and went to Heli, who perceived the Lord had called the youth. Go sleep, said he to him; and if thou hear the voice again, thou shalt answer, Speak,

Lord, for thy servant heareth. Samuel retired to take his rest, and upon hearing himself called by name for the fourth time, answered in the words that Heli had commanded him The Lord then informed Samuel of the heavy judgments which were soon to fall upon the high-priest and his family, in punishment of sins that were too enormous to be expiated by the sacrifices they offered. He declared that he could no longer bear the sinful negligence of a father, who, knowing the disorders, and seeing the profane excesses of his two sons, had contented himself with a gentle reprimand, when a just zeal for the honour and sanctity of God's altar required the most exemplary severity. Heli was very pressing the next

morning to know what the Lord had said. Samuel showed a great unwillingness to speak, and nothing but Heli's importunity could have prevailed upon him to impart the melancholy secret. Heli humbly submitted to the divine decrees, and with the deepest regret for his past misconduct, became sensible, that to fulfil the duties of a father, it was not enough to be singly good, that he moreover ought to have endeavoured to instil goodness into his children: he acknowledged his neglect, and resigned himself to the punishment thereof.

Heli, says St. Gregory, has many imitators both in the church and private families. Pastors silently behold the disorders of their flocks, which they ought to correct; and parents, either from indolence or false fondness, suffer those passions to grow up in their children, which ought to have been checked at their first appearance. Such a neglect tends to the ruin of their souls, and draws down God's displeasure, both upon themselves and their children.

A.M. 2888.] *Heli's Punishment.* [A.C. 1112.
1 KINGS, iv.

THE sins of the Hebrew nation were swelled to a great height, and the Philistines were the people whom God had chosen to be their scourge. Equally destitute of divine favours as of public virtues, the Israelites were torn to pieces by a calamitous war, their armies put to flight, and their country plundered. In times of public calamity, they had often humbled themselves under the hand of God, and by repentance recovered his former friendship. But now they only thought of carrying the ark into the camp, as if they meant to force Almighty God to their assistance, or to let the most sacred emblem of their religion become a prey to their enemies. Almighty God, whose sanctity is not to be sported with, and whose justice is not to be controlled by the sham of religion, saw the ark advance, but was not, on that account, the more propitiously inclined towards his people. The two sons of Heli, Ophni and Phinees, attended the procession to their ruin; for such attendants were more likely to hasten, than the ark was to stop, the stroke that God had prepared for the punishment of sinners. When they reached the camp, the army gave an universal shout of joy, and new courage seemed to animate the drooping Israelites The Philistines on the other hand grew dejected, and dreaded the mighty arm of the high God of Israel. But when their first alarms had subsided, they began to encourage one another, resumed their former vigour, and rushed out to battle with such impetuosity, that they bore down all before them. Ophni and Phinces were killed, with thirty thousand of the common men; the rest saved themselves by a shameful flight, and left the ark in the hands of the Philistines. Heli, in the mean time, whose sightless and decrepid age rendered him a moving object of compassion, had seated himself before the door of his house, facing the highway, and was waiting with impatience to hear the event: his fears foreboded no good, his troubled heart beat with anxiety for the ark of God. A Benjamite, who had escaped from the field of battle, passed by, and told him that the Israelites were routed with great slaughter, that his two sons, Ophni and Phinees, were amongst the slain, and the ark taken by the enemy. At the mention of the ark, the poor old man fell backwards from his seat, broke his neck, and died upon the spot.

From such visible strokes of divine justice, it appears how severely God punished an abuse of holy things, and how grievously he is provoked at the sins of those who, by a purity of manners conformable to the sanctity of their character, ought to stay the arm that is lifted up to chastise the sins of others. By the capture of the ark we see that it is not merely in the name, or in the holiness of a thing, that we are to trust for the divine protection; we must by the integrity of our lives make ourselves worthy of those graces which he has annexed to a right use of his holy institutions. God takes under his special protection none but those who deserve it by their virtues, and honour him by their actions.

A.M. 2888.] *Idol of Dagon.*—1 Kings, v. [A.C. 1112.

Although the ark of God seemed to be fallen into a stateof disgrace, and stripped of those honours which had hitherto surrounded it, yet never did its glory appear with greater lustre, than while it remained amongst the Philistines. It was carried from the field of battle into the town of Azotus, and placed in the temple of Dagon. This is an emblem of every sacrilegious attempt that is made to set up the worship of God and the worship of devils in the same heart. But God admits of no rival in his service: being but one, the supreme and sovereign Lord of all things, he will not give his glory to another: Dagon was not permitted to stand before the ark. Thrown by divine power down to the ground, it lay flat upon its face, and in that disgraceful posture was found by the Azotians, when they entered the temple next morning. With great concern they lifted up the helpless log, and put it back to the place from whence it had fallen. Dagon was as little able to preserve his station a second time, as he had been the first. He was found next day not only flat upon the floor, but also clipped of his hands and head, which were

broken off, and lay at some distance from the trunk. The arm of God then extended itself from the idol to the idolators themselves. The inhabitants of Azotus were suddenly struck with a painful sore, which hindered them from sitting down, while swarms of mice over-ran and destroyed the country. The miserable Azotians saw there was something more than natural in these chastisements, and that the insult offered to the ark was undoubtedly the cause. Being no longer able to bear the avenging hand of God which lay so heavy on them, they took the resolution of sending away the ark into some other town within their territories. They removed it from one town to another; but wherever they went, they carried with it the scourge of God upon the inhabitants. The whole country was in the deepest consternation; a general fear prevailed that the ark would be the destruction of them all, if it remained much longer amongst them. They consulted their soothsayers and wise men upon the subject, and by their advice agreed to send it back to the Israelites, and to accompany it with presents as an atonement for the sin they had committed against the God of Israel. Therefore, according to the number of their provinces, they ordered five golden figures of one sort, and five of another, representing the two sorts of plagues they had been scourged with, to be prepared and placed in a casket by the side of the ark, as soon as the carriage was ready to convey it away.

Thus were the proud Philistines humbled; thus, by a standing monument of their own weakness, they acknowledged the power of that God who stands in need of no human assistance to triumph over his most obstinate enemies. The joy they felt at seeing themselves masters of the ark, was quickly changed into mourning, and the evils that succeeded, filled them with the apprehension of a scourge still more dreadful; such is the troubled state of every guilty conscience. The joy of iniquity is but short; the pleasure of sin is either extinguished by succeeding pain, or embittered by remorse. If the sinner remains insensible of the temporal punishments by which God admonishes him of his duty, he then with reason may apprehend those greater punishments which await the impenitent in another world.

A.M. 2888.] *The Ark sent back*—1 KINGS, vi. [A.C. 1112.

IN consequence of the resolution taken to send back the ark, the Philistines had ordered a new wain to be made for the purpose, and two kine, that had already calved, to be ready to draw it. The ark was laid upon the carriage, and the little casket, containing the ten golden figures mentioned above, stood by the side of it; the kine were yoked to, and left to take their way. The Philistines had carefully shut up the calves, and agreed that the motion of their dams should determine what judgment they had to form of the calamities they had felt since the ark had been amongst them. If, contrary to their natural instinct, the kine should go straight on towards the Hebrew territories, they then should conclude that the scourge had been from God; but if not, they, in that case, should take it as a sign that nothing had happened but by mere chance. God in this instance condescended to the weakness of those idolators, and by his special providence, directed the kine towards the confines of Israel. They went forward with one continued pace; instinct indeed made them low after their young, but it neither stopped nor turned them out of their way. With the like steadiness ought every Christian to pursue his way to heaven, being neither drawn aside by passion, nor retarded by terrene affection. The Philistian chiefs, full of astonishment, followed the ark as far as Bethsames, which was the first town in the Hebrew dominions, and there, for the first time, the kine stopped of their own accord. The Bethsamites were filled with joy at the sight of the ark, the loss of which for seven months had cast all Israel into the deepest mourning. But their joy was soon changed into tears; they wept under the same avenging rod, which had so severely chastised the Philistines. A prodigious crowd of people had assembled at the place; it was not a zeal for God's honour, it was an eager curiosity to behold and look into the ark, which had drawn them together; and on that account more than fifty thousand of them were struck with sudden death. The dreadful stroke made the survivors tremble; they had now learned a due respect for the sanctity of the ark, but were afraid of the consequences which its stay might cause amongst them. They informed the citizens of Cariathiarim, that the ark was arrived from the Philistines, and begged they would come and fetch it from Bethsames. The men of Cariathiarim came accordingly, and respectfully carried off the ark to Gabaa, where it was deposited in the house of Abinadab. Being in the place where God was pleased it should remain, the ark was no longer the cause of any such calamities as had fallen so heavily upon the Philistines and Bethsamites; but became an instrument of many blessings that flowed in upon the whole country.

Our blessed Redeemer, who was prefigured by the ark, desires nothing more than to shower down his graces upon mankind: the more liberal he is of his favours, the more he is provoked by the ingratitude of those who either despise or abuse them. The Bethsamites seemed in some sort to honour the ark, by the joy they showed at its being brought amongst them; but their joy arose from a wrong motive. Their own, not God's honour, was the object of their joy: their pride was flattered to see themselves possessed again of the ark, while the observance of the law that was contained within it, made no part of their concern. With the like indiscretion, says St. Gregory, many Christians presumptuously approach the body of our Lord in his holy sacrament, and so perish in the presence of the Holy of Holies. Full of spiritual pride they go to the holy table without being duly prepared; with an unworthy disposition of soul they receive the immaculate Lamb of God, and thereby incur the guilt of everlasting death at the sacred source of life itself.

A.M. 2888.] *Defeat of the Philistines* [A.C. 1112
1 KINGS, vii.

AFTER the ark was recovered out of the hands of the Philistines, the state of affairs in Israel began to wear a more pleasing aspect. The Israelites had been humbled into a sense of their duty; God relented in his wrath; Samuel, a faithful priest and prophet, was appointed to judge and govern the nation; and no pledge more expressive of his friendship did God ever give to his people, than by giving them so able and so sage a leader. Actuated with a true zeal for God's honour and the nation's good, Samuel began by exhorting the people to a real conversion of their hearts from vice. He represented to them the infidelity of their past conduct, the enormity of their idolatries, and the necessity of doing penance: he promised them on the part of God, not only pardon of their sins, but also victory over their enemies, if they would destroy their idols, and adore the only true and supreme Lord of heaven and earth. The people heard him with attention, they were moved, they promised to do better, they in effect began by demolishing the idols of Baal and Astaroth. Upon these marks of repentance, Samuel appointed them to meet him at Masphat a town in the tribe of Juda, where he would pray for them. They obeyed his summons on the day he mentioned, which was a day of fasting and humiliation; they appeared in the garb of true penitents, they confessed their crimes, they bowed themselves down in prayer before God, they implored forgiveness, and conjured the Lord to accept the holocaust which Samuel, his faithful prophet, was going to offer for them. In the midst of these religious exercises, they were suddenly informed, that the Philistine army was in full march against them. The very name of an enemy from whom they had received so many defeats, alarmed and terrified them; they earnestly entreated Samuel to redouble his prayers, on which their safety depended. The Philistines in effect having been informed that the Israelites were assembled at Masphat, thought it a fair opportunity to cut off the whole nation at a stroke: accustomed to success, which they had vainly attributed to themselves, they marched on as to a certain victory, little thinking that the God on whom all things depend, was now reconciled with his people

Samuel was offering the sacrifice; the Philistines came up and began to attack. At that moment loud claps of thunder rolled from the seat of God, which spread such a terror through the Philistine army, that they immediately turned their backs, and fled off in the utmost confusion. The Israelites vigorously pursued, and gained a complete victory. Fortune from that day declared in favour of the Israelites; they recovered all the towns they had lost; and as long as Samuel was at their head, neither the Philistines nor any other enemy durst molest them in the field. Peace was restored, public virtues flourished, and Samuel for twenty years governed the Hebrew nation with prudence and the affections of a father. But as he advanced in years, the glory of this pleasing prospect gradually declined. Infirmity of age had made him unequal to the weighty charge; he communicated a share of his authority to his sons; but the sons had no share of their father's virtues. Avarice and self-interest presided at the councils of these young men, and directed their decisions in the administration of justice. This conduct of Samuel's sons gave the Israelites too plausible a pretext for proposing a change in their form of government. They wished to see themselves governed by a king, like other nations. The name and pageantry of a king pleased and flattered them; they petitioned Samuel to give them a king. Samuel, who fancied that this extraordinary petition arose from some personal dislike they had conceived against him, made his complaint to God. It is not with thee, replied Almighty God, it is with me that they are dissatisfied: not thee, but me they have rejected; they choose not that I should reign any longer over them. Explain to them the rights and great power of the king they ask for, and if they still insist upon it, grant them their request. The holy prophet made his report to the people, and they chose to have a king over them, like other nations.

We wonder, say the holy fathers, how the Israelites could prefer the government of men to that of God, and yet we express no concern at the conduct of Christians, who choose the prince of darkness for their king and leader, in preference to Jesus Christ. Though they are his members, and he their head, with the Jews they cry, We will not have him tc reign over us; while to the infernal tyrant they say if not in words, at least in effect, Thou art our king, and we thy subjects; we no longer make a part of the fellowship of Christ; we neither respect his councils, nor obey his commands: our own will is the law we follow; we admit of no restraint but such as we choose to submit to. Such is the language expressed in the lawless conduct of many Christians now-a-days.

A.M. 2909.] *Saul anointed King.* [A.C. 1091

1 Kings, ix.

Almighty God having consented to the request that his people had made, of being governed by a king, made choice of Saul in the following manner: Cis of the tribe of Benjamin, having lost his asses, sent his son Saul to look for them. Saul wandered for some time about the country from place to place without receiving any intelligence. Despairing of success, and being anxious lest his father might grow uneasy at his stay, he thought of returning home, when his servant advised him to go to Samuel, the man of God, who had the gift of seeing and resolving the doubts of those who went to consult him. The holy prophet by divine revelation had learned, that Saul was the man destined by Almighty God to be the first king of Israel; he therefore received him into his house with greater respect than is usually paid to a common stranger; he entertained him very hospitably, and kept him all night. In the morning he accompanied him part of the way home, and that he might be under no restraint in communicating to him the secret designs of God, he desired the

servant might be sent on before them
out a small vial of oil, and pouring it up
anointed and saluted him king; and to c
acted by the authority and dictation of A
had chosen him to be the prince of Israel, he
particular occurrence that he should meet w
home. When thou shalt come near to Rachel
he, thou shalt meet two men who will inform th
asses are found, and that thy father is only anx
thee. A little further on thou shalt see a troop of
coming down from the hill, with instruments of music
them: the spirit of the Lord shall seize thee at the same
thou shalt prophesy with them, and be changed into ano
man. Every circumstance happened as Samuel had foretc
Saul might now be looked upon as the most fortunate of me
he had been in quest of his father's asses, and had found a crown. Samuel convened the tribes at Masphat, and informed them that since they had rejected God, and instead of him had chosen to have a king for their protector, they must proceed by lots, to know who the person was. The lot first fell upon the tribe of Benjamin; then upon the family of Metri; and lastly upon the very person of Saul. Thus the event confirmed what had already passed in private, and indisputably proves that God presides over, and directs the lot of all men. The name of Saul was immediately echoed through the tribes. Saul was called upon to make his appearance, but Saul was not to be found; he had absented himself from the assembly, and lay concealed at home. Messengers were sent to fetch him: as soon as he arrived, Samuel presented him to the people, and desired they would observe the majestic figure of the man whom God had chosen for their king; for Saul was a graceful personage, tall in stature, and a comely mien: his very appearance commanded respect, and all the people cried out, God save the king! The satisfaction seemed general; some few there were, and they were the sons of Belial, who expressed their disapprobation. Saul took no notice of their disloyalty at the time; for Saul then was humble, and seemed far from being elated by his good fortune. Happy had he been, if he always had behaved with the same moderation. His subsequent conduct made it soon appear how hard it is to unite humility and dignity together, and how uncommon to see a dignified person truly humble

int out the election of Saul, as a subject
›n for those who are raised to the highest
.s in life. Whatever the preferment may
rch or state, they never must forget the
.r Christian profession: no elevation of rank
:xempt them from the duties of humility. They
uselves the followers of a crucified God: to be
.h Christ, they must not be ashamed to bear their
ut if, like Saul, they exalt themselves, and forget
d that raised them, they then may tremble, lest they
, humbled and finally reprobated, like him, in punish-
. of their pride.

.M. 2911.] *Jonathan and his Armour-bearer.* [A.C. 1089.
1 KINGS, xiv.

SAUL, soon after he began his reign, was engaged in a war against the Philistines, who had renewed their attacks with greater violence than ever. The two armies lay encamped within sight of each other, frequent skirmishes passed between them, but no decisive stroke was given on either side. Jonathan, the king's son, a youth full of vigour and of great personal courage, grew tired of these slow proceedings. He knew that it was as easy for the Almighty to overthrow a whole army by the hand of one man, as by the arms of thousands. Full of this confidence in God, and pushed on by the activity of his own genius, he stole out of the camp with no other attendant than his armour-bearer, and climbing over rocks that seemed almost inaccessible, threw himself within the enemy's lines. He attacked and slew the first that came to oppose him, his armour-bearer seconded his efforts, and they both performed such prodigies of valour, that they spread terror and confusion through the whole camp of the Philistines. The Israelites observing that, and Saul conjecturing from the absence of his son what the matter was, put his troops in motion. Being naturally impetuous in his actions, and eager in his pursuits, he bound himself and his whole army by an oath, not to eat of the least thing before evening, till he had been revenged of his enemies. He rushed forward to pursue the victory which Jonathan had begun; the Philistines, in great confusion, turned their arms against one another, took to their heels, and endeavoured to save themselves through a forest. The victorious Israelites pursued them with great slaughter, and though the trees on every side were drooping with honey, yet so sacred was the respect which the men had for their oath, that not one of so numerous a host durst take so much as a single drop. Jonathan only, who had heard nothing of his father's oath, being spent with fatigue, dipped the end of his rod in a honey-comb, and caught a slight refreshment as he passed along. Towards evening the army was ordered to halt, that they might breathe awhile, and renew their vigour to pursue the enemy at night. Saul, curious to know the success of this expedition, consulted God, but received no answer. This silence on the part of God he immediately attributed to some one of his men, who, in violation of his oath, had eaten before the time, and hastily swore that he should die for it, though it were Jonathan himself. The lots were ordered to be cast, and the offence fell upon Jonathan. Saul asked him what he had done. I have tasted but a little honey, replied Jonathan, with the end of my rod, and for so small a thing must I lose my life? Saul had sworn it, and insisted upon its execution. But Jonathan was the people's favourite: charmed with his gallant behaviour that day, and resolved to stand by him at all events, they rescued him out of his father's hands, and preserved his life.

Upon the danger to which Jonathan was exposed for having taken a little honey, the holy fathers remark how dangerous a thing it is, to pursue the deceitful sweets of worldly pleasures. Sin, to the sensual man, seems oftentimes as sweet as honey, or the honey-comb. It pleases for a time, says St. Ambrose, but there lurks a sting behind, and its wound is deadly: for a moment's pleasure, Jonathan infallibly would have suffered death, if the glorious success of his past actions had not recommended him to the people's favour, and reversed the sentence which his father had pronounced against his life.

A M. 2930.] *Reprobation of Saul.* [A.C 1070

1 Kings, xv.

Saul having checked the insolence of the Philistines, turned his victorious arms against the Moabites, the Ammonites, the kings of Edom and Soba: the success of his warlike enterprizes made him respected both at home and abroad, and he ruled with an absolute authority over his subjects of Israel. Having quieted his enemies about him, he was ordered by Almighty God to extend his conquests, and pour his vengeance upon the Amalecites. The Amalecites were an idolatrous, perfidious nation, the sworn enemies of the Hebrew people, whom they had attacked and attempted to destroy upon their march out of Egypt. Samuel, therefore, in the name of God, commanded Saul to destroy their whole race, without reserving so much as the least thing that belonged to them. In obedience to this order, Saul put himself at the head of two hundred thousand men, and marched against that devoted people. But so far was he from complying with the letter or the spirit of the order, that he undertook to interpret it as he pleased. He defeated their forces, slew the common people, but spared their king Agag; he reserved moreover the fattest of the flocks, took to himself the most precious of the spoils, and destroyed only the refuse. Provoked at so glaring a prevarication, the Lord commanded Samuel to go and declare to Saul, that he was sorry for having made him king. Saul, little solicitous about the glory due to God, had already erected to himself a triumphal arch on Mount Carmel, to celebrate the victory which he had tarnished by his disobedience. Being told that Samuel was coming to the camp, he advanced to meet him, and with the boldest assurance began to tell him how gloriously he had defeated the Amalecites, and how faithfully he had executed the orders of the Lord. What means, then, the voice I hear of flocks and herds, replied the prophet? They are what the people have reserved for sacrifice, answered Saul. What! will the Lord, said Samuel in the ardour of his zeal, will the Lord accept of sacrifice made in direct opposition to his commands? Better is obedience than victims: the fat of rams he will not regard, whilst his word is disobeyed. To rebel is in his sight like the sin of enchantment, and to disobey, like the crime of idolatry. The prophet represented to the unhappy king the great goodness God had shown him; how he had drawn him out of obscurity, and placed him upon the throne; how he had chosen him preferably to every other man, and raised him to honours which he never could have merited. Forasmuch, therefore, as thou hast preferred thy private interest to his glory, continued Samuel, and hast rejected the word of the Lord, the Lord in his turn hath rejected thee; he hath rent the kingdom of Israel from thee, and transferred it to thy neighbour, better than thee. Saul was touched with remorse, and cried out, I have sinned. If his heart had accorded with his lips, or had his words been the faithful sign of an unfeigned sorrow, they might have softened the rigour of the sentence: in the mouth of an impenitent prince, those words were no more than an insignificant sound. Saul, more eager to receive honours of men than the pardon of his God, desired the prophet to honour him before the ancients of the people, and accompany him back to the place, that he might adore the Lord his God. Samuel said he would not return with him, since he had wickedly rebelled against the Lord: he turned himself to go away, when Saul hastily caught hold of his cloak to stop him, and begged he would not depart in that abrupt manner Samuel therefore consented to follow him to the place of adoration, ordered Agag to be brought forth, and hewed him into pieces before

the Lord. This done, he departed into Ramatha, sorely lamenting the unhappy Saul, whom from that time he visited no more unto the day of his death.

Saul, before this, had incurred God's displeasure by a similar act of disobedience, when, being eager of battle, and seeing the enemy approach, he hastily, and contrary to order, presumed to set fire to the sacrifice which Samuel was going to offer. The holocaust was still smoking, when the prophet came to the camp. The king advanced to make him his excuses, and said, necessity had compelled him to act as he had done. Samuel reprehended him for his foolish presumption, and condemned the rashness of an action which forfeited him his crown, and prevented it from descending to his children. So true it is, that no action, however plausible it may outwardly appear, can ever please or deserve a reward in the divine sight, as long as it is done, either upon a bad motive, or contrary to the order that God has established.

A.M. 2934.] *Election of David.* [A.C. 1066.
1 Kings, xvi.

Saul having forfeited his crown, as we have seen, by his disobedience, another king, by divine appointment was soon after anointed his successor. Samuel was the person whom God employed to perform the ceremony. Samuel by revelation knew that Bethlehem was the place, and that Isai's was the family, which was to furnish a king for Israel. Thither he was to go, and consecrate the man whom God should show him. But as an undertaking of that nature seemed likely to give umbrage to the present king, and to provoke his resentment, the prophet was inspired to take such secret measures as might prevent every dangerous consequence. He pretended an obligation of offering sacrifices at Bethlehem, unsuspected took his victim, and set out. Being come to the place, he invited Isai to bring his sons, and partake with him in the sacrifice. Isai was the son of Obed, and had eight sons; he took the seven eldest with him to wait upon the prophet. Samuel fixed his eyes upon each of them as they came, and took particular notice of the eldest, who for his majestic figure seemed worthy of a crown. But it is not the outside of man, it is the heart that God is chiefly attentive to. The seven sons of Isai therefore passed before Samuel, without any heavenly intimation being given in favour of any one of them. The prophet then asked Isai, if he had no other son. Isai said he had, but that he was young, and at that time employed in taking care of his sheep. Samuel desired to see him. David, for so he was called, was immediately sent for and introduced. Samuel at first sight knew him to be the chosen prince, rose up, and poured the holy unction upon his head. From that moment the spirit of God departed from Saul, and rested upon David. David

was in the flower of his youth, of a fair and comely countenance, meek and gentle in his disposition, and a good musician. Saul being unhappily abandoned by Almighty God, whom he had first abandoned by his disobedience, was possessed by an evil spirit, which vexed him in a cruel manner, and at certain intervals worked him up into a perfect frenzy. This misfortune, which was the punishment of his past ingratitude, and the presage of his future downfall, proved the beginning of his rival's greatness. His frantic fits at times rose to such violence, that they became intolerable. His officers, out of compassion, advised him to look out for some skilful musician, who, by the strains of melody, might quell the rage of passion, and soothe his soul to peace. David, for his talents in music, as well as for the qualifications of his person, was preferred before all others; and so admirably well did he know how to make use of the talents he was master of, that he worked himself into great favour, and became the king's armour bearer. Whenever Saul was agitated by the evil spirit, David played upon the harp. With powerful and pleasing art the musician so tempered the sweet variety of his harmonious strains, that he commanded the affections of the soul, and charmed the transports of passion into reason.

The melody of David's harp, as some of the fathers remark, represents that sweet and engaging demeanour which should distinguish the peaceful minister of the gospel. Pleasing and assuasive as the strains of harmony, ought to be their discourses, whether they strive to allay the rage, or dispel the fears of a troubled mind. David himself, as St. Gregory observes, stood afterwards in need of the mild reproofs of Nathan, to be freed from the sin that enslaved him. The advantage which he reaped from that prophet's wise remonstrances, was real and lasting. The comfort which he himself administered to Saul by the melodious sounds of his harp, was but short; nor could it hinder that unhappy prince from attempting to take away his life. The psalms of this inspired king, have at present a more powerful influence upon soul that is well disposed to hear or read them. For, as St. Austin observes, nothing can be equal to the divine harmony of those sublime truths which are contained in the Psalms of David; and nothing can so powerfully contribute to drive away the spirit of pride from our hearts, and awaken them to the voice of heaven.

A.M. 2942.] *Victory of David over Goliah.* [A.C. 1058.
1 KINGS, xvii.

A FRESH war was begun between the Israelites and Philistines. The two armies lay encamped upon two neighbouring hills, with a narrow valley between them. Saul commanded in person, but seemed not forward to engage the enemy. Goliah, a Philistine of gigantic size, but of more gigantic pride, advanced between the two armies, and in the most opprobrious and insulting terms challenged the bravest of the Israelites to come out, if he durst, and decide the war with him by single combat. Shame and indignation stung the Israelites, to see themselves treated with such contemptuous insolence; but so enormous was the giant's bulk, and so tremendous was the aspect of his armour, that no one had the courage to advance against him. David had left his attendance upon Saul, and resumed the care of his father's flocks: three of his brothers having engaged in the king's service, he was sent by his father Isai with provisions for them in the camp. He found the armies ranged in order of battle, ran to inquire after his brethren, and saw the great Philistine coming forth, as he did every day, to defy the arms of Israel. The Israelites trembled with fear, and shrunk back from the face of danger. David was grieved to hear so insolent a defiance given to the host of the living God, and what grieved him more, to hear it given with impunity. For though Saul had promised great riches, and his daughter moreover in marriage, to any man who should slay that uncircumcised Philistine, yet of all the host there was not one bold enough to accept the challenge. David at that time was in about the three and twentieth year of his age, and being animated with a laudable zeal for the cause of God and the honour of his country, offered to enter the lists against an enemy, whom every one besides seemed to be afraid of. His eldest brother hearing him talk in that strain, reprimanded him for his presumption, and told him with a sneer, that he had better go home and handle his shepherd's crook, than remain an idle spectator of the war. The reproof did not abash the generous youth; it seemed to animate him the more; he publicly declared, that with the king's permission he would engage the mighty Philistine, and by the help of God lay him flat upon the ground. His words were reported to Saul: Saul desired to see him. Being introduced to the king, David expressed the manly purpose of his heart, and begged leave to go and fight against the Philistine. Saul considered the great inequality between a young unexperienced shepherd and an old gigantic warrior, and was unwilling to expose his crown and dignity to so doubtful an issue. Let no man's heart be dismayed in him, said the youth; I have exercised my hand against the savage beasts; I have pursued and struck a lion and a bear that came to devour my father's flocks; I slew them both; and by the divine succour I will slay in the same manner this uncircumcised Philistine, who has been so hardy as to curse the host of the living God; and by his death I will take away the reproach of Israel. Saul gave his assent, saying, Go, our Lord be with thee; and forthwith invested him with his own armour, his helmet, sword, and coat of mail. David never had been accustomed to such accoutrements, which upon trial he found were more cumbersome than useful: he put them off, and desired to have no other than the shepherd's weapons, which he knew much better how to use, his staff and sling. Goliah seeing the beardless youth advance with a sling in his hand, scornfully asked him, if he was coming to beat a dog? He despised and cursed him, threatening to throw his carcass to the beasts and fowls of the air. Thou comest against me, replied David, with a sword and shield; but I come to thee in the name of the Lord of hosts. It is his battle I fight; he will deliver thee into my hands: I shall strike thee, and take away thy head, that all the earth may know there is a God in Isreel. Having said this, he took a stone out of his shepherd's scrip, fixed it in his sling, and with a whirl drove it full against the giant's forehead. Down fell Goliah flat upon his face. David that instant ran up, and with the Philistine's own sword severed his head from his

body, to the joy of the Israelites and deep dismay of the Philistines.

This victory of David over Goliah, is an admirable figure of that which Jesus Christ, by the humility of his cross, gained over the audacious pride of Lucifer. The holy fathers look upon the tall Goliah, as the very image of pride, the most formidable enemy that the people of God have to engage with; it is an enemy that remains even after they have got the better of bears and lions, that is to say, of other sins the most enormous. The same saints remark, that pride is not to be defeated by human power, any more than Goliah was by the arms of Saul. David conquered with his sling and stone: by the first we understand the cross of Christ, and by the second the efficacy of his holy grace, on which our strength and victory depend.

A.M. 2942.] *Triumph of David.* [A.C. 1058.

1 Kings, xviii.

With Goliah fell the strength of the Philistine army. They abandoned their camp at the fatal blow, and in wild disorder began to make the best of their way home. The shouting Israelites rushed across the vale in pursuit of their flying enemies, and drove them with great slaughter as far as the gates of Accaron. The joy and surprise of the victors on this occasion were equally great; with surprise they beheld the escape they had made from the frightful danger that had threatened them; and with joy they extolled the courage of the man who had so gallantly preserved their lives at the risk of his own. Saul himself admired the fortitude of this young warrior, and informed himself more particularly of his history and family. Jonathan, his eldest son, was taken with the magnanimity of a youth, who by a single action had far outdone the great achievements which he himself had performed against the same enemy. Far from being envious of David's good fortune, or jealous of the praises that were given him from every quarter, he honoured his deserts, and invested him with his own arms and princely ornaments. Such an act of generosity was not lost upon a young man who was naturally good and generous in his disposition. Jonathan and David loved and esteemed each other; and from that time their mutual attachment became so strong, that there seemed to be but one soul and one heart between them. The joy for David's victory was not confined to the king's court or to the army; it spread from one extremity of the kingdom to the other; every rank, every sex and age of the people concurred in honouring the triumph of their hero: when he returned from victory, the women ran out of the cities to meet him, dancing and singing his praises in a general concert of vocal and instrumental music. Such sounds of acclamation rising on every side, and re-echoed through the nation, seem to have prefigured the songs of praise and jubilation which the different churches throughout the world were one day to sing, in honour of Christ's triumph over sin and death. Flattering as these honours were to David at that time, they became the source of much future trouble, and exposed him to many a danger which must infallibly have deprived him of life, if his prudence had not been equal to his courage. Very unlike his generous son, Saul grew jealous; he was piqued to see another man more honoured than himself; he swelled with envy to hear it sung, that David had killed his ten thousands, while Saul had killed but a thousand. This comparison provoked his spleen, and the distinction made in favour of David fired him with a desire of revenge. A mortal hatred rooted itself in his heart, and prompted him to destroy the man whom he had hitherto considered as one of the most deserving of his subjects, and to whom he actually stood indebted for the preservation of his crown.

Of the various passions which human weakness is subject to, envy, says St. Chrysostom, is one of the most fatal and most common. It rages through the church and state; it makes no distinction of persons; it insinuates itself into the breasts of all who have any pretensions to be taken notice of; it is secretly nourished in the heart, and yet miserably torments the heart that nourishes it. The very appearance of merit in another is enough to make it shoot its sting; and the more shining that merit is, the more envenomed is its malice. It allows no rest to those who are infected with its poison. It seldom admits of any cure; it lurked in the veins of Saul as long as he lived. The most deserving are commonly the chief objects of its rancour. The rays of virtue that enlighten the good, are a burning torment to the envious.

A. M. 2943.] *Saul's Attempt against David.* [A. C. 1057.
1 Kings, xix.

Saul's animosity against David grew daily more and more violent; the evil spirit continued still to vex him, and David soothed him with his harp. As the sweet musician was one day playing, according to his usual custom, the frantic prince made a sudden push at him with his lance, David, who was apprised of the king's malice, and never off his guard against the attempts he made upon his life, saw the motion of his arm, and happily avoided the stroke. Saul was convinced that the virtuous youth was under the divine protection, observed how prudent he was in all his ways, and concluded that every attempt to surprise him would be ineffectual; he therefore dismissed him from his attendance, and gave him a considerable command in the army. To men, who saw not into the king's intention, David might thereby seem to have gained the royal favour: Saul intended nothing less than his ruin. By a murderous design, in which David himself was afterwards too successful against Urias, he resolved to expose him to the sword of the Philistines. He had promised, as has been mentioned, to give his daughter in marriage to the conqueror of Goliah. Envy had made him unfaithful to his promise, and Merob, his eldest daughter, was married to another man. Nor had David, indeed, ever claimed her; for being conscious of his lowly birth, he thought himself unqualified for an alliance with the king's daughter. But a mutual affection springing up between him and Michol, Saul's second daughter, he altered his mind, and wished to become the king's son-in-law. Saul was no stranger to their inclinations, and offered to consent to their marriage, upon condition that he first killed him a hundred of the uncircumcised Philistines. David readily accepted of the condition, as though it had been meant to do him honour, led out his little troop to battle, attacked and defeated the Philistine army, of which he killed no fewer than two hundred men with his own hand. Flushed with success, he hastened back to Saul, numbered the trophies of his victory before him, and claimed Michol as the crown of his conquest. Saul was vexed to see the youth return triumphant from the field, where he hoped to have seen him slain: he was witness to the wisdom with which David conducted himself in all his actions; he perceived his fame and favour with the people increasing daily; he both feared and hated him. It had been natural to suppose, that his animosity might have been extinguished, or at least abated, when he made him his son-in-law. But the rancour of Saul's heart was incurable; he made no secret of his murderous design; he spoke to his servants and son Jonathan to second him in the bloody attempt. Sitting one day in his house with a lance in his hand, he was suddenly seized by the evil spirit that haunted him, struck at David as he was playing upon the harp, and tried to nail him to the wall. David happily escaped the stroke and fled from the king's presence. Jonathan, who felt for both his father and his friend, did all he could to make them reconciled; he reasoned and expostulated with his father upon the injustice of his proceedings against an innocent man who had done him no injury; he urged every argument that the tenderest affection of a friend, and the most dutiful respect for a father could suggest; all to no purpose. Saul in the night time sent a guard to surround David's house, and to kill him as soon as he should make his appearance in the morning. Michol, who loved David as much as her father hated him, was upon the watch, and defeated the cruel order, by letting him secretly down from a window. To amuse the guard while her husband escaped, and to make them believe that he was sick, and unable to rise, she dressed up a statue, which she laid upon the bed, and covered with clothes. The innocent deceit had its effect: David went off unpursued, and retreated to Samuel's house in Ramatha. Saul being told how his scheme had failed through the contrivance of his own daughter, called her to an account for what she had done, and despatched his sergeants to seize on David, even in the prophet's house. The sergeants found a troop of prophets standing before Samuel, grew inspired at the sight, and beginning to prophesy like them, forgot their errand. Saul upon that sent other messengers, who returned prophesying in like manner; and as the same thing happened a third time to others of his men, he resolved, in a transport of anger, to go himself into Ramatha. The spirit of the Lord came also upon him as he went along, and in spite of premeditated malice, he continued prophesying and singing with the rest all that day and night: from whence arose the proverb, What! is Saul amongst the prophets?

From these facts it appears, that the potentates of the earth have no other power than what they hold from God, who either indulges or restrains them in the exercise of it as he pleases. He at his nod either raises or depresses them; he suffers them to reign no longer than is conducive to his designs: he laughs at their feeble efforts, and at his own time rescues from their hands whomsoever he decrees to save.

A.M. 2944.] *Jonathan and David.* [A.C. 1056

1 KINGS, XX.

DAVID perceiving the obstinacy of Saul's malice against his life, began to think of leaving the country. Jonathan was in the deepest concern for the safety of his friend, and being unwilling to be severed from his company, begged he would not condemn himself to a foreign banishment, before he was thoroughly informed of the king's disposition. A solemn day was near at hand, when the king was to dine in public with his officers. Every one was there except David: David's seat stood vacant, and the king seemed much displeased: Jonathan offered to make excuses, which did but exasperate his father's spleen, and convinced him, that from Saul no peace was to be expected. He had promised David to let him know how the king stood affected, and agreed upon the sign that he was to make him. David was to lie concealed behind a stone, which stood up in a certain field, where Jonathan appeared by appointment with his bow and arrow, under the pretext of shooting at a mark. Jonathan shot his arrows near the stone, and by the words he spoke to

the page whom he sent to pick them up, signified to David that he must fly to save his life. The boy brought the arrows to his master, ignorant of what was doing. Jonathan gave him his arms, and bade him to carry them back into town. When the boy was gone, David rose from behind the stone, and falling flat upon the ground, thrice made his obeisance to Jonathan. They met and embraced each other; they tenderly wept, and renewed their promise of mutual friendship as long as life should last. With great reluctance they parted from one another; David was the more afflicted, and Jonathan bade him go in peace.

David was now bereft of every necessary of life; reduced to the condition of a banished man, he thought no refuge so secure as among the ministers of God's altar; he retired to the house of Achimelech the high-priest. Achimelech expressed great surprise at seeing him come alone. David pretended some pressing business, which required great expedition, and which had prevented his bringing any provision with him. Achimelech had no other than show-bread to offer him, which none but priests were allowed to eat of. David's distress was very urgent; necessity, he thought, exempted him from that ceremonial law: he took of the holy bread, and Jesus Christ in his gospel has approved his conduct He also, for his defence, took the sword of Goliah, which was there, and the high-priest, with a goodness which afterwards cost him his life, gave him every other assistance that lay in his power. One of Saul's officers happened to be there at that time, and thinking it a fair opportunity of making his court to the king, gave immediate information of what he had seen. This wicked courtier was by birth an Idumean, and known by the name of Doeg. Upon that information Saul in his rage sent for Achimelech, whom he accused of

high treason, as having conspired with David against his life. The virtuous priest, not conscious to himself of having done any thing more than what charity and a due respect had prompted him to do for the king's son-in-law, began to plead in defence of his own innocence, and spoke freely in commendation of David's honour and fidelity to his prince. Saul was more irritated than appeased by the pontiff's speech, and ordered him to be put to death upon the spot. Achimelech stood accompanied with eighty-five other priests, in their sacerdotal robes. Their sacred character inspired respect into the king's servants, who refused to execute their master's orders; and Doeg was the only man hardy enough to imbrue his hands in the blood of those venerable priests of the Lord. This execution was followed by the ruin of Nobe, one of the priest's cities. Abiathar, the son of Achimelech, escaped from the massacre, and informed David of what the tyrant had done. David was sorely grieved at the relation, and humbly considered himself as the cause of that bloodshed He was no longer safe in the king's dominions; he fled for refuge amongst the enemies of his country, and threw himself into the hands of Achis, king of Geth. Geth was not a place of safety for David, where his achievements were so well known; he was soon discovered to be the man who had slain their great champion Goliah, and had infallibly been sacrificed to the resentment of the citizens, if he had not with great presence of mind counterfeited the fool, and passed himself off as a madman.

The holy fathers consider the prudence of David, in counterfeiting the fool on this occasion, as a figure of that imaginary folly which the Gentiles once imputed to the cross of Jesus Christ, but which, according to St. Paul, surpasses the height of all created wisdom. The true followers of Jesus Christ have never been ashamed of such an imputation from a self-conceited world. It is enough for them to be accounted wise by God, whatever they may pass for in the opinion of men. By experience they know that what is by worldly men often accounted folly, is in the eyes of God the height of wisdom; and what the wisest of the wicked often adopt in practice, is little better than the depth of folly.

A.M. 2945.] *David and Abigail.* [A.C. 1055.

1 KINGS, XXV.

DAVID's situation was become truly deplorable, and his life most wretched. Always in danger of being either betrayed or assassinated, he was driven from the society of men, and obliged to shelter himself in woods and mountains. Being closely pursued by an implacable and active enemy, he skulked from place to place, from one wilderness to another, creeping into caverns and the dens of wild beasts. Yet even there he was upon the point of being taken and delivered into the hands of Saul, as it happened to him in the desert of Ziph. At the hazard of his life, he had but just time to slip down the rock, from whence he fled into the desert of Maon. That was his place of refuge more than once, where, being closely pursued, he had not only enemies, but also hunger to struggle with: he saw himself and his trusty followers, who had joined him to the number of about six hundred, in danger of perishing for want of necessaries. There lived in the neighbourhood a man of the name of Nabal, possessed of great riches and numerous flocks, but rough of temper, and savage even to cruelty. To this man David applied himself in his distress: he sent to him ten of his followers, to beg that he would relieve the wants of a distressed company, who had done him no injury. When they came to Nabal's house, which was upon Mount Carmel, they humbly represented their distress for want of provisions; they told him that David, the son of Isai, was their leader, and merited some return for the friendship he had shown to his shepherds in the desert. Nabal rudely answered, that he had no provisions for them, that he knew nothing of them or their leader; but that the country was over-run with slaves, who were trying to escape from their masters. David was exasperated at so injurious an answer; an answer which he had little expected, and much less deserved: besides the refusal, which he thought unjust, it expressed a contempt which he resolved to punish. He ordered his men to gird on their swords and follow him; he laid aside his natural meekness, and meditated a stroke which must have ended in the destruction of Nabal and all his family, had it not been prevented by the discreet and virtuous Abigail. Abigail was the wife of Nabal, a woman as amiable for her prudence, as her husband was odious for his roughness: she being informed of David's hasty approach to repay Nabal for his abuse, went out to meet him with presents and plenty of provisions. As soon as they met, she accosted him in so submissive and so engaging a manner, that

she at once mollified his anger, and disarmed his revenge. Nabal knew nothing of his danger till it was past. Abigail told him of it next morning, and related all she had done to save him. The man was so affected at the account, that he fell sick, and died ten days after. David made a proposal of marriage to the widow, which she at first modestly declined, and then consented to.

Abigail, by the prudent remonstrance she made to David in his anger, is a model of discretion, in teaching us to sooth and pacify the sallies of passion both in ourselves and others; and David by the deference he paid to her advice, sets a rare example of moderation to those who have received provocation. To listen to advice, and stifle resentment, is but too often termed a mark of weakness and dishonour. But nothing surely so becomes the dignity of man, as to make passion give way to reason; and to a Christian nothing is more honourable than to desist from a pursuit which can no longer be carried on consistently with charity and justice.

A.M. 2947.] *David's generosity.* [A.C. 1053.
1 KINGS, XXVI.

IN the midst of these troubles that disgraced the kingdom of Israel, Samuel died in the ninetieth year of his age. He was a man of unshaken virtue, faithful to God, and loyal to his prince; whose faults he never flattered, and for whose misfortunes he daily wept. To him are attributed the books of Judges and Ruth. His death was lamented by all the people of Israel. Saul in the interim persisted in his attempts against David with unrelenting violence, and was wasting the strength of his kingdom against a harmless man, whom he fancied to be his enemy. Being informed by his spies, that he was come back to the wilderness of Ziph, he marched at the head of three thousand men, and encamped round the hill where he supposed his rival to lie concealed. David by a singular exertion of courage, which could only come from God, resolved to visit him in his tent. With a single attendant called Abisai, he went down under the covert of a dark night into Saul's camp, and penetrating into the royal pavilion, found Saul and his officers asleep. Abisai whispered in his ear, that he had his enemy now lying at his mercy, and that with one stroke he might put an end to all his sufferings. David had too much generosity to commit so base an action, and was too well principled in the duty of a subject to his sovereign, to strike, or to suffer Abisai to strike, the Lord's anointed. He contented himself with the king's lance and goblet, which he took away, and carried with him back upon

the hill. Being there beyond the reach of any weapon, he called with a loud voice upon Abner, the general of Saul's army, and jocosely rallied him for the incomparable care he took of his royal master. Saul awoke at the sound, and hearing David's voice, rose up: he called after him with a smoothness of expression, which denoted some abatement of his fury; he spoke in a gentle accent, and styled him his son. David began in a submissive manner to expostulate with the king, why he harassed himself in the pursuit of a harmless man, who, with respect to him, was no more than a little flea? and whether it became the mighty king of Israel to pursue so insignificant a subject as he was, like a trembling partridge, upon the mountain's top? If the Lord in his anger, said he, hath stirred you up to commit these violences against one of your most faithful servants, may he accept my sacrifice: but if any evil counsellors have pushed you on to act as you do, whoever they may be, they are accursed in the sight of our Lord. To a remonstrance so just and conclusive, Saul had no reply to make; he only said he had sinned and acted foolishly; he owned himself indebted to him for his life, begged he would return, and promised to give him no future disturbance. David sent him back his lance, and concluded with a prayer, hoping that, as he had spared the life of Saul, so the Lord would spare his, and free him from distress.

The holy fathers are unanimous in their praise of David

on this occasion. St. Ambrose speaks in raptures of him, who, having it in his power to free himself at once from the persecution of a tyrant who sought his life, chose to remain exposed to continual death, rather than lift his hand against the anointed of the Lord. The gratification of his revenge for the evil treatment he had received, the immediate possession of a crown, the insurance of his life from danger, were strong inducements to the action; but the love of virtue, and conscious duty, had a more powerful influence upon David; his fidelity to God and his king, was grounded upon principles that were unshaken and invariable. His motive was disinterested and pure; from Saul he expected no return of gratitude; he had experienced none. He once before had shown the same generosity, when Saul, unarmed and alone, entered the cave where he and his men lay concealed; he offered no violence to the king's person, he restrained his followers from laying hold of him, he contented himself with a slip of his cloak, which he softly cut off, as a mark that he could as easily have taken away his life. Though Saul admired that forgiving generosity of David's temper at the time, yet his animosity soon flamed out anew, and prompted him to commit fresh violences against his meek benefactor. David, in pardoning his enemy, is the more deserving of our praise, as such a pardon of injuries had not then been sanctified by tho example, or taught by the word of an incarnate God: and his example ought to make those Christians blush, who fancy they may push their resentments against the members of Jesus Christ, to what violence and to what lengths they please.

A.M. 2949.] *David divides the spoils of Siceleg.* [A.C. 1051.
1 Kings, xxx.

David soon found that Saul was not to be depended upon, and that his life was in constant danger. Self-preservation forced him to throw himself once more into the hands of Achis, the king of Geth. Achis, though a Philistine had principles of generosity, and knew how to feel for the distressed. He received the illustrious fugitive with great marks of kindness, and gave him the town of Siceleg for his residence. Hostilities had been renewed between the Israelites and Philistines, and Achis insisted upon David's accompanying him to the war. David, by that means, was reduced to the sad alternative, either of disobliging his generous benefactor, or of fighting against his lawful sovereign. In such embarrassed circumstances he was at a loss how to act, when the Philistines themselves luckily drew him out of his difficulty. They thought an Israelite was not to be trusted in an expedition against his fellow-citizens, and therefore obliged Achis to dismiss him from the army. Achis reluctantly delivered their commands to David, which he softened with expressions of esteem, and made him his excuses upon the necessity he was under of satisfying the Philistine chiefs, who would not suffer an Israelite to accompany them to battle. David was no sooner extricated out of one difficulty, than involved in another. During his absence in the Philistine camp, a roving party of the Amalecites had plundered Siceleg, and set fire to the houses. Every thing of value was carried off by the plunderers, the children and the women were made prisoners, amongst whom were the wives of David and his followers. The men were so sensibly afflicted at this disaster, that not knowing which way to turn themselves, they threw the blame upon their leader, and threatened to stone him to death. David, though abandoned by his partizans, was not abandoned by his own fortitude: he put his trust in God, and with six hundred warriors set off in pursuit of the robbers. Success, he knew, depended upon expedition; he therefore continued his march with such vigour, that two hundred of his men were not able to keep pace with him. He left them behind, and pushing on briskly with the rest, came up with the enemy as they were enjoying themselves over their booty, little thinking of an attack. David fell furiously upon them; a bloody carnage ensued, which lasted till the evening of the next day, when not a man of the Amalecites was left alive, excepting those who escaped by the help of their camels. The victors recovered all, and even more than they had lost. Upon their return, a dispute arose, whether they who had not shared in the dangers of the field, should have their share in the booty; and the decision being left by common consent to David's arbitration, he judicially pronounced in their favour. This decision passed afterwards into a law, and was strictly adhered to in every future division of the spoils of war.

Similar to this is the spiritual economy of the church, in

an impartial communication of prayers and merits between its component members. And a comfortable reflection it is, for such of the faithful as have not either the talents or the strength to perform great actions, or to bear hard labours in the divine service. Enlisted under the same banner of Jesus Christ, they all concur with one another in the profession of the same faith; they all share in the same spiritual treasures; and to each one is impartially measured out the reward, not according to the strength of bones, or the rank of worldly honours, but according to his real deserts in the eyes of God. Charity and zeal may equal the little with the great, and render the weak more deserving than the strong; for with God there is no exception of persons.

A.M. 2949.] *Death of Saul.*—1 Kings, xxxi. [A.C. 1051.

David, by the refusal he met with from the Philistine princes, of letting him serve in their army, was even more fortunate than he imagined at the time; he was thereby prevented not only from fighting, but also from conquering against his country; for in that day's battle, Saul and his sons were slain, and Israel put to a shameful flight. That miserable prince had been long left by the spirit of God, and turned over to his own. Racked with the stings of a guilty conscience within, and pressed by the attacks of a furious enemy without, full of apprehensions, and anxious about the event, he sought in despair to know from the devil what he did not deserve to learn from God. He disguised himself, and went to consult the noted sorceress of Endor. When he came there, he told her she must raise up the ghost of Samuel. The woman being afraid of the severe laws which Saul had lately made against the dealers in magic art, refused to act, till he had promised on oath, that no harm should befall her for the thing she was about. Emboldened by the solemn promise he made her, she then began her enchantments; and, behold, before she had finished, the ghost of Samuel unexpectedly appeared: as soon as she saw him, she understood that the person who consulted her was Saul in disguise. Apprehensive of the severest vengeance, she began to tremble for her life. The king bade her not fear, and asked her what she saw. By the description she gave of the dress and awful figure of

the phantom, Saul knew it to be Samuel, and bowed out of reverence to the ground. The ghost then said, Why hast thou troubled my repose? Why dost thou ask of me what thou knowest already? The Lord hath left thee, and is gone over to thy rival. He will now do to thee as thou hast heard heretofore from my mouth; he will sever thy kingdom from thee, and give it to David; thee and thy Israelites he hath delivered into the hands of the Philistines; to-morrow thou and thy sons shall be amongst the dead. Saul forthwith fell all along the ground, for he was frightened with the words of Samuel, and there was no strength in him. The woman raised him up, gave him a refreshment, and dismissed him as soon as he had strength to go. The wretched prince walked away with a sorrowful heart, black with despair, and full of his approaching destiny. The fatal day was at hand; the two armies of Israel and Philisthim stood arrayed for battle on the mountains of Gelboe. The signal being given, the Israelites shrunk back from the enemy, and Jonathan and his two brothers were slain; the whole weight of the battle then fell upon Saul; an arrow from a Philistine's bow gave him a deadly wound: covered with disgrace, and still breathing, he commanded his armour-bearer to stab him; which the armour-bearer refusing to do, he caught hold of his sword, and setting the point against his breast, fell upon it, and expired.

Such was the exit of unhappy Saul, the first king of Israel. By an act of violence against his own life, he put an end to the long and barbarous violences which he had wantonly been guilty of against others. Happy might he have been, if he either had continued in a private station, or only had retained the same humble sentiments which he carried with him to the throne. Guiltless as the child of a year old, he began his reign; but in that happy disposition he reigned no more than two years. Elated with power, and dazzled with the splendour of a crown, he grew imperious and violent. He set off with a promising show of an auspicious reign; he fell before he had far advanced; and at last finished by a death which rendered him a frightful example to all succeeding ages. The holy fathers considered Saul under the same predicament in the old law, as they do Judas in the new. Both had been particularly chosen by God himself, and both were rejected; the first for his pride, the second for his avarice. They both fell from a station the most dignified; both, in despair, ended their days by self-murder. No call, no station of life, be it what it may can exempt a man from the weakness of human nature. No man is secure from temptation. The most elevated in dignity, says St. Ambrose, and the most steady, as they may seem, in the way of virtue, ought to be always fearful, and always upon their guard, lest they fall. A suppliant hope in God, and an humble diffidence of themselves, are necessary means to preserve the grace of final perseverance.

A.M. 2949.] *Lamentations of David.* [A.C. 1051.

2 Kings, i.

The death of Saul, and total overthrow of his army, was a subject of universal triumph amongst the Philistines. They took possession of the field of battle next day, and finding the king's corse amongst the slain, stripped him of his armour, and cut off his head, which they ordered to be carried about, and shown through their land, to convince the people of his death. His armour they dedicated to Astaroth, and his head they fastened up in the temple of Dagon. David in the interim, who had not less reason to be glad than they, was very differently affected. Far from rejoicing at an event so tragical in itself, though so advantageous to him, he shed tears of real sorrow. In a mournful canticle, which he composed on the occasion, he pathetically deplores the melancholy fate of Saul, the anointed of the Lord. in a strain still more moving, he laments the untimely fall of

Jonathan, whom he affectionately styles his brother and most loving friend. He invites the daughters of Israel to throw aside their gay attire, pour out their tears with him, and mourn over the helpless slain. Then, as if the place had been accessary to the disaster, he prays that neither the rain nor the dew of heaven may fall upon the mountains of Gelboe, where the shield of the valiant is cast away, where Saul lies trodden on the ground, as though he had not been anointed with oil. Oh! tell it not in Geth, tell it not in Ascalon, lest the daughters of the Philistines exult, lest the daughters of the uncircumcised rejoice! David did not content himself with these effusions of his grief in private, he expressed himself by his actions to the public. He thanked the citizens of Jabes Galaad, who had taken up and interred the bodies of Saul and his unfortunate sons. The first account of this fatal overthrow was brought to David in Siceleg, by a young Amalecite, who pretended to have been present at the king's death, and was in hopes of ingratiating himself by the relation of a story, which he embellished with several circumstances of his own invention. I came by chance, said he, to the mountain of Gelboe, where I found the king oppressed with anguish, and leaning upon his spear. At my approach he called out, and bade me free him from the distress he was in: wherefore knowing that it was impossible for him to live after the stroke he had received, I complied with his desire. I killed him; I took the diadem from his head, and the bracelet from his arm, which I have brought hither to thee, my lord. David rent his garments at the sad report, asked the Amalecite how he had dared in

that manner to lift his hand against the Lord's anointed, and ordered him to be put to death in punishment of his crime.

The throne being vacant, and David knowing himself to be the man who was to fill it, consulted the Lord to know how he was to act in this emergency, and where to go. The Lord bade him return to Hebron, the capital city of Judea: he went, was publicly anointed king, and acknowledged by that tribe. The other tribes being influenced by Abner, the late king's chief minister, acknowledged Isboseth, a son of Saul, for their king, and thereby divided the nation into two parties. A civil contest for the crown began between the two competitors; David appointed Joab to be his general, while Abner, with great abilities, supported the interest of Isboseth. The dispute was carried on with the loss of many lives for seven years, when Isboseth was traitorously murdered by two assassins, who carried his head to David. David was no more inclined to encourage murder in these two traitors, than he had been in the young Amalecite, and therefore ordered them to be treated in the same manner. Far from insulting an enemy in his fall, or from rejoicing at the advantage which he was to reap by it, he considered and felt for the wrongs that his enemy had suffered from the hands of his assassins; and thus, by a double instance of his justice, he convinces us, that he not only had the meekness to forgive the injuries, but also the generosity to honour the memory of his inveterate enemies. He put to death the Amalecite who had declared himself guilty of the death of Saul, and he executed Rechab and Baana for having stabbed Isboseth his son.

A.M. 2956.] *Sudden death of Oza.* [A.C. 1044.

2 Kings, vi.

By the death of Isboseth, David became the peaceable possessor of the crown of Israel, without a rival: the tribes unanimously acknowledged his undoubted right, and voluntarily submitted to his authority. The flame of civil discord being thus happily extinguished, the force of the nation was no longer divided, and the Israelites being again united under one head, had no other than the common interest to pursue. David resolved to make use of the power which God had placed in his hands, against the ancient enemies of his country His first expedition was against the fortress of Jerusalem, which was inhabited by the Jebuseans, and never had sub mitted to the Hebrew yoke. This fortress, which stood within the walls of the city, upon Mount Sion, was so advantageously situated, that it seemed to bid defiance to the force that could be brought against it; the garrison insulted David for an attempt which they deemed rash, and told him, the very blind and lame of the place would be enough to repel his attacks. But there is nothing so arduous, which true courage, supported by the arm of God, cannot overcome. David at that time had an army composed of heroes; to encourage them to victory, he promised the command to him who should first strike the Jebusean, and gave orders for a general assault. Joab was the first that mounted upon the wall; the troops rushed on after their general, and the city was added to the conquests of Israel. David took possession of the castle of Sion for himself, repaired the old buildings, and erected new ones round about upon the hill, which from his name was thenceforward called the city of David. Gratitude to God for his success, made him turn his thoughts upon the public duties of religion. The ark of God had for many years lain in a state of obscurity in the private house of Abinadab. The pious king's intention was to restore its first lustre: for that purpose he prepared a magnificent pavilion for its reception upon mount Sion, within the precincts of his own palace. Notice was given for a public translation of the ark, and the people were ordered to attend. They assembled to the number of thirty thousand; a new wain was made, the ark laid upon it, and Oza, the son of Abinadab, appointed to drive the oxen. The procession was conducted with that solemn show of religious magnificence which became the piety of a great king. David thought it not beneath his royal dignity to play upon the harp, being accompanied by the numerous choirs of musicians, whose joyful and harmonious sounds enlivened the country as they passed along. Every thing seemed to conspire to the public jubilee, when an unlucky accident interrupted the procession, and suddenly threw the minds of all into a melancholy consternation. One of the oxen began to kick, and made the ark lean on one side; Oza thinking it to be in danger of falling, hastily stretched out his hand, and held it. The Lord was provoked at the rashness of his action, says the Scripture, and struck him dead upon the spot. The spectators were seized with dread; David himself was terrified, and durst not proceed in his design of lodging the tremendous ark within the precincts of his palace. He deposited it in the house of Obededom, a virtuous Levite, where it remained for three months.

The dreadful judgment that befell Oza, for rashly laying his hand upon the ark, leaves no room to doubt of the awful respect which is due, and which God rigorously requires to be paid him in the things that regard his holy service. In the law of grace, infinitely more holy is the altar of Almighty God, than was the ark, under the law of Moses. An irreverence shown to the things of which the ark was no more than the figure, is of more enormous guilt; and its punishment, though not attended with visible strokes of divine vengeance, is infinitely more to be apprehended.

A M. 2956.] *The Translation of the Ark.* [A.C. 1044.
2 Kings, vi.

The visible blessings which God showered down upon Obededom, in consideration of the ark being under his roof, dispelled the king's fears, and made him wish to share in the divine favours. At the end of three months from Oza's death, David re-assumed his first design of translating the ark to Jerusalem; and to guard against every accident of the kind that had happened before, he considered in what manner Moses had directed the ark to be carried, whenever it should be necessary to remove it from one place to another. He found upon examination, that none but priests and Levites were permitted to approach it, and that it was not to be drawn by beasts, but carried upon men's shoulders. He therefore ordered the Levites to attend in ceremony on the day appointed, pacific sacrifices to be prepared, and every arrangement made suitable for the solemnity. Sacred canticles of his own composition were set to music, and skilful musicians appointed to perform with instruments and voices. The ark of the covenant was brought forth by the sons of Levi, who advanced with it upon their shoulders through a prodigious crowd of spectators, who lined the road; the ground streamed with the blood of victims, which were immolated to the living God, while hills and dales resounded with the strains of vocal and instrumental harmony. Dressed in a linen garment, such as the prophets wore, the king played upon his harp, and danced with all his might before the ark, as it moved along, till he came to Mount Sion. Michol was at the palace window waiting for the procession, and seeing her royal consort without his robes of state, and dancing in the crowd, despised him in her heart for his devotion. When the ceremony was over, she ran to meet him, and in a strain of irony said, that it was nobly performed, that it was a glorious sight, to see the king of Israel stripped of his royal robes, and dancing like a buffoon before his subjects. David, whose sentiments of religion were too well grounded, says St. Ambrose, to be shaken by a woman's ridicule, meekly answered, The Lord hath selected me from amidst the meanest of his servants, and hath preferred me to thy father. From God I received my crown, and through his mercy I am peaceably possessed of the kingdom of Israel: for which reason I will humble myself still more and more before him. I wish to be always little in my own eyes, and it shall be my glory to be thus on a level with the lowest of my subjects.

Thus did this holy king, says St. Gregory, lay aside the marks of royalty, that he might give scope to his piety. Forgetful of his dignity, forgetful of his victories, which had made him great in every one's eyes but his own, he not only humbled himself, but was also willing to be humbled by others. His example is a pattern of true devotion and humility; it teaches all Christians, of whatsoever rank, never to be ashamed of the duty they owe to God, and never to imagine that they vilify or degrade themselves by submitting to the external practice of religious worship. To be afraid of demeaning themselves by a public performance of their Christian obligations, is to be ashamed of the cross of Christ. If an irreligious world should try, like Michol, to laugh them out of their duty; with a noble disdain, like that of David, let them despise the impious raillery, and remember the sacred dignity to which God has raised them, by adopting them for his sons, and making them members of his church

The sublime idea that David entertained of the majesty of God, and the zeal he had of promoting the divine worship, made him think that the honours he had paid to God, in translating his ark to Mount Sion, fell far short of what were still due. He reflected that the ark of God had no better covering than that of skins, whilst he himself was lodged in a palace of cedar; he therefore traced in his mind the plan of a stately temple, which he resolved to build to the Lord of hosts. He communicated his design to the prophet Nathan; and Nathan, though he scarcely approved of it, was inspired to tell him, that such a plan should not be executed till after his death; that from his seed should arise a son, who should build a house to the Lord, and that the throne of his kingdom should be established for ever. David humbly acquiesced, and with acts of thanksgiving resigned himself to God for the accomplishment of his divine promises. To make his subjects happy in the interim, and to free them from the disgraceful burden of paying tribute to other princes, became the object of his laudable ambition. He took care to have impartial justice administered at home, while he asserted his own just rights abroad by force of arms. In the wars he waged, he gloried not like other kings in the number of his chariots and horsemen; his trust was in the Lord his God; prayer was his shield against the weapons of his enemies, and victory crowned his warlike expeditions. The Idumeans, the Philistines, the kings of Moab and Soba, the people of Amalec and Syria, were humbled by him, and made tributary to the crown of Israel. Notwithstanding the success that attended David's arms, Hanon, king of the Ammonites, had the imprudence not only to reject his friendship, but also to provoke his enmity. Hanon was a young, inexperienced prince, and son of Nass the late king of Ammon, from whom David had received many good services during Saul's persecutions. David wished to cultivate the same friendship with the son, as had subsisted between the father and him, and with that view sent ambassadors to compliment him upon his accession to the throne. Hanon suffered himself to be persuaded by evil counsellors, that the king of Israel's design was not to honour, but to betray the kingdom of Ammon, and that the ambassadors were no more than spies, sent to discover the strength and nature of the country. Under that persuasion, the rash prince let himself be led astray, and without considering the consequences, seized upon the ambassadors, shaved one-half of their heads, clipped away half their garments, and bade them be gone. The report of this shameful treatment was quickly carried to David, who sent to condole with his servants for the disgrace they had suffered, and to desire they would stop at Jericho, till their beards should be grown again. His next care was to wipe off the dishonour, which this affront to his ambassadors had thrown upon himself and the whole Jewish nation. He ordered Joab to put himself at the head of his army, and to march against the enemy. The Ammonites had foreseen this stroke, and provided against it; they had sent to their allies, and hired what forces they could out of Syria. Such troops as had no other interest than their pay to fight for, were not an equal match for the veteran troops of Israel. Joab, whose experience was equal to his courage, attacked and defeated them. Hanon did not despair; but recruiting his forces with new vigour, brought another formidable army into the field. Against an enemy who had such resources, David thought it advisable to march in person, and by his presence animate the Israelites to battle. They came to a general engagement; the Ammonites were routed with great slaughter; seven hundred of their armed chariots were destroyed, with their combatants; forty thousand of their foot and as many horses fell in the field of battle, and fifty-eight thousand more fled before the Israelites. A victory so complete discouraged the neighbouring nations from lending any further succours to the king of Ammon: the Syrians laid down their arms, and submitted to the conditions prescribed by the conqueror. The young Hanon was then convinced of the imprudent step he had taken; he saw his kingdom reduced tc the brink of ruin, through the advice of his wicked counsellors, and his own credulity. The rise or the fall of empires often turns upon the nice point of good or bad advice. Happy is the prince, who, being master of the affections of his subjects, has the discernment to choose, and the resolution to support, those who are both capable and willing to serve him well.

THE Ammonites, notwithstanding their late overthrow, were still restless; some of them refused to lay down their arms, and Joab was ordered to march against them. David in the mean time remained at Jerusalem, where amidst the sweets of domestic repose he met with a more fatal stroke than ever he had to fear in the field of war. He was one day walking upon the platform of his palace, about noon, and looking round him, happened to cast his eye upon a woman, as she was bathing herself upon a terrace opposite to him. He beheld and coveted: he asked who she was, and being told that she was called Bethsabee, the wife of Urias, he sent for her. The opening features of her beauty, as she approached, added fresh fuel to his flames; he yielded to the wicked desires of his heart; he solicited her consent to the sin of adultery, and obtained it. Bethsabee went home, and conceived: as her pregnancy advanced, she began to consider and apprehend its consequences. She knew how severe the law was against a crime of which she knew herself guilty. The absence of her husband was a convincing proof of her infidelity; her guilt could not lie long concealed, but must necessarily become its own discoverer. Under those circumstances she let David know the situation she was in. David immediately despatched an order to Joab for Urias to be sent home. Urias came, and as if he had been only wanted to give some account of the war, the king asked him several questions concerning the general and his army. He seemed satisfied with Urias's answers, bade him go home to sleep with his wife, and ordered plenty of meat to be sent after him. The hardy soldier, having no suspicion of the king's design, never thought of going to his own house, but threw himself down to sleep before the palace gate. David was informed of it, sent for him again, and pressed him to go home. Urias made him this noble reply: The ark of God is lodged in nothing better than a tent; the warriors of Israel and Judea rest upon the bare earth; Joab the general and all his army lie exposed in the field; and shall I make merry, and sleep with my wife? No, my liege, I will not do it. David however kept him a day longer, and made him eat and drink plentifully in his presence, hoping by this means to soften him into compliance. Urias was inflexible, he passed the second night as he had passed the first upon his couch, and went not into his own house: upon which the king took the resolution of adding a second crime to the first; to cover the shame of his own guilt, he resolved upon the murder of the innocent and brave Urias. In other circumstances David's natural goodness of heart would have prompted him to reward the man for his behaviour, which on that occasion determined him to sacrifice his life by the sword of Ammon. He sent Urias back with a letter to Joab, and in that letter commanded Joab to place Urias in the front of the battle, and there leave him. The murderous order was literally executed; Urias fell by the sword of the Ammonites, and Joab sent a particular account of his death to David. David received the message with as much seeming unconcern, as though he had no share in the horrid murder. Bethsabee mourned, as was the custom, for her husband's death; when the time of her mourning was past, she became the king's wife, was introduced into his palace, and bore him a son, the issue of adultery.

The fall of David into two atrocious crimes, is a deplorable instance of the instability of man; it proves that the most holy and most virtuous are never above the reach of temptation. However great their sanctity may seem, and however tried their virtue may have been, they still retain the tincture of that frail earth, out of which they were first formed. Such an instance of human infirmity must necessarily alarm the minds of thinking men; they who stand, can never promise themselves security; and the weak must tremble, when they see the strong thus overthrown. The crime of David is recorded in Holy Writ, not as an excuse for sin, or as an example to be followed, but as a caution, that all may be upon their guard, lest by presuming too much they chance to fall into the like misfortune.

A.M. 2970.] *David's Repentance.* [A.C. 1030.
2 Kings, xii.

David, who by a weakness inherent in human nature, had fallen into the abyss of sin, stood in need of more than his own natural force to enable him to rise. So malignant was the wound he had received in his soul, that he seemed as unconcerned at his guilt as though he were not conscious of what he had done. For a whole year he remained unmindful of his duty, and forgetful of his God; neither repenting, nor suing for forgiveness of his crime. God in his mercy beheld him with an eye of pity, and sent Nathan his prophet to him. Nathan, whose prudence was equal to his zeal, saw how delicate a point he had to manage: his prince was to be made sensible of his duty, and yet not offended; the truth was to be enforced, and the sinner roused from a state of insensibility, and yet nothing said that might exasperate the king's temper. The prophet then began, as though he meant no more than to inform the king of a certain rich man, who having his friend to entertain, would not kill any sheep or oxen of his own, of which he had plenty, but took from a poor man his favourite and only ewe, which he ordered to be killed and prepared for his own table. The very mention of an action so unjust and cruel, raised a laudable indignation in David's breast, who had no suspicion that the case regarded himself. Blind to his own cruelty and injustice, he pronounced the rich man's condemnation, and in that pronounced his own. He deserves to die, said the king, whoever the man may be, who has done so base an action. You are the man, replied the prophet; you are he whom the Lord has anointed king

of Israel, whom he has delivered from the hands of Saul, to whom he has granted victory, power, wealth, and a peaceable possession of the throne of Israel and of Juda: but for these and still greater favours that the Lord has in store, what return have you made? How have you repaid them, and in what manner have you testified your gratitude? Was it in the embraces of an adulteress? in the murder of Urias? or in the marriage of Bethsabee? For this cause the sword shall be drawn within the wall of your own house, and from your own children evils shall arise, to punish the contempt which you have put upon the Lord. The king's heart was touched; his conscience witnessed the justness of Nathan's reproach; he acknowledged the truth, and was not displeased to hear it. Without asking, as St. Austin observes, how a subject could thus presume to scrutinise the actions, and arraign the conduct of his prince, he listened in humble silence, and for the moment forgetting himself to be a king, acknowledged himself a sinner; more sincere than Saul, he cried out, I have sinned. He expressed no more than what he felt; he expressed the real sorrow of a contrite heart. In the spirit of repentance he humbly submitted to the chastisement which Nathan, on the part of God, prophesied against him and his family. Overwhelmed with grief, and yet borne up by hope, as St. Chrysostom takes notice, he resigned himself to sufferings, as the only means of atoning for his sin, and obtaining forgiveness. David was no sooner made sensible of his guilt, than he exerted all the powers of his soul to blot it out; he never ceased to shed the tears of penance, till he ceased to live. David in his fall, says St. Ambrose, has been imitated by many; in his repentance, but by few.

A.M. 2972.] *Afflictions of David.* [A.C. 1028.
2 KINGS, xiii.

DAVID soon began to feel the punishments which Nathan had pronounced upon him: these punishments were a temporal satisfaction due to the divine justice, even after the guilt of sin had been remitted by contrition. The first stroke of justice that fell upon the guilty king, was the death of his little son by Bethsabee. He was fond of the guiltless infant, he prayed that its life might be prolonged; he added tears and fasting to his prayers; but God's decree was not to be reversed. The stroke was after that extended to his other children. His daughter Thamar was ravished by her brother Amnon; and Amnon in revenge was murdered by his brother Absalom, at an entertainment which the murderer had prepared for his brothers, as a cover to his design. Absalom, upon this, was obliged to fly from his father's anger, and condemned himself to a voluntary banishment for three years. Being master of much cunning, and a great dissembler, he gained Joab's confidence, and by his mediation having recovered the king's good graces, became as much a favourite as ever he had been before. The goodness of a fond parent ought to have insured a mutual return of affection from the son. But goodness has seldom any influence upon a bad heart. The ungrateful son was no further sensible of his father's goodness towards him, than as it enabled him to promote his own ambitious designs. He had fixed his eye upon the crown, and entertained himself with the hopes of taking it from his father's brow, to place it upon his own. Full of that wicked project, he began to wind himself into the affections of the courtiers and officers;

he affected great popularity, promised what great things he would do to serve his people, if he were only king; he gained Achitophel, David's prime counsellor of state; by subtle arts and flatteries he seduced many of the king's servants from their allegiance, and increased his party by degrees, till he thought himself sufficiently strong to make good his pretensions. Under the pretext of a vow, which he said he had made during his banishment in the town of Gessur, he asked his father's leave to go to Hebron. Upon his arrival at that city, he erected the standard of rebellion, and declared himself king. Great were the numbers that flocked to his banner. The news of an insurrection, so unexpected and unnatural, shocked the good king to such a degree, that he knew not whom to trust, or what measures to pursue. He had no more than six hundred guards to oppose against the rebels, and was afraid of being besieged in his own city: too feeble to resist, he had no prospect of saving himself but by flight. His policy was to gain what time he could, and give his subjects an opportunity to show themselves in his defence. With that design he called together the few faithful friends he had about him, marched out of Jerusalem, passed over the torrent of Cedron, and made his retreat up the mountain of Olives. As he approached Bahurim he was met by Semei, one of Saul's kindred, who reviled him in the most abusive language, and threw stones at his followers. His followers

wished to revenge the insult as it deserved. But the humble penitent, who considered this revolt of his subjects as the effect and punishment of his own revolt against God, not only forbid any hurt to be done to the reviler, but with all patience received his insults, as from the ministers of divine justice. Absalom in the interim made a triumphant entry into Jerusalem with Achitophel by his side, the prompter of his schemes, and director of all his motions. By this traitor's advice he erected a public tent, and in the face of the sun violated his father's wives. It was a crime of the most atrocious nature; but it was a chastisement due to the injury that David himself had offered to Urias, and what had been particularly specified by the prophet Nathan. In all his afflictions the humble prince saw how proportioned his chastisement was to the nature of his sin; how visible the wicked disorders of his family resembled the past disorders of his soul; and how justly his own ungrateful rebellion against God was now punished by the rebellion of his son and subjects against their king. By experience he became convinced, that the greatest grace God can show a sinner, is not to spare him here, that he may spare him eternally, as St. Austin says. For the malignity of sin cannot, consistently with justice, be suffered to go unpunished; the measure of divine justice must some way or other be completed; sooner or later full atonement must be made, either in this life or in the next. To make full satisfaction, and to deserve a full discharge, the sinner has no other choice, than by a voluntary submission to such chastisements as God shall please to inflict upon him.

A.M. 2981.] *Death of Absalom.* [A.C. 1019.
2 Kings, xviii.

Absalom being master of the royal city consulted his council of war in what manner he should pursue this first stroke of his good fortune. Achitophel, the most able of his counsellors, was for vigorous measures; and had his advice been followed, it must have ended in the total ruin of the king, who had not yet drawn his troops together. But a superior wisdom presided over those deliberations, and directed them to a better end. Chusai, who was secretly in David's interest, being called upon by Absalom to deliver his opinion, differed from Achitophel, and refuted his advice. He represented the danger of driving men at once into despair; that a small body of desperate warriors, such as David's were, was capable of great achievements, and not to be reduced by force; that Absalom's party, being but lately formed, could not have that steadiness which is requisite to carry a difficult attack; and if some of them should chance to fall in the attempt, that the rest might grow disheartened, and turn the scale of war against him. This opinion prevailed, and Achitophel for once was not attended to. This slight, as he thought it, had such an effect upon the mind of that haughty minister, that he immediately went home, and by a violent death put an end to his life. Chusai contrived to give David notice of the dispositions that Absalom was making to march against him, and advised him to cross the river Jordan. David followed the advice, and having drawn a respectable body of troops together, resolved to give the rebels battle. His innate courage prompted him to lead them on in person;

but his trusty officers, who knew how much depended on a life so precious, would not suffer him to expose it in the field. He yielded to their reasons, and gave the command to Joab, with the strictest orders to preserve the life of Absalom. Absalom had taken the field with an army much superior in number to that of the royalists. The two armies came to an engagement in the forest of Ephraim: the rebels were defeated, twenty thousand of them remained dead on the spot, and the rest, with Absalom, endeavoured to save themselves by flight. Absalom was remarkable for a long flowing head of hair, and being hurried away by the confusion he then was in, rode under a thick spreading oak to avoid the enemy; his hair entangled itself in the boughs, and his mule going on,

left him hanging in that condition. He was discovered by some of the royal party, but out of deference to the king's order, no one presumed to lift his arm against him. Joab was informed of his situation, and hastened to the spot. Void of that delicacy of sentiment which his men had expressed, he took three lances in his hand, and struck them all into the heart of the unhappy prince, as he hung. The head of the rebellion being thus cut off, he ordered the signal to be given for a retreat, and no more blood to be spilled. Messengers were immediately despatched to give the king notice of his success. David's first question was, whether his son Absalom was safe? And being told that he was dead, his countenance fell, and the tears gushed from his eyes. The untimely fall of a darling, though rebellious son, damped the joy of victory; he shut himself up in his apartment; and the day so glorious to his arms and so advantageous to his subjects, was changed into mourning. Joab, who had expected to see the people rejoicing for the success he had in suppressing the rebellion, took great offence at this behaviour of the king. With the freedom of a brave, but rugged soldier, he broke in upon his sovereign, and reproached him for the little concern he seemed to have for his friends and faithful subjects. He told him how ill this grief became him on the day of triumph; that it shamed the faces of his victorious servants, who had saved his life, and the lives of his sons and daughters; that he seemed to love none but those who hated him; that his nobles were by this convinced how little he cared for them, and how pleased he had been if they, instead of Absalom, had perished in the field: he moreover added, that if he did not rise and show himself to the satisfaction of his faithful servants, they were ready to abandon him, and that before the end of the night he would not have so much as one man remaining by his side. Compelled by these harsh remonstrances of Joab, the king arose and sat in the gate: the people flocked around to see him, and professed their allegiance. But notwithstanding these public testimonies of his loyal subjects, David's breast still heaved with sorrow at the remembrance of his slaughtered son Absalom. The ingratitude, the treachery, rebellion, the murder, and the incests of an unnatural son, could not extinguish the first flame of a father's affection. David was still fond of Absalom, and in shedding his tears over the breathless corse, bitterly lamented the more lasting death of the soul.

A.M. 2981.] *Death of Siba.*—2 KINGS, xx. [A.C. 1019.

THE death of Absalom put an end to the rebellion: the men of Juda and Israel strove to out-do each other in honouring their king, whom they accompanied in great crowds on his triumphal return to Jerusalem. They who had been the most active against their sovereign in his disgrace, were the first to profess their allegiance after victory. It is what self-interest usually inspires into every traitor, when he finds himself too weak to do more mischief. Conscious of his guilt, and apprehensive of punishment, Semei amongst the rest came to throw himself at the feet of his much injured prince. The appearance of that insolent rebel raised an honest indignation in the breasts of all who saw him; they begged the king would give them leave to revenge his outrageous insults, and to wash off the stain in the reviler's blood. The meek and penitential disposition of the king's mind would not suffer him to grant any such request, nor permit the glory of his victory to be tarnished by the death of any one of his subjects. Miphiboseth, the son of Jonathan, clothed with the garb of misery and distress, presented himself at the same time. He came not to implore the royal clemency on account of any crime he had done; for to him David had declared himself a friend for his father's sake, and confirmed his title to the family inheritance of Saul his grandfather; he came to demand justice against his servant, whose name was Siba. This wicked man during the late troubles had persuaded David, that Miphiboseth his master entertained hopes of recovering the crown which Saul had lost, and for that purpose was soliciting the favour of the people of Jerusalem. David, who was not then at leisure to examine into the grounds of that accusation, supposed the story to be true, and dispossess d Miphiboseth of his estate, and gave it to his faithless servant. It was to recover this estate, and to clear his character, that Miphiboseth then appeared before the king. He was happy enough to justify his own conduct, and to detect the imposture of his servant; but, through a strange fatality too often attending kings and men in power, he could prevail upon David to restore no more than half of his estate; the slanderer was allowed to remain in quiet possession of the other half. Miphiboseth could not forbear showing some little displeasure at the treatment he received, though he peaceably acquiesced in the king's decision. Siba being thus secured in the enjoyment of his ill-gotten wealth, made use of it to plunge the nation back into the frightful horrors of a civil war. Being naturally bold and turbulent, he sounded the trumpet of revolt, and by his discourse persuaded all the tribes, excepting that of Juda, to take up arms against the son of Isai; for so he contemptuously styled the king. David, who by the past had been taught to fear the consequences of every popular commotion, exerted himself with vigour to quash the evil, if he could, before it should rise to any height. He sent for Amasa, whom he had resolved to employ on this occasion in the place of Joab, ordered him to collect what troops he could, and to march in three days' time against the rebels. Amasa was slow in his operations; David grew uneasy at this delay, and apprehending the advantage which an active enemy might draw from it, ordered Abisai and his brother Joab to lead their part of the troops into the field. Joab was ready at a moment's warning, though much out of humour on account of the preference which had been first given to Amasa. He put his army into motion, and Amasa joined him upon the march. As they had been always friends, Amasa went up to salute him, without the least suspicion of any ill-will that Joab had against him. Joab returned his civility with an equal show of friendship; but as he embraced him with one hand, treacherously stabbed him with the other. Siba fled at the approach of an army which had been used to conquer, and shut himself up in the town of Abela. Joab pursued him, and laid close siege to the place, being determined not to leave it till he had the traitor in his possession. A woman from the rampart asked him why he thus turned his arms against the cries of Israel; he answered, that his arms were pointed at none but Siba,

the ringleader of the rebels: she reported his answer to the people of the city, who by her persuasion cut off Siba's head, and threw it over the wall. Joab wanted nothing more; he immediately raised the siege, and peace was restored to Israel.

Joab was a gallant officer, and had rendered great services to his king and country. His character exhibits one of those ambitious men, who are not afraid of exposing their lives in a battle, who will execute their prince's orders with a becoming promptitude and courage, but will at times make it appear, that they have likewise their own glory and personal interest in view. Though Joab's fidelity, in what regards the essential service of his country, cannot be impeached, yet his inattention to please, his rudeness of behaviour, and boldness of speech to the king himself, made him a very troublesome though loyal subject. The murder of Abner and Amasa in cold blood, and the barbarous assassination of Absalom, whom he had express orders to spare, are indelible blots in his character. But notwithstanding all his defects and insolence, David left him to command his armies as long as he lived. With the spirit of an humble penitent he bore the insults of a rude subject, reflecting that he himself, for the sake of gratifying a lawless passion, had outrageously insulted the Sovereign of the universe, from whom he had received nothing but favours and unmerited preferment.

A.M. 2988.] *David chastised by pestilence.* [A.C. 1012.
2 Kings, xxiv.

Scarce had David begun to breathe from those public and domestic evils, which had wearied him ever since his sin with Bethsabee; scarce had he begun to taste the sweets of peace, when he fell into new troubles, and experienced fresh calamities. The penitent and the virtuous David still was man, still exposed to temptation and liable to sin. He had first been led astray by lust; his vanity now seduces him into a second fault. Vanity is a subtle vice; it is to be apprehended even by the best of men; it inspired David to learn the number of his subjects. Joab opposed it as an idle project, and very justly said, that for a prince it was enough to beg the blessing of God upon his subjects, without being inquisitive to know their number. But the king was positive: he nominated the commissioners, who for near ten months were employed in running over the whole country, and registering the inhabitants. By the lists delivered in by Joab to the king, it appeared that the number of the Jewish people amounted to thirteen hundred thousand fighting men, five hundred thousand of which were comprised in the single tribe of Juda; though Joab seems not to have given in the real number, which, according to the book of Chronicles, amounted to near three hundred thousand men more, besides those of Levi and Benjamin, who were not numbered; because, as the Scripture says, Joab unwillingly executed the king's orders. David had satisfied his vanity; he knew the number of his subjects, and saw his folly: he stood in no need of a prophet, as he did before, to make him sensible of the sin he had committed. Stung with remorse he publicly acknowledged himself guilty, and humbly besought the Lord to pardon him. Unmindful of his royal dignity, unless it was to humble himself at the reflection of its having led him into temptation, he thought of nothing but repentance: the prophet Gad came to him on the part of God, not to declare the pardon of his sin without his first being punished for it, but to propose which of the three punishments he would choose,—famine, war, or pestilence. The penitent king judging it more expedient to fall into the hands of God, than into the hands of men, chose pestilence. The pestilence

began, and raged with such violence, that in three days' time it carried off no fewer than seventy thousand persons. To see such numbers of his subjects so suddenly snatched out of life on his account, David was more sensibly afflicted, than if the whole punishment had fallen singly upon himself. Penetrated with the most tender feelings for his suffering people, he wept and prayed the whole time. It is I, said he to Almighty God, it is I who have sinned: I have done the evil, and why do my people suffer? Rather turn thy anger, O my God, and let thy vengeance fall upon me. Such was the king's prayer: the fervour that accompanied it, extinguished the divine anger; the exterminating angel stopped his hand, and the evil ceased.

By this example we see, and the holy fathers remark the same, that as Almighty God sometimes punishes his people for the sins of those by whom they are governed; so he often spares for the sake of those who strive by their prayers to disarm his justice and obtain his mercy.

A.M. 2989.] *Solomon, King.*—3 Kings, i. [A.C. 1011.

David was now almost worn out with sufferings and infirmities of age. His visible decline of life awakened the expectation of his aspiring sons. They had all their eye upon the throne, and no one was without hope. Adonias, the eldest of the brothers, seemed determined to be beforehand with the rest. This ambitious prince having taken care to engage in his interest some of the leading men in the kingdom, prepared a splendid entertainment for his friends, that they might take their opportunity to proclaim him king. Nathan had intelligence of the plot, and being interested for Solomon, whom the king intended for his successor, communicated it to Bethsabee, advising her to go immediately to the king, and remind him of his promise in favour of her son. She readily followed his instructions, and while she was yet speaking to David concerning his successor, in came the prophet, as if it had been by chance, and respectfully begged to know, if by his royal will Adonias had been called to the throne? Alarmed at the question, David gave immediate orders for his son Solomon to be anointed and enthroned. Sadoc the high-priest, and Nathan the prophet, lost no time in the execution of this order. The ceremony was solemnly performed in Gihon, and Solomon, by sound of trumpet, was proclaimed king, before any of the adverse party had the least suspicion of it. By this stroke Adonias saw an end put to his schemes at once; his partisans abandoned him to save themselves, and he a suppliant criminal fled to the altar, as his only refuge. Solomon pardoned him for what was past, and promised that no harm should befall him, as long as he remained within the bounds of duty. David in the interim was hastening towards his end; a deadly chill had benumbed his limbs, and no covering of clothes could keep him warm. Abisag, a comely virgin in the bloom of youth, was chosen out to nurse and cherish the decrepid king, and sleep in his bosom. David perceiving the time of his dissolution was drawing nigh, called to him his son Solomon, and gave him such instructions as he judged necessary for his future conduct in the government of the realm: he recommended to him a religious observance of the law, as it is written in the book of Moses, a fidelity in his duty to God, and equity in the administration of justice amongst his subjects: he moreover gave him a solemn charge to build a temple to the Lord the God of Israel, which he had much desired, but had not been permitted to do himself, telling him that he had already prepared materials, workmen, and money for the building: he concluded with some instructions of a private nature relative to Joab and Semei; after which he slept with his forefathers, in a good old age, full of days, and riches, and glory, and was buried in his own city, which henceforward became the burying-place of the kings of Juda.

Semei at first experienced great lenity from the new king, but his disobedience at the end of three years drew upon him the punishment which had been long due to his former insolence. The innocent blood of Amasa and Abner had for many years cried for vengeance against Joab. The conspiracy of this general with Adonias against the present king, called down the stroke at last, which the late king had suspended during his own life. For Adonias, after the demise of his father, had resumed his pretensions to the throne, and had demanded Abisag in marriage. Solomon saw into his designs, and cut off his pretensions at once by depriving him of life. Some time after, Almighty God appeared to Solomon in a dream, and promised to grant him whatever favour he should ask. Solomon turned his thoughts upon the favours which his father David and he already received from the divine hand, and considering himself now raised to a dignity, which the higher it was, exposed him the more to difficulties, he saw that great prudence would be requisite to the right government of a great people, and therefore begged God to grant him wisdom. His choice proved him worthy of the gift he asked. God was pleased with his petition, and to a wisdom superlatively greater than had yet been, or should be granted to any man besides, he added riches and glory superior to what any king had possessed before him.

By the example of this wise prince, Christians are instructed what in their choice they are to esteem, and what to prefer. Riches, honours, and the pleasures of life may well constitute the wish of an idolater, or of an infidel, who knows no other happiness than what affects his senses; but on a Christian truly wise, who considers the dignity of an immortal soul, those transient objects make no lasting impression. Being taught from his earliest years, that he has been created not only to serve, but to possess the God whom he adores, he aims at riches, honours, and glory, infinitely more excellent than what this world can give. He aspires to the kingdom of heaven; he studies the virtues that must gain him his Creator's love, and entitle him to a crown, which no rust shall ever tarnish, and no time consume. To seek the kingdom of God, and his justice, is the perfection of true Christian wisdom; and true wisdom is the source of every other good gift, that descends to us from the Father of lights.

A.M. 2991.] *Decision of Solomon.* [A.C. 1009.
3 KINGS, iii.

SOLOMON immediately began to display the talents with which God had blessed him: an occasion offered, in which he gave such a specimen of his wisdom, as excited the admiration and gained him the esteem of all his subjects. Two women of evil fame came before him to beg he would decide a matter of dispute between them. This woman and I, said one of them to the king, dwelt in the same house, where both of us within the space of three days were separately delivered of a male child. She unfortunately happened to smother hers in the night, as she lay asleep. She arose silently out of bed undiscovered, stole from me my babe, leaving her own dead child in the place of it. In the morning when I awoke, I rose with an intent to give my infant suck, and to my surprise found a dead child by my side. I fixed my eyes upon the breathless body, and considering him more diligently when it was clear day, I plainly saw that the infant was not mine. To this the other woman made reply, by charging her with a malicious falsehood, and claiming the living child as her own. They both went on for some time to dispute the matter with an equal degree of positiveness, the one as strenuously denying what the other as strenuously affirmed. Nothing could be collected in favour of one side more than of the other; no information could be gathered from any witness; the accident had happened in a private house and under the cover of a dark night. To discover the truth under such perplexing circumstances, required the sagacity of a Solomon, who, by his conduct on this occasion, showed himself possessed of a wisdom which saw into the secrets of all nature, not only with respect to plants, trees, and animals, as the Scripture testifies of him, but also with respect to men, by diving into the deep recesses of the human heart, and disclosing the hidden movements of a mother's love. The king having sent for a sword, ordered the child to be divided in two, and half to be given to the one, and half to the other. The pretended mother stood silent on hearing the sentence, while the other, melting into tears of tenderness for her help-

less infant, earnestly cried out, I beseech thee, my lord, give her the child alive, and do not kill it. Nature there spoke, and palpably discovered her to be the true mother of the child. Solomon therefore ordered him to be delivered to her. This decision gave universal satisfaction, and all Israel admired the wise ingenuity of the king.

Disputes must inevitably happen, when men are influenced by different principles, and have a different interest to pursue, and in those disputes the like difference of conduct will soon appear, as appeared between the two mothers in their pretensions to the surviving child. The man who is blinded by jealousy or self-love, often attributes to his neighbour the very evils of which he himself has been the cause; he cares but little what disturbance he may give, or into what confusion he may throw his neighbours, as long as he either gains his ends, or prevents his rival from gaining his: while the good Christian, whose principle is charity, is as moderate in his proceedings, as he is steady in his claim. Void of animosity, he pursues his right, that justice may be done; but when that right can no longer be insisted upon without injuring the innocent, he drops his pursuit, and consoles himself for whatever loss he suffers, in the testimony of an upright conscience.

END OF THE FOURTH AGE.

FIFTH AGE OF THE WORLD.

FROM THE FOUNDATION OF SOLOMON'S TEMPLE, 2992, TO THE END OF THE JEWISH CAPTIVITY UNDER CYRUS, 3468, CONTAINING THE SPACE OF 476 YEARS.

A.M. 2992.] *Temple of Solomon.* [A.C. 1008.
3 KINGS, vi.

THE reign of Solomon was a reign of peace and of every temporal felicity. The immense riches of the prince flowed in upon his subjects, and each one, as the Scripture says, reposed without fear under the shade of his own vine and fig-tree. Gold was in such plenty, that no man concerned himself about it, and silver was as common as the stones that lay heaped upon the ground. All the effusion of magnificence which the greatest princes have at any time displayed, falls far short of that which the Scripture relates of king Solomon. For the daily supply of his table he had upwards of a thousand bushels of fine flour, according to the computation of measures, and double that quantity of common meal; thirty oxen, and a hundred sheep; besides a prodigious multitude of stags, roe-bucks, buffles, and fatted fowls. He kept forty thousand stalls of horses for his chariots, and twelve thousand for the saddle, all regularly fed and arranged in the fairest order. The peace that smiled over all the land, was both the cause and the consequence of this surprising plenty. Being thus blessed with peace, and free from the very apprehensions of war, Solomon resolved to execute the designs which his religious father had minutely described and earnestly recommended to him before he died; it was to build a temple in honour of the living God. He made an agreement with Hiram, king of Tyre, to supply him with firs and cedars for that purpose from Mount Libanon: he called out the ablest workmen and artificers of his own subjects, to the number of thirty thousand: eighty thousand men were set to hew out stones and shape them for the masons, and seventy thousand more were constantly employed in carrying the materials as they were wanted: besides these, there were three thousand three hundred overseers, who had nothing else to do, but to inspect each department, and direct the whole. The dimensions of the temple contained three score cubits in length, twenty in breadth, and thirty in height: a porch was erected in the front, twenty cubits long, ten broad, and one hundred and twenty high. Adjoining the walls round about the temple, lay several courts and ranges of chambers of three stories one above another, for different uses. A cedar partition from top to bottom, with two folding doors, richly carved and gilt, divided the grand dome into two equal parts; the first of which measured forty cubits in length, and was called the sanctuary; the second measured twenty cubits, and was called the holy of holies. The inside of both divisions was covered with cedar and deal planks, twenty cubits high, embellished with carvings in relieve gilt, and wrought with cherubims, and palm trees, and divers figures that stood projecting out of the wall. The ceiling was carried up from thence with cedar boards, in the form of an arch, rising ten cubits in the centre. The floor was paved with beautiful and precious marble, the walls and ceiling both of the oracle and sanctuary were plated with the purest gold, and the plates were fastened on with nails of gold. Solomon laid the foundation of the temple in the fourth year of his reign, and completed it in the eleventh, which was the twenty-ninth of his age, and three thousandth of the world; being the first happy man who erected a temple to the true God; a temple so rich and upon so grand a scale, that the world at that time had seen nothing comparable to it.

Happy had Solomon been indeed, says St. Ambrose, if he

had, at the same time, been careful to ground himself in the virtue of humility; but, after having built a temple of stones and timber in his youth, he, in an advanced age, shamefully profaned the living temple of his own body. By an example the most deplorable, he is a warning to those Christians who content themselves with some of the shining works of virtue, as if nothing more were wanting to make them really good: the ground of true virtue, in which consists the happiness of man in this life, as St. Austin remarks, is to be humble. Solomon, in the midst of worldly greatness, fell into disgrace with his Creator, and by the subsequent shame of unbridled lust, tarnished the glory of his former deeds.

A.M. 3000.] *Furniture of the Temple.* [A.C. 1000.
2 Chron. iii. iv.

The images of two cherubims, ten cubits high, made of olive wood and overlaid with gold, were set in the midst of the inner temple. They stood upright, facing the sanctuary, with their wings stretched forth in such a manner, that one wing of each cherub touched the opposite wall, and the other two wings joined one another in the midst of the temple, each wing being five cubits long. A veil of violet, purple, scarlet, and silk, decorated with cherubims, richly wrought, hung against the partition that enclosed the holy of holies. In the sanctuary stood the altar of incense, which was made of cedar covered with gold, and ten golden candlesticks, five and five on each side, with their lamps to give light before the oracle. There were moreover ten tables, covered with gold, for the loaves of show-bread, censers also and vessels for the perfumes, bowls and mortars of pure gold, and vast quantities of other sacred furniture for the divine service. In the court before the temple was the brazen altar of holocausts, ten cubits high, twenty long, and as many broad. Ten large lavers of brass, curiously graven and ornamented with festoons and figures of different animals, stood five and five on each side, for the convenience of washing all such things as were to be offered in holocaust. On the right side, over against the east towards the south, was placed the molten sea, so called on account of its prodigious size: it was made of founded brass, measuring ten cubits from brim to brim, five in height, and thirty in circumference. It was supported by twelve brazen oxen, of which three looked to the east, three to the west, three towards the north, and three towards the south: the use of this immense laver was for purifying the priests before the daily performance of their sacerdotal functions. A vessel of this sort, but of much inferior size, had by Moses been made of copper, and placed between the altar and the tabernacle, that the priests might there wash their hands and feet, as often as they went in and out of the sanctuary. Hence it is imagined, that whenever the sacrifice of incense was offered, the priests approached barefoot to the altar of perfumes, and were therefore bound by a special law to purify themselves in the sacred laver, under pain of death.

From this external purity, which was required as a necessary preparation for those ancient sacrifices, that were no more than a figure of that which was to come, it is easy to conclude, what purity, both of body and soul, God expects from those who are his priests, and the ministers of his altar in the law of grace. For since it is almost impossible for them, while they converse with men, as St. Gregory observes, to be wholly spotless in their actions and affections, which are indicated by the hands and feet, they must have recourse to the purifying laver of compunction and humility of heart, that their souls may be cleansed from sin; that they may never approach the holy altar, nor partake of the sacred mysteries, but with respect, and, as far as human frailty will permit, with a purity resembling that of angels.

A.M. 3001.] *Dedication of the Temple.* [A.C. 999.

3 KINGS, viii.

WHEN Solomon had finished the temple, and furnished it with every requisite both for use and ornament, he prepared for the solemnity of its dedication. To render the ceremony as awful as he could, he published an order for his subjects to attend on the ninth day of the seventh month. All the ancients of Israel, the heads of families, and princes of the tribes obeyed the summons. They advanced to the city of David, on Mount Sion, where the ark of the covenant had been placed by that religious king; the priests respectfully took it up, and the Levites carried the vessels, and all other furniture that had been in the tabernacle of Moses. The king himself walked in procession before the ark, which was carried upon priests' shoulders, and set down in its place in the holy of holies, under the wings of the cherubims. There was nothing in the ark besides the two tables of stone engraven with the ten commandments, which Moses put there on Mount Horeb, when he came out of the land of Egypt. When the priests were out of the sanctuary, the Levites and singing men under the directions of Asaph, Hemen, and Idithun, began to play upon their cymbals and psalteries, and harps, on the east side of the altar, and with them a hundred and twenty priests sounding with trumpets. The air resounded far and near with the loud concerts of voices and instruments, and when they began to sing to words, *Give glory to the Lord, for he is good, for his mercy endureth for ever*, the house of God was filled with a cloud, nor could the priest stand to minister on account of the cloud. Upon which Solomon said, the Lord promised that he would dwell in a cloud; and turning his face towards the people, blessed the whole multitude of Israel, as he stood upon the brazen scaffold which he had set up upon that occasion, in the middle of the temple before the altar of the Lord. Then kneeling down, and lifting up his hands towards heaven in fervent

prayer, he begged the Almighty to shower down his choicest blessings upon the people of Israel, to grant the petitions of those who should come into that temple to adore him, and to let his anger be appeased by the repentance of those who should there confess their sins to him. He earnestly besought the divine goodness, that the people might there find an assured refuge in the day of affliction, a safe defence against the fury of their enemies, and a comfortable resource from every calamity of pestilence and famine; that he would look graciously upon his humble supplicants, and grant every kind of happiness to those who should at any time call upon his name in that holy place. The king had no sooner ended his prayer, than fire came down from heaven, and consumed the holocausts, and the majesty of the Lord filled the temple. The whole assembly fell prostrate upon the ground at the sight, and adored and praised the Lord, *because he is good, and his mercy endureth for ever*. The festivity lasted fourteen days, during which time Solomon offered no fewer than twenty-two thousand oxen, and one hundred and twenty thousand rams, in sacrifice to the living God.

The holy fathers, in their reflections upon Solomon's magnificence on this solemn occasion, remark how incomparably great is the respect due to our Christian churches, wherein resides the very truth of which the Jewish temple had nothing more than the shadow. For let us open the heavens, and look into the heaven of heavens, says St. Chrysostom, we shall find nothing more holy, nothing greater, than what Jesus Christ himself has placed upon our altars.

A.M. 3013.] *Queen of Saba.*—3 KINGS, x. [A.C. 987.

As soon as Solomon had completed and consecrated his temple to Almighty God, he began to build a palace for himself, which he planned and finished in so grand a style, that it became a subject of admiration to the many that flocked to see it. Solomon was in quiet possession of the whole tract of country, which Almighty God had promised to the race of Abraham, and not an enemy was near to disturb his peaceful reign. From distant nations, from all kingdoms of the earth, strangers came to see the works, and to hear the wisdom of a man, who was universally looked upon as the wonder and glory of his age. Of the many foreigners whom fame and curiosity drew to Jerusalem at that time, the queen of Saba was the most distinguished. The accounts she had received of the wonderful king of Israel, were so far above her conception, that she was determined to see whether the reality of his greatness bore any proportion with what report had spread abroad concerning him. With a noble train of attendants, she began her journey from the extremity of the south, and brought him presents worthy of her own and Solomon's magnificence: a hundred and twenty talents of gold, and vast quantities of precious stones and perfumes. She entered the royal city, she viewed the palace and the temple, she stood astonished at the richness and boldness of the architecture; but when she came to hear the wisdom of

the king's discourse, and considered with what depth o. knowledge he reasoned upon every subject, she seemed in a manner transported out of her herself. The dignity of divine worship, the splendour of the court, the number of the king's officers, and the regularity of his family, added much to her surprise: she owned that her expectations had been far surpassed, and that public fame, which so often magnifies, had here fallen far short of the reality. She seemed to envy the happiness of those who were employed in the service of so great a prince, and were near enough to catch the wisdom that dropped from his lips. Being then convinced of what she never could have believed if she had not seen, she took her leave to return into her own country, loaded with royal presents far more precious than those she had brought.

The arrival of the queen of Saba from the south, to view the wonders and to hear the wisdom of king Solomon, is mentioned by our blessed Saviour in his gospel, as a warning, lest she one day rise to condemn us before the judgment seat of Almighty God. She went to hear the wisdom of a man, subject to infirmities and liable to errors like herself, and happy did she pronounce them, who were permitted to approach his person. Christians have God himself for their master; it is Jesus Christ, the increated Wisdom of the Father, whom they hear; they have his unerring word for their rule of life, and the kingdom of heaven for their recompense: inexcusable therefore is their conduct, if in their actions they prefer men to God, the wisdom of the world to that of Jesus Christ, the enjoyment of the earth to the happiness of heaven.

A.M. 3023.] *Fall of Solomon.*—3 KINGS, xi. [A.C. 977.

THE glorious beginnings of Solomon's reign were sullied by a disgraceful end. By a fall still more deplorable than that of his father, he convinces us, that man never can rely with security upon himself; but the more elevated his station is, the more diffident he ought to be of his own abilities. The heart, which for many years had been the temple of the Holy Ghost, began to be most shamefully polluted by the love of women. Solomon, the once cherished favourite of God and man, fell from one abyss into another; bereft of his wisdom, he sunk from the depth of lust into the gulf of idolatry. He married no fewer than a thousand wives; seven hundred of them had the title and rank of queens. Though a plurality of wives was at that time permitted by the law, yet such an excess in the number, especially of idolatrous women, was expressly forbidden. Solomon had chosen to himself wives from Egypt, from the country of Moab and Ammon; and so blind and violent was his passion for them, that at their request he ordered different temples to be erected to their different idols. Astharhe, the goddess of the Sidonians, Camos, the idol of Moab, and Moloch, the idol of Ammon, not only had their temples, but received worship from Solomon himself. A conduct so unaccountably criminal in a wise man, now fifty years of age and upwards, drew upon him God's severest indignation. Almighty God appeared to him, not as he had done twice before, to approve his actions or to grant him favours, but to denounce heavy judgments upon him for his crimes. He told him that his kingdom should be divided, and the greater part of it given to his servants; but that in consideration of his father David, this division should

not take place till after his death. Jeroboam, the son of Nabat, was the servant here pointed at, and Solomon knew it by what had passed between him and the prophet Ahias. That prophet having met with Jeroboam in the field, took his cloak and divided it into twelve parts, of which he bade him take ten, as a mark of the division God was about to make of the twelve tribes of Israel, in punishment of the king's infidelity: Jeroboam was a man of good natural abilities; and entrusted with a public employment under Solomon; but having met with some contradiction, lifted up his hand against the king. After such insolence, he had no clemency to expect from his provoked sovereign, and being pursued by the ministers of justice, saved himself by a precipitate flight into Egypt. Solomon reigned forty years over Israel with great magnificence: he slept with his forefathers in the fifty-ninth year of his age, and was buried in the city of David; leaving the world in doubt, whether his memory be more worthy of praise or censure, whether he died the friend or enemy of his Creator, the object of his love or hatred. The holy Scripture informs us of his sin, but makes no mention of his repentance: whether he repented or not, no one can positively say; some think he did, and that in his book of Ecclesiastes is expressed the sorrow of his heart for having sinned, and the vanity he found in all his sinful pursuits.

Be that as it will, however fatal to himself the fall of Solomon may have been, it cannot fail of being serviceable to those who view it with the eyes of faith. It must inspire a contempt of all the world can give; the greatest affluenc of riches, pomps, and pleasures, cannot satisfy an immortal soul, nor make her happy. Worldly enjoyments never were possessed so abundantly by any man, as by Solomon; and no man ever was so thoroughly acquainted with their vanity and empty promises. Vanity of vanities, is the sentence he has pronounced upon them; all is vanity and affliction of mind, unless it be to love God, and to serve him alone.

A.M. 3029.] *Counsellors of Roboam.* [A.C. 971.

3 KINGS, xii.

SOLOMON, to defray the vast expenses he was at in his buildings and manner of living, had burdened his subjects with heavy taxes. Upon his death, Roboam, his son and successor, received an humble petition from the people, praying for relief. The young king took three days to consider of it, during which time he assembled his council of state to deliberate what answer he should make. The most experienced counsellors, who had been employed by the late king, agreed in opinion, that the way for a prince to establish his power, and to make himself master of his subjects, was to gain their affections by lenient measures in the beginning, and therefore advised Roboam to give a favourable answer to his people upon the subject of their petition. To a prince in the vigour of youth, giddy with his present power, and unconcerned about what might be the consequence, this advice was not welcome. He addressed himself to the young men, who had been brought up with him, and were ready to flatter him with the advice that was agreeable to his own notion. Young and inexperienced in the art of governing, he adopted the false system of his flatterers, and answered the deputies of his people in very imperious language: instead of lessening, he harshly threatened to add still more to their present grievances, and instead of whips to beat them with scorpions. The sacred historian observes, that this imprudent prince was by the secret judgments of God permitted thus to act, and thus to hasten on the execution of what Ahias had foretold to Jeroboam. For Roboam's answer to the deputies was no sooner made public, than the people broke out into an open revolt, and vowed never to submit themselves again to so lawless a master. The prince upon this seemed sensible of the false step he had made, and sent Aduram, one of his principal officers, to appease the tumult before it should rise too high. But the flame of sedition was now kindled: Jeroboam, who was come back from Egypt, had been active in blowing up the coals: Aduram was no sooner seen than stoned to death, and it was but by flight that the king escaped out of their hands. In this ferment the people of all Israel, that is to say, ten of the tribes, withdrew from their allegiance to the house of David, and chose Jeroboam for their king. Roboam fancied that he had strength sufficient to bring them back to their duty, and that by force of arms they might be compelled to acknowledge his authority. With him there remained the tribes of Benjamin and Juda, which last was by far the most considerable. He raised an army of a hundred and eighty thousand men, with an intention to pursue his just rights; but an inspired man, whose name was Simeias, unexpectedly came to him, and on the part of God forbade him to proceed against Jeroboam and his brothren of Israel, because nothing had happened in this revolution of affairs, but as God himself had said.

Thus, through the indiscretion of a young king, began the long and fatal division of the Israelites among themselves; thus, within the narrow limits of a single nation, were erected the two distinct nations of Juda and Israel. In this remarkable epoch of the sacred history, it appears that God disposes of the state of nations as he pleases, and that on him depends the fate of kings no less than that of other men. The most wise of men left his crown to an imprudent son, and the irregularities of Solomon's advanced age were visibly punished by the folly of Roboam's youth. The foolishness of Roboam, in preferring the opinion of his young companions to the sage advice of his old counsellors, bears an exact resemblance with the misfortune of those, who will listen only to such advisers as are either not capable to direct them right, or not honest enough to dissuade them from what is wrong.

A.M. 3030.] *The disobedient Prophet.* [A.C. 970.

3 Kings, xiii.

Jeroboam, seeing himself master of the ten tribes of Israel, adopted a system of politics, which is but too often followed by such Christians as make religion subservient to their interest. The impious king was persuaded, that should he let his subjects go to perform the public duties of religion in the temple of Jerusalem, they would, by degrees, have less respect for him, and perhaps return to the allegiance of their former sovereign; he therefore ordered two golden calves to be made, one of which he set up in Bethel, and the other in Dan, and divine honours to be paid to them, as to the God who had brought them out of Egypt. To them he erected two stately altars, and in the worship of his idols he strove to imitate the form that was observed in honour of the true God. He himself was the grand performer of his superstitious ceremonies. As he was one day standing upon the altar of Bethel, and offering incense to his idol, a prophet from Juda came, and in the name of God thus cried out against the altar: Altar, said he, a child of the house of David, by name Josias, shall be born, and he shall immolate upon thee the priests of the high places, who now burn incense upon thee, and he shall burn men's bones upon thee; and as a testimony of the truth I utter, the altar shall forthwith be rent, and the ashes that are upon it shall be poured out. The altar that instant split asunder, and Josias king of Juda literally fulfilled the prophecy three hundred and fifty years afterwards. Jeroboam, instead of profiting by this miraculous admonition, grew furious, and called upon his guards to take the prophet into custody. In the violence of his rage, he stretched forth his hand against the man of God, and it withered; nor was he able to draw it back again. Disarmed at the stroke, he changed his threats into prayers, and became an humble supplicant for his cure. By the prophet's prayer the king recovered the free use of his hand as miraculously as he had lost it. He acknowledged the favour, and invited his benefactor home to dine with him, which the prophet positively declined, upon the account that God had expressly forbid him either to eat or to drink in that place. The man of God departed homeward, and was soon after overtaken by an old prophet, who dwelt in Bethel. The old prophet having been informed by his sons of what the man of God had done that day in Bethel, immediately resolved to bring him to his house; he therefore went after him, and found him sitting under a tree: he courteously saluted and invited him to dine; the prophet of Juda replied, that the Lord had forbidden him to eat or drink the least thing in that place; upon which the man of Bethel said, I also am a prophet, and have been admonished by an angel of the Lord to follow and to bring thee back to Bethel, that we may there eat and drink together. The prophet of Juda let himself be persuaded; he returned with the other to Bethel, and as they were sitting together at table, the man of Bethel was inspired to reprimand him for his disobedience, and to tell him since he had returned and eat, contrary to the command of God, that his bones should not be buried in the sepulchre of his forefathers. The prophet of Juda rose up and departed: he had not gone far, before a lion met and killed him in the way. The old man, being told of

the accident, went and found the lion standing over the dead body, which he immediately took up, and carried back to Bethel, where he buried it, and ordered his own bones after death to be buried in the same grave. Thus the prophecy was both spoken and fulfilled the same day.

As one sin is oftentimes the punishment of another, St. Gregory thinks that the disobedience into which the prophet of Juda fell, may have been the consequence of some secret vanity he had felt in seeing himself privileged with the gift of miracles. Nothing is so apt to blind the understanding, as a vain conceit of one's self; and that perchance may have misled the prophet first to interpret, and then to break the order he had received. Being deceived by the invitation of a prophet of Bethel, he came to an untimely end; by a violent but passing death, he paid the punishment due to his disobedience, that his soul by suffering might be cleansed from guilt, and be prepared for a life of endless happiness.

JEROBOAM enjoyed little peace in his new acquired kingdom, which was not to be maintained but by hard struggle and perpetual bloodshed. After a troublesome reign of two and twenty years, he finished a wicked life by an unhappy death. His name is never mentioned in holy Scripture but with detestation, on account of his having set up the worship of idols, which was followed by all the kings, his successors in the throne of Israel, till an end was put to that kingdom by the Assyrians. Nadab, a prince equally wicked, succeeded his father, and reigned two years, when he was deprived both of his crown and life by Baasa. Baasa pursued the same violent method to secure the crown, that he had employed to get it: he cut off every branch of Jeroboam's stock, and by that bloody stroke executed the very sentence which the inspired Ahias had some years before pronounced against Jeroboam, in punishment of his idolatry. Having thus fixed his family, as he thought, in the throne of Israel, he declared war against Asa, king of Juda. Asa had lately succeeded his wicked father Ahias, who reigned but three years after the death of his father Roboam. The piety and zeal for religion which distinguished Asa's reign drew down the blessing of God upon his arms, and was the source of many glorious victories, which the armies of Juda gained against their enemies: for he had almost continual war with Israel, and the Israelites were not able to stand against him in the field. Baasa, after a cruel and turbulent reign of twenty-four years, died, and left the crown to his son Ela. This prince began his reign by the murder of Jehu, a holy prophet, who had denounced the same heavy judgment against Baasa's family, as Baasa himself had inflicted upon the family of Jeroboam. Ela reigned no more than two years; for Zambri, who was captain of half the cavalry, formed a conspiracy, and murdered him as he was sitting at table in the governor's house of Thersa, and declared himself king upon the spot. Zambri's treason was no sooner known in the camp, than Amri, who commanded the army, was chosen king by universal consent. Amri refused not the sceptre, which the unexpected favour of the people put into his hands. Being naturally brave, he marched directly against his antagonist, who had shut himself up in the city of Thersa. Zambri finding himself closely besieged by a resolute and active enemy, and seeing the city in danger of being taken, shut himself up in the royal palace, which he set fire to, and perished in the flames seven days after he had traitorously imbrued his hands in the blood of his lawful sovereign.

Zambri died in his sins, says the holy Scripture, and by the tragical end he made, has shown the world how odious a tyrant is both to God and men. This man, who might have been happy, had he been content to move within the bounds in which his fortune first placed him, became unhappy the very moment that the desire of lawless power carried him beyond his sphere. The title and the crown which he had acquired by the murder of his royal master, could not give him peace of mind; tortured with remorse, and hurried away by despair, he condemned himself to the flames, and thus became the self-executioner of a criminal, equally impious against God as he had been cruel to his prince.

A.M. 3092.] *Elias fed by Ravens.* [A.C. 908.
3 KINGS, xvii.

AMRI being peaceably possessed of the kingdom of Israel, bought the mountain of Somor, on which he built a city for his royal residence, and called it Samaria. After a wicked reign of twelve years, he had his son Achab for successor on the throne. This prince having married Jezabel, a daughter of the king of Sidon, brought in the worship of Baal, the Sidonian idol, and became like the very worst of his predecessors in the kingdom of Israel. It was in this king's days that the great Elias appeared, and began to exert the power he had received, of working the most stupendous miracles in support of the true religion. To punish the tribes of Israel for their crimes, which were at that time swelled to an enormous height, and to make them mindful of the God whom they had abandoned, the prophet by his prayers shut up the heavens from giving any rain for three years. This long drought caused a dreadful famine over the land: whilst others felt the punishment due to their sins, the prophet was miraculously supported by the divine hand, which fills every creature with benediction. His place of residence was at first near the torrent Carith, where the ravens brought him bread and meat every morning and evening, and he drank of the

pure stream. The spring being at last dried up, he was directed by Almighty God to go to Sarephta, a town of the Sidonians, where a widow woman would provide him with what was necessary. As he came near the town, he found a poor woman picking up a few sticks; he asked her for something to drink; she went to fetch him a draught of

water, and as she was going on towards her own house, he called after her to bring him also something to eat. She answered him, that a handful of meal and a little oil was all she had for the support of herself and son; that she was going to dress it for them both, that they might eat and die. The holy man comforted the woman in her distress, bade her first go and make him a little cake of the meal and oil she had, and after that to make for herself and son; for that neither the one nor the other should fail, as long as the drought continued. The widow went and did as the prophet told her. Both he and she and her family ate, and from that day the pot of meal did not waste, nor was the oil diminished. She was happy, though of an idolatrous country, to entertain a prophet of the living God under her roof, and by rendering him a service which was refused him in the land of Israel, she prefigured the future faith of the Gentiles succeeding the incredulity of the Jews. But the death of her only son happening soon after, changed her joy into sorrow. The prophet was moved at her misfortune, and having a faith in God equal to his compassion for the distressed mother, undertook to raise the child to life again. He took the breathless corpse out of the widow's arms, carried it to his room, laid it upon his bed, and stretched and measured himself upon the child three times, and cried to the Lord, and said, O Lord my God, let the soul of this child, I beseech thee, return into his body. The Lord heard the voice of Elias; the child revived; Elias took him down to his mother, and said, Behold thy son liveth.

In this instance, Elias is a bright example of that benevolent charity which all good men owe and pay to one another. To condole with our suffering brethren, to grieve with the afflicted, to comfort the distressed, to stoop to their relief, to become little with the little, and weak with the weak, as far as can be done without yielding to sin, is the exercise of that Christian charity which teaches us to love our neighbour as ourselves. To become all to all, that he might gain all to

Christ, was the practice of St. Paul, and still is the study of those holy men, who, according to their station in life, are zealous to promote the service and glory of their Creator.

A.M. 3096.] *Sacrifice of Elias.* [A.C. 904.

3 KINGS, xviii.

WHILE the prophet Elias lay safe in his retreat under the widow's roof at Sarephta, Achab and Jezabel made diligent search after him, with a design of putting him to death, as the cause of the heavy disasters that distressed the nation; but not being able to discover where he was, they wreaked their vengeance upon the priests of the Lord, and a dreadful persecution was commenced against them. Achab at that time had for the intendant of his palace, a man of extraordinary virtue, called Abdias, who, to screen as many as he could from the fury of their persecutors, had concealed no fewer than a hundred prophets in caves, where he privately supplied them with all the necessaries of life. This holy

man, as he was ranging the country, to see if he could find any grass for his horses and mules, met Elias, who by divine inspiration had left his retreat. The prophet bade him go and tell his master that Elias was there. Abdias was afraid of undertaking the commission, being in doubt whether the prophet might not fly off in the mean time, and thereby expose him to the king's displeasure. Elias assured him by the Lord of hosts, that his resolution was to see the king that day. Abdias therefore informed Achab of it, and Achab

N

came to meet Elias. As soon as he saw him, he with a stern severity exclaimed, Art thou he who troublest Israel? To whom Elias, with a spirit of zeal and fortitude not to be daunted by threats, nor silenced by contempt, answered, It is not I who trouble Israel: it is you, O prince; it is the house of your father, who have left the true God, and sacrificed to Baal. Nevertheless, call together the people of Israel, continued he, send for the prophets of Baal, and let them meet me upon Mount Carmel. Achab, in compliance with his request, sent to the children of Israel, and gathered together the prophets upon the mountain. Elias came according to agreement, and addressed himself to the Israelites in the following manner: How long will you be divided in your choice, O men of Israel? How long will you hang in suspense between the two? If the Lord be God, acknowledge him; but if Baal, then follow him. Of the prophets of the Lord, I am here the only one: and behold of the prophets of Baal there are four hundred and fifty. Let two bullocks be given us; let them take one, and me the other; let them dress theirs, and lay it upon the altar; I will do the same with mine: but let no fire be put under either. We will each in our turn call upon the God whom we respectively adore, and he who shall answer by sending down fire from heaven to consume the holocaust, shall be acknowledged for the true and only God. The people with one accord approved of the proposal. The prophets of Baal began in the first place to prepare their victim; they laid it upon the altar, and called upon Baal from morning to mid-day, but received no answer. You called not loud enough, said Elias to them; Baal does not hear you: strain your voices higher, your god is perhaps asleep, or on a journey, or talking, or at an inn. Piqued at the prophet's raillery, they exerted themselves anew, they bawled aloud, they leaped over the altar, they cut themselves with knives and lancets, but could get no answer from Baal. The hour of mid-day was elapsed; Elias called the people to him, and bade them repair the old stone altar of the Lord, which had been once there, but was then broken down; he drew a gutter round it, piled up the wood in order, and laid his disjointed victim on the top. This done, he ordered water to be brought and poured upon the pile, till it was thoroughly soaked, and the gutter filled with the running stream. The hour appointed for the sacrifice being come, the prophet in a solemn prayer addressed himself to the God of Abraham, Isaac, and Jacob, that he would manifest his glory to the children of Israel, and convince them that he was the Lord their God. He had no sooner spoke than the fire of the Lord fell, and consumed not only the holocaust, but

the whole pile, and the very stones of the altar. The evidence of the miracle answering exactly to the prophet's proposal, left no room for any doubt or reply: the people fell flat upon the ground, and confessed that the Lord was the only God. Then seize upon the prophets of Baal, cried out Elias, and let not one escape; his order was obeyed, and the impostors suffered immediate death, as their crimes deserved. The prophet then prayed to God a second time, that he would open the heavens, and let his showers fall again upon the earth. The clouds, as he prayed, began to gather, and scarce had the people time to reach the town of Jezrahel, before a copious fall of rain ensued.

This story of Elias, say the holy fathers, displayed the force of truth in the strongest colours, and marks out the influence it has upon the minds of men. Borne up by that confidence which his conscience gave him, Elias stood firm in his duty to God, though alone and surrounded by a whole nation of his enemies. In his person we see verified the saying of St. Jerome, that truth for its support wants but few defenders; no number of opponents can either hurt or shake it.

A.M. 3097.] *Flight of Elias.*—3 Kings, xix. [A.C. 903.

The wicked Jezabel, being told by Achab, how her prophets had been put to death, sent to let Elias know, that before the end of four and twenty-hours, he should experience the same fate. The holy prophet trembled at the threat, and fled out of the territories of Israel to Bersabee of Juda. There he dismissed his servant, and went forward one day's journey into the desert. By this sudden vicissitude of courage and timidity in so great a prophet, we see, says St. Gregory, how inconstant man is of himself amidst the various incidents of life, and how soon, after the most heroic actions, he falls back, if not strengthened from above, into his natural state of despondency and weakness. Elias having escaped into the lonely desert, spent with fatigue, and oppressed with anguish of mind, sat himself down under a juniper-tree, and begged of Almighty God to take him out of life. He laid himself down to sleep upon the ground, and an angel of the Lord appeared and woke him, saying, Arise and eat. He

opened his eyes, and saw a loaf and a pitcher of water placed near his head: he ate and drank, and composed himself to sleep again. The angel came a second time, and bade him eat again, because he had a great way to go. The prophet rose up, and being strengthened with that miraculous bread, which, by the commentators of Holy Writ, is considered as an emblem of the blessed Eucharist, which nourishes our souls with spiritual life during our pilgrimage on earth, he continued his journey for forty days and forty nights together, till he came to the mountain of Horeb, where he concealed himself in a cave. There he received an order from Almighty God to repair back through the desert to Damascus, where he should anoint Hazael, king of Syria; he was also ordered to anoint Jehu to be king of Israel, and Eliseus to be prophet. In obedience to this order, Elias left the mountains of Horeb, and in his way towards Damascus, found Eliseus ploughing with twelve yoke of oxen in a field. He spread his mantle over him as he had been commanded, and made him a prophet. Eliseus feeling himself changed, as it were into another man, left the oxen and ran after Elias, saying, Let me only go, and take my last farewell of my father and mother at home, and I will follow thee. Elias said, Go, and return back, for that which was my part, I have done to thee. Eliseus returned, took a yoke of the oxen he was ploughing with, invited the people to partake with him in the feast, then rose up and professed himself the follower and inseparable disciple of Elias.

Eliseus, says St. Ambrose, left his father to follow Elias, from whom he experienced every kindness, and every benefit of a father's love. Being the studious imitator of his master's virtues, he became his heir and successor in the gift of prophecy and miracles. Thus in the Old Testament, as well as in the New, we have the brightest patterns of perfection formed in the school of those excellent masters, who by the lustre of their virtues have drawn others to copy their example. In the law of grace we have this advantage above those of the ancient testament, that we see the path of virtue traced out to us, not only by the men of God, but also by a God-man. Jesus Christ, in the actions he performed, as St. Austin remarks, so tempered the actions of his divine and human nature together, as to place the imitation of his virtues within the reach of our weak capacities. We profess ourselves his followers, and the imitators of his virtues, and great at the last day must be our confusion before the whole world, if we shall appear to have acted in contradiction with ourselves, and be found destitute of those ornaments of humility, self-denial, and patience, which are essential to the character of a Christian.

A.M. 3105.] *Piety of King Josaphat.* [A.C. 895.
2 CHRON. xvii.

WHILST the wicked Achab reigned in the kingdom of Israel, and Jezabel his wife concurred with him in every excess of impiety, the crown of Juda had passed from Asa to his son Josaphat. Asa in his general conduct had been a religious prince, and distinguished himself by many heroic actions: he banished the worship of idols, built cities, and restored good order among his subjects. During his reign, Zara the Ethiopian invaded the territories of Judea, with a million of men; Asa collected his troops, and trusting in the hand of God more than in the force of his arms, drove the invaders back with great confusion and a total overthrow of their vast army. But being afterwards attacked by Baasa, king of Israel, he did not show the like fortitude. Unmindful of the power which had rescued him from the hands of the Ethiopians and Lybians, he made an alliance with the king of Syria. Almighty God was displeased with his conduct, and sent the prophet Hanani to tell him, that since he had placed his confidence in the king of Syria, and not in the Lord his God, wars from that day should arise against him. The truth was disagreeable to a man who had acted contrary to it: Asa, notwithstanding his piety, ordered the prophet to be imprisoned, and many of his subjects who had displeased him, to be put to death. The Scripture moreover blames him, when he was sick, for relying more on the skill of physicians, than on the help of God's hand. Thus, after having merited for many years the character of a just and pious prince, he finished his reign by a mixture of actions that were either injurious to God or cruel to his subjects. After a reign of one and forty years, he was succeeded by his son Josaphat, a prince not less distinguished for his religious than for his kingly virtues. He pursued the path that David had traced out to him. His great zeal for religion endeared him to Almighty God, and was the source of boundless blessings, that flowed in both upon himself and his people. Not satisfied with the bare orders that his father had given for no more sacrifices to be made to Baal, he struck at the very root of the evil, and demolished the groves and places of superstitious worship, that had been made upon the tops of mountains. And as ignorance is commonly the cause of abuse in religious matters, he dispersed through the towns of his dominions virtuous priests and Levites, who should explain the law to his subjects, and teach the observance of it. With this attention to the duties of religion, Josaphat joined an unwearied application to promote the welfare of his people, and to provide for the security of his kingdom against the attacks of foreign powers. In the art of governing he surpassed all his predecessors, and by that means made himself not only respected, but feared by the neighbouring princes. Constant success attended his arms, whenever he was compelled to turn them against the enemies of his country. In the person of this prince, God seems to show that he takes a pleasure in heaping honours and glory upon them, who are faithful in their duty of honour and respect to him. For God honours those who honour him, and covers with contempt those who contemn him.

A.M. 3107.] *Death of Achab.* [A.C. 893.
3 KINGS, xxi., xxii.

THE sins of Achab and Jezabel were now rising to their full height: the murder of the innocent Naboth completed their just measure. This inoffensive man, of the town of Jezrahel, was possessed of a vineyard, which he had inherited from his ancestors, but which, unfortunately for him, lay adjoining to the king's palace. Achab was desirous of converting it into a garden, and offered either to purchase or exchange it for something better. But Naboth was particularly fond of a spot which he had inherited from his forefathers, and would by no means consent to part with it. Naboth's refusal gave the king great uneasiness; insomuch that in a fit of fretful indignation he threw himself upon his bed, and refused to eat. Jezabel, observing the violent agitation of his mind, desired to know the cause, and upon telling her what it was, scornfully replied, Well dost thou reign, and great is thy sway in the kingdom of Israel, if thy power extends not to Naboth's vineyard: I will procure it for thee. She therefore wrote a letter in the name of Achab, sealed it with his signet, and sent it to the ancients and chief men of Jezrahel, with orders that they should suborn two false witnesses, to prove that Naboth had spoken blasphemy against God, and treason against the king. The order was no sooner received than executed. Naboth was called upon to clear himself of a crime which he had never thought of: it was in vain to plead; the witnesses were prepared to swear, as they had been directed: Naboth was declared guilty, condemned, and stoned the same day. Jezabel in triumph ran to acquaint the king, that he might go and take peaceable possession of Naboth's vineyard, for that Naboth was dead. Achab immediately hastened to the spot: Elias, by the command of God, met and accosted him

in these words: Thou hast slain Naboth, thou hast possessed thyself of his vineyard: but in the very place where the dogs have licked the blood of Naboth, they shall lick thy blood also; thy race, like that of Jeroboam and Baasa, shall be rooted out, and Jezabel shall be devoured by dogs in the field of Jezrahel. Achab engaged soon after in a war against the Syrians, and thereby hastened his destruction. Josaphat, who had married his son to Athalia, one of Achab's daughters, accompanied him to battle. This religious prince being unwilling to engage in an enterprise of that importance without consulting God, Achab ordered four hundred of his prophets to attend, who unanimously agreed in the answer that they knew would flatter their master. But this did not satisfy the king of Juda; he desired to know, if no prophet of the Lord was to be found. Achab answered there was one; but one whom he could not hear, because he never promised him any thing that was good. Josaphat begged he might see and hear what he had to say. The prophet was then sent for: it was the good Micheas, who being uninstructed in the art of evil flattery, contradicted every thing that the false prophets had said, and foretold, that the unsuccessful war should end in Achab's death. Achab ordered him to be carried off immediately to prison, to be there fed with the bread of affliction and water of distress, till his return in peace. If thou return in peace, replied the prophet, the Lord hath not spoken by me. The king was struck at the prophet's words, and in consequence put off the ensigns of royalty, not to expose himself in the field more than was necessary; for he knew the king of Syria's resentment was levelled principally against him; and in effect orders were given to the Syrian troops to direct their chief attacks against the king of Israel's person. The two armies advanced to give each other battle. The princely equipage which distinguished Josaphat alone above the rest, drew the whole weight of the battle that way, and he actually had fallen by the sword of the Syrians, if he had not declared aloud who he was. To such extremity of danger was a well-meaning prince exposed, in consequence of the alliance which he had made with a wicked one. By a random shot from a Syrian bow, Achab was mortally wounded in his chariot; a stream of blood gushed from the wound; he ordered his charioteer to drive him out of the field of battle, and he died at night. His chariot was drawn to the pool of Samaria, where it was washed, and the dogs licked up his blood, as the Lord had spoken. So inevitable is the stroke that God has once decreed against the crimes of men! The most potent monarchs, when their time is come, are as little able to resist, as the least of their subjects: in the hour of their prosperity they may thunder at others, says St. Austin, but the God of heaven, when he pleases, hurls down the vengeance which is due to their impiety; and then it is, that they who, according to the words of holy Scripture, appeared like gods upon the earth, are no more than dust and ashes before the Lord.

A M. 3108.] *Elias taken up to Heaven.* [A.C. 892.

4 Kings, ii.

Achab being slain in the manner we have related, was succeeded on the throne by his son Ochozias. This prince, who inherited both his parents' vices, and trod in their footsteps, lost his life in the second year of his reign by an accidental fall from a window. Being in great danger from the bruise he received, he sent to consult Beelzebub, the god of Accaron, whether he were to live or die. It was an insult the most abominable to the God of Israel, that a king of the Jewish nation should have recourse in his distress to the prince of darkness. Elias, on the part of God, met the king's messengers, and told them that Ochozias should not rise from the bed on which he lay, and that since he had sent to consult Beelzebub, as if there were no God in Israel, he should most certainly die. The messengers returned, and gave an account to the king of the man they had seen, and of the things he had said. By the description of his dress and person, Ochozias knew it to be Elias, and instantly ordered a captain with a company of fifty men to go and apprehend him. The captain went up to him, as he was sitting upon the top of a hill, and imperiously commanded him to come down to the king. Elias answered, If I be a man of God, let fire come down from heaven and consume thee with thy men: and it did so. The king sent another company, composed of an equal number of men, to the holy prophet. The captain delivered his orders with the same disrespect as the former, and perished by the same fate. The captain of a third company being sent upon the same errand, proceeded more cautiously: he presumed not to approach so near to the man of God; but stood at an awful distance, and in the most respectful terms begged, that he would condescend to return with him to the king. The holy prophet complied with the officer's request, and being admitted into the king's presence, repeated to him the fatal sentence of death, which happened soon after. This is the last public action that is related of Elias. The time appointed for his translation from earth to heaven was at hand: his disciple Eliseus had a knowledge of it, and was determined not to let him out of his sight. Elias tried three different times to retire from him, as if he wanted to be alone, and Eliseus each time declared that he would not leave him. They came to the banks of the Jordan: Elias smote the waters with his cloak, and the divided stream opened them a passage to the other side. Being gone over, Elias bade his disciple ask some favour of him before they parted. Eliseus asked him for his two-fold spirit of prophecy and miracles. That is a thing not easily to be granted, replied Elias; nevertheless, if you see me as I ascend towards the heavens, you shall obtain it. They went on walking and discoursing together, when, behold! a fiery chariot and fiery horses on a sudden parted them asunder; Elias slipt into the chariot, and was carried up in a whirlwind

towards heaven, and Eliseus saw him. As he mounted, hr let fall his mantle, as his last and only legacy to his deas disciple, who stood looking and calling after him. Eliseu, took up the mantle of Elias with respect, and received it, says St. Chrysostom, as a precious armour, that was to cover him, as it had covered his master, against the attacks of his powerful adversaries. Vested with a coarse and homely cloak, he bore the badge of that Christian poverty of spirit which is a sure fence to those who possess it, against the alluring temptations of a wicked world. This humble poverty of spirit is the source from whence the true disciples of Jesus Christ draw the greatest spiritual blessings; with this they live content, and envy not the rich their pomps and shining vanities.

A.M. 3108.] *First Miracles of Eliseus.* [A.C. 892.
4 Kings, ii.

Eliseus began immediately after the miraculous translation of Elias, to give convincing proofs that he was fully possessed of the gift he had asked for. The first exertion of his power was upon the waters of the Jordan. He had seen his master divide the stream as they came along, and in his return expected to do the same. He struck the waters with the mantle of Elias, which he had in his hand, but the waters did not divide. His faith was not dejected; he struck the river a second time, and with an animated confidence exclaimed, Where is now the God of Elias? The waters, as though they had been sensible of the prophet's power, instantly divided hither and thither, and the prophet passed over on dry ground between them. Some of the inhabitants of Jericho, who stood over against him, saw the wonder he had wrought, and being thereby convinced that the spirit of Elias was given to Eliseus, they advanced to meet him, and received him with a religious respect. He remained some days in the city, during which time the citizens represented to him, that notwithstanding their delightful situation, the waters of Jericho were very bad, and their soil barren, and therefore begged that he would make use of his miraculous power in their favour. The prophet listened to this request: he bade them bring him a new vessel with some salt, which being brought, he went out and cast the salt into the spring which supplied the town with water, assuring them, that God would henceforward heal both the unwholesomeness of the waters and the barrenness of the soil. The effect followed the prophet's promise. The efficacy of his words, says St. Ambrose, acted not only upon the superficial stream that flowed along the ground, it also penetrated into the hidden channels, healed the very source, and communicated the blessing of life to future generations. For by rendering the waters wholesome, Eliseus preserved the lives of thousands, who became the fathers of a posterity which would, otherwise, have never sprung to light. This, according to the same holy father, was a figure of that wonderful change which Jesus Christ has since effected in the morals and belief of men throughout the world. Into the midst of nations tainted with the corruption of sin, he has sent his apostles, whom he calls the salt of the earth, to heal them of their past sterility, and to make them fertile in good works. This miracle of Eliseus, which was so salutary to the town of Jericho, was followed by another which shows him to have been animated with the very spirit of Elias. In his way to Bethel, one of the seats of Jeroboam's calf-worship, he met with some boys of the town, who, perceiving him to be bald, began to insult and impudently miscall him. Eliseus looked back, and denounced the wrath of God upon them. He had scarcely spoken the words, when, behold! two bears came out of the neighbouring forest, and destroyed two and forty of the wicked boys.

We may with reason say on this occasion, what St. Austin said on another; that the wrath of Eliseus was a prophetic wrath, which even then marked out the misfortune of those untoward children of the church, who wickedly laugh and mock at the cross of Christ. There are many such, says the holy doctor; and though we see not the bears tearing their bodies into pieces, yet we know, that more deplorable is the secret havoc made in their souls by merciless devils, to whom they make themselves a prey, on account of the mockery and insults that they offer to Jesus Christ, by their loose maxims and immoral lives.

A.M. 3109.] *Other Miracles of Eliseus.* [A.C. 891.
4 Kings, iii., iv.

Ochozias, the king of Israel, was succeeded by Joram, his second brother, a wicked prince, though in a less degree than his parents Achab and Jezabel. For although he took down the statues of Baal which his father had set up, yet he still retained Jeroboam's worship of the golden calves. Having declared war against the Moabites, for refusing him the annual tribute which they had paid to his predecessors, he entreated the king of Juda to aid him with his troops. Josaphat, on account of the friendship that subsisted between them, headed an army to his assistance, and the king of Edom joined them in the expedition. They directed their route round the Dead Sea, through the dry and barren desert of Idumea: no enemy appeared: they marched on for seven days without any opposition, when the army began to suffer for want of water. It was a distressing situation; the king of Israel dreaded the worst of consequences, and fancied nothing could prevent their falling into the hands of Moab. Josaphat inquired if no prophet of the Lord was there to pray for them, and was told of Eliseus, who poured water upon the hands of Elias. The word of the Lord is with him, said Josaphat: the three kings went immediately to him, and Joram was the first to request his mediation in their favour. The request of a prince whose superstition led him, on every other occasion, to consult the prophets of Jeroboam, was not likely to obtain any extraordinary blessing from the God of Abraham. Go to the prophets of thy father and mother, said Eliseus to him: what have I to do with thee? Were it not for the respect I have for Josaphat, the king of Juda, I should not have regarded thee, nor hearkened to thy request: but bring me hither a musician. A musician came, and as he began to play, the prophet grew inspired. Make the channel full of ditches, said he, for it shall be filled with water that you may drink: the Lord will moreover deliver Moab into your hands. Next morning a copious stream, without wind or rain, poured itself along the desert, and the country flowed with water. The Moabites being informed that three kings were upon their march through the desert to invade them, had hastily drawn their troops together, and stood upon the borders of their country ready to receive them The rising sun spread its blushing rays upon the surface of the new stream, which the Moabites perceiving, and fancying to be blood, concluded that the kings had disagreed among themselves, and turned their swords against one another. Full of that notion, they confusedly hurried on to collect the spoils of a victory, as they thought, already gained to their hand. They advanced to the very camp of Israel. The Israelites received them sword in hand, unexpectedly attacked and defeated the whole army. Elated with their good fortune, they vigorously pursued their victory, stormed the enemy's cities, and laid waste the country.

Eliseus did not confine his miraculous power to those circumstances only, where kings and armies were to be saved from ruin; he made the poor the objects of his charity, and interfered for the relief of private families. A poor widow being oppressed with debt, and threatened by her creditor with the seizure of her two children, applied for relief to the holy prophet. The prophet asked her what she had left, and she answering, nothing but a little oil, he bade her borrow all the empty vessels she could find among her neighbours, and to fill them with her oil, which should never cease to run

as long as she had an empty vessel to receive it. The effect answered her wishes: the oil was multiplied sufficiently to satisfy her creditor, and still enough remained for her own and children's use.

This miracle, says St. Gregory, marked the plentifulness of divine grace, which the Holy Ghost has since diffused upon the church of Christ. It is our duty, says St. Bernard, to pray daily for a share of this holy oil; but if we would choose to receive any considerable portion of it, we should be careful to keep our hearts void of all sensual and terrene affections; for the unction of the divine Spirit replenishes those vessels only which it finds empty. Vain is the thought and idle is the attempt, to unite God and the world, the spirit and the flesh together; they both war against one another. No one can at the same time run after the pleasures of the earth, and taste of the sweets of heaven.

A.M. 3110.] *Naaman healed of his Leprosy.* [A.C. 890.
4 Kings, v.

Eliseus, in the different excursions that he made through the country, often passed by the town of Sunam, where a virtuous woman had, by her husband's consent, furnished a little room for his use, and gave him a friendly welcome as often as he came. In return for these charitable services, the prophet bade his servant ask her if he could procure her any favour from the king. She answered, none. What then can I do for her? replied the man of God. Do not ask, said Giezi, for she hath no son. She shall have a son, answered Eliseus, and shall conceive this very day. The event verified the prediction. The mother was happy in her son, till his untimely death made her more disconsolate, than if she had never known what it was to be a mother. She laid the breathless boy upon Eliseus's bed, and hastened to Mount Carmel, his usual place of residence, to relate her misfortune, and open the anguish of her mind to the holy man. Eliseus sympathised with her in her sorrows, comforted her with hopes, and directed his man Giezi to go with his staff, and raise the child to life. Giezi had not the faith of his master, nor the virtues requisite for so great a work. He laid the prophet's staff, as he had been directed, upon the child's face, but the child did not rise. The prophet therefore went in person to the woman's house; he stretched himself, in imitation of Elias, at full length upon the body of the child; he prayed; he called life into him that was dead, and restored him to his mother. The power of working great miracles accompanied Eliseus wherever he went, and acquired him a great name, not only amongst the Jews, but likewise amongst foreign nations. Naaman, the great favourite of the king of Syria, and the general of his armies, was infected with an inveterate leprosy: various prescriptions for his cure had been tried, to no purpose. Fortunately for him, he had in his family a Jewish girl, who often signified to his wife, her mistress, that she was sure the general would recover his health, if he would only go to the wonderful prophet in the land of Israel. Naaman followed the advice, and obtained letters from his royal master to Joram the king of Israel. Joram received the letters, and finding in them, that the king of Syria requested the cure of his servant Naaman, he began to rend his garments, and to ask, whom the Syrian took him for; was it for a god, who had the power of healing leprosies? Eliseus had intelligence of the matter, and privately desired Joram to send the general to him, that he might know there was a prophet in Israel. Naaman therefore, with a train of attendants, came to the prophet's gate. The prophet, without so much as going out to see or salute him, sent his servant to tell him, that to be healed, he must go and wash himself seven times in the river Jordan. Naaman, who had expected to see the prophet come and invoke the name of the Lord his God, and heal him by touching the affected part, was offended at the message, and in a rage turned his chariot to return into Syria; upon which his attendants began to remonstrate, that since the prophet had promised him his cure upon so easy a condition, as was that of washing himself in the Jordan, he ought certainly to comply. The general could not disapprove of so reasonable a remonstrance: he went to the Jordan, washed himself seven

times in the stream, and his flesh became as clean as that of a little child. Cleansed from his leprosy, he returned with all his train to Eliseus, and made him an offer of the rich presents which he had brought, but which the prophet would not receive. Giezi was a stranger to such generous principles: the self-interested servant followed Naaman as he went away, and by a lie, unknown as he imagined to his master, obtained from him the value of two talents of silver. Eliseus, who had the gift of knowing absent things, as though they had passed before his eyes, called his servant to a severe account for what he had done, and told him that as he had shared of Naaman's money, he should also share in his disorder. Giezi was that instant covered with a leprosy.

Naaman's cure, says St. Ambrose, is an emblem of the grace by which the new-born Christian is purified from the internal leprosy of sin in the waters of baptism. Naaman had the happiness not only to recover his corporal health, but what is infinitely more valuable, to partake also of the knowledge of salvation, and become a zealous adorer of the true God. Eliseus would accept of none of the precious gifts he offered him, and thereby sets an example of that amiable disinterestedness, which ought to animate every Christian in the offers of charity towards his neighbour: he gave gratis, what he had gratis received. The just severity he showed in punishing the covetousness of his servant, is a warning for all masters and persons in authority to be upon their guard, lest by suffering or conniving at the sins committed by their servants and dependants, they make themselves also partakers of their guilt.

A.M. 3116.] *Siege of Samaria.*—4 Kings, vi. [A.C. 884.

Eliseus had requested and obtained the twofold gift of prophecy and miracles; he shone both in the one and the other. In a war between the kings of Israel and Syria, the Syrians seem to have relied more upon art than upon force. Frequent ambushes were laid, in which the king of Israel must have been surprised, if Eliseus, by the supernatural knowledge he had of things, had not given him timely notice. The king of Syria, perceiving that his schemes were constantly discovered to his enemy, undoubtedly concluded that he had some traitor near him. But being assured that Eliseus was the man who defeated all his stratagems, he detached a body of his troops to take him. Eliseus was then at Dotham; the Syrians invested it by night, which the prophet's servant perceiving when he rose in the morning, gave himself and master up for lost. The holy prophet bade him not fear: he assured him that there was a more numerous and more powerful host at hand ready to protect them, and by his prayers obtained of God, to let his servant see the celestial army that stood arrayed for their defence upon the mountain.

The same prayer which opened the servant's eyes, shut those of the Syrians. Almighty God, at his request, struck them with blindness; Eliseus went out to meet them as they advanced, and told them that they had mistaken their way, and were come to the wrong city; that if they would follow him, he would conduct them to the place, and to the man they wanted. They agreed to follow him, for they saw not where they were; and he led them straight to Samaria. When he had them in the middle of the town, he prayed that their eyes might be then opened, and discover to them the situation they were in. Joram was inclined to put them to the sword; but the prophet representing to him, that he had no right to use such violence against men who had not been taken according to the rules of war, he consented to let them have a refreshment of meat and drink, and to be sent back to their master. This act of generosity did not disarm the malice of the Syrian king. Being implacable in his animosity against the Israelites, he drew his troops together, and laid siege to Samaria. By the length and closeness of the siege, the Samaritans were reduced to such extremities, that they ate of the most disgustful things, not to perish by famine! an ass's head and a certain measure of pigeon's dung, was sold at an exorbitant price: the common provisions of life could not be had for money. Then it was that happened the melancholy story of a woman, who having killed and feasted upon her own child, came to throw herself at the king's feet, demanding justice against her neighbour. The king desired to know the subject of her complaint. A neighbouring woman and myself, said she, being forced by necessity, agreed to kill and eat our own children. We began with mine; we boiled my son, and eat him: she promised to produce hers the next day, but now refuses to perform her promise, and has concealed him. Joram rent his garments through grief at the sad relation: racked with despair at the sight of the evils, for which there appeared no help, he put on a rough hair-cloth next his skin; he mortified his flesh, but turned not his heart from sin: void of the humble sentiments of a contrite heart, he directed his spleen against the holy prophet Eliseus, whom he made answerable for the distresses of Samaria, and therefore commanded one of his officers to go and strike off his head.

Such are the dismal effects of a fretful and impatient pride in a man who permits himself to be once cast down by immoderate affliction. Joram was distressed by his misfortunes, but not humbled; diffident of the divine goodness, he abandoned himself to despair, and sent an assassin to kill the prophet, who by his sanctity prorogued the fall of Samaria. Christians who balance the evils of the present life in the scale of divine faith, make a very different use of the afflictions they meet with; because whatever pain they suffer, they reflect that their sufferings are still less than their sins deserve. Trained to trials in the school of Christ, they humble themselves under the powerful hand of God, whom they are taught to consider, not as a judge delighting in the punishment of his enemies, but as a tender father wishing to reclaim his children from sin; and therefore patiently submit to the chastising rod, because they know he chastises whom he loves, and only strikes because he loves.

A.M. 3116.] *Predictions of Eliseus.* [A.C. 884.

4 KINGS, vii.

ELISEUS, by the spirit of God, knew the orders that Joram had given to take away his life. He was sitting with the ancients in his own house; he ordered the door to be shut against the king's messenger that might come, for he also knew that the king himself would quickly follow. In effect the king came, and as he made his complaint of the extreme distress to which Samaria was then reduced, the prophet consoled him with the promise of a speedy relief: At this time to-morrow, said he, a bushel of meal within the gate of Samaria shall be had for a stater, that is, for less than half a crown. Upon which one of the chief courtiers said that could not possibly be, though the Lord should make flood-gates in heaven: Nevertheless thou shalt see it with thine own eyes, replied the prophet, and yet shall not taste thereof. The following night an alarm was given in the Syrian camp, that an enemy was in full march to attack them. Their fears made them fancy that they actually heard the clash of arms, and the sound of chariots rushing to war: in the hurry of their fright, they concluded it to be an army of auxiliaries that the king of Israel had taken into his service, and ran pell-mell out of their tents, being only solicitous to escape with their lives through the dark. The Israelites remained pent up within their walls, ignorant of this confusion amongst their enemies. But four leprous men, who resided near the gate, seeing no prospect of an end being put to the siege, thought they had better trust themselves to the enemy's mercy, than remain to perish there by famine. They went over to the Syrian camp, and to their great surprise found it abandoned. Their first concern was to satisfy the rage of hunger; for they saw themselves in the midst of plenty, and not an enemy near to molest them. When they had satisfied their craving appetite, they ranged from tent to tent, and began to make a collection of the gold and silver spoils that tempted them on every side. They then spoke to one another upon this unaccountable departure of the enemy, and concluded that it would be looked upon as an unpardonable crime in them, not to inform the distressed citizens of these good tidings before morning: they therefore ran back to the town-gate, and informed the guard of the discovery they had made. Joram suspected some stratagem, and ordered his men to keep close within the walls, till he had learned what was become of the enemy. He had five horses still left: he ordered two of them to be mounted and sent to reconnoitre. By the quantities of plate and precious raiment that lined the high-ways, the flying Syrians were traced as far as the river Jordan; which being told in Samaria at the return of the two spies, the citizens poured out in crowds to the camp, from whence they carried off such heaps of riches and provisions, that at the very hour foretold by Eliseus the day before, a bushel of meal was sold for a stater in the gate of Samaria: and to verify the second part of the prediction, the incredulous courtier who had laughed at the prophet's promise, being stationed at the town-gate by order of the king, was trodden to death by the throng: he lived long enough to see, but not to taste of the promised plenty.

It is impossible, says St. Ambrose, not to adore God in the wonders he performs. The whole extent of futurity is always present to his view, and to his faithful servants he discovers as much of it as is conducive to his adorable ends. He miraculously interposed his divine power in favour of a city, which he set free at the very time that its destruction was thought to be inevitable. He cast a sudden panic into the insulting Syrians, he scattered their numerous army like dust before the wind, and four discarded lepers were the messengers of

Samaria's delivery. Amidst the joyful transports of a people so unexpectedly snatched from ruin, only one man was hurt: a great one of the world was trampled under foot by the vulgar crowd; a dishonourable death was the punishment of his disrespect to God's holy prophet. For God beholds the disrespect which is shown to the ministers of his holy word, as shown to himself; he links their honour and his own together: whoever despises them, despises him.

A.M. 3120.] *Jezabel devoured by Dogs.* [A.C. 880.
4 Kings, ix.

During these transactions in the kingdom of Israel, Josaphat had been succeeded in the crown of Juda by his son Joram. This unhappy prince inherited no share of his father's virtues; for in wickedness he resembled the kings of Israel, because, says the sacred text, he had for his wife a daughter of Achab. He murdered his brothers, and introduced the worship of Baal amongst his subjects. The punishment of these crimes was the loss of Edom, which revolted and became independent of the crown of Juda. He was likewise struck with a long and painful illness, which put an end to his short and miserable reign. His son Ochozias succeeded him both in crown and vices. This young king maintained the close friendship and alliance that his father had always observed with the king of Israel, whom he aided and accompanied in the war he had upon his hands against the Syrians. The time that the Lord had fixed for the utter extirpation of Achab's race, as Elias had foretold, was at hand. The fasting and the haircloth in which that wicked prince had humbled himself, when the prophet forewarned him of his doom, had moved Almighty God, as the text expresses, to put off the full completion of his punishment to the days of his son Joram. Those days were now come, and the prophet's sentence against Jezabel was carried into execution. Joram had received a dangerous wound in battle, and was carried to the town of Jezrahel to be cured: his friend and nephew Ochozias, the king of Juda, went to see him. In the mean time while Jehu, who was an officer in the army, and had already been anointed king of Israel, being as impatient of delay as he was ambitious of a crown, and being moreover encouraged by the officers of the army, resolved upon a stroke that should put him in immediate possession of the throne he had in view. He marched off with a troop of soldiers towards the town of Jezrahel. The sentinel at his approach gave notice that an army was in sight. Joram sent out two different messengers, one after the other, to know what the matter was. But as neither of them returned to give him any account, he ordered his chariot to be prepared, being determined to go and meet the troop in person: Ochozias the king of Juda, attended him in another chariot. Jehu was now advanced as far as the field that once belonged to the unhappy Naboth. There the two kings, Joram and Ochozias, met him. Joram asked if his intentions were peace, and finding by Jehu's answer, that no peace was to be expected, he turned about and fled off, crying out to Ochozias, that they were betrayed. Jehu that instant bent his bow, and shot him between the shoulders: the arrow went through his heart, and he fell dead in his chariot. The bloody corpse was by Jehu's orders immediately cast out into the field, and there left to the dogs, according to the word of the Lord spoken by Elias. Ochozias drove a different way, but was soon overtaken and mortally wounded. He fled to Magaddo, and there died. His servants laid him upon his chariot, and carried him to Jerusalem, where he was interred in the sepulchre of his forefathers, in the city of David. Jehu marched on to Jezrahel, and Jezabel began to tremble for herself. She had no resource but in the artifices of her sex. She therefore decked her head, and painted her face with all the art she was mistress of; she stood looking out of a window upon the street, and called aloud to Jehu as he

rode along. Jehu looked up, asked who she was, and bade the eunuchs that were by, throw her headlong down. The wall was sprinkled with her blood as she fell, and her body was trampled on by the horses' hoofs. No one durst presume to take up the corpse, till Jehu, in consideration of her being a king's daughter, gave orders for her burial. When they came to take up her body, they found nothing of its remains, but the skull and extremities of her hands and feet; for the dogs had devoured the rest, and the prediction of Elias was literally fulfilled.

Such was the end of that unhappy woman, who by her violence had served as an instrument in the hand of God for the chastisements of a sinful people. She was not ignorant of the truth, says St. Ambrose, and yet strove to suppress it: being bent upon the support of those false prophets who flattered her, she never ceased to persecute the true prophets of the Lord. Her presumption, says this holy father, induced her to decide and regulate every thing that concerned religion and the divine service: her strong passion was to blot out every remaining mark of the true religion, and by a just judgment of God, scarce any remains of her mangled body could be discovered after her death.

A.M. 3120.] *A dead man raised to life.* [A.C. 880.
4 KINGS, xiii.

JEHU was not less violent in the measures he took to secure the crown of Israel to himself, than he had been active in acquiring it; and while, from a principle of policy, he used that violence for the sake of promoting his own ends, he became the executor of God's decrees against the house of Achab. He extirpated the male issue of that wicked race, according to the prediction of Elias; and the heads of no fewer than seventy of Achab's sons, were sent to him in baskets by the citizens and chief men of Samaria. Being thus settled without any visible competitor in the throne, he undertook to exterminate the worship of Baal, which Jezabel had introduced, and strenuously promoted. An enterprise of that nature he thought might be attended with some tumult and confusion, should he proceed by slow degrees, or openly avow his intention. He therefore artfully disguised his design, and made the idolatrous prophets believe that he was more zealously devoted to Baal than Achab himself had been. He proclaimed a festival in honour of Baal, and sent through his kingdom to require their attendance in the temple of their god. Of them all not one failed on the day appointed: they entered the temple of Baal, which they filled with their numbers from one end to the other. Jehu commanded his soldiers, who were already prepared to fall upon them, not to let so much as one escape. The soldiers executed his orders, demolished the temple, broke the idol into pieces, and converted the place where it stood into a house of office. This zeal that Jehu showed against the worship of Baal, was acceptable to God, who in reward thereof promised, that his sons should sit upon the throne of Israel to the fourth generation. Happy had he been if he had gone one step further, and established the true religion upon the ruins of idolatry; but unfortunately for himself and subjects, he retained the idolatrous worship of Jeroboam's golden calves, which, after a reign of eight and twenty years, he transmitted to his son Joachaz. Joachaz was perpetually harassed by the calamities of war, which were poured upon his kingdom by Hazael, the king of Syria. Hazael, as we have seen, had been anointed king by the express command of God himself, and was now employed to scourge the sins of Israel. By the advantages he gained, and by the devastations he made in the country, he left Joachaz no more than fifty horsemen, ten chariots, and ten thousand foot, the scanty remnant of his numerous armies. Joachaz was not reclaimed by misfortune; after a wicked and inglorious reign of seventeen years, he died in his sins, and had for his successor his son Joas. About the beginning of this king's reign died the great Eliseus. Joas, wicked as he was, had a veneration for the holy prophet, and made him a visit upon his death-bed. The prophet promised the king victory against his enemies, in reward of his charity: he bade him shoot an arrow out of the window that looked against Syria, and to strike the ground with his javelin. The king struck the ground thrice: Eliseus was displeased that he had not struck it oftener. Three times only shalt thou strike thine enemies, said he; if thou hadst struck the ground six or seven times, thou then hadst pursued the Syrians to destruction. Eliseus died, and the glory for which he had been so renowned on account of his miracles during life, accompanied him even to the tomb. For in the same year of his death, some inhabitants of the country were carrying a dead man to be buried, and being suddenly terrified at the appearance of a roving party of Moabites, they hastily threw him into the grave of Eliseus. The dead body no sooner touched the bones of the holy prophet, but the man came to life, and stood upon his feet.

Great, no doubt, says St. Ambrose, is the miracle by which a dead body is restored to life; it is what we justly admire in the saints, and in Jesus Christ himself; but the resurrection of a soul from the death of sin to a life of grace, is infinitely more worthy of our attention. When the body thus revives, it is soon to die again; such a life is no more than the beginning of another death: but the life that the soul recovers, by being called from the state of mortal sin, is the beginning of a life that never ends; its happiness is to be with God in everlasting glory. To be recalled from the grave like Lazarus, is a privilege which no one is to expect; but to rise by repentance from the slavery of sin to the friendship of Almighty God, is the hope of every sinner. It is a work which no one of himself can do; it is the effect of the life-giving grace of Jesus Christ. By this supernatural grace alone we are enabled to rise after our fall, and his grace is never wanting to those who are serious in their endeavours to deserve it.

2 CHRON. xxiii., xxiv.

UPON the death of Ochozias, king of Juda, who was slain by Jehu, as has been related, his mother Athalia, a wicked and ambitious woman, seated herself upon the throne, in prejudice to her grand-children, whom she ordered to be secretly put to death. The royal children, in consequence of this cruel order, were all murdered, excepting Joas the youngest, whom Josabeth, the sister of Ochozias, and wife of Joiada the high-priest, stole out of the nursery, and secreted in the temple. Athalia enjoyed the power she had usurped, during the space of six years, when Joiada being weary of her tyranny, thought it time to acquaint the Jewish nation that there was a prince of the blood-royal still alive, to whom the crown and their allegiance were due. He had taken care to gain the officer of the guards beforehand; he had engaged the Levites and the chiefs of the families of Juda in his interest; he had taken every precaution necessary to support his undertaking; he then set the crown upon Joas's head, and proclaimed him king by sound of trumpet. The people testified their approbation by loud shouts of joy; Athalia was alarmed at the sound; she rent her garments; but hoping that her presence might awe the people back to their obedience, she ran from the palace to the temple, where she had the confusion to see the young Joas arrayed with the ensigns of royalty, and surrounded by the princes. She cried out, Treason! treason! and the high-priest commanded the cap-

tains and chiefs of the army to lead her forth beyond the precincts of the temple, where, without any effort made for her defence, the sword put an end to her life and usurpation. Every thing after her death seemed to promise peace and prosperity to the kingdom of Juda. Joas in his youth retained a grateful respect for the virtuous Joiada, to whose fidelity he stood indebted for his crown: he willingly listened to his instructions, and governed himself by his advice. He was shocked to see the ruinous condition to which the impiety of Athalia had reduced the house of God: it had not been repaired for years; it was exhausted of its treasures, which had been either squandered away or misapplied to the temple of Baal. He wished to see it restored to its primitive lustre; but his treasury was not in a condition to answer the expense. A proclamation was therefore made in Juda and Jerusalem, that every man should bring to the Lord, the money which Moses had appointed to be paid by the Israelites, when they were in the desert; and a chest was placed by the right side of the altar, to receive the money and voluntary contributions that were brought by the people for the repairs of the temple. Workmen were immediately set to work, stone and timber provided to make every necessary repair of the house of the Lord, and all the expenses defrayed with the money that was taken out of the public chest: whatever money remained besides was employed about the sacred vessels. Piety and religion flourished as long as Joiada lived. He died in the hundred and thirtieth year of his age, and on account of the eminent services he had done his country, was interred among the kings of Juda. Soon after his death, a very different face of things was seen in Juda. A crowd of wicked flatterers immediately beset the throne; their servile adulation pleased a weak prince; they wound themselves into his favour, and undid all that the wise and virtuous Joiada had done. It is commonly the fate of kings to adopt the sentiments of those who surround them. Joas became the very reverse of what he was before: Joas, guided by Joiada, had taken great pains to repair the temple, and re-establish the honour of Almighty God; Joas, surrounded by impious flatterers, set up idols and adored them. This roused the zeal of Zacharias, who had succeeded his father Joiada in the dignity of high-priest. With a holy liberty he represented to the king and his courtiers the nature of their offences, and how odious their abominations were to the God of their religious forefathers. His representation had no other effect than that of his own martyrdom; for Joas, without respect either to the father or the son, of whom the first had restored him to his throne, and the latter was now exhorting him to an indispensable act of duty, sentenced Zacharias, the son of Joiada, to be stoned to death; which was executed in the great court between the altar and the

temple. The holy priest patiently submitted to the sentence, and amidst his sufferings only begged that the Lord would see and do him justice. His prayer was heard; the reign of an ungrateful king became more miserable in the end, than it had been happy in the beginning. Within a twelvemonth after he had set up his idols, and murdered the high-priest, the Syrians broke in upon him, and with a handful of men routed an infinite multitude of Jews, because they had forsaken the Lord the God of their fathers, says the sacred text, and on Joas they executed shameful judgments. Full of pains and diseases, Joas dragged out a wretched life, till, in punishment of the murder of Zacharias, the son of Joiada, he was assassinated in his bed by two of his own servants, after a reign of forty years. They buried him in the city of David, but not in the sepulchre of the kings, his predecessors.

The end of this unhappy prince must naturally awaken the attention of those, whose station in life exposes them to the flattery of false friends. The language of a man who pours his incense where he has an interest to pursue, or favour to hope for, cannot be too carefully guarded against: it is always to be suspected. A flatterer is a stranger to sincerity; he fawns and praises, he smiles and caresses, with no other view than to gain his own selfish ends; deceit is his practice, and interest his motive. Flattery is the sure mark of a base disposition; it betrays a weakness both in him who gives and him who takes it.

A.M. 3197.] *The Prophet Jonas.*—JONAS, i. [A.C. 803.

JOAS was succeeded by his son Amasias. This prince, like his father, began his reign in prosperity, but ended with disgrace. Having vanquished the Idumeans in battle, he took away their idols, and set them up in his own dominions. This impious conduct drew upon him the displeasure of Almighty God. He was in his turn vanquished by Joas, king of Israel, taken and led a prisoner into his own city of Jerusalem. He remained in confinement till the death of Joas, when he recovered his liberty, reigned for some years, and was at last murdered by his own subjects. Joas being master of the city of Jerusalem, demolished a great part of the wall, and carried away with him the treasure of the temple to Samaria. The king having checked the Syrians by the several victories that Eliseus had promised him, and recovered the cities which his father had lost, left his son Jeroboam to carry on what he had so prosperously begun. Jeroboam, the second of that name, was a wicked but a valiant prince; by his abilities and success in war he restored the kingdom of Israel to its ancient territories, and confined the Syrians to the limits of their own empire.

Under this king lived the prophet Jonas, well known for his mission to the city of Ninive. The humble prophet thought himself unequal to an undertaking of that importance, though called to it by God himself: hoping to escape the arduous task by flight, he embarked on board a ship that was bound for Tharsis. But vain are the schemes of men, when formed in contradiction to the decrees of God. A violent storm arose at sea, and the ship was in the utmost danger of being lost. The trembling mariners shuddered with fear, and cried aloud on their God to save them. They began to lighten the vessel by throwing part of the cargo overboard; they bewailed their misfortune, and concluded that their present distress must be owing to some one of the crew, who by his sins had provoked the divine anger. Jonas, conscious of his disobedience, had retired apart into the lower part of the ship, where he fell asleep. The captain called him up, and bade him pray for their escape. The mariners had recourse to lots, in order to find out the cause why the present evil had befallen them; they cast the lots, and the lot fell upon Jonas; Jonas frankly owned himself guilty, told them who he was, and why he had tried to fly from the face of God. He declared himself ready to resign his life for the safety of the rest; that to calm the sea and save themselves from shipwreck, they must take and throw him in, as he knew it was on his account that they had been overtaken by the storm. The mariners stood astonished at his candid confession, admired his generosity, and the fortitude of his mind. Unwilling to hasten the death of a man who seemed so worthy of life, they plied their oars, and stretched every nerve to weather the storm, and regain the shore; but seeing their utmost efforts were to no purpose, and their danger increasing every moment, they made pity give way to fear, and threw the prophet into the sea. The sea that instant soothed its waves, and the tempest ceased. Kind Providence, ever mindful of his servants, would not suffer Jonas to perish, who, to save the lives of others, had thus generously made a sacrifice of his own. A huge fish was at hand to receive

him as he fell. Shut up in the whale's belly Jonas continued three days and three nights, not only safe from harm, but also master of his thoughts and reason; so that he there composed an admirable hymn of thanksgiving to the Lord, his great preserver and deliverer. The fish spewed him out upon the shore, alive and unhurt. From the jaws of death he came forth in a most wonderful manner; the lively figure of Jesus Christ, who in the same, though infinitely more glorious manner, was to rise from the tomb and bowels of the earth, triumphant over the powers of death and hell.

A.M. 3197.] *Penitence of the Ninivites.* [A.C. 803.
JONAS, iii.

ALMIGHTY GOD repeated his first orders to Jonas, commanding him to rise and go to Ninive. Of the many prophets who had been employed in the ministry of God's word, Jonas was the first who preached to the Gentiles, and in that became the representative of Jesus Christ, from whom the grace of salvation flows both upon Jew and Gentile. The prophet being taught by affliction to submit himself to the divine will, made no further objection against the command that was given him, but immediately set forward to perform it. Ninive was the capital of the Assyrian empire, a city so great and extensive, that it was a three day's journey to go through it. Jonas advanced one day's journey through the

streets, declaring to the citizens, who flocked to hear him, that by the end of forty days Ninive should be no more. A threat so terrible and so urgent drew the attention of his hearers, and threw a deadly consternation through the whole city. Conscious of crimes the most enormous, the Ninivites knew they deserved the severest judgment: they gave credit to the prophet's words, and humbled themselves before the Lord. With a true disposition of repentance they proclaimed a general fast; from the highest to the lowest, the little and the great, they clothed themselves with sack-cloth, that as all had sinned, all likewise might repent, and by a general penance obtain a general pardon. The king was no less alarmed than his people; he equally believed the prophet: he descended from the throne, laid his royal robes aside, put on a coarse sack, and sat himself down upon ashes, as a mark of his repentance. He likewise published an order, that neither man nor beast should eat or drink the least thing; that all his subjects should turn from their evil ways, and with united prayers and tears should strive to draw down the divine mercy. Who knows, said he, but God may take compassion on, and pardon us. He may perhaps reverse his threats and save us. The king's hopes did not deceive him. Almighty God only waited for the repentance of a sinful people to grant them pardon. He foresaw their penance; he employed his threats to gain it. Moved by the cries, and softened by the tears of a repenting city, he did not execute the sentence which he had inspired his prophet to denounce; out of regard to their penitential works he reserved the Ninivites, to punish the crimes of the unrepenting Israelites. This example of the citizens of Ninive is recorded in Holy Writ, not only to show the merit of fasting and penitential works, but also to encourage sinners to a true repentance: it is mentioned by our blessed Saviour himself, and it will cover those Christians with confusion, who, notwithstanding the threats pronounced by Jesus Christ in his gospel against sinners, persist in their evil courses, till the days of pardon and repentance are no more.

A.M. 3197.] *Jonas's complaint.*—JONAS, iv. [A.C. 803

JONAS being sensible that the destruction of Ninive was prevented through the repentance of its inhabitants, began to be afraid of passing for a false prophet. Instead of rejoicing, as he ought, at the prospect of so many thousands being preserved from present destruction, and preserved by his own happy concurrence, he let himself be depressed with grief; he prayed to die rather than to live, because the event did not turn out as he had expected. He went out of the city, and at some distance from it having made himself a bower, to screen his head from the scorching sun, he there sat himself down under its shade, and waited to see what would befall the city. Almighty God, who not only sees, but frequently stoops to the weakness of men, that they may become more sensible of his goodness towards them, caused an ivy-tree to grow up during the night, which spreading its matted branches over the bower, formed a close shelter against the rays of the sun. The prophet was overjoyed to see it in the morning; but his joy was only for that day; for at night the same divine power that had raised the tree, destroyed its sheltering foliage; a little worm, prepared by the hand of God, struck the ivy, and it withered. When the sun was risen, a hot and burning wind heated the air, the sun beat upon the head of Jonas, and he was scorched with the excessive heat. The loss of his ivy made him more impatient, and in the depth of his affliction he again wished to die. Then it was that the anguish of his soul disposed him to comprehend the truth which the Lord was pleased to make him sensible of. Thou art afflicted, said Almighty God to him, and thinkest thou hast reason, because the ivy is dead; yet thou didst not contribute either to plant or to make it grow; it went away as quickly as it came; in one night it grew up, and perished in the next. Thou grievest at the destruction of a thing which thou didst but begin to enjoy; and shall I not be moved at the destruction of a city so great as Ninive? There are more than a hundred and twenty thousand persons, who know not their right hand from their left, and ought I to be insensible of their misfortune, or ought I not to have mercy and to spare?

A.M. 3263.] *Impiety of Achaz.*—4 Kings, xvi. [A.C. 737.

After Amasias was slain, as we have said, by his own subjects, Ozias his son, who is called Azarias, at the age of sixteen mounted the throne of Juda. He was a prince of great abilities, which he employed for the good of his subjects and increase of religion, till towards the end of his life he forgot his station, and attempted the sacred functions that were peculiar to priests. Being elated by the long prosperity which had accompanied his reign for upwards of fifty years, he trespassed upon the rights of Aaron's priesthood, and presumed to offer incense upon the altar of perfumes. Azarias the high-priest, with eighty attendants of the sacerdotal order, repaired immediately to the temple, and represented to him the rashness of his attempt. The king was deaf to all Azarias said; he stood with the censer in his hand, and threatened aloud to kill any man that should offer to interrupt him in the ceremony; he over-awed the spectators with fear, when, behold! the marks of a spreading leprosy began to appear upon his forehead. The priests immediately ran up, and thrust him out of the sanctuary; he himself was glad to get out of sight as speedily as he could, to conceal his shame, which was the punishment of his pride. Being no longer worthy to converse with, or to be seen by men, he shut himself up in a private apartment, and resigned the reins of government to his son Joathan. Joathan was an excellent prince, and possessed of every quality that constitutes a great and virtuous king. He reigned no more than sixteen years, when he was succeeded by his son Achaz, the worst of men that had yet disgraced the crown of Juda. Vicious by nature, and by principle addicted to the superstitions of the kings of Israel, he cast statues to Baal, and renewed the abominations of idolatry, even in the holy city. He took down the great laver, and removed Solomon's brazen altar; in the place of which he erected another, made after the fashion of an altar he had seen at Damascus. He shut up the temple, he purified his son by fire, according to the rites of the Gentiles; he offered sacrifices and burnt incense upon the hills, and under every green tree. Urias the high-priest temporised with the king in every act of impiety, so that the infection spread through the whole nation. In punishment of this universal corruption, the kingdom was most miserably torn to pieces, and plundered of its riches by the kings of Israel and Syria. No less than a hundred and twenty thousand of the troops of Juda were slain in one day, and two hundred thousand women and children, with an immense booty, were carried away to Samaria. Far from becoming better by these dreadful strokes of divine justice, Achaz still plunged himself and his people into fresh calamities, by an alliance that he made with Theglathphalasar, the king of Assyria, to whom he made his kingdom tributary. He stripped the temple and his own palace of their costly furniture and treasures, to purchase the friendship of this new ally, from whom he received no help; for the Assyrian monarch having only his own interest in view, plundered every thing that came in his way, whether it belonged to Juda or to Israel. He made himself master of all the lands of Israel that lay on the east side of the Jordan, and led the inhabitants away with him into Assyria. This was the beginning of that fatal captivity, which was soon to put an end to the whole kingdom of Israel. But this did not alarm the wicked Achaz; the more he was chastised, the more reprobate he grew: he attributed his losses, not to the divine hand which scourged him for his crimes, but to a superior power in the Syrian idols. He therefore immolated victims to the gods of Damascus, set up their statues at the corner of every street in Jerusalem, and built them altars in the cities of Juda, where he ordered frankincense to be burnt in their honour. Provoked by such outrages, God would no longer bear with his impiety: by an untimely death he snatched him out of life, in the thirty-sixth year of his age, and the sixteenth of his reign.

The impiety of this abandoned prince is a shocking spectacle of the depravity of human nature; and the obstinacy with which he resisted every admonition that was sent to make him sensible of his crimes, is a proof that obduracy of heart is the greatest punishment which happens to a sinner on this side of the grave: final impenitence is the beginning of that painful reprobation which shall never end.

A.M. 3282.] *Destruction of the kingdom of Israel.*—4 KINGS, xvii. [A.C. 718.

JEROBOAM the Second swayed the sceptre of Israel with great temporal felicity for one and forty years, when, after an interregnum of eleven years, it descended to Zacharias his son. Zacharias was the fourth generation from Jehu, and the last who was to reign of that family, according to the prediction made by the Lord to that usurper. He reigned but six months, being slain by Sellum, who after one month's usurpation lost both the kingdom and his life, by the violence of Mahahem. Mahahem reigned ten years, and was succeeded by his son Phaceia, against whom Phacee, the son of Romelia, formed a successful conspiracy, and seized upon the crown. Phacee was the king who made so destructive a war upon Achaz, the impious king of Juda. After a reign of twenty years he was deposed and murdered by Osee, one of his subjects, and the last of the kings of Israel. The period fixed for the duration of that distracted kingdom was now run out: its subjects had for ages been a lawless and incorrigible people; no end could be put to their idolatrous crimes, but by a dissolution of their empire. Of all the kings who reigned in Israel from the time that Jeroboam first divided the Hebrew people into two kingdoms, to its final dissolution, there is not one whom for his wickedness the inspired writer does not absolutely condemn. They walked in the footsteps of their wicked founder Jeroboam; they adored his calves; they consecrated groves and places upon the hills for their superstitious sacrifices; they proscribed the ceremonies of the Jewish law, and adopted those of heathen nations; they, in fine, abandoned the God who had brought their fathers out of the land of Egypt, and bent their knees to idols of their own workmanship. To reclaim them from their evil ways, and to bring them back to the religion of their forefathers, Almighty God never ceased to admonish them, either by temporal calamities, or by the preaching of his prophets. The magnificent temple of Jerusalem was a standing monument of the worship they had left; but neither the zeal of Elias, nor the miracles of Eliseus, nor the temple of Solomon, had any effect upon those degenerate Israelites; therefore the Almighty determined to pour out the vengeance with which he had long threatened them; he determined to root them out of the land which he once had given them, and to make them vagabonds upon the face of the earth. Soon after Osee, their last king, had seized upon the crown, Salmanazar, the king of Assyria, and son of Theglathphalasar, invaded the kingdom of Israel, and conquered it. Osee was permitted to retain his regal dignity, upon condition of paying tribute, and acknowledging himself a vassal to the Assyrian monarch. This was an indignity to which he resolved to stoop no longer than necessity obliged him. He secretly applied to the king of Egypt for help against the Assyrians; which Salmanazar was no sooner apprised of, but he came back with a more powerful army than before, and laid siege to Samaria. The city held out against his attacks for three years, and upon its surrender, the whole kingdom of Israel submitted to the conqueror. To prevent all future revolts, Salmanazar collected the inhabitants together, put them under the direction of proper leaders, and transported them into the territories of the Medes and Assyrians. The Israelites from thence spread themselves by degrees into the northern part of Asia, and neither they nor their posterity ever returned into their own country, which was given to other inhabitants sent from the province of Asia. Thus an end was put to the kingdom of Israel by a total ruin of the ten tribes that composed it, two hundred and fifty-four years after it had been first severed from that of Juda.

A.M. 3286.] *The virtues of Tobias.*—Tob. ii. [A.C. 714.

Amongst the many thousands of Israelites who were led away by Salmanazar into Assyria, there was one, who for his virtues is distinguished from the rest, and whose history is recorded in holy writ for the instruction of after ages. He was of the tribe of Nephthali, by name Tobias. From his very childhood he showed a wisdom superior to his age, being prudent in his words, and grave in his deportment. He never suffered himself to be led astray by the crowds of those who ran to adore the golden calves of Jeroboam, but went regularly, as the law prescribed, to adore the God of Israel in the temple of Jerusalem. Being blessed with a son, he thought it his great duty to be careful of his education, and to instruct him betimes in the fear of God. In this virtuous man the change of circumstances and country made no alteration of principles and conduct: with the same steadiness he walked in the same path of virtue; he made it his study and his practice to give all the comfort and assistance he could to his fellow captives. To console the afflicted, to help the sick, and to bury the dead, were the daily exercises of his charity. Such virtues merited him a reward even in this life: he had full leave from the king to go where he should think fit; a leave it seems not granted to the rest of his countrymen. His usual residence was at Ninive; but he freely went from one part of the country to another, as his charity and neighbour's necessity called him. Being at Rages, a town belonging to the Medes, he found a poor man of his own tribe, called Gabelus, in great distress, and as by the king's bounty he had money at his disposal, he lent him ten talents of silver, taking his promissory note for the payment. After the death of Salmanazar, Sennacherib succeeded to the crown This prince being exasperated at the destruction of his army in Judea, of which we shall have the account in the history of king Ezechias, was resolved to revenge himself upon the captive Israelites, whom he persecuted by various kinds of cruelty, putting many of them to death, and leaving their bodies without burial. These fresh sufferings of his brethren redoubled the good Tobias's activity in their service. Sennacherib, to whom the virtues of humanity seem to have been even hateful, was offended at his charity, and gave orders for him to be put to death, and his goods confiscated. This forced the holy man to fly, not to lose his life. He found a safe retreat among his friends, of whom he had many, and by the tyrant's death, which happened soon after, he recovered his goods and former liberty. His charity was no longer restrained by fear, nor did the dangers and the hardships he had undergone, abate his zeal for the service of his neighbour. In the midst of an entertainment which he had made for his friends, it was told him that an Israelite had been just slain in the street; he immediately rose from table,

fetched away the corpse, and concealed it in his house till night, when he buried it. His friends put him in mind of the danger he had but lately escaped, and said that his zeal was indiscreet. Tobias, who had a greater regard for God than for men, would not let himself be talked out of his duty, nor would he suffer a dead body that came in his way to be unburied. Being one day more than usually tired with his pious labours, he chanced to lay himself down for a moment's rest near the wall of his house; a swallow had made her nest above, and the hot dung happening to fall upon his eyes as he lay exposed, deprived him of his sight. It was a misfortune the most grievous that could have befallen him; it severely tried his patience, but did not shake his constancy in virtue. As he had been always active in doing good to others, as much as he could, so he was scrupulously nice not to concur in any thing that might do them any wrong. His wife Anna, by the earnings of her labour, had saved enough to buy a kid, and had brought it home, unknown to Tobias. He heard the little animal bleat, and not knowing how it could come thither, asked his wife if it was not stolen. Anna thought herself injured by such a question, and began to revile him in very sharp and unbecoming language. Tobias, patient as Job, heard in silence; he made no reply, but with his other sufferings, offered this also to Almighty God, in atonement for his sins, and the sins of his nation: for in all his affliction he humbled himself beneath the hand of God, from whom he resignedly received them; he was thankful for past favours, and being no longer able to serve his neighbour, he gave himself to prayer, and as having nothing more to do with life, he begged Almighty God to receive his soul in peace.

Christians who read this history of Tobias, may justly admire, when they find such virtues practised in the midst of an idolatrous people, and practised by a man, who under the discouragement of censure and reproach from his nearest friends, had no example of Jesus Christ to excite, and no gospel to enlighten him. When they view the demeanour of this holy man more minutely, and compare it with their own, they then may blush at the wide disparity between themselves and him, as the holy fathers remark: the piety and patience of Tobias is a subject of emulation to the zealous Christian: to the slothful, a subject of confusion.

A.M. 3300.] *Young Tobias and his Angel.* [A.C. 700

TOBIAS, v.

TOBIAS, thinking that his prayers for a speedy release from the toils of life were heard, and that his death was near, gave to his son, the young Tobias, his last instructions; they were the instructions of a good father to an only son, the result of reason, and the dictates of true piety; such as every parent ought to recommend frequently to his children during life, and enforce at death. He charged him to be ever dutiful and attentive to his mother, to fear God, to guard against all sin, especially pride and impurity; to give alms according to his abilities; to advise with some prudent friend in every business of importance; and to be always diligent in holy prayer. After this he informed him of the money which was due to him from Gabelus, and which he desired him to receive. This debt he had never mentioned to his son before, and mentioned it only now from a principle of justice, that his son might not lose what belonged to him. The young man listened with dutiful respect to his aged father, and received his instructions, as spoken by a man endowed with the wisdom of God. He promised to comply with every injunction, as far as he was able; the only difficulty that occured, was how to recover the ten talents from Gabelus, of whom he knew nothing more than his name. The father told him, he must look out for some faithful guide, to show him the way to Rages, and carry with him Gabelus's own hand-writing, as a proof of the debt. The obedient son went forth to look out for such a person, and meeting with a comely young man in the appearance and equipage of a traveller ready for a journey, civilly saluted him, little thinking that under such a disguise was concealed an angel, whom God, by a special providence, had appointed for his guidance and protection. He asked him who he was, and from whence, and whether he knew the way into the country of the Medes. The angel replied, that he was one of Israel, and well acquainted with the roads of the country; that he had been at Rages, and knew Gabelus. The young Tobias was overjoyed at his good fortune in meeting with a stranger so qualified and willing to attend him; he introduced him to his father, who was equally pleased at the candour and friendly promises of the comely youth, who called himself by the name of Azarias, that is to say, the help of God. Azarias comforted the good old man, who sat bemoaning his misfortunes in being no longer able to see the light of heaven, assured him of a speedy cure from God, and promised to conduct his son to Gabelus at Rages, and to bring him home again. Raphael therefore, the archangel, under the shape and name of a travelling Israelite, began to direct the steps of young Tobias with peculiar care; which has been always looked upon as a specimen of that which our guardian angels have over us, and is a perfect model of that tender solicitude, which every pastor ought to show in taking care of his respective flock. Tobias bade his father and mother farewell, and set off with his guide towards the country of the Medes, and the dog followed him. They travelled on together, till they came to the river Tigris; Tobias sat himself down upon the bank to wash his feet, when, behold! a monstrous fish darted from the stream, as at its prey, to devour him. Struck with affright, he called upon his guide, who bade him take the fish by the gill and draw him ashore. He did so. The angel moreover told him to take out the entrails of the fish, and lay up the heart, the liver, and the gall, as useful in medicine, and proper to drive away all kind of evil spirits. They roasted part of the flesh, the rest they salted, and carried with them as much as might serve them till they arrived at Rages. When they came within sight of the town, his guardian informed him that they must lodge with one Raguel, a kinsman of his tribe, who lived in the country, and had an only daughter, whom he should demand in marriage. Tobias was startled at the proposal, for he knew that she had been already given to seven different husbands, one after another, who, by the devil's malice, had been all killed the very first night after their marriage. He dreaded the like misfortune; and what affected him still more, he was afraid lest such an accident befalling him, might also cause the death of his dear parents. Azarias reasoned away his fears, and assured him that the devil's power extended only over those who, without any respect for God, were guided more by sensuality than by reason in their choice and use of matrimony. He then taught him in what manner he was to sanctify his marriage, and concluded, by giving him such instructions as deserve the serious consideration of those who engage in the marriage state.

A.M. 3300.] *Old Tobias recovers his sight.* [A.C. 700.

TOBIAS, xi.

THE young Tobias, according to the angel's direction, went to Raguel's house, where, though an entire stranger, he met with a friendly welcome. Raguel thought he discovered in the young man, the features of his kinsman Tobias, and asked them if they were acquainted with him. The man you inquire after, replied the angel, is this young man's father. Raguel immediately threw his arms round his neck, and kissing him, with tears said, a blessing be upon thee, my son, because thou art the son of a good and virtuous man. Anna his wife, and Sarah their daughter, likewise wept. When the first salutations were over, he ordered an hospitable entertainment to be prepared. As soon as the dinner was ready, he desired them to sit down: Tobias took that opportunity of making his proposals to Raguel, and solemnly declared that he would neither eat nor drink in his house, unless he would first promise to grant him his daughter Sarah in marriage. Raguel knew not what answer to make; for though he approved of the match, yet he durst not give his consent, knowing what had happened to her former husbands. As he therefore stood in suspense without making any answer, the angel assured him, that his daughter had, by a special providence, been reserved for Tobias, and therefore no one hitherto could have her. Raguel had no further doubt; he took the right hand of his daughter and gave it into the right hand of Tobias, saying, the God of Abraham, and the God of Isaac, and the God of Jacob, be with you, and may he join you together, and fulfil his blessing in you. The matrimonial contract was then taken down in writing: they made merry, and blessed God. When they retired at night into the chamber prepared for them, Tobias carefully observed every direction which Azarias had given him; he took out of his bag part of the fish's liver, and broiled it upon the

coals, that by its smoke it might chase away the evil spirit: he exhorted the virgin to join prayer with him; because, being the children of saints, and not being joined together like heathens, who know not God, they were thus to pass the three first nights in holy prayer and continence. Raguel in the interim expected nothing less than the death of Tobias, and had already ordered his grave to be prepared; but being agreeably surprised in the morning to find him safe and sound, he filled up the grave, and gave free scope to the transports of his joy. Tobias had his thoughts still turned upon his parents; he knew how uneasy they would be about him; the delay caused by his marriage was unavoidable, and after that his business with Gabelus must be done. He opened his mind to Azarias, and Azarias undertook to transact that affair for him without any further loss of time. He took the note from him, went to Rages, received the money, and brought Gabelus with him to the feast. Gabelus wept for joy to see the son of his friend and kind benefactor: he embraced and kissed him. Tobias now began to be very solicitous about his parents: he pressed Raguel for his consent to return home. Raguel was charmed with his filial piety, delivered to him his daughter, with half his substance in hand for her present portion, and promised the other half after his own and wife's decease. He and Anna his wife took their last farewell with the kindest expressions of love and tenderness; they kissed their daughter with tears in their eyes: they recommended to her to love her husband, to honour her father and mother-in-law, to preserve order in her family, and to be particularly watchful over her own conduct. The good parents of Tobias were all this while in great anxiety about their son, whose absence began to seem very long. His mother went every day to the top of a hill, to see if she could descry him coming; she at last perceived him, and ran with great haste to impart the joyful tidings to her husband. The dog also, that had been the faithful attendant upon his master's steps, ran before, and by fawning and wagging his tail, confirmed the welcome news. The old father, who was blind, rose up, and giving a servant his hand, ran stumbling on to meet his son: they eagerly embraced each other; they poured out the tears of gladness into one another's bosom, and when they had adored and given thanks to God, they sat down together. The young

Tobias produced the gall of the fish, as the angel had told him, with which he rubbed his father's eyes, and restored

him to his sight. He then gave him a faithful account of all that had happened in his journey: his spouse arrived a few days after with his stock and money, and nothing more was wanting to complete the happiness of Tobias's family. Their first concern was to reward their faithful guide, to whose services, under God, they attributed their good fortune: they offered him one-half of their acquired substance. The angel then thought it time to let them know who he was: he told them that his name was Raphael, one of the seven spirits that constantly attended before the throne of God; that he had been commissioned by Almighty God to accompany the son in that visible manner; that he had invisibly offered up prayers to the Lord; that works of charity and devotion, fasting and alms-deeds, joined with prayers, were very acceptable in the eyes of God. He recommended to them a perseverance in the same holy practices, gave them his blessing, and vanished out of sight. Struck with religious awe, they fell prostrate upon the ground, where they remained for three hours in silent prayer; when they rose up, Tobias the father began to proclaim the praises of Almighty God for all his works, and, in a prophetic style, rehearsed the great wonders which he was afterwards to accomplish in his church.

The venerable Tobias, who had seen such scenes of human misery, both in and after the destruction of his country, lived two and forty years after he recovered his sight, and died in a good old age, past a hundred. He left behind him a faithful imitator of his piety, the young Tobias, who to all succeeding ages is set forth as a perfect image of that obedience and respect which is due from children to their parents. He is a bright example to married persons, teaching them by what virtues they are to sanctify themselves in the marriage state, and with what attention they ought to instruct and educate their children, that the virtues of the fathers may, with their names, be transmitted by descent to the latest posterity.

A.M. 3289.] *Ezechias, King of Juda.* [A.C. 711.

4 Kings, xviii.

Whilst the miserable Israelites were scattered through the Assyrian empire, and groaning in captivity, the kingdom of Juda, which had been reduced to the brink of ruin under the wicked Achaz, began to recover itself under the pious Ezechias, who succeeded his father six years before the destruction of Israel. Ezechias was a religious prince, of whom the Scripture gives this testimony, that amongst the kings who swayed the sceptre of Juda, either before or after him, there was not his equal: just by principle, and prudent in his conduct, he steadily adhered to the law of God, from which he never departed either to the right or to the left. Under his auspices a new face of things was seen over the whole kingdom of Juda: where impiety and superstition prevailed before, true virtue and religion flourished. He set open the gates of the temple, which his father Achaz had shut; he ordered the priests and Levites to sanctify themselves, that they might be worthy to purify the sanctuary, which had been profaned. The table of show-bread, the altar, and the sacred vessels were restored; the ancient ceremonies of religious worship were renewed, and holocausts offered to the Lord amidst the solemn sounds of vocal and instrumental music. He cut down the sacrilegious groves, removed every object of superstitious worship, and, amongst other things, broke to pieces the brazen serpent, which from Moses's time had been respectfully preserved, but by abuse was at last become a subject of scandal to the people. For the encouragement of the Levites to attend their sacred functions, he renewed the laws respecting the payment of tithes and first fruits. Such public virtues, and such zeal for the divine service, endeared him to Almighty God, who blessed his undertakings with success, and crowned his arms with victory. For Ezechias exerted himself not only in repairing the ruins of his kingdom, but also in re-establishing the dignity of the crown. He recovered the cities that had been dismembered from Juda, broke the growing power of the Philistines, and restrained them within the borders of their own narrow territories. Achaz had made himself and kingdom tributary to the Assyrians: it was an indignity which Ezechias would not stoop to. Roused with a laudable indignation to see the glory of Juda thus fallen, he rallied his broken forces, shook off the Assyrian yoke, and rendered himself an independent monarch. Under this religious king lived the great Isaias, his director in all his doubts, and comforter in all his pains; for he had many difficulties to struggle with, and the powerful enemies he had upon his hands made him sometimes diffident and doubtful of the event. But being strengthened by the counsels of that enlightened prophet, he defeated the efforts of his adversaries, and soared above the alarms of his own fears. Happy is the prince who disdains not to hearken to the advice of a prudent man, and happy was Isaias in having a king, who knew how to profit by the advice he gave him. Hence the holy fathers make this remark, that a king who truly fears God, will not easily quarrel with the true servants of God, and will think himself more happy in paying a due respect to the ministers of God's holy word, than in receiving the servile honours of flatterers.

A.M. 3291.] *The Prophet Isaias.* [A.C. 709.

Isaias was descended of the royal race of Juda: he began to prophesy in the reign of king Azarias, which he continued to do through the succeeding reigns of Joathan, Achaz, and Ezechias; till being upwards of a hundred years old, he was at last martyred by the impious Manasses. This seer, renowned for his singular piety, for his inimitable style and divine eloquence, for his knowledge and clear insight into futurity, ranks in the first place amongst the prophets He speaks so explicitly, and with such precision, of Jesus Christ and his church, that he seems to write more like an historian, penning down the account of past or present transactions, than a prophet who is foretelling the far distant events of ages yet to come. Amongst the many visions that he had, the following is one of the most awful. The Almighty appeared to him in full majesty, and, to use the expression of

St. John, he saw the glory of God sitting upon an elevated throne, environed with a troop of melodious seraphims, who, with heavenly voices, incessantly proclaimed the sanctity of the Lord of Hosts. The canticle they sung is borrowed by the church, and is daily chanted with solemnity before the canon of her liturgy. Awed by a reverential fear, and measuring his own littleness with the majesty of what he beheld, Isaias durst not presume to open his mouth, nor with unhallowed lips proclaim such holy mysteries. The celestial spirits saw the humble sentiments of his heart, and one of the seraphims that stood near the throne of God, flew to him with a burning coal in his hand, which he had taken up with a pair of tongs from the altar. The angel touched the prophet's lips with the fire, and pronounced him purified from the stain of sin. The prophet upon that offered himself to go and announce to the people of Juda whatever the Lord should please to command. In this, as the holy fathers remark, Isaias instructs the preachers of the gospel, with what purity of manners and intention they ought to undertake the sacred ministry, and how earnestly they ought to pray, that God would purify their lips and hearts, and, by his grace, make them fit to explain his holy word to men. According to the Hebrew tradition, Isaias finished his life, by being sawed in two during the persecution of Manasses. His death was precious in the sight of God, and seems to be particularly specified by St. Paul in his epistle to the Hebrews. There, speaking of the virtues and sufferings of the ancient prophets, the apostle says, that they patiently endured their torments, and, upon the hopes of rising to a better life, joyfully resigned the present, when they found it could be no longer held consistently with their duty to the Lord Almighty. They suffered mockeries and stripes; they were bound in chains, and imprisoned; some were stoned and cut asunder; some died by the sword, whilst others, of whom the world was not worthy, were left to wander through deserts, in distress, in want and misery, loaded with afflictions, and driven into mountains, into the dens of wild beasts, and into caverns of the earth.

Ecclesiasticus, before St. Paul, had also pronounced the panegyric of Isaias. Ezechias, says the author of that book, did what was right in the eyes of God; he walked in the ways of David his progenitor, under the direction of Isaias, the great and faithful prophet. At this prophet's word the sun retreated backwards in its course, and he lengthened the king's life. Being enlightened by the great Spirit of God, he saw into the deepest recesses of futurity, and comforted those who wept in Sion. He foretold what was to happen in the end of ages; he disclosed the most hidden secrets, and declared them long before the time. To these encomiums of Isaias and his fellow prophets, nothing more can be added; they are the encomiums dictated by the Spirit of God himself. For Jesus, the son of Sirach, and St. Paul, were the instruments to write what God had inspired.

A.M. 3291.] *Defeat of Sennacherib* [A.C. 709.

4 Kings, xix.

Sennacherib, the king of Assyria, being greatly exasperated against Ezechias for refusing to pay the tribute which his father Achaz had promised to Salmanazar, marched a powerful army into the kingdom of Juda, took many of the fortified cities, laid a heavy tax upon the country, and obliged Ezechias to purchase peace at an enormous price. He drew off his troops, according to the articles of agreement, but, by a breach of faith, sent back Rabsaces with a strong army to take possession of Jerusalem. Rabsaces, in a style the most imperious and insulting, summoned the king of Juda to surrender; he magnified the conquests made by the Assyrians, saying what kings they had conquered, and what countries they had subdued; he lastly represented how rash it would be in Ezechias to think of resisting the conqueror, whom no power, whether human or divine, was able to contend with. Ezechias rent his garments through grief at hearing such language, put on a penitential sack, and retired into the house of God to seek consolation by holy prayer. He sent to let Isaias know the anguish of his mind, and beg the assistance of his prayers and advice against the evils that threatened him. The prophet hastened to comfort his prince, exhorted him to put his confidence in God, and promised that a speedy message should make his enemy retire from the holy city. And in effect Rabsaces retired soon after, to join the king of the Assyrians, who was employed in the siege of Lobna. News was there brought to Sennacherib, that Tharaca, king of Ethiopia, was upon the march with a great army to attack them, upon which he despatched a messenger to Ezechias with a letter full of threats and blasphemy, to try if he could frighten him into submission. The holy king had recourse to God by prayer, as before: being in the temple, he produced the threatening letter of Sennacherib, and spreading it before the Lord, he thus prayed aloud: Lord God of Israel, who sittest upon the cherubims; Thou, who alone art the God of kings and of all the earth, incline thine ear and attend: open, Lord, thine eyes and see: hear what Sennacherib has said. For he hath blasphemed thy holy name. He hath indeed destroyed the other nations of the earth, and hath thrown their gods into the flames; for they were but graven gods, and made by the hands of men. But thou, O Lord our God, who madest heaven and earth, save us from his hand, that all the world may know that thou art the Lord, the only God. A prayer so ardent and so full of faith did not fail of its effect. Isaias sent to tell him that his prayer was heard, that the Assyrian king should not enter into the city, which God had resolved to save for his own and for David his servant's sake, but should ingloriously return by the way he came. Blinded to his ruin, Sennacherib returned to besiege Jerusalem, not doubting but it must fall an easy conquest to his arms. But in the night an angel went forth from the Lord, and passing through the Assyrian camp, destroyed a hundred and eighty-

five thousand of the army. When it was light Sennacherib saw the numbers of the slain: his pride and boasting were at an end; he thought no more of the conquest of Judea, but struck with terror and confusion he made the best of his way back to Ninive, leaving the Jews at full liberty to sow and reap their fields, as Isaias had promised them three years before. Divine vengeance pursued him even there: he began to vent his revenge upon the Israelites, when his two sons unexpectedly put an end to his life a few weeks after his return, by assassinating him in the temple of his idol.

Sennacherib, by the manner of his death, paid the tribute due to the justice of God, whose majesty he had insulted, and whose power he had blasphemously defied. Almighty God, in one night's time, and by the hand of one angel, swept away the collected forces of a vast empire; and if he did not involve the king in the general ruin with his army, as he formerly did Pharaoh, it was, says St. Jerome, because he reserved him for the sword of his own children. The impiety of the king against God was severely punished by the impiety of the sons against their father.

A.M. 3291.] *Ezechias restored to health.* [A.C. 709.

4 KINGS, XX.

EZECHIAS, at the time that he was straitened by the army of Sennacherib, fell dangerously ill. Being fond of life he prayed earnestly to God for his recovery. The prophet Isaias, in a visit that he made him upon his bed of sickness, admonished him to set his house in order, and prepare for death. Afflicted at the doleful summons, the king turned himself round towards the wall, and wept. But his lively faith made him still hope in the divine goodness; he persisted still to pray, and his prayer was for a longer life. The prophet had left him, and was gone as far as the middle of the court, when he felt himself suddenly inspired to go back and tell the king, that in consideration of his prayers and tears the Lord had granted him a reprieve; that in three days he should be able to make his appearance in the temple, and that fifteen years more were added to his life. The king begged him to exhibit some visible sign in confirmation of these promises, upon which the prophet wrought the celebrated miracle on the dial of king Achaz, in making the shadow of the index to go ten degrees backwards from the point it

was then advanced to. The fame of Ezechias's great and virtuous actions had spread itself through different kingdoms. Berodach Baladan, the king of Babylon, sent him presents and letters of congratulation upon the recovery of his health. An embassy from so great a monarch did not a little flatter the king of Juda. Pleased with the honour that was done him, he took a vanity in showing to the Babylonian ambassadors his riches, the gold and silver vessels, the shining treasures of the temple and royal palace. Almighty God, who beholds the inmost recesses of man's heart, saw the vanity of the prince and checked him for it. He sent Isaias to acquaint him, that since he was pleased the Babylonians should see his treasures, they should be all carried to the city of Babylon, and that his children, as well as others of the royal race of Juda, should serve as eunuchs in the court of Babylon. This prediction began to be verified in part very soon after Ezechias's death, which happened at the end of the fifteen years that had been granted him, after a glorious and religious reign of nine and twenty years. He was succeeded by his son Manasses, a boy of twelve years old. This prince, unfortunately bereft of his father at an age too tender to be his own guardian, grew up in vice, and in wickedness surpassed the worst of his predecessors. He undid all that his father had done; he seduced his subjects into the abominations of Achab; he sacrificed to Baal; he adored the whole host of heaven; he renewed the filthy enormities of the ancient Amorrheans, and set up an idol in the very temple. By his order the streets of Jerusalem flowed with innocent blood, and amongst the other victims of his cruel tyranny fell also the prophet Isaias, equally venerable for his sanctity as for his grey hairs. These and the like crimes provoked Almighty God to denounce against Jerusalem the vengeance which he had already executed upon Samaria, to erase the city, and to deliver the remnants of his people into the hands of their enemies. The Babylonians soon after invaded Judea, Manasses was defeated, taken prisoner, bound in fetters, and carried off to Babylon. The miseries he there suffered, however painful in themselves, became to him the spring of real happiness. Afflictions gave him understanding; he acknowledged the justice of God in his punishment, became a true penitent, and by his humble prayers obtained not only the pardon of his crimes, but also a release from his imprisonment. Being restored to his kingdom, he endeavoured, by public virtues, to repair the evils which he had caused by public crimes. He reigned five and fifty years. Manasses knew, says the sacred text, and acknowledged the Lord to be truly God. He confessed his omnipotence, which sovereignly disposes of the things below; he adored his justice, which spares not even kings themselves; he extolled, in fine, his goodness, which hears the prayers, and pardons the sins of the penitent.

JUDITH, V.

DURING the reign of Manasses, and after his release from captivity, as seems most probable, the kingdom of Juda was invaded by a formidable army of Assyrians, under the command of Holofernes. The rise and fall of empires is in the hand of God, who at certain moments raises one nation to chastise the sins of another nation, till the conquerors themselves deserve by their crimes to suffer the same vengeance in their turn, of which they had been the instruments before. The kings of Assyria were at that time permitted to extend their conquests, for the punishment of those whom they subdued. Nabuchodonosor, who is carefully to be distinguished from the king of that name who reigned in Babylon, had formed a project of reducing the nations round to his obedience, and of making himself an universal monarch. For that purpose he raised an immense army, which he put under the command of Holofernes, with orders to conquer every kingdom in the West. Holofernes fancied that no power upon earth would be able to stand against him. His troops, like a torrent, over-ran the earth; towns, provinces, and kingdoms were swept away, as he marched along: his very name struck terror into all, before he came near them; for he plundered and destroyed every thing, where the least opposition was made to his progress. Ambassadors arrived from all parts to make their submission to him, upon the terms that he was pleased to prescribe; and notwithstanding the servile honours they paid him, it was with the greatest difficulty they were suffered to live, after being deprived of their liberties and fortunes. The provinces of Mesopotamia, Cicilia, Syria, and Lybia, had submitted to the conqueror. The trembling Jews saw the storm coming fast upon them: they cast their eyes upon the holy city and the temple, and being sensible that every human effort they could make, would be insufficient to defend them, they endeavoured by prayer and fasting to engage the God of armies in their favour. In him they hoped as their only refuge, and in him they solely trusted for success in the warlike preparations they were making. Holofernes being informed of their resolution, was enraged to think that a people could exist hardy enough to oppose his arms. He desired to know who that people was; when Achior the general of the Ammonites, who was come to surrender himself to the Assyrians, began to recount the origin and progress of the Jewish nation; he discoursed of the power and majesty of the God whom they adored, related the wonders he had wrought at sundry times in their defence, and concluded, that every effort to subdue them would be ineffectual, unless they had forfeited the divine protection by their sins. Holofernes thought himself injured by such a speech; he wondered how any man could imagine, that a nation unarmed and unmanned, as he supposed the Jews to be, would be able to resist the great Nabuchodonosor; he commanded Achior to be bound in chains for his bold discourse, and sent into the city of Bethulia, there to wait his doom with the inhabitants of the place. Achior related to the Bethulians how exasperated Holofernes was; how he had vowed their destruction, and what vengeance he threatened, as soon as he could storm their city. The Bethulians humbled themselves before God, being resolved to make the best defence they could; they redoubled their prayers with a holy confidence in God, and comforted Achior, with the hope of seeing Bethulia triumph over the vain boast of Holofernes.

A.M. 3338.] *Fortitude of Judith.* [A.C. 662.

JUDITH X.

BETHULIA was situated amongst the mountains of Galilee, a city strongly fortified both by art and nature. Holofernes, at the head of an army, consisting of a hundred and twenty thousand foot, and twenty-two thousand horse, advanced to besiege it. The vast superiority of his numbers was enough to damp the most intrepid resolution of men, who had trusted in any other than the divine power. The Bethulians took up their weapons with a strong reliance on the Lord of Hosts, and defended themselves with surprising vigour, till Holofernes cut off the conduit, and possessed himself of the springs that supplied the town with water. Their courage then sunk, and their former resolution failed them. Nothing but murmurs and cries of despondency were heard in every quarter; their cisterns were dry, no succour was expected: finding themselves in distress, they cast the whole blame upon their chiefs, for not having made their peace at first with Holofernes, and declared aloud, that it was better to die at once by the sword, than to drag out life by a lingering death. Ozias, who commanded in the town, did and said all he could to console and rouse them: they were not inclined to hear him, and tumultuously insisted upon his surrendering the city immediately to the enemy; and it was but by his tears and entreaties, that he prevailed upon them to wait five days longer, promising to comply with their request, if within that time no succour should appear. Then it was that Judith began to show herself. Judith was a widow woman of more than ordinary virtue; from the time of her husband's death, she bid adieu to the finery of dress; and though possessed of a plentiful fortune and pleasing beauty, had consecrated the remainder of her days to devotion and penance. In the present distress of her country, she felt herself pushed on by a secret impulse to make some generous effort for the common good. She resolved upon an enterprise the most hazardous and singular; it could only be suggested by that divine Spirit, which inspired her with a fortitude equal to the danger; it was to visit Holofernes in his tent. She sent to the ancients Chabri and Charmi to come to her house, and having reproached them for their despondency in pretending to prescribe a time for the divine mercy, she told them that she had formed a plan for their delivery, and begged their prayers for its success. She mentioned not what her intention was, and dismissed them. As soon as they were gone, she shut herself up in her oratory, prostrated herself upon the ground, and by fervent prayer implored the divine blessing. She rose up full of confidence, put off her widow's weeds and clothes of penance, and adorned herself with all the graces that the richness and ornaments of dress could give. The purity of her intention sanctified the action, and God himself, says the sacred text, added to her beauty. Being attended by her maid, to whom she gave a bottle of wine and bread for their provision, Judith went praying along the street, till she came to the town gate, where Ozias and the ancients were waiting to give her their blessing, and wish success to her undertaking. She passed through the gates, and hastened down the hill towards the Assyrian camp about break of day, when the advanced guard perceived her coming. Being struck with her incomparable beauty, they took and conducted her to the tent of Holofernes their general. Holofernes was captivated at the very sight of her charms, bade her not fear, and asked the motive of her coming. She replied, that it was to fly from a city which she saw was on the brink of ruin, because its inhabitants, by their crimes, had provoked the wrath of God, and were, therefore, abandoned to the sword of their enemies. Holofernes interpreted Judith's words according to the pride of his own heart, and admired her wisdom, in which she seemed to excel as much as in beauty: he allotted her a separate tent, and gave orders that she should be respectfully supplied with every thing she wanted, and be at liberty to go in and out when, and as often as she pleased. She returned his courtesies with thanks, excused herself from eating of the meat he offered her, saying, that she had brought her own little provision with her, and could eat of nothing but what was allowed her by the law she professed. Thus, unawed by human respect, and unshaken by fear, Judith, in the midst of danger, and in the camp of her enemies, forgot not her duty to God, nor her obedience to his holy law.

A.M. 3338.] *Triumph of Judith.* [A.C. 662.

JUDITH, xiii.

JUDITH made use of the liberty she had received from Holofernes, of going in and out of her tent to adore her God; she went forth every night into the vale of Bethulia, bathed in the fountain, and returned, praying to the Lord God of Israel, that he would direct her steps for the delivery of his people. On the fourth day Holofernes appointed his chief officers to sup with him, and sent an invitation to Judith, that she would consent not only to eat and drink in joyfulness, but also to dwell with him: for he was deeply enamoured with her beauty. Judith, being in hopes that it might give her an opportunity of accomplishing the design she had in view for the good of her country, did not reject the proposal, but decked herself out to advantage, and repaired to the general's tent. The general was unusually gay on the occasion, and drank more plentifully than ever he had done before. When it was grown late the officers retired, and left Holofernes and Judith in the tent together.

Oppressed with sleep and wine he lay upon his bed; she rose up, and standing before the bed for some time, prayed to God in silence; with tears in her eyes she conjured him to strengthen her arm, and to second her endeavours in the service of her country. Armed with fortitude above her sex, she advanced to the bed's head; there hung the sword of Holofernes; she took it down, and drew it out of the scabbard; then lifting up her eyes to heaven, she twisted her hand in his hair, and at two strokes severed his head from the body. She wrapped up the head in his own rich canopy; and having taken some time to recover herself from the agitation she was in, went out and gave it to her maid, who

was waiting at the door of the pavilion. They then walked off together as they had done the three foregoing nights, and unsuspectedly passing through the guards, directed their steps towards the vale of Bethulia. When they came to the town gate, Judith called upon the watch to let them in. Judith's voice was no sooner heard than the ancients were called, and the whole city was in motion to receive her. By the light of torches they conducted her to a high place in the town, where silence being proclaimed, she began to harangue and exhort them to return thanks to God, for the protection he had given them by her arm, producing to public view the trophy of her victory, the head of Holofernes: a horrid spectacle to the eyes of humanity; but of joy and triumph to the citizens of Bethulia. Ozias and the ancients vied with each other in the praises of a woman, who had thus saved their lives and liberties at the peril of her own. Achior was desired to approach, and to view the head of the tyrant, who, in contempt of the God of Israel, had proudly devoted him and the Bethulians to a cruel death. Achior threw himself at the feet of Judith, professed his belief in the God whom she adored, and declared himself a Jew. Judith having thus acted her part, gave the citizens notice that they must now act theirs, and be ready to sally forth at sun-rise upon the enemy, with as much noise and clamour as they could. The Assyrians were alarmed with the unusual vigour of the besieged, who had hitherto kept themselves close within their walls; they ran to awake their general, and found the mangled trunk of a man weltering in his blood, without a head. There was nothing to be seen but confusion; nothing heard but yells of despair throughout the camp: being under no command, the Assyrians began to fly different ways, as their frights and fears dispersed them. The Hebrews pursued them with incredible slaughter, and notice being given to the neighbouring towns, the whole country was immediately in arms to demolish the flying enemy. An immense spoil was shared amongst the conquerors, and public rejoicings for the glorious victory were continued for three months. Joachim the high-priest, with all his ancients, went from Jerusalem to Bethulia to see and honour the woman, whom they styled the glory of Jerusalem, the joy of Israel, and honour of the people. Far from being elated by the encomiums they gave her, Judith remained as humble in her own eyes, as she was great in theirs: in a sublime canticle she proclaimed the praises of God, who had given her victory, and to whom she gave the glory. She retired back to her domestic oratory, made her servant free, resumed her private practises of prayer and holy fasting, and never after passed the threshold of her door, but on the solemn festivals of the year, when she appeared abroad with great glory.

Admirable is this history of Judith in all its circumstances. By an event which surpasses whatever fabulous historians have invented to display the courage of their heroes, we see that God is the protector of those who fear him, and that invincible are they who know how to put their trust in him. A single woman, by her unparalleled fortitude, defeated one of the most formidable armies that was ever set on foot; she alone preserved Bethulia, and rescued the whole country from destruction. But what makes Judith still more worthy of our admiration is, the victory she gained over herself. To prayer and fasting she joined the virtue of chastity all the days of her widowhood; and when the victory she had gained over Holofernes, had set her up as the object of public commendation, she hastened back within the walls of her private oratory, as though she were a stranger to her own merit, and humbly retreated from the face of her fellow-citizens, as though she had done nothing to deserve their praise.

A.M. 3374.] *Piety of King Josias.* [A.C. 626.
4 KINGS, xxii.

KING Manasses was succeeded by his son Amon, who imitating the impiety, but not the repentance of his father, died by the hands of his own servants, after a miserable reign of two years. The untimely death of Amon vacated the throne for his son, whose name, the celebrated Josias, the prophet had for ages before announced to the world. This prince was inclined to deeds of goodness from his earliest years, nor to his latest breath did he ever deviate from the path he had taken. As soon as he was of an age capable of acting for himself, for at his father's death he was but eight years old, he began by exterminating the idols of Baal, which had been set up in the country. His zeal was not confined within the bounds of his own kingdom; he extended it to a great part of the territories that had been once possessed by the unhappy Israelites, and endeavoured to establish the true religion amongst those idolatrous inhabitants who had succeeded to their possessions. Many altars and profane groves had been left still standing in the principal towns of Manasses, Ephraim, Simeon and Nephthali: he destroyed them all, broke the idols into pieces; and strewed the fragments upon the tombs of those who had immolated to them; he dug up the bones of those devoted priests who had once sacrificed to the calves of Jeroboam, and burned them upon the altar at Bethel. When he had done this, he set about repairing the temple, which by profanation and neglect had fallen greatly to decay. Then it was that Helcias the high-priest, in examining into things himself, found the book of Deuteronomy, written by the hand of Moses, which he delivered to Saphan the scribe, who carried it to the king. It was read aloud, and upon hearing the dreadful threats that God there utters against those who shall depart from his holy law, Josias rent his garments, and commanded Helcias to go and consult the Lord for him and the remnant of Israel and Juda, concerning the evils with which they were threatened in the book that was found. There lived at that time in Jerusalem a holy woman called Holda, and noted for the spirit of prophecy. Helcias, in obedience to the king's commands, went to consult her, and received for answer, that the threats contained in the sacred volume should with the utmost rigour be executed upon Jerusalem and the sinful inhabitants thereof; but because the king of Juda had been moved with the fear of God, and had humbled himself by penance and true contrition of heart, that the weight of God's wrath should not fall upon that place, till after he was peaceably deposited with his ancestors in the tomb. Upon the report of that answer, Josias called the ancients of Juda and Jerusalem together in the temple, and read to them the book of Deuteronomy from the beginning to the end. When he had done, he made a solemn covenant with Almighty God, and engaged himself to perform the things that were written in the book which he had read. Standing up in his tribunal before the whole multitude, he promised from his heart to observe all the divine precepts, and by his pressing exhortations persuaded his subjects to make the same promise. The exhortations and example of that good king, had such an effect upon the people, that they swerved not from their duty as long as he lived; and unfortunate was it for his kingdom, that he was not blessed with a longer life. Going out unadvisedly to battle against Nechao the king of Egypt, he received a wound, of which he died, after a godly reign of one and thirty years.

Almighty God hastened to draw this religious prince out of the midst of iniquity, says St. Ambrose, that he might not behold the calamities which were going to be poured down upon the kingdom of Juda. Josias had exerted the most active zeal, not only to abolish the remains of idolatry, but also to renew the exercise of true religion through his dominions; he celebrated the feast of the passover with a solemnity unknown to any of his predecessors; by his exemplary piety he teaches kings and persons in authority, that their first duty is to God; that while they expect to be obeyed themselves, they must see to have a due obedience paid to God; and that both by word and example they must enforce at least the same respect for the divine commands, as they do for their own. To the humble docility with which he listened to the book of Deuteronomy, the Scriptures attribute the felicity of this prince. The same disposition of an humble, docile heart, ought we to carry with us, as often as we go to hear, or sit ourselves down to read the word of God; a disposition to learn and practise what it teaches.

A.M. 3398.] *Siege of Jerusalem.* [A.C. 602.
4 Kings, xxv.

Judea, being deprived of her last good king, mourned as for the loss of a common parent. The wicked conduct of Joachaz, the son and successor of Josias, made all good men more sensible of their loss. The prince, who had no pretensions to the crown by birth, gained it by favour of the people, and at the end of three months lost it by the hand of Nechao king of Egypt. For Nechao in his return from the war which he had undertaken against the Assyrians, coming to Jerusalem deposed the miserable Joachaz, whom he carried with him in chains to Egypt, and appointed his elder brother Eliacim to reign in his place. Eliacim, better known by the name of Joakim, reigned eleven years, and though he had the advantage of many living prophets to point out the path of virtue, he nevertheless plunged into the depth of wickedness. The prophecy of Jeremiah being read to him, he cut it into pieces with a penknife, and threw it by scraps into the fire, on account of the threats it contained against him. The Spirit of God commanded Jeremiah to pen down the same prophecy in another volume, and to add still new threats to the former. Threats had no effect upon the heart of a hardened sinner; the measure of Juda's crimes was completed; the chief priests and people plunged into the most shameful abominations of the Gentiles, polluted the house of God, and scorned every messenger that was sent to remind them of their duty. The long injured mercy of Almighty God calling them to repentance, was then turned into justice, and Babylon was the scourge appointed by God, to reduce the inhabitants of Juda to the state to which Ninive had reduced those of Israel. Nabuchodonosor with a powerful army laid siege to Jerusalem, which he took by capitulation, made Joakim his prisoner, bound him with chains, and carried him with Daniel and other noble youths, and part of the sacred vessels, to Babylon. This happened in the year of the world 3398, and from that year is dated the first of the seventy years' captivity that the Jews endured in the country of Chaldea. Joakim seems to have recovered his liberty again, upon his promise of paying true allegiance and a yearly tribute to the Babylonian monarch. But breaking his oath by an open revolt at the end of three years, he again fell into the hands of the Chaldeans, from whom he received the just punishment of his crimes, by a violent and disgraceful death. Joachin, *alias* Jechonias, his wicked son, succeeded him for three months, when Nabuchodonosor snatched him from his throne, and carried him bound in chains away to Babylon. His mother, his wives, his children, and chief nobles of the kingdom, were sharers with him in his captivity: the treasures also of the temple, and the golden vessels, which Solomon had finished with so much art and magnificence, were at the same time transported to Babylon. In Judea little more remained besides the shadow of a kingdom, and some sad remains of its former grandeur. A merciful God seemed unwilling to inflict the last stroke upon his chosen people; he permitted their power to sink by degrees, that the sight of present calamities, and the gradual approach of greater evils might awaken them to repentance. Sedecias, the uncle of Joachin, and son of Josias, was invested with the title and appearance of king, under Nabuchodonosor. He was a worthless prince, averse to every thing that was good, deaf to the exhortations of Jeremiah, and buried in vice. The body of the people imitated the example of their prince; they defiled the land with pagan crimes, they insulted the prophets, and laughed at the divine threats. Sedecias in the ninth year of his reign revolted against the king of Babylon, and his revolt brought on the punishment due to his other crimes. Nabuchodonosor led a formidable army against him, and blocked him up in the city of Jerusalem. Though beset with the terrors of war without, and pinched with the miseries of famine within, the besieged vigorously defended themselves for two years. A wide breach was at last made in the wall, and the town carried by assault: the wretched Jews had nothing to trust to but flight and the victor's clemency. Sedecias escaped by night and fled towards Jericho. But being overtaken and brought back, he was presented to Nabuchodonosor, who executed severe vengeance upon him. Having ordered his sons to be massacred before his face, he plucked out his eyes, loaded him with irons, and carried him away captive to Babylon. Nabuchodonosor having thus taken not so much his own as the Almighty's revenge upon a stiff-necked people, returned in triumph to his own country, leaving Nabuzardan his general to complete the ruin of Judea. His orders were to throw down the walls of Jerusalem, to demolish the temple, the royal palace, and the rest of the houses; to strip the inhabitants of every valuable effect they had, and transport them to Babylon, so that none should remain except the poor husbandmen, who were necessary to cultivate the vineyards and plough the land.

Such was the dismal state to which Jerusalem was reduced in punishment of her sins. Such was the fall of that once happy city, and with such energy of expression is her devastation described by Jeremiah, in his Lamentations, that one must have lost the sense of feeling not to sympathize with the prophet in his grief. Holy is our grief, and salutary is our affliction, says St. Austin, when to a sincere detestation of sin we join our tears of compassion for the suffering sinner.

A.M. 3417.] *Destruction of the kingdom of Juda.*—4 KINGS, XXV. [A.C. 583.

NABUZARDAN executed the orders of his royal master with a severe hand. The destruction of every thing both great and sacred in Jerusalem was completed; amongst the miserable inhabitants that were collected for their transmigration into the country of Babylon, was the prophet Jeremiah. Nabuchodonosor, out of respect to his eminent sanctity, had given special orders about him. Nabuzardan had also a great reverence for the holy man, and left it to his choice, either to accompany the captives or remain in his own country. Compassion for the distressed husbandmen, who were left without help or counsel, determined the prophet to choose the latter. But his presence was of little service to men who were too headstrong to profit by advice. The appointment of Godolias to be their governor excited their jealousy; they refused to submit to his authority; they rose up and murdered him and his attendants in the town of Maspha. When they had committed the rash action, they began to consider and to dread the consequences: they reflected that Godolias had been appointed by Nabuchodonosor, and that the murder they were guilty of would be looked upon as a treasonable insult against the royal authority. The fear of punishment made them unanimously resolve to abandon the country, and fly into Egypt. Jeremiah endeavoured to calm their fears, and to dissuade them from their purpose, promising, that if they staid, no harm would befall them; but if they went, that they should every one of them perish in the land, which, like their own, was already destined to destruction. Notwithstanding that, they still persisted in their first resolution; their fears of the Chaldeans made them deaf to reason, and they unfortunately concluded, that there was no other way to preserve their lives, than by retreating into Egypt.

Thus was Judea abandoned by the remaining part of its natives, and reduced to a lonesome desert; thus was the plummet of the house of Achab, and the cord of Samaria, stretched out upon Jerusalem, as the Lord had long threatened; thus was the kingdom of Juda blotted out, and the degenerate Hebrews driven from the land, which had been given to their forefathers as an inheritance for ever, if they had remained faithful to the Lord their God. Jeremiah had used his endeavours to make the people sensible of their crimes, and exhorted them to avert the stroke of divine vengeance by a timely repentance. Being actuated with true zeal, he sought their salvation, not their praise; he flattered not their sins; he spoke not what might please, but what he thought might instruct and rouse them; and when he found that neither his representations nor his exhortations had any effect upon men who were running headlong into ruin, he admonished them to be upon the watch against the corruption of Babylon, lest in the midst of idolaters they might forget the religion of their ancestors, and adopt the superstition of the Gentiles.

JER. xxxviii.

JEREMIAH not being able to persuade that miserable remnant of the Jews whom Nabuchodonosor had spared, to remain in their own country, was forced to accompany them into Egypt, where, according to the Hebrew tradition, he fell a martyr to their resentment, for having reprehended them for their idolatry. Jeremiah was of the sacerdotal race, and noted amongst his contemporaries for great holiness of life. Being sanctified from his mother's womb, he was in the early years of his youth called to the ministry of God's word, and began to preach by the time he had attained the fifteenth year of his age. He was favoured with many revelations relative to the future misfortunes of the Jews. In his style and manner of expression, he is, of all the prophets, the most pathetic, as appears from his Lamentations. He saw the holy city of Jerusalem over-run with vices, which he knew would end in the ruin of his country, and therefore never ceased to admonish his fellow-citizens of the impending calamities which God, in his anger, had prepared for the punishment of an impenitent people. His zeal displeased the wicked, and excited the animosity of the great. Jeremiah saw the storm of persecution gathering round him: he saw his enemies prepared to take away his life, but was not daunted; he heard their threats, but did not shrink from his duty; being ready to seal with his blood the truths he uttered, the violence of his persecutors made him more animated and vigorous in his public discourses. The wicked princes of the people would

hear him no longer; they applied to Sedecias for leave to throw him into a cistern of deep mud. The king, though an admirer of the holy prophet, weakly yielded to their request, which was immediately put into execution; and Jeremiah must in a short time have been stifled, if the king had not, upon the representation of one of his officers, quickly ordered him to be taken out.

St. Jerome seems to wonder how a man, alone and unsupported as Jeremiah was, could stand against so many powerful adversaries; the holy doctor then corrects his surprise, dives into the cause of that wonderful effect of the prophet's fortitude, and ascribes it, not to the abilities of man, but to the omnipotence of God. For in the first page of Jeremiah's book we find, that God had promised to endue him with such resolution and fortitude of mind, as should enable him to stand unshaken, like a column of iron, or a wall of brass, against the attacks that should be made against him. He was assured of the divine protection, and from thence arose his force and confidence. From the same source also springs that magnanimity and undaunted courage, which we so deservedly admire in the martyrs and other saints of God. In this sense St. Cyprian says, that a man of God, that is, a man who, with truth upon his lips, has the love of God in his heart, and the fear of God before his eyes, defies the keenest rage of human malice: such a man may be deprived of life, but he cannot be overcome.

A.M. 3420.] *The Prophet Baruch.*—Bar. ii. [A.C. 580.

The prophet Baruch, however distinguished for his noble birth, was more illustrious for his piety. Drawn by the love of virtue, he bade adieu to every worldly advantage, to become the disciple of Jeremiah, whose secretary he was, and inseparable companion in his labours. He was the faithful interpreter of his master's will, and delivered the divine mandates to a sinful nation, with a magnanimity equal to that which we so much admire in the conduct and writings of Jeremiah himself. In the painful hardships which that holy prophet had to undergo, either in the discharge of his ministry, or from the malice of his enemies, Baruch never left him, being always ready to share in his sufferings, and to help him by his services, as far as he was able. Amidst the heavy trials which, in the old law, were a figure of those heavier labours that the ministers of the gospel were to undergo in the new, he movingly expresses how his mind was affected at the evils which he either saw in others, or experienced in himself. Alas! unhappy man as I am, says he in the depth of his affliction, why does the Lord thus send me grief upon grief? I pass all the days of my life in groans, and my growing sorrows leave me no repose. Such were the complaints of a man labouring under the load of adversity. Many of the sufferings which he had to bear, and which made the subject of his complaints, were the consequence of his attachment to Jeremiah. The persecutions that were raised against the one fell likewise upon the other; but nothing could ever make him break off the connection, or depart from his venerable master, as long as he lived. He remained his faithful attendant in life, and became the zealous imitator of his virtues after his death. He succeeded him in instructing and exhorting the people to their duty; his discourses breathe the same ardent zeal, but are tempered with expressions of profound humility. Behold the manner in which he addresses himself to Almighty God: "Hear, Lord, our humble prayers, and put an end to our captivity for thy own sake: draw us from the depth of our afflictions, that the world may know thou art the Lord our God. From thy holy habitation, O Lord, cast down thine eyes of pity on us; vouchsafe only to incline thine ear, and graciously hear us. Open thine eyes and see, for the dead who are shut up within the tomb, and whose souls are severed from their bodies, shall render neither honour nor glory to thy name. It is the living, who bend beneath the weight of their chastisements, who humble themselves in fasting and in mourning, whose eyes are grown dim with weeping, and whose hearts are rent with sorrow, that shall give glory to thee, O Lord, and make thy justice be revered." Hence, to all Christians who are the disciples, not of prophets only, but of a crucified God, it is obvious to conclude, that in their sufferings they must be humble as well as patient: for if patience be the perfection of charity, humility is the sanctification of patience, which is the support and preservation of every other virtue.

The twelve Minor Prophets.

Isaiah and Jeremiah, with Ezekiel and Daniel, are called the greater prophets; but why they are so called, no other reason can seemingly be given, than that they are more diffuse and voluminous in their prophecies than others. For all prophecy is equally from God, and whether it be long or short, it always is a supernatural gift of the Holy Ghost. Besides the four we have mentioned, there are twelve others, who being not so extensive in their writings, are commonly called the minor prophets. The time in which they flourished includes, from the first to the last, about four hundred years: for they lived not all at once, but were sent at different periods by a merciful Providence, to oppose the torrent of impiety, and to rouse the faith of an offending people. Baruch is not ranked by name in either class; for the prophecy which now bears his name, was for a long time supposed to have been the work of Jeremiah, and in effect is yet believed to have been mostly dictated by him, though penned by Baruch after his death.

In the order of time, the first of the minor prophets seems to have been Jonas, of whom mention has been already made, and he began to prophesy when he was very young. For he foretold the conquest which Jeroboam, the second king of Israel, was to make against the Syrians, by restoring the borders of Israel from Emath to the sea. This was under the reign of Amasias, king of Juda, about 823 years before Christ. This prophet's mission to the city of Ninive was of a later date.

Osee prophesied under Ozias, Joathan, Achaz, and Ezechias, kings of Juda, and continued preaching for near a century, having begun about 815 years before Christ.

Amos prophesied in the 25th of Ozias, king of Juda, about 780 years before Christ.

Abdias, though he has made no mention of the time in which he lived, seems to follow close upon the two last-mentioned prophets.

Michcas prophesied in the reign of Joathan, king of Juda, and expressly specified Bethlehem for the place of our blessed Saviour's birth, 750 years befor the time.

Nahum prophesied after the ten tribes were carried into

captivity, and foretold the destruction of Ninive. He lived under Ezechias, king of Juda, about 713 years before Christ.

Joel, although it be not specified in what reign he preached, seems to have lived under Manasses, king of Juda, and foretells the great evils that were coming upon the people for their sins, about 680 years before Christ.

Sophonias lived in the reign of Josias, son of Amon, and pronounced a woe upon the sinful city of Jerusalem, about 630 years before Christ.

Habacuc was contemporary with the prophets Jeremiah and Daniel, foretold the invasion of the Chaldeans against Judea, and lived to see his prophecy fulfilled, 600 years before Christ.

Aggeus prophesied 520 years before Christ, and was zealous in encouraging the Jews to rebuild the temple after their return from Babylon.

Zacharias lived at the same time with Aggeus, that is, a little before the Babylonian captivity. He speaks very clearly of Jesus Christ, of the conversion of the Gentiles, and of the flourishing state of Christ's Church.

Malachias prophesied after the temple was rebuilt, and is the last of the prophets. For from his time no prophet appeared, till John the Baptist, according to his prediction, rose from the desert to prepare the way for the great Messias.

All these holy prophets, as is evinced by their writings, were animated with the same spirit, and with the same energy inveighed against the wickedness of their times. In the most explicit and decisive terms they speak of the promised Messias, the father of the future age, and Saviour of the world. And the Messias, who by the mouth of these prophets thus announced himself to the world so long beforehand, has convinced mankind that he had a self-existent Being, before he took flesh and dwelt amongst us; and that the time at which he chose to become man, was fixed by his own free will. For prophecy, according to Scripture itself, is one of the most convincing proofs we have of the Divinity. It can belong to none but God to comprehend the boundless extent of ages, and in his eternity to behold the future as intimately present to him as the past. Therefore one of the holy prophets, in insulting the idols of the Gentiles, confidently said: Tell us the secrets of futurity, and we will say, you are Gods.

EZECHIEL, i.

EZECHIEL, the son of Buzi, of the priestly race, was inspired by Almighty God, in the country of Babylon, to instruct and comfort his fellow captives by his prophetic visions, which are conveyed in a style equally mysterious and sublime. In the fifth year of the captivity of king Joachin, with whom he had been led away out of Juda, eleven years before the total destruction of Jerusalem under Sedecias, being upon the bank of the great river Chobar, or Euphrates, he perceived a whirlwind rising from the north, and a great cloud fraught with fire, which enlightened the atmosphere around. In the midst of the fiery cloud appeared four living creatures, who, in shape and body, had the likeness of a human figure; but their heads and feet were of a very singular appearance. For each one had four faces in an opposite direction, looking towards the four points of the heavens; the face of a man was on the fore-part of all the four, the face of a lion on the right, on the left was the face of an ox, and behind was the face of an eagle rising somewhat higher. They had four wings, one on every side, and under each wing a hand, resembling that of a man; their legs were straight, and the sole of their foot was like that of a calf. Two of their wings covered each one's body, and the other two were extended and lifted up, as it were, ready for flight. Whenever they moved, and they moved as the impulse of the Spirit directed them, their motion was straight forward, and they ran and returned like flashes of lightning; neither did they turn about when they went, each one having his face always pointing forward. Their whole figure glowed with the appearance of burning coals, and bright flaming lamps. By the side of each cherubim (for the prophet tells us that he knew them to be cherubims) stood a wheel with four faces, of an immense size and dreadful appearance, shining like the chrysolite stone, and having their circles full of eyes. Each of the four wheels was a compound figure of two wheels set across one another, and so formed as to run with equal volubility towards any one of the four points of the world, without the necessity of turning. For the same divine Spirit which actuated the living creatures, also actuated the wheels, and they all stood still or moved on in the same proportion and velocity together, as the Spirit of life impelled them, forming, as it were, a magnificent chariot, in which the Almighty rode. For over the heads of the living creatures was expanded the likeness of the firmament, resembling crystal, and above the firmament a throne shining like the sapphire-stone, and on the throne was the appearance of a man, glowing like resplendent brass from his loins upwards, and from his loins downwards like shining fire. At the sight of this awful vision, Ezechiel fell upon his face: the Lord bade him rise, and announce his judgments to the children of Israel. The prophet rose in obedience to the divine command, and remained seven days in affliction with his people, when the Lord ordered him to go into the plain, where he showed him the same mysterious vision a second time. The term fixed for the total ruin of Jerusalem was in the interim hastening on; the remaining part of its inhabitants plunged into fresh crimes, and their hearts were hardened in iniquity. In the sixth year of king Joachin's captivity, Ezechiel saw the glory of the Lord a third time, being elevated in spirit to Jerusalem. The four living creatures and the wheels were exhibited to him in the same manner as he had seen them upon the banks of the Euphrates. He, moreover, saw six champions in armour, advancing to destroy the sinful city, and beside them a man clothed in linen, whom the Lord commanded to take off the burning coals which were in the midst of the wheels between the cherubims, and to pour them out upon Jerusalem. And after that the cherubims lifted up their wings, and the wheels with them, and the glory of the Lord departed from the midst of the city, and rested upon the mountain of Olives. The prophet saw it no longer, and was restored, in spirit, to the land of Chaldea.

The images exhibited in this vision to Ezechiel, were calculated to impress upon the minds of the Jewish people, a lively and respectful idea of the majesty of God, whom they had been used to consider as sitting upon the cherubims. To strike with awe, and to deter them from sin, the prophet described the Lord as coming forth to chastise them in his wrath, and was represented by the whirlwind and fiery cloud arising from the north; for Babylon, from whence the Almighty poured vengeance upon his faithless people, lay to the north of Jerusalem.

EZECH. xxxvii.

EZECHIEL was inspired, as has been seen, to declare the severe judgments of Almighty God to the impenitent Israelites, in the figurative language of sublime prophecy. The vision, in which he saw the heavy chastisement prepared by an injured Deity, not only against the Jewish nation at that time, but also against a sinful world in the latter days, are mysterious and alarming. He was likewise favoured with other visions, which were calculated to instil comfort into the afflicted, and to exhibit the pleasing effects of the divine goodness to a repenting people. In the twenty-fifth year of his captivity, he was transported, in spirit, to one of the high mountains in Judea, where he saw the temple of Jerusalem restored to its ancient splendour, and the glory of the God of Israel entering into it again, by the same eastern gate through which he had seen it depart, according to the appearance which had been shown him twenty years before, in the vision of wheels and cherubims near the river of Chobar. The re-establishment of the Jewish nation had some years before been displayed to him in his extraordinary vision of the bones. He was taken up by the spirit of God, and set down in the midst of a plain, which was scattered over on every side with a prodigious number of dry bones. After he had been led round, and had surveyed the horrid spectacle at leisure, the Lord commanded him to bid those bones unite again, and resume their former state. The prophet spoke as he was commanded, in the name of God,

by whom all things live, and to whom nothing is difficult. He commanded the dry bones to hear him, and as he prophesied, behold, a great commotion, with a rustling noise began amongst them: bones approached to bones, each one fixing itself in its respective socket; the nerves and muscles were stretched out upon them; flesh grew over, and they were clothed with skin, so that nothing but life was wanting to renew and perfect their former being. O son of man, said the Lord God of Ezechiel, bid the spirit come from the four winds, and blow upon the dead that they may live again. Ezechiel spoke, and at his word the spirit came into them, and they lived, and they stood upon their feet, an exceeding great army. Almighty God was then pleased to explain the vision to his prophet, and informed him, that the bones were the house of Israel, who, upon the destruction of their city, thought their hopes were lost, and their existence entirely cut off: but that he would open their graves, that he would raise and bring them back into the land of Israel, where they and their children's children shall dwell; that his servant David should be their prince for ever, that his tabernacle should be with them, that he would be their God, and they should be his people; that the nation, in fine, should know that he was the Lord, the sanctifier of Israel, when his sanctuary should be in the midst of them for ever.

Thus did Almighty God console his people in their distress; thus did he assure them of his pardon upon their repentance, and thus did he promise to lead them back out of their captivity, and restore them to their country, as it effectually came to pass some years after under the conduct of Zorobabel. This consolatory promise of Almighty God, was not confined to the bare re-establishment of the Jewish people in the land of Israel; it included also those greater blessings which were to extend to all nations throughout the world, by the establishment of the Christian church. Founded in a covenant of peace between God and his people, and cleansed from sin in the blood of Jesus Christ, the son of David, according to the flesh, the church, as one undivided fold, was then promised by the divine Spirit, that it should multiply and flourish, under one shepherd, to the end of the world.

A.M. 3410. *The Prophet Daniel.* [A.C. 590.
DAN. i. xiii.

AT the time that king Joakim first fell into the hands of Nabuchodonosor, Daniel, a youth of the royal blood of Judea, was, with many others, carried away to Babylon, When they were brought thither, he, with three other virtuous and comely youths, whose names were Azarias. Ananias, and Misael, was chosen out by Nabuchodonosor's order to be instructed in the language and manners of the Chaldeans. Asphenez, the master of the eunuchs, committed them to the care of Malafar, a principal officer at court, who had orders to see them daintily nourished with provisions of meat and wine from the king's table, that at the end of three years they might be fit to appear before the king. The religious youths being afraid of eating any thing that was forbidden them by the law, earnestly entreated Asphenez not to insist upon their tasting any thing besides water and legumes. Asphenez, however willing to indulge them, was apprehensive lest such a diet, instead of nourishing, might make them look pale and meagre, which he knew would displease the king. Daniel, therefore, made his application to Malafar, and begged they might be allowed to try their meagre diet only for ten days. Malafar consented, and at the end of the term there appeared upon their cheeks a more fresh and more healthy bloom, than in any of the other children, who had been pampered with the king's delicacies. Hence we see, how much God is pleased with a well-regulated abstinence, according to the order which he has established, and that it is not so much in the food we take, as in the blessing which he gives it, that the nourishment of life consists. The four Hebrew children were presented to the king at the end of three years, and were found so well accomplished, that in science and wisdom they far surpassed the natives of the country. Daniel distinguished himself even above his companions; he shone with superior talents, and began to be known for his gift of prophecy, which he discovered very early in life, in the affair of the chaste Susanna.

Susanna was the daughter of Helcias, a religious man, amongst the Jewish captives, and married to one Joakim, who, for his riches, was distinguished amongst his countrymen, and to whose house they resorted to have their private contests decided by the two judges, whom the Babylonians permitted them to choose every year. Susanna, by her religious parents had been timely instructed in the law of God, and received an education conformable to its precepts. To this pious education the holy fathers attribute the virtues of her riper years. Her prudent and chaste conduct had acquired her a reputation which all admired, and which none but the two wicked elders, who were appointed judges that year, would have attempted to rob her of. As they frequented Joakim's house, they fixed their eyes upon his wife, and fell in love with her; for the comeliness of her features were equal to the chastity of her mind. They observed, that when the people departed at noon, Susanna went every day to take a private walk in her husband's orchard, where there was a bathing-place. They were as yet ignorant of each other's secret designs, but happening one day to meet in the same place, and for the same wicked purpose of watching an opportunity to meet with Susanna alone, they discovered their passion to one another, and agreed to concur together in pursuing it. They stole one day privately into the orchard, and lay concealed. Susanna, suspecting nothing of their being there, went, as usual, to take her walk; it was a hot day, and the coolness of the stream invited her to bathe. She bid the two maids that attended her, fetch the oil and washing balls, and carefully shut the doors of the orchard. The maids did as they were ordered, and went out by a back door. They were no sooner gone, than the two elders suddenly arose, and running up to Susanna, made their criminal proposals, and pressed her consent, saying, that if she refused, they would bear witness of her having sent away her maids, that she might sin in private with a young man they had discovered with her. The virtuous Susanna sighed, and said, I am straitened on every side; for if I do this thing, it is death to me, and if I do not, I shall not escape your hands; but it is better for me to fall guiltless into your hands, than to sin in the sight of God. With that she raised her voice, and, as loud as she could, cried out for help. The elders also cried out at the same time: full of malice and vexation, they ran to the orchard gate, and declared to all they met, that they had surprised Susanna in the act of adultery; that they had found her with a young man, whom they had attempted to secure, but for want of help had been forced to let go. An accusation was then lodged in form against the innocent Susanna, and she was cited to take her trial next day before the people.

A.M. 3410.] *Chastity of Susanna.* [A.C. 590.
DAN. xiii.

SUSANNA'S family were all in tears; her friends stood blushing with shame, and covered with confusion: they had been long acquainted with her character, and knew it to be the very reverse of what she was then accused of. She was carried to the place of trial: the two elders were already there, her judges, witnesses, and accusers. She stood before them modestly covered with her veil, which those wicked men commanded to be drawn from her face, that so at least

they might be satisfied with her beauty. Her friends and acquaintance wept. She poured forth a flood of tears, and lifting up her eyes to heaven, as the witness of her innocence, placed her confidence in the Lord. The two elders rising up in the midst of the people, laid their hands upon her head, stated the charge, and related a fictitious story of their own to prove it. The people being swayed by their authority, and imposed upon by the venerable appearance of their hoary locks, condemned her to death, upon no other evidence than that of her iniquitous accusers. As soon as sentence was given, Susanna with a loud voice called upon God, to whom the most hidden things are known before they come to pass, and solemnly declared, that false witness had been borne against her; that she was innocent, and should die guiltless of the crime which was maliciously forged by her enemies. Her cries were heard by the Lord, though disregarded by men. As she was led to be put to death, Daniel, a young boy, being moved by the impulse of God's holy spirit, cried aloud, I am innocent of the blood of this woman; return to judgment, ye children of Israel, for they have borne false witness against her. Though single and unsupported in the middle of a furious crowd, says St. Bernard, Daniel raised his voice in favour of oppressed innocence, and publicly protested against a sentence which he knew to be unjust. He had the people and the judges against him; but he rather chose to expose himself to the censure of men, than by a guilty silence betray his conscience in the sight of God. The people were struck, and returned in haste to the place of judgment. The old men invited Daniel, since God had given him the honour of old age, to sit down among them. Daniel told the people to separate the two old men, that he might examine them apart. His advice was followed; he questioned them separately about the place, and asked under what tree they had seen the pretended crime committed. They had not been aware of that question, nor prepared their answer; the one contradicted what the other had affirmed. The forgery by that means was detected; the adulterous judges were convicted of perjury and slander, and

condemned to suffer the punishment to which they had just before condemned the chaste and innocent Susanna.

The holy fathers speak in a very high strain of Susanna's

virtue; she may be justly styled the honour of her sex, while the two elders will be always detested as the disgrace of men. Being judges, and advanced in life, their age and office gave them great sway amongst the people, and that sway they made use of to oppress the innocent, for a crime of which they alone were guilty. Admirable, on the other hand, is the fortitude that Susanna showed in the attack they made upon her. Alone, and destitute of every succour but what she hoped from God, she was suddenly assaulted by two men, who solicited her to an action which her heart detested: they promised her life and secrecy if she consented, public shame and death if she refused. Susanna being thus reduced to the alternative, either of consenting to sin, to save her reputation and life from danger, or of sacrificing both to preserve her innocence, she did what the love of virtue inspired her to do; she turned her thoughts to God, in whom her heart had confidence, as the Scripture expresses. She considered him present, as the judge and witness of her conduct; her resolution was to preserve her soul from guilt, to retain the favour and friendship of her Creator; resigned to whatever the malice of men could do against her, she chose to secure herself a life that should never end. Her steady virtue therefore received the divine blessing; her innocence was cleared; her husband and friends gave praise to God her protector, and her chastity is become a pattern to all succeeding ages.

A.M. 3417.] *Nabuchodonosor's Dream.* [A.C. 583.

DAN. ii.

THE manner in which Daniel had acquitted himself in saving the life of Susanna, gained him great credit in the sight of the people; his fame from that day forward began to increase, and he was soon after called forth to shine in a more conspicuous sphere of life. A skill more than human in interpreting of dreams, such as formerly paved the way to Joseph's preferment in Egypt, was the occasion of Daniel's rising to the highest dignities in Babylon. But Daniel's talent was still more excellent than that of Joseph, inasmuch as Daniel discovered not only the meaning of the dream, but also the dream itself. Nabuchodonosor had dreamed a dream, of which he remembered nothing more than that he had been terribly alarmed. He sent for the wise men and astrologers of his kingdom, to tell him what it was. They all declared it to be impossible for any man upon earth to divine what another man had dreamed of, and that none but the gods themselves, whose conversation was not with men, could satisfy the king's demand. Nabuchodonosor grew furious at their answer, and in his wrath gave immediate orders that all who had the name of wise men should be put to death. The order was hastened into execution: Daniel and his three companions, Ananias, Azarias, and Misael, were reputed in the number of wise men, and accordingly sought for to be put to death. They had not yet heard of the extraordinary and cruel decree which the king had passed for that purpose, and remained ignorant of their danger, till the very man who had the execution of the order informed them of it. Daniel went immediately to the king, and begged he might have some time allowed him to consider upon and resolve his intricate question. Being indulged in his request, he came back to his companions, desired them to join with him in prayer, to the Father of lights, and that very night the whole mystery was revealed to him in a vision. He presented himself next day before the king, and offered not only to relate, but to interpret the dream, which none of the wise men of Babylon were knowing enough to find out. Nabuchodonosor seemed to express some doubt whether Daniel himself would be able to satify his demand, but desired to hear what he had to say. Daniel then began: Being in your bed, O king, you began to think what revolutions might happen in after-times, and he

to whom no mystery is unknown, showed you the things that are to come. You saw in your sleep a tall and bulky statue of a horrible aspect standing before you. The head of the statue was of gold, the breast and arms of silver, the belly and the thighs of brass, the legs of iron, and the feet partly iron, partly clay. You saw it standing in that manner, till a stone, which, without the help of human hands, was cut from a mountain, struck it on the feet, and crumbled the whole into dust; after that the stone itself became a great mountain, and filled the whole earth. Such, O king, was your dream, and this is the interpretation of it. The golden head of this huge statue denotes you and your empire. To you shall succeed a second, but less empire of silver, which shall be followed by one of brass, till the fourth of iron shall arise and break down all before it. But as the statue's feet were partly iron and partly clay, so shall this kingdom be parted within itself, when from God a fifth kingdom shall be established, which shall extend itself over the whole earth, and which no power shall ever overturn, and no length of ages ever put an end to. Nabuchodonosor listened with attention to the wonderful narration, stood astonished at the prophet's wisdom, and at the conclusion of his discourse bowed respectfully down to do him homage, confessing his God to be the God of gods, and the Lord of kings. Daniel was immediately loaded with honours and royal favours; he was created prince over all the provinces of Babylon; and at his request, his three Hebrew companions, whose names were changed into Sidrach, Misach, and Abdenago, were appointed to preside over the public works in the particular province of Babylon. This department required their attendance in the country, while Daniel, now called Balthasar, was constantly about the king's palace.

A.M. 3417.] *The Hebrews in the fiery furnace.* [A.C. 583.
DANIEL, iii.

THE three young Hebrews soon found, that in their elevated station they had much envy and malevolence to struggle against. The Babylonian nobles thought themselves disgraced by those honours which were bestowed on strangers, and watched every opportunity of revenge. Nabuchodonosor had set up a golden statue of an enormous size, and by a public edict commanded the nobles and chiefs of his kingdom to come to the dedication of it, and to adore it, under pain of death. The day appointed for the ceremony was at hand; the Chaldean princes, the captains and governors of the provinces, repaired to the plain where the statue stood; the music began to play, and at the sound all fell prostrate, as they were ordered, to adore it. Ananias, Azarias, and Misael, did not attend: their absence was taken notice of by their enemies, who eagerly seized that occasion of venting their spleen, and of accusing them of disobedience to the king. The king sent for them; he stormed and threatened to cast them into the fiery furnace, unless they complied with his edict, like the rest of his subjects. The three youths were not to be moved by such threats; full of faith and holy confidence, they steadily replied, that the God whom they adored, was able to deliver them from every evil that the king's hand could throw upon them; but, if it was his divine will to let them suffer, that they were ready for the worst, and the king might know that they would not adore his statue, nor any of his gods. Irritated by an answer which he did not expect, and which his pride could not brook, Nabuchodonosor ordered them to be bound, and cast into the burning furnace, which on that occasion was made seven times more hot than usual. The order was immediately executed: the three Hebrews were bound by the feet, and cast into the flaming furnace, clad as they were with their

robes and garments. They fell down amidst the flames harmless, whilst the men who cast them in, were burned to death,

Then Azarias standing up, raised his voice in the name of all three, and called upon the God of their forefathers for protection. Almighty God sent his angel to their relief; the angel struck off their bonds, and fanned them with a most refreshing breeze, as he walked to and fro with them amidst the surrounding flames. Full of admiration and gratitude for this miraculous interposition of the divine power, they all three, as with one voice, began to sing a sublime hymn of thanksgiving, in which they invited the whole creation to join them in proclaiming the praises of the Most High. The king's servants in the interim ceased not to throw in brimstone, pitch, and tow, to feed the flames, which burst out and consumed such of the Chaldeans as were near the furnace. The spectators stood astonished; Nabuchodonosor rose in haste to behold the holy youths in the furnace, and as he approached saw with them a fourth personage, whose form was like that of an angel. Struck with astonishment, he went to the door of the furnace, and said, Sidrach, Misach, and Abdenago, servants of the Most High God, come forth! They came out immediately; the Babylonian chiefs flocked round to examine them, and found that the fire had no power on their bodies, that it had neither touched their garments, nor singed so much as a single hair of their head. Then Nabuchodonosor broke forth in praise of the great God, who had so wonderfully delivered his three faithful servants, and published an edict, by which he made it death for any one who should dare to blaspheme the God of Sidrach, Misach, and Abdenago; and them he promoted to new dignities in the province of Babylon.

The three Hebrew youths, thus tried and thus protected in the fiery furnace, exhibit a lively image of the saints, as the holy fathers remark, in their various trials of affliction. An angel of the Lord descended with them into the furnace, and the fire consumed nothing that belonged to them besides their bonds; they felt a cool and refreshing comfort from the flames, which burst out with vehemence upon their tormentors. So it happens in the persecutions of the saints. Whenever persecutors vent their spite, whether by tortures, or by penal laws, the sharpest pain recoils back upon themselves, while the objects of their malice are repaid with consolation in their sufferings for a good cause. Afflictions only hurt the body, they purify and perfect the souls of God's chosen servants: the unction of the Holy Ghost allays their outward pains, and fills their hearts with inward joy.

A. M. 3434.] *Nabuchodonosor's Chastisement.* [A.C. 566.
DANIEL, iv.

The good fortune that attended Nabuchodonosor in his warlike expeditions, had added Egypt to his former conquests. Victory made him insolent; his immense riches, and vast extent of empire, inspired him with such notions of his own excellence, that he fancied himself to be something more than mortal. But as a proof to all succeeding ages, that the greatest potentates, in spite of their prosperity and splendid opulence, are still but poor and feeble men, God was pleased to chastise that haughty monarch in a manner the most humiliating. Nabuchodonosor in a dream saw the heavy stroke that was prepared to lower him, though he could not comprehend it. Perplexed and terrified at the mysterious vision that was shown him, he consulted Daniel, of whose enlightened knowledge and superior wisdom he had been already witness, and begged him to interpret his dream, which he related as follows: In my sleep, said he, I saw a flourishing tree, which seemed to lift its head above the clouds, and to spread its branches from one extremity of the earth to the other. It was luxuriantly clothed with comely leaves and loaded with delicious fruit. The animals of the earth were nourished under its shade, and the birds of the air made their dwelling in its boughs. The form of some heavenly watchman descended from above, who with a loud voice cried out: Cut down the tree, lop off the boughs, and scatter the fruit thereof; but leave the stump of its roots, and let it be tied with a band of iron and brass; for seven revolving seasons let it be wet with the dew of heaven; let his heart be changed from man's, and let his portion be with beasts, amongst the grass of the earth. Daniel listened attentively to the king's narration, till he had heard the whole: he remained silent for a whole hour, fixed, as if with thought, and much troubled in mind, till at the king's command he thus began to explain: The tree, my liege, which you saw, is yourself, whose greatness reaches to the heavens, and whose power extends to the boundaries of the earth. The words of the holy watchman express the sentence which the Most High hath pronounced against you. For you shall be driven from the society of men, your dwelling shall be with beasts and the wild inhabitants of the forest, you shall eat grass like an ox, you shall be exposed to the dew of heaven, till at the end of seven years you shall be convinced, that the Most High ruleth over all kingdoms here below, and disposeth of them as he pleaseth. But as the root of the tree was suffered to remain, so shall your kingdom still remain to you, after you shall have known that all power is from heaven. Wherefore be not displeased at my advice, which is, that you redeem your sins by almsdeeds, and your iniquities by being merciful to the poor: God may perhaps forgive your offences. Nabuchodonosor did not profit by the advice. At the end of twelve months, as he was walking in his palace, and priding himself upon the great achievements by which he had raised Babylon to its present pitch of grandeur, he heard a voice from heaven repeating to him the sentence of his chastisement, as before pronounced by Daniel: he was immediately struck by the hand of God; a beast's heart was given to him, and he ran away from the company of men to eat grass like an ox, and be exposed to the dew of heaven for seven years. During that time his hair grew out like the plumage of an eagle, and his nails became like the claws of a bird of prey. At the end

of seven years he lifted up his eyes to heaven, and he was restored to his senses. Being sought for by his nobles and magistrates, he was reinstated in his kingdom and former glory. Cured of his pride, and convinced of the justice of that divine power which had humbled him to the earth, he published a decree, in which he related these wonders which the Most High had wrought towards him, that all nations of the earth might know, that the God of Daniel was the true and only God of the universe.

Such was the chastisement which God inflicted on Nabuchodonosor for his pride. That haughty monarch had exalted himself with great insolence against the Almighty: he was therefore degraded from his throne, and driven out to dwell with wild beasts in the forest. Similar to that is the disgrace which every sinner incurs before God, when in contradiction to reason he follows the impulse of his passions, and quits the fellowship of the saints, to run after the objects of his sensual appetites. He is then rightly compared to irrational beasts, says the Psalmist, and is made like unto them. To rise from so deplorable a state, let him lift up his eyes to heaven as Nabuchodonosor did: God rejects not the sighs of the penitent; he is ready to pardon and to spare, whenever his mercy is implored with sincerity and truth.

A.M. 3442.] *Idol of Bel and the Dragon.* [A.C. 558.

DANIEL, xiv.

NABUCHODONOSOR did not long survive his re-establishment in the kingdom of Babylon. He was succeeded by his son Evilmerodach, as it is generally thought, who seems to have been a friend to the captive Jews; for upon his accession to the throne, he not only released king Joakim from prison, in which he had been confined seven and thirty years, but also treated him with a respect suitable to his royal dignity. Daniel enjoyed the same honours under Evilmerodach, as he did under his predecessor. Far from growing remiss in his duty to God by the favours he enjoyed at court, the holy prophet employed his power to destroy the worship of idols, and promote that of the living God. The favourite idol of the Babylonians was called Bel, to whom they affected to pay great respect, though the notions they had formed of his godship were pitifully low and sensual. They fancied him to stand in need of daily food for his existence, which they plentifully supplied him with. A magnificent temple had been built in his honour; thither they repaired to pay him their devotions, thither they every day sent him for his support many measures of the finest flour, forty sheep, and a proportionable quantity of wine. The priests of this idol entered by night through a subterraneous passage, which they had secretly contrived, and by carrying off the provisions, made the ignorant people believe that they were eaten by Bel. Even the king himself was imposed upon by the gross imposture, and went every day to worship Bel in the temple. He invited Daniel to accompany him: Daniel was too enlightened and steady in his worship of the true God, to comply with the king's request. The king asked him why he would not adore Bel? Because I acknowledge no artificial gods, replied the holy man; I worship none but the living God. The king was surprised that Bel should not be thought a living god, since he daily consumed such quantities of meat and drink. Daniel smiled, and said, that a god which was nothing but clay within and brass without, could not want either meat or drink. The king in anger called for his priests, and threatened them with death, if they did not tell him what became of the meat which was set every day before the idol. If it is consumed by Bel, said he, Daniel shall die, for having blasphemed against him. Be it done according to thy word, replied Daniel. The king, therefore, with Daniel, and the priests of Bel, seventy in number, entered the temple, together. Let the meats be set upon a table, said the priests, let the wine be prepared, the door then shut, and sealed with the king's ring; and if in the morning they are not found to have been eaten by Bel, we shall suffer death; but if they are, let Daniel then die who has spoken against us. The priests went out, the king set the meats before Bel, and Daniel commanded his servants to bring ashes which he sifted all over the pavement before the king; and going forth they shut the door and departed, after having sealed it with the king's ring. The priests entered by night, according to custom, with their wives and children, through a private passage, and there consumed or carried off the whole provision. The king rose early in the morning, and Daniel with him. Eager to know the event, he repaired straight to the temple, and examined the seal, which he found untouched and whole. As soon as he had opened the door, he cast his eyes upon the table, and seeing the provisions gone, cried out, Great art thou, O Bel, and there is no deceit in thee! Daniel laughed, and held the king from passing the threshold, until he had observed the pavement, and beheld the footsteps of men, women, and children, that were imprinted in the ashes. The king upon examination found private doors, through which they entered, and being resolved to strike at the root of the imposture, ordered the priests, with their wives and children, to be put to death, delivering Bel into the power of Daniel, who destroyed both the idol and the temple.

Daniel had scarce disabused the king of one error, when he fell into another equally gross: for a monstrous dragon being found in the same place, the superstitious Babylonians set him up for a god instead of Bel, and adored him. The

king endeavoured to persuade Daniel to join with them in their adoration, since he could not say of this as he had said of Bel, that he was not a living god. Daniel answered, that he adored the Lord his God, the creator of heaven and earth; that this other was no living god; and that by his permission he would kill the dragon without sword or club. The king having granted him leave, he made up a composition of pitch, grass and hair, which he rolled into lumps and gave to the dragon. The dragon swallowed them, and burst asunder; upon which Daniel exclaimed, Behold him whom ye worshipped! The essential service that Daniel rendered to the king and people of Babylon, by disabusing them of their errors, ought to have received some recompense; it met with none; it was repaid with enmity and persecution, the usual portion of the saints, in return for the good they wish and do to ungrateful men.

A.M. 3442.] *Daniel in the Lions' Den.* [A.C. 558.
DANIEL, xiv.

THE grandees of Babylon, being exasperated at seeing their deities destroyed, resolved to be satisfied with nothing less than the death of him who had destroyed them. They gathered round the king in a tumultuous manner, and insisted upon Daniel's being delivered into their hands, threatening to destroy him and his house if he refused to comply. They told him that he was become a Jew, that he had demolished Bel, that he had slain the priests and killed the dragon. Terrified at their insulting menaces, the king yielded to necessity, and abandoned Daniel to their resentment. The people no sooner had the prophet in their power, than they cast him into a den, where seven hungry lions stood ready to devour him. To make the animals more greedy of their prey, they were kept fasting, and during the time that Daniel was confined amongst them, were deprived of their daily food. But the Lord, who had saved the three youths in the fiery furnace, forgot not Daniel in the lions' den. By the ministry of an angel he not only shut up the lions' mouths, but also provided him with food, in the very place where he had been thrown for food to the ravenous animals. There was at that time in Judea a prophet called Habacuc. This virtuous man had prepared a mess of pottage and broken bread for the reapers, and was going with it into the field, when behold, an angel presented himself in the way, and bade him carry it to Daniel in the lions' den at Babylon:

Habacuc replied, that he did not know where Babylon was: upon which the angel took him by the hair of his head, and conveying him in that wonderful manner through the air, set him down at the mouth of Daniel's prison. Habacuc called upon him by name to take the dinner which the Lord had sent him. Daniel thankfully received it, and the angel in a moment restored Habacuc to the spot in Jewry from whence he had brought him. Daniel had now passed six days with the lions; on the seventh day the king came to the den, not so much to set the prophet free as to lament his death.

He looked into the cave, and seeing him not only sound, but likewise full of life, with ecstacy exclaimed, Great art thou, O Lord, the God of Daniel! He ordered the holy man to be taken out that instant, and the promoters of his intended death to be thrown in, where the lions devoured them in a moment, before him. The king, who was witness of the fact, then said: Let all the inhabitants of the universe revere the God of Daniel; for he is the Saviour, and he it is who performs prodigies and wonders upon the earth; who hath delivered Daniel out of the lions' den.

Ecclesiastical writers observe, that if, in imitation of the Babylonian king, the laws of retaliation were properly enforced, the world would soon be cleared of all rash and false accusers; nor should we see the innocent so often sacrificed, nor the slanderer so shamefully encouraged. But such evils are permitted, says St. Gregory, for the good which an all-seeing God knows how to draw from them. By such trials he polishes the virtues of his saints, by sufferings he strengthens their fidelity in his service, and adds new lustre to their crown. Thus Abel's innocence was tried by Cain's malice; thus was Jacob's patience proved by Esau's violence, and David's meekness perfected by the persecution of Saul.

A.M. 3444.] *Vision of Daniel.*—DAN. vii. [A.C. 556.

EVILMERODACH reigned no more than two years, and had for successor his son Baltassar, the last of the Chaldean kings. In the first of this king's reign, Daniel gives us an account of a vision he had, in the following manner: I was in my bed, says he, and behold, I saw the sea agitated by the four jarring winds of heaven, and from the sea came forth four monstrous beasts, differing in the shape one from another. The first was like a lioness, with the wings of an eagle. I beheld, till her wings were plucked off, and she was lifted up from the earth, and stood upon her feet as a man, and the heart of a man was given to her. The second beast resembled a bear, with three rows of teeth in its mouth, to which it was said, Arise and devour much flesh. The third had the appearance of a leopard, that had four heads and four wings, like the wings of a bird. The fourth beast was of a more terrible aspect than any of the other three. He was exceedingly strong, and had great iron teeth, eating and breaking in pieces, and treading down the rest with his feet. He had ten horns, in the middle of which sprung another little horn, at the appearance of which, three of the first horns were plucked up: this horn had eyes like the eyes of a man, and a mouth which uttered big words. Such was the first scene exhibited to the prophet's view, and to this succeeded another, in which the Ancient of days, God himself, appeared upon his throne of glory, surrounded by thousands and thousands of ministering spirits. And behold! with the clouds of heaven came, as it were, the Son of Man, to whom the Ancient of days gave honour, and power, and empire, which shall never end. I trembled with respectful fear, continues Daniel: but being eager to know the meaning of what I saw, I approached near one of the heavenly attendants, and asked him what these things were meant to signify. The four beasts signify four kingdoms, replied the spirit, which shall rise upon the face of the earth. I then desired to be informed of some particulars concerning the fourth beast, which appeared so dreadful and different from the otner three; and the angel told me, this fourth beast is the fourth kingdom, which shall give laws to the universe; the power of this kingdom is greater than any that went before. It shall devour the whole earth, and shall tread it down and break it in pieces. The ten horns of this kingdom are ten kings who shall reign therein. After them shall arise another king, more powerful than the former, and he shall bring down three kings. He shall open his mouth in blasphemies against the Most High; he shall cast the saints of God under his feet, and shall proudly think that he has the power to alter times and laws at his discretion. But his power shall be soon broken, not to rise again: for no longer than a time and times and half a time shall the just be delivered into his hands. The Ancient of days shall then come, and give judgment to his saints on high. The time and times and half a time is a mysterious expression, found also in the Revelation of St. John upon the same subject, and signifies a year and years and half a year, that is, three years and a half. The four great kingdoms here mentioned by the prophet, are universally understood to be the four great monarchies of the Assyrians, Persians, Greeks, and Romans, and the last horn arising amidst the ten upon the fourth beast, to denote the power and reign of Antichrist for three years and a half.

Daniel two years after was favoured with another vision, in which he was apprised of several particular circumstances, relating to the second and third, that is, the Persian and Greek empires. And in a vision which he had in the third year of Cyrus, he was carried by the same prophetic spirit through the history of the Persian kings, of Alexander the Great, and his successors in the Grecian empire, and of the wars and persecutions that they were to raise against the people of God, till the Roman arms should prevail over them who had conquered before. Daniel speaks of these memorable revolutions in a style so clear and intelligible, that Porphyry, the great enemy of Christianity, not being able to dispute the truth of his words, has represented them as written by an historian who related past events, lest he should be obliged to confess that one sovereign God of the universe, who alone can give his prophets an insight of things which are yet to come.

But the most remarkable and the most important of

Daniel's prophecies, is that in which he specifies and determines the precise time when Christ the prince was to come, and the Saint of saints to be anointed.

In the first year of the reign of Darius the Mede, whilst he was pouring out his fervent prayers for the Jewish people, and considering the seventy years during which their captivity was to last, according to the prediction of Jeremias, he saw the angel Gabriel coming towards him. Because thou art a man of desires, said the angel to him, I am come to tell thee, that the seventy weeks upon thy people are shortened, that iniquity may cease, that everlasting justice may be brought, and prophecy be fulfilled. Know, then, that from the date of the order which shall be published for the rebuilding of Jerusalem unto Christ, the prince, there shall be seven and sixty-two, that is, sixty-nine weeks; and after this, viz., in the middle of the ensuing week, Christ shall be slain, and the victim and the sacrifice shall fall; and the people who shall deny him, shall not be his: there shall be in the temple the abomination of desolation, and the desolation shall continue even to the end.

Hence it appears, that as the chief circumstances of our blessed Saviour's life, to wit, his birth of a pure virgin, his miracles, his passion, death, and resurrection, had been revealed to the prophet Isaias, so to the prophet Daniel was now shown the precise time when these prophecies were to be accomplished. The prophet's weeks are, by all interpreters of the holy Scriptures, understood to include years for days; so that sixty-nine weeks of years, amount to the number of 483 years. The grant for rebuilding the walls of Jerusalem was made by Artaxerxes, in the twentieth year of his reign, which was the 3548 of the world. Now, if to 3548 we add Daniel's weeks of years, 483, we shall bring it to 4031, which, according to the vulgar computation, was the year in which Christ our Lord was baptized by St. John, and began to announce himself to the world, three years and about three months before he died upon the cross for our redemption.

A.M. 3466.] *King Baltassar's Condemnation.* [A.C. 534.

DANIEL, V

BALTASSAR the king made a sumptuous feast for a thousand of his nobles, and every one drank according to his age. Being elevated with wine, he ordered the sacred vessels which Nabuchodonosor had taken out of the temple at Jerusalem to be brought in; and he and his officers, and his wives and concubines drank out of them: they drank wine, and sung the praises of their idols and graven gods. In the height of their profane mirth, there appeared the fingers, as it were, of a man's hand, writing some unintelligible words upon the

wall over against the great candlestick. The king beheld the joints of the hand that wrote: his countenance grew pale, his heart throbbed, his knees, through fear, struck one against the other, guilt and remorse troubled his very soul. He cried aloud for his wise men to come and explain away his fears. They came; he promised great honours to any of them that should interpret to him the meaning of the mysterious writing: they looked at it; they stood perplexed and puzzled where to begin; they knew not how to read, much less explicate the unintelligible characters; the king's trouble increased; his nobles were in the utmost consternation. The queen being told what had happened, went to the banquetting-room, and endeavoured to calm the king's mind: she mentioned Daniel, whom, on account of his superior wisdom, Nabuchodonosor had appointed prince of the wise men. Daniel was immediately introduced: the king promised to honour him with a purple robe and a golden collar, and to create him the third man in his kingdom, if he would only read the writing, and declare the interpretation thereof, which the wisest of his Chaldeans were not able to do. The holy prophet answered, Keep thy rewards to thyself, and reserve thy gifts for others; the writing I will read thee, O king, and show thee the interpretation thereof. Nabuchodonosor, your father, was a great and illustrious prince; but when his heart was lifted up, and his spirit hardened into pride, he was degraded from his throne, driven from the company of men, made to dwell with the wild asses, and to eat grass like an ox, his body being wet with the dew of heaven, till he humbly submitted to the dominion of the Most High. You also have exalted yourself against the God of heaven, you have profaned his sacred vessels, you have to his dishonour extolled your molten gods, which can neither see nor hear you. For this reason the hand, by his omnipotent decree, hath written your condemnation in these three words, Mane, Thekel, Phares. For this is the meaning of them: Mane, God hath numbered the days of thy kingdom, and the number is now finished. Thekel, Thou art weighed in the balance, and art found to be under weight. Phares, Thy kingdom is divided, and given to the Medes and Persians. Baltassar, although he heard his doom in the interpretation he received, nevertheless honoured the interpreter, and according to his promise, promoted Daniel to the dignity of being third man in his kingdom, little thinking that his kingdom was to end that very night.

Cyrus, who commanded the Persian army for his uncle Darius the Mede, was then before the walls of Babylon, and having opened himself a way, which the Babylonians did not suspect, into the city, he surprised king Baltassar in his palace at night, and by his death put an end to the Chaldean empire. The sudden and unforeseen stroke that carried off the wicked Baltassar at an hour he the least expected, ought to be a warning, says St. Jerome, to all those Christians, whose sinful excess and impenitent lives expose them to the daily risk of being surprised by a like untimely end.

A.M. 3466.] *Daniel a second time in the Lions' Den.*—DAN. vi. [A.C. 534.

THE revolution that extinguished the race of Chaldean kings in Babylon, opened the way which God had appointed for the re-establishment of the Jewish people. Daniel enjoyed the same favours under the Persian, as he had under the Babylonian kings. Darius respected him as a man replenished with the Spirit of God, and having already made him one of the three first princes of his kingdom, began to think of appointing him commander-in-chief over the whole empire. This partiality for a Hebrew captive piqued the Persian nobles; they envied him his honours, became jealous of his power, and resolved to do all they could to procure his disgrace. They laid their counsels together, and deliberated in what manner they should proceed against the holy man. For Daniel was so faithful to his trust, and so irreproachable in his whole conduct, that there was no room for suspicion, and no grounds for any criminal charge against him. They had observed his inviolable attachment to the law of God, his steady piety and assiduity in prayer. There they were in hopes of surprising him into their snares, there they resolved to attack him, but yet in so artful a manner, as to let no one know or suspect their design. They presented themselves before the king, whom they had incensed with their flatteries, and extolled as the sovereign source from whence all favours and gifts were derived, and ought to flow; they persuaded him to publish an imperial decree, by which it was ordained, that whosoever, during the space of thirty days, should presume to offer any prayer or petition either to God or man, except to the king, should be cast into the lions' den. Darius, who was flattered with the proposal, and saw not into its design, confirmed and published the decree, which after that could be neither altered nor transgressed by any man whatever with impunity. Daniel, who was a man of holy desires, paid no attention to that strange ordinance. Preferring the law of God to that of men, he retired at his usual hour three times every day into his chamber, where, opening the window which looked towards Jerusalem, he knelt down and worshipped God in fervent prayer. His enemies suspecting what would happen, were upon the watch to surprise him; they found him praying and making supplication to his God; they hastened to the king, reminded him of his edict, lodged a formal accusation against Daniel, the Hebrew captive, for having transgressed it, and insisted upon his being cast into the lions' den. The king was much grieved: he interested himself in behalf of the accused, and laboured till sun-set to deliver him out of their hands. The nobles perceiving the king's designs, and being determined not to give up their point, positively declared that, according to the laws of the Medes and Persians, no royal decree could be revoked or dispensed with; that Daniel had offended, and must therefore suffer as the law expressed. The king could resist no longer: Daniel, by his command, was brought forth and cast into the den of lions. A stone was laid upon the mouth of the den, which the king sealed with his own ring and that of the nobles, that no further violence might be offered to the holy prophet: for he hoped the lions would respect, and the God of heaven deliver him. Darius retired to his palace, would suffer no meat to be set before him, and laid himself down without taking any supper. Sleep fled from his eyes, and he could take no rest; he rose early in the morning, hastened to the den, and with a mournful voice called out, Daniel, servant of the living God, hath thy God been able to deliver thee from the lions? O king, live for ever, answered Daniel; my God hath sent his angel, and hath shut up the mouths of the lions, and they have not hurt me. The king in a transport of joy commanded him to be taken out of the den, and his accusers to take his place. Those men therefore who had accused the holy prophet, were brought with their wives and children, and being thrown into the den, the lions caught them as they fell, and broke their bones in pieces. Darius then published a decree, that all within his empire should honour and revere the living and eternal God, who had so wonderfully freed his servant Daniel from the lions' den.

Daniel's example in the duty of prayer, says St. Jerome, ought to be imitated by all Christian people, that God in his mercy may preserve them from becoming a prey to enemies infinitely more fierce and powerful than lions. Sin, says the holy Scripture, has the teeth of a lion; its bite is fatal to the soul, and its wound is death; the devil, like a roaring lion, is always upon his round, says St. Peter, seeking whom he may devour. Our deliverance from such enemies is the effect of God's special grace, which in his ordinary providence he grants only to those who ask it.

Afflictions of Job.—Job, i.

Job, so well known for his humble patience, united in himself two things which are seldom found in the same person, great virtue and great riches. The Scripture does not tell us when the holy man lived; but he is supposed to have been the great grandson of Esau, and contemporary with the father of Moses: the text says, he dwelt in the land of Hus, a plain and upright man, fearing God and declining from evil. He had seven sons and three daughters, whom he carefully instructed in their duty to God, and educated in the principles of charity and union amongst themselves. He rose early in the morning every eighth day, and offered sacrifice for each one of them, that they might not only be purified from sin, but also sanctified by the divine blessing. Satan, who is always upon the watch to tempt and seduce mankind, was vexed to see such virtues practised, and such happiness enjoyed, by a mortal inhabitant of the earth. He did not know what motive the holy man might have in all that outward show of good; whether the temporal felicity and worldly wealth which surrounded him, might not possibly be the ground of his piety to God, and make him thus active in the divine service. Being bent upon doing whatever mischief he was able, he asked the Almighty leave to strip Job of his possessions, not doubting but adversity would make him break out into acts of impatience, and provoke him to blaspheme like other men. Almighty God, who knew the unfeigned goodness of his servant's heart, and who was also willing to humble Satan's pride, by showing him how impotent his malice was against a good man, aided by divine grace, gave him the leave he asked. Satan immediately began to try his utmost malice, and as if he meant to make the holy man despair at once, poured out afflictions on him like a torrent, which by flowing in at once should allow him no time to recollect or arm himself against them. Four different messengers, one immediately upon the back of another came to inform Job of his accumulated misfortunes; that his herds were driven away by the enemy, his flocks killed by lightning, his servants slain, and his children crushed to death by the house falling upon them, as they sat at table. Job heard the melancholy tale, and though the sharpness of the stroke pierced his very heart, as appears by the rending of his garments, yet he uttered no complaint. With an humble resignation to the divine will, he fell prostrate on the ground, adored, and said, Naked I came out of my mother's womb, and naked shall I return to my mother earth: the Lord hath given, the Lord hath taken away; as it hath pleased the Lord, so it hath been done: let his name be for ever praised. Thus the trials which were designed by Satan to destroy, served but to confirm and strengthen the patience of the holy man. The malicious fiend, however, did not desist, but presented his petition to the Almighty a second time; for his power against the saints goes no further than God is pleased to let it; and his petition was to afflict Job's person. For the confusion of Satan's malice, the Lord granted him his request, with an express reserve not to hurt his servant's life. Satan therefore went and struck Job's body with one continued ulcer, from the top of his head to the sole of his foot. In that sore condition the

holy man left his house, and seated himself upon the dunghill, where with a shell he scraped off the corruption and the worms that swarmed from his ulcerous body. Of all his worldly goods nothing was then left him but his wife, and she not for his comfort. She upbraided him for his simplicity, bid him blaspheme God, and die. Job bore the lash of her bitter tongue with the same patience as he bore his other sufferings, and only made her this short answer: Thou talkest like one of the foolish women: if from the hand of God we have received good things, why should we not receive likewise evil? Job in all this sinned not by word; and the more nearly united to him the person was who reviled him, the more severe was the trial, and the more exemplary is his patience.

Friends of Job.—Job, iv.

Job being reduced to the piteous condition in which the sacred writer has described him upon the dunghill, met moreover with other trials, that seem to have affected him more sensibly. Three of his friends, who in the book of Tobias are styled kings, came to visit and condole with him in his misfortunes. But far from receiving any comfort from them, he was reduced to the disagreeable necessity of defending himself against their false and insidious reasoning. Amidst the evils he endured, his solid comfort was, the uprightness of his heart, and consciousness of his past innocence. He received his sufferings as trials to purify his virtue, like gold in the furnace; he considered the shortness of human life, and consoled himself with the thought of a future resurrection. I know, says he, that my Redeemer lives, that in the last day I shall rise from the earth, and that with these very eyes I shall behold God my Saviour. This was the faith, this the hope of holy Job, and this his three friends endeavoured to deprive him of. They strongly maintained to him, that his sufferings could be imputed to no other cause than his own guilt: according to the narrow notions of earthly men they concluded, that as his chastisement was grievous, grievous also must have been his crimes: nor did they content themselves with the simple proposal of their erroneous maxims, they strove to maintain them by sophistical arguments, and clothed their slanders with an air of plausibility. Job stood in need of all his patience to support himself under this trial: he refuted their calumnies by solid reasoning, he asserted and proved his own innocence, he tried to convince them of their mistake, and adduced every argument to set them right. But they were not willing to be informed, and by their obstinacy we see how dangerous a thing it is to be misled by prejudice, and how hard a thing it is to remove an impression which has been once entertained. For having suffered themselves at first to be drawn aside by a false appearance, that seemed to favour their erroneous notions, they would not afterwards believe, but that the sufferings of their friend were the sufferings of a criminal. God himself condescended in the end to justify the innocence of his injured servant. He showed his indignation against the falsity of those pretended friends, treated their principles as folly, and declared that he would not pardon them their sins, but at the request of him whom they had wickedly endeavoured to stigmatize with guilt.

Hence we are to learn, say the holy fathers, never to judge ill of the good and virtuous, on account of the disadvantages of life under which they may chance to labour: our judgment of another's goodness is not to be regulated by the riches and worldly honours of which he may be possessed. The true state of things is often very different in itself from what appears to our outward senses. They who seem the happiest in the opinion of a deluded world, are frequently miserable within themselves, and despicable in the sight of God; and those whom the world despises and rejects as unworthy of its notice, God honours with his friendship, and ranks amongst his saints. Job lived long enough to see his character fully justified, even in the opinion of a sensual world. In the latter part of his life, he was blessed with health and riches in greater abundance than he had ever enjoyed before. In those darker ages of the world, such visible rewards seemed necessary for the encouragement of virtue; but since the Son of God has become man, and has borne our pains, the enlightened Christian raises his notions higher. Not by his senses, but by faith, he forms his judgment of the recompense which is due to good and evil. Though left under the pressure of sufferings even to the end of life, he is neither staggered in his faith, nor dejected in his hope. He considers those only as real evils, which destroy the life of the soul, that is, sanctifying grace, and sets his heart on no other riches than what are invisible and eternal.

END OF THE FIFTH AGE

SIXTH AGE OF THE WORLD.

FROM THE END OF THE BABYLONIAN CAPTIVITY, 3468, TO THE BIRTH OF JESUS CHRIST, 4000; COMPREHENDING THE SPACE OF 532 YEARS.

A.M. 3468.] *Temple of Jerusalem rebuilt.* [A.C. 532.
1 ESDRAS, i.

THE wrath of God against the Jewish people being appeased, and the term of their seventy years' captivity being complete, Cyrus, the glorious conqueror and monarch of the East, published an edict, by which he granted leave to all the Jewish nation to return into their own country, and rebuild the temple. He likewise gave an order at the same time, that the sacred vessels formerly brought thither by Nabuchodonosor, should be takeu out of the royal treasury of Babylon, and given back to be used in the divine service, for which they were first designed. In consequence of this edict, upwards of forty-two thousand Jews put themselves upon their march back into Judea, under the conduct of Zorobabel, the son of Salathiel, and grandson of king Joachin, or Jechonias. Upon their arrival at Jerusalem, they erected a temporary altar for their daily sacrifices, till the temple, which they were preparing to rebuild, should be finished. Trees of cedar were brought from Libanus by the Tyrians and Sidonians, as Cyrus had ordered; masons and hewers of stone were hired; Levites were appointed to hasten on the work of the Lord; and the foundations of a new temple laid with great solemnity and loud demonstrations of joy. Vested in their sacerdotal attire, the priests stood with trumpets in their hands, and the Levites with cymbals, ready to sound the praises of Almighty God in hymns of jubilation and thanksgiving, according to the manner of David, king of Israel. While the masons fixed the foundation stones, the priests and Levites joined in chorus, which was heightened by the acclamations of crowding spectators. The young people burst out into peals of joy, whilst the chief of the fathers and the ancients wept, to see how far the outlines of the new edifice fell short of the old. The Samaritans, the ancient enemies of Juda and Benjamin, being informed that the children of the captivity were building a temple to the Lord the God of Israel, addressed themselves to Zorobabel and the ancients of Juda, that they also might be admitted as partners in the work; but their request not being complied with, they did all they could, both by open force and secret intrigue in the court of Persia, to interrupt the building and frustrate its design. Cyrus was not to be prevailed upon to alter the decree which he had once published in favour of the Jewish people: but after his death, Cambyses, his son, let himself be prevailed upon by the repeated slanders of the Samaritans, so far as to forbid the Jews to proceed any further; and a stop was put to the building, till the second year of his successor, Darius Hystaspes. This prince being disabused of the calumnies which had been thrown out against the Jewish people, and informed of the edict which Cyrus had once given in their favour, ordered the building of the temple to be resumed; he even contributed towards the expense, and in the sixth year of his reign, the temple was entirely finished, and dedicated with great solemnity. The Jews in Judea, having thus formed their re-establishment, continued to strengthen themselves under the protection of the kings of Persia, Darius, Xerxes, and Artaxerxes. In the seventh year of the reign of Artaxerxes they were joined by a fresh body of their brethren from Babylon, under the conduct of Esdras, a virtuous and learned priest. Esdras had made the law of God his particular study, and sedulously conformed his practice to the sanctity of its precepts. He went with full powers from Artaxerxes to visit Judea and Jerusalem, to carry the silver and gold which the king and others had freely offered to the God of Israel, to deliver the holy vessels that were given for the use of the temple, to regulate the sacrifices, and observe the rights of the God of heaven, to appoint judges and magistrates, to punish vice, and establish good order in the republic. When Esdras arrived at Jerusalem, he found with great concern, that the first comers of the Jews had intermarried with the inhabitants of the country: he dreaded the consequence of those alliances, and therefore, after he had related to them his commission from the king, had prayed and fasted for their sin, and delivered the sacred vessels which he had brought with him, to the ministers of the temple, he convened the people, and represented to them how contrary to the holy law those profane marriages were, and how necessary it was to break them off. The people were convinced by his discourse, and with one accord solemnly promised to dissolve the present, and to make no future marriages with the idolaters of the land.

The connexions formed between the Jews and those pagan women, are, according to the holy fathers, a lively image of what is done by those Christians who adopt such maxims, and form such connexions in life, as are inconsistent with the sacred promises they made to God at baptism. And as the offspring of those mixed marriages confounded the Hebrew language with that of Azotus and Moab, by using the words sometimes of one and sometimes of the other; so this motley sort of Christians seems willing to unite the spirit of Jesus Christ and of the world together, wishing to obey them both, and to speak the language both of the one and of the other. But as Esdras convinced the Jews, that they could not remain the people of God, at the same time that they sought an alliance with their enemies; so every Christian must own the force of this evangelical truth, that no one can serve two masters at the same time; he cannot divide his heart between God and Mammon. God, who created the whole man, requires nothing less than his whole service.

A.M. 3495.] *Queen Esther.*—ESTH. iv. xv. [A.C. 505.

WHILST a part of the Jewish people were re-establishing themselves in Judea, the remaining part in the provinces of Babylon ran great risk of being totally destroyed. The mighty Assuerus, as he is called in the Book of Esther, and is thought to be the same person as Darius Hystaspes, had a favourite courtier, whose name was Aman. Every mark of honour and royal favour was bestowed upon this haughty man, to whom all the king's servants about court were commanded to bend the knee. The king's court was then at Susan. Aman received that servile homage from every one excepting Mardochai the Jew. Mardochai was one of the captives whom Nabuchodonosor had carried away with king Jechonias to Babylon. This man having distinguished himself by the discovery of a plot which two eunuchs had formed against the king's life, had an apartment appointed him in the palace, and the king made him presents for the information he had given. Aman was exceedingly angry to see Mardochai refuse him an homage which the other chief servants of the king servilely paid him, and knowing him to be a Jew, resolved that not only he, but his whole nation, should feel the weight of his resentment. He took an opportunity of representing to the king, that the Jews were an insolent, lawless people, who by their religious tenets embroiled the state, and disturbed the peace of his subjects; that it was not safe to let them live, and that for the good of the empire they ought to be utterly extirpated. The credulous prince implicitly believed what his favourite told him, and gave him full power to act as he pleased in that affair. Aman had all he wanted: he drew up an edict, to which he affixed the king's seal, and peremptorily commanded, that on the thirteenth day of the twelfth month, every Jew throughout the Persian dominions should be massacred, without distinction of age or sex. The publication of this cruel edict threw the Jews into the utmost consternation; they saw no resource but in God, whose mercy they implored by prayer and fasting. Through every town in the different provinces where the order was published, great were the lamentations and cries of the oppressed people bemoaning their unhappy destiny.

Almighty God in his goodness had already provided for their safety by the means of Esther. This incomparable woman, who was niece to Mardochai, had succeeded to the place of queen Vasthi. Vasthi, by an act of disobedience, had incurred the king's displeasure, and was on that account divorced and deposed from her royal dignity. After her divorce, officers were sent through the different provinces, to seek for beautiful maidens to bring them to Susan, that the king might choose one of them to be his queen, instead of Vasthi. Of the many fair rivals who appeared, Esther pleased him the most, and fixed his choice. The charms of her mind were still more excellent than those of her beauty. She had from her tender years been educated by Mardochai, her father's brother, who after the death of her parents had adopted her for his daughter. With the same docility as when she was a little one, she continued to respect his precepts, and to regulate her whole conduct by his advice. Her marriage with Assuerus was celebrated with a princely magnificence. The king set the royal crown upon her head, made her his queen, and honoured her with every mark of

favour and distinction which love and esteem prompted him to bestow upon the most amiable of women. He knew nothing of her family connexions: for Mardochai had charged her to make no mention hitherto of her country and people. But as the day fixed for the execution of Aman's bloody edict was drawing near, he told her it was high time to declare herself, and to exert the influence she had upon her royal consort for the preservation of her people. She humbly remonstrated, that to go into the king's inner court without being sent for was a capital offence, and to appear before him without his order would certainly be her death, except the king should hold out his sceptre to her in token of clemency. Mardochai replied, that divine Providence had perhaps raised her to the crown, that she might be ready to succour her distressed brethren at this time; that when a whole nation was upon the edge of destruction, she ought to think of saving other lives besides her own; that if she chose notwithstanding to be silent, God would employ other means for his people's safety, but that she and her father's house should perish.

Esther yielded to his reasons, and resigned herself to the will of heaven. She only desired, that he and the other Jews in Susan would join with her in prayer and fasting for three days, after which she promised to go to the king and risk her life for theirs. The three days were spent in acts of the most fervent devotion: on the third day Esther put on her royal apparel, took two maids with her, and entered the king's apartment. With a mind full of anguish and fear, that lay hidden under the graces of a cheerful countenance, she passed through the doors in order, till she came into the king's presence. The king was seated upon his throne, glittering with gold and precious stones: surprised at the unexpected appearance of his queen in that place, he gave her a look which seemed to show displeasure. She sunk down with fright, the colour left her cheeks; pale and faint, she rested her weary head upon her handmaid. God at that moment changed the king's spirit into mildness; he started from his throne, and ran in haste to raise her up. He took her in his arms till she came to herself, and caressed her with these words: What is the matter, Esther? I am thy brother, fear not, thou shalt not die; the law was not made for thee; come near and touch the sceptre. And as she made no answer, he laid the golden sceptre upon her neck, and kissed her, saying, Why dost thou not speak to me? I saw thee, my lord, as an angel of God, said she, and my heart was troubled for fear of thy majesty: for thou, my lord, art admirable, and thy countenance is full of graces. And while she was speaking she sunk down, and was near fainting a second time. The king was in great distress; his servants came round to comfort him: he bade her ask whatever she pleased, and he would grant it, though it were one half his kingdom. Esther only begged that the king would please to come that day, and bring Aman with him, to the banquet which she had prepared for them. The king graciously consented, and sent immediately for Aman.

A.M. 3495.] *Triumph of Mardochai.* [A.C. 505.

ESTHER, vi.

THE king went with Aman to Esther's banquet according to his promise, and being in the height of good humour, pressed the queen to tell him what request she had to make, promising her to grant whatever she would ask. If I am thought worthy of the king's notice, said Esther, I only beg that he will bring Aman with him again to-morrow, and I will then open my request to him. Aman went away in high spirits, and passing by the king's palace, saw Mardochai sitting at the gate. Mardochai took no notice of him, nor did he so much as move from his seat, or show him the least respect. Aman was exceedingly chagrined, returned home to meet his wife and friends, and opened to them the vexation of his soul. Though I am blessed with children, said he; though I flow with wealth; though I am honoured by the king, and preferably to all others invited to dine with the queen; yet I think it nothing, as long as I see Mardochai sitting before the king's gate. His wife and friends advised him to prepare a gallows for Mardochai, and solicit an order for his execution next morning, so that he might accompany the king with joy to the queen's banquet. The advice pleased him, and he ordered a gibbet fifty cubits high to be erected at his own door that afternoon. The king at night not being able to sleep, commanded the annals of his reign to be brought and read to him; and as they were reading, they came to that place where it was written how Mardochai had discovered the treason of Bagathan and Tharas, the eunuchs who plotted the king's death; upon which Assuerus interrupted the lecture, and asked what reward Mardochai had received for that important service. It was answered, none at all. Aman was at that very hour standing in the court, ready to prefer his request against Mardochai as soon as he could gain admittance. The king being told that Aman was there, ordered him to come in, and immediately asked him, what ought to be done to the man whom the king was desirous to honour? Aman, not imagining that royal honours could be intended for any one beside himself, readily answered, that the happy man ought to be clothed with royal robes, to have the crown set upon his head, to be mounted upon the king's own horse, and in that state to be conducted through the streets by the first nobleman of his kingdom, who should hold the bridle, and proclaim aloud as he went along, Thus shall the man be honoured whom the king is pleased to honour. Go then, said the king, and see that thou punctually perform very part of it to Mardochai the Jew. Aman had no choice: he durst not reply, nor could he oppose the order dictated by himself Then, to the astonishment of all Susan, did the humble Mardochai suddenly appear invested with the most splendid honours that a Persian monarch could bestow upon a subject; whilst the haughty Aman walked as an attendant, bowing and proclaiming the honours of a man whom he had destined to the gallows for not having bowed to him. Aman having performed this painful task, made haste into his own house, swelling with vexation, and covered with confusion. He told his wife and friends what had befallen him; they had no comfort to give him, but expressed great apprehensions of some more fatal stroke in reserve. If Mardochai, said they, be of the Jewish race, this is but the beginning of thy downfall: thou art too weak to stand against so powerful an adversary; thou canst not resist, thou shalt fall in his sight. Their words were in a few hours verified: as they were yet speaking, the king's servants came to call him to the queen's banquet. How sweetly, but how powerfully, God disposes of all things to effect his designs, either for the punishment of the wicked, or for the protection of the good!

A.M. 3495.] *Punishment of Aman.* [A.C. 505.

ESTH. vii.

THE king and Aman went the second day to banquet with the queen; and when the king was warm with wine, he said, What is thy petition, Esther, that it may be given thee? Though thou ask the half of my kingdom, thou shalt have it. Then Esther, who, by deferring to make her petition, had

made the king more eager to hear, and more earnest in his promise to grant it, laid aside the appearance she had hitherto put on of mirth and cheerfulness, and, in the mournful accents of a supplicant, humbly begged, that if she had found favour in his eyes, the king would only please to suffer her and her people to enjoy the common light, which the malice of her enemies was ready to deprive them of. If we had been only sold for slaves, said she, and been permitted to drag out life in chains, I then should not have presumed to complain, but have bemoaned our fate in silence; but now, since we are destined to the slaughter, it is a cruelty, it is a disgrace, which rebounds upon the king himself. The king stood amazed, and being ignorant of the affair, asked what and whom she meant. The queen then pointing at Aman, said, He is the man, he is our enemy, who, by an abuse of the royal favour he enjoys, has published an edict for the massacre of the whole Jewish people, whose only crime is their religion and fidelity to God. Assuerus, who had a fund of natural goodness, was shocked at the horrid scene into which Aman's pride and his own credulity had almost betrayed him. His indignation rose, he left the room, and retired to a shady walk adjoining the palace. Conscious of his guilt, and apprehensive of the danger his life was in, Aman took that opportunity of the king's absence to throw himself at Esther's feet, as she lay reclined upon her couch, and to implore her protection. The king came back into the room, and seeing Aman in that posture before the couch, exclaimed in wrath against the traitor, as guilty of offering violence to his queen, and sentenced him to death. An officer standing by mentioned the gibbet that he had prepared for Mardochai the day before: hang Aman upon it, said the king: the order was instantly obeyed; and thus, by a just judgment of God, the criminal suffered the very same punishment, which he had maliciously planned against the innocent.

To the great commendation of Assuerus, St. Ambrose remarks, that this mighty monarch thought it no dishonour to acknowledge his mistake, as soon as he discovered it; he desisted from a measure which he found to be unjust; he saw his easy temper had been wickedly imposed upon, that his friendship had been turned to the abuse of his authority, and his name employed to stain his honour with the effusion of innocent blood. He punished the guilty as he deserved, and drew the innocent from the gulph of despair. In a second declaration, contradictory to that which Aman had sent abroad, he made known the very great esteem he had for the Jewish nation, and promoted Mardochai to the same posts of honour that Aman his enemy had enjoyed before So truly verified was the sentence of our blessed Saviour, in which he has since declared, that every one who exalts himself shall be humbled, and whoever humbles himself shall be exalted.

A.M. 3548.] *Walls of Jerusalem rebuilt.* [A.C. 452.
2 Esd. ii.

Assuerus, or, as he is otherwise called, Darius Hystaspes, left the crown of Persia to his son Xerxes, of whom the Scripture mentions nothing more than his name. Xerxes was succeeded by his son Artaxerxes, surnamed Longimanus, a great favourer and protector of the Jews. This prince in the seventh year of his reign, as we have seen, sent Esdras to Jerusalem, with full powers to establish laws, and form the manners of the Jewish people. He employed the Jews in his own court, amongst whom was a holy man called Nehemias, who served him in the capacity of cup-bearer. Nehemias is commended in the sacred writings for his prayer and fasting, and the love of his country; for he was of Jewish extraction, and considered himself as an exile, driven by misfortunes from the country of his ancestors. He omitted no opportunity of inquiring after his countrymen in Judea, and of informing himself of the true state of their affairs. He had the comfort to learn, that by the zeal of Zorobabel and Esdras, the republic there had assumed a regular form of government, that the temple was rebuilt, and the observance of the law enforced amongst the people: but it grieved him beyond measure to hear of the ruinous condition in which the walls of Jerusalem still lay. His charity made him lament the evils which he wished to see redressed, and a heavy gloom sat upon his brow, which betrayed the sadness of a troubled heart. The king, as he received the wine from his hand, observed the melancholy looks, and kindly asked what troubled him. How is it possible, my liege, replied the humble man, not to be sad, while the sepulchre of my forefathers, while the city of Jerusalem is desolate, and the gates thereof lie consumed with fire? What is thy request? said the king. If it seem good to the king, answered Nehemias, I beg it may be permitted me to visit the city where my forefathers lie interred, and to rebuild the walls, thereof. He promised to return within a limited time, and upon that condition the king graciously granted him his request, and dismissed him with letters of recommendation to the governors of his country beyond the river, and particularly to Asaph, the keeper of the royal forest, to furnish him with timber, that he might cover the gates of the tower of the temple. This was the twentieth year of Artaxerxes' reign, and from this epoch begins the date of Daniel's seventy weeks of years. Nehemias being come to Jerusalem, took three days to review the broken walls and ruins of the city, before he mentioned the design and grant he had to repair them. Then calling together the priests, magistrates, and nobles, he told them how much he had felt, and how he grieved at their desolate and defenceless situation; encouraged them to rise and build up the walls of Jerusalem, and produced the royal license which, through the divine mercy, he had obtained from Artaxerxes for that purpose. The joyful citizens immediately set all hands to work they measured out the whole into different portions, which they undertook by companies; the heaps of rubbish were cleared away, every breach in the wall was closed, the gates and towers began to rise. The work was carried on with the greatest success and expedition, when the Samaritans, and other hostile neighbours of the Jewish nation, assembled to stop its progress. Nehemias then found it necessary to arm a part of the citizens, and to place a guard, day and night, to defend the workmen against the attacks of their enemies. By the redoubted efforts of human industry, to which the Almighty gave a blessing, the works were completed in less than two months, and Jerusalem again was girted round with walls and bulwarks.

Nehemias is an example of that active zeal, which ought to animate every Christian in his duty both to God and man. His undertaking to repair the holy city, threw him into those circumstances in which St. Paul describes himself to have been, when he says, that he saw nothing but struggles from without and alarms within. For while he had the open force of an armed enemy to repel from the walls, he had to defeat the secret artifices of a venal tribe, who were bribed to terrify the citizens with false predictions, and make them desist from their undertaking. Nehemias, by the sagacity of his genius, and the vigour of his resolution, triumphed over both. He taught the Jews how to use the trowel and the sword together, and in his whole conduct so happily united the virtues of fortitude and prudence, as to appear neither too bold on one hand, nor too timid on the other.

A.M. 3828.] *Chastisement of Heliodorus.* [A.C. 172.
2 Mac. iii.

Jerusalem being in some sort restored to its ancient splendour, the Jews from that time enjoyed a long and prosperous peace, with the free exercise of their religion, under the king of Persia, till an end was put to that empire by Alexander the Great. This renowned conqueror of the East had been figuratively shown to the prophet Daniel in two different visions, first under the appearance of a winged leopard with four heads, and then under the appearance of a goat with four horns; by which emblematical figures, not only his rapid conquests and great power are expressed, but the division also of his empire into four kingdoms, which sprung up under as many of his captains, to whom he parcelled out his extensive territories. This prince died about the year of the world 3680, and in the partition of his conquests the kingdom of Asia fell to the share of Seleucus, under whom and his successors Judea continued to enjoy their full liberty, till the reign of Antiochus Epiphanes, whom Daniel, in the eighth chapter, seems to point out for his cruel persecution of the Jews, and profanation of the holy temple. The general peace had indeed suffered some interruption under Seleucus Philopater, his brother and predecessor in the throne of Syria.

Philopater had a great esteem for Onias the high-priest, on account of his singular piety, and although an idolater, furnished an annual revenue to provide victims for sacrifice to the living God; but upon the information of one Simon, who had been made overseer of the temple, that great sums of money were deposited in the treasury, over and above what was necessary for the sacrifices, he sent Heliodorus, his commissary, with orders to fetch them away. Heliodorus, upon his arrival, signified the king's orders to Onias the high-priest. Onias told him that the monies in question had been deposited in his hands for the benefit of poor widows and orphans, that he was but the administrator of them, and could not deliver them up. Heliodorus replied, that it was not in his commission to examine how and for what purposes those monies had been there deposited, but to carry them to his master. The whole city upon this was flung into the greatest consternation; the people, with Onias at their head, fled for refuge to the throne of God, whom they besought with ardent prayers, that he would defend them against all violence, and not suffer his sanctuary to be plundered of its treasures. Their petition was heard. Heliodorus advanced as far as the entrance of the temple, fully determined to seize by force, what he could not obtain without it. The soldiers who accompanied him, were by the power of God suddenly struck with dread, which cast them to the ground, and deterred them from executing their leader's commands. For there appeared to them a man on horseback, clad in golden armour, and the horse on which he sat, reared and violently struck his fore feet against Heliodorus, while two comely young men, in rich attire, standing on either side, scourged him incessantly with rods that they had in their

hands. Heliodorus dropped down speechless upon the ground, where he lay, till he was taken up and carried off in a sedan chair. His friends immediately addressed themselves to the good Onias, humbly begging that he would call upon the Most High to grant life to the man, who was seemingly in the agony of death. Onias being apprehensive lest the fact might be misrepresented, and the miraculous effect of God's power be construed into treason against the king, consented to their request, and by his prayers saved Heliodorus from death. The two heavenly young men, still standing by the side of Heliodorus, said to him: Return thanks to the priest Onias, for on his account our Lord hath granted thee life; and since thou hast received this visible chastisement from God, declare to all men the great and wonderful works of his divine power: having said this, they both disappeared. Heliodorus joyfully fulfilled the injunctions that were laid upon him, and returned to Seleucus. Seleucus was unwilling to renounce his claim to the sacred treasures, and advised with him about sending some other person to fetch them away; upon which Heliodorus frankly declared, that if he had any enemy or traitor in his kingdom, whose death or punishment he wished, he might send him thither, where the power of God undoubtedly resided, for the chastisement of all who should presume to approach the holy place with a design of doing evil to it.

A.M. 3834.] *Signs in the Heavens over Jerusalem.*—2 Mac. v. [A.C. 166.

Upon the death of Seleucus, his brother Antiochus, surnamed Epiphanes, or the Noble, took possession of the throne. This man was the son of Antiochus the Great, and became a barbarous persecutor of the Jewish nation. He seems to have been raised to pour out vengeance upon a sinful and perverse people. The good Onias was possessed of too many virtues to remain unmolested in a city, where the principles of ambition and venality publicly prevailed. He had a wicked brother called Jason, who, grasping at power, subverted him in the dignity of the priesthood. Jason became high-priest by dint of money, in the room of Onias, and by an additional sum obtained the king's license to erect a school, in which the Jewish youths were instructed in the manners and vices of the Gentiles, and trained up in the games and exercises of the heathen heroes. This wicked man had not long enjoyed his ill-gotten power, before he found a rival in Menelaus, the brother of Simon, who had been the first promoter of Heliodorus's attempt upon the treasure of the temple. Menelaus, of the tribe of Benjamin, and therefore disqualified for the priesthood, supplanted Jason by the same evil practices which Jason himself had so successfully employed against Onias. For honours and dignities, even the most sacred, were then bestowed upon the worst of men, as they had money to purchase them. To supply himself with the sums he wanted, Menelaus had seized upon and sold some of the rich vessels belonging to the temple. Such profanation afflicted the holy Onias, who was still permitted to live: from his private retreat at Antioch, he reprimanded Menelaus for his sacrilegious impiety, and therefore fell a victim to his revenge. The death of the holy priest was lamented by all good men, and honoured with the tears of Antiochus himself. Onias was honoured by the king, from whom he had received the greatest injustice, while Menelaus was undermined by those whom he thought his fastest friends. He was turned out of the post of honour by the intrigues of Lysimachus, his brother, and only recovered it again by force of bribery. Thus was the Jewish republic miserably torn into factions; thus was order banished from the state; the priests no longer attended to the service of the altar; things sacred and profane were confounded together; no attention paid to the laws, either human or divine; Jerusalem was polluted with the blood of her own citizens, and dreadful times came on, which seem to have been foreboded by the tremendous signs which for forty days were seen over the holy city. There was the appearance of soldiers glittering in golden armour; a multitude of men was seen in helmets with drawn swords, troops of horsemen moving to and fro through the air, shaking their shields, and encountering one against another. Such unusual signs filled the minds of men with dreadful alarms, and all most earnestly prayed that these prodigies might turn to good. In that general consternation of the people, Jason thought it a fair opportunity of recovering his former dignity; he was, moreover, encouraged to that undertaking by a report which prevailed of Antiochus's death in Egypt: he therefore entered the city with an armed body of men, and glutted himself with the blood of his fellow-citizens. But he carried not the point he aimed at; for Antiochus had been successful in his expedition against Egypt, till the Romans interrupted him in his conquests, which drove him to wreak his indignation on the Jewish people. He marched an army to Jerusalem, with a view of reducing it entirely to his obedience. The different factions of the citizens, tearing one another into pieces, gave him an easy conquest; he took the city by storm, and, as he was cruel by nature, and grown insolent with success, deluged the streets with human blood. In the space of three days that his fury raged, without giving any quarter to man, woman, or child, there were fourscore thousand of the people massacred, forty thousand made prisoners, and as many sold for slaves. Menelaus led the king into the temple, from whence, with impious hands, he took the sanctified vessels, and rifled the holy treasury: and though he added blasphemy to sacrilege, in contempt of the living God, no such judgment befell him as had befallen Heliodorus. For the sins of the people had at that time provoked Almighty God to chastise them by the hands of their enemies, and they had no Onias to intercede in their behalf. The anger of Almighty God never appears so terrible, as when he suffers his enemies to domineer, within the sanctuary, and profane his very altar; for no holiness of the place can give a sanction to the sinfulness of its inhabitants, and no sanctuary shall screen them from the vengeance which their sins deserve.

A.M. 3837.] *Martyrdom of Eleazar.* [A.C. 163.
2 Mac. vi.

Antiochus having made himself master of Jerusalem, raged with all the fury of a tyrant against its miserable inhabitants. He appointed governors more cruel than himself, who plundered and afflicted the people in his absence, and at the end of two years sent Appollonius, with a great army, to slay all the men who had attained the age of manhood, and to sell the younger sort, with the women, for slaves. The view of Antiochus was to destroy the race, and extirpate the religion of the Jewish people. Not long after he sent another of his generals from Antioch, to compel the Jews to depart from the laws of their forefathers and of God. Then was the holy temple defiled with all sorts of revelings and impurities; a statue of Jupiter Olympus was erected therein, men were dragged by the king's officers to offer sacrifice to the heathen idols, and orders given for every one to be put to death who should refuse to follow the pagan rites. Then was misery to be seen. Two women, for having circumcised their children, were publicly led through the city, with their infants hanging at their breasts, and cast down headlong from the walls: while others were burned alive in caves, where they assembled to keep the sabbath. Such cruelties so terrified the generality of the people, that scarce any one had the courage to profess himself a Jew. Many however, when publicly called upon to declare their sentiments, bravely stood the severe trial, and ended their lives by martyrdom. Amongst these glorious champions was Eleazer, a chief scribe, whose piety and grey hairs rendered him truly venerable. Being apprehended by the king's officers, and, in contempt of the law, being violently pressed to eat swine's flesh, which they thrust into his mouth, he vigorously resisted, and preferred a glorious death to the dishonourable terms of life. He went on cheerfully towards the place of execution, when they who accompanied him, being moved with compassion and respect for his age, took him aside, and begged he would consent to let some legal meat be set before him, that by eating of that, at least, he might seem to comply with the king's order, which would be enough to save his life. The venerable old man was not to be imposed upon by such pretexts of friendship. He considered the unblemished character he had hitherto maintained through life, the testimony he owed to truth, and the respect due to the law of God in those particular circumstances, and rejected their proposal with a nobleness of soul that was natural to him. I would rather die, said he, than do what you counsel me. Such dissimulation becomes not these grey hairs. God forbid that I should ever sully the purity of my former life by such a stain, and thereby give occasion for young men to imagine, that Eleazar, at the age of four-score and ten, has renounced the religion of his forefathers, and consented to the superstition of the pagans. Miserable should I be indeed, if the poor remains of declining life could tempt me to prevaricate in so shameful a manner. For, although I were to escape the judgments of men for the present, yet neither alive nor dead shall I escape the hand of the Almighty. It is, therefore, better for me to die courageously at once, than, by a disgraceful compliance, appear unworthy of my old age: so by example, I shall teach my fellow-citizens, that the laws of God are to be preferred to those of men; that the duties of religion are to take place of worldly interest, and even of life itself. This noble and generous answer was attributed to a stubborn pride by his pretended friends, who thereupon turned their professions of kindness into injuries. Eleazer was forthwith carried to the place of execution, where by a

glorious death, he left, not to the young men only, but to the whole nation, an example of the most heroic fortitude. By his conduct he teaches us with what caution we ought to avoid whatever may be a subject of scandal to the weak, and in what manner we are to give glory to God, by a sincere confession of the truth.

A.M. 3837.] *Martyrdom of the Machabees.* [A.C. 163.

2 Mac. vii.

The venerable Eleazar was soon after followed by a youthful band, who signalized their courage by a much severer conflict. They were seven brothers, commonly known by the name of Machabees. Antiochus himself presided at their martyrdom, and being enraged to see such constancy in an age so tender, he stretched every nerve to terrify and torture them into a compliance with his impious demands. He condemned them all to undergo the same torments one after another, that the sufferings of the foregoing might intimidate the next. The eldest was first called out, in the presence of his mother and the rest of his brethren, to enter upon the bloody combat. The executioner cut out his tongue, chopped off the extremities of his hands and feet, drew off the skin of his head, and then cast the mangled body into a large frying-pan, where the remains of agonizing life were consumed by a slow fire. The first being thus barbarously slain, the second and the rest were successively tormented and slain in the same manner. Each advanced in his turn, each with the same manly fortitude bore the tyrant's tortures, and each with the same steady perseverance triumphed over his savage inhumanity.

They adored the decrees of God, who was pleased to make this trial of their faith; they readily submitted to the torments in punishment for their sins; they cheerfully resigned a life which they hoped to receive one day again by a glorious resurrection. And, as if the sight of sufferings had inspired them with fresh courage, they told the tyrant that he was not to fancy them abandoned by their God; that it was impious folly in him thus to fight against the Almighty; that he was but a passing scourge in the Almighty's hand, and would himself soon feel the vengeance already prepared for his chastisement. Antiochus would willingly have pardoned them their reproaches, if he could but have got the better of their fortitude. Six of the brothers had gloriously conquered by their death; the seventh only remained, the youngest of them all, and him the tyrant hoped to gain by caresses and fair promises. He promised him his friendship, wealth, and happiness, if he would only abjure the laws of his forefathers; and when he perceived that his words made no impression, he called the mother, and desired her, if she had any fondness left for an only surviving son, to disabuse him of his error, and by her advice preserve his life. The incomparable woman, who to a mother's tenderness joined a manly fortitude of mind, despised the tyrant's solicitations, and in derision promised that she would advise her son since he desired it. Wherefore, bending towards the amiable young man, she exhorted him in her native tongue, that he would have pity on her who had borne him nine months in her womb, who had suckled and brought him up to that age; that he would not fear the tormentor, but look up to God, the Creator of heaven and earth, and all things in them; and that he would courageously follow the glorious example of his brethren, that so, by the divine mercy, she might be worthy to receive them all again in life eternal. Animated with fresh resolution the young man interrupted his mother, as she was yet speaking, and called upon the executioners to renew the combat. Why do you hesitate? said he: for whom do you stay? Behold me fixed in the resolution of obeying the law; nor will I disobey God, to obey the king. The tyrant foamed with rage to see himself thus mocked and defeated: with fiercer barbarity than he had shown against the other six brothers, he discharged his fury upon the seventh, and tortured him to death. The illustrious mother, having nothing more to fear for her sons, followed them with redoubled vigour, in their victorious career, and with them laid down her own life on the same day, in the same glorious cause.

The holy fathers are diffusely eloquent in their encomiums on this incomparable woman. From her, as from the source under God, was derived the flow of virtuous magnanimity which so distinguished her sons. With a more than manly firmness she beheld them in their torments, and exhorted them to die. Those endearing arts and caresses which many mothers often misapply to other purposes, were by her made use of solely for the real advantage of her children. The tender feelings of a mother were, by the activity of her faith, directed beyond the enjoyment of present happiness; her desire was to see them in that blessed abode where she might receive them again, without the fear of losing them for evermore. By her example she teaches Christian parents what sentiments of piety, what principles of religion they ought to inspire into their children; and in what manner, when called upon, they are to give those to God, whom they have received from God. For whether they live, or whether they die, they solely belong to God: as long as they live, they should live to God; and when they die, they ought to be designedly parted with, as a precious pledge that can be no longer kept than is agreeable to the divine will.

A.M. 3837.] *Generosity of Mathathias.* [A.C. 163.
1 Mac. ii.

During the scene of desolation which stained the land of Juda with the blood of its best citizens, Mathathias, a valiant and religious man of the sacerdotal race, retreated with his family into Modin, a small town situated upon a hill; the former residence of his ancestors; there, with the deepest anguish, he considered over and bewailed the misfortunes of his country. Why have I been born, said he, to see this affliction of my people, this desolation of the holy city? She is fallen a prey to her enemies, her temple is profaned, her treasures plundered, the vessels of her glory in the hands of foreigners, her beauty and ancient splendour is extinguished; the spoils of Sion are carried off, to enrich the barbarous nations of the earth. Full of these melancholy reflections, Mathathias sat mourning over his country, covered with sack-cloth and bathed in tears. Many other Jews had also taken refuge at Modin, but were not long suffered to remain unmolested; for the king's deputies pursued them thither, and insisted on their abandoning the law of God, and sacrificing to idols. Mathathias had the grief to see many of his countrymen yield to the fear of suffering, and apostatise from the religion of their forefathers. The king's officers used every argument to persuade him into a compliance with the edict; they made him offers of money, honours, and preferment, which he rejected with a generous disdain, and publicly declared that though all nations should consent to obey Antiochus, and every man of the Jewish people should depart from the faith of their forefathers, yet neither he nor his brethren, nor his sons, would pay obedience to an edict that was incompatible with the law of God. As he spoke these words, there came a Jew, in the sight of all, to offer sacrifice upon the altar which was there erected to Antiochus's idol. Mathathias saw and was grieved, his reins trembled, and his wrath was kindled according to the judgment of the law.—*Deut.* xiii. With a zeal like that of Phinees, he slew not only the Jew who was offering idolatrous sacrifice, but also the officer who had compelled him to it, and immediately left the town, summoning his fellow citizens who had any zeal for religion, to follow him into the desert. His five valiant sons, John, Simon, Judas, Eleazar, and Jonathan, were the chief who followed him: they retreated to the mountains, where they endeavoured to shelter themselves from persecution, till, being joined by the most courageous and zealous of the people, their numbers swelled into an army, strong enough to face their enemies in the field. Mathathias led them on against the king's troops, whom he forced to retreat before him, and to fly for safety beyond the boundaries of Judea. He scoured the whole country, as he marched along with his victorious followers, overturned the profane altars that he met with, and restored to the inhabitants the free exercise of their religion. But death cut him short, before he had time to finish what he had so prosperously begun. Before he expired, he called his sons to him, and in this manner expressed to them the noble sentiments of his soul: Now it is that the anger of the Lord lies heavy upon his people; the proud domineer, and threaten our nation with ruin. You, therefore, O my sons, arm yourselves with zeal for God's law, and be ready to die in its defence. Call to mind the glorious actions of your forefathers, and let their example spur you on to the pursuit of glory. Joseph, in spite of his brother's envy, became the lord of Egypt; David triumphed over the persecutions of Saul; Ananias, Azarias, and Misael, were delivered from the fiery furnace, and Daniel from the lions' den. Thus through every age it appears that God never abandons those who place their confidence in him. Therefore, fear ye not the violence of a sinful man, who, notwithstanding the present blaze of glory that surrounds him, is no more than dust, and a worm of the earth. He glories in his might to-day, and to-morrow he shall be no more; for he shall again return into the dust from whence he was first taken, and his vain conceits shall perish with him. Such were the last sentiments of Mathathias, by which he endeavoured to infuse into the breasts of his gallant sons the same holy zeal that burned in his own; he gave them his blessing, and was laid to his forefathers, in the town of Modin.

A.M. 3838.] *Judas Machabeus.*—1 Mac. iii. [A.C. 162.

Mathathias, in the last instructions that he gave his sons, had singled out Simon for his prudence, and Judas for his warlike valour; he had recommended to them that the first should aid them by his counsels, and the second should command the army. Void of jealousy, and only zealous for the public good, they religiously complied with their father's will. Judas, surnamed Machabeus, in accepting of the command, promised his brethren that he would do his best to answer the good opinion which his father had been pleased to express of him, to discharge the trust which they had consented to repose in him. Eager to complete what his father had but just begun, he girded himself for battle like a giant, says the sacred historian, and buckled on his sword, which was a shield to the whole army. He rushed to war, and in his acts was like a lion, and like a lion's whelp roaring for his prey. In forming his army, he made choice of those men only who had never bent their knees to the idols of Antiochus; for he relied chiefly upon God for victory, and religiously concluded that a wicked multitude would be more likely to draw down a curse upon his arms, than help him to conquer. He therefore collected those together whom the dread of torment had dispersed: with those he formed a body of six thousand chosen men, and with these he thought himself a match for all the forces that the Syrians could bring against him. His study was to infuse his own sentiments into the minds of his soldiers, and to inspire them with the same confidence in God. He represented to them, that God alone is the Lord of hosts; that on him alone they were to rely for success; that by prayer and fasting they must render him propitious to their arms; that under his all-powerful protection they had nothing to fear from the thousands of a pagan enemy; for that God alone held the balance of victory, and could turn the scale as easily in favour of a small as of a great number. Thus Jonathan, the son of Saul, routed the camp of the Philistines: thus Ezechias was delivered from the army of Sennacherib. Nor did he doubt but the Almighty had the like mercy still in store for him; that the cries of the afflicted, that the blood of the innocent, that the prayers of the penitent, would disarm his divine justice against Juda, and turn his vengeance upon the insolent foe, who had defiled the temple with idols, and Jerusalem with blood. And to make his followers still more resolute and united in their undertaking, he ordered it to be proclaimed through the camp, that all they who were afraid of facing the enemy, or who had any private interest to pursue, or domestic business to call them home, should instantly retire, and leave him with the rest, to conquer for their religion and country.

Thus did Judas Machabeus prepare himself to fight the battles of the Lord; thus did he spirit up his followers to feats of glory, and teach them how they were to conquer. The zeal, the piety, the faith and resolution of this Hebrew chief well deserve the notice of all Christians, who have a much more important undertaking upon their hands. The life of man, says holy Job, is a warfare upon earth. We have our souls to save, we have heaven to gain; and heaven can be gained only by those who are eager and vigorous in the pursuit. The strong united powers of the world, the flesh, and the devil, surround us on every side, and oppose our progress. With them there is no peace to be expected; we must fight, we must strive to conquer too, before we can be crowned. For this we must be equipped with the spiritual armour of God, without whom we can do nothing. Unable of ourselves to advance a single step, we must endeavour, by humble prayer, to obtain from Jesus Christ those succours of his holy grace, which alone can invigorate our efforts, and render them successful.

A.M. 3838.] *Victories of Judas Machabeus.* [A.C. 162.

Judas Machabeus having prepared himself for war in the manner we have said, directed his first attack against Appollonius, who commanded a great army of infidels in Samaria. He gained a complete victory, slew Appollonius with his own hand, and stripped him of his sword, which he ever after used in battle, as long as he lived. For from this time Judas was in perpetual war with the Syrians, nor was it by the death of one general, or by the overthrow of one army, that the Syrian power could be broken. Upon the death of Appollonius, Seron took the field with a numerous army, not doubting of success, and promising himself great honour from the defeat of a general whose name was become the talk of foreign nations. Seron's boasted promises of victory ended in a total overthrow, which covered him with confusion, and crowned his adversary with new glory. The news of those two battles fired Antiochus with a fresh desire of revenge; the disgrace that had fallen upon his arms, made him eager to wash it out. Though he drained his treasury of money, and his kingdom of men, he resolved to set on foot another army, which would defy every attempt, and baffle every power that Judas could bring against it. The state of affairs requiring the king's presence in Persia, Lysias, the viceroy of Syria, was entrusted with the management of this expedition against Judea. An army of forty thousand foot, and seven thousand horse, under the command of Ptolemy, Nicanor, and Georgias, three of his most able generals, marched into the Jewish territories. The sight of so formidable an army struck a panic into the desponding Jews. Judas saw the evils that were pouring in upon him, and exerted his abilities to repel them. By word and example he animated his troops against an enemy who had nothing to trust to but their numbers and weapons, whilst they, the chosen people of God, had all the heavenly host to defend them. He admonished them to prepare for battle by prayer and fasting; he reminded them of the wonderful protection God had shown their forefathers in ancient times, and how glorious it was to fight for the sacred laws of God and the liberties of their country. Having thus dispelled their fears, and warmed their courage for battle, he led them on against the Syrians, whom he charged with such intrepidity, that he broke and routed their whole army. This stroke reduced Lysias almost to despair; he was afraid the miscarriage of the war might be attributed to his neglect, and therefore resolved to command the next campaign in person. He drew together all the recruits he could during winter, and in spring led an army of sixty thousand foot and five thousand horse into the heart of Judea. Judas was there ready to receive him, gave him battle, defeated and forced him to retreat with great loss to Antioch.

Judas having no enemy upon his hands, turned his thoughts upon repairing the devastations which the Gentiles had made in the country. His first object was the house of God; for he was afflicted to see the sanctuary desolate, the altar profaned, the gates burned, and in the courts shrubs grown up as in a forest. He began by appointing priests of an unblemished character for the performances of the sacrifices; he cleansed the holy place and the courts, threw down the altar on which the idol of Jupiter had stood, and built a new one, which was dedicated with great joy and religious festivity. Then were the sacred veils hung up again, and the holy vessels renewed; the golden candlesticks, the altar of perfumes, the table of show-bread restored to their places, and every other thing provided for the divine service.

Thus did Judas pass the winter months, till the service of his country called him forth again into the field. The neighbouring nations had taken offence at his repairing the temple, and conspired the destruction of his people. The Idumæans, the Amorrheans, and Ammonites, rose in arms against him, and great forces appeared in the field on the side of Galilee, in Galaad, and beyond the Jordan. Judas, with a rapidity of success which distinguished him for a favourite of heaven, chosen to fight and conquer for the defence of Israel, scoured the whole country, and discomfited his enemies wherever he met them. He stormed their fortresses, reduced their cities, and frequently routed their numerous armies, without losing so much as a single man. For the Lord of hosts was with him, and holy angels visibly protected him more than once in battle.

In an attack he made upon Georgias, the governor of Idumæa, some of his soldiers fell, because they had forfeited the divine protection; for when he came to bury them, he found under their clothes some pagan donaries, which they had taken, contrary to the law, at the sacking of Jamnia 2 *Mac.* xii. The religious chief was grieved at the sin his men had been guilty of, but still hoping that they might find mercy, on account of the piety they had shown in dying for their country and religion, made a collection of twelve thousand drachms of silver, which he sent to Jerusalem, that prayer and sacrifice might be made for them. Holy, therefore, says the sacred text, and salutary is the thought of praying for the dead, that they may be loosed from their sins. For to sins already remitted, as the fathers unanimously teach, and it appears in Nathan's speech to king David—2 *Kings*, xii.—a temporal punishment is sometimes reserved; and from that punishment Judas hoped, by prayer and sacrifice, to release his deceased friends and fellow warriors.

A.M. 3841.] *Death of Antiochus.*—1 Mac. vi. [A.C. 159.

During these transactions in Judea, Antiochus had undertaken an expedition against Elimas, a rich and strong city in Persia. The inhabitants knowing that nothing but the desire of plunder had invited the king to attack them, defended themselves with great resolution, and forced him to make a precipitate retreat into the province of Babylon. Here, covered with confusion at his disgrace, he was informed of the bad fortune which had likewise attended his arms in Judea. Vexed with rage, and sickening with grief, to see himself thus baffled in his projects, he vowed revenge against the people who had thrown such dishonour on him, publicly declaring that he would reduce Jerusalem to a heap of ruins, and make it a common burying-place of the whole Jewish nation. But God, who sees the heart, and knows how to check the pride of man, struck him with an incurable and painful plague in his bowels, which soon reduced him to the grave. He, however, mounted his chariot, and breathing revenge against the Jews, ordered his servants to drive on with the utmost expedition. The arm of God stopped him short in his career. Being thrown from his chariot, he was bruised in a terrible manner; and being no longer able to bear the motion of a carriage, he ordered himself to be put in a litter, not to interrupt his journey. Thus the king, who was replenished with pride above the measure of man, says the holy Scripture, who to himself seemed to rule even the waves of the sea, and to weigh the heights of the mountains in a balance, was in a moment humbled by the manifest power of God, which struck him to the ground. Loathsome worms swarmed out of every part of his body, the stench of which became insupportable to his attendants, to himself, and the whole army. For his flesh rotted and dropped from his bones, while his bowels were tortured with exquisite pains, in punishment of the cruelties with which he had so unmercifully racked the bowels of others. The growing tortures of his body, joined to the vexations of his mind, rendered his situation every hour more and more lamentable. He then began to reflect within himself, and to confess his great misery. The remembrance of the evils which he had done in the holy city of Jerusalem, added keen remorse of conscience to his other pains; he acknowledged the justice of the stroke that laid him thus low. It is just, said he, to submit to God; nor is it for man to equal himself to God. Then, as if he had some glimmering hope of softening the rigour of divine justice into mercy, he promised Almighty God, that he would treat Judea with clemency equal to his former severity; that he would make the city free, and put her citizens upon the same footing with those of Athens; he promised to furnish the holy temple with every necessary expense for the sacrifices, to make himself a Jew, and in every part of the earth to proclaim the power of God. All this he promised by word of mouth; and wrote, moreover, a letter to the Jewish nation, full of seeming friendship and esteem. But the just judgment of God was come upon him, says the sacred text; despairing of life, Antiochus prayed to the Lord, from whom he was not likely to obtain mercy, and thus ended a wicked and miserable life by a more miserable death.

Such was the exit of Antiochus the noble. The show he made of a death-bed repentance, proves both the deceitfulness and ineffiacy of a sorrow which is extorted only by pain, and comes not from the heart. Repentance deferred to the last hour, though accompanied with all the verbal protestations of Antiochus, is not to be relied upon. A Christian who, by a deliberate neglect, throws himself into that extremity, has no better grounds for his hope of pardon, than had that reprobate king. The grace of dying well is, in the common course of providence, granted to those only, who by a virtuous life endeavour to obtain it. The sentence of St. Austin upon this subject deserves our notice: Do you desire to die well? says he: you then must live well: for whoever leads a good life cannot meet with a bad death. A good death is the recompense of a good life.

A.M. 3841.] *Courage of Eleazar.*—1 MAC. vi. [A.C. 159.

THE death of Antiochus Epiphanes ended not the war, nor the calamities of the Jewish people. The Syrian generals still strove to subdue the country for their new king Antiochus Eupator, who succeeded his father both in his crown and antipathy against the Jews. Judas Machabeus headed his victorious troops against them, and in different battles vanquished Georgias, Timotheus, and Lysias. Humbled by his defeat, Lysias became an advocate for peace, and a truce was agreed on between the king and Judas Machabeus: but no lasting peace could be expected, where traitors among the Jews themselves were ready to sell their country to the common enemy. Men jealous of the power and envious of the glory which Judas had so justly acquired in the field, invited Antiochus to come to their assistance, and to deliver them from the tyranny of a man who over-awed his fellow-citizens, and hindered them from submitting to the king of Syria. Antiochus, upon that information, called together his friends and the captains of his army, raised all the men he could at home, took foreign troops into his pay, and collected an army of a hundred thousand foot, and twenty thousand horse, with which he invaded Judea. The appearance of an army, not less formidable for the glittering armour, than for the numbers of its men, was enough to strike terror into the most brave; and what rendered it still more formidable, were two and thirty elephants, trained to war, and bearing each upon his back a strong wooden tower, garrisoned with two and thirty warriors. Judas Machabeus was not daunted at the sight; with his usual courage and confidence in God, he led forth his troops to battle: he fought, he slew great numbers of the enemy. Eleazar, his younger brother, signalized himself by a very singular act of magnanimity. The valiant youth having observed an elephant more remarkable than the rest for his size and glittering armour, and not knowing but Antiochus might be upon the back of him, generously resolved to sacrifice his life for the sake of finishing the war, if he could, with one stroke. He cut his way through the thickest of his enemies, till he reached the elephant, the object he had in view. He threw himself between the feet of the monster, and standing under it, vigorously thrust his sword into his belly. Down fell the beast, and crushed the conqueror to death in the very act of triumph. Such feats of uncommon bravery gave Antiochus no great encouragement to carry on the war: and on the other hand, Judas seeing how difficult it was to maintain the field against so numerous a host, thought it prudent to retreat to Mount Sion. The king went to attack him, and was repulsed. Provisions grew scarce in the land, as it was the Sabbath year, and the king at the same time received intelligence that his presence was necessary to quash a rebellion which Philip the governor had raised at Antioch; therefore, by the advice of Lysias, he granted an honourable peace to Judas Machabeus, and retired with his army into Syria.

A.M. 3842.] *Death of Judas Machabeus.* [A.C. 158.
1 Mac. ix.

Antiochus did not long survive the treaty which he had made with Judas Machabeus. Demetrius, the son of Seleucus, having escaped from Rome, where he had been detained as a hostage in the room of his uncle Antiochus Epiphanes, declared himself king, and being well supported in his claim, he deprived his cousin, Antiochus Eupator, both of the crown and life. This revolution in the kingdom of Syria had no sooner taken place, but some discontented Jews began to make their court to the new king, by slandering the fame and virtues of Judas Machabeus. Amongst these enemies of their country the chief was Alcimus, a wicked and ambitious man, whom the king nominated to the high-priesthood, as a reward for his treachery, and employed as the minister of his designs against Judea. This Alcimus being joined with Bacchides in the command of a great army, did as much mischief to the people of Judea by his hypocrisy, as by open violence. For under the name and sanction of high-priest, he seduced many from their duty, and plunged them into rebellion against the laws of God and of their country. Judas exerted himself with such activity against them, that he forced them to relinquish their enterprise, and to retreat with dishonour into Syria. The miscarriage of this expedition against Judea, determined Demetrius (1 *Mac.* vii. and 2 *Mac.* xiv.) to employ Nicanor, one of his principal lords, who was an active general, and sworn enemy to the Jewish nation. Nicanor, at the head of a powerful army marched into the very heart of Judea, and defeated Simon with the troops he had under his command; but dreading the valour and superior abilities of Judas Machabeus, declined meeting him in the field, and solicited his friendship. Judas, who wished to spare the effusion of human blood, listened to his proposals. They entered Jerusalem together, and lived on amicable terms with one another, till the wicked Alcimus seeing himself thus disappointed in the hopes of the high-priesthood, accused Nicanor to Demetrius of being his enemy's friend. Nicanor, being then afraid of incurring the king's displeasure, resolved to seize the first opportunity of taking Judas by surprise, and of sending him prisoner to Antioch. Judas happily discovered and prevented his design. They, therefore, broke off their treaty of friendship, put themselves at the head of their respective troops, and came to a battle, in which the Syrians were worsted with the loss of near five thousand men. Nicanor, upon the defeat, became outrageous, and being joined by an army from Syria, proudly boasted of his mighty power, and threatened to destroy the temple, unless Judas were delivered into his hands. Judas, whose trust was in God, assembled and exhorted his troops to battle, with all that manly fortitude for which he was so remarkable, and fervently intreated the Almighty to send his holy angel to their defence, as he had formerly sent him against Sennacherib, and in one night had slain one hundred and eighty thousand of the Assyrian army. Almighty God heard his prayer, and comforted him with an apparition of the holy priest Onias, and the prophet Jeremiah. Jeremiah presented him with a golden sword to destroy the enemies of Israel, and Onias told him, that Jeremiah the prophet of God was a lover of his brethren, and prayed much for the people and holy city. Judas related this vision to his soldiers, who were exceedingly encouraged thereby; they marched full of confidence to battle; five and thirty thousand fell of the Assyrians, among whom was Nicanor himself, and a complete victory was won. Judas commanded Nicanor's head and right arm, which he had insolently lifted up against the temple, to be severed from his body, and carried to Jerusalem. His tongue, moreover, which had uttered blasphemies against the Most High, was cut into small pieces, and given to the birds.

This victory was the last of Judas Machabeus. Demetrius raised fresh troops, and poured in new armies upon the conquerors, who began to be wearied by the length, and disheartened by the labours of war, to which they saw no end.

Most of Judas's men declined the service; all to eight hundred abandoned him in the field, and they that remained exhorted him to a prudent retreat. No, let us rise, said he; let us march to meet our enemies: though the rest are shrunk away, we may still be able to maintain our ground. God forbid we should ever fly from the face of our adversaries: it would be shameful to turn our backs upon them whom we have so often vanquished. If our time is come, let us die like men in the defence of our country. With this resolution, he led out his little troop against an army of two and twenty thousand Syrians, commanded by Bacchides and the wicked Alcimus. It was fought with great obstinacy from morning till evening: Judas forced the enemy's right wing, and put it to flight; but pursuing them too far, he was attacked by those in the left wing, that closed in upon him: there, overpowered by numbers, he as gloriously fell as he had bravely fought. His brother took his body, and buried it with their father's, in the city of Modin.

A happy death, after a life of heroic virtues, is the term which every Christian ought to have constantly in view. Never to degenerate from the sublime thoughts of the sons of God, never to stoop to actions that disgrace the noble character of a Christian, and never to shrink back from the divine service, should be his principal and unvarying resolution. No human respects or fears, no appearance of difficulties, ought to dishearten him in the undertaking. He has God for his witness, and the helper of his endeavours. The struggle lasts not long; his labours will soon end; the glory that awaits his victory is everlasting. The only thing he has to fear while life remains, is lest he should fear any thing more than Him, who is his protection upon earth, and his reward in heaven.

A.M. 3843. *Jonathan High-Priest.* [A.C. 157.

1 MAC. ix.

AFTER the death of Judas Machabeus, his brother Jonathan was chosen by general consent to supply his place, and to fight the battles of Israel. He collected the broken troops of the republic together, formed them into an army, and retreated into the desert of Thecua, judging it more advisable to harass the enemy by frequent skirmishes, than to risk the fortune of his country in a pitched battle. This prudent plan of operations had the desired effect: for by the vigorous defence he made when attacked, and by the many advantages he seized to attack in his turn, he forced Bacchides, who commanded the Syrians against him, to evacuate the country, and subscribe to articles of peace. Jonathan having nothing more to fear from foreign enemies, began to restore good order among his subjects at home, and to repair the evils which had been occasioned by the war. His power was respected, and his friendship courted by the very prince, who, a little before, had been his implacable enemy. For a young competitor of the crown of Syria had lately started up in th person of Alexander Bales, the son of Antiochus Epiphane and made Demetrius totter upon his throne. These two rivals divided the power and affections of the Syrians equally betwixt them; and each of them being sensible that the scale of the empire must turn to whichever side Jonathan should incline, they both solicited his friendship. Jonathan gave fair words to them both, though his inclination biassed him in favour of Alexander. Alexander, in effect, defeated his antagonist, whom he slew in battle, and possessed himself of the crown of Syria. He treated Jonathan with great respect, acknowledged him to be the high-priest of the Jewish nation, and invited him to the city of Ptolemias, where he was to receive the king of Egypt, and espouse his daughter. Jonathan accepted the invitation, and that he might appear of some consequence before two such mighty kings, he went in great state, carrying with him magnificent presents for Alexander, for he knew that some factious Jews were gone before to lodge their complaints against him. Alexander received him with every mark of honour and esteem; and they who came to be his accusers, had the confusion to see him confirmed in his high dignity, and seated upon a level with the kings themselves. Alexander soon after met with an untimely end; for the late Demetrius had left a son of the same name, who being supported by Ptolemy, king of Egypt, laid claim to the crown of Syria, and by the murder of Alexander entered into actual possession of the kingdom. This prince had sent his general Appollonius with an army into Judea, to repay Jonathan for the part he had taken in favour of Alexander. The revenge he meditated, ended in his disgrace.

Jonathan gave Appollonius battle, and put his army to flight. Demetrius, thus perceiving that no advantage was likely to be reaped from the enmity of a man so versed in the art of war, resolved to court his friendship. Peace, therefore, being restored to the two nations of Syria and Judea, the people breathed for some time, till the war was again renewed by Tryphon. Tryphon was an officer of Alexander's party, and having his eye upon the crown of Syria, declared himself against Demetrius, and proclaimed Antiochus, the young son of Alexander, king in his stead. Jonathan sent three thousand valiant warriors to Antioch for the support of Demetrius, his friend and ally: these troops executed the commission they were sent upon, with so much vigour, that they slew in one day no fewer than a hundred thousand of Demetrius's enemies, and thereby put him again in peaceful possession of his kingdom. But Demetrius soon after breaking his faith with Jonathan, and being defeated by Tryphon, forced the Hebrew chief to declare in favour of the young Antiochus, who was crowned and acknowledged king at Antioch. Tryphon having thus strengthened his interest among the Syrians, thought he had now no other obstacle than Jonathan's attachment to Antiochus, that could hinder him from taking the crown from his prince's brow, and setting it upon his own. He, therefore, formed a scheme to put Jonathan out of the way. Treachery effected what no force of arms or money could have done. Under the specious show of friendship, Tryphon invited Jonathan into the town of Ptolemais. Jonathan imprudently believed him to be sincere, disbanded his army, and trusted himself with no more than a thousand attendants in one of the strong towns of his natural enemies. He had no sooner entered into Ptolemais, than the gates were shut, he traitorously taken, and his followers put to the sword. Such was the fatal consequence of trusting himself to a pretended friend, whose interest it was to betray him.

Fortitude, though a cardinal virtue, is not the only virtue requisite for our conduct in life. Without prudence we shall often run ourselves into straits, from which no fortitude will be able to save or extricate us. Our blessed Saviour tells his followers to unite the prudence of the serpent with the simplicity of the dove: this will teach us not to deceive; that will make us wary against the deceits of others. To deceive, or to be deceived, says St. Jerome, is unworthy of a Christian: the one argues a want of discretion, the other a want of fidelity to God and man.

A.M. 3861.] *Simon High-Priest.* [A.C. 139

1 Mac. xiii.

Of the five gallant sons of Mathathias, Simon was the only one left for the defence of Judea in her distress. Simon waited not for an invitation to serve his country; having shared in all the labours, and in all the dangers that his brothers had undergone in the public service, he voluntarily stepped forward, and offered himself to his fellow-citizens. You know, said he to them, what great battles I and my brethren and my father's house have fought in defence of our holy laws and sanctuary; you are witnesses of the distresses we have felt; my brethren have lost their lives in the service of Israel, and I am left alone. Far be it from me to spare my life in these times of public trouble, for I am not better than my brethren. I will avenge my nation, and the sanctuary, and our children, and wives; for the heathens have collected their forces together, and from mere malice meditate our ruin. Simon's words infused a generous ardour into the breasts of the people; they chose him for their leader in the place of Judas and Jonathan, bade him fight their battles, and promised to do whatever he should order. Simon lost no time, drew an army together, finished the fortifications of Jerusalem, and took the field against Tryphon, who was advancing with a numerous army towards the confines of Judea. Tryphon had not expected to meet with such a force, or to find a general so ready to oppose him. He, therefore, sent deputies to Simon, pretending that he had only detained Jonathan on account of money which was due from him to the king's treasury, and promised to release him, upon condition that a hundred talents of silver were paid for his ransom, and his two sons sent as hostages for his good behaviour. Simon knew the deceitful language, and suspected the traitor's design was to destroy both the father and his sons, after he had received the money for his ransom; but being apprehensive, lest he might incur the displeasure of the Jews, if he should not do his utmost to set Jonathan at liberty, punctually fulfilled the conditions that were required on his part. The event soon showed that his suspicions had not been ill-grounded; for the perfidious Syrian was no sooner possessed of the sum he wanted, than he slew Jonathan, with both his sons, and then marched away into his own country.

Simon's endeavour to save his brother's life having proved ineffectual, he resolved to honour him after death. Having recovered the dead body out of the enemy's hands, he carried it to Modin, and there deposited it with the remains of his renowned father and brethren: he erected over them a magnificent monument, as an honorary tribute due to the memory of those illustrious chiefs, who had so eminently distinguished themselves in the defence of God's people: his motive was to honour the merit of the deceased, not to flatter the vanity of the living. Simon governed the Jewish nation with great wisdom and steadiness for eighty years, when one Ptolemy, his son-in-law, being instigated with a wicked desire of power, conspired against, and deprived him of life. His death was universally lamented by the people, and his remains were, with due honour, interred at Modin, in the monument which he himself had erected to his family predecessors.

Such was the end of the illustrious Machabees, whom God, in his singular providence, raised up to fight his battles; and with them ends the history of the Old Testament. Those five glorious brothers, being all animated with the same spirit, and inflamed with the same zeal in the midst of perils, for the service of God and their country, exhibit a bright example to the champions of the New Law, which succeeded soon after. They teach their Christian successors, with what intrepidity and zeal they are to stand forth in the cause of virtue and religion, how unbiassed by private interest, how united amongst themselves, how free from envy and ambition, how indefatigable, how active in their undertaking, how dependent on God for success. Amidst the constant hurry and alarms of war, they always found time for prayer, and by their prayers obtained the divine blessing upon their arms and country.

Simon was succeeded both in the sacerdotal and civil power by his son John, who, from a victory he gained over the Hyrcanians, obtained the surname of Hyrcanus. Hyrcanus left the sovereign power to his son Aristobulus, who assumed the crown and title of king. Hence, the regal sceptre was transmitted from one to another of the Jewish nation, till Herod, by the means of Mark Antony, obtained it of the Roman people, and was acknowledged king in Jerusalem. Herod being an Idumæan by birth, and consequently of a foreign race, in him the sceptre of Juda failed. A leader of Jacob's line no longer presided over the Jewish people; the term foretold by the holy patriarch to his son Judas for the coming of the Messiah, the expectation of nations, was then at hand. In the thirty-seventh year of King Herod's reign, which was the four thousandth of the world, Jesus Christ, the eternal Son of God, was, for us men, born in Bethlehem, a town of Juda.

END OF THE SIXTH AGE, AND OF THE OLD TESTAMENT.

THE HISTORY

OF

THE NEW TESTAMENT.

SEVENTH AGE OF THE WORLD.

FROM THE COMING OF JESUS CHRIST TO THE END OF TIME.

St. Matthew the Evangelist.

BEFORE we enter upon the historical narration of facts in the New Testament, it may not be thought superfluous to give some account of the four Evangelists, who were inspired to write them. The four Gospels, as they are called from the names of their sacred writers, are, in fact, four books of the same and one individual Gospel of Jesus Christ, who teaches us therein the truth, and the way to eternal life. Of the four evangelists, St. Matthew is the first in order, who of a publican became an apostle. He wrote his gospel in Jerusalem, at the request of those Jews who had embraced the

Christian faith, according to St. Jerome; or, according to St. Epiphanius, in consequence of an order from the apostles themselves. He wrote it not in Greek, but in the Hebrew or Syrian language, as Eusebius in his history, and several holy fathers affirm. St. Jerome, moreover, adds, with Eusebius, that Pantinus, in his mission among the Indians, found an original copy of St. Matthew's gospel, written in Hebrew, which he brought to Alexandria, and which in his time was kept in the library of Cæsarea. This original is since lost, but the Greek translation of it has been carefully preserved. Who the author of this translation was, we cannot precisely tell: some of the fathers attribute it to St. John, others to his brother St. James. St. Matthew, according to the remarks of St. Austin, seems to have had the humanity of Jesus Christ chiefly in his eye, and therefore sets off with a genealogical account of his royal descent from David, and in the progress of his gospel exhibits to us the chief transactions of his life upon earth. For this reason he is not so sublime, either in his style or sentiment, as St. John, who frequently treats of the mystery of the blessed Trinity, and discourses of the divinity of Jesus Christ. The manner, therefore, of St. Matthew's writing seems more adapted to the capacity of the faithful in general, because he enters into a more particular detail of those actions and instructions in which Jesus Christ was pleased to accommodate himself to our weakness, and to place the example of his virtues within the reach of our imitation. Although it belongs not to us to seek out reasons, and to form conjectures about the secret designs of God, in inspiring four different men to write the same gospel, yet this we may say, that the will of Jesus Christ is, to have his holy law written in the hearts, and expressed in the interior life of all Christians, that their exterior actions may exhibit the visible characters of that invisible charity which he desires to see imprinted in our souls. The design of Jesus Christ was not simply to instruct us by his written word; it was, moreover, to excite in his followers a desire of copying his actions, when they should read or hear the example he had given them; so that the lustre of his virtues, as well as the truth of his doctrine, might be perpetuated from age to age, not in the dead letter, but in the living actions of the faithful. However commendable it may be to read the gospel with respect and attention, yet the knowledge of it will avail us nothing without the practice of what we read: for the most perfect knowledge of every evangelical truth will never make us the true disciples of a God-man, unless we comply with those sacred precepts, and in our lives trace out those religious virtues which he has taught us: then it is, and only then, that we become the images of the life of Jesus Christ, as Jesus Christ both is, and always was, the perfect image of his Father. It is not certain in what year St. Matthew wrote his gospel, but it is generally thought to have been about the year forty-two, that is, about eight years after our blessed Saviour's ascension into heaven.

St. Mark the Evangelist.

Of Mark frequent mention is made in the Acts of the Apostles, and in the Epistles of St. Paul. But it is not clear who that Mark was; whether the evangelist, as St. Jerome seems to think, or another of the same name, whom St. Peter mentions at the end of his first epistle, and call his son. However that may have been, the constant tradition is, that the evangelist was the Mark who preached the Christian faith in Egypt, and founded the church of Alexandria, the second metropolitan in the world. Most of the holy fathers seem to agree in opinion, that St. Mark wrote his gospel at Rome, conformably to the information which he received from St. Peter, and at the request of the Christians there, as Eusebius informs us. For that celebrated historian having related the wonderful success which accompanied St. Peter's preaching at Rome, adds, (*Lib. 2, c. 15.*) that they who heard him were so charmed with the excellency of his doctrine, that they desired to have it in writing: the important truths that fell from the mouth of the holy apostle excited their piety, and made them wish to refresh their memory by reading at their leisure what they had heard him speak. They, therefore, addressed themselves to Mark, the disciple of St. Peter, and by their entreaties prevailed upon him to pen down the evangelical history which bears his name. It was written under the inspection, and published by the approbation of St. Peter, who on that account was thought by some, as Tertullian says, to have been the author of the work. St. Austin and St. Jerome, with most of the holy fathers, are of opinion that Mark wrote his gospel in Greek, though by the style and frequent Hebraisms that occur in his writings, he seems to have been a native of Judea, and more familiar with the Hebrew than the Greek idiom. He, for the most part, sticks close to St. Matthew in his narration of facts, often makes use of the same words, and in many places does but abridge the history. He alters, indeed, the order of the narration at times, adds some new circumstances, and relates several entire facts of which St. Matthew makes no mention. He says nothing of St. Peter's walking upon the sea, nor of the high commendations he received from our blessed Saviour, upon hi confessing him to be the Son of God, but is very particular in the circumstances of his denying his divine Master; which St. Chrysostom attributes to the great humility of that apostle, who guided his disciple's pen. The same holy doctor asks, why, of the four that were appointed to write the history of Jesus Christ, no more than two were chosen out of the sacred college of apostles? For St. Mark, as well as St. Luke, were only disciples; the first of St. Peter, and the latter of St. Paul. To which he answers, those holy men were not moved by the desire of human praise in any of their undertakings, but that the sole glory of God and advantage of the church directed them in their thoughts and actions, as the Holy Ghost inspired. St. Mark wrote his gospel about the third year of Claudius, as it is thought, that is, about the forty-third year of our Lord. His diction is concise and expressive, his periods are concluded with a pleasing and elegant simplicity.

St. Luke the Evangelist.

St. Luke was a native of Antioch, the capital city of Syria, the companion of St. Paul in his apostolical excursions, and styled by him the beloved physician and his fellow-labourer. When or how he became a proselyte to the Christian religion is uncertain. What he has written in his gospel he learned from those who, as he himself says, were from the beginning eye-witnesses and ministers of the word; for he was not conversant with our blessed Saviour, as St. Matthew and St. John were. By a special disposition of the divine wisdom, it was ordained, says St. Austin, that the evangelical history should be written by two men, who had not seen the things they relate; to the end we might learn to submit our understanding in obedience to divine faith, whether it be communicated to us by an apostle, or only by a disciple of an apostle. For the certitude of truth which is contained in the holy gospels, rests not upon the ground of human evidence, which at most can afford us nothing more than a moral certainty; it rests upon the special assistance of the Holy Ghost, who could not inspire the sacred penman to write any thing but what was true. God is truth itself: he cannot be deceived in what he sees, nor can he deceive us in what he reveals. In the gospel, therefore, every fact is equally certain, and the doctrine equally true, whether written by an evangelist or by others: for the writers were equally inspired, and what they say is undoubtedly the infallible word of God. The esteem which St. Luke was in, spread from one church to another, on account of his gospel, which St. Paul approved and recommended; and great, says St. Ambrose, must have been the merit of this evangelist, who was so highly commended by the great apostle of the Gentiles. What induced him to write his gospel was the rash presumption of some other writers, who had obtruded their own compositions upon the public, and had gravely given out their own fabulous relations for the true history of Jesus Christ. To prevent the mischief that might arise from thence, he diligently informed himself of the real truth from those enlightened apostles who had been acquainted with our blessed Saviour from the beginning; he collected a circumstantial account of the things which Jesus Christ had said and done, and published it for the instruction of the faithful. He has expressed himself with a greater purity of language than the other evangelists; for he was well versed in the Greek tongue, as St. Jerome remarks, and in that language he wrote both his Gospel, and his Acts of the Apostles. There is great elegance and perspicuity in his style, an eminent sublimity of thought, accompanied with that genuine simplicity which characterizes the work of an inspired writer. He is thought to have written his gospel about the year of our Lord fifty-three; his Acts were not finished before the year sixty-three. He lived in a state of celibacy to the eighty-fourth year of his age, and, as the church says of him, always carried about in his body the mortification of the cross, for the honour of the divine name: so that, if his death was not signalized by the actual effusion of his blood in testimony of the true faith, as the holy fathers seem to doubt, we may at least say of him, in the words of St. Jerome, that his life was a long and continued martyrdom.

St. John the Evangelist.

St. John was a native of the town of Bethsaida, the son of Zebedee, and brother of St. James, surnamed the Greater. Being unmarried, and in the flower of his youth, he was called to the apostleship, in which state he remained a virgin to his death, as St. Jerome relates. The virginal purity of his body and mind made him the beloved disciple of his divine Master, says the same father: that it was which rendered him more worthy of Jesus's love; this entitled him to the privilege of resting his head in the bosom of our Lord at his last supper; in consideration of this, Jesus Christ, in his agony upon the cross, recommended his Virgin Mother to him, in whom there was a resemblance of chastity and holy love. After the descent of the Holy Ghost, he preached the faith in Asia Minor, where he founded the different churches, which he continued to direct by his apostolic authority as long as he lived, having fixed his metropolitan seat at Ephesus. Being called to Rome, he was condemned by the Emperor Domitian to be cast into a cauldron of boiling oil; but being miraculously preserved, and coming out more fresh and vigorous than he entered in, says Tertullian, he was banished into the island of Patmos. Here he was favoured with those heavenly and mysterious visions, which he has so wonderfully described in his book of Revelations. After the death of Domitian he returned to Ephesus, where he was engaged to write his Gospel, about the year ninety-eight. Cerinthus and Ebion having impiously asserted, with great scandal to the new Christians, that Jesus Christ had no existence before that which he received from Mary, and was consequently no more than a pure man, all the bishops of Asia Minor, as well as the deputies from several other churches, addressed themselves to St. John, as the most able and best qualified to refute so blasphemous a heresy. St. John's zeal for the honour of his divine Master, made him readily consent to undertake the task. It was a task of the utmost importance to the church; a task superior to the talents even of an apostle without the special direction of God's holy Spirit; and, therefore, to draw down the divine blessing upon his undertaking, he desired them to join with him in prayer and public fasting. Almighty God seems to have rewarded their piety with ample effusion of light upon the holy evangelist. Full of the holy Spirit, and animated by the dignity of his subject, St. John pointed his style much higher than any one of the other three evangelists, and in a strain the most sublime, began by establishing the divinity of God's eternal WORD. St. John, says the learned St. Austin, in his comments upon the gospel, was in a special manner made choice of to unfold the divinity of Jesus Christ. The other three evangelists seem to walk with Jesus Christ upon the surface of the earth, and their progress relate the actions of his mortal life; while St. John, like an eagle, soars aloft above the clouds of human understanding, and penetrating into the bosom of the Father, fixes his eye upon the divine WORD, the co-eternal Son of God, without being dazzled by the rays, or overpowered by the glory of infinite majesty. To record the sentences, and to pen down the sublime instructions of his divine Master, seems to have been the application of this evangelist more than of any other. For whilst the others dwell chiefly upon those actions of our Saviour which serve to regulate the manners, and direct the conduct of our lives, St. John is eager to supply their omissions of those more exalted truths which contain the mystery of the blessed Trinity, the equality of three divine persons, and the glory of a life to come. And we cannot but observe, adds the same holy doctor, that though the desire of establishing the most elevated points of doctrine made him first take up his pen, yet the love we owe our brethren, after the example of Jesus Christ, is what seems to animate him through all his writings; and though the object he had in view was to prove the divinity of Jesus Christ, yet of all the sacred writers he is the only one who has represented to us his humility in washing the disciples' feet: by which he undoubtedly insinuates to us, that the most sublime knowledge of religion ought ever to be accompanied with the virtues of charity and humility.

Annunciation of the Blessed Virgin.—Luke, i
[A.M. 4000.]

When the plenitude of time was come that God had fixed from eternity to shower down his blessings upon mankind, by giving them a Redeemer, the angel Gabriel was first deputed to Zachary, a holy priest, whose wife was Elizabeth, one of

the daughters of Aaron. The heavenly messenger came to tell him that he should have a son, whose name should be John, and whose birth should be a subject of joy to many in Israel. Six months after, Almighty God deputed the same angel to a virgin whose name was Mary, residing in Nazareth, a city of Galilee. Mary had been espoused to a holy man called Joseph, a descendant of the house of David. The divine Providence had in a special manner presided over those nuptials, which provided the Virgin with a guardian and protector of her purity. For with the same sentiments of virtue, and in the same dispositions of mind, says St. Austin, both Mary and Joseph entered into a mutual engagement of joining the marriage state with a state of virginity, of which the world had not seen an example. Almighty God honoured this alliance with an issue which was to set open the gates of heaven, which for ages had been shut against us by the crime of our first parents. Mary was the woman destined by Almighty God to crush the serpent's head, as it is written in the book of Genesis, c. 3, and it was to obtain her consent, that God then sent his angel to Nazareth. The angel found her alone, as St. Ambrose

observes, and respectfully said unto her, *Hail! full of grace, the Lord is with thee; blessed art thou amongst women!* The humble virgin was disturbed at the angel's salutation, and trembled with fear, lest, as Eve had been deceived by the serpent, she also might be misled by a similar delusion. She considered the sense and import of his words, and thereby gives us an admirable example of discretion, which teaches us not to be too hasty in consenting to a proposal, before we understand the nature of its obligation. The angel saw the trouble of her mind, and to appease it said, Fear not, Mary; for you have found favour with the Lord. He then opened the subject of his commission, and told her that she should conceive and bring forth a son, and call his name Jesus; that he should be great, even the Son of the Most High; that he should sit upon the throne of David; that he should reign in the house of Jacob, and that of his kingdom there should be no end. The Virgin listened to the angel with great attention; she heard the wonderful things he promised, but desired to know how it could possibly be done, because she was a virgin. It was not an idle curiosity, but a mark of her submission to the divine will; nor was it a want of faith, but an intimation of the chaste purpose of her mind, which induced her to ask the angel that question. The angel, in reply, assured her, that no concurrence of man was requisite for what the sole power of the Most High, with her consent, would operate within her; that by the ineffable virtue of the Holy Ghost, she should conceive, bear a son, and still remain a pure virgin. It is what the prophet Isaiah, c. 7, had expressly foretold. But to convince the Virgin that nothing was impossible to God, the angel, moreover, told her what had happened to her cousin Elizabeth in an advanced age, who, notwithstanding the many years she had been reputed barren, had miraculously conceived, and was six months gone with child. The Virgin having thus received the information she desired, and being told the manner in which the mystery was to be wrought within her, gave her consent. In terms the most humble and submissive, terms that expressed the holy disposition of her heart, she said: Behold the handmaid of the Lord: let it be done to me according to thy word.

The angel, having thus happily completed his commission, returned to heaven, and the wonderful mystery of the Incarnation took place that instant. For Mary had no sooner given her consent, than the Son of God, the second Person of that most adorable Trinity, by an invisible and inexplicable operation of the Holy Ghost, took flesh and *became man* in her womb, without the least detriment to her virginal integrity. That was the happy moment in which the work of man's redemption was begun; that was the moment when an incarnate God unlocked the source of those plentiful graces, which were to flow for the salvation of mankind, to wash our souls from sin, and to sanctify them for eternal life.

Visitation of the Blessed Virgin.—Luke, i.
[A.M. 4000.]

Mary was no sooner become the mother of a God incarnate, than she hastened to pay a visit to her cousin Elizabeth. With a cheerful alacrity which should always accompany the performance of a good action, she set out upon a long and toilsome journey into the mountainous part of Judea, to congratulate her cousin upon the happy event of her being six months gone with child. When she came to Zachary's house, she entered in, and without mentioning the pre-eminence of her own maternity, humbly saluted Elizabeth. Elizabeth no

sooner heard the Virgin's voice saluting her with the sweet tidings of peace, than she felt her infant exulting for joy within her womb. Thus John the Baptist, before he could see to point him out, became the first adorer of Jesus Christ upon earth, and by the impression he then made upon his mother, entered upon the office of Precursor to our Lord, even before he was born. Elizabeth seemed at a loss how to express what she felt upon this extraordinary interview inspired by the Holy Ghost she cried out: Blessed art thou amongst women, and blessed is the fruit of thy womb! and whence is it that the Mother of my Lord should come in this manner to me? Mary, who was not to be outdone either in the sentiments or in the expressions of humility attributed nothing of her unparalleled greatness to herself, but gave the whole glory to God her Saviour. Unable, as it were, to contain the flowing tide of gratitude that filled her soul at the thought of God's goodness towards her, she

burst out into that excellent canticle, the *Magnificat*, which may be justly styled the eulogy of the humble, and confusion of the proud. Mary remained with Elizabeth about three months, till the Baptist was born and circumcised, as seems most probable, and then returned to her own house at Nazareth.

Mary teaches us by her conduct on this occasion, not to seek the applause of men by the services we do them, nor to make a boast of the good we have done, or of the gifts we have received. If Almighty God in his goodness imparts to us the power or the talents to assist our brethren, to him only we are to give the glory; to ourselves nothing is due but the confusion for having either neglected our talents, or not employed them to the best advantage.

A.M. 4000.] *Birth of Jesus Christ.* [A.D. 1.

LUKE, ii.

THE favours of Almighty God to his saints are oftentimes accompanied with trials of affliction; and this the Blessed Virgin experienced upon her return to Nazareth. For her pregnancy beginning to appear, St. Joseph her husband was disturbed at the mystery, which he knew not how to account for. He had observed nothing in his spouse which was not conformable to the strictest rules of the most immaculate virtue; he had a high opinion of her sanctity, and being a just man, and unwilling publicly to expose her, thought of putting her away privately. Under this perplexity of mind, and undetermined what to do, he fell asleep: when, behold,

during the silence of the night, God sent an angel to comfort and free him from his doubts. Joseph, son of David, said the angel to him, be under no apprehensions concerning Mary thy spouse; for that which is conceived in her, is of the Holy Ghost: she shall bring forth a son, and thou shalt call his name Jesus; for he shall save his people from their sins. By this heavenly message, Joseph was more convinced than ever of the unparalleled perfections of his spouse, and he teaches us by his conduct, how cautious we ought to be in the steps we take, and in the judgments we form with respect to our neighbour, and how great our obligation is to judge favourably of the good and virtuous, notwithstanding the unfavourable circumstances that may appear against them. Joseph gave implicit credit to the angel: in the eyes of men he became the reputed father of Jesus Christ, of whom his virgin spouse was really the mother.

Mary having almost gone her full time seemed to wait the day of her being brought to bed at Nazareth, and yet the prophet Micheas, c. 3, had expressly said that from Bethlehem should come forth the leader to rule the people of Israel. The hand as well as the eye of Almighty God reaches from end to end, through the whole extent of times and places: in his wisdom he so disposes all things, that he most powerfully but sweetly makes his creatures subservient to his designs, even while they seem to take their ordinary course.

After many long and violent struggles for superiority among the Roman chiefs, the whole world was then in peace, under the command of Augustus Cæsar, the Roman emperor. That mighty prince, being ambitious to know the precise number of his subjects, published an edict, by which all in their respective provinces were commanded to repair to the town of their ancestors, that their names might be there enrolled by the proper officer. In obedience to that edict, Joseph, with his spouse, was obliged to go to Bethlehem, his paternal town of residence; for he was of the house and family of David. A long journey in December, when short days, and the wintry season incommoded the most sturdy traveller, was necessarily attended with great inconveniencies to a delicate woman in Mary's condition. But Mary in the emperor's edict adored the hand of God, and respectfully submitted to his divine pleasure, being persuaded, that whenever he makes his will known, whether by an angel, or man, his substitute, he is with equal cheerfulness to be obeyed. Being come to Bethlehem, they found the inns and public places of reception already full, for great was the recourse of strangers at that time. In vain did Joseph seek through the town for a night's lodging: no one would admit, no one shelter him under his roof. They were forced to be content with a stable, where they screened themselves as well as they could against the inclemency of a winter's night. This was the place, and these were the circumstances, in which the divine Redeemer chose to appear. When the night had finished

half its course, and the whole creation lay hushed in silence, when the hour was come for the Eternal Word to be born in time, the undefiled and ever immaculate Virgin brought forth her first-born Son, wrapped him up in swaddling clothes, and laid him in the manger. There, unknown to the world, and rejected by his own chosen people, shivering with cold, and destitute of the common solaces of life, Jesus lay in an open stable, the outcast, as it were, of men, though he had the whole universe at his disposal. By choice he began to dwell amongst us in a state of humility, of poverty, and sufferings, and by that has shown us, what judgment we are to form of the pride, of the magnificence and pleasures of a sinful world. Nothing, say the holy fathers, can give us an instruction equal to this wonderful humiliation of the Son of God: by the profound humiliation of Jesus Christ in the stable of Bethlehem, we are more powerfully moved to adore his infinite power, than by all the shining beauties we admire in the universe. The state of helpless infancy to which an omnipotent God had been pleased to stoop, ought daily to remind us, that we always stand more in need of the divine help, than a new born child does of the help of men.

Shepherds at the crib in Bethlehem.—Luke, ii.
[A.D. 1.]

Jesus Christ was no sooner born, than he began to make himself known, not to the learned doctors, or mighty princes of the people, who were little qualified to learn the humility of an incarnate God, but to a few holy and illiterate shepherds, whose simplicity made them little in their own eyes, and disposed them to know the hidden mysteries of the Divinity. For in the neighbourhood of Bethlehem there were shepherds standing upon the watch, to guard their flocks from the dangers of the night; and their watchfulness points out a duty incumbent upon those who wish to know and follow Jesus Christ. As a token of the great Light which was now risen to dispel the shade of death, a beaming brightness shone from the heavens, and behold an angel of the Lord approached! Struck at the awful appearance, the shepherds trembled with exceeding fear. Fear not, said the angel; I am come to bring you tidings of great joy, which shall likewise extend to all the people: for this day is born to you a Saviour, who is Christ the Lord, in Bethlehem, in the city of David. You will know him by the sign I give you: you will find the infant wrapped round with swaddling clothes, and laid in a manger. The heavenly messenger was not ashamed of the infant state to which an omnipotent God had now humbled himself for the love of man, and, therefore, confidently described the marks by which the great and wonderful Messiah was to be discovered. As soon as he had delivered his message to the shepherds, he was joined by an innumerable troop of other celestial spirits, praising God, and saying, Glory be to God on high, and on earth peace to men of good will. The shepherds had now forgot their fears; they spoke with confidence, and invited one another to go as far as Bethlehem, that they might see the wonder which God had wrought. The evangelist observes, that they went with speed: for Jesus Christ is not to be sought with indifference, nor is he usually found by the slothful. When they came to the place, they found Mary and Joseph, and the divine infant lying in a manger, as the angel had described him. Far

from being scandalized at the meanness of his appearance, they were filled with admiration; they saw and believed; they spoke with raptures of the mystery to others, who were equally astonished at the things they heard.

Mary, in the mean while, was fixed in silent thought upon her son; she caught attentively the words that were spoken of him, and laid them up carefully in her heart. Though mother of the Word Eternal, she disdained not to listen to the words of illiterate shepherds, and gives thereby an unexceptionable reproof to those self-sufficient Christians, who, being proud of their worldly wisdom, disdain to consult or hear those spiritual pastors, whom God has appointed to teach them the ways of truth. The word of God, whether it be heard or read by us, is the ordinary channel through which Almighty God conveys the knowledge of salvation to us; we cannot receive it with too great respect, nor be too careful in laying it up within our hearts. Faith comes by hearing, and it is by frequently receiving, and attentively considering the instructive lessons of salvation, that faith is kept alive and nourished in our souls.

Circumcision of Jesus Christ.—LUKE, ii.
[A.D. 1.]

ON the eighth day after the divine infant was born, the Blessed Virgin and St. Joseph circumcised him as a descendant of Abraham; and in this exhibit a bright example of that holy simplicity, which teaches us not to dispute about the law of God, but to fulfil punctually what it ordains. A law that had been given to Abraham, as a sign of his faith in Him who was to come, they knew could not oblige the Messiah himself; a law, by which the stain of original sin was washed out in the blood of him who received it, through the future merits of a God-man, they knew could not be for him who had no sin, and by whom all sins were remitted; yet they waited not for any new order to enforce their obedience; they submitted to the law as they found it; they were too docile to pretend an exception where God had made none, and too humble not to conform to the common practice. But if the Blessed Virgin and St. Joseph appear so worthy of our admiration for their religious submission to the law, how far more admirable is the example of Jesus Christ himself? For, besides the pain which attended the operation, he would also take upon him the disgrace, and bear in his flesh the mark of a reputed sinner. Being by nature incapable of the least blemish, he would, notwithstanding, suffer the punishment of sin, to make us sensible of its enormity. When we consider how the innocent Jesus at that tender age began to bleed, and to bleed on our account, we ought to blush at our guilty delicacy, which persuades us, either to explain away the force of our Christian obligations, or shun the trouble of complying with them. The humility of a God stooping to the low condition of a sinner, ought to shame us of our pride, and make us eager to expiate, by sufferings and humiliations, the guilty cause for which the divine Jesus suffered. Sufferings and humiliations pave the way to real glory. It is what happened to Jesus Christ—it is what will happen to the zealous imitators of his virtues. In submitting to the painful and humiliating ceremony of circumcision, the blessed infant merited the adorable name of Jesus: a name the most glorious, and expressive of his saving power. He abased himself by an act of humility the most profound; for which reason, as St. Paul says, God hath exalted him, and hath given him a name above all other names that in the name of JESUS every knee shall bow, in heaven, on earth, and in hell; and every tongue confess, that JESUS is the Lord.

A devotion towards this sacred name began with the church itself; it ought never to be pronounced but with respect. From generation to generation, parents have taught their children to confide in this holy name, and repeat it with a lively faith, mixed with love, that they may obtain the blessing of salvation, promised by St. Paul to those who shall duly call upon it. For in calling upon Jesus, our Saviour God, we publicly declare, that through him alone, and not from ourselves, the grace of salvation comes. The name was brought from heaven by an angel: the Father himself gave it to the divine infant, even before he was conceived in the Virgin's womb. It, therefore, is our duty not to rob him of the glory which he has thus received: we should be careful not to hinder him from being a SAVIOUR to us: with profound humility let us lay open the wounds of our souls before him, that the merits of his life and death may heal and save us.

Adoration of the Kings.—MATT. ii.
[A.D. 1.]

SCARCE had the birth of Jesus Christ been announced to the Jews by an angel, when the unusual apparition of a star manifested it also to the Gentiles. The nations that had sat for ages in the darkness of infidelity, were admonished by a miraculous light, that a king was born for the salvation both of Jews and Gentiles. This new star appeared in the East; but of the many to whom it appeared, we know of none who profited by it except the sages, as they are called in holy Scripture. They were kings, as we learn by tradition, and three in number. Being eager to find the king, who was so manifestly indicated to them, they lost no time in forming doubts and difficulties, but prepared their presents, the tokens of their faith and piety, and began their journey towards Jerusalem, as the star directed them. They entered the royal city without disguise, they made no secret of their intention; within the hearing of a jealous prince, they declared they were come to pay their adorations to a new-born king of the Jews, and desired to know where he might be found. Herod, who knew he had no other title to the crown of Judea, than what the Romans gave him, was much more alarmed at this inquiry which was made after another king. The Jews, who, according to their carnal notions of things, imagined that the long expected Messiah was to restore their earthly kingdom to its ancient splendour, were in commotion at the news, and the whole city of Jerusalem seemed in an uproar. Herod called together the priests and doctors of the law, to inform him of the place where Christ was to be born. The conduct of those Jewish doctors on that important occasion was most unaccountable, and will to endless ages show how undeserving they were of a mercy which then offered itself to them. They told the king that Bethlehem was the place where he might find the infant: they cited him the very passage out of the prophet, but maliciously suppressed the latter part of the prophecy, which would have informed him, that no temporal crown could be the pursuit of Him, who was from the beginning, and whose coming forth was from the days of eternity. Herod having thus received from the doctors the information he wanted, sent for the sages:

he told them to come privately to him, and having diligently learned from them the precise time of the star's appearance, he civilly dismissed them towards Bethlehem, with a strict charge to bring him back an account of the child when they had found him, that he also might go, as he pretended, to adore him. The sages, upon leaving the city, saw the star again, which they joyfully followed, till they came to Bethlehem. It there stopped its course, and rested over the house, where the object of their adoration lay. They entered the house,

and there found the child, with Mary his mother. Full of faith, and wholly bent upon the adorable object of their hope, they fell upon their knees, opened their treasures, and with the same humble homage of their hearts that was expressed in the bending posture of their bodies, presented him their mysterious offerings of gold, frankincense, and myrrh. When they had finished their acts of adoration, they thought of returning back to Herod, having no suspicion of his murderous designs. But God admonished them in their sleep not to go near the tyrant, and they went another way into their own country.

Thus it was, says St. Austin, that Jesus Christ made himself known to some, whilst he concealed himself from others; being ardently sought after and adored by strangers, he was sinfully neglected by his own people. The faith of the enlightened Gentiles discovers to us the strange infidelity of the Jews. The knowledge which the Jews drew from the holy Scriptures, only served to render them the more criminal; they made no use of the extraordinary lights they had received from God, they thereby forfeited those precious graces, which were taken from them and given to the Gentiles. Christians who are careless of the divine gifts, have the same fatal judgment to apprehend: a similar neglect draws after it a similar chastisement; darkness succeeds to light, and an obduracy of heart ensues. The miraculous star, says the same father, had disappeared long ago: having once pointed out the Messiah, it has not since that time been seen: the light of the gospel shines in its stead. Those who are as diligent as the sages were, in following this unerring light, will as surely find their Saviour, and reap with them the fruit of their past labours. Whatever marks of infidelity they may observe in others, if they are sensible of God's great goodness in having called them into the admirable light of the true faith, gratitude will make them faithful to the grace of their vocation, a pious zeal will make them ready to perform the duties of it, and a desire of being happy will teach them to adore their Saviour in spirit and in truth.

Purification of the Blessed Virgin.—LUKE, ii. [A.D. 1.]

AT the end of forty days Mary repaired to Jerusalem, that she might there satisfy the two-fold precept of her own purification, and of the child's presentation in the temple, according to the law of Moses. She knew indeed, that her virginal purity had been rendered more bright by the divine virtue of her Son; she knew from the words of the law, that the obligation did not concern her; but she also knew, that the public was not then acquainted with her singular privileges; she had seen her Son submit to the law of circumcision, and therefore would admit of no exemption, that should publicly distinguish her from the rest of her sex. In memory of what happened to the first-born of Egypt, when the Israelites were delivered from thence, the Levitical law ordained, that every first-born son of the children of Israel should be consecrated to the Lord, and then redeemed by the offering of some living creature, which for the rich was a lamb, and a pair of pigeons or two turtle doves for the poorer class. Mary, though descended from the kings of Juda, stood as an humble hand-maid of the Lord, with a pair of doves, and Jesus in her arms. There lived at that time in Jerusalem, a good old man, called Simeon, who being adorned with every religious virtue, was waiting for the consolation of Israel. By a secret inspiration of the Holy Ghost, he came to the temple at the very hour that Jesus was brought thither by his parents, for he had received a promise from the Holy Spirit

that he should not depart out of life, before he had seen the anointed of the Lord. Being illuminated by the interior light of faith that filled his soul, he took the divine infant into his arms, and burst out into a transport of praise and holy joy. Now, my God, said he, now thou mayest dismiss thy servant in peace, since, according to thy word, mine eyes have seen the Saviour of the world; since thou hast revealed the Light, which shall shine not only on the Jews, but upon every nation in the universe. The Blessed Virgin and St. Joseph listened with admiration to the venerable old man, who blessed them, and continued to prophesy what should happen to the Son, and what a sword of grief should pierce through the Mother's soul. A pious widow whose name was Ann came up at the very moment, and added to the prophecies that Simeon had begun. Ann was a perfect model of virtue to all in her situation of life; after having lived seven years with her husband, she became a widow, and consecrated the remainder of her days to prayer and fasting, being then eighty-four years old. The example of her virtues was the more admirable in her age, which was as corrupt and as licentious to the full, as ever disgraced the Jewish nation. It teaches us, that in the midst of a corrupt world Christians should never be off their guard; that they cannot be too diligent in the duties of a well-ordered piety, lest they forget their character, and become reprobates by the force of bad example.

The presentation of the child Jesus by his mother in the temple, is an instruction to Christian parents the most important and essential; for as there can be nothing in life more dear to parents than their children, so nothing in reason ought to engage their attention more, than to procure them real happiness. For this, it is their duty to recommend them frequently to God, to pray devoutly for them, and to put them in the way of obtaining the divine blessing. Their innocence and their timely instruction in Christian piety, is a precious treasure committed to their care, of which God will one day demand an exact account. It is a charge of the utmost consequence, both to themselves and children; a charge which cannot be duly fulfilled without steady application. A certain tenderness of feeling, which unfortunately leads some parents to indulge their children's humours, and to flatter their pettish inclinations, is a mistaken fondness; it is but a selfish love, and a real cruelty to those whom they think they love.

Flight into Egypt.—MATT. ii.
[A.D. 1.]

HEROD was impatient for the sages' return from Bethlehem, till finding they had slighted the charge he gave them, and were gone home another way, he was hurried into a transport of anger, which deluged the country with innocent blood

By an act, the most inhuman that ever was done by the worst of tyrants, he has shown the world what his intention was, when he so diligently interrogated the sages, and so strictly ordered them to bring him back an account of the child they were in quest of. But God, who laughs at man's presumptuous folly, silently defeated the tyrant's malice, and made his bloody cruelty instrumental to the glory of the innocent. An angel in the night informed Joseph of the murderous design that Herod had upon the child's life, and admonished him to save both him and the mother by a speedy flight into Egypt. Joseph in this instance is a perfect model of that prompt obedience, which every Christian owes to the commands of God. He was commanded to rise that moment, to leave his native country, and fly off with the child and his mother, not towards the sages, or to any friendly nation, but into Egypt, amidst the idolatrous and natural enemies of the Jewish people. The tender age of the infant, the delicate complexion of the Virgin mother, seemed to require every comfort that his own private dwelling could have afforded. But that slender comfort was to be given up; it was dark night, and no time to be lost in making provision for a long and laborious journey. The faithful guardian of the Word incarnate rose upon the first notice that was given him, punctually fulfilled every tittle of the order, took the child and his mother, and set off for Egypt, uncertain when or whether he should ever return or not. The love he bore to Jesus, the desire he had of serving him to the extent of his power, softened every hardship, and made him forget the labours of an unexpected banishment.

The divine Jesus might have rendered himself invisible, or by a visible exertion of his power might have disarmed Herod, as he did Pharaoh in ancient times; but he chose to fly, for the encouragement of those who were afterwards to suffer banishment for his sake; by his own example he would instruct his followers, that in the heat of persecution they may laudably fly to save their lives, in hopes of some future good. Herod began to rage with all the violence that jealousy, heightened by disappointment, could inspire. With a cruelty that would have shocked the most savage barbarian, he gave orders for every male child that had been born within the two last years, in and about Bethlehem, to be killed. To such barbarous shifts was the ambitious monarch driven by

his politics! An innocent babe, he knew not who, made him tremble upon his throne; he tried his utmost skill to find him out, he drenched the country with harmless blood to make sure of his destruction, he filled the air with the shrieks and lamentations of disconsolate mothers, that he might draw out the enjoyment of a crown to a somewhat greater length. But no honours purchased by such crimes could give any real enjoyment. His cruelty heaped confusion upon himself, whilst it opened the gate of happiness to those who felt its stroke: nor could it rage beyond the bounds that God had set it; amidst the thousands of slaughtered innocents, He alone escaped, who alone was aimed at.

No malicious efforts of the wicked can ever frustrate the decrees of God; their hatred or their love become, as he pleases to direct, the instruments of his holy designs; the whole world combined with all the powers of darkness, can never stop the execution of what an omnipotent Providence has once decreed. If once assured of the divine will, we have but to follow it without fear: if in the station of our duty we have any thing to suffer, we suffer for justice sake. Herod's cruelty became the glory of the innocents: his sword could hurt their body only; their souls were sanctified by the effusion of their blood; their memory through every age is celebrated on earth; they reign eternally with God in heaven.

Jesus amidst the Doctors.—LUKE, ii.

[A.D. 12.]

JESUS CHRIST remained no longer in Egypt than was necessary to avoid the sword of his persecutors. Upon the death of Herod, an angel of the Lord appeared again to Joseph, as the head of the family, and bade him return into the land of Israel. With the same ready deference to this second order, as he had paid to the first, St. Joseph began his journey back into his native country. Being informed that Archelaus had succeeded his father in the kingdom of Judea, and fearing for the safety of the divine treasure which he carried with him, he avoided the territory of Judea, and went by divine admonition to Nazareth, which was situated in the province of Galilee, from whence our blessed Saviour was called a Nazarean, as the prophets had foretold. The evangelists make no mention of what Jesus did from the time of his infancy to that of his baptism, except one thing, which happened when he was twelve years of age. Besides that interior homage which the Blessed Virgin paid to God within the secret closet of her heart, she punctually performed those public duties of religion which were in practice at that time: she went regularly every year with Jesus and Joseph to Jerusalem, at the feast of Easter, that she might perform her devotions in the temple, as the law directed. On one of those occasions it happened, and it was in the twelfth year of Jesus's age, that she lost her son. For the eighth and last day of the festival being over, she set out with her spouse to return to Nazareth, the child Jesus remaining in Jerusalem without their knowing it; they thought he had been in company with their kinsfolks and acquaintances, who were returning homeward on the same day. But when they met at night, the child was not to be found. The afflicted parents therefore not finding him, went back next morning to Jerusalem, and sought him there. With great anxiety and grief of mind they made diligent search after him, but had not the comfort to find him. On the third day as they entered the temple, behold! Jesus was sitting among the doctors of the law, asking them questions, and answering in his turn, to the great astonishment of all that heard him. Mary forgot her griefs the moment she saw her Son: the very sight of her divine Jesus

filled her soul with transports of joy, and she said: Son, why hast thou done so to us? behold, thy father and I in sorrow have been seeking thee. And why were you seeking me? replied the son: did you not know that I was to be where the business of my Father called me? The answer admitted of no reply: it is pointed full at those worldly parents, who unhappily try to divert their children from the service of their Creator.

The history of Jesus's life from this period to the thirtieth year of his age, is comprised by the evangelists in this short sentence—He went down with them to Nazareth, and was subject to them. It is the sentence which St. Austin dwells much upon in his instruction to children; a sentence which teaches them at once to know, and to love the obedience which they owe their parents. Jesus, says St. Luke, advanced in wisdom, and age, and grace with God and men.

The whole creation, says St. Austin, was subject to Jesus Christ; and Jesus Christ, whom all things obey, was obedient to his parents. Parents also have their lesson of instruction in this history. The anxiety which the Blessed Virgin expressed in seeking her Son, teaches parents how they are to act, when their children leave them, not to employ themselves in the business of their heavenly Father, as Jesus did in the temple, but to lose themselves in the labyrinths of a licentious world. It behoves them to use every serious endeavour that they think expedient, to bring the delinquents back to a sense of their duty; it behoves them to enter the house of God with a spirit of Mary, to seek and pray for the salvation of those whom they have brought into the world for no other end, than that they may hereafter be happy with God in heaven.

Baptism of Jesus Christ.—MATT. iii.
[A.D. 31.]

IN the fifteenth year of the reign of Tiberius Cæsar, while Jesus was still private in the city of Nazareth, John the Baptist began to preach aloud to the people: Prepare ye the way of the Lord, and make straight his paths; for every valley shall be filled, every mountain and hill shall be made low, and all flesh shall see the salvation of God. The holy prophet being inspired by the Lord, went forth from the desert, where he had lived for some time more like an angel than a man, and preached to all, as he went along through the country of Judea. The people flocked from Jerusalem and the other towns to hear his exhortations. In terms the most persuasive he exhorted them to do penance, and as a sign of their repentance he baptized them in the river Jordan; by which he strove to dispose their minds for the more perfect baptism of Him, whose precursor he was. The austerity of his life, and the lustre of his virtues, gained him the confidence and attention of his hearers: he was listened to as a wonderful servant

of God, and respected as a great prophet. The people in general had conceived so high an opinion of his sanctity, that many began to doubt whether he were not the Christ, who, from the testimony of the ancient prophets, was expected about that time. While the inhabitants of Judea thus crowded round the Baptist to hear his doctrine, and to be baptized by him in the Jordan, Jesus himself came from Galilee, being thirty years of age, and presented himself before John to be baptized, as though he had been a sinner, like the rest of men. The Baptist stood astonished at this profound humility of the Son of God, and refused to pour the water on his sacred head, till he was first assured, that so it

became them to fulfil all justice: in obedience to his blessed Lord, by whom he wished rather to be baptized, he at last consented to perform the holy ceremony, of which he deemed himself unworthy. Jesus being baptized, forthwith came out of the river, and the Eternal Father, who delights in exalting those who humble themselves, gave honourable testimony of him before the multitude. For, behold! the heavens opened, and the Holy Ghost, in the mystic shape of a dove, visibly descended upon the head of Jesus, and a voice at the same time was heard to say, This is my beloved Son, in whom I am well pleased.

The glory of Jesus Christ, as the holy fathers remark, is founded in humility. An incarnate God humbled himself before man, that he might thereby repair the injury which man, by aspiring too high, had offered to the Eternal Father. Jesus, the most exalted of men, put himself upon a level with the lowest: though impeccable by nature, and the very source of innocence, he disdained not the character and appearance of a sinner; whilst we, sinners as we are, affect the show of innocence, and vainly strive to appear better than we are.

Jesus Christ in the Wilderness.—MATT. iv.
[A.D. 31.]

As soon as Jesus was baptized, he began by example to teach those who, in process of time, were to be baptized in his name, what virtues they are to study, what trials and temptations they are to expect. He retired, or, as the text expresses it, he was led by the Holy Spirit into the wilderness, where, far from the noise of men, he addicted himself to silent prayer and fasting for forty days together, and was then tempted by the devil. That haughty spirit not being able to persuade himself, that a God could lie concealed under the form of such human weakness, and yet doubting, as it seems, in what sense he was to understand the voice which had declared him to be the Son of God, resolved to try if he could draw the secret from him. For this purpose he assumed some corporeal form, and artfully concealing, as he fancied, the malice of his intention, addressed himself to Jesus in these words: If thou art the Son of God, command these stones to be changed into bread. Our blessed Saviour, who would not gratify the tempter's curiosity by an external sign of his divinity, answered him from the book of Deuteronomy, c. viii., Not in bread alone doth man live, but

in every word that proceedeth from the mouth of God: by which answer our blessed Lord not only baffled the design of his infernal enemy, but has also given us an instructive lesson, not to be afraid of exposing our lives to famine, or to any other inconvenience in the divine service, but to be chiefly solicitous for that spiritual life which is nourished by the word of God, by holy prayer, and those other helps which the Eternal Word has instituted. Satan, perceiving the little prospect he had of succeeding in a barren wilderness, where no tempting object appeared to excite the senses, by a permissive power from God, took our blessed Saviour, and conveyed him to one of the pinnacles of the temple. If thou art the Son of God, said he, cast thyself down; for it is written, God hath appointed his angels to take care of thee, and to bear thee up in their hands, lest thou chance to dash thy foot against a stone. With the same holy weapon which he had so successfully applied just before, Jesus Christ defeated his enemy a second time, and cited another passage out of the same book of Deuteronomy, c. vi., where it is said, Thou shalt not tempt the Lord thy God. This second rebuff provoked the devil's anger, at the same time that it confounded his pride. He hitherto covered his malice under some show of respect, as if he were speaking to the Son of God; he then threw off the mask, and spoke in a style that denoted nothing but the empty boast, and lying promises of a fallen angel. He carried our Saviour to the summit of a high mountain, from whence he showed him the kingdoms of the earth, with the shining riches and magnificence thereof: all this, said he, I will give thee, if thou wilt fall down and adore me. The presumptuous spirit promised more than he could perform; a single sentence discomfited him in a moment: Avaunt, Satan, said Jesus Christ; for it is written, Thou shalt adore the Lord thy God, and him only shalt thou serve. Satan departed that instant, and angels came and ministered to the Lord.

The temptations which Jesus Christ was pleased to undergo in the wilderness, have been considered by his followers as a subject both of consolation and instruction. By example, he has taught them how to fight against their spiritual enemies, and to conquer too: the struggle may be painful while it lasts; heavenly comforts soon succeed. Let us love retirement, say the holy fathers; let us fast and pray, and the devil cannot hurt us. With a lively faith, let us meditate upon the word of God, and it will furnish us with an impenetrable shield against the fiery darts of our enemy. Let us put our trust in Jesus Christ, the vanquisher of our enemies, and temptations will but serve to strengthen our virtues and increase our crown.

Marriage at Cana in Galilee.—JOHN, i. ii.
[A. D. 31.]

WHEN Jesus Christ had spent forty days in the exercise of private devotion, and by that had taught his followers in what manner they ought to prepare themselves for public action in the divine service, he left the wilderness, and began to manifest himself to the world. He directed his way to the river Jordan, where his precursor was still preaching and

baptizing. The Baptist saw him coming, and exclaimed, Behold the Lamb of God! behold Him who taketh away the sins of the world! Two of John's disciples, one of whom was Andrew, were particularly struck at the words they heard, and wished to be acquainted with the person of whom their master gave so singular a testimony. They took an opportunity to follow Jesus, as he went away, and asked him

where he lived. Jesus invited them to come and see; they accordingly accompanied him to the place of his abode, and remained with him that day. Andrew, in his return back, met Simon, his brother, and telling him that he had found the Messiah, introduced him to Jesus. Jesus fixed his eye upon Simon, and told him that he should be called Cephas, which is to say Peter. From that time the number of Jesus's followers began to increase, and his name was much talked of in the country, though he had not yet wrought any public miracle in testimony of his divine mission. Being at Cana, a town in Galilee, he and his disciples were invited to a marriage feast: Mary, his mother, was also there. During the entertainment the wine failed, which being observed by the Blessed Virgin, she mentioned it to Jesus, whose power she knew was equal to his charity. The answer she received might, perchance, be constructed into a refusal by any one less acquainted than Mary was with the designs of her divine Son: she told the waiters to do what Jesus should direct them, and it quickly appeared that her request was granted. There stood six stone pitchers, containing each of them two or three measures. Jesus bade the waiters fill them with water, and they filled them up to the brim: he then ordered them to pour out, and carry some of it to the chief steward

of the feast. The steward tasted it, and being ignorant of the wonderful change it had undergone, expressed his surprise to the bridegroom, who, contrary to the common custom, as he thought, had kept his good wine to the last.

This was the first miracle, says St. John, by which Jesus manifested his glory, and strengthened the faith of his disciples; and it was wrought at the request of Mary, the mother of Jesus. The different sorts of wine that were produced on this occasion, the one by the bridegroom, and the other by Jesus Christ, mark the different delights of a spiritual and of a worldly life. Worldly pleasures seem pleasant to the taste of carnal men; they flatter the senses, they amuse and entertain while they last, but they last not long; they are soon drained out with life, and often leave a bitter emptiness behind them. The pleasures of a spiritual life are sweetened by the grace of Jesus Christ, and convey to the soul an inexpressible satisfaction, a solid and lasting peace, such as is not to be found in the turbulent joys of sinners. When a devout soul has once begun to taste the sweets of such a peace, she shuts her eyes to those objects which cannot be pursued with innocence; she reposes in the calm of an upright conscience, she keeps her last end constantly in view, she relishes only the things of God, and breathes after a happiness that shall never be exhausted.

Nicodemus.—JOHN, iii.
[A.D. 31.]

THE first miracle of our blessed Saviour was soon after followed by many more, which raised a high opinion of him amongst the people, and spread his reputation through the country. The rich as well as the poor, the learned and ignorant, became informed of the extraordinary things that Jesus said and did. Nicodemus, a principal man among the Jews sought a conference with him in private; for, being

afraid of declaring himself the public follower of a teacher who was likely to meet with great opposition, he came to Jesus by night: he saluted him with the honourable appellation of Master, and frankly confessed that the evidence of his miracles left no room to doubt of his being sent by God for the instruction of mankind. Our blessed Saviour expressed no notice of the encomiums he received from the Jewish doctor, and though he knew him to be a man of learning and repute amongst the Pharisees, he nevertheless entertained him upon those more humble subjects of doctrine, which are most opposite to the conceits of human pride: he spoke to him of the necessity of humility, and a docile obedience to the heavenly truths, positively declaring that unless a man should be born anew, he could have no part with him in the kingdom of God. Nicodemus, with all his learning, was at a loss to know what Jesus meant, and asked how it were possible for a man to return into his mother's womb, and be born anew. For the knowledge of that learned doctor of Israel extended not beyond the dead letter of the law, as St. Augustin observes, nor could the utmost stretch of his reasonings dive into the depth of divine faith. Our blessed Saviour explained to him the nature of the second birth, which was to be in water and the Holy Spirit. The Spirit, said he, breathes where it pleases, and of himself no man can tell from whence or whither it goeth. Nicodemus owned his ignorance concerning those spiritual matters, and was convinced that human reason, however capable of understanding the motives of credibility, can never comprehend the secrets of those sublime truths which it is obliged to believe. The ineffable mystery of the divine and human nature united together in one person, the exaltation of the Son of Man upon the cross, the great love which God has shown to men, since, to make them eternally happy, he did not spare his only begotten Son, were points which our blessed Redeemer proposed to Nicodemus for his belief, as necessary for his eternal welfare. But men, said he, prefer darkness to light; conscious of their evil deeds, they shun the light, not to see their guilt: fond of their ignorance, they studiously avoid the instructions that might otherwise help them to discover the truth, and correct their errors. Nicodemus was sincere in his search after truth; he found it, and embraced it. A fear of what the world would say, made him ashamed at first of appearing in the company of Jesus Christ by day; he came to consult him by night. He had the courage afterwards not only to declare himself publicly, but also to plead for his divine Master before the council, and to express his disapprobation of the bloody sentence which condemned him to the cross. Nor did he relent either in his courage or in his love for Jesus, after the ignominy of his passion: he assisted Joseph of Arimathea in taking down the sacred body from the cross; he helped to embalm and lay it in the sepulchre.

From these progressive steps which Nicodemus made in the way of virtue, the holy fathers take occasion to say, that we are not immediately to despair of those timid souls who dare not at first declare themselves in favour of the truth. Great allowances must be made for human weakness; we must know how to counsel the doubtful and compassionate the feeble. Reflection, perchance, may dissipate their fears, and give them courage; in secret silence they may consider the eternal truths; the grace of God may, at the same time, work within their souls, and inspire them with fortitude; so that they may no longer fear or blush to show themselves in the cause of Jesus Christ.

The Samaritan Woman.—John, iv.
[A.D. 31.]

The frequent miracles that accompanied the preaching of our blessed Saviour drew vast numbers after him, and his followers became much more numerous than those of the Baptist. The great precursor had finished the great object of his mission; he had baptized, he had preached, he had pointed out the Messiah to his hearers. A desire of reclaiming sinners from their evil courses had first drawn him from his retreat in the desert, and the same desire then drew him to Herod's court. That prince had a great esteem for the holy man, whom he loved and revered as a prophet: he took a pleasure in hearing him discourse; he did many good things by his advice, and patiently bore his reproofs upon the subject of an incestuous marriage which he had contracted with his brother's wife. The adulteress would suffer no control: fired with lust, and instigated by the jealous Pharisees against the Baptist, she first procured his imprisonment, and then his death. Our blessed Saviour perceiving the ferment which agitated the people's mind on that account, retired for a time out of the confines of Judea, into Galilee. In his way he passed through Samaria, near the town of Sichar, where he had an interesting conversation with a Samaritan woman, who came to fetch water from Jacob's well. Spent with heat and the fatigue of his journey, Jesus was resting himself upon the well when the woman came. He was thirsty, though his thirst seems to have been more mysterious than natural, and he asked her to let him drink. The woman was surprised to hear herself accosted by a native of Judea, for the Jews had no communication with the Samaritans, and said, How dost thou, being a Jew, ask of me to drink, who

am a Samaritan woman? If thou didst but know the gift of God. replied our blessed Saviour, and who the person is who desires thee to give him water to drink, thou perhaps would have asked of him, and he would have given thee living water, of which whosoever drinketh shall not thirst for ever. For the water that I will give, shall become a perpetual fountain, springing up into life everlasting. She desired he would give her of that water, that she might not thirst, nor be obliged to come to the well again. Our blessed Saviour made no answer to her petition, but changed the discourse, mentioning some past actions of her life, by which she discovered him to be a prophet; she, therefore, desired him to tell her which of the two temples, whether that in Jerusalem or that upon the mountain of Garizim in Samaria, was the true place of divine worship. Jesus answered, that the time was at hand when adoration should be no longer paid to God either in the temple of Jerusalem, or on the mountain of Samaria, and that the true adorers should adore the Father in spirit and in truth. We know the Messiah is coming, said the woman, and he will instruct us in all these matters. He is already come, said our Saviour, and I am he. The woman upon that, left her pitcher, and hastened into the town to inform them of the wonderful prophet she had found. The citizens went forth to see and invite him into the town. He accepted of their invitation, remained two days amongst them, and many believed in him.

The holy fathers admire the condescension of our blessed Saviour on this occasion, in which he disdained not to enter into conversation with a Samaritan woman, upon a subject the most important, and to impart to her the whole secret of the new law. He informed her and all mankind, that true piety consists not in an empty name, nor in the mere performance of some outward ceremony in the temple of Jerusalem, or on the mountain of Samaria, but in an unfeigned goodness of heart, which adores the Father in truth. How sacred soever those material edifices may be, which are dedicated to the divine service, more sacred are the living temples of the souls and bodies which have been consecrated to God in baptism. They then become the dwelling of the Holy Ghost, and through the grace of Jesus Christ, we ought to take care that they always remain so, by rendering to God the sincere homage of our actions and desires, in the true spirit of religion.

The Storm appeased.—Matt. viii.
[A.D. 31.]

Jesus, upon his arrival in the province of Galilee, began to preach publicly, and to exhort his hearers to do penance, because the kingdom of heaven drew near. He visited the town of Capharnaum, and sought by his holy word to open the eyes of its blind inhabitants; but they obstinately rejected the light that was offered them; they preferred error to truth, and by an abuse of divine goodness, rendered themselves more criminal than they were before. They stopped their ears against the exhortations that were made

them, and refused the evidence of miracles that were wrought for their conviction. For in the confirmation of his heavenly doctrine, our blessed Saviour, during his stay amongst them, healed the centurion's servant, who lay at the point of death; he cured St. Peter's mother-in-law of a scorching fever; he

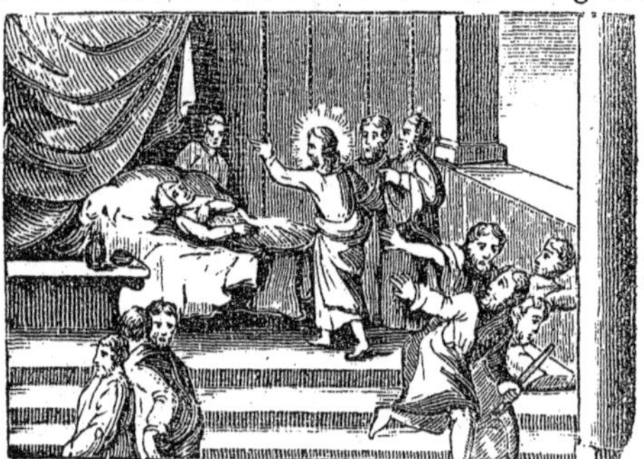

delivered many from the evil spirits that had possessed them; and all that were sick he restored to perfect health. The fame of these miraculous cures, which the ungrateful citizens of Capharnaum did not duly attend to, brought vast crowds of people thither from other parts of the country; some to hear his doctrine, some to see his miracles, and others to beg redress in their corporal infirmities. This concourse of people naturally flattered the disciples, who thought themselves sharers in the honours and respect that were paid to their divine Master. For by this time there were many who followed Jesus Christ, and publicly professed themselves his disciples. Wherefore, to train them by degrees to the labours and hardships that are inseparable from the divine service, and to convince them that they were not to follow him upon the motives of worldly advantages and popular applause, he took them into a boat, and put off to sea. He composed himself to sleep, and in the interim a violent storm arose, which covered the boat with waves, and threatened them with an approaching shipwreck. Terrified at the danger, the disciples ran to Jesus and awakened him, saying, Save us, Lord, or we perish. He rebuked them for their fears and

want of faith; then, rising up, he commanded the winds and the sea, and behold! a great calm presently ensued. The disciples lost their fears, and wondering exclaimed, Who is this? for even the winds and sea obey him!

The vessel on which our blessed Saviour was embarked, is, according to St. Austin, an emblem of the church, which amidst the troubles of a wicked world, is, as it were, beaten by the waves of a boisterous sea. She seems at times to be so violently tossed and agitated by the storms of adversity, that if Jesus Christ had not promised to be always with her, we should be inclined to think her lost. Almighty God permits such storms to rise, lest the calm enjoyment of the world might make us forget the heavenly country to which we always ought to steer. By those trials he intends to rouse our sleeping faith, to awaken our confidence in him, and to remind us of his promised protection: for at the same time that he forewarns us of the tribulations we must unavoidably meet with, he also tells us not to fear. Having provided us with a bark wherein to work our passage through this stormy world, he knows how to conduct us safe into the wished-for port. No shipwreck is to be apprehended by them who seek their protection from God by holy prayer. The more violent the trial is, the more earnest ought to be our prayer. If Jesus Christ is with us, what shall we fear? If God is for us, what harm can we receive? Our chief apprehension ought to be, lest our diffidence in God, or our remissness in prayer, may render us less deserving of our Saviour's goodness.

The Demoniac cured.—MARK, V.
[A.D. 31.]

JESUS CHRIST having shown his disciples that the boisterous elements were under his command, went ashore on the other side of the water, in the country of the Gerasens, where he gave a convincing proof, that his power over the infernal spirits was not less absolute. Of the many demoniacs that are mentioned by the evangelists, there is one whom St. Mark has described more particularly: and the description gives us an idea of the power and dismal tyranny which the devils were at that time permitted to exercise upon the bodies, as well as the souls of men. This miserable man being transported out of himself by the spirit that possessed him, had stripped off his clothes, and bursting from confinement, ran wild and naked through the country. No human force could tame, and no chains were strong enough to bind him. He skulked among the tombs of the dead, and roved about the mountains, howling day and night, and tearing his flesh to pieces with the stones. His fierce and savage yells frighted every body from the place where he was. Happening to be near the spot where our blessed Saviour came on shore with his disciples, he ran and adored him, crying with a loud voice, What have I to do with thee, Jesus, the Son of the most high God? I adjure thee by the name of God, that thou torment me not. For Jesus had commanded him to come out of the man; and to be compelled to obey the commands of a God-man, was a tormenting thought to the proud spirit. Jesus asked him his name: not because he was ignorant of it, say the holy fathers, but because he would impart to his followers a knowledge which should strike them with a profitable fear. The spirit answered that his name was Legion, because they were many; and he entreated our blessed Saviour not to drive him out of the country, but to permit him to enter into the herd of swine that was feeding on the mountain. It was granted, and the swine, to the number of two thousand, being instantly possessed by the whole legion, ran headlong down the precipice into the sea and were drowned. The fact was immediately divulged through the country, and crowds of people flocked to the place, where they were astonished to see the man who had been troubled by the devil, now clothed and sitting like a lamb at the feet of Jesus. Penetrated with a grateful sense of the mercy he had received, the poor man would willingly have remained with his divine deliverer; but Jesus bade him return home to his friends, and publish the wonderful favour God had done him.

This demoniac, according to the holy fathers, exhibits a striking figure of those unhappy sinners, who, by a habit of vice, fly from the fellowship of the saints, strip themselves of the robes of sanctifying grace, and sit naked in the state of deadly sin, far from those heavenly mansions which have been purchased for them by the blood of their Redeemer. Hurried away by the violence of lawless passions, they run wild in the pursuit of sensual enjoyments, forget their last end, and break every moral and religious tie that tends to restrain them in the desires of their corrupt hearts. Wallowing in the mire of animal delights, and rushing headlong into the gulph of endless perdition, they stand in need of a miracle of grace to free them from their wretched slavery, and restore them to the peace which no man can enjoy, as long as he is at variance with God.

The Paralytic.—MATT ix.
[A.D. 31.]

OUR blessed Saviour re-embarked at the request of the Gerasens, and returned to the coast of Capharnaum. Notwithstanding the many wonders which Jesus Christ had wrought in and about the town of Capharnaum, we read but of one person that was converted there, and that was Matthew the publican. This man, by following the divine call, became an apostle, while the rest of his fellow-citizens remained in their incredulity, and thereby became more guilty in the sight of God, than the ancient inhabitants of Sodom and Gomorrha. Drawn by the sweet attractives of divine grace,

Matthew left his lucrative employ to accompany Christ the Son of God. Happy with himself, on account of the favour he had found with his Creator, he wished to see the same grace extended to others of his acquaintance. For that purpose he invited Jesus to his house, and many publicans and sinners sat down with him at table. The Pharisees, who professed the minutest nicety in their external observance of the law, affected to be scandalized, and asked the disciples, why their master eat and drank with publicans and sinners. Jesus heard what they said, and made them this reply: For them who are well there needeth no physician; the sick only want the physician's help: go, therefore, and learn the meaning of the sentence, *I will have mercy and not sacrifice*, for I am not come to call the just, but sinners.

While our blessed Saviour remained at Capharnaum, he wrought a noted miracle in favour of a paralytic. The sick man being too infirm to be taken out of bed, was carried to the house where Jesus was: not being able to gain admittance on account of the throng, his friends hoisted him up as he lay upon his bed, and uncovering the roof of the house, let him down into the room before our blessed Saviour's feet. Jesus was pleased with this testimony of their faith. encouraged

the sick man to be of good heart, and told him his sins were forgiven him. The Scribes and Pharisees who were present, secretly construed the words into blasphemy, as expressing a power in man which belonged solely to God. Jesus, to whom their most secret thoughts were as perfectly known, as though they had been declared by word of mouth, suddenly asked them, if it were not as easy for him to tell the man that his sins were forgiven him, as to bid him rise from his bed and walk. And to convince them that he had the power of doing both the one and the other, he said to the paralytic: Rise, take up thy bed, and walk. The paralytic rose, and the spectators, full of admiration at the miracle, returned thanks to God, who had given such power to man.

Christians have daily occasion to admire the same power, and to thank God for the same goodness, which he still continues to mankind. Jesus Christ, as man, had received from his Father the power of forgiving sins, and that power he has imparted to his delegates in the sacred ministry. By that singular privilege, which he communicated to his apostles on the very day of his resurrection, Jesus Christ has raised the priests of his church above the common rank of men: by that he entrusts them with a power which he has not granted even to the angels; by that he has appointed them to be judges and physicians of our souls; by that they become our spiritual fathers, and from them we receive a more happy generation, than we have received from our corporal parents; by that they are qualified to instruct and direct us to eternal life; they speak and determine in the name, and by the authority of Jesus Christ, whose ministers they are. It is our duty to hear, to respect, and honour them: it is to them we must have recourse as often as we stand in need of being loosed from our sins.

Election of the Twelve Apostles.—LUKE, vi.

[A.D. 32.]

WHEN our blessed Saviour had employed upwards of twelve months in preaching, baptizing, and working miracles, he began to manifest his care for the establishment of his church through all succeeding ages. Out of his numerous followers he selected twelve, whom he purposed to employ in the conversion of the Gentiles. Having once chosen them from the common class of believers, he, by a second election, raised them to a superior class amongst his disciples; by which he clearly intimated, that the virtues he expected from them, were to be of a much higher perfection than those he expected from the rest of his disciples. By this sublime vocation the apostles became the domestic companions, and familiar friends of their blessed Lord, living with him under the same roof, and eating at the same table. This let them into the secrets of our blessed Redeemer's hidden life; this gave them an opportunity of conversing more intimately with him, and of being witnesses, not only of his public, but also of his private virtues. To them he opened himself more freely, and explained at large those points of doctrine and morality, which he communicated to the people in parables. To inform his church of the manner and dispositions he would have her observe in the future election of her ministers, Jesus Christ retired to a lonely mountain, where he watched and prayed the whole night. When it was day he called his disciples round him, out of whom he selected twelve, and named them apostles, viz., Simon surnamed Peter, Andrew his brother, James and John, Philip and Bartholomew, Matthew and Thomas, James the son of Alpheus, and Simon who is called Zelotes, and Jude the brother of James, and Judas Iscariot, who became a traitor.

Jesus sat down in the midst of them, and made that admirable discourse which is recorded by St. Matthew, and contains a clear abridgment of the whole gospel. He sets off in direct opposition to those maxims which are generally adopted in the world, and pronounces those happy, who by men are commonly accounted unhappy. He shows how imperfect the ordinances were of the old law, in comparison of what he should exact from his followers in the new; that unless their virtues should be more full than those of the Scribes and Pharisees they could not enter the kingdom of heaven; that he should require perfection from them, not only in their outward actions, but also in their very thoughts and desires: that it should not be enough to have the appearance or the knowledge of virtue; that a shining outside might, indeed, satisfy the eyes of men, but that no outward show, without real goodness of the heart, would be acceptable to God. Therefore, in the sequel of his discourse, he insists upon an upright and a pure intention, which is, as it were, the eye that enlightens and directs the body of their actions. He tells them to strive by virtuous deeds, to lay up for themselves a treasure in heaven, which no rust or moth can consume, and no length of time destroy; that where their treasure is, there also will be their hearts; that their first concern must be to seek the kingdom of God and fulfil his commands; that to prevent a solicitude and anxious care about the goods of this world, their heavenly Father will provide them with every necessary in life, and crown them after death with eternal glory; that as they have but one supreme Master to serve, their service cannot be divided between two, and that to serve God and the world together is a thing impossible.

From these established principles, as they are laid down by the great Master of perfection, it appears that the end of the Christian law is, to repair the old man, and to perfect the new. A purity of intention, and a sincere desire of pleasing God, should animate a Christian in all he does and in all he desires. To abstain from bad actions in public, that he might have the appearance of being good, was enough for a Pharisee, whose ambition was to gain the applause of men: but by a Christian, who reflects that he is ever in the presence of an all-seeing God, the object to be aimed at and pursued is, real virtue, which teaches him not to rest in the outward letter of the law, but to sanctify each action by the inward purity of his motive.

Christ upon the Mountain.—Matt. v. vi.

[A.D. 32.]

Our divine Teacher, in his discourse to the people upon the mountain, descends from general principles to particular, and specifies the virtues which he expects to see in his faithful followers: a purity of intention, a desire of pleasing God in all things, a fraternal love, meekness, pardon of injuries, diligence in prayer, a serious endeavour at salvation, a perfect observance of his commandments, and a cleanness of heart, free not only from deadly sins, but also as much, as may be, from those lesser transgressions, which tarnish the beauty of the soul, and lead her by degrees towards the eternal precipice. For whoever is unfaithful in little things, will be likewise unfaithful in greater things; and if he slights venial faults, he will fall insensibly into the most enormous. It, therefore, is no trivial matter, it is an important part of Christian duty, which our blessed Saviour speaks of, when he so explicitly condemns every deliberate motion of anger in the heart, and so rigorously forbids even the desire of an object

which we cannot lawfully enjoy. The Jews chiefly sought to please the eyes of men, who judge by what they see; the followers of Christ must seek to please the eyes of God, who beholds the heart. To shun the track of disgraceful crimes, requires no great effort from a sober man; but to stifle the desires that flatter corrupt nature, and to break every unruly passion, in obedience to the law, is the exercise of Christian fortitude. To love a friend or benefactor, is the result of natural reason; it is no more than what heathens do; but to love our enemies, and to do good to those who persecute and slander us, is the virtue of Christ's Gospel. It is what Christ teaches us in his very first sermon; it is what he strongly insists upon; it is what he renders unto us, ..e to our heavenly Father, who showers down his favours upon the undeserving, and makes the sun equally rise upon the good and the wicked. To do as we would have others to do to us is another grand principle which our blessed

Saviour has marked out for our conduct in life; and if it were once adopted in practice, as well as in speculation, we should hear no complaints of one neighbour against another; no injuries, no slanders, no calumnies, no rash judgments. Rash judgments are severely condemned by our blessed Lord. In the heart of man, there often is a natural inclination to judge others, and the judgments we form, are oftentimes as rash as they are unjust. For the same self-love which lurks within us, inclines us as much to magnify our neighbour's faults, as to diminish our own; blind as hypocrites, we discern not the most glaring misdemeanors in ourselves, whilst we descry the slightest defects in our brethren.

If we did but oftener reflect upon that dreadful judgment, which all must one day undergo, we should not be so hasty to judge our brethren, say the holy fathers; much less should we make their faults the subject of our conversations. If the duty of fraternal charity has not force enough to check our rashness, fear at least ought to furnish us with motives sufficient to put us upon our guard. The way to find mercy before the judgment-seat of Christ, is to show it now. For in the same weight and measure as we deal with others, Jesus Christ will deal with us. Judge not, that you may not be judged: condemn not, and you shall not be condemned.

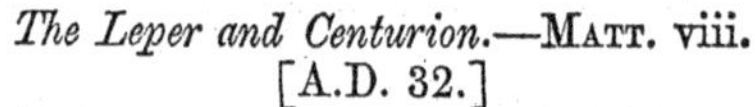

The Leper and Centurion.—MATT. viii.
[A.D. 32.]

OUR blessed Saviour having finished his discourse upon the mountain, went down into the plain, being attended by his disciples, and the numerous crowds that followed them. A leper saw him coming, and being actuated by a lively faith and hope of being healed, respectfully approached and prostrated himself before him. Like an humble supplicant, he did but intimate the nature of his complaint, and for his cure resigned himself entirely to the will of Him whose power he confessed: it is the example we are to follow, as often as we pray. He only said: Lord, if thou wilt, thou canst make me clean. And Jesus, stretching forth his hand to touch him, answered: I will; be thou healed. The will of God is the source of every grace that we receive; the leper was that instant cleansed: but to teach the due subordination which the law prescribed to superior powers, our blessed Lord bade him go and show himself to the priest, and offer the gift, as it was ordained by Moses.

Jesus went to Capharnaum, where he was desired to show his healing power in favour of a centurion's servant. The centurion, though a Roman, had a high opinion of Jesus Christ, and thought himself unworthy of approaching him in person. He had done many good services to the Jewish nation, and made himself many friends amongst the citizens of Capharnaum: to them he communicated his distress on account of his sick servant, and begged they would intercede in his behalf with Jesus. The ancients of the Jews undertook to present his petition, and at their request our blessed Saviour went towards the centurion's house. The centurion, whose humility equalled his faith, deemed himself unworthy to receive, or even to speak to so great a guest; he desired some of his friends to meet Jesus, and to say in his name: Lord, I am not worthy that thou shouldst enter my roof; say but the word, and my servant shall be healed. The words are very expressive of the sentiments which the centurion nourished in his heart; they received the approbation of our blessed Saviour himself; they are adopted by the Catholic Church in the administration of the holy eucharist, wherein the same Lord is truly and verily received by the faithful. Humility inspired the diffident Roman to employ the intercession of his Jewish friends, whom he thought more worthy than himself of Jesus's favours. It is the example we follow, when, to obtain the divine blessings, we address ourselves to God's more deserving friends, both in heaven and on earth, whose prayers are more likely to be heard than ours. The centurion's request was granted through the mediation of his friends, and Jesus healed his servant upon the spot where they met him.

This charitable concern which the centurion showed for his dying servant furnishes the holy fathers with an opportunity of putting all Christian masters in mind of the care which they are obliged to take of their servants, especially when they are sick; it is a duty which they owe them in charity; to neglect their domestic servants, either in their spiritual or in their temporal distress, is, in the apostle's language, to be worse than infidels. Masters never should forget that they also have a Master in heaven, to whom the poor are as dear as the rich, and with whom there is no exception of persons. If they expect to be mercifully dealt with by Almighty God, they should remember to be kind to those whom he has placed in their service.

The Widow's Son of Naim.—Luke, vii. [A.D. 32.]

The miraculous power which Jesus Christ had frequently exerted in favour of the sick, extended also to the dead. The first person restored to life, that we meet with in the gospel, was the daughter of Jairus, a ruler of the synagogue Jairus, it seems, neither had the faith nor the humility of the centurion; for he asked Jesus to come to his house, and thought it necessary that he should lay his hand upon the deceased, to raise her again to life. Our blessed Saviour was pleased to comply with Jairus's request, went to his house, bade the multitude retire, that were mourning round the corpse, took the maiden by the hand, and she rose up. The fame of this miracle was quickly spread through the whole country.

Our blessed Lord, in one of his excursions through Judea, went to a city called Naim; and when he came near the gate, behold, the corpse of a young man was carried out amidst the crowd of a numerous attendance to be buried. He was a widow's only son, snatched out of life in the flower of youth. Bathed in tears, the disconsolate mother attended the funeral procession. Jesus saw her distress, was moved with compassion, approached and told her not to weep. She made no answer; the tears in abundance streamed from her eyes, and silently expressed the anguish of her heart. He advanced and laid his hand upon the bier: they who carried it stood still, and Jesus with emphasis exclaimed, Young man, I say to thee, Arise! Awaked, as it were, by the powerful call, the young man instantly arose, and began to speak.

The spectators stood amazed, and glorified God, saying a great prophet hath risen amongst us, and God hath visited his people.

To men who extend not their thoughts beyond what strikes their outward senses, it may seem, as if our blessed Saviour had met the funeral by chance, as it came out of the gates of Naim; but to the true believer it is evident, that nothing less than a premeditated design to raise the dead carried him thither at that particular time. For, as the holy fathers observe, in their comments upon this passage, nothing happens by accident in this world; all is directed by a watchful and unerring Providence, and what short-sighted mortals call chance, is the certain effect of a cause permitted to act by the deliberate designs of God. The holy fathers, moreover, consider the love which the mother bore for an only son, as a figure of that tender love which the church has for her children: with the warmest affection she embraces each one in particular, as if he were the only one: and with the hopes of seeing them hereafter raised to eternal life, consoles herself amidst the cares and afflictions that must necessarily befall her in this vale of tears. The spiritual death of many of them is a subject to her of continual sorrow. With a heavy heart she sees her thoughtless children snatched from her arms by unruly passions, and hurried away by a train of sins towards the fathomless abyss. She mourns their misfortune, and implores the pity of her heavenly spouse, that he may raise them again by his powerful grace. With that hope she comforts herself in her afflictions, and with a longing desire expects the hour, which is to restore her repenting sons to life again. The repentance of a sinner gives joy not only to the church on earth, but also to the saints and angels who are in heaven: for there is joy in heaven upon the repentance of every sinner.

Mary Magdalene.—Luke, vii.
[A.D. 32.]

The surprising and frequent miracles of Jesus Christ being rumoured through Judea, and the country round about, the people were struck with a reverential awe, and proclaimed him a great prophet. John the Baptist, who was, during this time, in prison, judged it a favourable opportunity to convince his disciples that Jesus was the true Messiah, and, therefore, sent two of them, as from himself, to ask him whether he was not the person whom the prophets had foretold, and the Gentiles expected for their salvation. The conduct of our blessed Saviour on that occasion is very remarkable. He knew how jealous those disciples were of their master's reputation, and how much afraid lest any one should be thought greater than the Baptist; he, therefore, chose to say nothing that might give them uneasiness, or increase their jealousy; he spoke by his works, and wrought many miracles in their presence: then bade them return, and tell John what they had seen. When they were gone, Jesus began to commend the Baptist for his unparalleled virtues, for his fortitude, for his unshaken constancy, and penitential life. He also spoke to the people upon the necessity of doing penance, which was to open to them the kingdom of heaven; for the kingdom of heaven requires violence, says he, and the violent bear it away. Woe be to the citizens of Corozain and Bethsaida; woe be to the town of Capharnaum, who have rejected those graces, and remain insensible at those miracles, which long ago would have moved the heathenish inhabitants of Tyre and Sidon to do penance in sack-cloth and ashes. Bethania was more happy in the illustrious conversion of Magdalene, a noted sinner in the city. This woman, who became henceforward as famous for her piety as she had hitherto been infamous for her disorderly life, came to Jesus when he was at dinner in the house of Simon the leper. With a forwardness which was only excusable from the goodness of her intention, she rushed into the room, and coming behind, near to Jesus' feet, threw herself upon the ground to kiss and embrace them; then bathing them with

her tears, she perfumed them with a precious ointment and wiped them with her hair. Simon, who was of the Pharisean sect, began to think it very extraordinary that Jesus Christ, if he were a prophet, should not know the woman to be a sinner; or, if he did, that he should let her come so near to him. But he soon found how presumptuous he had been in forming such judgments in his heart, and by the answers he gave to our blessed Saviour's questions, was forced to own his mistake. Jesus bade him observe the humble services which Magdalene had done him since she entered the room, commending her for the fervour of her charity, and the activity of her faith, and declared that many sins were forgiven her, because she had loved much! he told her to depart in peace.

Mary Magdalene, say the holy fathers, is the perfect model of a true penitent; from her heart she detested the past irregularities of her life; she bade adieu to sin, with a firm purpose never to relapse again. In the work of her conversion, she employed the very things which she hitherto had made subservient to the works of sin; her hair, her ointments and perfumes, the past incentives of her passions, were piously sacrificed to the exercise of penance. Abandoned as she had been to habitual vice, she became pure in the sight of God, as soon as the fire of charity sanctified her penance, and refined her affections from the dregs of sin.

Parable of the Sower.—MATT. xiii.

[A.D. 32.]

OUR blessed Saviour had one day sat himself down on the sea-shore, vast crowds of people gathered round, and as they pressed upon him he stepped into a boat, and from thence made a long discourse to them as they stood upon the shore. He chose to convey his instructions chiefly in parables, and figures, according to the use and style of language in those countries. Amongst other parables he proposed that of the sower, which he distinguished into four parts: A husbandman, said he, went forth to sow his seed, of which

some went beyond the bounds of the field upon the highway, where it was either trodden under foot by travellers or eaten by the birds. In the explication of this first part of the parable, as he delivered it afterwards in private to his apostles, our blessed Saviour says that the seed is the word of God, and that they by the way-side are the hearers who forget the word almost as soon as they have heard it. For the devil comes immediately, and, either by his own wicked suggestions, or by his agents, as so many fowls of the air, takes away the seed of salvation from their hearts, lest it should there quicken their faith, and produce the fruits of eternal life.

The second part of the parable is that in which the seed is said to fall upon a rock, where meeting with no depth of soil, it is burned up by the sun, almost as soon as it begins to spring. And these are they, says Christ, who at first seem pleased with the word of God, but having no great fund of goodness, forget it in the time of trial, and fly back at the approach of temptation. Such persons are very apt to deceive themselves, and their illusion is this: the pleasure which they seem to find in receiving the word of God, makes them fancy that they want nothing more to produce the fruit of godliness in their souls; little thinking that a heart which is not softened by compunction, and improved by works of piety, is incapable of producing any lasting good. The third part of the parable is that in which the seed is said to have fallen among thorns; the thorns grew up and choked it. Such is the misfortune of those, says our Lord, whose thoughts are taken up with the concerns of this world. They, indeed, hear the word of God; but the cares of life, their restless desires, and wordly pursuits, stifle the growth of virtue in their souls and prevent its fruit. On a heart thus entangled and perplexed with deceitful riches, the sacred word of God, whether written or delivered by his ministers, has but little or no effect. The fourth and last division of the parable marks the different produce of that part of the seed which fell upon good ground. In some the increase was a hundred grains for one, in some it was sixty, and in others only thirty. Such are the different degrees of goodness which the word of God produces in the hearts of the faithful, according to the dispositions it there meets with. If the heart is but singly good it will not show itself by many heroic actions, and if not cultivated with continual care, it will be in danger of growing bad. For which reason it is our duty to strive and pray daily, that we may become more and more perfect in the increase of charity and good works.

It is by patience that we reap the fruit of our endeavours; it is by taking pains that we advance in virtue; by sufferings and by labour in the divine service, our charity becomes more vigorous. Charity is, as it were, the root of Christian piety; from thence all other virtues draw their life, their nourishment, and beauty; the more vigorous the root, the richer will be the fruit it produces. Watered by the dew of heavenly graces, it will shoot up into an increase of those shining virtues which adorn the church, and distinguish each industrious member in his respective state and calling.

Decollation of St. John.—MARK, vi.
[A.D. 32.]

ALTHOUGH the doctrine of our blessed Saviour was so pure in its principles, so conformable to reason, so confirmed by miracles, and so pleasing in its promises of eternal glory, yet few embraced it. A general incredulity and obduracy of heart prevailed in the cities of Judea, and in no city more than in that of Nazareth. It was natural to imagine, that the Nazareans would have thought themselves in some sort honoured, by the fame of one who had lived and grown up among them, and that they would have cherished him, as the most valuable of their citizens. Their behaviour was diametrically the opposite. They had seen and conversed with him from his youth; they knew no learning that he had acquired; in his figure they discovered nothing that set him above the common level; in his mother and relations they beheld no title that distinguished him from the poorer class of the people. To his doctrine therefore they would give no credit, nor would they allow his miracles which they had not seen. The great reputation which Jesus had acquired amongst others, made them jealous, and their jealousy grew into a violent antipathy against him. They laid hands upon him, and led him to the steep point of the rock on which their town was built, with an intention to throw him headlong down. But the hour for Jesus to die was not yet come, and no human malice could advance it. He slipped out of their hands, and walked away through the midst of them. This perverse incredulity of the Nazareans hindered Jesus from working any miracles amongst them, excepting the cure of some of their sick, which he did by imposing his hands upon them. On his return from Nazareth, he was informed of John the Baptist's death.

It has been already mentioned, that St. John was cast into prison on account of the reprimand he gave to king Herod, for his incestuous connexion with Herodias, the wife of his brother Philip. Herodias had often solicited the king to have him put to death, and the king as often refused to consent, not only from a principle of esteem for the holy man, but likewise from a fear of the people's resentment, who venerated the Baptist as a wonderful prophet. But Herod's imprudence betrayed him soon after to commit the bloody deed. He celebrated his birth-day with great mirth and magnificence; a grand entertainment was prepared, and the chief men of Galilee were invited to attend; the daughter of Herodias was introduced before the company, and desired to dance. The manner of her performance so pleased the king, that he hastily promised upon oath to give whatsoever she should ask, though it were half his kingdom. The girl immediately left the room to consult her mother what she should ask. Go and ask for the head of John the Baptist, replied the adulteress. The girl ran back to Herod, and desired that he would forthwith give her on a dish the head of John the Baptist. Struck at the unnatural request, the king was sorry for the rash promise he had made, but, out of respect to the company, resolved to keep his oath, not to displease the daughter of Herodias. He therefore ordered

an executioner to go forthwith to the prison, and cut off the Baptist's head. The head was given in a dish to the girl, and the girl presented it to her mother.

Thus was the great precursor of our Lord impiously slain in the vigour of life; thus was John murdered by the sword of Herod, who had always admired and esteemed him for his purity of doctrine and sanctity of morals. Herod fell not all at once into the enormity of guilt; by gradual steps he had advanced towards the depth of crimes; one excess had led him on to another; a lustful passion opened the way to incest, and incest plunged him into murder. Herod was permitted to take away the life of St. John the Baptist, greater than whom no prophet had ever risen amongst the sons of women. The life of that holy man was sacrificed to the capricious revenge of a wicked woman; it was sacrificed for a dance. Hence we see, says St. Gregory, in what light we are to consider this mortal life, which is so liable to misfortunes, and so miserably harassed by the suspicions, by the hatred and the slanders of wicked men. It is to a future life that we should constantly look up; a life which neither the tongue of slander, nor the sword of persecution can affect. Tyrants may rage and threaten; pain may crumble these mortal bodies into dust; but a passing death will open us an entrance into that heavenly kingdom, where the blessed know no change and fear no decay.

Miracle of the Loaves and Fishes.—MATT. xiv.

[A.D. 32.]

OUR blessed Saviour, upon the death of John the Baptist, retired with his apostles into the wilderness. In his unerring wisdom, by which he sweetly assigns all things to their appointed times and places, he deemed it expedient to withdraw from the public, at a time that his miracles began to be the subject of inquiry at court. Herod, the son of a jealous father who had sought to destroy Jesus amongst the slaughtered innocents, was curious to know who the man could be who appeared so powerful in word and work; and while some said, he must be Elias or one of the prophets, he vainly fancied him to be the Baptist risen from the dead. Jesus left them to their groundless conjectures, and crossed the lake of Genezareth, to conceal himself with his apostles in the desert. When he came to the opposite shore, he found a multitude of people, who had gone round by land, and were resolved to accompany him, for the sake of hearing his instructions, and of seeing his miracles. They proceeded in a body together, and advanced some way into the desert. The day began to decline: the apostles came to their divine Master, and advised him to dismiss the people, that they might provide themselves with something to eat. For they were still fasting, and had brought no provisions with them; the place being a desert and no town near. Jesus bade his apostles produce their slender store, and asked what it was; they answered, only five barley loaves and two fishes. Divide the multitude into companies, replied our Saviour, and make them sit down upon the grass. Then taking the bread into

his hands, and lifting up his hands to heaven, he blessed the loaves and fishes, and gave them to his disciples to distribute. In the act of distribution, both the bread and the fishes were so wonderfully multiplied that they were more than sufficient to satisfy the whole multitude, which amounted to five thousand, besides women and children. They all eat till they were satiated, and of the fragments that remained there was still enough to fill twelve baskets.

The holy fathers consider these five thousand men, as a figure of those Christians who quit the world, in desire at least, to follow Jesus Christ through the desert of this life. Their pleasing conduct presents us with an admirable picture of those virtues which distinguish the perfect members of Christ's church. Attached to the company of their divine Master, they attentively listen to his eternal truths, they seek no earthly comfort but dependently upon his will. The union amongst themselves is so perfect, that they seem to make but one man, being all warmed with the same zeal, and animated with the same spirit, in pursuit of the same end. They are happy in the presence of Jesus, their Lord and Saviour, they persist in his service without being tired, and joyfully bear whatever labours and difficulties they meet with, rather than fail in the fidelity which they owe to their Creator. Resigned to the divine will, they trust to the fatherly goodness of a God-man in their present wants; they know he has numbered the hairs of their heads, not one of which falls to the ground without his permission; they remember it is he who feeds the birds of the air, and that he never abandons those who are serious in their endeavours to serve him. With such sentiments of faith and holy confidence they persevere to the end, and deserve thereby to receive the reward of their patience.

Saint Peter upon the waters.—MATT. xiv.

[A.D. 32.]

THE wonderful multiplication of the loaves and fishes, impressed such a sense of gratitude upon the hearts of the people, that they were for setting the crown upon their benefactor's head, and making him king. But our blessed Lord, who, by example as well as by word of mouth, came to teach his followers not to seek, much less to intrude themselves into worldly dignities and honours, fled from them, and concealed himself in a neighbouring mountain. When it was grown dusk, and the people were dispersed, the disciples went back to the sea-shore. For he had told them to take the boat, and return without him to Bethsaida. This he did, as the event showed, to convince them of their weakness in the absence of their divine Master, without whom they could do nothing. They had no sooner put to sea than a storm arose, and the boat was violently tossed by the foaming waves. They plied their oars, they exerted all their might, and struggled with the contrary wind the whole night. Our blessed Saviour saw them from the shore, but seemed in no great haste to help them. About the break of day he advanced towards them upon the surface of the deep, and came near the boat, as if he meant to pass them. The spectacle was new to the disciples: not knowing how any one could walk upon the waters, they took it for a ghost, and screamed out for fright. Jesus upon that spoke to them, and said, Fear not; it is I. Peter was the first to know his Master's voice, and being as regardless of danger, as he was confident of the divine succour, immediately replied, Lord, if it is you, bid me come to you upon the waters. Jesus said, Come. Peter that instant threw himself out of the boat, and to the great astonishment of the rest, walked as steadily upon the rolling billows, as though he had trod on solid ground. He went boldly on, till he came near to our blessed Saviour, when perceiving the wind was high and the sea rough, he lost courage and began to sink. Terrified at his situation, he cried out. Save me,

Lord; and Jesus stretched forth his hand and took hold of him, saying, Thou man of little faith, why dost thou doubt? He entered with him into the boat; the wind fell, and they rowed ashore.

The holy fathers, who consider all the words and actions of our Saviour as full of mystery, ask the question, why he would permit his apostle to sink, after he had expressly commanded him to come forth upon the waters. It was, say they, to convince him by experience, that his life and being depended on the saving hand of God; it was to check that forward boldness which seems to have been blended in his natural disposition, lest it might make him vain and presumptuous. A certain degree of fearfulness is conducive to our spiritual good; it helps to make us humble and diffident of ourselves; it is founded in the knowledge of our own inability; and this knowledge tells us, that for the success of our undertakings, we must solely depend on God, who lets us down and draws us up again as he pleases. Of all those who have the happiness to believe in Christ, there is not one who has not, and does not daily receive from his divine hand, greater favours than St. Peter did, in being preserved from the watery deep. There are other storms more fatal to our souls; there are other gulphs and other waters of perdition, from which we stand hourly in need of being saved by the grace of our Redeemer: without his supporting hand, we long time since had sunk beneath the evils that surround us.

Jesus the living Bread.—JOHN, vi

[A.D. 32.]

THE Jews who had followed Jesus into the desert, having lost sight of him, and knowing that his disciples were gone across the lake, returned to Capharnaum, where they were surprised to find him. They asked him when and how he came. Jesus, without taking notice of their inquiries, told them they only followed him for the sake of the bread which they had miraculously shared in the day before, and from thence took occasion of mentioning a much more excellent bread, which he promised to give them for their nourishment to eternal life. For I am the Living Bread, which came down from heaven, said he, and this is the bread which I shall give; it is my flesh, for the life of the world, and whosoever eateth thereof, he shall live for ever. The incredulous Jews not being acquainted with a doctrine so spiritual and sublime, called it a harsh saying, and disputed with one another, how it were possible he could give them his flesh to eat. But notwithstanding their cavils, our blessed Lord positively asserted the point in question, and in terms still more explicit, thus confirmed what he had just told them: *Verily, verily, I say unto you, unless you eat the flesh of the Son of Man, and drink his blood, you shall not have life in you. He that eateth my flesh, and drinketh my blood, hath life everlasting: he abideth in me and I in him. For my flesh is truly meat, and my blood is truly drink. This is the bread which cometh down from heaven, not like the manna, of which your fathers eat and died. He that eateth this bread shall live for ever.* Many therefore of the Jews who were present, and even some of the disciples, took offence at these expressions, and were scandalized at the doctrine they conveyed; and because they did not understand how Christ could really give them his flesh to eat, and his blood to drink, refused to believe, and left him. According to their carnal notion of things, they concluded that Jesus meant to give them his flesh to eat, and his blood to drink, not concealed under the pure appearances of bread and wine, but in a disgustful manner, like the flesh of a dead man, says St. Austin, or a piece of meat from the shambles And therefore to disabuse them of that gross mistake, our blessed Saviour told them, that flesh inanimate and separated from the spirit would profit nothing, but that the flesh which he should give them was quickened by the spirit, and should quicken them. Having given that explanation of the manner in which he promised to communicate his body and his blood, as he did verily and indeed at his last supper, he returned to the twelve, and asked them if they would also leave him. Upon which St. Peter, with his wonted zeal, made answer, To whom, Lord, shall we go? Thou hast the words of eternal life: we believe and know thee to be Christ the Son of God.

Our blessed Lord perceiving the minds of the people were exasperated against him, on account of his doctrine, withdrew from that part of the country, and retired towards the confines of Tyre and Sidon. Notwithstanding the desire he seemed to have of being there concealed, he was discovered by a Chananean woman, whose daughter was possessed by an evil spirit. She came and earnestly besought him to have pity on her: he made her no answer: she redoubled her prayers, crying aloud for relief: the apostles interceded in her behalf, and Jesus said, that he was sent only to those who were perishing in the house of Israel. Not discouraged at the refusal, the woman pushed forward and cast herself at the feet of Jesus, saying, Lord help me. Jesus told her it was not fit to take the children's bread and give it to the dogs. Yes, Lord, said she, with an humble confidence, even

the dogs are permitted to eat of the crumbs that fall from their master's table: I ask no more. Then Jesus, overcome, as it were, by her pious importunity, made answer, O woman, great is thy faith; be it done as thou desirest: and her daughter was cured from that hour.

Our blessed Saviour, says St. Chrysostom, refused at first to listen to the petition of this Chananean woman, that by her example he might instruct us, with what faith, humility, and perseverance we ought to pray. To make his servants the more sensible of his mercy, and the more eager to obtain it, he often seems to pay no attention to their prayers, till he has exercised them in the virtues of humility and patience. Ask, says he, and you shall receive: knock, and it shall be opened to you.

Transfiguration of our Lord.—Matt. xvii.

[A.D. 33.]

Our blessed Saviour, after some stay in the confines of Tyre, returned into Galilee, where he wrought many miraculous cures of the infirm and lame, of the blind and dumb. After that he visited the borders of Cæsarea, which was a town situated near the springs of the river Jordan, and subject to Philip, the brother of king Herod. Being on the way thither, and conversing with his apostles as they went along, he asked them, Whom do the people say I am? Some say you are John the Baptist, answered the apostles, and some Elias; others again say that you are Jeremias, or some one of the ancient prophets. But you, said our blessed Saviour, whom do you say I am? Simon Peter, without a moment's hesitation, made answer and said, Thou art Christ, the Son of the living God. Blessed art thou, Simon Bar-Jona, replied our Saviour; because it is not from the dictates of flesh and blood, but by the revelation of my heavenly Father that thou hast learned this truth. And I say unto thee, because thou art Peter, which is to say a rock, that upon this rock I will build my church, and the powers of hell shall never prevail against her. To thee also I will give the keys of the kingdom of heaven, and whatsoever thou shalt bind or loose on earth, shall be also bound or loosed in heaven. Such is the solemn promise which Jesus Christ then made to St. Peter of constituting him the head of his church, which, like a great fabric, being built on him, as on a firm rock, he assures him shall never fail. Nor by any fault which that

apostle committed afterwards, was Jesus ever provoked to retract the promise he had once made. But lest a promise so flattering and extensive might render that apostle too elate, he humbled him soon after by a rebuke the most severe. For Peter being not yet initiated in the mystery of the cross, endeavoured to dissuade his divine Master from exposing himself to the ignominious treatment that awaited him in Jerusalem. Satan, replied our Saviour (for so he called him, to make him sensible of his error in opposing the divine will), go back, thou art a scandal to me; thou dost not yet relish the things of God. For he who will save his life shall lose it, and he who shall lose his life for my sake shall find it. If any man will come after me, let him deny himself, take up his cross, and so follow me.

Six days after this, Jesus called aside three of his apostles who seem to have been greater favourites than the rest, and went with them to a high mountain, which is generally thought to have been the mountain of Thabor in Galilee. He there composed himself to pray in their presence, and, as he prayed, his body was transfigured into the appearance of a glorified body: his face shone with resplendent brightness like the sun, and his garments became white as snow. Moses and Elias appeared at the same time, and discoursed with him upon the subject of his future passion in Jerusalem. St. Peter, in a transport of joy at what he saw, cried out, Lord, it is good for us to remain here: if thou wilt, let us make three tents, one for thee, one for Moses, and a third for Elias. And as he was speaking, behold! a bright shining cloud spread itself over them, and from the cloud issued forth

a voice, saying, This is my beloved Son, hear ye him. The three apostles, at the sound, fell prostrate on their faces, and remained trembling on the ground till Jesus came, and, with a gentle touch, bade them rise and not fear. He then went down with them from the mountain, but strictly charged them not to say a word of what they had seen, till the Son of Man should be risen from the dead.

This mysterious transfiguration of our Lord, was one of the means he made use of to confirm the faith of his apostles, and to convince them, in a manner the most sensible, of his divinity; and, in effect, St. Peter has mentioned it in one of his epistles as a convincing evidence of that eternal truth. Jesus Christ, by exhibiting to his favourite apostles the figure of a glorified body, was pleased to give them a foresight of that happy change which the bodies of his elect shall put on at the general resurrection: by that he inspired them with fresh zeal in his service; by that he animated them with new courage to undertake and suffer great things for his holy name; by that, in fine, he showed them how transcendent the glory is of that supernatural happiness, which shall reward the light and momentary tribulations that the just here undergo for God's sake.

A Child the model of Humility.—MATT. xviii.

[A.D. 33.]

As our blessed Saviour came down from the mountain, he saw a crowd of people gathered round his other disciples, who were endeavouring, without effect, to cast the devil out of a young man, brought to them by his father, in Jesus' absence. The father, perceiving Jesus as he approached,

ran to meet him, and humbly besought him to have pity on his unhappy son, and to deliver him from the evil spirit that tormented him. Jesus heard, and granted him his petition. Then came the disciples secretly to Jesus, and asked why they had not been able to relieve the young man, since he had given them power over the infernal spirits. It was on account of your incredulity, replied our Saviour; for if you had but faith, you might move mountains: this kind of devil was not to be removed but by prayer and fasting. They walked on towards the city of Capharnaum, which for two years had been our Saviour's chief place of residence: he spoke to them, as they went along, upon his approaching death and resurrection. His language was a mystery to the disciples, nor did they understand what he meant: they began some other subject of discourse, and disputed apart with one another, which amongst them seemed to be the greater man. When they reached Capharnaum, the tax-gatherers came to St. Peter, and asked him if his Master did not pay the tribute-money? St. Peter answered, that he did, and went straight to the house of his master's abode. As soon as he entered, Jesus prevented him, and asked from whom it was that the princes of the earth received tribute; whether from their children or from strangers? From strangers, replied Peter: the children then are free, said our Saviour; but that we may not scandalize them, go to the sea. and take the first fish that comes to hand: upon opening its mouth, you will find a piece of money, which you shall pay to the officer for us two. In this instance our blessed Lord instructs his followers to comply with the well-regulated duties of social life, and to obey those civil powers that are established for the good of the community.

The apostles being met at our Saviour's dwelling, he asked them what they had been disputing about as they came along: they made him no answer. He therefore sat down, called them round him, and in order to cure them of their vain notions of preferment in his service, said: Whoever amongst

you would wish to become the first, let him demean himsel as the last, and behave as if he were the servant of all. And to give them as distinct an idea as was possible of that humble spirit which he desired to infuse into their souls, he brought forward a little child, and placing him before them said, that unless they become like unto that little one they shall never enter into the kingdom of heaven.

Humility is a virtue essentially requisite for salvation: repugnant as it is to human pride, it must be studiously cherished, if we pretend to a place in the kingdom of Christ. It is of the utmost consequence to check that strong inclination by which we are led to think highly of ourselves, to grow impatient of restraint, and to run after every object which either flatters our vanity or feeds our ambition. The only ambition worthy of a Christian is, to rival the perfection of the saints by a holy life, to aim at a crown of immortal glory amongst the angels, and to aspire to the happiness of being exalted by our heavenly Father in his kingdom. We are born and have been baptised for greater things than to become slaves to base passions of corrupt nature. However shining may be the talents, wealth, and titles which make one man appear greater than another in the eyes of his fellow creatures, it is humility, it is charity, and the other gospel virtues which constitute the real goodness of a Christian, and render him truly great in the sight of God. The comparison of a little child, as it is applied by our blessed Saviour, strikes at the root, and checks the very sap of pride. To enable us to form some judgment of ourselves, and to see what place we deserve amongst the followers of Jesus Christ, let us look into our hearts, and there search for the dispositions of the tractable little child. Humility of sentiments, innocence of manners, a docile submission and obedience to God in his substitutes and precept, must form the character of every Christian who means to enter through the narrow gate into everlasting life.

The ten Lepers.—LUKE, xvii.

[A.D. 33.]

THE feast of tabernacles being near, the apostles pressed their divine Master to go into Judea, and made use of arguments to persuade him to it. They considered it as a fair opportunity of showing himself at Jerusalem, and of displaying his miracles to the world; they said some of his followers were wavering in their faith, and required the evidence of miracles to fix them in his service. Jesus had quitted Judea, as we have seen, upon the death of John the Baptist, and he knew the Jews sought to put him also to death; he therefore told his apostles that his time was not yet come, nor would he accompany them amongst his enemies. Wherefore, as they wished to be at Jerusalem for the beginning of the festival, they set off without him; he remained some days in Galilee, and then followed them, but in a private manner, and unattended by any of his disciples. He passed through the middle of Samaria, and coming to a certain town of the country, was discovered by ten lepers, who, standing at a distance, and raising their voice in a suppliant manner, begged he would have mercy on them. Jesus pitying their condition, bade them go and show themselves to the priests. The lepers went in obedience to his command, and in the way were suddenly made clean. Struck at the miracle, one of them immediately began with a loud voice to proclaim the praises of Almighty God, ran back to his divine benefactor, and, throwing himself at his feet, returned thanks for the

blessing he had received. Jesus asked him, if there were not ten who had been cured, and what was become of the other nine. For of them all, says St. Luke, this was the only one who returned to give glory to God, and he was a Samaritan. Jesus bade him rise, commended his faith, and dismissed him.

The reproach which our blessed Saviour cast upon the nine lepers for not coming to thank him for the mercy he hath shown them, proves how much he is displeased with the vice of ingratitude. Ingratitude, says St. Bernard, dries up the fountain of piety, stops the flow of divine grace, and hinders the hand of God from showering down the favours he has in store for his deserving friends. No favour from God, say the holy fathers, ought to be received without the deepest sense of gratitude: gratitude in return for one favour, is the surest way to receive a second. Gratitude is a part of our Christian duty; it is a pleasing virtue, and the characteristic of a good heart. It is not enough to observe a silent respect for our benefactors, or to content ourselves with the inward satisfaction we feel upon some extraordinary favour they have done us. The nine ungrateful lepers were undoubtedly sensible of the notice which Jesus Christ had taken of them, admired his goodness and rejoiced at their cure, but they returned no public thanks, they showed no exterior signs of a grateful heart; their memory is therefore branded with infamy to future ages, that Christians may from thence conceive a just horror of ingratitude, which renders them odious to God and man. Happy is the man, says St. Bernard, who is never weary of returning thanks to God for the daily benefits he receives; who, considering himself as a stranger in this world, acknowledges every act of kindness as a favour the more gratuitously bestowed, since of himself, without the grace of his merciful Redeemer, he can merit nothing but contempt and punishment.

The Woman taken in Adultery.—John, viii.

[A.D. 33.]

Jesus made no stay at Samaria, but went straight on to Jerusalem. Upon his arrival there, he found the Jews strangely divided in their opinions about him: some maintained him to be a good man, others not: they had looked for him on the first day of the feast, and not finding him, many called him a seducer of the people. When the time of the festival was half over, for it lasted eight days, Jesus appeared publicly in the temple; and, sitting down to instruct the people, drew the eyes and attention of all upon him. They admired the heavenly doctrine that flowed upon his lips, and stood astonished at the manner in which he delivered himself. For they knew he had never been initiated in the study of the law, nor been ever taught in the school of human learning. He gave full scope to his zeal, and spoke his sentiments so freely that the people wondered to see the Pharisees remain silent; and some even began to doubt whether the scribes and elders had not at last acknowledged him for the true Messiah: many of the people believed in him, and paid him great respect on account of the miracles he wrought. The Pharisees swelled with envy—nor would their pride suffer them to stand inactive any longer—they sent their officers to apprehend and bring Jesus before them. But Jesus' hour was not yet come; the officers were so charmed with his discourse that they made no attempt to seize him, and returned as they came: being reprimanded by their masters for not having executed their orders, they made no other answer than, that no man ever spoke like him. Jesus returned at his own hour to the mountain of Olives, to pray.

and came betimes next morning into the temple, where he resumed his instructions to the people. The Pharisees with pain beheld the success that attended his preaching, while some styled him the prophet, and some the Christ: being bent upon his ruin, they watched every opportunity that seemed favourable to their invidious design, and left no stone unturned to slander his reputation, and destroy his credit amongst the people. They had surprised a woman in the fact of adultery; they led her away to the temple, presented her to Jesus, and asked him what he would have done to her. Their intention was to traduce him before the public; to accuse him of cruelty if he condemned her, and of violating the law if he acquitted her. For the law of Moses ordained, that every woman convicted of adultery should be stoned to death. Our blessed Lord, who saw through the malice of their hearts, bowed himself down as they continued asking him, and with his finger wrote upon the ground. They repeated the question, and insisted upon an answer. Jesus raised himself up, and said, Let him that is without sin amongst you cast the first stone at her: then stooping down again, wrote as before on the ground. The Pharisees upon that sneaked away one by one, and left the

woman standing in the midst. Jesus raised himself up, and asked her if any had condemned her; and she answered, no one: neither shall I replied he; depart in peace, and beware thou sin no more.

By this example our blessed Saviour teaches us to look into ourselves, and to examine our own conduct rather than censure that of our neighbour. Men oftentimes have a horror of gross sins, that strike their senses, and take no notice of internal sins, which are perhaps more monstrous in the eye of a pure spirit. The sin of the rebel angels in heaven, and the sin of our first parents in paradise, were undoubtedly more heinous than that of the adulteress. It is unpardonable in a Christian, harshly to censure and condemn his brother, because he has fallen into a fault of which he himself is perhaps innocent. It would better become him to humble his soul before God, by whose mercy he has been hitherto preserved from falling into sins still more enormous; which, considering the instability of his heart, he knows not how soon it may be his misfortune to commit. If we expect to be treated with lenity in our misfortunes, we should not forget to show that lenity to others. Lenity is one of the most effectual methods to make the delinquent sensible of his fault. The lenity that Jesus Christ showed upon this occasion, had without doubt a more salutary effect upon the adulteress's mind, than all the severity of the Mosaic law. It is the spirit of lenity and charity which the church, in imitation of her spouse, has adopted with regard to her children; she turns her back upon none, however grievous their sins may be; she beholds them with the eye of a tender mother; she invites them to their Christian duties; she stands with open arms to receive the penitent, and absolves them from their guilt the moment she is assured of the sincerity of their repentance.

The Man who had been born blind.—JOHN, ix.

[A.D. 33.]

OUR blessed Saviour having silenced the Scribes and Pharisees by an answer they did not expect, continued his instructions to the people, and expressly told them, that he was the light of the world, and that none who followed him should walk in darkness. He expostulated with his enemies, why they showed such spite and used such violence against him. Is there one amongst you, said he, who can convict me of having done evil? If you are the descendants of Abraham, why do you not perform the works of Abraham? If I have spoken nothing but the truth to you, why do you not believe me? Why do you seek my life? Abraham did not so.

Abraham your father was exceeding glad to see my day of coming into the world; for before Abraham had a being, I am. I come from above; I am not of this world; I honour my Father, who is with me; I always do his will, and speak the truths he hath imparted to me. But you understand not my words, nor do you hear, because you are not of God; for who is of God heareth the words of God. The Jews in answer reviled him with abusive language, and took up stones to throw at him. But Jesus withdrew from their presence, and retired out of the temple.

Jesus, as he passed along, saw a beggar who had been blind from his birth. The disciples asked him to what cause, whether to the man's own, or to his parents' sin his blindness was to be attributed. Neither to the one nor the other, replied our Saviour, but that the glory of God may be manifested in his cure: I am the light of the world. Having said that, he spat upon the ground, and with his spittle moistened the dust into clay, which he spread upon the eyes of the blind man, bidding him go and wash in the pool of Siloe. This man went and washed, and came back seeing: and it was the Sabbath-day. The miracle was quickly divulged through the city, and became the subject of public talk. Every one who had known the man, and had seen him sit begging in the street, was curious to ask him in what manner he had recovered his sight. His answer was, that a certain man, called Jesus, had made clay with his spittle and anointed his eyes, and sent him to wash in the pool of Siloe; that he went and washed, and saw. The man was carried before the Pharisees, to whom he gave the same account. The Pharisees were unwilling to believe the fact, which was so much to Jesus' honour: they reasoned differently upon it; some said that no good man would ever have made clay upon the Sabbath, whilst others more justly observed that none but a good man could give sight to the blind. They asked the man what he thought of the person that had cured him. He is, undoubtedly, a prophet, replied the man. Provoked at this answer, they pretended to call the miracle in question, and to doubt whether he had ever been blind. They sent for his parents, of whom they desired to know whether this was their son who is said to have been born blind, and how he came to see. The parents, afraid of being brought to trouble on that account, answered with great caution: they only said, that he was their son, and had been born blind; but that how and by what means he had recovered his sight they were wholly ignorant; that if they wanted to be satisfied on that point, they had but to ask their son, who was of an age to answer and to speak for himself. They therefore, called the man again, and dictated the answer they would have him make: speak out, they cried, and give glory to God, for we know this man is a sinner. Whether he be a sinner or not, replied the beggar, I know not; but this I know, that I was blind, and now I see. Why, what did he do to thee, said they, and how did he open thy eyes? I have already told you, said the man, and you have heard it. Why would you hear it again? will you also become his disciples? They, therefore, reviled him saying, Be thou his disciple; we are the disciples of Moses. To Moses we know God has spoken; but as for this man, we know not from whence he is. That is truly wonderful answered the beggar; you know he hath opened mine eyes, which he could not have done unless he were from God; for God granteth not such favours to sinners: for, from the beginning of the world, it hath not been heard that any man ever opened the eyes of one born blind; and unless this man were of God, he could not do anything. The Pharisees upon that observed no farther measures with him; they cursed him for pretending to teach them, and cast him out of the synagogue. Jesus hearing of the disgrace which was cast upon the poor man for his constancy in professing the truth, put himself in the way of being met by him, and asked him if he believed in the Son of God? The man desired to know who he was; and being informed that it was He who was speaking to him, he readily professed his belief, prostrated himself at the feet of Jesus, and adored him.

Thrice happy, say the holy fathers, was the man who through his corporal blindness discovered the true Light which enlightens every man that cometh into this world. He became not the adorer only, but also the defender of Jesus Christ against his enemies; unshaken by their threats, he boldly declared the truth, and silenced their captious arguments against it. The Jews cast him out of their synagogue, but Jesus received him into his communion, and made his heart the living temple of the Holy Ghost.

The good Samaritan.—Luke, x.

[A.D. 33.]

After the cure of the blind man, St. John, *ch.* x. relates what our blessed Saviour told the Jews relatively to his church, which he represents as a congregation of believers, called together by himself into one fold. Into this fold no one enters but by him who is the door, Jesus Christ, himself: he is the Sovereign pastor of our souls; he has spared no labour in seeking that which was lost; he has sacrificed his ease, and laid down his life for the salvation of his flock. He, therefore, calls himself the good shepherd, who, with the tenderness of a father, watches over and defends his fold; while the mercenary hireling flies at the approach of danger, and abandons his flock to be dispersed and worried by the wolf. He continues the allegory, and, speaking of other sheep who were to enter in and compose his fold, which he makes but one under one shepherd, he specifies the character of docility and obedience which distinguishes his flock from every other flock, and says, that they who are his, know his voice, and follow it; that he knows them, and they know him;

that he calls them by name, and they obey; that he goes before them, and they follow. Having thus inculcated that mutual duty which subsists between the spiritual shepherd and his flock, our blessed Saviour next explains the nature of that universal charity which links all men together, and makes them neighbours to one another.

A doctor of the law came up, and with an assuming air

asked him, what was the great commandment of the law. Jesus answered with his usual brevity, that it was to love God above all things, and his neighbour as himself. And who is my neighbour? replied the doctor. Jesus answered him in the following parable: A certain traveller being on the way from Jerusalem to Jerico, fell into the hands of thieves, who, after having robbed him, grievously wounded and left him half dead upon the ground. A priest who was accidentally travelling the same way, found the man lying in that condition, but made no stop nor offer to assist him. A Levite passed by soon after, and showed as little feeling as the priest. At last came a Samaritan, who being moved with compassion for the poor man in that forlorn situation, went to his relief, dressed and tied up his wounds, conveyed him to a public house, recommended him to the host, and gave him money to procure everything necessary for his recovery. Now, which of these three seemeth to thee, said our blessed Saviour, to have been a neighbour to the wounded traveller? It was he, no doubt, replied the doctor, who gave him his assistance. Go, therefore, subjoined our Saviour, and do thou in the like manner.

From this incident it appears, that a follower of Jesus Christ is not to restrain his charity, or to exclude any man in distress from the acts of his benevolence, no matter what his country may be, or what his profession in life: he is created according to the image of God, he is redeemed by the blood of Christ, and his present necessity claims a right to our assistance, if we are able to give it. Charity is compassionate and benign; it is not confined to a particular kingdom or climate, nor appropriated to any one set of men, exclusive of another; it embraces all mankind. The charitable Samaritan no sooner found his neighbour in distress, than he went to his relief; not content with a barren pity, such as the priest and Levite might have felt, he stopped to comfort and assist him: he set aside every other business for the present moment, and exerted his charity at the hour it was wanted: the next hour might have been too late. The opportunity of doing good is never to be neglected: a work of mercy well-timed is undoubtedly acceptable both to God and man.

Martha and Mary.—Luke, x.

[A.D. 33.]

Besides the twelve apostles whom our blessed Saviour had chosen from the number of his followers, he chose also seventy-two others, who are known by the special name of disciples. These he likewise employed, though in an inferior degree, as his coadjutors, in doing good to men. He sent

them before him two and two together, to the different places which he intended to visit. They faithfully acquitted themselves of their respective functions, without being jealous of the twelve who had been raised to a station above them. They are the prototypes of those inferior ministers in the church, who with due subordination to their episcopal superiors, have their share in the work of the holy ministry, according to the rank and power which is given them. The seventy-two disciples were sent by their divine Master with a power to preach, to cast out devils, and to cure diseases. On a certain occasion they returned with great joy to tell him, that in virtue of his holy name the impure spirits were subject to them. Our blessed Saviour saw the spark of vanity which was rising in their hearts, and checked it immediately, by telling them that he had seen Satan fall like a flash of lightning from heaven: I have given you the power, said he, to work miracles; but do not rejoice on that account; rejoice that your names are written in the book of life. You are happy in being privileged to see and hear the things you do; many of the prophets and ancient kings wished for the same privilege, but had it not. Jesus then, by a special impulse of the Holy Ghost, returned thanks aloud to his Father, for having revealed to the humble those sublime mysteries which were hidden from the proud and wise. After he had finished these discourses, he retired into a certain town, where he was received by Martha, the sister Mary. These two sisters lived together in Bethania, and .ten, as it seems, had the happiness of being visited by our lessed Saviour. Mary placed herself at his sacred feet, and there silently listened to the truths he spoke, while Marth was busily employed in preparing something for him to eat

Martha was displeased at Mary for leaving her to do the work alone, and made her complaint of it to Jesus. Jesus was far from interrupting Mary in her laudable attention to the word of God; but spoke in her defence to Martha, and said, that she gave herself much unnecessary trouble, while Mary had chosen the better part, which should not be taken from her.

From hence the holy fathers conclude, that though some must necessarily apply themselves to the external works of charity and justice, without which no society can be maintained, they nevertheless are the most happy who pass their days in holy retirement, free from the cares of worldly business, and employed in the exercises of a spiritual life. Nothing in appearance could be more becoming the servant of Jesus Christ, than to prepare him a repast; yet Christ preferred the repose of Mary to the employment of Martha. One thing is necessary, said Jesus to Martha; and that the saints have considered as spoken to themselves—to save their souls they thought was the only necessary thing they had to do, and that they strove to do with all their might. Whatever else seemed to draw their attention from that necessary business, they either carefully avoided, or made subordinate to it. They were careful to sanctify the works of an active life with a pure intention; they joined the two sisters together; the activity of Martha, and the prayer of Mary was their alternate exercise: thus they always kept the essential point in view, and thus they always happily succeeded in that one, that important, and that necessary affair, for which only they lived.

Folly of Riches.—Luke, xii.

[A.D. 33.]

Our blessed Saviour having expressed his approbation of a contemplative life, in the person of Mary Magdalene, declared the advantage and necessity of prayer, for all who are engaged in the exercises of an active life. He instructed his disciples in the method of praying, and in a set form of words, made for their daily use a most holy prayer, which is called the Lord's Prayer: he moreover told them how necessary it was to pray not to fall into temptation; that they ought to pray with a lively faith and a firm hope; that they ought to knock and persevere till they receive their petition, for that his Father will refuse them nothing which they shall ask in his name. A petition in the name of Christ our Saviour, says St. Austin, is that which hath eternal salvation for its object. A petition for the superfluous goods of life, for power, wealth, or honours, therefore, is not the petition which Christ has promised shall be granted. Such things oftener hinder our salvation than promote it. They naturally nourish our pride, and furnish self-love with every material for its own indulgence. Therefore it is not for such things that our blessed Saviour would have his disciples pray; they are beneath the wish of a Christian who has his thoughts fixed upon the endless joys of heaven. Be not anxious, as the Gentiles are, says he, about your raiment or your food. Behold the birds of the air and the lilies of the field. The same providence of the Father watches over you; he knows your wants, and will supply them: make it your first care to love and honour him. Beware of all covetousness, for it is not in the enjoyment of worldly possessions that the happiness of life consists. In confirmation of this truth, he proposed the parable of a rich man, who, seeing the plentiful crops that his lands produced, was at a loss to know what he should do with them. How must I manage, said he to himself, and where am I to store up my heaps of corn? Why, this will I do: I will pull down my present barns, and build up larger. There I will lay up my stores, and say to my soul, Behold, my soul, thou hast great plenty of everything, thou hast goods to last thee for many years; enjoy thyself at ease, eat, drink, and be merry. Such were the vain conceits of that man, when God unexpectedly said to him: Fool, thy soul shall be taken from thee this very night; and who then shall possess thy treasure.

In this parable our blessed Saviour shows his followers what a folly it is to place their happiness in the enjoyment of worldly wealth. Riches, that may be lost at any hour, and must be parted with in death, cannot make a Christian happy; they may flatter his senses for a while, they cannot satiate the cravings of an immortal soul. The rich man is styled a fool by our blessed Saviour, not because he had acquired his riches by any undue methods, but because he flattered himself with the thought of enjoying them for many years, little thinking that death was to snatch him from them that very night. If Christians did but oftener reflect upon the moment which, sooner or later, must separate them from all their worldly connexions, they would learn to turn their thoughts towards heaven, and to fix them on those heavenly riches which nothing can take away. But, unfortunately for them, the mortality of their present state, and the uncertain hour of their departure hence, is seldom the subject of their reflections. No one scarce considers it as he ought; and yet it is a consideration the most obvious and the most profitable. Jesus Christ knew the importance of it, and as his desire is that all men should be saved, he commands all to be constantly upon the watch, lest they chance to be surprised by death, as by a thief in the night. One of the most salutary practices of true piety is, to entertain the mind with a frequent meditation of death: it was the practice of holy David; I meditated, said he, in my heart, and the years of eternity I had present in my mind.

The Prodigal Son.—Luke, xv. [A.D. 33]

The Son of God, who had so often exhorted men to repentance, was pleased to show, by different parables, how acceptable the repentance of a sinner is to God, and what joy it gives to the blessed citizens of heaven. At one time he expresses it by the joy of a shepherd who has recovered his lost sheep, and at another, by the joy of a woman calling her

neighbours to come and congratulate with her, for having found the piece of money she had lost. But the most expressive and most moving comparison our blessed Lord makes upon the subject, is that of the Prodigal Son. A certain man, says he, had two sons; the youngest of them was eager to become his own master, and asked his father to give him the fortune that fell to his share. Being indulged in his request, he left his father's house a few days after, and travelled into a foreign country. He there fell into bad company, and by his prodigality and debauchery soon spent his fortune. From a state of affluence and ease he sunk into the opposite extreme of poverty and want; and what added to his misery, the country was sorely pinched with famine. To save himself from starving, he was compelled to look out for service, and actually hired himself to a man, who sent him to take care of his swine at a farm-house. His condition there was truly lamentable; for nobody gave him anything to eat, and he was reduced to the necessity of feeding upon the husks which were thrown to the swine. The wretchedness of his situation made him begin to think: he entered into himself, and in the anguish of his heart exclaimed, Alas! how many servants are there who abound in plenty in my father's house, while I am here perishing with hunger! I will rise and return to my father; I will confess to him the grievousness of my offence; I will own myself no longer worthy of being called his son, and will offer myself to be admitted as one of his menial servants. With these sentiments of humility and sorrow, he rose up and returned

towards his father's house. His father saw him coming when he was yet a great way off, and being moved to tears of joy and compassion at the sight, ran to meet and embrace him. Covered with confusion, and penetrated with keen remorse for having departed from so good a father, the son cried out: Father, I have sinned against heaven and before you; I no longer deserve to be called your son. Such unfeigned marks of a contrite and humble heart, moved the indulgent father, not only to forgive, but also to restore him to his former favour. The servants were ordered to bring forth the richest robe for his attire, to put a ring upon his finger, and shoes upon his feet. The fatted calf was killed, and great rejoicings made on the occasion. The elder son, who had been out in the field, heard the music and dancing, as he came near the house, and asking one of his servants what it meant, was displeased, and refused to go in. His father went out to invite him; the young man's jealousy was raised, and thus he expressed it to his father: I have been always dutiful to you, said he; I have never disobeyed your commands, and yet you have never given me so much as a kid make merry with my friends; whereas, this your profligate son, who has squandered his substance away with harlots, no sooner appears, than the fatted calf is killed for his entertainment. Son, replied the father, thou art always with me, and all I have is thine. But it was fitting we should thus rejoice for thy brother—since he was dead, and is come to life again; he was lost, and is found.

This parable is so fully expressive of what it is meant to express, say the holy fathers, that nothing more can be added to it. The wretchedness that follows an abandoned sinner, and the satisfaction that accompanies a true penitent, are fully displayed. The unfortunate young man no sooner became sensible of the miserable state he was in, than he resolved to quit it. He had foolishly departed from his father's house; he was admonished of his folly by the misfortunes he fell into; conscious of his guilt, he repented, and returned to his father, with a firm purpose never to stray from him any more. Let us rise from the state of sin in the same manner, let us return to God with all our hearts, and we shall experience the same mercy from our heavenly Father, who tenderly loves us. Let us only repent, like the prodigal son, for having left our father's house, and we shall, like him, rejoice to see ourselves restored to our former state of grace and friendship with the Almighty God. To the passing confusion which may attend a confession of our guilt, succeeds a peace and pleasing joy which no sinful enjoyment of the world can give.

The Rich Glutton.—LUKE, xvi.

[A.D. 33.]

OUR blessed Saviour on a former occasion having declared how hard it was for a rich man to enter into the kingdom of heaven, shows, in the parable of the rich glutton, what misery a man entails upon himself by the abuse of riches. There was a rich man says he, clothed with purple and silk, who feasted sumptuously every day. Before his door lay a poor man whose name was Lazarus, full of sores, begging for the scraps which fell from his table, but which no one had the charity to give him. The dogs came and licked the beggar's sores, which he patiently permitted them to do, humbly submitting to receive whatever comfort it pleased God to send him in his sufferings. Lazarus bore his pains with patience; he made no complaint, nor did he murmur at the treatment he received from man. Death soon put an end to his afflictions; his soul being purified by the sufferings he had patiently borne, was carried by angels into Abraham's bosom. The rich man died also; but as his state during life

had been different from that of Lazarus, so different likewise was his situation after death. He was buried in the deep abyss of hell, from whence, lifting up his eyes, he saw Abraham afar off, and Lazarus in his bosom. From the midst of tormenting flames he called upon Abraham, begging of him to compassionate his sufferings, and to let Lazarus come to his relief. Being exquisitely tormented by the piercing fire, he asked for a drop of water to cool his tongue. Abraham bade him remember that he had wickedly indulged himself in the enjoyment of good things during life, while Lazarus had been beset with sufferings and evils; Lazarus was therefore now comforted and he tormented. Thus, not being able to obtain so much as the smallest comfort for himself, he desired Abraham at least to let Lazarus go to his father's house, and admonish his five brothers, who were still living, lest they might come into the same place of torments. They have Moses and the prophets for their instruction, said Abraham; if they will not hearken to them, neither will they believe though one should go to them from the dead.

In this parable, our blessed Saviour points out the two opposite terms to which a different use of God's creatures leads the different classes of mankind. By a mistaken world afflictions are styled the evils of life, though to the humble Christian they pave the way towards endless happiness; while riches are esteemed a blessing, though so dangerously connected with real misery. The sufferings of Lazarus were short; the joy that succeeded was eternal. The momentary pleasures of the rich man were but the prelude to everlasting torments. After death he found as little pity from Abraham as Lazarus in life had found from him. The time of mercy was then no more. Happy are the suffering poor, if they are only careful to use the advantages which their humble station gives them for their improvement in virtue. Poverty with all its attendants, borne in longanimity and patience, is a source of endless blessings for the world to come. Unhappy are the affluent rich, if they make not a Christian use of what they have received. To comfort the distressed, and to help the needy, is the privilege of being rich; and happy are they who so use their privilege; the way to draw upon themselves the compassion of their heavenly Father is, to show compassion to their poor brethren.

The Pharisee and the Publican.—LUKE, xviii.

[A.D. 33.]

UPON the chair of Moses, said our blessed Saviour to the people, sit the Scribes and Pharisees; therefore, whatever they shall tell you to do, observe and do it; but according to their works, do ye not; for their works correspond not with their words. Full of themselves, they seek the first places at all public entertainments; they love to be saluted in the streets, and affect to be called Rabbi; if they perform the external work of the law, it is that they may be seen and praised by men: they are full of malice and deceit within; if they give alms to the poor, it is with a trumpet sounding before them; if they fast, they take care to let others know it; if they pray, it is at the corners of the streets, and in public places, that all may see them. It is against such pharisaical hypocrisy that our blessed Lord cautions his followers. He tells them to be content with being obscurely good; to seek the approbation of their heavenly Father who sees the hidden intention of their hearts; to let the light of their good works be no farther seen in public, than that men may be drawn thereby to imitate the good they see, and to give the glory thereof to God; he therefore recommends to them to be cheerful when they fast, not boast of their alms-deeds, or make an affected show of devotion.

To humble the pride of those who entertained high conceited notions of themselves while they despised others, our blessed Lord proposed the parable of a Pharisee and a publican. Two men, said he, went into the temple to pray, the one a Pharisee, the other a publican. The Pharisee

standing bolt upright gave thanks aloud to God, because, unlike to the rest of men, he was neither an extortioner, nor a thief, nor an adulterer, nor such as even the publican behind him; but that he fasted twice in the week, and paid the tithes of all he possessed. With very different sentiments from these, the publican stood far below; conscious of his unworthiness, he durst not so much as lift up his eyes to heaven; he knocked his breast and only spoke these words: O God, be merciful to me a sinner.

Having thus proposed the parable, Jesus Christ declares how different his thoughts are from ours, and how elevated his judgments are above those of men. The pompous show of piety in the Pharisee, may have attracted the eyes of men; it provoked the displeasure of Almighty God: the publican, to vulgar eyes may have seemed an object of contempt; his humility rendered him acceptable to Jesus Christ; for Jesus embraces the humble, and rejects the proud. Humility is the foundation of Christian piety; without humility every other virtue is no more than show, a glittering appearance of something good, without the reality. A prayer dictated by pride became a sin in the Pharisee; prayer, united with an humble contrition of heart, justified the publican.

Workmen of the Vineyard.—MATT. XX. [A.D. 33.]

THE Hebrew people, from the time of their great patriarch Abraham, were the only happy nation which Almighty God, had adopted for his own, which, as a chosen vineyard, he had fenced in with wholesome laws, and cultivated with peculiar care. What could I do more for my vineyard, which I have not done? says he, by the mouth of his prophet: I expected it would produce me grapes, and it has yielded nothing but wild and sour fruit. The master sent his servants at different times to the dressers of his vineyard, as it is in the parable, to admonish them of their duty; they abused and beat his servants; he sent them his only son, and him they cast out, and barbarously put to death. What had the master then to do with these wicked murderers, says our Saviour, but to destroy them in their turn and to set out his vineyard to other husbandmen more industrious and faithful. O Jerusalem, Jerusalem, who hast killed the prophets, and hast stoned to death those who were sent to thee, thou must answer for the blood thou hast unjustly spilt: the day will come when thy enemies shall surround and cast thee down, nor of thy stately buildings shall they leave so much as one stone upon another. From this incredulous and perverse generation the kingdom of heaven shall be taken away, and given to a nation which shall yield the fruits thereof in due season. To confirm this promise made in favour of his church, which, after the reprobation of the Jews was to be planted amongst the Gentiles, our blessed Redeemer spoke the following parable:

The kingdom of heaven, said he, is like to the master of a family, who went out betimes in the morning to hire workmen for his vineyard. He agreed with them what wages they should have, and set them to work. About the third hour of the day he went out again, and finding others standing in the market-place idle, he told them also to go into his vineyard, promising to each a recompense proportionable to his work. He did the same at the sixth and ninth hours of the day. Going out, moreover, about evening, and meeting with others still unemployed, he asked them why they stood there all the day idle. Their answer was, because no one had hired them: he, therefore, bade them go, like the rest, into his vineyard, with a promise of rewarding them according to their deserts. When the day was over, he commanded his steward to call the workmen together and pay them their hire. The last comers were called upon in the first place, and, though they had worked but one hour, received each of them the same wages as the master had promised to the first. They who had been set to work in the morning, imagining that when it came to their turn they should receive something more, were much disappointed to find no increase made to the pay they had agreed for, and received it with great murmuring against the master. These last, said they, have worked no more than an hour, and in their

pay are made equal to us, who have borne the burden and heat of the day. Friend, said the master to one of them, I do thee no wrong. Didst thou not agree with me for a day's wages? Take what belongs to thee, and go thy way. It is my will to give the last the same I give to thee. Am I not master in this, to do as I please? or is thine eye to be jealous because I am good? So shall the last be first, and the first last. For of the many that are called, only few are chosen.

This parable has afforded ample subject for the holy fathers to exhort all Christians to shun idleness, as displeasing to God, and to labour diligently in the affair of their salvation. Men are born and appointed to labour in the service of Almighty God, each one according to his state and calling. Let each one be diligent in performing that part of the task which is allotted him, and he will receive his due recompense; for God will give to every one according to his works. However unequally the goods of fortune may seem to be divided here, we are not to murmur at the secret disposition of divine Providence; it is not for this world we have heen created, nor is it in this world that we expect our reward. The reward of an eternal inheritance above is what we expect from God, to whom alone all our actions should be ultimately referred. For God, in the next life, rewards nothing but what is done for him in this. From him alone we receive the power of doing good, and when he rewards us for the good we have done, it is not so much our deserts as his own gifts that he crowns.

Lazarus raised to life.—John, xi.
[A.D. 33.]

The Scribes and Pharisees seeing themselves aimed at in these parables of our blessed Saviour, used all their art to surprise him in his words, and to draw some expression from him that might furnish them with a subject of accusing him to the people. With that view they sent to ask him, whether it were lawful to pay tribute to Cæsar? Should he say it was, they were ready to cry him down as an enemy to the liberty of his country; and should he say it was not, king Herod's men were at hand to accuse him of treason against the Roman emperor. Jesus, to whom the thoughts of men were as fully

known as their actions, said, Why do ye tempt me, ye hypocrites; show me the coin of the tribute; and they showed him a Roman penny. He asked them whose image it was that was stamped upon it. They told him it was Cæsar's; give then to Cæsar what belongs to Cæsar, said he, and to God what belongs to God. The Pharisees swelled with vexation to find themselves thus baffled; and what vexed them still more, they saw that the fame of Jesus Christ was increasing daily by the miracles he wrought, of which the most celebrated was that of raising Lazarus from the dead.

Lazarus was taken dangerously ill in Bethania, and his two sisters, Martha and Mary, gave notice of it to Jesus, hoping that he would come and heal him; for they knew that Jesus loved both them and Lazarus. Upon receiving the message, our blessed Lord made answer, that this sickness of Lazarus was not to death, but for the manifestation of his and his Father's glory. He seemed in no haste to go near him, but remained two days longer in the place where he was. Lazarus died in the mean time. Jesus then told his disciples he must return into Judea: they endeavoured to persuade him from going where he had lately been in danger of being stoned to death. Our friend Lazarus is dead, said he, and I must go to raise him up: I am glad, for your sake, I was not there, that you may believe; but let us go to him. Then it was that St. Thomas expressed a fortitude of mind worthy of himself, and of every follower of Jesus Christ. Let us also go, said he, and die with him. When Jesus came with his disciples to Bethania, he found that Lazarus had been four days in his grave. Martha no sooner heard that Jesus was come, than she went out to meet him. Lord, if thou hadst been here, said she, my brother had not died. Thy brother shall rise again, said Jesus. I know he will rise at the last day, replied Martha, and now I also know, that whatsoever thou wilt ask of God, God will give it thee. I am the resurrection and the life, said Jesus; he who believeth in me, although he be dead, shall live, and whoever liveth and believeth in me shall not die for ever. Dost thou believe this? Yes, Lord, answered Martha, I believe thou art Christ, the Son of the living God; and having said that, went to call her sister Mary, who remained sitting with her friends that were come from Jerusalem to condole with her upon her brother's death. Martha whispered in her ear that Jesus was come and called for her. Mary quickly rose up and went towards him; for Jesus still remained in the place where Martha had met him. The Jews, who did not hear what Martha whispered, thought that Mary was going, in the hurry of her grief, to weep over her brother's grave; they rose up and followed her. When she came to Jesus, she threw herself at his feet, and pouring forth a torrent of tears, said: Lord, if thou hadst been here, my brother had not died. Her friends around were also melted into tears: Jesus likewise wept, and was much troubled. He asked where they had laid him; they desired him to come and see. He therefore went groaning in spirit to the sepulchre, which was a vault, with a stone laid over it. Jesus ordered the stone to be taken off: Lord,

by this time he stinketh, said Martha, for he has been dead four days. Did I not tell thee, replied our Saviour, that if thou believe, thou shalt see the glory of God. They then took the stone away: Jesus lifted his eyes to heaven, and having addressed his Father in a short but fervent prayer, cried with a loud voice, Lazarus, come forth; and presently he who had been dead came forth, bound as he was, hands and feet, with winding-bands, and his face tied round with a handkerchief. Loose his bands, said Jesus, and let him go.

The holy fathers consider this resurrection of Lazarus, as a figure of the spiritual resurrection of a soul from the state of sin. Jesus Christ approaches the sinner by his holy grace; he calls upon him by his holy word; he warms him into a sincere regret for his past sins; he animates him with a strong purpose of amendment by the infusion of his holy spirit; he unbinds him by the power which he has given to the ministers of his church, and bids him go to lead a new life. Such is the wonderful work which the Saviour of our souls produceth in the order of grace. The tears, the sighs, the groans, and prayer of Jesus Christ at the tomb of Lazarus, indicate the difficulty there is in resuscitating a soul that has been long dead by a habit of mortal sin. But however great the difficulty may be, the sinner who is desirous of life, and willing to concur, ought never to despair, when he considers how powerful and how good his Redeemer is.

Zacheus.—Luke, xix.

[A.D. 34.]

The Pharisees were soon told of the surprising miracle which Jesus had performed in Bethania, and, being stung with envy at the credit he had acquired thereby, assembled in council to deliberate what measures they should take against him. If we let this man alone, said they, for they did not deign to call him by his name, all the world will believe in him. The great miracles he does will draw the whole nation after him; the jealous Romans will come and destroy us. Upon this, Caiphas, who was the high-priest for that year, took up the discourse and said, You know nothing, neither do ye consider that it is expedient for you that one man should die for the people, that the whole nation may not perish. Caiphas, in giving this advice to the Jews, said more than he understood, and in quality of high-priest prophesied that Jesus should die to save all nations of the earth. Therefore from that day they watched every opportunity that could forward their iniquitous designs. Jesus knew their intentions against his life, and walked no longer openly amongst them, but retired towards the desert into a town called Ephrem, where he abode with his disciples. His stay there was not very long; for the approaching festival of Easter called him back to Jerusalem, where the Pharisees had already given orders for his being apprehended as soon as he should appear. Our blessed Lord took his twelve disciples apart, and said to them, Behold! we are going to Jerusalem, and the Son of M shall be betrayed to the chief priests, and delivered to the Gentiles to be mocked, and scourged, and crucified; and on the third day he shall rise again. He was followed by a great multitude, and when he came near to Jericho, Zacheus, a ~ich and principal man among the publicans, had a great desire to see him. Being low of stature, and not able to approach on account of the crowd, he ran forward and climbed up into a sycamore tree, that overlooked the way. When Jesus came to the place he

looked up, and bade him quickly come down, because he intended to abide with him that day in his house. Whenever God calls, no delay is to be made: if his first call be not answered, he may not call again. Zacheus lost not a single moment: he made haste down, and joyfully received the Son of God into his house. The people were not a little surprised, and all murmured at seeing Jesus go to the house of a man who was a reputed sinner. But Zacheus was no longer a sinner in his heart; he had renounced his wicked practices, and standing in humble posture before our Lord, declared the resolution he had taken, of distributing one-half of his goods to the poor, and of making restitution with the other half to those he had wronged. Jesus upon that pronounced him a true son of Abraham, and declared him to be in the straight path to salvation.

The holy father look upon Zacheus as the model of a true conversion. To some it may seem as if Zacheus had prevented Jesus Christ, and made the first advances towards his justification. But, in fact, Jesus Christ by his secret graces had first touched his heart, and the visible attempts that Zacheus made of coming to Jesus, were the effects of those invincible desires which the divine mercy had already stirred up within him. Zacheus gave to the poor no more than one-half of his goods, because God accepts not of the alms which are not our own to give: for as much of the other half as he had unjustly acquired, was not his, but the property of those he had wronged. The quadruple satisfaction he made to his injured neighbour is a mark of the sincerity of his repentance: he struck at the very root of that passion which had hitherto been predominant in his heart, and thereby began his conversion upon a solid and lasting foundation. When the chief obstacle that opposes a sinner's return to God is once removed by a sincere repentance, his advancement in virtue becomes easy. If a neighbour has been maliciously injured, either in his goods or reputation, he must be indemnified as far as the offending party has it in his power: however difficult the task may seem to the proud and covetous heart of man, the obligation is indispensable; the sin is not remitted, says St. Austin, unless restitution be made of what was taken away.

Triumph of Jesus Christ.—JOHN, xii.

[A.D. 34.]

OUR blessed Saviour advanced from Jericho to Bethania, where he arrived six days before the great feast of Easter. Lazarus and his two sisters received him with great marks of joy and pious gratitude, and a supper was prepared for him in the house of Simon the leper. *Mark*, xiv. 3. Martha waited, and Lazarus was one of them who were at the table with him.

Mary, in the interim, took a pound of rich and odoriferous spikenard, with which she anointed his feet, and wiped them with her hair. Judas, the traitor, murmured at such waste, as he was pleased to call it, and said she had better have sold the ointment, and given the price of it to the poor: but Jesus commended her piety, and bade them not molest her, since she had thereby anticipated the duty of anointing his body before his burial. The report of Jesus being come to Bethania, was quickly carried to Jerusalem, and many of the Jews flocked thither to see not only him, but also Lazarus, whom he had raised from the dead. The Pharisees were more and more exasperated to see such honours paid to Jesus Christ; they observed that Lazarus was the cause why many were induced to believe in him, and, therefore, thought of putting him likewise to death. Jesus left Bethania the next day, and having advanced as far as Mount Olivet, sent two of his disciples into an adjoining village, where he told them they would find an ass standing with her colt. Untie them, said he, and lead them hither; and if any one shall offer to hinder, or to ask you questions, tell him the Lord wants them, and forthwith he will let them go. The two disciples went immediately to the village, and found an ass, as he had said, standing with her foal; they untied them, and being asked by some that were standing by, why they did so, answered as Jesus had directed them: no one then offered to hinder them, and they brought away the colt, spread their garments, and set Jesus upon the back of him. Jerusalem at that time was thronged with foreign Jews, who were come from different parts to keep the feast of the passover. These people being informed of the wonderful miracles which Jesus had wrought, and hearing of his approach towards the city, crowded out to meet and conduct him in triumph: with branches of palms and olives in their hands, they walked in procession before and after him, rending the air with peals of joy and acclamation. Then were fulfilled the words of Isaiah, saying, Tell ye the daughters of Sion, *Behold thy King cometh to thee, meek, and sitting upon an ass.* Some strewed the way with their garments as he came along, some cut down the boughs of trees, while the multitude cried out, *Hosannah to the Son of David! blessed is he who cometh in the name of the Lord: Hosannah in the highest!*

The holy fathers write in the most exalted style of this triumph of Jesus Christ: by this, say they, Christ anticipated the triumph of his resurrection, as in his last supper he anticipated the mystery of his passion. In vain did the Pharisees and elders rage, in vain did the Jewish chiefs form their cabals against the Lord, and against his Christ. The people yielded to the force of truth, and ran out in shoals to grace the triumph, and proclaim the praises of the Messiah. Many also of the chief men believed in him, but on account of the Pharisees durst not declare their belief, lest they should be turned out of the synagogue: for they loved the glory of men more than the glory of God, says St. John.

Zeal of Jesus Christ.—MARK, xi.

[A.D. 34.]

JESUS rode on in triumph, amidst the joyful shouts of numerous attendants, till he came near the gates of Jerusalem, when the sight of that unhappy city drew tears from his eyes. With tears of compassion he bewailed the blindness of a people, shutting their eyes against the light which offered itself to them: he wept for the misfortunes of a city which would not know the day of her visitation, nor receive the gifts that appertained to her peace; he saw her upon the point of completing all her former crimes, by putting him to death: and foretold the ruin that should soon overtake her in punishment thereof. He beheld the final impenitence of that stiff-necked people, says St. Gregory; and in the temporal destruction of their city, deplored the final reprobation of their souls. The citizens were all in motion at his approach: they asked who was coming amidst such a train of followers, and were answered, that it was Jesus the prophet, from Nazareth of Galilee. Jesus had no sooner entered into Jerusalem, than he went to the temple, which he found crowded with the tables of money-changers, and the chairs of them who sold doves. He was provoked to see such traffic carried on in a place which had been solely consecrated to the divine service, and in which nothing ought to be allowed that did not immediately regard the worship of Almighty God. Moved with zeal for his Father's honour, he expressed a holy anger against the profane abuse, overturned the chairs and tables, and drove the buyers and

ellers away, telling them that the house of God was a house of prayer, and ought not to be thus converted into a den of thieves.

The active zeal which our meek Saviour showed against the profanation of his Father's house, ought to put every Christian upon his guard against all unseemly behaviour in the place of divine worship. Our churches are infinitely more holy than the ancient temple of Jerusalem; they are in a special manner sanctified by the presence of God, who dwells therein, as on his throne; the word of God is there read and heard; the praises of God are there sung; the offering of prayer and sacrifice is there made. Wherefore, to frequent those holy places with any other view than that of honouring the Supreme Being, to make them the seat of idle talk, of jest, of laughter, of curiosity, and sloth, is an abuse frequently condemned by the holy fathers, as an insult offered to Almighty God in the very sanctuary. Jesus Christ, who exerted such zeal for his Father's honour in the temple of Jerusalem, cannot be indifferent to the dishonour that is shown him in a Christian church, by the daily irreverence of those who profess themselves his followers and adorers: nor can we doubt but he will one day do himself justice, and punish the offence with the severity it deserves.

The Wedding Garment.—MATT. xxii.

[A.D. 34.]

OUR blessed Saviour, from the time of his public entry into Jerusalem till he was betrayed by Judas, spent the day in the temple, and about evening retired to Bethania, to pray in the Garden of Gethsemani. The people were up betimes every morning to receive him, and to hear his exhortations; and so diligent were they in their attendance, that the Pharisees durst not presume to execute the design they had formed of seizing him by open violence. Our blessed Redeemer, by the force and eloquence of his doctrine, sought to convince and gain the hearts of his enemies; but, finding them hardened against his holy word, he confirmed the threat he had uttered more than once before, of transferring the gift of faith from them to the Gentiles. And, lest the Gentiles might grow vain at seeing themselves preferred before a people who, for so many ages, had been the favourites of heaven, he took care to inform them that the choice made in their favour was not to be attributed to any precedent merits of their own, but to the gratuitous mercy of Almighty God who called them; he strongly inculcated the necessity of corresponding with the divine gift more faithfully than the Jews had done, lest, like them, they might also forfeit the grace of their vocation. This instruction he conveyed to them in the following parable:

The kingdom of heaven, said he, is like to a king, who made a marriage for his son. A public entertainment was prepared, and notice given for the invited to come. The invitation was strangely neglected, and no one came. The king sent his servants round a second time to exhort the invited to come, and tell to them that his beeves and fatlings were killed, and every other preparation made for their reception. This second invitation was no better received than the first. They all went their ways, one to his farm, another to

his merchandize, while others even insulted the king's servants, and put them to death. Provoked at their outrageous conduct, the king ordered a body of troops to march against the murderers, whom he totally destroyed, and burned their city to the ground. That being done, he bade his servants go forth into the highways, and call all they should find to the marriage-feast, that the places of the unworthy might be filled up. The servants speedily obeyed their master's orders: they called in all they found, and the hall of entertainment was crowded with a numerous assembly of good and bad mixed together. When they were placed at table, the king

went in to see them, and perceiving one amongst them not clothed with a wedding garment, he asked him how he came hither without his proper dress. The man made no reply; upon which the king told his servants to bind him hand and foot, and to cast him forth into outer darkness, where there shall be weeping and gnashing of teeth. For many are called but few are chosen.

The drift of this parable is, to show that the Jews had been first invited to believe in Jesus Christ, and upon their refusal, the Gentiles were called in to take their place. The king is Almighty God; his son is Jesus Christ, who by his incarnation espoused the church; the feast is his sanctifying graces in this life, and glory in the next. His servants are the prophets, and other ministers of his holy word. To make ourselves worthy of the graces which God invites us to receive, we must correspond by our own endeavours; and when we approach these mysterious nuptials, at the table of our Lord, the least thing we can do is, to appear in a robe suitable to the sanctity and majesty of him who invites us. This nuptial robe, according to the holy fathers, is the robe of innocence and justice, without which we have nothing to expect, but to be turned out of the number of God's elect, and cast into the dark abyss. For the fate of the unhappy man in the parable, according to St. Austin, indicates the misfortune of those who neglect to adorn their souls with virtues, who enter into eternity without having the white garment, which at their baptism they were to carry unspotted before the tribunal of Christ. Happy is the man who shall be always upon the watch against his master's coming, and careful to keep his garments whole and clean, as it is said in the Revelations, that he may not be put to the blush at appearing in the state of nakedness and shame.

Parable of the Talents.—Matt. xxv.

[A.D. 34.]

Before our blessed Lord would put an end to his preaching, he deemed it necessary to forewarn the world of the rigours of his justice. In the parable of the five wise and five foolish virgins, he informs us that however holy our state of life may be, we must still be diligent and watchful in every duty; that though our actions may shine as bright as lamps to the eyes of men, we shall not be admitted into heaven unless our charity, like oil, nourishes the flame, and gives life to our

faith. By the parable of the talents, as it is related by St. Matthew, he leads us into the knowledge of many other important truths. A certain man, says our Lord, going to take a long journey, called his servants to him, and distributed his goods amongst them. To one he gave five talents, to another two, and to a third, one, according to each one's natural capacity. The two first employed themselves in such a manner, that by their industry they doubled the talents which each of them had received. The third tied his talent up in a handkerchief, and hid it in the ground. The master returned some time after, and called them all to an account. The servant who had received five talents, offered them back, with an addition of five more, which he had gained by his

diligence. Well done, thou good and faithful servant, said the master, because thou hast been faithful over a few things, I will place thee over many; enter into the joy of thy Lord. Next came the servant who had received two talents, and as he had made an equally good use of his time, was rewarded equally with the first. The third then presented himself before his master, and said, Sir, I knew you to be a hard man, and expect to reap where you have not sown. Under that apprehension, I therefore went and hid your talent in the ground; behold, here it is. The master upon that said to him, O wicked and slothful servant, I judge thee by thy own words; for if thou knewest that I reap where I have not sown, why didst thou not place my money in the banker's hands, that at my return I might have received it with profit? The idle man had nothing to allege in excuse for his negligence; upon which the master, having first ordered the talent to be taken from him and given to the other who had ten, condemned him as an unprofitable servant, to be cast into utter darkness, where he was doomed to weep and gnash his teeth, far from the light of heaven and the presence of his Creator.

By the talents, the holy fathers understand the gifts of grace and nature, which Almighty God bestows upon his servants in such proportion as he thinks fit. To some he gives more, to some less; but to all he gives with a view that they may faithfully employ whatever they receive, to his honour, and their own improvement in virtue. It is of the use and improvement which we make of God's gifts, that we shall be demanded an account at the end of life. It will profit us nothing to have made no bad use of our talents or not to have lost them: nothing is more fatal than to stifle the graces, and to bury the gifts of God; we must absolutely improve them, to be saved. To whom much has been given, of him much will be required.

The Last Judgment.—MATT. XXV.
[A.D. 34.]

OUR blessed Saviour finished his discourse to the people, by announcing to them the terrors of the last judgment. The supine negligence of men in the affair of salvation, and their great negligence to do their duty upon the nobler principles of love, made it necessary to rouse their attention by suggesting the motives of fear. The great and bitter day will come, when the mysterious ways of Providence shall be disclosed to the open view of men and angels, and to each one shall be assigned the everlasting lot that his works deserve. The day will be ushered in with the most foreboding signs of calamity and misery, which shall make men wither away with fear, at the expectation of evils which shall then come upon the whole world. For there shall be signs in the sun, moon, and stars; the earth shall tremble, and the powers of heaven shall be shaken. An angel will sound the dreadful trumpet, which shall be heard from the highest heavens down to the nethermost abyss; and a voice will cry: Arise, ye dead, and come to judgment. In the twinkling of

an eye, the dead will rise from their graves, and stand before the tribunal of Christ, who will judge every one according to his works. Surrounded by myriads of angels, the Son of Man will then appear coming in a cloud with great power and majesty. In a moment he will separate the good from the bad, as the shepherd separates his sheep from the goats; the sheep he will place on his right hand, and the goats on his left. To the first, he will say, Come, ye blessed of my Father, and possess the kingdom which has been prepared for you from the beginning of the world: for I was hungry, and you gave me to eat; I was thirsty, and you gave me to drink; I was a stranger, and you took me in; I was naked, and you clothed me; I was sick, and you comforted me; in prison, and you visited me: for whatever you have done of this kind to any of my little ones, you have done it to me. Then he shall turn to them on his left hand, and say, Depart from me, ye cursed, into eternal fire, which was prepared for the devil and his angels; for you gave me neither to eat nor to drink; nor have you relieved me in any other distress in which you saw me. And when they shall say, At what time, Lord, have we seen you in distress, and have not succoured you? he will answer, As long as you did it not to one of these least, you did it not to me. The just shall then go into everlasting life, and the wicked into everlasting punishment.

Such shall be the end of that tremendous day. How dreadfully surprised will the reprobate then be! and how different will be their thoughts from what they are at present! The wicked are, by a merciful Redeemer, sentenced to endless torments for having neglected the duties of fraternal charity; from whence it is evinced, that to be saved, we must not only abstain from evil but also do good. To compassionate our brethren in their sufferings, and to help them in their corporal and spiritual wants, is a Christian duty. They are the mystical members of Christ's body; whatever charity we do, or refuse to them, Christ looks upon as done or refused to himself. Blessed are the merciful, for they shall find mercy. The best grounds we can have to inspire confidence in the divine mercy, is the exercise of charity towards our brethren.

The Last Supper.—MATT. XXVI.

[A.D. 34].

THE time fixed from eternity for the world's redemption was upon the eve of its accomplishment: it was the middle of Daniel's seventieth week of years, when, according to the prophecy, Christ was to be denied by his people, and put to death. Judas Iscariot, one of the twelve, had already bargained with the Pharisees for a certain sum of money to betray him into their hands. Jesus perfectly knew what was to happen to him; he foresaw the malice and contrivance of the plots that were laid against his life, and permitted them to take their course, for his time was now come: he freely met the danger, and concealed himself no longer from his enemies. But before he suffered, he would eat the Paschal lamb with his disciples, for the last time. He directed them to a certain house in the city, where he told them to prepare the supper in a large dining-room, which the man of the house should show them. They went, they found every thing as he had said, and there they prepared the Passover. At the appointed hour in the evening, Jesus sat down, and the twelve apostles with him. Most earnestly have I desired, said he, to eat this Paschal supper with you, before I suffer. For from this time I will not eat it, till it be fulfilled in the kingdom of God; nor will I drink of the fruit of the vine, till the kingdom of God come. Take the chalice and divide it amongst you: you have continued with me in my temptations, and I dispose to you, as my Father hath disposed to me, a kingdom, that you may eat and drink at my table in my kingdom, and may sit upon thrones, judging the twelve tribes of Israel.

Our blessed Lord hath promised his disciples (*John*, vi.) that he would give them the living bread, which was his flesh, for the life of the world, and this was the day, the very eve of his passion, fixed for the fulfilling of his promise. Knowing that his hour was come, when he should pass out of this world to the Father, and having loved his own who were in the world, he loved them unto the end. When the supper was therefore done, says St. John, he rose from table, laid aside his garments, and having girt himself round with a towel, poured water into a basin, and began to wash his disciples' feet. After he had washed, and wiped them with the towel with which he was girt, he took his garments,

and sitting down again, said to them: Do you know what I have done to you? If I, your Lord and Master, have washed your feet, you also ought to wash one another's feet: for I have given an example for you to follow. Having said that, he was troubled in spirit, and declared that one of them would betray him. The disciples were alarmed, and asked who the traitor was. It is he, said our Lord, to whom I shall offer a morsel of bread dipped in the dish; and he offered it to Judas Iscariot: Judas having taken it, immediately went out; and it was night. Jesus, therefore, being at table, after he had washed his disciples' feet, took bread into his sacred and venerable hands, blessed, broke, and gave it to his disciples,

saying, Take and eat, *For this is my Body.* After that, he, in like manner, took and blessed the cup, which stood with wine in it upon the table, bidding them all to drink of it, saying *This is my blood of the New Testament, which shall be shed for many unto the remission of sins*, and then added, *Do this for a commemoration of me.* By which last words he empowered and commissioned his apostles, and their successors in the priesthood, to do and consecrate the same, and thereby verified the prediction of the Psalmist, who styled him a priest for ever, according to the order of Melchisedech. This is the clean oblation, which the prophet Malachy said, should be offered to God in every place, from the rising to the setting of the sun; and this is daily offered in the church of Christ, throughout the world, by the ministry of the priests, to whom he has given the power to do what he did at his last supper; that is, to consecrate the bread and wine in his name and to change them into his Body and his Blood.

The sacrament of the Body and Blood of our Lord, is a mystery so sublime and incomprehensible to human weakness, that nothing but the clear and express word of God could induce us to believe it. But since Jesus Christ himself so positively tells us, says St. Cyril of Jerusalem, *This is my Body, This is my Blood*, who will dare to call his word in question, or doubt whether his body and his blood be really there? At Cana he had changed water into wine, and at his last supper he changed wine into blood. For under the appearance of bread he gives us his body, continues the holy doctor, and under the appearance of wine he gives us his blood. (*Catachesi. Mystagog.* 4.) What was bread before the consecration, says St. Ambrose, becomes the Body of Christ after consecration, and his body is truly there. Before the words of consecration, the body of Christ was not there; but he spoke, and there it was. For to God, who by his word made the world out of nothing, nothing is impossible. Hence, the chalice which we bless, says St. Paul, is it not the communication of the blood of Christ? and the bread which we break, is it not a participation of the body of our Lord? Therefore, whosoever shall eat this bread, or drink of the chalice of the Lord unworthily, shall be guilty of the body and blood of our Lord.

Jesus in the Garden of Gethsemani.—MATT. xxvi.

[A.D. 34.]

AFTER Judas was gone out to concert measures with the Pharisees for the execution of his treacherous design, our blessed Saviour made an admirable discourse to the eleven that remained. In words the most pathetic and expressive of his love, he exhorted them to a steadiness in the divine service, and to a perfect love of their neighbour, as the distinctive mark of their being his disciples. Let not your heart be troubled, said he; because I go to the Father and will prepare a place for you: for in my father's house there are many mansions. You believe in God, believe also in me. I will not leave you orphans; I will come again, and will take you to myself; that where I am, you also may be. If you love me, keep my commandments; he who loveth me, shall be loved by my Father, and I will love him; whatsoever you shall ask the Father in my name, that will I do. Peace I leave with you; my peace, such as the world cannot give, I give unto you. I will ask the Father, and he will give you another comforter, the Spirit of Truth, who shall abide with you, and teach you all things.

He addressed himself in a particular manner to St. Peter and informed him of the devil's malicious designs against him; but I have prayed, said he, to the Father for you, that your faith may not fail. He likewise admonished them all of the great trial they would meet with that very night; and how they would fly and forsake him in the middle of his enemies. St. Peter, who did not then know himself, answered with his usual confidence, that whatever the rest might do, he at least would not abandon him, but was ready to accompany him even to prison, and death itself. He spoke the generous disposition of his heart, but relied too much upon his own strength; he had not yet learned to mistrust his weakness, and therefore our blessed Saviour told him, that before the crowing of the cock he should thrice deny him. Jesus Christ after that made a most fervent prayer to his eternal Father, not only for his apostles, but also for them who, through their word, should believe in him; which when he had done, he went forth with his disciples, and passing over the torrent of Cedron, retired, according to his custom, into the Mountain of Olives. His eleven disciples followed him to the place called Gethsemani, where he bade them stop, while he should go into the garden to pray, as he had often done before. He took with him Peter, James, and John, his three favourite apostles, to be the witnesses of this last scene of his bitter passion. For then it was that he began more sensibly to feel the infirmities of human nature; then it was that all our griefs and miseries flowed in with full tide upon him. Overwhelmed with sadness, he told his disciples his soul was sorrowful even unto death; he bade them stay there and pray, that they might not sink under the temptation. He then withdrew from them to the distance of a stone's throw, and kneeling down said; Father, if it be possible, let this cup pass from me; but if that cannot be without my drinking it, let thy will be done, not mine. He rose up, came to his disciples, and found them asleep. He upbraided Peter for not being able to watch one hour with him, commanded them to watch and pray against the temptation, and retiring again repeated the same tender prayer, in the same submissive words, to his heavenly Father. Full of concern for his dear disciples, he soon after visited them again, and found them still sleeping, for their eyes were heavy; he left them, went back again, and prayed a third time, saying: my Father, if this chalice may not pass away, but I must drink it, thy will be done. The anguish of his mind increased still more and more, which threw him at last into a bitter agony. Thick drops as it were of blood, gushed through the pores of his body and trickled down upon the ground. In the midst of this distress he was comforted by an angel; and, notwithstanding the violent agitation of his soul, he prayed the longer.

This mysterious agony of the Son of God is a subject of astonishment to the holy fathers: on one hand, they contemplate Jesus Christ, the splendour of his Father's glory, and the figure of his substance, sorrowful and trembling at the prospect of his ensuing passion; and, on the other, behold his martyrs meeting their torments with magnanimity and joy. But since he has taken upon himself our infirmities, and has borne our sorrows, Jesus Christ has become the fortitude of the saints. Encouraged by his example, and strengthened by his grace, the zealous Christian joyfully submits to hardships and distresses, as he has seen his Redeemer do before him. In the time of trial and temptation, prayer is his refuge; it is his best and only comfort; it is taught him by the word and example of Jesus Christ in the garden of Gethsemani. Poor, and exercised in labours from his youth, Jesus is ready to do and suffer still more, according to the divine decrees; he makes no prayer but in conformity to his Father's will, and offers himself to drink the bitter cup which was prepared for him, becoming obedient for us unto death, even the death of the cross.

Jesus taken by the Jews.—Matt. xxvi.

[A.D. 34.]

After our blessed Lord had ended his prayer, he came to his disciples for the third time, and said, Arise, let us go, the traitor is at hand; and while he was yet speaking, behold, Judas, at the head of a rude rabble with lanterns, clubs, and swords, entered the garden. It was a place well known to the traitor, for he had frequently accompanied his Master thither, when he went to pray. The soldiers did not know Jesus, and might have easily mistaken another for him if Judas had not agreed to give them a signal: the signal he agreed upon was a kiss: whomsoever I shall kiss, said he, that is the man; hold him fast. The traitor, therefore, upon entering the garden, went straight to Jesus, and saluted him with a kiss. Friend, said our blessed Saviour to him, for what art thou come? Is it with a kiss that thou betrayest the Son of Man? The multitude drew near, and Jesus, knowing all that was to happen, advanced to meet them. With a voice that bespoke his divinity, he asked them whom they wanted; and they answering, Jesus of Nazareth, he said, I am he. His words struck terror into them, they instantly drew back, and fell to the ground. From this single circumstance it appears that Jesus submitted to his enemies, not

for want of power, but by the free consent of his own will. He asked them a second time whom they wanted, and they repeated, Jesus of Nazareth. I have already told you, said he, that I am the person; if, therefore, you seek me, let these go their way unhurt. In the midst of danger Jesus seemed regardless of himself, and only anxious about his friends; and disdained not to become a supplicant for his disciples' safety, whilst he abandoned his own to the discretion of his enemies, as the executioners of his Father's will. St. Peter made some efforts to defend his divine Master, drew his sword, and striking at Malchus, a servant of the high priest, cut off his right ear. That was not the zeal nor the defence which our blessed Saviour required at that time: unwilling to give the least cause of complaint to his enemies, he miraculously healed the servant's ear, and reprimanded his apostle for having struck him. He stood not in need of human arms, when at his request the Father had legions of angels to defend him. The tribune, therefore, and his band laid hold of Jesus and bound him. Meek as a lamb which is led to the slaughter, he only said, that they came armed with swords and clubs, as if they had a robber to secure: that he had sat daily amongst them teaching in the temple, and no one had offered to touch him; but that it was now their hour, and the power of darkness. His disciples then left him and fled, like a scattered flock, which by some cruel stroke is bereft of its shepherd.

Jesus before Caiphas.—MATT. XXVI.
[A.D. 34.]

JESUS, being abandoned by his disciples, was dragged along by his enemies into the city, and led before Annas, the father-in-law of Caiphas, the high-priest for that year. Annas did not detain him very long, but sent him, bound as he was, to Caiphas' house, where the scribes and elders were assembled. The high-priest began to question him concerning his disciples and his doctrine. Jesus answered, that he had spoken openly to the world; that he had always delivered his doctrine in the synagogue and in the temple, and had taught nothing which was not publicly known; that he need only ask the people, and they would inform him of the things they had heard. Upon that, one of the servants who were standing by gave Jesus a blow, saying, Is it so thou answerest

the high-priest? To which Jesus meekly replied, If I have spoken wrong, tell me in what: if well, why dost thou strike me? The chief-priest and whole council were fully resolved to procure his death; but to proceed with some outward form and appearance of justice, an accusation was to be brought against him, and witnesses produced in support of the charge. A mercenary crowd appeared, ready to swear as they should be directed; but the evidence they gave was inconsistent and contradictory: amongst other accusations of their own forging, two false witnesses declared they had heard him say he could destroy the temple of God, and in three days' time build it up again. Jesus was silent. Caiphas rose up, and asked him if he made no reply to the charge which these witnesses had brought against him. Jesus was still silent. Upon which the high-priest adjured him in the name of the living God, to tell him whether he were the Christ or not. Jesus then answered, If I tell you, you will not believe me; and if I ask you, you will neither answer nor let me go. Nevertheless, I say to you, hereafter you shall see the Son of Man sitting on the right-hand of the power of God, and coming in the clouds of heaven. Art thou then the Son of God? they all cried; and he answered, So you say, and I am. The high-priest hearing that, rent his garments and cried out, He hath blasphemed; there needs no farther proof; you have heard the blasphemy from his own mouth: what is your opinion? They all exclaimed, He is guilty of death and immediately left the court. Then it was that the soldiers and insolent rabble began to insult and torment the innocent Jesus. They tore off his beard and hair; they spat upon his face; they mocked and buffeted him for their diversion; they blindfolded his eyes, and in derision bade him guess who it was that struck him. Such was his treatment during the whole night.

St. Peter had followed his divine Master at a distance, from the garden of Gethsemani, and being desirous of seeing what the event might be, procured admittance into Caiphas' house. As he was standing amongst the servants, warming himself at the fire, a servant-maid came up and asked if he did not belong to Jesus of Nazareth. Peter no longer felt the courage or the zeal he had shown to defend his master in the garden, he trembled at the woman's voice, and denied him; and immediately the cock crew. He was again asked the same question, and again he not only denied his master, but moreover added, that he did not even know any such man. About an hour after a servant of the high-priest, and kinsman of Malchus, whose ear Peter had cut off, declared that he had seen him with Jesus in the garden: and others said, that his very language betrayed him, and proved him to be a Galilean. Peter then began to swear, and most solemnly protest that he did not so much as know the man they spoke of. The cock crew at that moment. Jesus at the same time turned round and looked at him. Peter then remembered what Jesus had told him after supper: stung with shame and remorse, he immediately went out, and wept bitterly

The fall of the great apostle is a striking instance of human weakness. Wonderful is the conduct of Almighty God, in permitting the man to fall whom he had chosen to be the head and chief pillar of his church. Peter's sin was not the result of a corrupt heart; it sprung from cowardice, not malice. He soon recollected himself, and eagerly seized the first grace that called him back to repentance. He rose the moment he became sensible of his fall: his actions spoke the unfeigned sentiments of a contrite heart. I hear not the voice of St. Peter lamenting his fall, says St. Ambrose, but I see his tears. Happy tears! whose silent flow obtained the sinner's pardon.

Jesus before Pilate.—MATT. xxvii.

[A.D. 34.]

THE Jewish council met again betimes in the morning, to finish their murderous plan against Jesus, and the result of their debate was, to accuse him before Pontius Pilate, the Roman governor. Jesus, therefore, like a public malefactor, bound in chains, was led from Caiphas to the governor's hall, where the chief priests and scribes were at the gate ready to accuse him; for they would not enter under the roof of an idolater, lest they would be defiled, and become unfit to partake of their paschal ceremonies. Pilate, therefore, went out to them, and asked what accusation they brought against the man. They answered, in general terms, that if he were not a malefactor, they would not have brought him thither. Pilate

would admit of no such indeterminate accusation, but bade them take and judge him according to their own laws. The Jews replied, that they had no longer the power of sentencing any man to death, of which they had judged him guilty, and began to accuse him of crimes against the state. We have found this man, said they, perverting our nation, forbidding tribute to be paid to Cæsar, and saying that he is Christ the king. Pilate went into the hall again, and calling Jesus, asked him if he was a king. Jesus answered, I am; but my kingdom is not of this world: if it were, my servants would certainly strive to prevent my being delivered to the Jews. For this I was born, and for this I came into the world, that I might give testimony to the truth. What is the truth? replied Pilate: and without waiting for an answer, went out again to the Jews, and declared that he found nothing to condemn in him. The Jews being apprehensive lest the judge should acquit him, grew more earnest, and tumultuously cried out, that he had been stirring the people up to sedition through the whole country of Judea, from Galilee to Jerusalem. Upon the mention of Galilee, Pilate asked if Jesus were not of that province, and being told he was, sent him away to Herod, who was king of Galilee. Herod was at that time in Jerusalem, and having heard much of Jesus Christ, was glad of the opportunity he had long wished for, of seeing him, and hoped he would work some miracle in his presence. When Jesus came before him, he asked him a variety of questions, but receiving no answer, treated him as a simpleton, exposed him in a white robe to the mockery of his guards, and sent him back to Pilate. Pilate, upon that

called together the chief priests, the magistrates, and people, and told them that there was no grounds for the charge they had brought against Jesus; that Herod, also, was of the same opinion, and had sent him back uncondemned as he went. Pilate, therefore, tried every expedient to set Jesus free, without exposing himself to danger; for he plainly saw that the Jews had accused him out of mere spite and envy. At the Paschal time, it was customary for the governor to release some one of the prisoners, as the people should choose. There was in prison a notorious criminal, by name Barrabas, who in a seditious riot had committed murder. With this miscreant, the worst and most odious of men, Jesus was set in competition for the people's choice. Pilate asked them which of the two he should release, Jesus or Barrabas. Not him, but Barrabas, was the cry. It was in vain to represent the innocence of the one, and the guilt of the other. Away with him, they cried; give us Barrabas: away with Jesus to be crucified. Pilate was distressed; he knew not which way to turn, doubtful whether to resist or yield. He was in hopes of moving them to compassion, and of inducing them to ask for the release of the innocent when they should see him suffer: by a barbarous and wicked policy he condemned Jesus to be scourged. Jesus was, therefore, led into the Prætor's court, stripped and tied to a pillar, and a whole band of soldiers ordered out to glut their cruelty upon him.

Judas seeing the violence of these proceedings, and being racked with remorse at the heinousness of his treason, carried back the thirty pieces of silver for which he had sold his Master to the chief priests and ancients, saying, I have sinned in betraying innocent blood. What is that to us? said they;

look thou to it. Upon which he threw down the money in the temple, went his way, and hanged himself in despair. Judas Iscariot, from being an apostle, became the worst of reprobates. From being unfaithful to the divine grace, he at first became a murmurer against the honours done to Jesus Christ: his avarice then prompted him to sell his master to the Jews, and despair made him finish all his other crimes by suicide. The enemy of our salvation still tries by the same arts to lead men gradually from their duty, and to plunge them into vice. In the beginning he conceals the malice of his temptations; he discloses not the abyss into which he intends to throw them; he dresses up the sin in such deceitful colours, that its enormity is not seen before it is consented to. He then artfully removes the veil, and unfolds the crime in its blackest shape; he so magnifies the shape or the difficulty of penance, so exaggerates the rigours of divine justice, that he frightens the sinner from repentance, and drives him to despair. Not to fall into the dismal gulf, grievous sinners ought to dwell no longer upon the enormous crimes they have committed, than it may help them to repent; they ought by turns to relieve the mind, and look up to the divine mercy. God is always good and merciful to the repenting sinner: he who has suffered and died for sinners never rejects the sighs of an humble and contrite heart.

Behold the Man!—Matt. xxvii.

[A.D. 34.]

When the soldiers had satiated their barbarity with whips and scourges upon the body of Jesus, they proceeded to other acts of cruelty and insult. They wove a crown of sharp thorns and set it upon his head; they threw an old purple garment round his shoulders, and put a reed, by way of sceptre, in his right hand; they bent their knee in derision, as before a mock king; they spat upon him, they smote him

on the face, and taking the reed from his hand, they struck him on the head, saying, Hail! king of the Jews! The lamentable plight to which Jesus Christ was then reduced, moved the heart of Pilate, and he was in hopes that the sight of so piteous an object might also move the Jews. With that view he took him up into a conspicuous place, and showed him to the people, saying, Behold the man! Vested

with the crown of thorns and purple garment, Jesus was no sooner seen, than the cries of an enraged rabble were heard from every side, calling out, Crucify him! crucify him! Pilate pleaded for him, and asked what harm he had done;

he has made himself the Son of God, they cried, and according to the law he therefore ought to die. When Pilate heard this, he grew more and more alarmed: he entered into the hall again, and asked Jesus from whence he was; Jesus gave him no answer. Dost thou not speak to me, said Pilate, and knowest thou not that I have power either to crucify or release thee? Thou wouldst not have any power against me, replied our Saviour, unless it were given thee from above. The Jews continued crying out to Pilate, If thou release this man, thou art not Cæsar's friend. Pilate therefore led Jesus forth about the sixth hour and sitting down upon the judgment-seat, said to the Jews, Behold your king! Away with him! cried out the Jews, away with him! Crucify him! Shall I then crucify your king! said Pilate. We have no king but Cæsar, replied the priests; and whosoever maketh himself a king speaketh against Cæsar. These words awakened the fears of an ambitious courtier, who was not disposed to risk either his fortune or his favour with the emperor, for the sake of doing justice and protecting the innocent. He called for a basin of water, and, as if he could wash himself clean of the crime which he was going to complete, he washed his hands before the people, and declared himself innocent of the blood of that just man. Let his blood fall upon us and upon our children, cried the hardened Jews. Pilate then released Barrabas, according to their request, and delivered Jesus unto them to be crucified.

This weak but barbarous compliance of Pontius Pilate, against the dictates of his own conscience, is a melancholy proof of the sway which ambition and self-interest have over the minds of worldly men. The known innocence and sacred character of Jesus Christ, had little influence upon a man who was ready to make a sacrifice of every thing but his own fortune. Pilate had indeed some inbred notions of equity; he had naturally an inclination to protect oppressed innocence; but those honest sentiments were banished from his breast the very moment he was threatened with the emperor's displeasure; nor could they be recalled by any warning that his wife had been inspired to give him. Great resolution is necessary not to be drawn from our duty by a desire of pleasing men; a great struggle is required not to be borne down the torrent of our passions, when pushed by worldly fears and interest. The advice of friends, and our own reflections, are insufficient, without the grace of Jesus Christ, to aid and support our feeble efforts. Pilate had the grace, which was abundantly sufficient to have preserved him from the sin, but his own co-operation was wanting. It is our duty, therefore, to watch and pray, not only that we may receive the graces of Jesus Christ, but that we may be also faithful in co-operating with the graces we receive.

Jesus carries his Cross.—MATT. xxvii.

[A.D. 34.]

THE Jews having at length extorted the sentence which they had been so obstinately bent upon, carried it into immediate execution. They had already prepared a huge cross, the ignominious instrument of their barbarity: they laid it upon the shoulders of our blessed Lord, to carry to the mountain of Calvary, the place of their public executions. Two

thieves were condemned to be crucified at the same time; so that literally fulfilled were the words of Isaiah, saying, that he should be ranked with sinners. Jesus therefore went forth bearing his cross, burdened with our iniquities, as the prophet said, and carrying all the grief that a sinful world had heaped upon him. He went forth from the holy city of Jerusalem towards the mountain, amidst the hisses of an insulting multitude, that crowded round to be spectators of his sufferings. His sufferings of the morning had already drained his strength; he was too enfeebled to stand under the heavy cross, and to go on as fast as they would have him. Therefore, laying hold of one Simon of Cyrene, they made him take and carry the cross after Jesus, to the mount.

The cross, or the yoke of Christ, is borne by two: by Jesus Christ, and the Christian who suffers for Christ's sake. Simon the Cyrenean was engaged to help the Son of God in carrying his cross; God himself enables us to carry ours. By his grace he so strengthens us in our afflictions, that we not only bear them with ease, but receive them with a kind of inward satisfaction. Comforted by his example, let us resignedly submit to the cross that is laid upon us, and in silent penitence follow our divine leader to the holy mountain: he suffers us not to be loaded above our strength; by spiritual comforts he sweetens his service and makes the burden light.

Many devout persons, and amongst them the pious women who were unshaken in the service of Jesus Christ, followed him as close as they could, and by their tears and sighs expressed how much they shared in his sufferings. He turned about to them as he went along, not for the sake of receiving any consolation from them, for it is not to creatures we must turn in our affliction, but he turned to give them comfort. Ye daughters of Jerusalem, said he, weep not for me, but weep for yourselves and children. For the time will come when it shall be said, happy are the barren, and happy are the breasts which have not given suck. Men shall call upon the hills to cover them, and upon the mountains to hide them. For if to the green wood they do these things, what will happen to the dry? Such tenderness of affection, expressed by the Son of God in such circumstances to his faithful followers, cannot fail of moving every Christian who will seriously consider. If we only remember who Jesus is, what he suffers, and for whom, we shall be ashamed to complain of the slight and passing sufferings that fall to our share. Or should weak nature be still tempted to murmur or to grow impatient, we must then reflect that the sufferings of this life are but short: that if we share in the sufferings of our Redeemer, and bear them as we ought, we shall likewise share with him in his glory.

Jesus upon Mount Calvary.—MATT. xxvii.

[A.D. 34.]

JESUS being come to the top of Mount Calvary, on which he was to offer the great sacrifice of himself for the world's redemption, was immediately presented with a draught of wine mixed with gall: he did but taste and refused to drink it. He was then stripped of his clothes, stretched upon the cross, his sacred hands and feet bored through with nails, and

fastened to the wood. It was the sixth hour of the day, and a mournful darkness spread itself over the face of heaven. The cross was set upright, and fixed in the earth; the whole weight of his body bearing upon the bleeding wounds of his hands and feet; above his head was an inscription, written in Hebrew, Greek, and Latin, that all might know him to be Jesus of Nazareth, King of the Jews. On each side of him, as if he were of all malefactors the most notorious, was crucified a thief. He hung in the middle, an adorable spectacle to the world, to the angels, and to men; Jesus Christ, the mediator of peace between earth and heaven, bleeding and dying for the love of mankind. The people with unfeeling heart stood looking on, and the rulers with them derided him in his torments. They passed under his cross, scornfully wagging their heads, and exclaiming, Thou who canst destroy the temple of God, and in three days build it up again, now save thyself; if thou art the Son of God, come down from the cross, and we will believe thee. The chief priests and elders of the people turned his very miracles into a contempt of his power. He saved others they cried;

let him now save himself; he trusted in God, let God now deliver him if he will, for he said, I am the Son of God. Jesus thus insulted and blasphemed amidst his sufferings, sought no revenge; his thoughts were the thoughts of peace; breathing charity and benevolence for his cruel enemies, he cried, *Father, forgive them, for they know not what they do.* And one of the thieves who were hanging by him, blasphemed like the rest, saying, If thou be Christ, save thyself and us. But the other rebuked his wicked companion, and proclaiming the innocence of Jesus Christ, begged to be remembered by him, when he should come into his kingdom: Jesus answered him in these comfortable words: *Amen, I say to thee, this day thou shalt be with me in paradise.* Simeon's prophecy to the Virgin Mother was now fulfilled. Pierced with a sword of grief, Mary approached her agonizing son, and stood at the foot of the cross with John, the beloved disciple. Jesus looked down and saw them; with expiring voice he recommended them to each other: to his mother he said, *Woman, behold thy son;* and to John, *Behold thy mother.* To the afflictions which Jesus then suffered in every part of his body, nothing could be added but those of his soul. Covered with wounds from the sole of his foot to the crown of his head, he was truly that man of pains and sorrows, as Isaiah had described him. A single ray of the beatific vision which his soul always enjoyed, would have cheered away all his griefs at once, had he not miraculously suspended its influence at that hour, and denied himself every consolation that could sooth his bitter agony. The mysterious dereliction of our blessed Lord upon the cross, is a fitter subject for pious meditation than description. It was extreme; it forced this tender exclamation from him: *My God, my God, why hast thou forsaken me!* Jesus knowing that all things were now accomplished, said, *I thirst;* upon which the soldiers dipping a sponge into vinegar, and fastening it to a reed, put it to his mouth, and when he had taken the vinegar, he said, *It is consummated:* every circumstance which the prophets had foretold, relating to his mortal life and passion, was now fulfilled. Jesus Christ had hung near three hours upon the cross; his sacred humanity was spent with suffering; nothing more remained than to pay the last tribute due to his heavenly Father for the redemption of the world. The sun was eclipsed, and universal darkness sat upon the earth till the ninth hour; the earth quaked, the graves were opened, the rocks split asunder, and the veil of the temple rent from top to bottom. Jesus Christ at the last gasp, and in the agony of death, with a loud voice, exclaimed, *Father, into thy hands I commend my Spirit;* and saying this, bowed his head and expired.

The mystery of the passion and death of Jesus Christ upon the cross, is so far removed above the reach of human understanding, that unless the divine Spirit takes away the veil from our eyes, in vain we shall strive to comprehend it. Christ dies upon a cross, says St. Bernard, and thereby merits all our love; he gives us his holy Spirit and thereby excites our love. By the help of faith we may contemplate Jesus Christ crucified; but without the gift of his holy Spirit we shall not love him. Let us then with gratitude approach the tree of life, and with affection gather the fruit thereof. Since the Son of God was pleased to give us his life, there is no other mercy which we may not hope to obtain, through his blood and passion; for with him there is plentiful redemption.

Jesus in the Sepulchre.—MATT. xxvii.

[A.D. 34.]

THE wonderful sacrifice of the cross being accomplished, the prodigies and signs that accompanied it struck the spectators with religious awe; they changed their insults into sighs, and returned knocking their breasts, into the city. The centurion who commanded the soldiers upon the mountain had been particularly attentive to everything that had passed, and publicly declared the man whom he saw expire, to be truly the Son of God. The sacred body of our Saviour remained hanging upon the cross, till Pilate, at the request of the Jews, gave orders about it; for the next day being the great and solemn Sabbath of the Paschal week, the Jews petitioned Pilate, that the bodies might be taken down from their crosses and carried away that evening. The soldiers therefore went and broke the legs of the two thieves, to despatch them. When they came to Jesus and saw him already dead, they did not break his legs; and the words of Exodus, saying, You shall not break a bone of him, were fulfilled. But one of the soldiers with the thrust of a spear opened his side from whence there issued out blood and water. Joseph of Arimathea, a good and upright man, and a disciple of Jesus, went in boldly to Pilate, and begged the body of Jesus. Having obtained this request, he repaired straight to the mountain with Nicodemus, and took the

body of our blessed Lord, which they wrapped in fine linen, and perfumed with a precious mixture of myrrh and aloes, according to the custom of the Jews. There was a garden nigh, and in that garden a new monument proper for the interment of the dead, in which nobody had been yet buried. Thither they carried the sacred body of our Lord; there they decently laid it, and rolled a huge stone against the mouth of the sepulchre.

St. Chrysostom is charmed with the courage of Joseph and Nicodemus, who publicly declared themselves, on this solemn occasion, to be the disciples of Christ, which their fears had hitherto hindered them from doing. They set their fears aside; they forgot all human respect, when piety to their deceased Lord called for their service. They lost no time, they spared no cost, they carried their precious spices in profusion: happy was their lot in having the body of their dear Redeemer for the object of their charity. From the example of these holy disciples, St. Chrysostom exhorts his people to a practice of the like virtues; he tells them to provide perfumes for the body of Jesus Christ. For our poor and virtuous brethren, says he, are the living members of Christ; we piously and meritoriously pour out the odours of charity upon them, as often as we compassionate them in their sufferings, and relieve them in their wants. Some one or other of them daily stands in need of our help, and may be comforted by us: what we do to the least of them, we do to Jesus Christ himself.

Resurrection of Jesus Christ.—MATT. XXVIII.

[A.D. 34.]

THE Scribes and Pharisees were not satisfied, though they saw Jesus in the grave. They remembered what he had said about his rising again upon the third day, and although they did not believe the prediction themselves, yet they were afraid it might make some impression upon others. They pretended to suspect some design in the disciples of stealing away their Master's body, and of spreading a report of his being risen from the dead. Therefore, they desired Pilate that he would order a guard round the sepulchre, to prevent any one's coming near it for three days. You have a guard, said Pilate, go and dispose of them as you shall judge fit. They went immediately and made the sepulchre sure by setting a seal upon the stone, and placing the soldiers round. They fancied that by those precautions they should destroy the notion of Christ's resurrection; and by those precautions they established its belief beyond the possibility of doubt. Early in the morning of the third day, there was a great earthquake; for an angel of the Lord descended from heaven, rolled back the stone, and seated himself upon it. His countenance was as lightning, and his raiment as snow. The guards were struck with terror, and became as dead men. But, upon recollecting themselves, some of them went into the city and related to the chief priests what they had seen. The priests, alarmed at the report, assembled the council, and consulted together what to do. They agreed to stop the soldiers' mouths with money if they could, and to bribe them to say, that during the night they had fallen asleep, and Jesus' disciples came in the interim and stole away his body. The soldiers took the money, and conformably to their instructions, published the fictitious story, which was industriously spread amongst the people. Mary Magdalene and some other holy women, whose piety was never weary in the service of Jesus Christ, went betimes in the morning to perfume the dead body of our Lord. They asked one another, before they came to the place, how they should be able to roll away the stone from the entrance of the monument, for the stone was very great; but at their approach they perceived the stone was rolled back, and the entrance open. They saw an angel in the shape of a young man, clothed in white, who thus accosted them: Fear not, I know you seek Jesus of Nazareth, who was crucified; he is risen, as he said; he is not here; behold the place where he lay; go quickly and tell his disciples that he is risen and will go before them into Galilee, where they shall see him. The women immediately hastened to perform their commission, and upon their report, St. Peter and St. John repaired to the monument: Mary Magdalene went also back with them. They entered the monument, saw the linen cloths lying, and the handkerchief which had been about his head, wrapt up apart, but being able to discover nothing more, departed again to their home. For they were not yet sufficiently enlightened to understand the Scriptures concerning the resurrection. Mary Magdalene remained after they were gone, standing and weeping at the mouth of the sepulchre. Eager to find him whom she loved, she stooped down, and looking into the tomb, perceived two angels in white apparel, sitting one at the head and the other at the feet where the sacred body had lain. They asked her why she wept. Because they have taken away my Lord, said she, and I know not where they have laid him. She turned herself back, and seeing a man there standing unknown to her, took him for the gardener, and said, Sir, if you have taken him away, tell me where you have laid him. Jesus said, Mary! Mary knew him at the word, and in an ecstacy of joy, turning round, answered him, Rabboni; which is to say,

Master. Do not touch me, said Jesus to her, for I am not yet ascended to my Father, but tell my brethren that I ascend to my Father and your Father, to my God and

your God. The love and perseverance which the pious Magdalene expressed in seeing her Redeemer, made her worthy to find him. The mystery of a resurrection so glorious to Jesus Christ, and so interesting to us, is the confirmation of our faith, and the foundation of our hope. Jesus Christ died for our redemption, and is again risen for our justification. By this we know, that if we suffer with Jesus, with Jesus we shall also rise. The certain hope of a resurrection from the grave, to a state of immortality, is the Christian's comfort in affliction, and his encouragement in hardships. The light and passing tribulations of this world, if rightly borne, entail upon us an immense and eternal weight of glory in the next.

Disciples at Emmaus.—LUKE, xxiv.

[A.D. 34.]

THE holy women, in obedience to the angel's commands, being on their way from the monument to the disciples, were met by Jesus, who said to them, All hail! They went up, took hold of his feet, and adored him. He suffered them not to remain long there, but bade them go and deliver the message they were carrying to his brethren. Two of his disciples happened to be going on the same day to Emmaus, a small town between seven and eight miles distant from Jerusalem; they talked over the late transactions in Jerusalem as they walked along, when our blessed Saviour, in form and habit of a traveller, came up and joined them. He did not let them know who he was, but as any other traveller might

have done, desired them to tell him the subject of their discourse, and why they looked so sorrowful. To which one of them, whose name was Cleophas, made answer, Is it possible you should be the only stranger in Jerusalem not to know what has happened there within these few days. He asked them, What? and they replied, concerning Jesus of Nazareth. He was a great prophet, continued they, both in word and work, and we hoped he would have redeemed Israel. But our chief priests and princes caused him to be apprehended, condemned, and executed upon a disgraceful cross. This is the third day since his death, and we are at a loss to know what we are to expect or hope for. Some women of ours have been this morning to visit his tomb, and have alarmed us with their accounts. They could not find the body, but saw an apparition of angels, who informed them that Jesus was not to be sought amongst the dead, that he was not there; that he had risen, and was alive again. Upon this information, some of our brethren also hastened to the sepulchre, and found everything as the women had related. O foolish and senseless men! exclaimed our Saviour, how dull are you in your understanding, and how slow is your belief! According to the prophets was it not necessary that Christ should suffer all these things, and so enter into his glory? He then quoted to them the different passages of holy writ, which Moses and the prophets had spoken of him, and which he graciously interpreted to them. When they came near Emmaus, he made a show as if he had been going further on; they represented to him, that the day was too far spent for him to think of going any further that evening; they invited him to remain with them, they pressed, and in the end prevailed. Jesus therefore entered with them into a house, where being at supper he took bread which he blessed, broke, and gave to them. By that action, which the holy fathers think was a sacramental communion, the eyes of the two disciples were immediately opened; they saw and knew him, but enjoyed his company no longer, for he that moment vanished from their sight. They communicated their thoughts upon the matter to one another, and mentioned the glow their hearts were in while he explained the Scripture to them; they wished to impart the joyful tidings to their brethren as soon as possible and therefore set off that very hour back again to Jerusalem, where they found the eleven apostles with some others assembled together, to whom they related what had passed in the way, and how they had known him in the breaking of the bread.

From the circumstance of this history, we may gather how agreeable to Christ are the conversations of his followers upon pious and religious subjects. No subject is so worthy of a Christian's thoughts, as what God has done and suffered for us; and if we entertain a due sense of our Redeemer's love, we shall not be backward to express our gratitude; for out of the abundance of the heart the mouth speaketh. The two disciples discoursed as they walked along, upon the passion and resurrection of Jesus Christ. Drawn by their discourse, Jesus Christ joined their company, asked them questions, that they might repeat what they had said, expounded the Scripture to them upon that subject, enlightened their minds with new rays of faith, and warmed their hearts with a glow of piety and holy love.

Christ's Charge to St. Peter.—JOHN, xxi.

[A.D. 34.]

ON the same day of his resurrection, when it was late, and the chamber doors were shut where the apostles kept together for fear of the Jews, Jesus suddenly appeared standing in the midst of them, and said, Peace be to you. Seeing them in a fright and troubled, as if they saw a spirit, he asked

them why they were frightened, and why such thoughts arose in their hearts. Behold my hands and feet, said he; feel and see that it is I, for a spirit hath not flesh and bones, as you see me have. He therefore said again, Peace be with you: as my Father sent me, so do I also send you. After which he reathed upon them, and said, Receive ye the Holy Ghost: whose sins you shall forgive, they are forgiven; and whose sins you shall retain, they are retained. At his last supper, four days before, he had given to his apostles the power of consecrating his body and his blood in the sacrament of the holy Eucharist; and here he gave them a power to forgive sins in the sacrament of penance, and thereby completed their sacerdotal character. Thomas, one of the eleven, was absent when Jesus came, and being afterwards told by the other disciples that they had seen the Lord, would not believe them; and unless I shall see in his hands the prints of the nails, said he, and put my finger into the place of the nails, and

my hand into his side, I will not believe. After eight days Jesus came again to his disciples in the room, whilst the doors were shut as before, and saluted them with a Peace be with you. Thomas was then present; and as if it had been solely on his account that Jesus had come, he turned to him and said, Put in thy finger hither, and see my hands; bring hither thy hand, and put it into my side, and be not incredulous, but faithful. Thomas immediately exclaimed, My Lord, and my God! To whom our blessed Saviour said, Thou has believed, Thomas, because thou hast seen: happy they who have not seen, and yet believe.

Jesus Christ showed himself for a third time to his apostles, as they were fishing in the lake of Tiberias; and then it was

that he fulfilled the promise which he had made to St. Peter, (*Matt.* xvi.) of building his church upon him, as upon a rock, against which no storms of persecution, and no powers of hell ever should prevail. Simon Peter and Thomas, with the two sons of Zebedee and Nathaniel, and two other disciples, being fishing in the sea of Galilee, Jesus came and stood upon the shore, without being known by them. He called out, and bade them cast their net on the right side of the ship, where they would catch plenty of fish, for they had yet taken none. They cast their net as he directed, and by the wonderful capture they made, St. John knew it to be the Lord: upon which St. Peter girted his coat round him, and plunging into the sea, swam ashore. The rest came in the ship. As soon as they landed they saw hot coals lying, and a fish laid thereon, and bread. Jesus invited them to come and dine: no one presumed to ask him who he was, for they knew him to be the Lord. When they had dined, Jesus said to Simon Peter, Simon, son of John, lovest thou me more than these do? Yes, Lord, replied Peter, thou knowest I love thee. *Feed my lambs*, said Jesus; and asked him again, Simon, son of John, lovest thou me? Peter made the same answer as before, and Jesus repeated to him the same charge to *feed his lambs*. He said to him the third time, Simon, son of John, lovest thou me? Peter, full of humility and diffident of himself, was grieved to hear his Master ask a third time whether he loved him, and modestly replied, Lord, thou knowest all things, thou knowest that I love thee. Jesus then said, *Feed my sheep*.

To feed, in the style of holy Scripture, is to guide, rule, and govern, as St. Ambrose and others take notice: and to feed the lambs and the sheep of Christ, is undoubtedly to have the supreme spiritual power of governing and directing the whole flock of Christ in all matters belonging to faith. This is the charge which our blessed Saviour thrice repeated to his apostle, bidding him feed his lambs and feed his sheep; for this he changed his name into Peter, which signifies a rock, and for this he prayed that his faith might never fail. Upon this ground the spiritual supremacy of St. Peter and his successors in the pontifical chair has, in every age and in every country been reverenced and acknowledged by the holy fathers, as their writings show: namely, Tertullian, St. Cyprian, St. Leo, St. Jerome, St. Austin, St. Chrysostom, and the first General Councils, particularly that of Chalcedon.

Ascension of our Lord.—Acts, i.

[A.D. 34.]

Our blessed Lord remained forty days upon earth after his resurrection, appearing sometimes to all his apostles at once, and sometimes only to some, that he might thereby fully convince them of his being risen, and wean them by degrees from his corporeal presence. During that time, he instructed them in the nature and the use of those spiritual powers which he had imparted to them for the good of mankind. What those instructions were in particular, the evangelists do not mention. St. Luke in general terms says, that he spoke to them of the kingdom of God, which, according to St. Gregory, is his church upon earth. St. Matthew and St. Mark finish their evangelical history with these remarkable words of our blessed Saviour to his apostles, saying, To me is given all power in heaven and on earth ; go ye, therefore, teach all nations, baptizing them in the name of the Father, and of the Son, and of the Holy Ghost. He who shall believe and be baptized, shall be saved ; but he who shall not believe, shall be condemned. Teach them, therefore, to observe everything that I have commanded you ; for, behold, I am always with you, even to the end of the world.

Jesus Christ had now finished the work for which he came down from heaven and dwelt among us. He had enlightened the world by his doctrine, and redeemed it by his death ; by his miracles he had confirmed the truth of his revealed religion ; he had established his church, which he commands all to hear ; he had promised to assist his church with the Spirit of Truth to the end of ages ; he had appointed his vicar as an universal pastor, to preside over the church in his name and to feed his flock, both sheep and lambs, in his absence: nothing more remained than to take possession of that seat of bliss, which he had merited for his own sacred humanity and us. Therefore, on the fortieth day after his resurrection from the dead, he led his disciples forth to the Mountain of Olives, near Jerusalem ; he there gave them his last blessing and raised himself from the earth towards heaven. They fixed their eyes upon him, as he ascended through the air, till an intervening cloud received him out of their sight. By his own divine power he ascended into heaven, where he sits

at the right hand of the Father; being, as he always shall and ever will be, the same consubstantial and co-eternal God with him and the Holy Ghost in one and the same divine nature. The apostles kept their eyes still fixed on heaven, when two young men in white apparel came and asked them why they stood thus gazing at the heavens: the Jesus whom you have seen taken from you into heaven, said they, will in the same manner come again from thence to judge the living and the dead.

Trivial is the pomp of this vain world to a devout and fervent Christian, when he contemplates the glory of Jesus Christ, and considers the never-ending happiness of the citizens of heaven. Heaven is the object on which we ought to turn our eyes; thither ought our hearts and wishes to aspire. We never should forget, that the country to which we belong, that the bread which nourishes our souls, that the grace which supports our virtues, that the happiness which we hope to partake of, and the Head of which we are members, is in heaven. The spiritual treasures which we here enjoy, and the temporal advantages which we receive from creatures, are appointed us by Almighty God, as helps towards our last end. It was to open us an entrance into heaven that Christ shed his blood; it was to draw our hearts thither that he ascended before the last day. The heavenly princes were commanded to lift up their eternal gates, and the King of glory, the Lord of powers, entered into his kingdom, which he had acquired by his sufferings and death.

Descent of the Holy Ghost.—ACTS, ii.

[A.D. 34.]

OUR blessed Saviour, before his ascension, had commanded his apostles not to stir from Jerusalem, till they should be endued with the virtue of the Holy Ghost, whom he promised to send them. In obedience to that order they returned from Mount Olivet into the city, where they retired into an upper room, and persevered unanimously in prayer with the women, and Mary the mother of Jesus. During that interval St Peter began to exercise the prerogative of his apostolical supremacy; he informed his brethren, that according to the holy Scriptures they must fill up the place of Judas Iscariot who, by his traitorous prevarication, had fallen from the apostleship, and must, therefore, choose some one of them who had followed Jesus from the time of his baptism to the day of his ascension, and had been witness of his resurrection. Two were immediately nominated in preference to all others, Matthias, and Joseph, named the Just. To determine which of the two was to be preferred, they had recourse to lots, devoutly praying to Almighty God, that he would be pleased to manifest his will to them. The lot fell upon Matthias and he was consequently associated with the other eleven apostles.

When the time of Pentecost, that is to say, the term of fifty days after Easter, was accomplished, a sudden noise was heard, as of a mighty wind rushing from the heavens, which filled the whole house where the apostles were assembled. Over the head of each one there appeared the form of a fiery tongue, and all of them were immediately replenished with the Holy Ghost. From that moment they became endowed with the gift of tongues, and they spoke in different languages, as the Holy Ghost inspired. The apostles were no longer those timid and pusillanimous men who had hitherto trembled at every noise and skulked from danger; they rushed into the streets of Jerusalem and, in defiance of their enemies, preached the crucified Jesus. As soon as it was noised abroad, the people ran in multitudes together and were amazed to hear, each one, his own language spoken by Galileans. Jerusalem at that time was crowded with Jews, devout men out of every nation under heaven, who were come to celebrate the feast of Pentecost. Astonished to hear the apostles, in various tongues, speaking the wonderful works of God, they asked one another what it meant; while others, in derision said, that they were full of new wine. St. Peter

rose up with the eleven, to refute the calumny: in a pathetic discourse he informed his hearers, that what they saw and wondered at, was not the effect of wine, but of the Holy Spirit, which God had promised by his prophet Joel to pour out upon his people. He expatiated upon the miracles, the death and resurrection of Jesus Christ, in a language so inspired and persuasive, that no less than three thousand, upon conviction, embraced the true faith, and were baptized in the name of Jesus Christ, for the remission of their sins.

On that day of Pentecost, when the law of Jesus Christ took place of the law of Moses, the church, the new Jerusalem, as St. John speaks in his Revelations, descended from heaven, like a bride decked out to meet the bridegroom; and

Jesus Christ, the eternal priest according to the order of Melchisedech, erected a new temple to the honour of his Father. The mystery of the death and resurrection of a God-man was announced to the various inhabitants of the earth who were then at Jerusalem, that no nation under the sun might be ignorant of it. On that day Jesus Christ victoriously triumphed over those who had nailed him to the cross; he convinced them that all their schemes against him had been vain, and were made to serve as means to accomplish the designs of God. On that day he planted his apostolic church as an everlasting monument of his victory: to the latest posterity that monument shall stand, and defy every effort that either man or devils can raise against it. The Spirit of Truth, if the promises of Christ are, as no one doubts, infallible, shall abide with the church, and teach her all truth to the end of the world.

Cure of the Lame Man.—Acts, iii.

[A.D. 34.]

The multitude of believers in Jerusalem became every day more and more numerous. Being as unanimous in charity as they were in their belief, they no longer retained any possessions which were not devoted to the common service of their brethren, so that they had no poor amongst them. Addicted to prayer and the pious exercises of their religion, they were not swayed by passion, nor led astray by private views; their chief concern was to serve and honour God; they took their meat with gladness and simplicity of heart. The admirable holiness of their lives, conjointly with the preaching and miracles of the apostles, commanded respect from their fellow-citizens. Of the many miracles wrought by the apostles in confirmation of their doctrine, that was the most memorable which St. Peter did in favour of a lame beggar. The holy apostle went with St. John at the ninth hour to perform his devotions in the temple. They entered at the gate which was called the beautiful, where a cripple from his mother's womb lay unable to move without help. The poor man fixed his eyes upon the apostles, as if he expected an alms. St. Peter told him, that he was not possessed either of gold or silver, but that he would give what he had, and forthwith commanded him in the name of Jesus Christ, to rise and walk, taking hold of his right hand at the

same time, and lifting him up. The man that instant leaped upon his feet, stood firm upon his legs, and walked joyfully with the apostles into the temple, giving thanks to God for the favour he had received by their means. Struck with wonder and amazement to see the man so instantaneously cured, the people cast their eyes upon the two apostles, which St. Peter observing, said: Ye men of Israel, why do you wonder, and why do you look at us, as if by our own power we had made this man to walk? The God of Abraham, of Isaac, and of Jacob, has glorified his Son Jesus, whom the prophets foretold, whom the God of our Fathers sent amongst you for your salvation, out whom you and your rulers accused before Pilate, and crucified. But I know, brethren, that you did it through ignorance, or the Author of Life you never would have put to death. Repent, therefore, and be converted, that your sins may be blotted out. While he was thus speaking to the people, the priests, with the Sadducees and officers of the temple, came up, and being exasperated at the subject of their discourse, commanded silence, and took both him and St. John into custody. The great council of the Jews the next morning ordered the two apostles to be brought before them. Upon their appearance, they asked them by what power and in whose name they spoke and acted as they did. St. Peter answered, In the name of our Lord Jesus Christ; for there is no other name under heaven given to men, whereby we can be saved. He it is whom you crucified, whom God hath raised from the dead, and by whom this man hath recovered the use of his limbs. The man was present; every one saw him standing upright upon his feet; his cure was a fact not to be denied. They ordered the apostles to withdraw, and began to confer amongst themselves how they were to act in this case. They could not dispute the miracle, and to punish the apostles for having relieved a poor cripple, might cause a tumult among the people; they therefore agreed to exert their endeavours in suppressing the report, and to have nothing more said either of Jesus or of the miracle. Upon this conclusion they called in the apostles, whom they thought to terrify by menaces and to silence by authority, bade them begone, and be careful for the future not to speak nor teach in the name of Jesus. The apostles were not to be intimidated by such threats. We leave you to judge, said they in reply, whether it be right to hear you, rather than God. We cannot but speak the things which we have seen and heard. This answer of the apostles deserves to be well considered by every Christian; the maxim is indispensable in those circumstances where God commands one thing and man another: it can never be justifiable to obey men in preference to God.

Ananias and Saphira.—ACTS, V.

[A.D. 34.]

ST. PETER and St. John being acquitted by the Jewish council, went to find out their friends, whom they knew to be in great concern about them. They related how the whole affair had been conducted, and how it ended. The brethren with one accord lifted up their voice to God, in thanksgiving, and devoutly prayed that he would continue to protect his servants, and inspire them with confidence to resist the impious who had combined against the Lord and against his Christ. When they had finished their prayer, the place shook wherein they were assembled; they felt the invigorating effects of the Holy Ghost; they were filled with new courage, and they preached the word of God with confidence. The multitude of believers had but one heart and one soul. No one had anything belonging to him, which was not at the service of the community; and they who sold their lands or houses, brought the money and laid it at the apostles' feet to be distributed as the wants of particulars should require. Charmed by the example of such virtues and struck by the miracles of the apostles, great numbers flocked to the standard of Jesus Christ. St. Peter is celebrated by the inspired writer, as the chief and most active instrument in God's hand for those great achievements; his power of curing the sick seems to have had no bounds. The inhabitants of the country and cities round about, brought forth their sick into the streets, and laid them on beds and couches, that the shadow, at least, of that illustrious apostle might reach them as he passed along, and heal their infirmities.

While the church thus smiled with success, and the joy of the Holy Ghost was diffused through the hearts of the faithful, a melancholy disaster alarmed them with the terror of God's righteous judgments. A certain man named Ananias, with his wife Saphira, had sold a field, and brought to the apostles a part only of the money which they had received for it, and laid it at St. Peter's feet as if it had been the whole sum. The inspired apostle knew the fraud which the unhappy man had committed, and thus upbraided him for it: Why, Ananias, hast thouyielded to the temptation of Satan? Why hast thou lied to the Holy Ghost, and fraudulently retained a part of the price for which thou hast sold thy land? Wert thou not at liberty to sell, or not to sell thy field, as thou shouldst think fit? It was thine own. And after thou hadst sold it, was it not in thy power to make thy promise or not? Why hast thou prevaricated in thy heart? Thou hast not lied to men, but to God. Thunder-struck at these words, Ananias fell down, and gave

up the ghost. The young men who were present, immediately rose up, and carried him out to be buried. About three hours after in came Saphira, having no suspicion of her husband's death. Tell me, woman, said St. Peter to her, whether you sold the land for so much? And she answering, Yes, he severely rebuked her for the wicked agreement she had made with her husband, and denounced the vengeance of God against her for having tempted him. Behold the men, said he, who have carried off thy dead husband to the grave, are at the door, and they shall carry thee out in the same manner. She that instant fell down before his feet and expired. The young men coming in and finding her dead, carried away the body and buried it beside her husband.

The sudden death of these two unhappy Christians is a manifest proof of the guilt which is contained in a breach of promise made to God. God declares that he hates rapine in a holocaust, and tells us to be faithful in rendering to him the vow we have made. The severe judgment which befel Ananias and Saphira, says St. Austin, ought to caution Christians against all such fraudulent proceedings, as are inconsistent with the truth and simplicity of the gospel. He calls their action a sacrilegious fraud, and St. Chrysostom says, it was a theft of what was consecrated to God. It matters not by whom the thing was given, whether by themselves or by any other: the moment it was appropriated to the divine service, it belonged to God, and no one after that could presume to destroy or take it to himself without sacrilege.

Martyrdom of St. Stephen.—ACTS, vii.

[A. D. 34.]

OF all the Jewish sectaries that opposed the progress of the gospel, the Sadducees were the most violent. Stung with envy to see the people so eager in embracing a new doctrine, they caused the apostles to be apprehended and cast into the common prison. In the night an angel of the Lord opening the doors led them out, and bade them preach next day to the people in the temple. The Jewish elders met in the morning, and sent their ministers with orders to bring the

apostles before them. The ministers repaired to the prison and unbarred the doors, but found no prisoners within: they went back and related how they had found the guard upon duty, the prison well secured, and the prisoners gone. The elders were thrown into the greatest confusion at this report and knew not what measures to take, when a person came to inform them that the men whom they had put in prison were then actually preaching in the temple. An officer was despatched to summon them. The apostles ready to obey every order of the magistrates that was consistent with their duty to God, followed the officer into the council. The high-priest reproached them with disobedience to the former orders which had been given them, not to mention the name of Jesus among the people, nor to disturb the public peace with any new doctrine. St. Peter answered in the same words as before, that God was to be obeyed preferably to men. The answer threw the council into a violent ferment; they swelled with rage, they stormed and threatened the apostles with instant death, when Gamaliel, a wise and prudent Pharisee. rose up to make them hear reason, and to calm their passions. With a soft and soothing eloquence he dissuaded them from acts of violence, and convinced them that they had no other measure to take than that of moderation; that if this new doctrine was the invention of men, it would of itself soon fall to naught; but if it sprung from God, that it would be rashness in them to oppose it. They agreed to follow his advice, and to dismiss the apostles, after having scourged and strictly charged them never to speak again in the name of Jesus. The apostles went from the presence of the council rejoicing, because they had been accounted worthy to suffer reproach for the name of Jesus. Their zeal was not damped by suffering, they preached daily in the temple, and from house to house ceased not to teach the faith and doctrine of Jesus Christ.

Soon after this, some discontentedness arose amongst the faithful themselves. The Jewish converts who were from Greece, murmured against those of Judea and complained, even to the apostles, that their widows were neglected. The apostles bade them choose out seven discreet and virtuous men, who should take upon them the management of those things, which they, in the daily ministry of the word, could not attend to. By common consent seven men were accordingly chosen; the apostles laid their hands upon them and ordained them deacons. The most eminent of these seven was Stephen, who to a natural greatness of soul united an ardent zeal for the cause of God. Full of the Holy Ghost, he exerted the force of that sacred eloquence which distinguished him above the rest, in instructing the people in the knowledge of salvation. His enemies strained every nerve to silence him, but were not able to resist the wisdom and the spirit that spoke by his tongue. They had recourse to violence: they suborned false witnesses to say that he ceased not to speak against the temple and the law, that he had blasphemed against God and Moses. He was summoned to appear before the council and answer to the charge which was brought against him. Stephen stood in the midst of the assembly: they all fixed their eyes upon him; for there was something so charming in his looks, that his face seemed as if it were the face of an angel. Being questioned by the high-priest, he entered into a short detail of the sacred history from Abraham down to that time: he upbraided them for their incredulity and obstinacy in resisting the Holy Spirit, and concluded by telling them, that like to their hardened forefathers, who had persecuted the prophets, they had made themselves the betrayers and murderers of the Just one, whose coming the prophets had foretold. His words cut them to the very heart: they gnashed their teeth at him through anger and desire of revenge. The holy Levite stood for some time silent, looking up steadfastly to heaven, and at last exclaimed, Behold! I see the heavens opened and the Son of Man standing on the right hand of God! Then the

Jews, as though he had uttered blasphemy, stopped their ears, and rushing furiously upon him, hurried him out of the city to a place where they stoned him to death. A young

man called Saul, kept the garments of those who stoned him. Stephen fell upon his knees, and whilst his enemies hurled their stones at him, most earnestly called upon Jesus not to lay the sin to their charge; and when he had ended his prayer, he slept happily in the Lord.

St. Stephen is the first of those innumerable martyrs, who have since shed their blood for Jesus Christ. The charity he expressed for his executioners in the very act of his martyrdom, shows him to be the true disciple of his divine Master. He had reprimanded his enemies with some degree of severity, but that severity was inspired by the love he bore them. He reproached their incredulity with zeal, but without bitterness. He was a dove, says St. Austin, whose anger had no gall. If he was strong in his expressions, it was to break the hardness of their hearts. At the same time that he glowed with zeal for their salvation, he offered up his blood to God for those who spilled it.

Samaritans Baptized and Confirmed.—Acts, viii

[A.D. 34.]

Upon the death of St. Stephen a grievous persecution commenced against the church at Jerusalem. Saul, an active zealot, distinguished himself* by his violences, entering into the houses of the faithful, and dragging away men and women into prison. A general consternation prevailed amongst the ministers of God's word; all, except the apostles, fled from the storm and dispersed themselves through the country of Judea and Samaria. The dispersion of the faithful contributed to the propagation of the gospel, for they preached the word of God wherever they went; and then it was, that the town of Samaria became acquainted with the name of Christ, by the ministry of Philip, one of the seven deacons. This holy man accompanied his preaching with many miracles; the Samaritans ran in crowds to hear him; they believed and were baptized. Amongst the number there was one Simon, a noted magician, who by his sorceries had long imposed upon the people; this man, after he had received baptism, attached himself particularly to Philip. The apostles being informed that the Samaritans had received the word of God, judged it necessary to provide them immediately with those spiritual helps, which Jesus Christ had appointed to confirm the faith of his followers against the terrors of persecution. St. Peter and St. John were deputed to go to Samaria for that purpose: when the two apostles came thither they prayed for the new converts, that they might receive the Holy Ghost; and no sooner did they lay their hands upon them, than they accordingly received the Holy Ghost. Simon observing the visible effects which ensued from the mysterious imposition of hands, was carried away by a wicked desire of performing the like wonder, and therefore offered money to the apostles, if they would grant him the power of conferring the Holy Ghost in the same manner. Keep thy money to thyself, said St. Peter, and let it perish with thee, since thou hast wickedly thought that the gift of God may be purchased with silver. Guilty of the same crime, and liable to the same curse, are they also who, like Simon, shall presume at any time to barter spiritual things for temporal.

The apostles returned to Jerusalem, and St. Philip was admonished by an angel to go towards the great road which led from Jerusalem to Gaza. When he came thither he saw a chariot going on, and in it an eunuch of great authority under Candace, the Queen of Ethiopia. This man had been to pay his homage to God in the temple of Jerusalem, and was upon his return home; he had the Scriptures open before him, and sat reading the prophecy of Isaiah. Philip was inspired to go up to him, and as he approached, distinctly heard what the eunuch said, for he read aloud. Do you think you understand what you read? said Philip to him. And how should I, replied the eunuch, unless I had some one to explain it to me. Come into the chariot and sit by me. The passage of the prophecy which he was reading, was this: *Like a sheep was he led to the slaughter, and as a mute lamb under the hands of his shearer, he opened not his mouth.* Is it of himself or of another that the prophet here speaks? said the eunuch. Philip then began, and instructed him in the belief and doctrine of Jesus Christ. The eunuch listened with attention, lost not a single word that was spoken to him, and being thoroughly persuaded of the truth he heard, asked, when they came to a certain water, what hindered him from being baptised. Nothing, answered Philip, if you only

believe. I do, replied the eunuch; I believe that Jesus Christ is the son of God: then commanding the chariot to stand still, and going down with Philip into the water, he was baptised. As soon as the ceremony was over, the Spirit of the Lord miraculously took away Philip, and the eunuch saw him no more. Happy in himself, and thankful for the grace which God had conferred upon him in so wonderful a manner, the eunuch cheerfully pursued his journey to Ethiopia; and Philip continued preaching the gospel through all the cities from Azotus till he came to Cæsarea.

Conversion of Saul.—ACTS, ix.

[A.D. 34.]

THE powerful effect of St. Stephen's prayer for his persecutors, appears in the conversion of Saul. Saul was a native of Tarsus in Cilicia, warm and violent in his temper, and, as he says of himself, a most zealous stickler for the traditions of his forefathers. He had signalized himself, as we have seen, in the persecution of Jerusalem, and from that time breathed nothing but blood and slaughter against the disciples of our Lord. Not satisfied with what he had already done against them, he applied to the high-priest for credentials which he easily obtained, and set out with full power to Damascus, to seize all he could find there of that persuasion, and to bring them bound in chains to Jerusalem. When he came near the town of Damascus, he was suddenly surrounded by a strong light from heaven, much brighter than the sun, and falling on the ground heard a voice speaking to him in the Hebrew tongue, Saul, Saul, why dost thou persecute me? Lord, who art thou? replied Saul. I am Jesus, whom thou persecutest, said he. Saul then trembled, and astonished cried out: Lord, what wilt thou have me to do? Rise up, said Jesus, go into the city, and there it shall be told thee what thou must do. The men who accompanied him stood amazed; for though they saw no one, they nevertheless heard the voice. Saul arose from the ground, and found, though his eyes were open, that he could not see. His attendants took him by the hand and conducted him to Damascus, where he remained blind for three days, without eating or drinking the whole time. There was at Damascus a certain disciple, named Ananias, whom our Lord in a vision ordered to go into the street which is called Straight, and to enquire at the house of Judas for one Saul of Tarsus. Ananias was startled at the order, and represented to the Lord what a violent man this Saul was, what cruelties he had committed against the saints in Jerusalem, and with what powers he was now come to Damascus. Nevertheless go thy way, said our Lord, for this man is to be a vessel of election, destined to carry my name before the Gentiles and kings, and the children of Israel Ananias went to the place appointed, and being introduced to the man he asked for thus said: Brother Saul, the Lord

Jesus, who appeared to thee in the way as thou camest, hath sent me hither, that thou mayst receive thy sight, and be filled with the Holy Ghost: he at the same time laid his hands upon Saul, and immediately there fell from his eyes something like scales. Saul at the moment recovered his sight, and rising up was baptized. He remained for some days with the disciples at Damascus, appearing at times in the Jewish synagogue, and publicly declaring Jesus to be Christ the Son of God. All who saw him stood astonished at the change, and wondered to hear the man speak so strenuously in support of the doctrines which they knew he came to persecute.

St. Paul, according to the account he gives of himself to the Galatians, remained not long at Damascus before he retired into Arabia. In that retirement he spent near three years, without any communication with the Jews, till he came back to Damascus. After his return he began to preach the faith of Christ, and addressed his discourses chiefly to the Jews, who not being able to withstand his arguments, and yet not willing to embrace his doctrine, sought to take away his life. Though he would have been happy to seal the truth by the effusion of his blood, yet in hopes of reserving himself for some greater good, by labouring for the salvation of others, he permitted his friends to let him down the wall in a basket by night, and so escaped out of the hands of his enemies. He went straight to Jerusalem, where he was known only by his former violences. The faithful had received no certain account of his conversion, and were afraid of coming near him, till Barnabas introduced him to the apostles St. Peter and St. James. As soon as the history of his conversion was known, he was received with open arms, and admitted amongst the disciples of Jesus Christ. His stay at Jerusalem was no longer than fifteen days; for his great zeal would not suffer him to remain either silent or inactive. He drew upon himself a persecution which must have ended in his death, if the brethren had not prevented it by sending him away to Cæsarea and Tarsus.

The conversion of Saul was once the joy of the church, and is still its consolation. The riches of the divine mercy are not limited; they are sometimes poured out upon the hearts even of the most obdurate. From being a violent persecutor of Christ's church, Saul became her zealous defender, and the successful propagator of her doctrine. The most habituated sinner, as long as life remains, is never to despair. The Almighty has his moments and his times of grace; he may strike and humble the sinner to the very earth; and happy will the sinner be, if, in the spirit of St. Paul, he as promptly answers, Lord, what wilt thou have me to do?

Cornelius Baptized.—Acts x.
[A.D. 39.]

WHILE Saul was preparing himself for the apostleship of the Gentiles, St. Peter wrought great wonders, and made many conversions amongst the Jews. The church was restored to peace; the faithful in Judea, Galilee, and Samaria, practised the most perfect virtues, and enjoyed the consolation of the Holy Ghost. St. Peter made his apostolical excursions through the country, visiting and confirming his little flock by word and work. At Lydda he healed Eneas, who for eight years had been confined to his bed by a palsy; and at Joppe, he raised to life a woman called Tabitha, who was remarkable for her alms to the poor. During his stay at Joppe, he was called by divine appointment to communicate the faith also to the Gentiles, in the person of Cornelius, a centurion in the Italian cohort. This man so much commended by the sacred historian for the regularity of his family, for his piety to God, and his alms-deeds to the poor. Being at Cæsarea, he was favoured one day with an apparition of an angel, who told him that God had heard his prayers, and accepted his alms; but that he must send men to Joppe, and

call to him one Simon, who was surnamed Peter, and lodged in the house of Simon, a tanner, by the sea side, by whom he would be informed what was moreover required of him. Almighty God might as easily have commissioned the angel to instruct Cornelius, as to bid him send for St. Peter. But it is his divine will, that a due respect be paid to those powers which he has established upon earth; and in seeking the instruction we stand in need of, he expects we should submit to ask it if those whom in his wisdom he has commanded us to hear. When the angel was departed, Cornelius called two of his servants, to whom he related the vision, and sent them to Joppe. They reached the town next day about noon. St. Peter at that very time was gone into an upper room of the house where he lodged, and being at his prayers, fell into an ecstacy of mind. He saw the heavens opened, and from thence a sort of vessel descending, like a great sheet, let down by the four corners, in which there was a variety of living creatures, of fowls, reptiles, and four-footed beasts. He heard at the same time a voice telling him to kill and eat. Far be it from me, replied the saint, to eat of any thing that is unclean: to whom the voice answered Call not that unclean which God hath purified. This was repeated to him three times over, and presently the vessel was taken up into heaven. Now, whilst Peter was doubting within himself what could be the meaning of this mysterious vision, the centurion's servants came to the house and enquired for him. The Spirit of God bade him go down to them, telling him they came by his orders. The apostle therefore went down to the men, and asked them what they came for. They made answer, that

Cornelius, a centurion, a just and virtuous man, being warned by an angel, had sent them to desire he would return with them to their master's house in Cæsarea. St. Peter detained the men that night, and set off with them next morning, in company of some of the brethren from Joppe. Cornelius, in the interim, had assembled his friends and acquaintances, waiting with impatience the apostle's arrival; and no sooner was he told of his being come, than he went out to meet and salute him, which he did with profound respect, according to the eastern custom, and bowed himself down to his feet. The humble apostle was disturbed at the extraordinary respect which the centurion paid him, and putting out his hand to help him up, said, I am but a man, undeserving of so much honour. He entered with them into the house, and seeing the many Gentiles who were there assembled, began to tell them how great an aversion a Jew had to visit or converse with Gentiles; but that God, by a special vision, had signified to him not to call any man unclean; that he had therefore obeyed their message, and desired to hear for what reason they had sent for him. The centurion then related his vision at full length, and concluded by saying, that all there present were ready to receive whatever commands the Lord should communicate to them by his mouth. St. Peter answered, that God was not a respecter of persons; that of whatsoever nation men might be by descent or birth, he excepted none from his mercy, as long as by faith and good works they sincerely sought to please him. After that he explained the doctrine, the life, the death, and resurrection of Jesus Christ, of whom the prophets had given testimony, in whom alone there was remission of sins, and whom the Father had appointed to be judge of the living and the dead. While he was thus speaking, the Holy Ghost descended upon all those who heard him: they were presently endowed with the gift of tongues, and began to glorify God; which determined the apostle to baptize them upon the spot. St. Peter after some days' stay at Cæsarea, went to Jerusalem, where he found himself much censured by the Jewish converts, for his communication with the uncircumcised Gentiles. The humble apostle did not pretend to silence them by authority; he saw their complaints arose from prejudice, and sought to set them right, by explaining the matter to them. He disdained not, says St. Gregory, to enter into the justification of his own conduct before his inferiors, and related to them his own and the centurion's vision. In confirmation of the fact, he referred them to the Jewish witnesses whom he had taken with him from Joppe, and concluded, that it did not behove him to withstand God, and refuse baptism to those who had received the Holy Ghost as well as they.

St. Peter delivered out of Prison.—Acts xii.
[A.D. 41.]

The favourable account which St. Peter gave of his excursion to Cæsarea, immediately silenced the objections of those who had been ready to find fault; the faithful were happy to see the Gentiles thus called to partake with them in the grace of eternal life, and exceedingly rejoiced when they were likewise informed of the great numbers who had embraced the faith at Antioch. Barnabas, a good man, as the Scriptures witness, full of faith and the Holy Ghost, was sent thither to promote the work which the grace of God had so happily begun. Upon his arrival he could not but rejoice at the pleasing prospect of religion: an extensive field was opened to his zeal! the harvest of souls was very great, the workmen few. He encouraged them to persevere in the happy course they had undertaken, and went to Tarsus in quest of Saul. He found him and brought him back to Antioch, where they employed themselves for a whole year in the service of the Lord; they preached, they instructed, they laboured with unwearied zeal, and had the consolation to see their labours crowned with success. The proselytes they made were very numerous, and each one vied with his neighbour in the study of good works: then and there it was, that the followers of Christ's doctrine were first distinguished by the name of Christians. About the same time there came prophets thither from Jerusalem, and amongst them one called Agabus, who foretold a great famine. The Christians were alarmed at the prophecy, and began to provide against the time of distress, which happened under Claudius. They collected considerable sums, which they put into the hands o Saul and Barnabas for the relief of their brethren dwelling in Judea. The church of Jerusalem was at that time sorely aggrieved by a persecution, which Herod, at the instigation of the Jews, had commenced against the faithful; the wicked king had already slain St. James, the brother of St. John, and was then meditating the death of St. Peter. Having caused him to be apprehended during the Easter time, he kept him in prison under a strong guard, till the holydays were over, when he intended to bring him forth to the people. The faithful were in the deepest consternation at the disastrous event, rightly judging that the welfare of the flock was closely connected with that of the pastor, and therefore day and night did they send up their most fervent prayers to heaven for his deliverance. The Almighty graciously heard their petition, and delivered his apostle on the very night that preceded his intended execution. Bound with two chains, St. Peter lay asleep between two soldiers in the prison, perfectly resigned within himself either to life or death, when the angel of the Lord came with great brightness to the place, and striking him on the side, said, Aris

quickly. That moment the chains fell off from the apostle's hands; he speedily arose, put on his sandals; threw his garment round him, and followed the angel through the first and second ward, till they came to the iron gate which led to the city. At their approach the gate of itself flew open, and they went on to the end of the street, where the angel left him. The saint then came to himself, for hitherto he seemed to have been in a dream, and said, Now I know that the Lord hath sent his angel, and delivered me from the hand of Herod, and from all the expectations of the Jews. Musing on the event, he came to the house of Mary, the mother of Mark, and knocked at the gate. Many of the faithful were there met to pray: a girl called Rhode hearing some one knock, went to hearken at the door, and immediately knew it to be Peter's voice; instead of letting him in, she ran back in a transport of joy to acquaint the company that Peter was at the gate. They told her she had lost her senses; but she positively assured them that so it was: still they would not believe her, and said it was his angel she had heard. Peter in the mean while continued knocking: they then went to the door, and on opening it saw him, and were astonished. He beckoned to them with his hand not to say a word, silently entered into the house, and gave them an account of what God had done for him. When he had finished his narration, he desired them to repeat it to James and the rest of the brethren, and hastened immediately out of the city, as privately as he could.

The wonderful release of St. Peter out of prison has been thought to be of such importance to the church, that she has instituted a day of thanksgiving to God on that account. She then experienced, as she has often experienced since, that God is the sovereign disposer of all things here below; that he sets what bounds he pleases to the power of tyrants; that he opens or shuts the prisons at his nod, and makes even the passions of men subservient to his will, in the execution of his unchangeable decrees.

Labours of St. Paul.—Acts xiii. &c.
[A.D. 44.]

St. Luke makes little mention of St. Peter after his miraculous deliverance out of prison, and fills up the remaining part of his history with the transactions chiefly of St. Paul. This holy apostle, soon after he had brought to Jerusalem the charitable collections made by the Christians of Antioch, was, by a particular inspiration of the Holy Ghost, ordained, with Barnabas, the apostle of the Gentiles; which was done by fasting and praying, and imposing hands upon them. Immediately after their ordination they directed their apostolical course to the city of Selucia, and from thence sailed into Cyprus, where they preached the word of God in the Jewish synagogues through the whole island, till they came to Paphos upon the coast. They there met with Sergius Paulus the pro-consul, a prudent man, who desired to hear them preach. Sergius was charmed with the doctrine he heard, owned himself convinced, and would immediately have embraced the truth, had it not been for the dissuasions of a Jewish magician, whose name was Bariesus, or Elymas. The apostle was grieved to see a bar put to the gospel by a false prophet of his own nation: full of the Holy Ghost he arraigned the magician for his hypocrisy, and denounced the wrath of God upon him, telling him that he should become

blind, nor see the sun for a time. The threat was no sooner spoken than executed: struck blind upon the spot, the impostor could no longer find his way about without some friendly hand to guide his steps. The pro-consul profited by the magician's misfortune, and as he admired, so he readily believed and embraced the doctrine of Jesus Christ. From this date we find the apostle of the Gentiles no longer called by the name of Saul, which from the pro-consul's surname, as it is supposed, was changed into Paul.

The two apostles sailed from Cyprus to Perge in Pamphylia, and from thence went to Antioch in Pisidia. St Paul, according to his custom, entered the Jewish synagogue, and in a long discourse established the doctrine and divinity of Jesus Christ. He was desired by many of his audience, as they went out, to speak again on the same subject on the next Sabbath. The jealous rulers of the synagogue, perceiving that he made many proselytes, rose up against him, and by the disturbances they raised, drove him and Barnabas out of the country. The apostles repaired to Iconium in Lycaonia, where they made many converts both of the Jews and

Gentiles. But a persecution being raised by the unbelieving Jews, they were soon after forced to fly to the cities of Derbe and Lystra. The miracle which St. Paul here wrought upon a man who had been a cripple from his mother's womb, made the superstitious heathens believe, that they were two deities in human shape that had come amongst them: they fancied Barnabas to be Jupiter, and Paul, for his eloquence of speech,

to be Mercury; the priest of Jupiter brought forth oxen, and crowned them with garlands before the gates, for sacrifice in their honour. The apostles ran in haste to the deluded multitude, tore their garments, and exerted their eloquence to convince them, that they were also mortal men like themselves, and that not to them, but to the sovereign Creator of the universe only, sacrifice was due. It was with great difficulty that the people were prevailed upon to desist. A few days after, so inconstant are the honours bestowed by an undiscerning multitude, the Lystrians started into the opposite extreme. Excited by the slanders of certain Jews who arrived from Iconium, they laid hands upon St. Paul, dragged him out of the town, where they stoned and left him for dead. When the barbarians were gone, he rose up and entered into the city. Next morning he set off with Barnabas to Derbe, visited the towns and provinces through which they had already passed, preaching, confirming, and ordaining priests whereever they went, and returned to Antioch in Syria. There they called the faithful together, to whom they related what great things God had done by their hands, and what a door was opened for the gospel amongst the Gentiles. On that occasion a difficulty was started by some Jewish converts, who contended that the ceremonies of the Mosaic law ought to be observed by those who were converted of the Gentiles. In a question of that nature, where men were strongly biassed by the prejudice of education, nothing could be decided by private authority. St. Paul therefore and Barnabas were deputed to consult the apostles and priests of Jerusalem upon that subject. It was in the year fifty-one. The apostles and bishops met in council; St. Peter, as president over all the rest, opened the subject of debate. After a full discussion of the matter, a decision was formed in the name of the Holy Ghost, and of all assembled, That the burden of the Mosaic law was not to be imposed upon their believing brethren of the Gentiles. The decision was received at Antioch with great joy and respect.

St. Paul remained some time at Antioch, when he invited Barnabas to accompany him in visiting the churches they had founded; but a dispute arising between them, whether John, surnamed Mark, should go with them or not, they separated, and St. Paul chose Silas for his companion. He visited the cities of Syria and Cilicia, where he had already preached the word of God, and coming to Troas was called by special revelation into Greece. At Lystra, he associated to himself a faithful disciple and companion of his travels whose name was Timothy. With him and Silas he passed through Phrygia and Galatia, and setting sail from Troas for Macedonia, came to Philippi. Here St. Paul having cast a Pythonical spirit out of a young woman, he and Silas were carriod before the magistrates, who ordered them to be scourged and cast into prison. The holy prisoners being at their prayers, a sudden earthquake shook the foundation of the prison, and set open the doors. The goaler went in, fell down at their feet, and was converted. The magistrates sent their sergeants next morning to let the prisoners go. St. Paul complained that being a Roman citizen, he had been illegally treated, and therefore would not depart till the magistrates themselves should come and dismiss them honourably. The holy apostle continued his journey to Thessalonica, where he preached with great success, till the violence of the Jews forced him to retire to Berea. He there met with the like persecution; wherefore leaving Silas and Timotny behind him, he went to Athens, where he converted Denis the learned Areopagite. From Athens he directed his course to Corinth, and to Ephesus, in the province of Ionia; in all which places he converted great numbers to the Christian faith, and established church discipline amongst them. The zeal of the great apostle seemed to quicken as he went; the more he suffered, the more his heart was on fire: the Jews persecuted him in every place he came to; but the more he was opposed, the more he strove to make Jesus Christ known and honoured amongst the nations

Sufferings of St. Paul.—ACTS xxii., xxiii., &c.

[A.D. 60.]

ST. PAUL allowed himself no rest; he never ceased announcing Jesus Christ, and him crucified, through all the different states of Greece and Asia Minor; from province to province, from one island to another, he passed with indefatigable labour, braving every danger by land and sea, as his pastoral solicitude for the different churches called him. When he could not visit them in person, he instructed, reprehended, and exhorted, as charity directed, by his epistles. The glory of God, and the salvation of souls, were the only objects that occupied the thoughts of that zealous apostle. Though he had great difficulties to struggle with, he was comforted to see his preaching seconded by the faith of thousands, and his endeavours perfected by the special grace of Almighty God. For it was not by himself, as he says, but by the grace of God with him, that he performed such wonders. The gift of miracles was so conspicuous in him, that even the handkerchiefs and aprons which had touched his body, healed the sick, and put the infernal spirits to flight. From visiting the churches of Asia, he was called to Jerusalem, where he foresaw great trials would befall him. For having been ordained the apostle of the Gentiles, the Jews of Jerusalem looked upon him as an enemy to their law and the holy temple. He had not been there many days before the city was in an uproar. They seized him in the very temple, dragged him forth, and amidst a riotous crowd of citizens were preparing to kill him, when the Roman tribune being apprised of the tumult, took with him a file of soldiers, and hastened to the place. The Jews being awed by the soldiers' presence left off beating the blessed apostle, and the tribune immediately laying hold of him, commanded him to be bound in chains, asking who he was, and what he had done. Some cried out one thing, some another; nothing was to be heard but clamour and tumult. The tribune therefore, not being able to learn anything for certain amidst such confusion, ordered his soldiers to lead off the prisoner to their quarters. The people followed with loud cries and insolence, demanding his death. The apostle asked the tribune's leave to speak to them; which being granted, he made a sign with his hand to the people, as he stood upon the stairs, and there being a profound silence, he began to harangue them in the Hebrew tongue. He gave them a clear and circumstantial account of his birth at Tarsus, and education at Jerusalem, of his doctrine, and zeal for the law of his forefathers, of his former violence against the Christians, of his conversion and mission amongst the Gentiles. They listened with great attention, till he mentioned the Gentiles; they then interrupted him, and cried out that such a man was not fit to live. The tribune conveyed him away within the quarters, ordering him to be scourged and put to the torture, that he might know why thus they cried out against him. When they had bound him, Paul asked the centurion, whether it was lawful to scourge a Roman citizen uncondemned. The centurion hearing that, went to the tribune and told him this man was a Roman citizen. Fearful of the consequences, the tribune was sorry for having bound him, came straight to the holy apostle, unloosed his chains, and appointed the next day for him to plead his cause before a council of the Jews.

The council was composed of two different sects, of Pharisees and Sadducees, who were equally as violent in temper, as they were opposite in opinion concerning the doctrine of spirits and a future resurrection. St. Paul took advantage of the disagreement of his judges, and professed himself of the Pharisean sect, in his belief and hope of the resurrection of the dead. The Council was thereupon divided in their judgments for and against him; the dispute grew warm, and the tribune being apprehensive lest Paul might be torn to pieces by them, ordered a guard of soldiers to go and bring him safe within the quarters. The Jews were not yet satisfied; their malice against the holy apostle was implacable, and more than forty of the most fiery zealots bound themselves by oath, neither to eat nor drink till they should see him dead. St. Paul received notice of this conspiracy from his sister's son, and acquainted the tribune with it, who, for his security, ordered a strong body of troops to escort him out of the town, and convey him to Felix the governor of Cæsarea. Felix at first sight discovered his innocence, yet being in hopes o. extorting money from him for his release, kept him two years a close prisoner, till Festus arrived to succeed him in the government of the province. The Jews presented a petition to the new governor, that he would order Paul to be sent from Cæsarea to Jerusalem. Had their request been granted, their design was to have assassinated him upon the road. The apostle knew their intention, and had no other way o. preventing its effect than by appealing to Cæsar. Festus promised him he should be sent to Rome. A few days after, king Agrippa came to salute Festus at Cæsarea: their conversation turned upon the subject of St. Paul; Agrippa had heard much of the wonderful man, and was eager to see him. Festus promised him he should both see and hear him. Next day the venerable prisoner was brought forth into the hall of audience, before the principal men of the city, and permitted to speak for himself. The holy apostle began by saying, how happy he was in being permitted to plead before Agrippa, and in the sequel of his discourse spoke with such strength and elegant simplicity of expression, that Agrippa told him in the end, he had almost persuaded him to become a Christian. He proved his innocence so much to the satisfaction o. all who heard him, that both Festus and Agrippa publicly declared, he might have been set at liberty, if he had not appealed to Cæsar. St. Paul was therefore committed to the care of Julius, a centurion, who had orders to conduct him to Rome. Having taken leave of his friends, he was put on board a ship with other prisoners, and after a long and perilous navigation, through boisterous winds and seas, was at last shipwrecked upon the coast of Malta. The ship went to pieces upon the rocks, the crew got safe ashore, where they experienced great humanity from the inhabitants. St. Paul having gathered a bundle of sticks, and having laid them upon the fire which was kindled to dry their clothes, a viper came out of the heat, fastened to his hand, and there hung: the barbarians from thence concluded him to be a murderer, whom the Divine justice had overtaken by land after having spared him at sea. But when they saw him shake off the venomous creature into the fire without receiving any hurt, they altered their opinion, and fancied him to be a god. The

apostle during his stay there employed his miraculous power in favour of the sick, and amongst others healed the father of Publius, who was governor of the island. At the end of three months he embarked again, and passing by several places landed at Puteoli, and from thence went to Rome. He there met with courteous treatment from the Romans, being permitted to remain unmolested in his own private lodging under a single guard, and to see whom he pleased. He remained a prisoner in that manner for two years, during which time he ceased not to preach the faith of Christ to all who came to see him, and made many converts, even of Cæsar's household, as we gather from his Epistle to the Philippians.

St. Luke here finishes his history of the Acts of the Apostles. Of all the holy fathers who have left us their comments upon St. Paul, St. Chrysostom seems to have carried his ideas of him to the highest point of panegyric. He speaks with raptures of his virtues, and displays the flowers of his golden eloquence, in setting forth the praises of a saint, the memory of whose sufferings gave him singular comfort and encouragement amidst the like trials, which he himself had to undergo in the cause of Jesus Christ

Epistles of St. Paul.

By his apostolic labours and preaching, St. Paul founded many churches in the different provinces which he enlightened with the doctrine of Jesus Christ, and by his epistles he either more fully instructed, or confirmed, those whom he had converted from their superstitious errors to the divine truths of Christianity. Of these epistles we have no less than fourteen, which have been carefully preserved and handed down to us by the Catholic Church, with the other inspired writings of the New Testament.

The first in point of time is that which he wrote from Corinth to the Thessalonians, about the year 52, as it is thought. Fearing lest they might be disheartened at the sight of persecution, he strongly exhorts them to shun all sin, and to remain steadfast in faith, that they may be found without blame at the coming of our Lord Jesus Christ. These words of the apostle, either through ignorance or malice, were interpreted by some as if the day of judgment was near at hand. The Thessalonians were alarmed, and the apostle, to calm their fears, wrote them a second epistle soon after the first, assuring them that a revolt must first happen, and Antichrist the man of sin be revealed, before Christ should come to judge the world. He tells them to keep and abide by the traditions which they had learned from him, whether by word of mouth or by his epistle. After this he wrote his epistles to the Galatians, as it seems, from Ephesus, in the year 55. The Galatians had learned the Christian faith from St. Paul, but after his departure from them were unfortunately seduced by some false teachers, who represented the apostle as a man of little consequence. They erroneously maintained, that the law of Moses was still in force, and ought to be observed by all. Against this error, as subversive of the gospel, St. Paul writes to them with all the plenitude of his power, which he had received from Christ, and pronounces anathema against any one who shall dare to preach to them a doctrine different from what he had taught them.

The year after, and from Ephesus as is probable, he wrote his first epistle to the Christians of Corinth. Corinth was the capital city of Achaia, where he had preached a year and a half, and had made many converts. The chief design of his epistle was to take away the dissensions that had spread amongst them, and to settle divers matters of ecclesiastical discipline. He teaches them in what manner the incestuous Christian was to be treated, speaks of sins against chastity, of the state of continency, which he prefers to that of matrimony, explains the duties of married people, the sacrament of the holy Eucharist, the different gifts of the Holy Ghost, and the mystery of the resurrection. Soon after this he wrote them a second epistle to congratulate them on the good use they had made of his former admonitions. In this epistle he comforts the afflicted with the hope of a future reward, reprehends the faulty, and in justification of his own conduct, as well as for their instruction against the slanders of some Jewish teachers, he expatiates upon the sufferings he had endured for his faith, and the singular graces God had bestowed upon him.

In the year 57 or 58 he wrote his epistle to the Romans, before he had yet been at Rome. The purport of his writing was to unite all the new Christian converts, whether they had been Jews or Gentiles, in the bonds of peace and perfect charity. For there were, it seems, warm disputes and contentions among them. The Jewish converts valued themselves upon their being the chosen people of God, the descendants of Abraham, and strenuously contended for the observance of the Mosaic precepts. The Gentile converts, on the other hand, reproached the Jewish people with their frequent infidelities against God, with their cruel persecutions of his prophets, and lastly with the murder of Jesus Christ, their Messiah. In their turn they also boasted of the great learning and science that had flourished among the Gentiles. The apostle then begins by showing, that neither the Jew nor the Gentile had reason to boast, but that both ought to humble themselves in the sight of God, the author of all good, that it was not on account of any merit of their own, but by the pure mercy of God, that they had been justified and called to the true faith; that it was not by any ceremonies of the Mosaic law, which now ceased to bind, nor by any precepts of the heathen philosophy, which was void of faith, but by a firm belief and steady practice of the religion taught by Jesus Christ, that they were to work their salvation. The last chapters of this, as well as of most of his other epistles, are a strong exhortation to all Christian virtues.

It is not known at what time, or from what place it was that he directed two epistles to Timothy, whom he had ordained bishop of Ephesus, and one to Titus, who was the chief bishop of Crete. The design is the same in all three, which is to instruct them and all bishops in their pastoral charge over their respective flocks. He likewise wrote a short epistle to Philemon, exhorting him to take back into favour his slave Onesimus, who had run away in debt, but was now become a Christian penitent, and ready to return to his master's service.

St. Paul was twice a prisoner at Rome on account of his faith. He seems to have been released from his first imprisonment in the year 62, and imprisoned again in the year 64. From his prison he wrote an epistle to the Ephesians, another to the Philippians, and a third to the Colossians. The style and subject of these three epistles are nearly the same. The apostle's intention was to strengthen the faith of his new converts, and to caution them against the seduction of false teachers.

His epistle to the Hebrews of Palestine is supposed to have been written in the year 63. To show the insufficiency of the old law, which was a figure or passing shadow of the new; to ascertain the divinity and everlasting priesthood of Jesus Christ: to prove, in fine, that justification and salvation was only to be hoped for through the grace and merits of Christ, is the sublime subject of this epistle. The three last chapters contain a pathetic exhortation to the practice of all Christian virtues, especially of faith, hope, patience, and fraternal charity.

Epistles of the other Apostles.

Besides the epistles of St. Paul we have seven others written by four apostles, viz. St. James the less, bishop of Jerusalem and son of Cleophas or Alpheus, St. Peter, St. John the Evangelist, and St. Jude, the brother of James above-mentioned.

St. Paul in his epistles to the Romans and Galatians, as we have seen, had not only declared that the Christian converts were exempt from the ceremonies of the Mosaic law, but that the ceremonies themselves, without true faith, were wholly unprofitable unto salvation. Simon the magician misconstrued the apostle's doctrine, as if no good works were necessary for salvation, but that faith alone was enough to save a man. Simon had his followers; for his doctrine flattered the human passions. To stop the growth of so pestilential an evil, St. James judged it necessary to address a general epistle to all his Christian brethren of the twelve tribes, about the year 62. After having shown that faith without good works is absolutely dead, and void of all saving power, he exhorts them to patience under their afflictions, to the exercise of fervent prayer, and a firm reliance on the grace and goodness of Almighty God. He tells them to resist their disorderly lusts and desires, as the occasions of sin, condemns the evils of the tongue, gives them wholesome advice against the vices of pride, vanity, and ambition, and enforces the sacramental rite of anointing the sick with holy oil.

St. Peter, as Eusebius and St. Jerome testify, placed his episcopal see at Rome, about the year of Christ 44, from whence soon after, as it seems, he wrote his first epistle to the converted Jews, that were dispersed through the countries of Pontus, Galatia, Cappadocia, Lower Asia, and Bithynia. His chief intention being to confirm them in the faith of Christ, and to instruct them in the practice of a virtuous life, he discourses in a most sublime and majestic simplicity of style upon the merciful dispensations of Divine Providence, in sending them a Redeemer in the person of Jesus Christ, the immaculate Lamb of God, and eternal Son of the Father. He exhorts them to acts of gratitude for so singular a mercy, encourages them with a prospect of an everlasting crown in heaven, to stand firm in their profession of the true faith under all trials, and gives them such lessons for a moral and holy life, as are applicable to every rank and order of men in the Church of Christ. A little before his death, about the year 65, he is generally thought to have written his second epistle, the purport of which differs not from the first. With a strength and nobleness of expression, he establishes the divinity of Jesus Christ, brands the evil practices of false teachers with the mark of reprobation, describes the final dissolution of the world by fire, and the awful coming of Jesus Christ in the last day to judge all men according to their works.

St. John the Evangelist has left us three epistles, written, as it is supposed, not long before his death. The first which is the chief, is addressed to the faithful in general. Its principal design is to confirm them in their belief of the divinity and incarnation of Jesus Christ, against Cerinthus and other heretics, who, by their blasphemous assertions, disturbed the peace of the church at that time. The style is concise, smooth, and expressive. The sentiments are such as characterize the beloved disciple of Jesus Christ, breathing the purest love of God and our neighbour. This pure love, that burned in his breast, sharpens his expressions against the enemies of Christ, in proportion as it sweetens them in favour of the friends of Christ. His second epistle is a short but nervous abridgment of the first. It is addressed to one Electa, a lady of note, whom he exhorts to hold no communication with those who, by their insidious and poisonous doctrines, would wish to seduce her and her children from the faith of Christ. His third epistle contains but a single chapter, written to Gaius, whom he warmly commends for his faith, charity, and hospitality.

St. Jude wrote the last epistle as it stands in the Testament, but at what time is uncertain. It is addressed in general to all who had embraced the faith of Christ. Its design is to give all Christians a just horror of the detestable doctrines and infamous practices of the Simonites, Nicolaites, and such heretics, who, having the name of Christians, were become a scandal to religion, and to all mankind. This epistle, in expression and sentiment, greatly resembles the second chapter of St. Peter's second epistle.

From the date of the apostolic writings, it is manifest that the Church subsisted many years without any written rule of faith: yet all that time the Church was no less the pillar of truth, no less guided by the Spirit of truth, and, consequently, no less to be heard, than she is now. Nay, were it not for her unerring authority, we could not be certain what is to be received as canonical Scripture, and what not. For the Scripture itself does not tell us what books have been inspired, and what have not. During the three first ages, before the Church decided, several of the epistles were doubted of, viz., that of St. Paul to the Hebrews, that of St. James, the 2nd of St. Peter, the 2nd and 3rd of St. John, and that of St. Jude. These apostolic writings could be no rule of faith at the time they did not exist; they could be no universal rule at the time they were doubted of; nor can they now be the only rule. For as St. Chrysostom remarks, the apostles did not deliver by writing all the things that were to be believed. We believe, for example, that there is an obligation of sanctifying the first day of the week instead of the seventh; but in this belief we are directed by the church alone. Saturday was the ancient Sabbath, Sunday is the new. This, by ecclesiastical tradition, we are taught to keep holy.

Revelations of St. John.—Apoc. i [A.D. 94.]

Although the Revelations of St. John are full of mystery, and obscure in themselves, yet the saints and interpreters of the holy Scriptures esteem them as a prophetic and instructive history of Christ's Church, from its first establishment upon earth to its final triumphant state in heaven. The first part relates to the particular churches that were founded in Asia Minor; the latter part regards the Catholic Church at large. The sacred intelligence is conveyed under the mysterious symbols of seals, trumpets, and vials. There are seven seals, to each of which corresponds a trumpet and a vial, and they denote as many periods of time, into which this last and seventh age of the world is subdivided. At the beginning of each period the Lamb is represented as opening one of the seals, which encloses the great events that are to befall the church during that period. An angel in consequence sounds the trumpet, to give the alarm as it were to mankind, on account of the evils that are going to ensue; while another angel pours out the vial of divine vengeance upon sinners, in punishment of the evils they have brought upon the church.

The apostolic prophet tells us, that being in the island of Patmos, whither he had been banished by the emperor Domitian, he was in the spirit upon the Lord's day, and heard behind him the shrill voice, as it were, of a trumpet, telling him to write down what he saw. He turned himself round, and beheld seven golden candlesticks, in the midst of which there stood a person like unto the Son of Man, clothed with a garment down to his feet, and girted round about the breast with a golden girdle. His venerable locks were as white as snow, his eye-balls flamed like fire, his feet like burnished brass, and his voice resembled the sound of many rushing waters. In his right hand he bore seven stars; from his mouth came out a sharp two-edged sword; his whole countenance shone like the sun. Struck at the awful

appearance, St. John fell down at his feet, as though he had been dead. The mysterious personage then laid his righ hand upon him, saying, Fear not; I am the First and the Last; and alive, and I was dead; and behold I am living for ever and ever. The seven stars you see in my right hand, represent as many angels or bishops of the seven churches in Asia, signified by the seven candlesticks. What you therefore see, write in a book, and send it to the seven churches. To the angel of Ephesus say, that I commend him for the labours he has endured, for his zeal against the deeds of the impious, and for his patience and suffering; but that I have something against him, for having fallen from his first fervour. Let him therefore reflect from whence he is fallen, and do penance. To the angel of Smyrna impart the words of consolation, amidst the sufferings of persecution and slander which he is forced to undergo. Let him prepare for new conflicts, and persevere as he has begun, faithful unto the end: I will give him the crown of life. Tell the angel of Pergamus, that his steadfast faith is acceptable to me, but that I expect him to show more vigour against the teachers of wicked doctrine: let him do penance, or I will come quickly to him. Tell the bishop of Thyatira that I see his charity to the poor, his fortitude in sufferings, and his fervour in good works; but that I have something against him because he suffers the false prophetess Jezabel to seduce my servants. Inform the bishop of Sardis, that he is dead in the sight of God, though he has the name of being alive; his works are imperfect. Let him do penance, and remember what talents he has received and what he has heard; else I will come and surprise him like a thief in the night. Let the angel of Philadelphia know, that I love him on account of his fidelity and patience in sufferings; that I will strengthen him against the hour of temptation, and make him a pillar in the temple of my God. In the last place, tell the Bishop of Laodicea, that I cannot bear him on account of his tepidity, and that I am ready to cast him from me: he thinks himself rich, and does not see that he is miserable, and poor, and blind, and naked. Let him therefore purchase of me the purest gold, that he may become rich, and provide himself with white garments, that the shame of his nakedness may not appear.

The judgments here passed by Jesus Christ upon those respectable prelates of the Church, are a subject of alarm to all Christians, who are upon their way towards heaven. Jesus Christ revealed to his beloved apostle, says St. Gregory, the good which those seven bishops had performed, and yet declared that they had penance still to do for the evils which had crept in amongst their good works. In the strictness of his justice he discerned the progress they had made in virtue, and noticed the degrees they had fallen from their first fervour. From amidst their shining actions, he distinguished each single fault, and let not pass any one speck that disfigured the beauty of their virtues. A single omission of duty, one neglect of vigour, when it was called for, provoked his displeasure; and nothing but a timely repentance could secure these most venerable and otherwise virtuous personages from being removed from their station, and seeing their crowns given to others. In this mysterious revelation, continues the holy pontiff, Jesus Christ informs us how little the most virtuous Christians have to glory in, and how great reason they have to humble themselves before God. If we only dive into our own hearts, and with an impartial eye survey the foldings of our conscience, we shall discover more than enough to confound our pride, and to give us a mistrust of all the good we can think ourselves possessed of.

Opening of the Heavens.—Apoc. iv.

From the first scene which was exhibited upon the earth to St. John, he was in spirit wrapt up to heaven. The heavens opened to his view, and a voice, like that of a trumpet, summoned him to come and see the things which were to happen in after times. Behold! a throne was set in heaven, and upon the throne one sitting, whose appearance was as the brilliant jasper and sardine stone. A bright rainbow, like an emerald, extended itself over the throne, and edged it round with a variegated crown of the most lively colours. In a circle round the throne stood four and twenty seats, on which there sat four and twenty elders, robed in white, with crowns of gold upon their heads. From the throne there issued out lightnings and thunders, and voices: before the throne were seven burning lamps, which are the seven spirits of God; far and wide, as if it were the floor of heaven, was expanded a boundless plain, resembling the glassy surface of a calm and transparent sea. In the midst and round about the throne stood four living creatures, full of eyes on every part of them. The first of these creatures had the resemblance of a lion; the second, of a calf; the third, of a man; and the fourth, of an eagle upon the wing. They ceased not day and night crying out, Holy Holy, Holy is the Lord God Almighty, who is, and who is to come! And whilst the four living creatures proclaimed that canticle of praise to Him who sat upon the throne, the four and twenty elders prostrated themselves before him, and laid their crowns at his feet, saying, Thou art worthy, O Lord our God, to receive glory, and honour, and power, because thou hast created all things, and for thy will they were and have been created. In the right hand of him who sat upon the throne, St. John saw a book, written on every side, and sealed with seven seals. A mighty angel advanced, and proclaimed with a loud voice, if any one was there worthy to open the book, and to loose the seven seals thereof: and no one was found. St. John upon that poured out a flood of tears, and one of the elders said to him, Weep not, for behold the lion of the tribe of Juda, the root of David, has conquered by his death, and merited the power of opening the book, and of loosing the seven seals thereof. St. John then looked, and saw standing in the midst of that celestial assembly, a Lamb with seven horns and seven eyes, resembling a victim that had been slain. The Lamb advanced, and took the book out of the hand of Him who sat upon the throne, and opened it: at that moment the four living creatures, and the four and twenty elders fell down before him; each one having in his hand a harp and golden vial full of fragrant odours, which are the prayers of the saints. They all began a new canticle of praise in honour of the Lamb, saying, Thou art worthy, O Lord, to take the book, and open the seals thereof: because thou hast been slain, and by thy blood hast redeemed us unto God out of every tribe and nation upon the earth. At the same time thousands and thousands of angels raised their voices in honour of the Lamb that was slain, and every creature which is in heaven, and on the earth, and in the sea, joining and singing benediction, and glory, and power to Him who sitteth upon the throne, and to the Lamb, for ever and ever: and the four living creatures said, Amen.

The holy fathers seem lost in admiration at the profound homage which the happy citizens of heaven pay to Jesus Christ, as St. John has described him under the emblematical figure of the Lamb. To him is given all power in heaven and on earth; the power of disclosing those mysterious secrets which had been sealed up in the bosom of the Divinity, and which none but a God-man could dive into. By his death and resurrection he has imparted to us a knowledge, of which the world was ignorant before: consequently, great is the obligation we are under of paying him our most grateful homage; wonderful are the secrets of his kingdom, which he has revealed unto us; and unremitting ought to be our endeavours to attain it. To join those heavenly choirs, and to sing the praises of our Creator eternally with them, is the object of our hope, and the completion of our purest desires.

The Seven Seals.—Apoc. vi.

The Lamb having received the book, began to exercise his power in opening the seven seals which were set upon it. Upon his opening the first seal, one of the living creatures cried out with a voice as loud as thunder, Come and see. St. John looked, and behold, a white horse, the emblem of triumph. His rider was equipped with a bow, and had a crown upon his head, like some mighty conqueror going forth in quest of victory. At the second seal there appeared another horse that was red, the baneful token of war. To him who sat thereon was given a great sword, and power to kindle bloody strifes amongst men, and to banish peace from the face of the earth. At the third seal there went forth a black horse, the representative of famine; and he who sat upon him, held a pair of scales in his hand. At his appearance a voice was heard, saying, Two pounds of wheat for a penny, and thrice two pounds of barley for a penny; but the wine and oil hurt thou not. At the fourth seal appeared a pale horse, the ghastly mark of pestilence. His rider was called Death, and Hell followed him. His power extended over the four parts of the earth, to destroy mankind by the sword, by famine, pestilence, and the beasts of the earth. At the fifth seal, St. John saw under the altar, the souls of them who had been slain for the word of God; and they cried with a loud voice to the Lord, holy and true, to justify their cause on earth. To each one of these a white robe was given, and they were told to rest awhile, till the number should be filled up of their brethren, who were to fall a sacrifice like them, in testimony of the truth. At the sixth seal, those deadly terrors ensued, which shall strike the wicked at the approach of God's avenging day. For there was a great earthquake, the sun became black as sackcloth of hair, the moon grew red as blood, and the stars from heaven fell upon the earth. The heaven itself shrunk back like a book, or a sheet of parchment that is rolled together; the mountains and the islands were shaken out of their places; the kings of the earth, the princes and mighty warriors, the rich and powerful, ran to hide themselves in dens and caverns of the earth. Overwhelmed with terror, they called upon the rocks and mountains to fall down, and screen them from the face of Him who sitteth upon the throne, and from the wrath of the Lamb.

Such is the description of those alarming images which were revealed to St. John. The dreadful display of Divine justice, and the terrors of the wicked at the expectation of evils that they fear, are exhibited in such striking colours, that we cannot but tremble at the imperfect glimpse we catch of them. The obscurity in which these truths are revealed at present, discloses enough to fix our faith, and at the same time excites our apprehension of something still more terrible than we can yet discover. I am persuaded, says St. Denis of Alexandria, that the revelations of St. John are as sublime in themselves, as they are unintelligible to men. Though I do not comprehend the words I read, yet I know they contain something great; the truth, though concealed in obscurity, is not less important. I pretend not to set myself up as a competent judge of these matters, nor do I measure them by the littleness of my own capacity; but trusting more to divine faith than to human reason, I firmly believe those revealed points, though above the reach of my weak comprehension. My respect for divine revelation is not lessened by its being obscured; I respectfully receive the truth which is revealed, and silently adore the mysteries which I cannot comprehend.

The Seven Trumpets.—APOC. viii.

WHEN the Lamb had opened the seventh seal, there was silence in heaven, as it were for half an hour. St. John then observed seven angels, each with a trumpet in his hand, standing in the presence of God; another angel came at the same time, having a golden censer, and placed himself before the altar. He was presented with incense, that he might offer of the prayers of all the saints, upon the golden altar which was erected before the throne of God. For by the incense the prayers of the saints were represented, and the smoking fragrance ascended up before God from the hand of the angel. The angel after that filled his censer with fire from the altar, and casting it upon the earth, there ensued great earthquakes, and thunders, and voices.

The seven angels then prepared themselves to sound the trumpet. At the sound of the first angel's trumpet, there fell upon the earth a storm of hail and fire, mingled with blood, which destroyed a third part of the earth and trees, and burned up all the green grass. The second angel sounded his trumpet, and, as it were, a huge burning mountain was thrown into the sea, a third part of the sea was thereby turned into blood, a third part of the creatures which had life in the sea died, and of the ships a third part likewise perished. At the blast of the third angel there fell from heaven a blazing star like a torch; and the name of that star was called wormwood; it fell upon a third part of the springs and rivers, the waters of which being poisoned in their source, became bitter, and many men died thereof. The fourth angel sounded his trumpet; and behold, a third part of the sun, of the moon, and of the stars, was smitten with darkness; so that the day and the night were deprived of one third of their usual light. At that moment an angel flew through the midst of heaven, crying with a loud voice, Wo, wo, wo to the inhabitants of the earth, by reason of the evils which the three other angels were ready to denounce.

By the exhibition of these awful scenes, as they were shown to St. John, it appears how dreadful the judgments are which an offended God will pour out upon those who will slight his justice and abuse his mercy. He warns sinners long beforehand of the severe punishment which awaits the impenitent in another world. He sends forth his angels, the ministers of his holy word, to rouse mankind out of the lethargy of sin, to awaken in them a respect for his sacred law, and a fear of offending him. He calls the sinner to repentance, he patiently waits his return; but he waits not beyond the term that his wisdom has fixed; he suffers not his patience to be abused with impunity; when the time of his mercy is run out, every thing then becomes subservient to his justice.

The Locusts.—Apoc. ix.

The fifth angel having sounded his trumpet, St. John saw a star fall from heaven to the earth, and to him was given the key of the bottomless pit. He opened the mouth of the pit, from whence a thick smoke arose, as from a burning furnace; and the light of the sun and the air was darkened. From the smoke of the pit there swarmed out locusts, which had the power of scorpions to vex and sting mankind. But their power was confined to those men only, who had not the seal of God upon their forehead; nor were they permitted to hurt the trees, or the grass, or any green thing of the earth. Neither had they a power given them over the lives of men: their power was not to kill, but to torment for five months; and the pain they caused, was like to that of a scorpion when he striketh a man. In those days, says the sacred text, men shall seek death and shall not find it; they shall wish to die, and death shall fly from them. The shape of those monsters was like to that of a war-horse prepared for battle. They wore on their heads a sort of glittering crown like gold; in their faces they resembled men, had the hair of women, and the teeth of lions. They were armed with iron breast-plates, and the noise they made with their wings, was like the rumbling sound cf many horses and chariots rushing on to battle. They had a tail like that of a scorpion, and in their tail a sting. They had over them a king, the angel of darkness from the bottomless pit, whose name was Abaddon, that is to say, the Destroyer. This was the first of the three last woes spoken by the angel. The sixth angel then sounded his trumpet, and from the four corners of the golden altar was heard a voice, saying to him, Let loose the four angels that are bound in the great river Euphrates. The four angels were accordingly loosed, who were prepared for an hour, and a day, and a month, and a year, to destroy the third part of men. Their preparations for war were immediately formidable: the number of their troops amounted to two hundred millions. St. John says, he saw their horses and their riders. Their riders were covered with breast-plates of fire, of hyacinth, and brimstone; the horses had heads like lions, and from their mouths issued forth fire, and smoke, and brimstone. The power of those horses was in their mouths, and in their tails; for their tails were like to serpents: they had heads, and with them they hurt. By them a third part of men was slain, and of those who survived, none repented of their sins, none refrained from the works of iniquity; nor did they cease from their idolatrous worship of devils and molten gods.

To the locusts and the horses, who are described by St. John to have such power in their mouths and tails, St. Gregory compares all hypocrites and false teachers. For these also under their lips have venom and a sting, with which they wound and hurt mankind: under the disguise of a glittering outside they walk abroad, and as they want neither art to flatter, nor abilities to please, work themselves by degrees into favour with the people and potentates of the earth, in order to gain their wicked ends. Thus it was that the Arians, like other sectaries of every age and clime, imposed upon the world, and maintained a formidable party against the church, till being broken by intestine jars an disputes of doctrine amongst themselves, they sunk at last, like insects into the earth again, from whence they sprung

The Mysterious Book.—Apoc. x.

St. John saw another mighty angel descend from heaven, clothed with a cloud, and crowned with a rainbow on his head; his face shone like the sun, and his feet were as pillars of fire. In his hand he held a little book, which was open; then setting his right foot upon the sea, and his left upon the land, he cried out as loud as is the roaring of a lion, and was answered by seven voices, that uttered their sentences in thunder. St. John was about to write the things which the seven thunders had uttered, when a voice from heaven bade him seal them up, and write them not. The angel, still standing upon the land and sea, lifted up his hand to heaven, and swore by Him who liveth for ever and ever, who hath created the heaven, the earth, the sea, and all things in them, that time should be no more; that as soon as the seventh angel should begin to sound his trumpet, the mystery of God should be finished, as he hath decl. .d by his servants the prophets. When he had said this, the voice again from heaven spoke to St. John, bidding him go and take the little book from the angel's hand. The apostle went and asked the angel, as he was still standing, to give him the book. Take it said the angel, and eat it up: in thy mouth it shall be sweet as honey, but when thou hast swallowed it, thou shalt find it bitter in thy bowels. Thou must prophesy again to many nations, to different kings and people. St. John received the book from his hand, and when he had eaten it found it both sweet and bitter, as the angel had assured him.

The little book mentioned in this revelation, is, according to the holy fathers, no other than the Holy Scripture, which furnishes our souls with food and nourishment. We cannot digest it of ourselves, nor can we comprehend what it contains, without the special grace and direction of Almighty God: he himself must deliver it to us by his angels, or ministers, as he did to St John, and once before to Ezechiel the prophet. We, then, eat that book, according to St. Gregory, when by the help of the Holy Ghost we relish and digest the sacred truths which it contains. To those who know what it is to taste the sweets of virtue, the sacred truths are sweet and pleasant; but to those who are addicted to sensual pleasures, the knowledge which restrains them is bitter and disgustful. It may also happen, says the same St. Gregory, that we experience within ourselves the same two contrary effects of sweet and bitter from the same knowledge. For the more we know of God, the more we know also of ourselves. Unless God enlighten us, there is nothing but darkness in us. Numberless defects, sins, and passions, lie concealed within our hearts, unknown to our very selves, till the light of the Holy Ghost shows them to us. Then it is that we begin, with bitterness of heart, to reflect on our past follies, and to beg with the Royal Prophet, that all our desires may henceforward be directed solely to the Lord. Let me know thee, my God, let me know myself, was the fervent prayer of St. Austin.

Death of the two Prophets.—Apoc. xi.

After St. John had taken the book, he was presented with a reed like unto a rod, and bid to rise and measure the temple of God, the altar, and them that adored therein; but not to regard the outward court, because it was abandoned to the Gentiles, who were permitted to trample the holy city under foot, two and forty months. My two witnesses, said the Almighty, shall prophesy a thousand two hundred and sixty days; they are the two olive trees, and the two candlesticks, standing before the Lord of the earth: out of their mouths fire shall flame, to devour their enemies who attempt to hurt them. To these is given the power to shut the heavens, that no rain may fall the whole time of their prophecy; they have a power to turn the waters into blood, and to afflict the earth with plagues, as often as they will: and when they shall have given full testimony of the truth, the beast that ascended out of the abyss shall be permitted to assault, to conquer, and to kill them. Their dead bodies shall be exposed in the streets of the great city, which is called spiritually Sodom and Egypt; it is the city where their Lord was crucified. Strangers of the tribes, of different tongues and nations, shall see their bodies lying for three days and a half, and not suffer them to be interred. The inhabitants of the earth shall rejoice over them, and make merry; they shall send presents to one another, because the two prophets are dead who sorely tormented them. The revelation of this history is thus far related in the prophetic style, as of a thing to come; but as in the divine sight there is no event, however far removed into futurity from us, but what is present or even past with respect to God, the narration goes on from this place, as of a past transaction. For after three days and a-half, says the sacred text, the spirit of life returned into the two prophets; they stood upon their feet, and great fear fell upon all who saw them. Summoned by a voice from heaven, saying, Come up hither, they mounted into a cloud before the face of their enemies, and went triumphantly to heaven. At that hour a violent earthquake was felt, by which a tenth part of the city fell down, and seven thousand men were slain; the survivors were seized with dread, and gave glory to the God of heaven. At that period the second wo was past, the third wo will come quickly. The seventh angel sounded his trumpet, and there were great voices in heaven, saying, The kingdom of this world is become our Lord's and his Christ's, and he shall reign for ever and ever. The four and twenty elders fell on their faces and adored God, saying, We give thee thanks, O Lord God Almighty, because thou hast taken to thee the great power: the nations were angry, and thy wrath is come; the time is come, when the dead shall rise and be judged, and thou shalt render to thy servants the reward of their labours, and to the wicked, who have corrupted the earth, punishment and everlasting destruction.

It is remarked by St. Austin, that as the church began, so she will likewise end in sufferings and persecution upon earth, that so she may be perfected for her triumphant state in heaven. For not only the two prophets of which the Apocalypse makes mention, but many more heroic saints in those latter days, shall suffer martyrdom with invincible patience. Though attacked by the infernal dragon with unbridled fury, they yet shall triumph through the grace of Him who suffers not his servants to be assailed with greater trials than he enables them to bear. The devil has no further power against us than Jesus Christ allows him: and Jesus Christ allows him no more than is necessary to try the patience, and to perfect the virtues of his elect.

The Beast of the Apocalypse.—Apoc. xiii.

The description of the beast that slew the two great prophets is drawn in the most frightful colors: St. John saw him emerge from the sea. It was a monster with seven heads and ten horns: upon his horns were ten diadems, and on his heads names of blasphemy. In shape he resembled a leopard, with a bear's feet and a lion's mouth. One of his heads, he saw, had been struck with a mortal wound, but the wound was then healed. His strength was enormous, and that strength he received from the dragon. The whole earth seemed to be in great admiration with the beast; they ran after him in crowds, they adored him, and lavished wonderful praises on him. He spoke great things; he opened his mouth in blasphemies against God, to blaspheme his sacred name and his tabernacle, and all the blessed citizens of heaven. Power was given him to make war upon the saints for two and forty months, and to overcome them: his empire was universal; it extended over all the nations of the earth, and all adored him, who had not their names written in the book of life. After that, St. John saw another beast coming up from the earth: this beast had two horns like a lamb, and spoke as a dragon. He executed the power of the former beast, and compelled the inhabitants of the earth to adore him. To this second beast was granted a power of performing great wonders, and seeming miracles, so as to call down fire from heaven. By these signs he seduced many from their duty to God; he gave life and speech to an image of the beast, which he caused to be made and set up as an idol, ordering them to be slain, who should refuse to adore. He shall oblige every one, both little and great, rich and poor, to wear a mark or sign of their submission to the beast; and no one should be allowed either to buy or sell, who has not this mark either in his right hand or upon his forehead: which mark shall be either in the name of the beast written at length, or the number of his name; for it is the number of a man, and the number of him is six hundred and sixty-six.

The eyes of St. John were drawn from these two frightful monsters, to behold the Lamb, that appeared standing upon Mount Sion, and with him a hundred and forty-four thousand chosen souls, who had his name and the name of his

Father written on their foreheads. They sung, as it were, a new song before the throne, and the heavenly arches resounded with joyful harmony. These are they, in whose mouth there was no lie, and who are not defiled with women; for they are virgins, and follow the Lamb whithersoever he goes; robed in innocence, they are without spot before the throne of God. This prospect was presently interrupted by an angel flying through the midst of heaven, and crying with a loud voice, Fear the Lord and give honour to him, because the hour of judgment is come. That angel was followed by two others, the first of which said, she is fallen, the great Babylon is fallen: and the other proclaimed aloud, that if any man should adore the beast and his image, and receive his mark either in his hand or on his forehead, the same shall also drink of the cup of God's wrath, and be tormented with fire and brimstone. They who shall be doomed to this punishment, shall have no rest by day or night; for the smoke of their torments shall ascend for ever and ever in the sight of his holy angels, and in the sight of the Lamb. Here is the patience of the saints, who keep the commandments of God, and the faith of Jesus: and a voice from heaven said, Blessed are they who die in the Lord, that they may rest from their labours, for their works follow them.

St. Gregory is diffuse in his remarks upon these two beasts of the Apocalypse: the second more especially makes him tremble. His outward figure is that of a lamb, but his language is the language of a dragon, deceitful aud poisonous. The description, says the holy doctor, gives us a faithful picture of those seducing hypocrites, who go about to draw men into perdition, and the snares of the devil. They spring from the earth, that is to say, they are engendered and exist by a power altogether earthly; they wear the appearance of a lamb, that unsuspecting mortals may not be afraid of coming near them; and when they have drawn them within their reach, they then entangle them in the serpent's fold, and kill them with their poisonous breath.

The Seven Vials.—Apoc. xv.

St. John says he saw another sign in heaven, great and wonderful. He saw seven angels holding in their hands the seven last plagues, which are the accomplishment of God's wrath. These angels coming out of the temple, for the temple of the tabernacle was there displayed in full view, received from one of the four living creatures seven golden vials, full of the wrath of God. A loud voice, at the same time, came from the temple, saying, Go and pour out the seven vials of God's wrath upon the earth. The first angel then went and poured out his vial upon the earth. A sore and grievous wound that instant fell upon those who had the mark of the beast, and had adored his image. The second angel poured out his vial upon the sea, which became like the blood of a dead man, and every living creature died therein. The third angel poured out his vial upon the springs and rivers, and they were changed into blood. The angel that presided over the streams, then said, Thou art just, O Lord, in thy judgments; for they have shed the blood of the saints and of the prophets; and thou in return hast drenched them with blood. Yea, answered another angel from the altar, O Lord God Almighty, true and just are thy judgments. The fourth angel poured out his vial upon the sun, which became thereupon exceedingly hot, and with its burning rays, scorched men to death. Parched with the piercing heat, sinners blasphemed God, and remained impenitent. The fifth angel poured out his vial upon the throne of the beast, and his kingdom became dark. Bitter pains and wounds afflicted his wicked partizans: they blasphemed the God of heaven; they knawed their tongues through pain, but did not penance for their sins. The sixth angel poured out his vial upon the great river Euphrates, the waters of which were immediately dried up, and made an easy passage for the kings to march from the East. Then from the mouth of the dragon, from the mouth of the beast, and from the mouth of the false prophet, St. John saw three unclean spirits coming out like frogs. For the infernal spirits shall work signs in those days, going forth to gather the kings of the whole earth to battle against the great day of Almighty God; and they shall be gathered together in one place, called Armagedon. The seventh angel poured out his vial into the air, upon which a tremendous voice was heard from the temple, saying, It is done. Dreadful flashes of lightning, mixed with loud claps of thunder, shot across the sky, and the earth shook in such a manner as had never been known before The great city was split into three parts, the cities of the nations fell, and the great Babylon was remembered in the vengeance of a just God.

Then came one of the seven angels to St. John, and said, that he would show him the great harlot, with whom the kings of the earth had sinned, and by the wine of whose prostitution the inhabitants of the earth had been intoxicated. The apostle, therefore, was taken away in spirit into the desert, where he saw a woman sitting upon a scarlet-coloured beast, which was covered over with names of blasphemy, having seven heads and ten horns. She was clothed in scarlet, ornamented with gold and precious stones, and held a cap in her hand. Upon her forehead was written the word Mystery; Babylon the great, the mother of the fornications and abominations of the earth; and she was drunk with the blood of the saints and martyrs of Jesus.

This wicked woman, according to the holy fathers, is an expressive figure of the world, which intoxicates the minds of men with the cup of sinful pleasure, and dazzles them with the glittering pride of life, till by its abominations it draws upon itself and them the stroke of God's severest judgments. The name of Mystery, which the harlot showed upon her brow indicates the blindness of worldly men, who sport away their time, heedless of the evils that hang over them. Full of the present enjoyment, they think not of futurity, and sit enchanted with their fancied happiness. But death soon must break the slender thread of life, and dissolve the charm. The mystery will be then unfolded; they will clearly see, that they have toiled through life to perish in the end; that by false pleasures or by real evils they have forfeited their title to the joys of heaven, and incurred the guilt of eternal pains

Ruin of Babylon.—Apoc. xviii.

After the mysterious prodigies already related, St. John says, he saw another angel coming down from heaven: great was his power, and his glory illumined the earth. With a mighty voice he cried, She is fallen, the great Babylon is fallen; she has become the habitation of devils, and the haunt of every unclean spirit. Of her poisonous cup all the nations have drank: with her the kings of the earth have committed fornication, and the merchants of the earth have been enriched with her luxurious delicacies. Wherefore go out from her, my people, said another voice, fly from Babylon, lest you become partakers of her sins and punishment. For her sins have reached unto heaven, and the Lord hath remembered her iniquities. Treat her as she hath treated you; pay her double for all her works, and in the cup which she presented to you, mingle unto her the double of what she gave. Multiply her sorrows, and heap torments on her in proportion to her pride and wantonness. For she said in her heart, I sit a queen, and am no widow, and sorrow I shall not see. She therefore in a day shall find herself overwhelmed with plagues, with death, with mourning, and with famine, and she shall be burned with fire. The smoke of her destruction shall be seen from afar: the kings of the earth, who were sharers of her sinful delights, shall weep and bewail themselves over her. But the fear of sharing in her torments shall keep them at a distance. They shall stand afar off, and exclaim, Alas! alas! that great and mighty city, Babylon, how in an hour is thy judgment come! The merchants also of the earth shall weep and mourn over her: for no man shall there traffic any more Her gold, her silver, her pearls, her precious stones, her fine linen, her purple, silk, and scarlet, her frankincense, her odoriferous woods, and every other costly commodity, are perished with her. The pleasures and magnificence of her riches, in which she formerly rioted, are now lost, never more to be recovered. The pilots and the mariners, as they sail along the sea, shall look at a distance, and pointing at the place of her conflagration, say, What city was ever equal to that great city, which poured out her riches into the bosom of the merchants: alas! how desolate is she become! how quickly is her greatness fallen! While the mariners, the merchants, and the kings of the earth thus wept over the sinful city, the citizens of heaven, the holy apostles and prophets, were invited to rejoice, for the judgment of God had passed upon her. A strong angel took up a huge stone, as it were a mill-stone, and cast it into the deep sea, saying, So shall the great Babylon be thrown down and appear no more. The sound of the harp and flute shall no longer hail the day of gladness in thee; in thee no artist shall be found; the light of a lamp shall not shine, nor shall the voice of the bridegroom and the bride any more be heard. For thy merchants were the princes of the earth, and by thy enchartments the nations have been seduced; the blood of the prophets, and of the saints, has been there spilled.

The lamentations of the mariners, of the merchants, and kings of the earth, weeping over the destruction of their favourite city, Babylon, are solemn, and expressive of the vanity of all worldly greatness. They remember the good things they had there enjoyed, and bemoan their loss: with deep regret they deplore their misfortune, not for having misplaced their affections, but for being no longer able to enjoy what they loved. Thus have the wicked toiled, says the wise man; thus have they wearied themselves in the path of iniquity; their pride and their riches have profited them nothing. As fools they erred from the way of truth; their hope vanished in a moment, like the smoke which is scattered before the wind. They passsed their lives amidst the plenty of good things upon earth, and in the twinkling of an eye went down to hell. With unavailing tears they there shall weep, and in despair shall gnash their teeth at the prospect of evils which shall never end.

The Dragon bound in Chains.—APOC. XX.

UPON the destruction of Babylon, the whole court of heaven, saints and angels, raised their melodious voices in singing Alleluias to their Almighty King, for the just judgment he had passed upon the great harlot. The heavens opened, and behold a white horse, and on the horse one sitting, who was called, *The Faithful and True.* His piercing eyes were as a flame of fire, and on his head were many diadems: his robe was sprinkled with blood, his name, THE WORD OF GOD. Clothed in fine linen, white and clean, the celestial armies followed on white horses. From his mouth proceeded a sharp two-edged sword, and on his garment, and upon his thigh, was written, THE KING OF KINGS, AND THE LORD OF LORDS! Then did St. John see an angel standing in the sun, and calling together the birds of the earth to feast upon the flesh of the slain. For the kings of the earth, with the beast at their head, had drawn their armies together to make war against him who sat upon the horse. The beast and his false prophet were taken and cast alive into the pool of fire, burning with brimstone. The rest were slain by the sword of the conqueror, and their flesh devoured by the birds.

When this scene was passed, an angel descended from heaven with the key of the bottomless pit, and a great chain in his hand. He laid hold of the dragon, the old serpent, which is the devil and Satan, and having bound him with the chain, cast him into the bottomless pit, and shut him up for a thousand years, that he might seduce the nations no more, till that time be accomplished. Placed on seats then appeared those holy souls, who never had adored the beast, or received his mark either on their foreheads or on their hands, but had given their lives in testimony of Jesus Christ, with whom they reigned a thousand years till the second resurrection, when they shall receive their full and complete happiness in soul and body. And when the thousand years shall be accomplished, Satan shall be loosed out of his prison for a little while. He shall then go forth to rouse to battle the nations that lie in the four quarters of the globe. Innumerable as the sands of the sea their armies advanced, under the command of Gog and Magog, to attack the camp of the saints, and to encompass the beloved city. But fire flamed from heaven and devoured them; and the devil who seduced them, was cast into the pool of fire and brimstone, where both the beast and the false prophet shall be tormented day and night for ever and ever.

St. John then relates how he saw a great shining throne, and upon it one sitting, before whose face heaven and earth fled away, and were seen no more. The dead had been summoned by a trumpet to rise and come to judgment. He saw them standing before the throne; the books were opened, and sentence pronounced upon every one according to his works. Hell and death were cast into the lake of fire, and with them all the rest whose names were not written in the book of life. This is the second death.

It is generally agreed, that St. John, in these last chapters of his Revelations, speaks of that dreadful persecution, which, through the power and instigation of the devil, shall be raised against the Christian Church by Antichrist, whom St. Paul calls the man of sin, and son of perdition. Hence we find the holy fathers and ancient interpreters of the sacred writings unanimous in their opinion upon the three following points: 1. That Antichrist can be but one determinate individual man. 2. That that individual man will not appear till towards the end of the world. 3. That he shall not reign under that denomination for any long time, namely but for two and forty months. Consequently, every application of these mysterious truths, calculated to support any private doctrine or party disputes, is purely arbitrary, and destitute of all foundation, both in the text of Scripture, and the writings of the fathers. The meek spirit of Christianity, and simplicity of the gospel, surely cannot teach us to restrain the word of God, and distort the obsure mysteries of prophecy to the purpose of railing at one another. The Revelations of St. John are full of heavenly wisdom; in terms the most clear, they unfold many important and instructive truths, which the most ignorant may understand, and the most simple cannot be deceived in. The majesty of Almighty God, and the power of Jesus Christ, as it is described by St. John, in the kingdom of his glory, the formidable attempts of Satan agains the elect of God, the dreadful terrors of the last day, the eternal torments of the reprobate in the lake of fire and brimstone, and the consummate happiness of the saints in heaven, are points on which we may profitably employ our thoughts, and which we cannot too attentively consider; they ground us in the principles of true Christian knowledge; they teach us what to fear and what to hope for; they animate our faith and awaken our charity; they fix our choice, and direct our practice in the purpose of a good life. Such is the fruit which our blessed Lord desires we should reap from the reading of his holy word, lest the restless cares of this life engage our hearts, and expose our souls to the danger of being untimely overtaken by the last day.

The New Jerusalem.—Apoc. xxi.

After the first heaven, and first earth, and sea had disappeared, as St. John says they did, when the Judge seated himself on his throne to judge the world, he saw a new heaven, and a new earth arise. He saw the holy city, the new Jerusalem, coming down from God out of heaven, decked with rich ornaments, like a bride prepared for the reception of her spouse; and he heard a voice from the throne, saying, Behold the tabernacle of God with men, and he will dwell with them: they shall be his people, and he dwelling in the midst of them shall be their God. He shall wipe away their tears from their eyes, and death shall be no more: nor shall mourning, nor sights, nor sorrow be any longer, for the former things have now an end. After that, one of the seven angels who had the vials, came to St. John, and taking him up in spirit o a high mountain, showed him the heavenly Jerusalem

coming down from God out of heaven. The holy city was crowned with radiant light, the brightness of God himself, and the lustre thereof was like to a precious stone. It was enclosed with a high wall, drawn in a quadrangular form of equal length on every side. The wall was built on twelve foundations, in which were engraven the names of the twelve apostles. The city had twelve gates, and at the gates twelve angels, three to the east, three to the north, three to the south, and three to the west; on the twelve gates were written the names of the twelve tribes of Israel, a name on each gate. The angel who conversed with St. John had in his hand a golden reed, with which he measured the city, the gates and the wall thereof, and the dimensions of the city were twelve thousand furlongs every way. The wall was built of jasper, but the city itself was of pure gold, transparent as the clearest glass. The foundations of the walls were ornamented with every sort of precious stone, and the twelve gates were so many pearls, each gate being made of one pearl. The streets were paved with polished gold, and the gates stood always open, it being one eternal day, which knew no night. The city had no need of the sun or moon to enlighten it; for the Lamb was the lamp thereof, and the glory of God diffused a transcendant brightness through every part. St. John saw no temple therein, for the Lord God Almighty and the Lamb were the temple. Nothing defiled shall ever enter into that holy place; nothing can be admitted there, which is tarnished with the least spot of sin; no one enters who has not his name first written in the book of life From the throne of God and of the Lamb, there flowed the river of life, of which the streams were as clear as crystal. On each side of the river, and in the centre of the city, grew the tree of life, bearing twelve fruits, and yielding its fruit every month; and its leaves were to heal the nations. There shall be no curse any more: but the throne of God and of the Lamb shall be eternally there, and his servants shall serve him. They shall behold him face to face; his name shall be written upon their foreheads, and they shall reign for ever and ever. After all these things had been shown to St. John by the angel, Jesus thus spoke to him: I have sent my angel to testify unto you tnese things, which must be done shortly. I am the root and the offspring of David, the bright and the morning star. Behold, I come quickly, and my reward is with me, to render to every one according to his works. I am Alpha and Omega, the first and the last, the beginning and the end. Blessed are they who wash their garments in the blood of the Lamb, that they may be worthy to enter into the city, and partake of the tree of life.

Such is the description which St. John has given us of the heavenly Jerusalem, and such is the pleasing picture that Jesus Christ has revealed, of the immense happiness which he has prepared for his elect. The images are drawn in such colours and with such materials, that while they place the objects of our wishes within the reach of our weak senses, they give us an idea of something still more exquisite which we cannot comprehend. For heavenly happiness in itself is such as no mortal eye can see, and no heart conceive. Good Christians always keep that holy city in view; thither their hearts aspire; thither their thoughts and affections tend. Knowing that the glory there, is in different degrees proportioned to their labours here, they willingly submit to the chisel of affliction, and joyfully bear the strokes of contradiction and suffering from a wicked world, that they may be worthy of the joys of heaven. They never forget the pool of fire burning with brimstone, which is so often mentioned in the book of Revelations, that the fear of sinning may not be extinguished. Thither they often look down with one eye, while the other is turned up to heaven, the eternal mansion of the blessed, that their souls may be animated with fresh nope, and quickened with new desires. Love but the goods which God has promised you, says St. Austin, and fear the evils with which he threatens you: with steady virtue you will then despise whatever promises and whatever threats this vain world can make you.

THE END.

CATALOGUE OF BOOKS

PUBLISHED AND FOR SALE BY

D. & J. SADLIER & CO.,

164 WILLIAM STREET, New York;

128 FEDERAL STREET, Boston;

CORNER OF NOTRE DAME AND ST. FRANCIS XAVIER STREETS, Montreal, C. E.

A Liberal Discount made to the Trade, Religious Institutions, Public Libraries, &c.

A.

ADELMAR, THE TEMPLAR. Cloth, - - - - $0 25
ALL FOR JESUS; or, The Easy Ways of Divine Love. By FABER, - - - - - - - - - 0 75
ALICE RIORDAN; or, The Blind Man's Daughter. By Mrs. SADLIER, - - - - - - - - - - 0 38
ALTON PARK, - - - - - - - - - 0 75
AILEY MOORE. 2 vols., - - - - - - - 0 75
ALICE SHERWIN; or, The Days of Sir Thomas More. 75 cents; gilt, - - - - - - - - - - 1 12

This is an Excellent Historical Novel of the time of the Reformation in England.

ART OF SUFFERING. Translated from the French, by E. BUTLER. 25 cents; gilt, - - - - - - $0 38
ALTAR MANUAL; or, Instructions for Confession and Communion. Cloth, - - - - - - - - 0 38
ART MAGUIRE; or, The Broken Pledge. By CARLETON, - - - - - - - - - - - 0 38
ANIMA DEVOTA; or, Devout Soul, - - - - 0 38
AUDIN'S LIFE OF HENRY VIII. 8vo., - - - 2 00
" " " LUTHER. 2 vols. 8vo., - - 3 75
ARCHCONFRATERNITY OF THE HEART OF MARY, 0 19
ARK OF THE COVENANT. By Rev. T. S. PRESTON, 0 38
ANGELICAL VIRTUE, - - - - - - - - 0 25

B.

BALMES' FUNDAMENTAL PHILOSOPHY. Translated from the Spanish, by H. F. BROWNSON. 2 vols. Cloth, $3 50; half morocco, $4; calf antique, - $4 50
BALMES ON EUROPEAN CIVILIZATION. 8vo., 2 00

BANQUET OF THEODOLUS, - - - - 0 50
BAINES' ESSAY ON DIVINE FAITH, - - - 0 75
BALLS AND DANCING. By ABBE HULOT, - - 0 38
BAXTER'S TENETS OF THE CATHOLIC CHURCH EXPLAINED, - - - - - - - - - 0 19
BENJAMIN; or, The Pupil of the Christian Brothers. Translated from the French, by Mrs. SADLIER. Cloth, 0 25
BERTHA; or, The Pope and the Emperor. By McCABE, - - - - - - - - - - 0 75
BIBLE AGAINST PROTESTANTISM. By Dr. SHEIL, 0 50
BIBLE QUESTION FAIRLY TESTED, - - - 0 38
BEAUTIES OF SIR THOMAS MORE, - - - 0 75
BEAUTIES OF THE SANCTUARY, - - - 0 50
BICKERTON; or, Emigrant's Daughter, - - - 0 50
BLAKES AND FLANIGAN'S. A Tale illustrative of Irish Life in the United States. By Mrs. J. SADLIER. 75 cents; gilt, - - - - - - - - - 1 13
BLIND AGNESE, - - - - - - - - - 0 38
BLANCHE. A Tale, - - - - - - - - - 0 25
BLANCHE LESLIE AND OTHER TALES. 6 vols. Paper, 75c. per doz., six in one; cloth, 38c.; cloth, gilt, - - - - - - - - - - 0 63
BOSSUET'S HISTORY OF THE VARIATIONS OF THE PROTESTANT CHURCHES. 2 vols. Cloth, 1 50
BOYHOOD OF GREAT PAINTERS. 2 vols. Cloth, 0 75
" " " Gilt, - - 1 25
" " " 2 vols. in 1, - 0 63
" " " " gilt, 0 88
BARTOLI'S LIFE OF ST. IGNATIUS. 2 vols., - 2 25
BLESSED SACRAMENT. By FABER, - - - 0 75
BROWNSON'S ESSAYS AND REVIEWS ON THEOLOGY, POLITICS, AND SOCIALISM. Cloth, $1 25; half morocco, - - - - - - - 1 75
BUTLER'S LIVES OF THE FATHERS, MARTYRS, AND OTHER PRINCIPAL SAINTS. 4 vols. 8vo. Illustrated with 25 fine Steel Engravings and four Illuminated Title Pages. Sheep, marble edges, $9; roan, marble edges, $10 50; roan, full gilt, $12 50; morocco extra, $14; morocco extra, beveled, - - 16 00

SADLIERS' *Edition is the most complete and best published.*

BUTLER'S LIVES OF THE SAINTS. Cheap Edition. 4 vols. Cloth, $5; roan, $6; bound in 12 vols., or Libraries, - - - - - - - - - - $8 00
BUTLER'S CATECHISM (as used in the United States), - - - - - - - - - - - 0 5
BUTLER'S CATECHISM FOR THE DIOCESE OF TORONTO,
BUTLER'S CATECHISM FOR THE ARCHDIOCESE OF QUEBEC, } Containing the large & small Catechisms bound together, 0 5
BRYANT ON THE IMMACULATE CONCEPTION, 0 50

C.

CATECHISM OF SCRIPTURE HISTORY, - - $0 50
" OF THE COUNCIL OF TRENT, - 1 00
" OF PERSEVERANCE, - - - 0 38
" OF AN INTERIOR LIFE, - - - 0 25
" OF THE HISTORY OF IRELAND, - 0 25
" DOCTRINAL AND SCRIPTURAL By COLLOT. Translated from the French, by Mrs. J. SADLIER. Half bound, 38c.; cloth, - - - - - - 0 50
" OF THE CATHOLIC RELIGION. Translated from the German of Rev. F. X. WENINGER. 12mo. Cloth, - 0 88
" FOR THE USE OF CATECHISTS. By PERRY. Cloth, 63c.; arabesque, - 0 75
" GENERAL. Approved by the National Council, - - - - - - - 0 3
" FOR THE DIOCESE OF BOSTON, - 0 3
" " " NEW YORK, 0 3
" BUTLER'S FOR U. S., QUEBEC AND TORONTO, - - - - - - 0 5
" FLEURY'S HISTORICAL. Abridged, 0 12
" DOUAY, - - - - - - 0 12
" OF THE CHRISTIAN RELIGION. By KEENAN, - - - - - - - 0 75
" DOCTRINAL. By KEENAN, - - 0 31

CAHILL'S (DR.) LETTERS AND SPEECHES, - 0 50

CATHOLIC YOUTH'S MAGAZINE. 3 vols., - - 2 25
" DOCTRINE PROVED FROM SCRIPTURE, - - - - - - - 0 38
" BRIDE. Translated by Dr. PISE, - - 0 50
" PULPIT. A Collection of Sermons. Cloth, - - - - - - - $2 25
" CHRISTIAN INSTRUCTED. By Bishop CHALLONER. Flexible, 25c.; cloth, - 0 38
" CHRISTIAN INSTRUCTED. By QUADRAPANI, - - - - - - - 0 25
" LEGENDS AND STORIES. Cloth, 50c.; cloth, gilt, - - - - - - - 0 75
" HYMN BOOK FOR YOUTH, - - 0 4
" HISTORY OF AMERICA. By McGEE, 0 50
" SUNDAY SCHOOL CLASS BOOKS, - 0 13
" MELODIES. By ROHR, - - - 0 25
" HARP. A Collection of Masses, Hymns, &c., - - - - - - - - 0 38

CAROLINE HENSON, - - - - - - - 0 19

CASTLE OF ROUSSILLON. A Tale of the Huguenot Wars. Translated from the French, by Mrs. SADLIER. Cloth, 50c.; cloth, gilt, - - - - - - - 0 75

CHALLONER'S HISTORY OF THE PROTESTANT RELIGION, - - - - - - - - - - $0 19
CHALLONER'S MEDITATIONS FOR EVERY DAY. 2 vols., - - - - - - - - - 1 50
CHALLONER'S MEDITATIONS. Abridged, - - 0 75
CHARITY AND TRUTH. By HAYWARDEN, - - 0 63
CHRISTIAN BROTHERS' FIRST BOOK READING LESSONS, - - - - - - - - - 0 6
CHRISTIAN BROTHERS' SECOND BOOK READING LESSONS, - - - - - - - - 0 13
CHRISTIAN BROTHERS' THIRD BOOK READING LESSONS, - - - - - - - - - 0 38
CHRISTIAN BROTHERS' FOURTH BOOK READING LESSONS, - - - - - - - - 0 63
CHRISTIANITY AND THE CHURCH. By Dr. PISE, 0 75
CHRISTMAS NIGHT'S ENTERTAINMENTS, - - 0 38
CHATEAU LESCURE. A Tale, - - - - 0 38
COBBETT'S HISTORY OF THE REFORMATION, 0 75

SADLIER'S *is the only complete Edition of* COBBETT *published.*

COBBETT'S LEGACIES TO PARSONS AND LABORERS, - - - - - - - - - $0 38
CONSIDERATIONS ON THE WORLD, - - - 0 38
COTTAGE CONVERSATIONS. By MARY MONICA, 0 50
CONSCIENCE'S TALES. 6 vols., viz.:
" CURSE OF THE VILLAGE, - - 0 75
" LION OF FLANDERS, - - - 0 75
" WAR OF THE PEASANTS, - - 0 75
" TALES OF OLD FLANDERS, - 0 75
" MISER, - - - - - - - 0 75
" DEMON OF GOLD, - - - 0 75
CONFEDERATE CHIEFTAINS. A Tale of the Great Irish Rebellion of 1641. By Mrs. J. SADLIER, - 1 25
CHOIR BOOK. Containing the Morning and Evening Service of the Catholic Church. By GERBET, - 2 00
CHAPEL CHOIR BOOK, - - - - - - - 0 50
CEREMONIAL OF THE CATHOLIC CHURCH, - 1 00
CON O'REGAN; or, Scenes from Emigrant Life. By Mrs. J. SADLIER. (In Press.) Cloth, 50c.; gilt, - 0 75
CONFESSIONS OF AN APOSTATE. By Mrs. J. SADLIER. (In Press.) 16mo. Cloth, 50c.; do., gilt, 0 75
COCHIN ON THE MASS, - - - - - - 0 75
CONFIDENCE IN THE MERCY OF GOD, - - 0 50
CROSS AND SHAMROCK, - - - - - 0 50
CALLISTA. A Tale of the Third Century. By Dr. NEWMAN, - - - - - - - - - - 0 75

D.

DAILY PRAYER. A Manual of Catholic Devotion. 18mo. Very large type. (In Press.) At prices from 75 cents to - - - - - - - - -	$10 00
DEVOUT COMMUNICANT. By BAKER, - - -	0 38
DEVOTIONS TO THE SACRED HEART, - -	0 50
DEVOTIONS TO THE SACRED HEART. By Father DALGAIRNS, - - - - - - -	0 50
DEVOTIONS TO THE SACRED HEART. 32mo., -	0 25
DE COURCY'S AND SHEA'S CATHOLIC CHURCH IN THE UNITED STATES, - - - - - -	1 50
DEVOTIONS TO CALVARY, - - - - -	0 38
DR. DIXON ON THE HOLY SCRIPTURES, - -	2 50
DUTY OF A CHRISTIAN TOWARDS GOD. From the French of Ven. LA SALLE, by Mrs. J. SADLIER. 38 cents; cloth, - - - - - - - -	0 50
DOUAY TESTAMENT. 16mo. Cloth, - - -	0 38
" " " Roan, gilt edges, -	0 75
DOUAY BIBLE. 12mo. Sheep, - - - -	1 00
" " " Roan, marble, - -	1 50
" " " Gilt edges, - - -	2 00
" " SADLIERS' Fine Imperial 4to. To which is added WARD'S ERRATA OF THE PROTESTANT BIBLE. Illustrated with 25 plates. At prices from $11 to - - - - - - - - - -	22 00
DOUAY BIBLE. SADLIERS' Illustrated Edition. With 17 plates. To which is added WARD'S ERRATA. At prices varying from $5 to - - - - - -	12 00
DOUAY BIBLE. SADLIERS' Small 4to. Printed on very fine paper, and Illustrated with 12 fine Steel Engravings. Imitation, gilt edges, - - - -	6 00
Morocco, extra, 12 plates, - - -	7 50
" " " " Clasp, - -	9 00
" " " " Beveled, -	8 50
" " " " " Clasp, -	10 00
" " Paneled, - - -	12 00
" " Medallion, tooled edges,	15 00
DOUAY BIBLE. SADLIERS' Extraordinary Cheap Edition. Small 4to. At prices from $2 25 to -	7 00
DOUAY, (HAYDOCK'S.) At from $14 to - -	25 00
" POCKET BIBLE. Roan, plain, - - -	1 00
" " " Roan, gilt, - - -	1 25
" " " Morocco, extra, - -	3 00

E.

EDMA AND MARGUERETTE. By Madame WOILLEZ,	$0 38
EDITH MORTIMER. By Mrs. PARSONS. Cloth, -	0 50
ELEANOR MORTIMER; or, The World and the Cloister. By AGNES M. STEWART. Cloth, - -	0 50

ELEVATION OF THE SOUL TO GOD, - - - - $0 50
ELINOR PRESTON; or, Scenes at Home and Abroad. By Mrs. J. SADLIER. (In Press.) Cloth, 50c.; cloth, gilt, - - - - - - - - - 0 75
EPISTLES AND GOSPELS FOR ALL THE SUNDAYS AND FESTIVALS, - - - - - - 0 19
EUCHARISTIC MONTH, - - - - - - - 0 38
EUCHARISTICA, - - - - - - - - - 0 63
EXERCISE OF FAITH IMPOSSIBLE EXCEPT IN THE CATHOLIC CHURCH, - - - - - - 0 38
EXPOSITION OF THE APOCALYPSE, - - - - 1 50
END OF CONTROVERSY. By Dr. MILNER, - - 0 50
ERRATA OF THE PROTESTANT BIBLE. By WARD, 0 50

F.

FABIOLA. A Tale of the Roman Catacombs. By Cardinal WISEMAN. 12mo. Cloth, 75c.; cloth, gilt, $1 12
FABER'S ALL FOR JESUS; or, The Easy Ways of Divine Love. Coth, 75c.; cloth, gilt, - 1 25
" GROWTH IN HOLINESS. Cloth, 75c.; gilt, - - - - - - - - - 1 25
" THE CREATOR AND CREATURE. Cloth, 75c.; gilt, - - - - - - - - 1 25
" THE FOOT OF THE CROSS. Cloth, 75c.; gilt, - - - - - - - - - 1 25
" SPIRITUAL CONFERENCES. Cloth, 75c.; gilt, - - - - - - - - 1 25
" THE PRECIOUS BLOOD. Cloth, 75c.; gilt, - - - - - - - - - 1 25
" TALES OF THE ANGELS, - - - - 0 38
" BETHLEHEM. (In Press.) Cloth, 75c.; gilt, - - - - - - - - - 1 25
FATHER LAVAL. By McSHERRY. Cloth, 50c.; gilt, - - - - - - - - - 0 75
" DRUMMOND AND HIS ORPHANS, - 0 38
" FELIX, - - - - - - - - 0 38
" JONATHAN; or, Scottish Converts, - - 0 75
" OSWALD. A Catholic Story. Cloth, 50c.; gilt, - - - - - - - - 0 75
" ROWLAND. By Dr. PISE, - - - - 0 38
" SHEHEY AND OTHER TALES. (In Press.) By. Mrs. J. SADLIER. Cloth, 50c.; cloth, gilt, - - - - - - - - - 0 75
FAITH, HOPE AND CHARITY. A Tale. Cloth, - 0 75
FAMILIAR INSTRUCTIONS. By Rev. J. CURR, - 0 19
FENELON ON THE EDUCATION OF A DAUGHTER, 0 50
FESTIVAL OF THE ROSARY. By Miss STEWART, 0 25
FIFTY REASONS WHY THE CATHOLIC RELIGION OUGHT TO BE PREFERRED TO ALL OTHERS. Cloth, - - - - - - - - - 0 19

FIRST COMMUNION. (Letters to the Young), - $0 38
FLEURY'S HISTORICAL CATECHISM. 4 parts, - 0 38
" " " Abridged, 0 12
FOURFOLD DIFFICULTIES OF ANGLICANISM, - 0 38
THE FOLLOWING OF CHRIST. New Translation, with Prayers and Reflections. With Supplement, containing Methodical and Explanatory Tables of the Chapters of the FOLLOWING OF CHRIST. Gilt edges, $1; English morocco, extra, $1 25; Morocco, super extra, $2 25; Morocco, flexible, beveled, $2 50. 24mo. edition, same type: Cloth, plain, 38c.; Roan, plain, 50c.; Roan, gilt edges, - - - - - 0 75
FLORINE. A Tale of the Crusaders. By McCABE, - 0 75
FLOWERS OF LOVE AND MEMORY. By Mrs. DORSEY, - - - - - - - - - - 0 75

G.

GARBET'S MORNING AND EVENING SERVICE OF THE CATHOLIC CHURCH. Containing a variety of Masses, Motettes, Hymns, &c., - - - $2 00
GALLITZEN'S DEFENCE OF CATHOLIC PRINCIPLES, - - - - - - - - - - - 0 38
GALLITZEN ON THE HOLY SCRIPTURES, - - 0 38
GARDEN OF ROSES AND VALLEY OF LILIES. By KEMPIS, - - - - - - - - - - 0 25
GOBINET'S INSTRUCTION FOR YOUTH, - - 0 75
GENEVIEVE. A Tale, - - - - - - - 0 38
GOTHER'S SINCERE CHRISTIAN, - - - 0 38
GOLDEN BOOK OF THE CONFRATERNITIES, - 0 38
" TREATISE ON MENTAL PRAYER, - 0 38
GRIFFIN'S COMPLETE WORKS. Edited by his Brother. 10 vols., 12mo. Printed on fine paper, and Illustrated with fine Steel Engravings:

1. THE COLLEGIANS. A Tale of Garryowen.
2. CARD-DRAWING. A Tale of Clare.
   THE HALF SIR. A Tale of Munster.
   SUIL DHUV. A Tale of Tipperary.
3. THE RIVALS. A Tale of Wicklow; and TRACY'S AMBITION.
4. HOLLAND TIDE, THE AYLMERS OF BALLY-AYLMER, THE HAND AND WORD, and BARBER OF BANTRY.
5. TALES OF THE JURY ROOM. Containing "Sigismund," "The Story Teller at Fault," "The Knight without Reproach," &c., &c.
6. THE DUKE OF MONMOUTH. A Tale of the English Insurrection.
7. THE POETICAL WORKS AND TRAGEDY OF GYSIPPUS.
8. INVASION. A Tale of the Conquest.

9. LIFE OF GERALD GRIFFIN. By his Brother.
10. TALES OF THE FIVE SENSES, and NIGHT AT SEA.

10 vols. Cloth, extra, per set, $10; half roan, $12 50; half morocco, $16; half calf, antique, $20; full morocco, antique, gilt edges, - - - - - $30 00

Any volume may be had separate, as each volume is complete in itself.

GREEN BOOK. By O'CALLAGHAN, - - - - - $0 50

H.

HASKIN'S TRAVELS IN ITALY, FRANCE AND IRELAND, - - - - - - - - - - - $0 50
HAY ON MIRACLES, - - - - - - - - 0 75
HAY'S SINCERE CHRISTIAN, - - - - - 1 50
" DEVOUT CHRISTIAN, - - - - - 1 50
HEROINES OF CHARITY. Containing the Life of Mrs. SETON and a number of others. 12mo. Price only 50 cents; gilt, - - - - - - - - 0 75
HISTORY OF IRELAND, Ancient and Modern. By Abbe MACGEOGHEGAN. Cloth, $2 25; half morocco, 2 50
HISTORY OF IRELAND, from the Earliest Period to the Emancipation of the Catholics. By T. D. MCGEE, M.P.P. 2 vols. (In Press.) - - -
HISTORY OF IRELAND. By MOONEY. 2 vols., - 3 00
" " " By MOORE, - - - 4 00
" " THE RISE AND FALL OF THE IRISH NATION. By Sir JONAH BARRINGTON. With 29 Portraits, - - - - - - - - - - 1 00
HISTORY OF THE IRISH REBELLION OF 1798, 0 50
" " " REFORMATION. By COBBETT, 0 75
" " " MISSIONS IN JAPAN AND PARAGUAY, - - - - - - - - - - 0 63
HISTORY OF THE WAR IN LA VENDEE. 6 plates, 0 75
HIDDEN TREASURE, - - - - - - - - 0 25
HUC'S CHRISTIANITY IN CHINA, TARTARY AND THIBET. 2 vols. 12mo., - - - - - 2 00
HUGHES' AND BRECKINRIDGE'S CONTROVERSY, - - - - - - - - - - - 1 00
HUGHES' AND BRECKINRIDGE'S ORAL DISCUSSION, - - - - - - - - - - - 1 50
HORNIHOLD ON COMMANDMENTS AND SACRAMENTS, - - - - - - - - - - - 1 25
HOLY WEEK, - - - - - - - - - 0 50
HOME OF THE LOST CHILD, - - - - - 0 38
HOURS BEFORE THE ALTAR, - - - - 0 25

I.

IDLENESS ; or, The Double Lesson. And other Tales. Translated by Mrs. SADLIER. (In Press.) 18mo. Paper, 15c. ; cloth, 25c. ; cloth, gilt, - - $0 38
IMITATION OF CHRIST. By KEMPIS, - - - 0 38
" BLESSED VIRGIN, - - - 0 50
IMMACULATE CONCEPTION. By Cardinal LAMBRUSCHNI, 50c. ; gilt, - - - - - - - 0 75
INSTRUCTIONS ON MATRIMONY, - - - 0 38
INTERIOR CHRISTIAN, - - - - - - 0 38
INDIAN COTTAGE. By Dr. PISE, - - - - 0 38
INTRODUCTION TO A DEVOUT LIFE. By St. FRANCIS DE SALES - - - - - - 0 38

J.

JOHN O'BRIEN. By Rev. Mr. RODDEN, - - - $0 50
JEW OF VERONA, - - - - - - - - 2 00
JOURNEE DU CHRETIEN. (French Prayer Book), 0 38
JOY OF THE CHRISTIAN SOUL. From the French, 0 19

K.

KENRICK, F. P., (Archbishop of Baltimore,) PRIMACY OF THE APOSTOLIC SEE VINDICATED, $1 50
KENRICK, F. P., VINDICATION OF THE CATHOLIC CHURCH, - - - - - - - - 0 75
KENRICK, F. P., JUSTIFICATION EXPLAINED, 0 75
" THEOLOGIA MORALIS. 2 vols., 4 00
" " DOGMATICA. 3 vols., - - - - - - - - - - - 6 00
KENRICK, F. P., THE PSALMS. With Notes, - 3 00
" JOB AND THE PROPHETS. With Notes, - - - - - - - - - - 3 00
KENRICK, F. P., THE PENTATEUCH. With Notes, 3 00
" HISTORICAL BOOKS. " " 3 00
KENRICK, P. R., (Archbishop of St. Louis,) OUR ANGLICAN ORDINATIONS, - - - - - 1 25
KENRICK, P. R., HOLY HOUSE OF LORETTO, 0 75
" NEW MONTH OF MARY, - 0 38
KIRWAN UNMASKED. By Archbishop HUGHES, - 0 06
KERNEY'S FIRST CLASS BOOK HISTORY, - 0 25
" COMPENDIUM OF HISTORY, - - 0 75

L.

LADY FULLERTON'S ELLEN MIDDLETON, - $0 75
" " GRANTLEY MANOR, - 0 75
" " LADY BIRD, - - - 0 75
" " ST. FRANCES OF ROME, - 0 50
LEGENDS OF THE BLESSED VIRGIN, - 0 50

LAW AND WILBERFORCE'S LETTERS, - - $0 19
LAMP OF THE SANCTUARY. A Tale, - - - 0 25
LAWRENCE; or, The Little Sailor, - - - - 0 38
LETTERS ON THE SPANISH INQUISITION. By De Maistre, - - - - - - - - - - 0 50
LENTEN MANUAL, - - - - - - - - 0 38
" MONITOR, - - - - - - - 0 38
LIGUORI (ST.) ON THE RELIGIOUS STATE, - 0 38
" " SPIRITUAL SUBJECTS, - - 0 38
" " ON COMMANDMENTS AND SACRAMENTS, - - - - - 0 31
" " PREPARATION FOR DEATH, - 0 50
" " LOVE OF CHRIST, - - - 0 38
" " WAY OF SALVATION, - - 0 38
" " HOURS OF THE PASSION, - - 0 38
" " VISITS TO BLESSED SACRAMENT, - - - - - - 0 38
" " ON PRAYER, - - - - - 0 25
" " CHRISTIAN VIRTUES, - - 0 63
" " MYSTERIES OF FAITH, - - 0 50
" " MEDITATIONS ON THE INCARNATION, - - - - - - 0 50
" " SPIRIT OF - - - - - 0 38
" " SPIRITUAL WORKS, - - - 0 50
LIFE OF CHRIST FOR YOUTH. Translated from the French, by Mrs. J. Sadlier. 18mo. Illustrated. Cloth, 50c.; cloth, gilt, - 0 75
" CHRIST. By St. Bonaventure, - - 0 50
" CHRIST AND HIS APOSTLES. From the French of De Ligney. Super royal 8vo. Illustrated. Cloth, $4; roan, marble, $5; roan, full gilt, $6; morocco extra, $7; morocco extra, beveled clasp, $8; paneled, $10; medallion, - - - - - - 12 00
" THE BLESSED VIRGIN MARY. To which is added the History of the Devotion to Her, and Full Meditations on the Litany. Translated from the French of Abbe Orseni, by Mrs. J. Sadlier. Super royal 8vo. 16 plates. Cloth, $4; roan, marble, $5; imitation, full gilt, $6; morocco, $7; morocco beveled, extra, $8; paneled, $10; Turkey extra, medallion sides, - 12 00

This is by far the most complete and the most interesting Life of the Blessed Virgin published.

LIFE OF THE BLESSED VIRGIN; or, Lily of Israel. 18mo. Cloth, 50c.; cloth, gilt, - - $0 75
" THE BLESSED VIRGIN. 32mo. Cloth, 25c.; cloth gilt, - - - - - - - 0 38

LIFE OF ST. FRANCIS OF SALES, BISHOP AND PRINCE OF GENEVA, - - - - $0 63
" ST. ALOYSIUS GONZAGA, - - - 0 38
" ST. BERNARD. By Abbe RATISBONE. Cloth, $1; cloth, gilt, - - - - - 1 50
" BISHOP MAGINN. By T. D. McGEE, - 0 75
" CARDINAL XIMINEZ, - - - - - 3 00
" BLESSED PAUL OF THE CROSS, - - 0 50
" BLESSED ANN OF JESUS, - - - 0 50
" ST. ANGELI MERICI, - - - - - 0 50
" ST. AGNES OF ROME, - - - - - 0 25
" ST. FRANCIS XAVIER, APOSTLE OF THE INDIES, - - - - - - - 1 00
" ST. IGNATIUS LOYOLA. By BARTOLI. 2 vols., - - - - - - - - 2 25
" ST. LIGUORI. 12mo. Cloth, - - - 1 00
" " 18mo. Cloth, - - - 0 25
" ST. CATHARINE OF SIENNA, - - 1 00
" ST. TERESA. 12mo. Cloth, - - - 1 00
" " 32mo. Cloth, - - - 0 25
" FATHER EPHRAIM, of the Order of La Trappe, - - - - - - - - 0 75
" ST. PATRICK AND ST. BRIDGET. Cloth, 0 50
" ST. ASSISIUM, - - - - - - - 0 38
" ST. FRANCIS OF ROME. By Lady FULLERTON, - - - - - - - - 0 50
" ELIZABETH OF HUNGARY. By the Count MONTALEMBERT. Cloth, $1; cloth, gilt, - 1 50
" SISTER CAMILLA, THE CARMELITE, - 0 50
" MRS. SETON. By Rev. C. I. WHITE, D.D., 1 25
" SISTER ROSALIE, - - - - - - 0 38
" ST. ROSE OF LIMA, - - - - - 0 50
" ST. ZITA, - - - - - - - - 0 50
" ST. JOSEPH. Taken from the Mystical City of God. Cloth, 50c.; cloth, gilt, - 0 75
" PRINCESS BORGHESE, - - - - 0 38
" ST. STANISLAUS, - - - - - - 0 38
" ST. LOUIS, - - - - - - - - 0 25
" RT. REV. JAMES DOYLE, late Bishop of Kildare and Leighlin, with his Letters on various subjects. Cloth, - - - - 0 38
" ST. MARGARET OF CORTONA, - - 0 50
" BISHOP BRUTE, the First Bishop of Vincennes. By Bishop BAYLEY. Illustrated. Cloth, - - - - - - - - - 1 25
" ST. BRIDGET, - - - - - - - - 0 38
" MARY MAGDALENE. By the Rev. T. S. PRESTON, - - - - - - - 0 38
" B. V. MARY. By Rev. T. JOSLIN, - - 0 75
" A MODERN MARTYR (Bishop BORIE), - 0 38

LIVES OF THE NINE MAGDALENES. Translated from the French. (In Press), -
" " EARLY MARTYRS, including the Life of Mary Magdalene. By Mrs. HOPE. Cloth, 75 cents; gilt, - $1 12
" " FATHERS OF THE DESERTS. To which is added the Life of Saint Mary of Egypt. By Bishop CHALLONER. Cloth, 75 cents; gilt, - 1 12
LINGARD'S HISTORY OF ENGLAND. 13 vols., - 10 00
" " " Abridged. 8vo., 2 00
LETTERS TO AN EPISCOPALIAN. By AUGUSTINE BEDE, - - - - - - - - - - - 0 75
LIONELLO. A Sequel to the Jew of Verona, - - 1 00
LITTLE TESTAMENTS OF JESUS AND MARY. Cloth, 13 cents; Embossed gilt, - - - - - 0 25
LAURA AND ANNA. A Tale, - - - - - 0 38
LORETTO; or, The Choice. By MILES, - - 0 50
LOSS AND GAIN; or, The Story of a Convert. By NEWMAN, - - - - - - - - - - 0 50
LOUISA WARDEN, - - - - - - - - 0 13
LITTLE SNOWDROP, - - - - - - - - 0 38
LITTLE ANGEL OF THE COPTS. 2 vols., - - 0 75
LORENZO; or, The Empire of Religion, - - - 0 25
LYRA CATHOLICA, - - - - - - - - 0 50

M.

MAGINN'S LETTERS TO LORD STANLEY. Paper, $0 13
MAGUIRE'S SERMONS. Cloth, - - - - - 0 50
MARY, STAR OF THE SEA, - - - - - - 0 38
MARTHA; or, The Hospital Sister, - - - - 0 38
MAGUIRE'S ROME; ITS RULER AND ITS INSTITUTIONS. Cloth, $1 25; cloth, gilt edges, - - 1 75

This is decidedly the best and most interesting work on Rome and its Institutions ever published.

MAUREEN DHU. A Tale of the Claddagh at Galway. By Mrs. SADLIER. (In Press), - - - - -
MARLE'S LIFE OF MARY QUEEN OF SCOTS, - $0 75
MANAHAN'S TRIUMPH OF THE CHURCH, - 1 25
MANNING'S (DR.) GROUNDS OF FAITH, - - 0 25
MANUAL OF THE SODALITY, - - - - - 0 25
" CONTROVERSY, - - - - - 0 63
" CEREMONIES, - - - - - 0 50
" SODALITY OF HOLY ANGELS, - 0 06
" ROMAN CHANT, - - - - - 1 50
" PIETY, - - - - - - - - 0 50
MARY THE MORNING STAR, - - - - - 0 38
McGEE'S (T. D.) HISTORY OF THE REFORMATION IN IRELAND, 0 75

McGEE'S (T. D.) HISTORY OF THE IRISH SETTLERS IN AMERICA, - - $0 50
" CATHOLIC HISTORY OF AMERICA, - - - - - - 0 50
" POPULAR HISTORY OF IRELAND. 2 vols. (In Press), -
" CANADIAN BALLADS, - - 0 50
" LIFE OF BISHOP MAGINN, - 0 75
" SEBASTIAN; or, The Roman Martyr. Cloth, 38c.; cloth, gilt, 0 63

MACGEOGHEGAN'S HISTORY OF IRELAND. Cloth, $2 25; half bound, - - - - - - - 2 50
MEMORIAL OF A CHRISTIAN LIFE. By LEWIS of Grenada, - - - - - - - - - 0 50
METHOD OF CONVERSING WITH GOD, - - 0 25
MILNER'S LETTERS TO A PREBENDARY, - 0 38
MISSION OF DEATH. A Tale of the New York Penal Laws. By M. T. WALWORTH. Cloth, 50c.; cloth, gilt, - - - - - - - - - - 0 75
MONTH OF MARY. 32mo., - - - - - - 0 25
MONTH OF MARY; or, Graces of. Cloth, - - 0 38
" " " " Roan embossed, 0 50
MORAL TALES. By SHERLOCK, - - - - - 0 38
MRS. HERBERT AND THE VILLAGERS, - - 1 50
MISSION AND DUTIES OF YOUNG WOMEN, - 0 38
METROPOLITAN ILLUSTRATED SERIES OF SPELLERS AND READERS. Compiled by a Member of the Order of the Holy Cross:

METROPOLITAN SPELLER AND DEFINER. 130 plates, - - - - - - 0 13
" FIRST READER. Illustrated, - 0 19
" SECOND " " - 0 31
" THIRD " " - 0 50
" FOURTH " With Biographical Notices of the Authors from whom the selections are made, 0 75
" FIFTH READER; or, Book of Oratory. (In Press), - - 1 00

The METROPOLITAN READERS *are selected principally from Catholic Authors, and are intended solely for Catholic Schools. They are the only Illustrated Series of Catholic Readers published in this country.*

MEMORIALS OF THE BLESSED. By FAIRBANKS, $0 75
MISSION BOOK; or, Manual of Prayers Calculated to Preserve the Fruits of the Mission. At from 38c. to - - - - - - - - - - - - 3 00
MYLIUS' HISTORY OF ENGLAND, - - - 0 75

N.

NEW LIGHTS; or, Life in Galway. By Mrs. J. SADLIER. Cloth, 50c.; cloth, gilt, - - - - $0 75
NEWMAN'S SERMONS TO MIXED CONGREGATIONS, - - - - - - - - - - 0 75
NEWMAN'S CALLISTA. A Tale of the Third Century. Cloth, 75c.; cloth, gilt, - - - - - - - 1 12
NOUET'S MEDITATIONS, - - - - - - 1 50
NORMAN STEEL, THE PRIEST HUNTER. By Mrs. J. SADLIER. (In Press), - - - -

O.

ONE HUNDRED SERMONS. By Rev. Father THOMAS, - - - - - - - - - - $1 25
ORIENTAL PEARL. A Tale. By Mrs. DORSEY, - 0 25
ORPHAN OF MOSCOW; or, The Young Governess. Translated from the French, by Mrs. J. SADLIER. Cloth, 50c.; cloth, gilt, - - - - - - - 0 75
ORATORY OF A FAITHFUL SOUL, - - - 0 38

P.

PATH TO PARADISE. A Manual of Prayers. At from 19c. to - - - - - - - $5 00
" OF PERFECTION, - - - - - - 0 50
" WHICH LED A PROTESTANT LAWYER INTO THE CHURCH, - - - - -
PAPIST REPRESENTED AND MISREPRESENTED, 0 13
PAROCHIAL AND SUNDAY SCHOOL LIBRARY. In 12 volumes. First Series. Each volume sold separately, or in sets of twelve. Fancy paper covers, 15c.; neat cloth, 25c.; cloth, gilt edges, 38c. Containing:

1. THE WONDERFUL DOCTOR. An Eastern Tale. By Canon SCHMID.
2. THE EASTER EGGS, THE BIRD'S NEST, AND TITUS AND HIS FAMILY. In 1 vol. By Canon SCHMID.
3. THE NIGHTINGALE, and THE INUNDATION OF THE RHINE. In 1 vol. By Canon SCHMID.
4. HENRY EICHENFELS, and THE FIRE. In 1 vol. By Canon SCHMID.
5. HOP BLOSSOMS, and THE CRAY FISH. In 1 vol. By Canon SCHMID.
6. THE JEWELS, and DIAMOND RING. In 1 vol. By Canon SCHMID.
7. THE WOODEN CROSS, and CHAPEL OF WOLFSBUHL. In 1 vol. By Canon SCHMID.
8. LEWIS, THE LITTLE EMIGRANT. By Canon SCHMI
9. THE LITTLE HERMIT. By Canon SCHMID.
10. CHRISTMAS EVE. By Canon SCHMID.

11. THE BLACK LADY, THE FOREST CHAPEL, and THE OLD CASTLE. In 1 vol. By Canon SCHMID.
12. MEMOIRS OF A GUARDIAN ANGEL. A Catholic Tale. Translated from the French.

PAROCHIAL AND SUNDAY SCHOOL LIBRARY. In 12 volumes. Second Series. Uniform in size and price with First Series, containing:

1. HAIL MARY; or, The Beauties of the Angelical Salutation. To which are added, DIVINE PROVIDENCE, NEGLECT OF PRAYER, and THE CHRISTIAN SERVANT. In 1 volume.
2. VALENTINE REDMOND; or, The Cross of the Forest. To which are added, HANS THE MISER, and PERRIN AND LUCETTA. In 1 volume.
3. THE ANGEL OF CONSOLATION. To which is added, THE INFIDEL'S DEATH-BED. In 1 volume.
4. THE ADOPTED SON. To which are added, THE ENVIOUS GIRL REFORMED, THE COPPER COINS AND THE GOLD COINS. In 1 volume.
5. ISABELLA; or, The Heroine of Algiers. To which are added, THE STRAWBERRIES, and THE FARM AND PRESBYTERY. In 1 volume.
6. LUCY LAMBERT; or, The Shrine of the Forest. By MARY M. KING.
7. LENT LILIES. A Tale. To which are added CORPUS CHRISTI AFTERNOON, and THE USHER'S HORSE. In 1 volume.
8. POOR FANNY; or, The Motherless Child who Found a Mother. By MARY MONICA.
9. THE LITTLE SNOW-DROP; or, the Unbaptized One. By CECILIA MARY CADDELL.
10. THE STEP-SISTERS; or, A Cure for Prejudice. To which is added a beautiful Play for little girls, entitled THE MAY QUEEN. By REBECCA V. ROBERTS. In 1 volume.
11. LUCY WARD; or, The Dweller in the Tabernacle.
12. RICH AND POOR; or, Lady Adela and Grumbling Molly.

POPULAR LIBRARY OF HISTORY, BIOGRAPHY, FICTION, AND MISCELLANEOUS LITERATURE. A Series of Works by some of the most eminent writers of the day. Edited by Messrs. CAPES, NORTHCOTE, and THOMPSON:

1. FABIOLA; or, The Church of the Catacombs. By his Eminence Cardinal WISEMAN. 12mo. Cloth extra, 75 cents; gilt, - - - - - - $1 13
2. THE LIFE OF ST. FRANCIS OF ROME. By Lady FULLERTON. 12mo. Cloth, 50 cents; gilt, 0 75
3. CATHOLIC LEGENDS. 12mo. Cloth extra, 50 cents; gilt, - - - - - - - - - 0 75
4. HEROINES OF CHARITY. 12mo. Cloth extra, 50 cents; gilt, - - - - - - - - 0 75

5. THE WITCH OF MILTON HILL. Cloth extra, 50 cents; gilt, - - - - - - - $0 75
6. PICTURES OF CHRISTIAN HEROISM. Cloth extra, 50 cents; gilt, - - - - - - 0 75
7. THE BLAKES AND FLANAGANS. By Mrs. J. SADLIER. Cloth extra, 75 cents; gilt, - - 1 13
8. THE LIFE AND TIMES OF ST. BERNARD. By Abbe RATISBONE. Cloth extra, $1; gilt, - 1 50
9. THE LIVES OF THE EARLY MARTYRS. Cloth extra, 75 cents; gilt, - - - - - - 1 13
10. HISTORY OF THE WAR IN LA VENDEE. By G. J. HILL. 12mo. Illustrated. Cloth, 75c.; gilt, 1 12
11. TALES AND LEGENDS FROM HISTORY. 12mo. Cloth, 63 cents; gilt, - - - - - - 0 88
12. THE MISSIONS IN JAPAN AND PARAGUAY. 12mo. Cloth, 63 cents; gilt, - - - - - 0 88
13. CALLISTA. A Tale of the Third Century. By JOHN HENRY NEWMAN. 12mo. Cloth, 75c.; gilt, 1 12
14. MANUAL OF MODERN HISTORY. By MATTHEW BRIDGES, Esq. 600 pp. 12mo. Cloth, or half roan, 1 00
15. ANCIENT HISTORY. By MATTHEW BRIDGES, Esq. Cloth, or half roan, - - - - - - - 0 75
16. THE LIFE OF ST. ELIZABETH OF HUNGARY. By the Count DE MONTALEMBERT. 12mo. Cloth, $1; gilt, - - - - - - - - - - 1 50
17. LIFE AND LABORS OF ST. VINCENT DE PAUL. A new, complete, and careful Biography. By H. BEDFORD, Esq. 12mo. Cloth, 50 cents; gilt, - - - - - - - 0 75
18. ALICE SHERWIN. An Historical Tale of the Days of Sir THOMAS MORE. 12mo. Cloth, 75c.; gilt, - - - - - - - - - - - 1 12
19. LIFE OF ST. FRANCIS DE SALES. By ROBERT ORMSBY, M.A. Cloth, 63 cents; gilt, - 0 88

PARABLES OF ST. BONAVENTURE, - - - 0 38
PAULINE SEWARD. A Tale by BRYANT, - - 1 25
PASTORINI'S HISTORY OF THE CHURCH, - 0 75
PICTORIAL NEW TESTAMENT, - - - - 1 50
PICTURES OF CHRISTIAN HEROISM. By Dr. MANNING. Cloth, 50c.; cloth, gilt, - - - 0 75
PIOUS BIOGRAPHY FOR YOUNG LADIES, - 0 38
POCKET MISSAL. At from 50c. to - - - 2 50
POOR MAN'S CATECHISM. Flexible, 25c.; cloth, 0 38
" " CONTROVERSY, - - - - - 0 38
POPE AND MAGUIRE'S DISCUSSION, - - - 0 75
POOR SCHOLAR. By CARLTON, - - - - 0 50
PROPHECIES OF ST. COLUMBKILL. Translated from the Irish. By O'KEARNEY, - - - - 0 38
PERRY'S INSTRUCTIONS FOR THE USE OF CATECHISTS. Cloth, 63c.; Arabesque, - - 0 75

PERILS OF THE OCEAN AND WILDERNESS, - $0 50
PRETTY PLATE. By Dr. HUNTINGTON. Cloth, 38c.; cloth, gilt, - - - - - - - - - 0 63
PIUS THE NINTH AND THE TEMPORAL RIGHTS OF THE HOLY SEE. By RHODES, - - - 0 38
PARADISE OF THE CHRISTIAN SOUL, - - 1 25
PROTESTANT'S TRIAL BY THE WRITTEN WORD, 0 38
" CONVERTED BY THE BIBLE AND PRAYER BOOK, - - - - - - - - 0 38
PURGATORY OPENED; or, Month of November, - 0 25
PRACTICAL PIETY. By ST. FRANCIS OF SALES, - 0 50
PROTESTING CHRISTIAN. Paper, - - - 0 13
PROPHET OF THE RUINED ABBEY, - - - 0 50

R.

RAVELLINGS FROM THE WEB OF LIFE, - - $0 75
RATISBONE'S CONVERSION, - - - - -
RED HAND OF ULSTER; or, The Fortunes of Hugh O'Neil. By Mrs. J. SADLIER, - - - - - - 0 38
RELIGION IN SOCIETY. With an Introduction. By Archbishop HUGHES, - - - - - - - 1 00
REEVE'S HISTORY OF THE CHURCH, - - 1 00
" HISTORY OF THE OLD AND NEW TESTAMENTS. With 230 cuts, - - - 0 50
" DISCOURSES, - - - - - - - 1 50
REVIEW OF FOX'S MARTYRS, - - - - - 2 50
RISE AND FALL OF THE IRISH NATION. By Sir JONAH BARRINGTON. With 29 Portraits, - - 1 00
RITUALI ROMANO EXCERPTA, - - - - - 0 50
RODRIGUEZ'S CHRISTIAN PERFECTION. 3 vols., 2 50
ROMAN MISSAL FOR THE USE OF THE LAITY. Plain, - - - - - - - - - - - - 1 00
ROTH'S LIFE OF NAPOLEON III., - - - 0 75
RULES OF THE ROSARY AND SCAPULAR, - 0 25
" OF A CHRISTIAN LIFE. 2 vols., - - 1 50
ROSE OF TANENBOURGH, - - - - - - 0 38
ROSEMARY; or, Life and Death. By Dr. HUNTINGTON. Thick 12mo. Illustrated. Cloth, $1 25; cloth, gilt, - - - - - - - - - - - - - 1 75
ROMAN CATACOMBS. By NORTHCOTE, - - 0 50
ROME AND THE ABBEY. By the Authoress of "Geraldine," - - - - - - - - - - 0 75

S.

SALVE FOR THE BITE OF THE BLACK VIPER, $0 25
SEGUR'S ANSWERS TO POPULAR OBJECTIONS AGAINST RELIGION, - - - - - - 0 38
SERAPHIC STAFF, - - - - - - - 0 19

SCHMIDT'S ONE HUNDRED TALES, - - - $0 38
SHANDY MAGUIRE. By PAUL PEPPERGRASS, - 0 50
SHEA'S FIRST BOOK OF HISTORY. Illustrated, 0 38
" ELEMENTARY HISTORY OF THE UNITED STATES, - - - - 0 25
" HISTORY OF CATHOLIC MISSIONS, - 1 75
SHIPWRECK AND OTHER TALES, - - - 0 38
SHORTEST WAY TO END DISPUTES. By Dr. MANNING, - - - - - - - - - - 0 50
SKETCHES OF O'CONNELL. By McGEE, - - 0 50
SINNER'S CONVERSION REDUCED TO PRINCIPLES, - - - - - - - - - - - 0 31
SINNER'S GUIDE. By LEWIS, of Granada, - - 0 75
SICK CALLS FROM THE DIARY OF A MISSIONARY PRIEST. By Rev. E. PRICE, - - - 0 50
SPAEWIFE. By the Author of SHANDY MAGUIRE. 2 vols., - - - - - - - - - - 1 50
SINCERE CHRISTIAN. By Bishop HAY, - - 1 50
SPALDING'S (BISHOP) MISCELLANEA. 8vo., - 1 50
" EVIDENCES OF CATHOLICITY, - 1 25
" LIFE OF BISHOP FLAGET, - - 1 00
" HISTORY OF THE REFORMATION IN GERMANY, SWITZERLAND, AND ENGLAND. 2 vols., - - 2 50
" Cheap Edition of the above in 1 vol. (In Press), - - - - - - 1 25
SPANISH TESTAMENT, - - - - - - 0 88
" PRAYER BOOK, - - - - - - 0 50
SURE WAY TO FIND OUT THE TRUE RELIGION, 0 19
SOUL UNITED TO JESUS, - - - - - 0 25
SPIRITUAL EXERCISES OF ST. IGNATIUS, - 0 50
" MAXIMS OF ST. VINCENT DE PAUL, 0 25
" COMBAT, - - - - - - - - 0 25
" DIRECTOR, - - - - - - 0 38
" CONSOLER, - - - - - - 0 25

SADLIER'S (MRS. J.) WORKS, ORIGINAL AND TRANSLATED.

" ALICE RIORDAN; or, The Blind Man's Daughter, - - - - - - - $0 38
" BLAKES AND FLANAGANS. A Tale of Irish Life in America, - - - 0 75
" RED HAND OF ULSTER; or, The Fortunes of Hugh O'Neil, - - - 0 38
" WILLY BURKE; or, The Irish Orphan in America, - - - - - 0 25
" NEW LIGHTS; or, Life in Galway, - 0 50
" THE CONFEDERATE CHIEFTAINS. A Tale of the Great Irish Rebellion of 1641. Cloth, $1 25; gilt, - - - 1 75

THE COTTAGE AND PARLOR LIBRARY.

SADLIER'S (MRS. J.) 1. THE SPANISH CAVALIERS. A Tale of the Moorish Wars in Spain. Translated from the French, by Mrs. J. SADLIER. 16mo. Cloth, 50c.; cloth, gilt, - - - - - - - $0 75

" 2. ELINOR PRESTON; or, Scenes at Home and Abroad. By Mrs. J. SADLIER. (In Press.) 16mo. Cloth, 50c.; cloth, gilt, - - - - - - - 0 75

" 3. BESSY CONWAY; or, The Irish Girl in America. By Mrs. J. SADLIER. 16mo. Cloth, 50c.; cloth, gilt, - - 0 75

" 4. THE CONFESSIONS OF AN APOSTATE; or, Scenes from a Troubled Life. By Mrs. J. SADLIER. (In Press.) 16mo. Cloth, 50c.; cloth, gilt, - - $0 75

" 5. CON O'REGAN; or, Scenes from Emigrant Life. By Mrs. J. SADLIER. (In Press.) 16mo. Cloth, 50c.; cloth, gilt, 0 75

" 6. MAUREEN DHU. A Tale of the Claddagh at Galway. By Mrs. J. SADLIER. (In Press.) 16mo. Cloth, 50c.; cloth, gilt, - - - - - - - 0 75

" 7. FATHER SHEEHY, and Other Tales. By Mrs. J. SADLIER. (In Press.) 16mo. Cloth, 50 cents; cloth, gilt, - - 0 75

" 8. NORMAN STEEL, THE PRIEST HUNTER, and Other Tales. By Mrs. J. SADLIER. 16mo. Cloth, - - 0 50

TRANSLATIONS.

" ORSINI'S LIFE OF THE BLESSED VIRGIN. At from $1 50 to - - $12 00

" DE LIGNEY'S LIFE OF CHRIST. At from $4 to - - - - - - 12 00

" LIFE OF CHRIST; or, Jesus Revealed to Childhood and Youth. Cloth, 50c.; cloth, gilt, - - - - - - - 0 75

" ORPHAN OF MOSCOW. A Tale, - 0 50

" CASTLE OF ROUSILLON. A Tale, - 0 50

" DUTY OF A CHRISTIAN TOWARDS GOD. Half bound, 38c.; cloth, - 0 50

" COLLOT'S DOCTRINAL AND SCRIPTURAL CATECHISM. Half bound, 38c.; cloth, - - - - - - 0 50

" BENJAMIN; or, The Pupil of the Christian Brothers. Cloth, 25c.; gilt, - 0 38

" THE BABBLER. A Moral Drama for Boys, - - - - - - - - 0 15

SADLIERS (MRS. J.) JULIA; or, The Gold Thimble. A Moral Drama for Girls, - - - - $0 15
" THE POPE'S NIECE, and Other Tales. (In Press), - - - - - - - 0 25
" IDLENESS; or, The Double Lesson. (In Press), - - - - - - - 0 25
" THE KNOUT. A Tale of Poland. 18mo., cloth, - - - - - - - - 0 50
SUNDAY MONITOR, - - - - - - - 0 38
STORIES OF THE SEVEN VIRTUES, - - - 0 38
ST. VINCENT'S MANUAL, - - - - - - 0 75
ST. AUGUSTINE'S CONFESSIONS, - - - 0 50
" " MEDITATIONS, - - - 0 38
SOUL ON CALVARY, - - - - - - - 0 50
SODALIST'S FRIEND, - - - - - - - 0 50
SUFFERINGS OF CHRIST. By Father THOMAS, S.J., 1 50
" OF JESUS, - - - - - - 0 38
SPANISH CAVALIERS. A Tale of the Moorish Wars in Spain. From the French, by Mrs. J. SADLIER. Cloth, 50 cents; cloth, gilt, - - - - - - 0 75
SONGS FOR CATHOLIC SCHOOLS. By Dr. CUMMINGS, - - - - - - - - - - 0 25

T.

TALES OF THE FIVE SENSES. By GERALD GRIFFIN, - - - - - - - - - $0 50
" AND STORIES OF THE IRISH PEASANTRY. By CARLTON, - - - - - 0 75
" OF THE FESTIVALS, - - - - 0 38
" OF THE SACRAMENTS, - - - - - 0 50
" AND LEGENDS FROM HISTORY, - - 0 62
TRAVELS OF AN IRISH GENTLEMAN. By THOS. MOORE, - - - - - - - - - - - 0 75
TREATISE ON GENERAL CONFESSION, - - 0 25
TRIALS OF A MIND. By Dr. IVES, - - - 0 50
THINK WELL ON'T. By Bishop CHALLONER, - 0 19
TEACHINGS AND STUDIES OF THE SOCIETY OF JESUS. By Abbe MAYNARD, - - - - 0 50
THE GOVERNESS. A Tale. By MILES, - - 0 38
THE KNOUT. A Tale of Poland. By Mrs. J. SADLIER, 0 50
THE TRIALS OF MAYBROOK. A Tale, - - 0 38
THE NEW GLORIES OF THE CATHOLIC CHURCH, 0 75
THE ROMAN VESPERAL, - - - - - - 0 75
THE VISITATION MANUAL, - - - - - 1 00
THE MINER'S DAUGHTER, - - - - - - 0 38
THE RACCOLTA; or, Book of Indulgenced Prayers, 0 50
THE LITTLE OFFICES OF THE BLESSED VIRGIN, 0 25
THE FLOWER BASKET, - - - - - - - 0 38
THE SAINTS OF ERIN, - - - - - - 0 50
THE YOUNG COMMUNICANTS, - - - - - 0 25

THE SACRAMENTALS. By BARRY, - - - $0 75
THE CHRISTIAN MOTHER, - - - - - - 0 25
THE POPE'S NIECE, and Other Tales. From the French, by Mrs. J. SADLIER. (In Press.) Paper, 15c.; cloth, - - - - - - - - - 0 25
THE SCAPULAR OF THE PASSION, - - - 0 38
THE VISION OF OLD ANDREW THE WEAVER, 0 38
THE BIBLE QUESTION FAIRLY TESTED, - - 0 38
THE SPAEWIFE; or, The Queen's Secret. 2 vols., 1 50
THE GRACES OF MARY; or, Devotions for the Month of May. Cloth, - - - - - - - 0 38
THE IRISH AGENT (VALENTINE McCLUTCHY). By WILLIAM CARLTON. Half bound, 50c.; cloth, - 0 75
THE URSULINE MONTH OF MARY, - - - 0 38
THE MONTH OF MARY. Translated from the French, by FABER, - - - - - - - 0 38
THE PROPHECIES OF ST. COLUMBKILLE, - 0 38

W.

WALSH'S ECCLESIASTICAL HISTORY OF IRELAND, - - - - - - - - - - - $3 00
WAY OF THE CROSS. With illustrations, - - 0 06
WARD'S CANTOS; or, England's Reformation, - 0 50
" ERRATA OF THE PROTESTANT BIBLE. Half bound, 50 cents; cloth, - - - 0 75
" TREE OF LIFE, - - - - - 3 00
WHITE'S CONFUTATION OF CHURCH OF ENGLANDISM, - - - - - - - - - - 0 75
WILBERFORCE ON CHURCH AUTHORITY, - 0 75
WILLY BURKE. By Mrs. SADLIER, - - - 0 25
WILLY RIELLY. By CARLTON, - - - - 0 75
WILLITOFT; or, The Days of James I. By McSHERRY, - - - - - - - - - - 0 75
WELL! WELL. A Tale. By Rev. M. A. WALLACE, - 0 75
WISEMAN'S (CARDINAL) LECTURES ON HOLY WEEK, - - - - - - - - 0 75
" CATHOLIC DOCTRINE, - - - 1 00
" REAL PRESENCE, - - - - 0 75
" SCIENCE AND REVEALED RELIGION. 2 vols., - - - - 3 00
" ESSAYS ON VARIOUS SUBJECTS. 3 vols., - - - - - - - 7 00
" SERMONS, - - - - - - - 0 25
" LAST FOUR POPES, - - - 1 00
" TOUR IN IRELAND, - - - - 0 75
" VINDICATION OF ITALY, - - 0 25
" HIDDEN GEM, - - - - - 0 75

Y.

YOUNG SAVOYARD, and Other Tales. Cloth, 38c.; cloth, gilt, - - - - - - - - - $0 63
YOUTH'S DIRECTOR, - - - - - - - 0 31
YOUNG CRUSADER. A Tale, - - - - - 0 38

STANDARD CATHOLIC PRAYER BOOKS.

☞ *The following Prayer Books are all printed on fine paper, in clear, bold type, beautifully illustrated, and for beauty of finish and durability of binding cannot be excelled. They contain all the necessary prayers used by Catholics, all carefully revised and issued under the approbation of the Most Rev.* JOHN HUGHES, *D.D. The most particular pains have been taken in the printing and binding of these Prayer Books.*

The most Complete and best got up Prayer Book Published in this Country is—

THE GOLDEN MANUAL. Being a Guide to Catholic Devotion, Public and Private. Compiled from approved sources. 18mo., 1041 pages. Illustrated with 12 engravings.

Neatly bound in sheep, 1 plate, - - - -	$0 75
Roan, plain, 1 " - - - - -	1 00
Embossed roan, gilt edges, - - - - -	1 50
Embossed roan, gilt edges, with clasps, - -	1 75
American morocco, gilt edges, 6 plates, - -	1 75
American morocco, gilt edges, 6 " with clasps,	2 00
English morocco, gilt edges, 8 " - - -	2 00
English morocco, gilt edges, 8 " with clasps,	2 50
Morocco, extra illuminated, 8 " - - -	2 50
Morocco, extra illuminated, 8 " with clasps,	3 00

Fine Paper, Illuminated Title, 12 *Plates.*

Morocco, beveled, - - - - - - -	3 00
Morocco, beveled, clasps, - - - - - -	3 50
Morocco, antique, - - - - - -	4 50
Morocco, antique, clasps, tooled edges, - -	5 50
Morocco, carved, tooled edges, with clasps, - -	8 00
Morocco, carved, tooled edges, with medallion, -	10 00
Rich velvet, clasps, - - - - - - -	6 00
Rich velvet, clasps and corners, with a case, -	9 00
Rich velvet, medallion on the side, - - -	10 00
Also, various styles, from $12 to - - -	20 00

THE WAY TO HEAVEN. A Select Manual of Prayers for Daily Use, compiled from approved sources. 18mo., 760 pages. Printed on superfine paper, and illustrated. To which is added the Epistles, Gospels and Collect for all the Sundays and Festivals of the Year.

Roan, antique edges, 5 plates, - - - -	1 00
Roan, gilt edges, 5 plates, - - - - -	1 25
English morocco, gilt edges, 5 plates, - - -	1 50
English morocco, gilt edges, 5 plates, clasps, -	2 00

Morocco, super extra, 5 plates, - - - - $2 25
Morocco, super extra, 5 plates, clasps, - - 2 75
Morocco, super extra, beveled, 9 plates, - - 2 50
Morocco, super extra, beveled, 9 plates, clasps, - 3 25
In rich velvet papier mache, and pearl binding, ranging in prices, from $5 to - - - - 20 00

WAY TO HEAVEN. 24mo. edition. Reduced prices.
Roan, embossed, plain, 2 plates, - - - - 0 38
Roan, gilt sides, - - - - - - - - 0 50
Roan, embossed, gilt edges, 4 plates, - - - 0 63
Roan, embossed, gilt edges, 4 plates, clasps, - 0 75
Roan, full gilt sides and edges, - - - - 0 75
Roan, full gilt sides and edges, clasps, - - - 0 88
Morocco extra, 6 plates, - - - - - 1 50
Morocco extra, 6 plates, clasps, - - - - 2 00
Morocco extra, beveled, flexible, 8 plates, - - 1 75
Morocco extra, beveled, flexible, 8 plates, clasps, 2 25
Velvet, with corners and clasps and case, - - 5 00
Velvet, with rims and medallion, - - - - 6 00
Velvet, with rims, corners, clasps, medallion, with case, - - - - - - - - - 7 00

THE GARDEN OF THE SOUL. A Manual of Fervent Prayers, Pious Reflections, and Solid Instructions. To which is added Bishop ENGLAND's Explanation of the Mass; and the Epistles, Gospels, and Collects for all the Sundays and Holydays of the Year. 18mo., 718 pages, finely illustrated.
Extra morocco, tooled edges and clasps, - - 4 00
Extra morocco, antique, tooled edges and clasps, 5 00
Extra morocco, clasps, gilt edges, - - - 2 50
Extra morocco, gilt edges, - - - - - 2 00
Imitation morocco, clasp, gilt edges, - - - 1 25
Imitation morocco, gilt edges, - - - - 1 00
Embossed morocco, gilt edges, - - - - 0 75
Strong roan, plain edges, - - - - - 0 50

This is an excellent book of devotion. The Epistles and Gospels and Bishop ENGLAND'S *Explanation of the Mass add greatly to its value; they alone are worth more than is charged for the whole book.*

LARGE PRINT PRAYER BOOK.

DAILY PRAYER. A Manual of Catholic Devotion. 18mo., finely illustrated. (In Press.)
Roan, plain, - - - - - - - - $0 75
Embossed, gilt edges, - - - - - - 1 25
Embossed, gilt edges, clasps, - - - - 1 50
Imitation, full gilt edges, - - - - - 1 50
Imitation, full gilt edges, clasps, - - - - 1 75
English morocco, gilt edges, - - - - 1 75

English morocco, gilt edges, clasps,	$2 00
Morocco extra,	2 25
Morocco extra, with clasps,	2 75
Morocco extra, beveled,	2 75
Morocco extra, beveled, clasps,	3 25
Morocco extra, tooled edges and clasps,	4 50
Morocco extra, antique, tooled edges and clasps,	6 00
Velvet bindings, from $5 to	10 00

This Prayer Book will be printed from very large type, and be illustrated in the most beautiful manner.

THE KEY OF HEAVEN. A Manual of Prayer. 24mo., illustrated.

Cloth,	$0 31
Roan, plain,	0 38
Gilt sides,	0 50
Imitation, full gilt edges,	0 75
Imitation, full gilt edges, clasps,	0 88
Morocco extra,	1 50
Morocco extra, clasps,	2 00
Morocco extra, beveled,	1 75
Morocco extra, beveled, clasps,	2 25
Morocco extra, tooled edges,	2 50
Morocco extra, tooled edges, clasps,	3 00
Morocco extra, tooled edges, corners and clasps,	4 00

THE PATH TO PARADISE. 32mo. Large edition, with 12 fine steel engravings.

Super extra morocco, beveled, flexible, clasps,	2 00
Super extra morocco, beveled, flexible,	1 50
Super extra morocco, clasps,	1 75
Super extra morocco,	1 25
Imitation morocco, 6 plates, gilt edges, clasps,	0 63
Imitation morocco, 6 plates, gilt edges,	0 50
Imitation morocco, 4 plates, gilt sides,	0 38
Cloth extra, 1 plate, plain,	0 25

THE PATH TO PARADISE. Beautiful miniature edition. 12 fine steel engravings.

Extra morocco, clasps, gilt edges,	1 50
Extra morocco, without clasps, gilt edges,	1 00
Imitation morocco, 6 steel engra'gs, full gilt edges,	0 50
Imitation morocco, 4 steel engravings, gilt edges,	0 38
Imitation morocco, 1 steel engraving,	0 25
Cloth extra, 1 steel engraving,	0 20

THE GATE OF HEAVEN; or, Way of the Child of Mary. A Manual of Prayers and Instructions, compiled from approved sources, for the use of Young Persons. Illustrated with 40 plates. 320 pp., 32mo. Fine paper.

Cloth extra,	0 21

Roan, plain, - - - - - - - - -	$0 31
Roan, gilt. - - - - - - - - -	0 38
Roan, full gilt, - - - - - - - -	0 50
Roan, full gilt, clasps, - - - - - -	0 63
Morocco extra, - - - - - - - -	1 00
Morocco extra, clasps, - - - - - -	1 50

THE POCKET MANUAL. A very neat Pocket Prayer Book. With 4 steel engravings. 48mo.

Cloth, gilt, - - - - - - - - -	0 13
Embossed, gilt edges, - - - - - -	0 25
Imitation Turkey, gilt edges, - - - - -	0 31
In tuck, gilt edges, - - - - - - -	0 38
Turkey morocco, - - - - - - -	0 50

THE ALTAR MANUAL; or, Instructions and Devotions for Confession and Communion. With Visits to the Blessed Sacrament, Devotions to the Sacred Heart of Jesus, and various other Devotions. From the "Delices des Ames Pieuses." Edited by EDWARD CASWELL, M.A. 432 pages, 18mo. Fine paper. and steel engravings.

Roan, marbled edges, - - - - - - -	0 75
Roan, gilt edges, - - - - - - -	1 00
Morocco extra, - - - - - - - -	1 75
Morocco extra, beveled, - - - - - -	2 25

THE ALTAR MANUAL. 24mo.

Cloth extra, - - - - - - - - -	0 38
Roan, plain, - - - - - - - - -	0 50
Roan, gilt, 4 plates, - - - - - - -	0 75
Morocco extra, 6 plates, - - - - - -	1 50

THE MISSION BOOK. A Manual of Instructions and Prayers adapted to preserve the Fruits of the Mission. Published under the direction of the Paulist Fathers. 18mo. 493 pages, illustrated.

Plain roan, - - - - - - - - -	0 50
Roan, full gilt, plain edges, - - - - -	0 63
Roan, embossed, gilt edges, - - - - -	0 75
Roan, embossed, gilt edges, clasps, - - - -	1 00
Imitation, full gilt, - - - - - - -	1 00
Imitation, full gilt, clasps, - - - - -	1 25
Morocco extra, - - - - - - - -	2 00
Morocco extra, clasps, - - - - - -	2 50
Morocco extra, beveled, - - - - - -	2 50
Morocco extra, beveled, clasps, - - - -	3 00

THE MISSION BOOK. 24mo.

Roan, plain, - - - - - - - - -	0 38
Roan, gilt sides, - - - - - - - -	0 50
Roan, embossed, gilt edges, - - - - -	0 63
Roan, embossed, gilt edges, clasps, - - - -	0 75
Roan, full gilt edges, - - - - - - -	0 75

Roan, full gilt edges, clasps, - - - - -	$0 88
Morocco extra, - - - - - - - - -	1 50
Morocco extra, clasps, - - - - - -	2 00
Morocco extra, beveled, - - - - - -	1 75
Morocco extra, beveled, clasps, - - - - -	2 25

THE RACCOLTA; or, Collection of Indulgenced Prayers. (Suitable for Confraternities and for Private Devotion.) Translated by AMBROSE ST. JOHN, of the Oratory of St. Philip Neri, Birmingham.

Cloth, - - - - - - - - - -	0 50
Roan, plain, - - - - - - - - -	0 63
Roan, full gilt, plain edges, - - - - -	0 75
Roan, embossed, gilt edges, - - - - -	0 88
Roan, embossed, gilt edges, clasps, - - -	1 00
Imitation, full gilt, - - - - - - -	1 00
Imitation, full gilt, clasps, - - - - - -	1 25
Morocco extra, - - - - - - - - -	1 75
Morocco extra, clasps, - - - - - -	2 25
Morocco extra, beveled, - - - - - -	2 00
Morocco extra, beveled, clasps, - - - - -	2 50

JOURNEE DU CHRETIEN. A very fine French Prayer Book, containing 630 pages, and 12 fine steel engravings. 24mo. Published with the approbation of the Right Rev. Dr. BOURGET, Lord Bishop of Montreal. Printed on fine paper.

Cloth extra, - - - - - - - - -	0 38
Imitation morocco, four steel engravings, gilt, -	0 50
Imitation morocco, six steel engravings, gilt edges,	0 75
Extra morocco, without clasps, gilt edges, - -	1 50
Extra morocco, clasps, gilt edges, - - - -	2 00

PAROISSIEN DES PETITS ENFANTS PIEUX. A beautiful French Prayer Book. Published with the approbation of the Right Rev. Dr. BOURGET, Lord Bishop of Montreal. 48mo.

Cloth extra, - - - - - - - - -	0 13
Roan, gilt edges, - - - - - - -	0 25
Roan, full gilt edges, - - - - - - -	0 31
Roan, tucks, - - - - - - - -	0 38
Morocco extra, - - - - - - - -	0 50

THE ROMAN MISSAL FOR THE USE OF THE LAITY. At from $1 to - - - - - - - 3 00

www.ingramcontent.com/pod-product-compliance
Lightning Source LLC
LaVergne TN
LVHW021104110826
845150LV00001B/167

* 9 7 8 1 4 2 5 5 6 5 3 3 6 *